69TH CONGRESS, 1ST SESSION
SENATE DOCUMENT NUMBER 95

ART AND ARTISTS
OF THE CAPITOL OF
THE UNITED STATES
OF AMERICA

By

CHARLES E. FAIRMAN

ART CURATOR
UNITED STATES CAPITOL

UNITED STATES
GOVERNMENT PRINTING OFFICE
WASHINGTON
1927

SENATE CONCURRENT RESOLUTION NO. 21

SUBMITTED BY MR. FESS

Resolved by the Senate (the House of Representatives concurring), That there be printed and bound as may be directed by the Joint Committee on Printing five thousand additional copies of Senate Document Numbered 95, entitled "Art and Artists of the United States Capitol," of which one thousand copies shall be for the use of the Senate, three thousand copies for the use of the House of Representatives, five hundred copies for the use of the Architect of the Capitol, and five hundred copies for the use of the Joint Committee on the Library.

Adopted: July 1 (calendar day, July 2), 1926.

INTRODUCTION

Nearly one hundred and thirty-four years have passed since the laying of the corner stone of the National Capitol by President Washington, September 18, 1793. During this long period of time the affections of the American people have clustered about the city of Washington, D. C., and the building occupied by the Congress for over a century and a quarter; the building typifying the permanency of American institutions and ideals, as well as the prosperity of the Nation.

It may not be safe to estimate the culture of a people by their progress in art attainments or art possessions. The necessities of those early years, the strict economy of those days, left but little for expenditure in art directions, and to have a roof for shelter was considered wiser than to possess paintings or sculpture. Works of art could be acquired at a later time when the necessities had been provided.

To present in a connected manner the development of the art of the National Capitol has been the purpose of this work. For years material has been collected not so much for the purpose of book writing as for the purpose of being informed to such an extent that intelligent help might be given to those in search of information concerning art matters relating to the Capitol Building. Many have advised the compilation of this information in a convenient form, and to their words of encouragement this work is due; their belief that I could tell the story of the art development of the Capitol in an acceptable manner has given the courage to attempt the necessary labor involved in the preparation of this volume, and to those who have made this work possible this book is dedicated.

My sincere thanks are tendered to those who have cheerfully assisted me in securing the many illustrations used in this work. The discovery that so many were willing to lend a helping hand has been a pleasure not easily forgotten.

CHARLES E. FAIRMAN.

WASHINGTON, D. C.,
September 15, 1927.

THE CAPITOL DOME AT NIGHT

As twilight fades, many batteries of electric lights are focused upon the Dome of the Capitol
The great white Dome is visible for many miles, sending the message
of the lighting of the way by the Government

{ IV }

DAVID LYNN

Architect of the Capitol (1923)

Courtesy of Buckingham

CHARLES E. FAIRMAN
Art curator of the Capitol

{ VI }

CONTENTS

LIST OF ILLUSTRATIONS

{ x }

{ XI }

ART AND ARTISTS OF THE CAPITOL
OF THE UNITED STATES
OF AMERICA

❧

CHAPTER I

EARLY ART IN THE CAPITOL

HEN Thomas Jefferson, the third President of the United States, was inaugurated on March 4, 1801, he became, by virtue of his office, a manager or chief superintendent charged with the construction and completion of the United States Capitol Building. When the seat of government was moved to Washington in the year 1800 there had been erected for the purposes of the Capitol a small rectangular building familiarly known as the Supreme Court section of the Capitol, and in this building was housed the United States Senate, the House of Representatives, the Supreme Court, the courts of the District of Columbia, and the library, now known as the Library of Congress. South of this building was a large vacant space, practically the extension of East Capitol Street. In this vacant space people passed to and from the western to the eastern portion of the city. Conveniently located in that section now occupied by the central portion of the Capitol were two wells which for many years furnished water to citizens residing in that vicinity, for the Capitol grounds were then occupied by homes.

South of this vacant space were the foundations of another building equal in area and intended to compare in cubic contents with the portion already erected and occupied. For some time after the inauguration of President Jefferson but little was done toward the erection of that southern building, now known as the Statuary Hall section of the Capitol, except that the foundation walls progressed slowly, and within the area of these walls there was built a one-story elliptical-shaped building of brick construction designed for the accommodation of the House of Representatives and known to the people of that period as "The Oven."[1]

President Jefferson brought for the tasks before him a well-equipped mind, architecture having formed a portion of his education. In fact, he was enough of an architect to know better than to attempt to carry on the work of the construction of the Capitol

---

[1] Report of James Hoban, Superintendent of the Capitol, of the work done at that building from the 18th of May, 1801, to the 14th of December, 1801:

"Elliptic room, south wing, 70 x 94 feet.

"The elliptic room has been carried up 2 feet 3 inches high, 4½ bricks thick, and 16 feet higher, 3½ bricks thick, with 16 niches and 16 arches to form an arcade.

"The girder and joist have been laid and floored, the building roofed, boarded and shingled, the ceiling covered, the walls and ceiling plaistered.

"The window frames and sashes, door frames and doors, finished.

"A gallery, on a semielliptic plan, has been put up, 120 feet long, with three rows of seats.

"A covered way has been built 145 feet long, from the north to the south wing, with two flights of steps, and three water-closets.

"James Hoban.

"The Commissioners of the Federal Buildings."

Contract price for the "Oven" was $4,789 (proceedings of the commissioners June 20, 1801).

without the assistance of the best talent in this country. He therefore appointed, on March 6, 1803, Benjamin Henry Latrobe, an architect of distinction whose work in other sections of the country had received favorable notice by the best of judges. Mr. Latrobe was then engaged upon other building and engineering projects and could not for some time take up his residence in Washington, and attended to his duties by visits to the city as occasion required his personal attention to such matters as could not be left entirely to the charge of his subordinate, who was known by the title of "clerk of the works." The plans for the Hall of the House of Representatives as developed by Mr. Latrobe required sculptural decoration, and at this time professional sculptors were unknown in the United States. In fact, the development of the art of sculpture was less advanced than that of painting. For some years the art of the painter as exemplified by such artists as John Singleton Copley, Benjamin West, Gustavus Hesseleus, John Smibert, Charles Willson Peale, John Trumbull, Rembrandt Peale, Patience Wright,

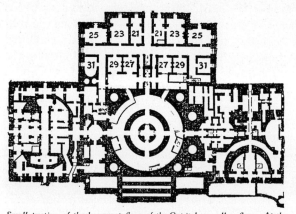

the modeler in wax, and her son, Joseph Wright, the portrait painter, had been well known to the American people. In sculpture there were a few examples, such as the works of Giuseppe Ceracchi, who had executed several busts of prominent Americans prior to the year 1795. There had been, since the year 1769, a statue of the Right Hon. William Pitt erected in Charleston, S. C.; while the tomb of Montgomery in St. Paul's Church, New York City, the work of Caffieri, executed in 1777, is called by some the first national monument erected in this country. According to Charles

Small portion of the basement floor of the Capitol, or cellar floor. At the right is the Supreme Court section, and at the left the section known as Statuary Hall. In the section at the left may be seen the outlines of an oval, the foundation of "The Oven," a temporary structure used by the House of Representatives before their occupation of the Hall of the House in 1807

Henry Hart there had been, at the beginning of the year 1800, advertisements of one James Traquair offering for sale busts of Washington, Franklin, Hamilton, and William Penn. It is stated that Traquair employed to do this work John Dixey, an Irishman of some ability as a sculptor, and Giuseppe Iardella, a skillful Italian carver, who had been brought over to America to carve sculptural decorations for the mansion of Robert Morris. But it appears that to the mind of Jefferson and to the mind of Latrobe this country did not possess the sculptors with the ability to execute the required work. Accordingly on March 6, 1805, Latrobe addressed a letter to Philip Mazzei [1] setting forth in detail the conditions existing and the requirement of trained sculptors for the work at the Capitol. The letter is so interesting that it is introduced in its entirety as contained in the journal of Benjamin Henry Latrobe. [2]

---

[1] Mazzei, Philip (mah-tzay-ee), Italian physician, born in Tuscany, 1730; died in Pisa, March 19, 1816. He studied medicine, practiced for several years in Smyrna, and from 1755 to 1773 engaged in commerce in London. In December, 1773, he came to Virginia, with several other Italians, to introduce the cultivation of the grape, the olive, and other fruits of Italy. He took an active part in supporting the movement for independence, and was the friend and correspondent of Thomas Jefferson; in 1779–1783 he was the agent in Italy to obtain Army stores for Virginia. He revisited the United States in 1785. Subsequently he was privy counselor for the King of Poland, and in 1802 received a pension from the Emperor Alexander of Russia. He was a zealous republican and an enemy to intolerance. He published "Récherches historiques et politiques sur Les Étas Unis de Amérique septentrionale," Paris, 1788.

[2] The journals or letter books of Latrobe are contained in 18 books covering a period of more than 20 years and dealing with wide variety of subjects. These books—which the author has had an opportunity of examination—are now in the possession of Ferdinand C. Latrobe, a great-grandson of the distinguished architect.

UNFINISHED SKETCH OF THE SENATE AND HOUSE WINGS OF THE OLD CAPITOL
Drawn by Benjamin H. Latrobe

WASHINGTON, *March 6, 1805.*

PHILIP MAZZEI, Esq.

SIR: By direction of the President of the United States I take the liberty to apply to you for your assistance in procuring for us the services of a good sculptor in the erection of the public buildings in this city, especially of the Capitol.

The Capitol was begun at a time when the country was entirely destitute of artists, and even of good workmen in the branches of architecture, upon which the superiority of public over private buildings depends. The north wing, therefore, which is carried up, although the exterior is remarkably well finished as to the masonry, is not a good building. For two or three years after the removal of Congress to this city the public works were entirely discontinued. In the year 1803, however, they were resumed, and under the patronage of the present President and the annual appropriations by Congress the south wing of the Capitol has been begun and carried on. It is now so far advanced as to make it necessary that we should have as early as possible the assistance of a good sculptor of architectural decorations. In order to procure such an artist the President of the United States has referred me to your assistance, and to enable you to make choice of the person most likely to answer our purpose I will beg leave to describe to you the nature of the work we require to be done. The principal sculpture required will be of twenty-four Corinthian capitals, two feet four inches in diameter at their feet, and open enriched entablatures, of 147 feet (both English measure) in length. There are beside five panels (tavole) enriched with foliage and an eagle of colossal size in the frieze, the distance between the tips of the extended wings being twelve feet six inches.

The material in which this is to be cut is a yellowish sandstone of fine grain, finer than the peperino or gray sandstone used in Rome—the only Italian sandstone of which I have any distinct recollection. This stone yields in any direction to the chisel, not being in the least laminated nor hard enough to fly off (spall) before a sharp tool. It may, therefore, be cut with great precision. The wages given by the day to our best carvers are from $3 to $2.50, or from about $750 to $900 per annum. They are considered good wages, but the workmen who receive them are very indifferent carvers and do not deserve the name of sculptors. My object is to procure a first-rate sculptor in the particular branch of architectural decorations. He should be able to model and bring with him another good though inferior workman as his assistant, to whom we could pay from $1.50 to $2 per day.

It is not my intention to confine you to these prices, but to leave it to you to do the best you can for the public interest both as to the excellence of the talents and the moderation in the wages of the person you may be pleased to select. Should you even (which I do not think improbable) find a man of superior

From a painting by Charles Willson Peale

PORTRAIT OF BENJAMIN HENRY LATROBE

Architect of the Capitol (1803–1817)

merit willing to come hither on lower terms than those we pay to our very indifferent carvers, it were well to contract with him at the terms with which he will be perfectly satisfied, as he may depend on receiving such an addition to his stipulated salary if his conduct merits it as will place him in proper relation as to salary as well as to abilities with our other workmen. There are, however, other qualities which seem so essential as to be at least as necessary as talents. I mean good temper and good morals. Without them an artist would find himself most unpleasantly situated in a country the language and manners of which are so different from his own, and we should have no dependence upon a person discontented with his situation. For though every exertion would be made on my part to make his engagement perfectly agreeable to him, the irritability of good artists is well known and it is often not easily quieted.

The American consul at Leghorn, who does me the favor to forward this to you, will provide all the expenses and make the arrangements necessary to the voyage of the persons you may select. I think it necessary that he should enter into a written contract to remain with us two years. We will pay all their expenses hither, their salary to commence on the day on which they shall be ready to leave Leghorn, and any reasonable advance to enable them to wind up their affairs at home should be made to them. Single men would be preferred, but no objection would be made to married man, whose family may come over with him. On expiration of the time, and should he choose to return, the expenses of the voyage will also be paid to him on his arrival again in Italy and not before. But this stipulation should not be made unless absolutely demanded. I have a further favor to ask which I hope will give you less trouble than the preceding. It is proposed to place in the Chamber of Representatives a sitting figure of Liberty nine feet in height. I wish to know for what sum such a figure would be executed by Canova in white marble, and for what sum he would execute a model in plaster (the only material I believe in which it could be brought hither), to be executed here in American marble from the model.

If Canova should decline the proposal altogether, as he must now be an old man, what would be the price of such a statue and such a model by the artist he should recommend as in his opinion the nearest to himself in merit?

Although I have not the honor to be personally known to you, I shall not take up your time by apologies for giving you this trouble.

The time is already approaching when our vines and our olives will spread your name and our gratitude over a great portion of our country. Let us also owe to your kindness the introduction of excellence in the most fascinating branch of art.

With true respect, etc.,

B. H. Latrobe.

As a result of this correspondence, Giuseppe Franzoni and Giovanni Andrei arrived in this country some time in February of 1806. We find reference to their arrival in a letter of March 3, 1806, from Latrobe to Lenthall, who was the "clerk of the works" at Washington. The reference is as follows:

Yours of the 25th. And so Franzoni and Andrei have arrived. I will trump all my Italian and write to them tomorrow to keep them in good humor. Among other letters received on Friday last I had one from Mazzei who procured them for us. He says that Franzoni is a most excellent sculptor and capable of cutting our figure of Liberty and that Andrei excells more in decoration. I wish they would go and seek clay for modelling. Andrews could tell them where to find it and then model one of our capitals. But I shall be with you in a week or ten days now.

The selection of sculptors by Philip Mazzei seems to have been a fortunate one. Giuseppe Franzoni was the son of the president of the Academy of Fine Arts at Carrara and a nephew of Cardinal Franzoni. A younger brother, Carlo Franzoni, came to this country subsequent to 1815. Both of the Franzoni brothers died in Washington.[3] It is quite evident that Giuseppe Franzoni was upon speaking terms at least with President Jefferson, and that he made a call upon the President soon after arriving in Washington is shown by the following letter:

Washington, *March 2, 1806.*

Sir:—I did not understand until told so by the servant at the door, that the articles of marble which you had left here, had been intended as presents to me. Be assured that I receive this mark of your good will as thankfully as if I could accept of it, but I have laid it down as a law to myself to accept no presents of value while I am in public office, and adherence to this rule is necessary for the tranquility of my own mind and it is necessary for the public good. These motives cannot fail to meet your approbation and to justify my request that you receive the objects back again, and with them the same thanks for the offer as if I had retained them. Be assured that I shall avail myself of every occasion of being useful to you, and accept my salutations.

(Signed) Thomas Jefferson.

Mr. Franzoni.

(From a letter in the Manuscript Division of the Library of Congress.)

---

[3] The Federal City, p. 86, by S. D. Wyeth.

In the Senate corridor, main floor, west end

PORTRAIT OF THOMAS JEFFERSON
Thomas Sully, painter

It is claimed by some of the descendants of Giuseppe Franzoni that soon after his arrival in Washington, being dissatisfied with the housing accommodations furnished by the Government, he purchased the dwelling afterwards known as 121 Pennsylvania Avenue SE. It is also claimed by the same descendants that Giuseppe Franzoni was the intimate friend of Jefferson, dining with him on Sundays, and that they are now in possession of several articles of value given by the President to Mr. Franzoni and his wife, including a silver sugar dish made to order for the President and given to Mrs. Franzoni as a Christmas present. Perhaps the impression which these Italian sculptors made upon

Mr. Latrobe, and which is confirmatory of their excellent character, is best shown by the inclusion of a letter of Mr. Latrobe to Philip Mazzei as follows:

WASHINGTON, *April 12, 1806.*

Signor MAZZEI.

SIR:—I am much ashamed that I have not before answered your very obliging letters, dated July 20, and Sept. 1st., but at the time I was in Philadelphia, and several circumstances occurred to prevent it, the principal of which was the illness and subsequent death of one of my children.

When I received your letters, Signors Franzoni and Andrei had not arrived, but they soon after landed in Baltimore, and came on hither immediately. As I was not here and none of my agents could speak Italian, they remained perfectly idle as to the public works, but amused themselves in making several small models, which better than any other recommendation proved them to be perfect masters of their art. Their conduct also during this period, won the favor of everybody and I have to thank you most sincerely for having so punctually attended to my request, that you would send out them of good morals, and of talent in their art.

Accept then, my very sincere acknowledgments of the favor you have done me particularly, and to the country at large, for I have no sort of doubt, but that the work which they will produce, will give a taste of art to our citizens of which at present, very few have the most distant apprehension.

Having only arrived here a few days ago, I have not been able to get our friends regularly to work as yet. Franzoni, however, has begun to make a model of an Eagle for the frieze of the Hall of Representatives, and Andrei, the capital of one of our columns.

It is fortunate that I still remember Italian sufficient to converse with them, although it is now more than 20 years since I spoke that language fluently. Enough however remains in my memory to understand them, and to be perfectly understood. I have already procured for them a house in which each family has two very convenient rooms, and a good kitchen and accommodations for a servant.

I have raised their wages to 170 dollars per month for both of them, and shall endeavor also to comply with your stipulation for house rent. I have completely furnished their house and as this was not stipulated, the increase of their wages will go to pay for their furniture.

In six months it will be paid for and then their whole salary will be free. All this I have explained to them in an Italian letter, no doubt not very grammatical, and yet a very intelligible one, for they appear most perfectly satisfied.

Nothing could be done more wisely than to have sent their wives with them. They are a pair of very good-humored little women, but they have the Florentine dialect in so strong a degree that I can hardly understand anything they say. It shall be my endeavor to make them as comfortable as possible, so as to induce them to keep their husbands in the country.

As to the Statue of Liberty, I fear we must for the present give up the thoughts of it, for the monies appropriated by Congress will not permit the expense of obtaining it even from Thorwaldsen. I cannot sufficiently express to you my thanks for the trouble you have taken on this occasion. When I am a little better acquainted with the talents of Franzoni, I shall be able to judge whether or no I can employ him on this project. The statue is indeed essential to the effect of my architecture, but I am already accustomed to deprive myself of much gratification, in employing the arts of sculpture and painting in my work, which I might easily procure in Europe, for it is a truth that Franzoni and Andrei are the only sculptors in America.

Accept once more my sincere thanks and expressions of my sincere respect.

Yours truly,

B. HENRY LATROBE.

I will write again when Franzoni and Andrei have been here a few months, and I can say more concerning them.

Additional information relating to the actual contract between the United States Government and Franzoni and Andrei is contained in the following copies of letters written in Italian and found in the copy books of Benjamin H. Latrobe, now in the possession of his great-grandson, Ferdinand C. Latrobe, who has obligingly had these letters translated for use in this work. The letters referred to are dated April 25, 1806; May 1, 1806, and December 1, 1806.

WASHINGTON, *April 25, 1806.*

Messrs. FRANZONI & ANDREI.

GENTLEMEN: When I wrote to Signor Mazzei, asking him for the favor to secure for us the assistance of your talents, I left to him the arranging of the details of the agreement, which would be drawn up between the U. S. and yourselves. In the written contract I have just received from him it is agreed that all your traveling and maintenance expenses—for yourselves and your wives—would be paid for by the U. S. until you land in America, and that a salary of 65 sequins per month would be paid to you for two years, beginning with October 1, 1805.

In a private letter, Signor Mazzei tells me that he promised to you—although this is not authorized in my letter to him—free lodging for the two years covered by the contract. These are the only conditions to which we are apparently bound.

Since the time, however, when Signor Mazzei was in America, food and labor have increased in cost; the salary he provided for you, perhaps, is not so generous as he intended it to be and you expected. For this reason, the President of the U. S., to give you a proof of his contention that you would be glad to live with us and to give us the advantage of your genius and your good will, has induced me to offer you better conditions than are written in your contract. It gives me much pleasure to be the medium of his generosity, especially since you have not complained nor asked any more than had been agreed upon.

The new conditions which will be accorded to you, will therefore be as follows: (1)—Your lodging, that is the same house in which you live, will be at the expense of the U. S. (2)—the monthly salary, for two, will be 70 sequins, equal to 85 dollars each per month, or $170. for two. (3)—All expenses for the purchase of furniture will be advanced by the U. S. in your account. And the increase in your salary of eleven sequins a month, will be deducted from your salary until the account is paid. (4) You are authorized to hire one or two apprentices to teach them the art of the sculptor. His or their salary will be paid into your hands and will be proportionate to their work and talents, on condition that you will provide his or their lodging and board. This ought to be a very advantageous condition for you.

I do not need to assure you of my great desire to make pleasant and profitable your engagement and your stay in America, to smooth the inconvenience of living where you cannot, for the time being, understand either the language or the manners of the people. And I have no doubt that your talents and your diligence will do honor to your characters and to my good opinion of your selves.

In writing this letter, because of lack of practice in the Italian language, I did not make use of the polite manner of addressing you with the third feminine person. I feared I might be too obscure in expressing my thoughts.

With much good will, I am,

B. HENRY LATROBE,
Public Architect of the U. S. in Washington.

WASHINGTON, *May 1st, 1806.*

Messrs. FRANZONI & ANDREI.

GENTLEMEN: All the accounts for expenses, furniture, maintenance, etc., have now been gathered and paid, with the possible exception of a few of minor importance, which you will please settle, if convenient, from your own salary.

Enclosed you will find your account with Mr. Munroe, the city superintendent, to whom all accounts concerning the city and public buildings are referred. Others will pay your salary, through Mr. Lenthal.

The addition of $25.70 to your salary will be deducted to pay the sum of $206.52 as I explained in my previous letter. This will last about eight months, after which you will receive the full salary of $170. Meanwhile there will be paid you $144.30 (equal to 65 sequins) as arranged with Signor Mazzei.

In order not to leave you without ready cash, Mr. Lenthal will pay you $100—for two, for the time past. The salary for May will be paid on the first of June, and so on, for the following months.

The account of Rhoads was so extravagant that 170 dollars have been paid by the U. S. in order to reduce your outlay from ten to six dollars a week each.

With much good will, etc., etc.,

B. H. LATROBE.

WASHINGTON, *December 1, 1806*

Messrs. FRANZONI & ANDREI.

GENTLEMEN: In order to have your bill to the Treasury paid in full, it is necessary to explain how were spent the $110. dollars which you received from Mr. Purviance, revenue collector at Baltimore, who sent your signed receipt to the office of the Superintendent of the City. Mr. Purviance is dead and cannot easily furnish the explanation that is wanting. All the moneys that were necessary for your expenses till you reached the city, will be paid by the U. S., but it is absolutely necessary in order to get a credit for those $110 dollars to make out an account in this form:

THE SUPERINTENDENT OF THE CITY DR. TO FRANZONI & ANDREI

For our expenses in Baltimore and for the journey and maintenance from the date of our arrival
    in Baltimore to the date of our arrival in Washington, on account of our salary........ $110

There is also another difficulty concerning the account of Mr. Appleton, because of the beds that were purchased in Leghorn for your trip. It will be necessary to write me a letter stating that Captain Kiddall has kept all those things and refused to turn over to you anything that had been used by you during the voyage.

I have also spent some 40 or 50 dollars for various things that were bought. I shall give the Superintendent an account of such expenses and they will be paid when it is convenient.

When these accounts are made up and paid, all your expenses will have been refunded and there will remain for you about 200 dollars for this month. In the future there will be the full salary of $170.00 dollars a month.

    With much good will,

B. H. L

The Italian sculptors, however, did not seem to be able to grasp the American point of view. This, no doubt, was difficult, owing to their training in a far different school of sculpture. The perplexities of the architect are shown by the following letters from Mr. Latrobe to John Lenthall and Charles Willson Peale:

PHILADELPHIA, Mar. 24, 1806.

Mr. JOHN LENTHALL.

DEAR LENTHALL: * * * I much fear that our friend Franzoni may be much above the carving of architectural decorations; if so, what can we do with him? In the first place he may model our eagle in order that we may be able to get at the embossment(?) of the stone. I would leave to his own management the disposition of this gigantic bird; in the first instance the tip of its wings ought at least to reach the centers of the columns. I think indeed they ought to cover the shafts; in the latter case they would cover 12' 6'' in width of the frieze; a good reason, however, occurs to stop them at the center, namely, that there is a joint; I shall bring with me the beak of an eagle which I am promised, or at all events a very good and measured drawing.

If Mazzei, however, has sent us a sculptor of animated nature only, he has not only acted contrary to my request, but was himself not aware of what he did; for he advises our Liberty to be carved at Rome (not I suppose from model there), but at least if copied here she might possess nothing of the antique.

As to writing Italian, I find I am very much out of the habit, but I will still attempt it to-morrow if possible; to-morrow, and to-morrow, and to-morrow, means never I suppose.

      *   *   *   *   *   *   *

WASHINGTON, April 18, 1806.

Mr. C. W. PEALE,
        Philadelphia.

MY DEAR SIR: You will say, and I am afraid with truth, that I never write to you but to give you trouble. At present I have really no other object but to lay myself under still greater obligations to your kindness than I am already.

In my design of the Hall of the House of Representatives, an eagle has become necessary as the principal decoration of the center of the Hall in the frieze.

(Here is given in the letter a sketch of the Capitals of two columns, and on the entablature an eagle with extended wings.)

We have here two most capital Italian sculptors lately arrived. One of them is now modeling an eagle, but it is an Italian, or a Roman, or a Greek eagle, and I want an American Bald-eagle. May I therefore beg the favor of you to request one of your very obliging, and skilful sons, to send me a drawing of the head and claws of the bald-eagle of his general proportions with the wings extended, and especially

CHARLES WILLSON PEALE

Self-portrait

Represented by the full-length portrait of George Washington, in the Senate wing (facing the painting of the Battle of
Chapultepec), and the portrait of Gunning Bedford, jr., in the House wing (facing the painting
of the First Reading of the Emancipation Proclamation)

{ 10 }

of the arrangement of the feathers below the wing when extended. The eagle will be fourteen feet from tip to tip of the wings, so that any glaring impropriety of character will be immediately detected by our Western members.

Let me beg of you to do me this favor. I want merely outlines, but as soon as possible. I should be truly thankful.

Yours very affectionately,

(Signed)   B. H. LATROBE.

The good offices of Charles Willson Peale seem to have resulted in the Americanization of the knowledge of Giuseppe Franzoni on the characteristics of the bald-headed eagle. Mr. Latrobe seems greatly encouraged in the result of Franzoni's efforts, as is shown by the following extract from his letter to President Jefferson under date of August 27, 1806:

* * * The frieze of which one half has been for some time set on the east side will then be completed without delay, including the eagle of which a considerable part is finished one wing being nearly complete and the body and the other wing formed, and I will venture to say that when it is completed there is not in ancient or modern sculpture, an eagle's head, which in dignity, spirit, or drawing is superior to Franzoni's. It is very superior to his model. Unfortunately, however, he was this morning seized with a spitting of blood, and being of a weakly constitution, and still weaker nerves, I fear we shall not be able to keep him long. He will want to return to Italy. * * *

Later information concerning the Italian sculptors is found in a letter from Latrobe to Philip Mazzei, dated December 19, 1806. This letter is valuable, as it tends to show that the father of Giuseppe Franzoni was reported to be a sculptor, and for the further reason that it refers to the birth of a daughter of the Franzoni family, probably the daughter who in after years, it is claimed, posed for her uncle, Carlo Franzoni, as the model for the female figure in the Car of History.

PHILADELPHIA, *Dec. 19th, 1806.*

Signor MAZZEI, *Pisa.*

DEAR SIR: On my arrival in this city about 14 days ago, I found on inquiring it was doubtful whether you have ever received my letter of the 12th of April and the 21st of May, 1806. They both were put on the same vessel, which was carried into Gibraltar and probably the letters were examined and forwarded. I therefore transmit duplicates of the same, and will forward triplicates and duplicates of the present letter by the next opportunity.

Our Italian sculptors continue to give us the utmost satisfaction. Franzoni was not very well for a few weeks in Summer but has been long entirely recovered. His wife has been brought to bed lately of a fine little American girl. They both appear perfectly satisfied with their situation, and we have every reason to make them so. Hitherto Franzoni has been only engaged with Eagles. He has finished a colossal Eagle in the Frieze of the Entablature of the Hall of Representatives 12' 6'' from wing to wing, and is now engaged on a free Eagle, also colossal for the Gate of the Navy Yard. This promises to be the most spirited Eagle I have seen in sculpture either modern or antique. When this is finished he will commence a group of seventeen female figures in which his talents will be more worthily employed. I shall endeavor by every reasonable encouragement to detain them in the country after their time is expired. One motive to induce them to remain will be to encourage the interests of their friends in Italy. I intend therefore to order all the Capitals of our principal columns of Franzoni's father, who I understand is a sculptor by profession in that particular line. I will endeavor with this letter to send to you the necessary drawing, venturing thus further to intrude upon the kindness you have already shown to us.

In our papers a paragraph has appeared, and has been copied into all the papers on the continent informing the public that Mr. Thorwaldsen was actually engaged in making for us a statue of Liberty of the colossal size described in my first letter. If this should be the case, which I hardly suppose *she shall be heartily welcome on her arrival:* but the President did not intend to incur the expense; and I had already looked to Franzoni for the best statue he could execute. I have seen enough of his talents to believe that he will not *disgrace* us by his Sculpture, but also that Canova & probably Thorwaldsen & Flaxman are his superiors in a great degree.

P. S. In settling the accounts of our Italian sculptors, I am at a loss whether your agreement with them included house rent or not. They assert, that although it is not stipulated in the contract, it was verbally agreed to by you. Wishing to give them every possible encouragement, I have no objection whatever to allow it, but it would facilitate much the passing of their accounts, if we had a statement of the fact, or otherwise, which I could produce. You say in one of your letters that you thought it a reasonable allowance to them.

Should it not be in my power to send you the drawing by the present opportunity, may I beg you to inquire of Franzoni's father for what price he will engage to deliver to you 50 Corinthian Capitals 3 ft. 6 in. high of the usual proportions and design and they may be in *two Blocks* each.

B. Henry Latrobe.

As the work progressed, the architect found other perplexing situations. It appears that although he had considered Franzoni one of the best of sculptors, he was not thoroughly pleased with the designs submitted by him. It had seemed in the plan for the decoration of the Hall of the House of Representatives that a statue of Liberty should be given a prominent position. The difficulties of securing from Franzoni such a statue as had been contemplated by Latrobe are shown by an extract from a letter written by Latrobe from Philadelphia December 31, 1806, to Lenthall, as follows:

* * * I am puzzled about Franzoni's blocks. By the bye, as I have told you before I do not like his model. It may be correct Symbology or emblematology to give Dame Liberty a club or shelalah, but we have no business to exhibit it so publicly. As to the beautiful picture of Peace, which is Canova's, of doves nestling in a helmet; it has no business there at all. I must have one arm close to her side resting in her lap. The other may be raised and rest on a wig or block or capped stick, (which is much more honorable than the wig block, as the cap is more honorable than the wig) for aught I care.

Your drawing is sufficient to enable me to study the thing, and probably in a day or two I shall give my final orders and reduce her ladyship in height to perhaps 7 feet sitting. * * *

Thus far but little has been said of the work of Giovanni Andrei. His work as a decorative sculptor related more particularly to the carving of the Corinthian capitals of the columns designed to support the frieze to which reference has heretofore been made. Possibly Andrei was not progressing as rapidly as the architect had hoped for, and the following extract from a letter from Latrobe to the President, dated at Philadelphia, January 6, 1807, would seem to indicate that it might be a matter of economy to have the capitals carved in Italy:

* * * I have within the past fortnight sent to Mr. Mazzei, duplicates of all my former letters, and have requested him to inquire of Franzoni's father the expense of one of the capitals of the size required for the Capitol. * * *

It should be understood that in the preparation of the Hall of Representatives a decided change had been made in the Thornton plan for this Chamber. Doctor Thornton had provided for a hall elliptical in shape, and Mr. Latrobe changed this design by providing in place of it two semicircles abutting on a parallelogram, the whole of this Hall covered with a flat dome supported by a colonnade of 24 columns standing on a wall some 7 feet above the floor of the Hall, beyond which were the galleries and lobbies. While the architect had contemplated columns of the Doric order, Mr. Jefferson ordered that Corinthian columns be used instead. It is proper to state, however, that positive orders were not often given by Mr. Jefferson. Suggestions, however, were made from time to time and differences reconciled in a friendly spirit which always existed between the President and the architect.

In the meanwhile Mr. Latrobe was not permitted to give his whole attention to the erection of the south wing of the Capitol. Unfortunately the north wing, although in a condition where it could be occupied upon the first session of Congress in this city in 1800, had become from various causes, the chief of which seemed to be faulty construction, sadly in need of repair. Some of the wooden beams were badly affected by dry rot. The

WILLIAM THORNTON

First Architect of the Capitol (1793–1802)

From a miniature painted by Robert Field, now owned by Mrs. Henry H. Flather, Washington, D. C.

plastering was sagging and in some places had fallen, the roof was leaking badly, and the construction of this portion of the building was of such character that it seemed to be impossible to repair except by the substitution of a new roof. On account of the necessary work required in the north wing, the occupancy of the south wing was delayed far beyond the expectation of the architect and all concerned. In a report made February 28, 1804, Mr. Latrobe had planned to have the hall completed and ready for permanent occupancy during the year 1805, but had modified this statement by suggesting that on account of dampness it might not be advisable to expect its completion until the fall of 1806. It does not appear, however, that the year 1806 was destined to see the completion of the Hall of the House of Representatives. In the year 1807 the Congress met in the month of October and occupied the new Hall of the House of Representatives. Mr. Latrobe stated in a report of March 23, 1808, that the south wing of the Capitol—

may be considered as finished except in the following particulars:

1. All the woodwork and walls require to be painted. The woodwork is only primed.
2. Of the twenty-four Corinthian columns of the Hall of Representatives, the capitals of only two are entirely finished; eight are in a state of forwardness; and fourteen are only rough hewn or bosted.
3. Only part of the cornice is finished.
4. The sculpture over the entrance is incomplete.
5. The enclosure of the lobbies is not yet finished.
6. All the chimney pieces of the principal story and two of the of the vestibules, ten in number, are wanting. * * *

This report also contains important information on the progress of the sculpture.

The sculpture which is still deficient can only be completed in the course of time. There are at present in the service of the United States two very skillful Italian sculptors, Messrs. Andrei and Franzoni whose talents are evident in their works. They and their pupil Somerville, one of our own citizens, will make very considerable progress during the next season and much other assistance can be obtained in the less difficult parts of the work.

The year 1808 was one of strict economy, based upon the advice of President Jefferson that no more work should be done than could be paid for from the appropriations available. This probably accounts for the very meager appropriation estimated for the work of the following year, as shown in the report by Mr. Latrobe, dated November 18, 1808:

SOUTH WING OF THE CAPITOL

To continue the work on the capitals of the column of the House of Representatives, to defray expense of repairs of glass, and minor repairs; to procure strong American glass for the large windows of the Hall, which have been imperfectly glazed, and independently of the convenience are liable to frequent breakage; and to put up ten deficient chimney pieces, will be required $6,000.
I beg leave to remark that this sum includes the salaries of the Italian sculptors engaged by contract in the service of the United States, and who, when no longer employed, are to be sent home at the public expense. The future annual expense of this wing will not exceed $5,000.

The year 1808 marked the arrival in Washington of a work of art, known as the Naval Monument, purchased by officers of the United States Navy to memorialize the losses of the Navy at Tripoli. The monument was brought to this country on the frigate *Constitution* and by an act of Congress approved March 13, 1808 (Stats. L., vol. 2, p. 476), the duties were remitted. This monument was erected at the Washington Navy Yard and remained there during the time when the yard was burned to prevent it falling into the hands of the British and some years later was removed from the navy yard to the west front of the Capitol, where it was located in a large pool, of which it formed the center.

The monument remained in this location until the year 1860, when it was taken down and reerected in the grounds of the Naval Academy at Annapolis, where it still may be seen.

It has previously been stated that Latrobe was an architect of distinction at the time when he was selected by President Jefferson to take charge of the construction of the south wing of the Capitol. It is interesting to give at this time an opinion relating to Latrobe from Rembrandt Peale, as published in volume 1 of the Crayon (1855):

When Latrobe had finished his beautiful edifice of the Pennsylvania Bank, then a rare architectural object in our country, he met a friend, whom he led to a spot in Second Street, as affording the most picturesque view of the building. "Friend Latrobe," said he, "thee may be proud of thy work, if thee will; but I am no friend of the Fine Arts—I am a friend of the coarse arts." This Latrobe thought was indeed a very *coarse* idea. Still it may not be amiss to remark that artists have done their country some collateral service. It was a portrait painter, Robert Fulton, that gave us the power of steam navigation. It was a portrait painter, S. F. B. Morse, that devised the magic electric telegraph. It was a portrait painter, C. W. Peale, that first made porcelain teeth for himself and a few friends, and I, though a portrait painter, lighted the first city with gas.

Although the foregoing is interesting, it seems strange that Mr. Peale has omitted to call attention to an invention of Charles Willson Peale, known as the polygraph. We are indebted for this information to an address delivered by John H. B. Latrobe, son of B. H. Latrobe, architect, before the American Institute of Architects in Washington, D. C., November 16, 1881. Concerning this invention, Mr. Latrobe states as follows:

The materials from which much of the foregoing has been prepared, have been furnished by the letter book and portfolio mentioned. That I should have letter books from a date that knew not press copy books or manifold writers needs an explanation that might be put into a foot note, were it not connected with one who if not an architect was an artist, a mechanician and a scientist, and in this way near of kin to the profession whose members are before me. I refer to Charles Willson Peale. About the year 1802, he invented what he called a polygraph, the essential parts of which were a light horizontal rod, with jointed sockets at each end, to hold common quill pens. This was connected with parallel motions; one travelling upon the upper part of the inclined desk, while the other was suspended from a frame above it, the two permitting the pen rod to move the width and length of a sheet of paper. Two of such sheets were held flat by spring bars at their upper edges. The movement of the two pens being made thus identical, while the left hand one held by the writer, wrote the letter the right hand one wrote a duplicate original which was placed in the desk drawer, until a sufficient number had accumulated to be bound and indexed. * * *

As it is claimed by some that President Jefferson invented the polygraph, the following letter from Latrobe to Charles Willson Peale would seem to establish Mr. Peale as the inventor:

WASHINGTON, *Feb. 22nd, 1804.*

CHARLES W. PEALE,
    Museum, Philadelphia.

MY DEAR FRIEND:—I was in hopes that before now I should have had the pleasure to give you at least a dozen orders for Polygraphs so many of my friends have talked about buying. At last however I can send you one but you will be obliged to break thro your law of not forwarding without the cash. It is for the President of the United States. It must be made as perfect as your best, but different in one respect. Instead of one drawer to draw out on the left hand, it must have two drawers each of half the length, one to draw out to the right the other to the left. It must have a binding frame and half a ream of paper as usual. Please to send it by the first vessel bound to Alexandria to the care of Mr. Lewis Deblois, Merchant Alexandria for the President of the United States, enclosing a bill of lading by post to Mr. Deblois. As soon as it arrives the President will send you the money. You had better write to him and enclose him a bill. I am ashamed to say that I had not the courage to ask it beforehand.

I have in the mean time lent the President my own Polygraph, much to mine and my wife's inconvenience, whom I have now restored to her former post of copying clerk. You will I am sure so far oblige me as to send me another of the most approved construction to New-Castle to be there on the 6th of

March at the latest. As the President U. S. receives that which you will make for him my old one will be sent to you from Alexandria. You will recollect that it is of the first construction with three bars. Tomorrow I hope to find you another order. Believe me most Sincerely yrs.

B. HENRY LATROBE.

P. S. I consider myself responsible to you for the amount of a Polygraph until you receive mine from the President and for all extra expense.
(From letter book of B. H. Latrobe (1804.), vol. 1. p. 75.)

While the letters of Latrobe, the architect, are exceedingly interesting, for the purposes of this book, dealing with the art and artists of the Capitol, it is sometimes necessary to use only such portions as seem appropriate for the subject of this work. The following letter is, however, given in its entirety:

WASHINGTON, *March 26, 1808.*

SIGNOR ANDREI: I am very sorry that I could not see you today; but it is not of much consequence; when you go to Baltimore, you will best learn what you have to do. You will arrive at Baltimore in the evening. Take a hack and go to the college. I have given you a letter to the bar-keeper (il primo maestro del oste) who will direct you to Mr. Godefroi, to whom I have given you a letter lives opposite the tavern at which you alight. Send the letter over to him; and if he is at home he will go with you. He is an excellent man and architect of the chapel.

I think you had better take a box of clay (una scatola de terra, per cominciargo) to begin with.
Yours truly,

(Signed) B. H. LATROBE.

The nature of the work referred to in this letter has not been definitely determined. It is known, however, that both Andrei and Giuseppe Franzoni worked at their profession for parties in Baltimore and for this service received $10 per day, and at this amount they became dissatisfied with the regular compensation received by them from the Government. Latrobe refers to this in a letter used later.

Later in the year Latrobe makes the following report to the President:

WASHINGTON, *Sept. 11, 1808.*

SOUTH WING

Franzoni has completed his sculpture both on the frieze over the entrance and the Speaker's chair. The figure of Commerce which is entirely new, is not, I think equal to the other three (Agriculture, Art and Science), though remarkably well finished. The eagle has also acquired more repose and correctness.

Mr. Bridport's ceiling will do him great honor. I fear the members will think it too fine, and I doubt not but that Mr. Randolph will abuse it. The contract is for $3,500 all expense included.[4] The columns proceed slowly in the completion of the capitals. We shall add only three to the number that are finished, but the capitals of all the pilasters are done. All the dentils of the cornice are cut, and much progress made in the enrichment of these members below the modillions. All the rosettes on the heads of the modillions are also finished.

All this work though it adds exceedingly to the general effect does not tell so well in detail and I have preferred executing it this year and leaving nothing but the capitals of the columns unfinished, because the necessity of the latter work is much more evident to the untrained eye, than of the former.

The workmen are also now engaged in moving the situation of the fireplaces from the back of the Speaker's chair to the 2d intercolumination of the right and left.

This improvement was distinctly pointed out by the experience of the last session. The crowding of the members behind the chair where they could not be seen was highly inconvenient. I shall also move the chair three feet further back. * * *

The completion of the south wing seems to have been retarded both by the nature of the work remaining to be done and the few employees retained upon this work. On

---

[4] The ceiling referred to was the ceiling of the Hall of the House of Representatives destroyed by the fire in this section of the Capitol at the time of the occupancy by the British troops August 24, 1814. It was the work of George Bridport, of Philadelphia, who afterwards (1817) in connection with his brother, Hugh Bridport, opened a drawing academy in the city of Philadelphia.

September 8, 1809, Mr. Latrobe in a letter to President Madison refers to the condition in the south wing of the Capitol as follows:

> In this Wing the only work to be done is to proceed in carving the capitals of the columns. Five of them are in hand and they will be about two-thirds finished before the next session. To finish them will be the work of about six years. * * *

It has before been mentioned that Mr. Latrobe seemed to be dissatisfied with the progress being made in the completion of his plans for the Hall of the House of Representatives. In a letter addressed to Thomas Munroe, a commissioner of public buildings and grounds, under date of September 14, 1809, he states:

> * * * As by their contracts the sculptors are to be provided with lodgings, I saw not any way of getting off unless money were laid aside from the present appropriation to pay for the whole year. I have however, made a preliminary arrangement, subject to your approval with Mr. Law since then, for a house on Capitol Hill (that formerly occupied by Capt. Rankin) to pay $200.00 if kept for a whole year, and $250.00 if quitted in a shorter period, which arrangement would probably answer your ideas best.
>
> As to the new arrangement spoken of, no such thing exists. On the contrary I have repeatedly told the sculptors both Franzoni and Andrei, that it was out of my power to alter their wages. That their agreement could be modified only by the President of the U. S. But as I have observed that since their trip to Baltimore, where for some very coarse sculpture they have received at the rate of $10.00 per day, they have not appeared satisfied, I have proposed that they should take their work by the piece. For the Senate Chamber six capitals are in hand to be carved, and as many for the House of Representatives.
>
> I had some conversation with Andrei as to the price at which he could afford to take these capitals, he paying the wages of the caster and assistants; but as it is evident that not one of them can be completed before the meeting of Congress, but that they must be put up unfinished, this arrangement has fallen through.
>
> Andrei although an incomparable artist [5] is the slowest hand I ever saw, especially in modeling, and in fact our clay models of his work have cost us more than the same things in marble. Therefore I have since your absence set him to model some things at home after working hours i. e. after six o'clock the price being fixed at $20.00. It would cost $50.00 in the common way.
>
> With Franzoni I have also agreed for a figure of Justice for the Court Room at $200.00. He works on it Sundays, and at night by a lamp. He will not finish it I fancy, these 6 or 8 months. Thus the public get the work done, and I take care that it is not done in working hours. At the same time these men whom it is very important to retain are comparatively satisfied. * * *
>
> I am far from believing that they will be spared by the next session. Franzoni has six figures as large as life in hand which will be without arms next session, and Andrei will not have half finished his capitals. They cannot be suffered to remain so. I will see you on Saturday. In the meantime believe me—
>
> > Very respectfully,
> >
> > > B. HENRY LATROBE.

The following letter gives the last information concerning the models for the statuary designed by Giuseppe Franzoni for the Hall of Representatives. Originals in high relief carved from these models were destroyed when the Capitol was burned by the British August 24, 1814.

C. W. PEALE, *Philadelphia*.

> MY DEAR SIR: By Captain Hand who sailed from Alexandria about a week ago, I send to the Academy of Arts four boxes containing the four figures of Agriculture, Art, Science and Commerce which are sculptured in alto relievo over the entrance of the Hall of Representatives here. They occupy 25 feet in length in the original and are rather larger than life filling the frieze of the center map of the colonnade. These are the original small models. I hope they will arrive safe. Commerce has lost a

---

[5] From a German art encyclopedia the following information is obtained: Andrei is credited with having made the balustrades of the high altar of the Church of Santa Marie Novella in Florence. It is also stated that he was brother-in-law and the instructor or teacher of Giuseppe Franzoni, with whom he came to Washington in 1806. The statement, therefore, of Mr. Latrobe that Andrei is an incomparable artist seems well founded.

2

{ 17 }

foot I fear.   I think I heard it crack in packing but it can be easily replaced with a little White lead. I fear *Lead* will be really the only way to put our Commerce *on foot* again.   I say let the boxes be brought up by Hand to the Academy, for it would be a pity if after having been carried by Hand all the way from hence, they would be ruined by being at last put into a dray.

They are packed in sawdust.   The limbs are relieved, and some entirely free.   Great care must therefore be taken in removing it.

Is Rembrandt really come home?

Love to all around you.

Yours truly,

B. H. Latrobe.

December 10th, 1808.

CHAPTER II

BURNING OF THE CAPITOL AND ITS RESTORATION

 N THE reconstruction of the north wing of the Capitol a vestibule was planned which now forms the vestibule leading to the law library of the United States Supreme Court. In this vestibule are six columns composed of cornstalks with the capitals modeled from ears of corn. Mr. John H. B. Latrobe in his address before the American Institute of Architects, previously referred to, states that these columns were modeled by Giuseppe Franzoni. We quote the following from a letter written by the architect, Latrobe, August 28, 1809, to Mr. Jefferson, who was then residing at Monticello:

DEAR SIR: I have packed up and sent to Richmond to be forwarded to Monticello, a box containing the model of the capital of the column of the lower vestibule of the Senatorial department of the North Wing of the Capitol, which is composed of ears of maize, on a short frustrum, raising it about four feet from the ground. It may serve for a dial stand; and should you appropriate it to that use, I will forward to you a horizontal dial in Pennsylvania Marble of the proper size. These capitals during the summer session obtained me more applause from the members of Congress than all the works of magnitude or difficulty that surround them. They christened them "the corn cob capital," whether for the sake of alliteration I cannot tell but certainly not very appropriately. * * *

Concerning these columns in the vestibule of the law library of the Supreme Court, there seems to be a clashing of authority. Mr. S. D. Wyeth, who in 1865 commenced the publication of a series of books under the general title "The Federal City" or "Ins and Abouts of Washington," attributes these capitals to Carlo Franzoni, a younger brother of Giuseppe Franzoni, who came to this country subsequent to 1815. He also attributes the allegorical group in plaster in the law library to Carlo Franzoni and fixes the date of its execution as 1817. This group is called Justice and Fame, and the question may properly arise as to whether this is not the composition of Giuseppe Franzoni, who was engaged in the modeling of a figure of Justice for the court room in 1809, as shown by the letter from Mr. Latrobe to Thomas Munroe of September 14, 1809, and previously referred to. We know, however, by the letter of Mr. Latrobe to Thomas Jefferson, dated August 28, 1809, that the capitals of this vestibule were modeled prior to August 28, 1809. It is difficult, however, to trace step by step the records of the art works of these early sculptors. This is due to some extent to the destruction of a great many public documents during the War of 1812. From this period there is great difficulty in identifying specific works upon which these sculptors were engaged. The manner in which accounts were kept at that time and the fact that payment for their services came from the general fund for the completion of the Capitol gives us little information with which to follow the progress of their different activities. We know from contemporaneous records that the architect, B. H. Latrobe, was made a fellow of the Pennsylvania Academy of Fine Arts in 1810, and that by invitation he delivered an address before the Society of Artists in the United States May 8, 1811, at Philadelphia. The address, while of a scholarly type, dealt largely with the history of art during the Grecian and Roman prosperity, and especially showing that art had flourished during the days of the Republic of Greece some centuries before the Christian era. In the course of his address the following language occurs:

I have, however, I fear, dwelt on this part of my subject to the fatigue of your patience; but if a conviction can be wrought, and diffused throughout the Nation, that the fine arts may indeed be pressed

THE "CORNCOB" CAPITALS

Designed by Benjamin H. Latrobe and executed by Giuseppe Franzoni in 1809

into the service of arbitrary power, and—like mercenary troops do their duty well while well paid—yet that their home is in the bosom of a republic, then, indeed, the days of Greece may be revived in the woods of America, and Philadelphia become the Athens of the Western world.

In the meanwhile the impending war with Great Britain had resulted in a condition of uncertainty throughout the country which made appropriations for the completion of the Capitol very difficult to obtain. The Capitol at this time consisted of two rectangular buildings with an open space between, the northern building being occupied by the Senate, the Supreme Court of the United States, and the Library of Congress; the southern building contained the Hall of the House of Representatives, a Chamber whose enrichment with sculptural decorations far exceeded any plans which had been made for the Chamber occupied by the Senate. Giuseppe Franzoni and Andrei were still at work, and the attachment which had existed for years between Latrobe and Thomas Jefferson remained unbroken. We introduce here another letter from Jefferson to Latrobe showing the completion of a medallion executed for Mr. Jefferson, the nature of which has not as yet been determined, and its location, if it still exists, is unknown:

MONTICELLO, *January 25, 1812.*

DEAR SIR: I was on a visit of six weeks to a distant place of mine when the elegant work of Messrs. Franzoni and Andrei arrived, and an attack of rheumatism, subsequent to my return has prevented till now my acknowledgment of it; and what acknowledgment can I make adequate to its merit? The one formerly contemplated is unworthy of a thought, and nothing in that line to which my resources are competent, would be its equivalent. Can there be the hope of any occasion ever occurring in which I can be useful to them, and make them sensible of the value I set on their exquisite medallion; of my thankfulness for it, and my wish for some occasion of rendering them any service in my power? Until this occurs I shall consider myself much their debtor, and as what has passed on the subject has always been through yourself, I must solicit through the same channel a conveyance of these sentiments to them with the assurance of my respect, nor am I at all unmindful how much it is to your good will that I owe this beautiful performance; but the occasions of being thankful to you have been so frequent that an expression of my sense of them can be but a matter of repetition, and as it is however, accept as a cordial offering and with it the assurance of my great respect and esteem.

(Signed)   THOS. JEFFERSON.

Mr. LATROBE.

Affairs a little later seemed to have been approaching a crisis. In an appropriation bill approved July 5, 1812 (Stats. L., vol. 2, p. 775), an appropriation is made for the payment of $2,500 for the compensation of the late surveyor of public buildings (Architect Latrobe) to the 1st of July, 1811, when his duties in that capacity ceased. There is also contained in the same appropriation bill the following:

SECTION 2. And be it further enacted, that a sum not exceeding one thousand dollars be, and the same is hereby appropriated for the purpose of enabling the President of the United States to return to their native country, the two Italian sculptors lately employed on the public building, and to close the original contract made with them on behalf of the United States.

It is somewhat singular that the following section of this same act authorizes the superintendent of the city of Washington to contract for the completion of the sculpture in the south wing under the direction of the President of the United States and appropriates $4,000 for this purpose. This condition admits of several conjectures, the most probable one being that the Government contemplated the closing of the contract with the Italian sculptors and completing the sculptural work in such a manner that less money would have to be expended than would be with Franzoni and Andrei continued in their employment. Although we are anticipating events which transpired later, it may be proper to say in this connection that however much these Italian sculptors may have desired to return to their Italian home they did not at this time do so. The war with

Great Britain had rendered ocean voyages decidedly unsafe, and for awhile they remained in this city where they had resided for the preceding six years.

A description of the Hall of Representatives as it was completed or partially completed before its destruction by the British August 24, 1814, is obtained from two different sources. Wyeth in his Federal City states:

> The Hall of Representatives was semicircular with a vaulted ceiling. Twenty fluted Corinthian pillars of sandstone supported the entablature. The American eagle carved in sandstone by Signor Giuseppe Franzoni ornamented the frieze over the Speaker's chair. On the opposite frieze was a group by the same artist representing Agriculture, Commerce, Art, and Science.
>
> Behind the Speaker's chair sat the figure of Liberty, with an eagle by her side, her right hand presenting the Constitution and in the left a Liberty cap. Her feet rested on a reversed crown and symbols of monarchy and oppression.

Another description of the Hall of the House of Representatives is found in the address of John H. B. Latrobe before alluded to. It is so interesting that it has been considered well worthy of quoting in its entirety:

> I can still recall, among the shadowy impressions of my earliest boyhood, the effect, approaching awe, produced upon me by the old Hall of Representatives. I fancy I can see the heavy crimson drapery that hung in massive folds between the tall fluted Corinthian columns to within a short distance of their base; and I remember, or think I remember, the low gilded iron railing that ran from base to base and over which the spectators in the gallery looked down upon the Members on the floor. I seem to see, even now, the Speaker's chair, with its rich surroundings, and the great stone eagle which with outspread wings, projected from the frieze, as though it were hovering over and protecting those who deliberated below. Of course, after so many years, it is not impossible that form and color have been given to the memories of a boy, nine years old at the time, by what he has since seen in the portfolios which were almost the picture books of his childhood. Be this as it may, however, there can be no question that the old Hall of Representatives was a noble room. Even the British officer who was ordered to destroy it is reported to have said as he stood at the entrance, "That it was a pity to burn anything so beautiful." In a letter from Mr. Jefferson to Mr. Latrobe, dated Monticello, April 14, 1811, he says: "I declare at many and all occasions that I considered you the only person in the United States who could have executed the Representative chamber, or who could execute the middle building on any of the plans proposed"; and again on the 20th of July, 1812, referring to a letter in which Mr. Latrobe had spoken of attacks upon him, Mr. Jefferson says: "With respect to yourself, the little disquietudes from individuals not chosen for their taste in works of art will be sunk in oblivion, while the Representative chamber will remain a durable monument to your talent as an architect."

After this but little was done in the way of appropriations except to provide for the repairs to the north wing of the Capitol. This section of the building seemed to be constantly in a condition requiring the continuous expenditure of money to remedy original construction. We must bear in mind that at this time these two widely separated portions of the Capitol Building were connected by a wooden passageway, so that the unoccupied space between the Senate and the House of Representatives might be crossed with as little discomfort as possible. This condition continued until the War of 1812, and that memorable day, August 24, 1814, which witnessed the destruction of the United States Capitol by its being set on fire by the British forces. Of the actual occurrence there is but little definite history. The annals of Congress referring to this event seem to be occupied almost wholly in an attempt to determine how it happened that the American forces were not able to check the British advance at the Battle of Bladensburg and by this failure permitted the capture and the burning of the Capitol. The best account of what transpired at the Capitol while occupied by the British is taken from Hazelton's "National Capitol, Its Architecture, Art, and History." The information from which this statement was originally obtained has not been identified.

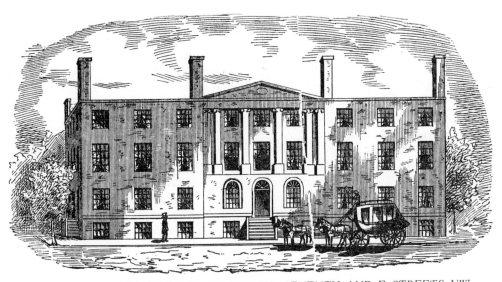

BLODGET'S HOTEL, NORTHWEST CORNER SEVENTH AND E STREETS NW.

*The first session of Congress after the Capitol was burned by the British August 24, 1814,
was held in this building, at that time used by the Post Office Department*

* * * On reaching the Capitol, the enemy detailed a body of men to take possession of the building. Admiral Cockburn incensed, no doubt, by the shot which killed Ross's horse, impudently ascended the rostrum in the House of Representatives, sprang into the Speaker's chair in his muddy boots, and, calling his battle-stained troops to order in mock parliament, shouted derisively: "Shall this harbor of Yankee Democracy be burned? All for it will say, Aye!" An unanimous cry in the affirmative arose from the soldiers, and the order was cheerfully given. By means of rockets, tar barrels found in the neighborhood, broken furniture, heaps of books from the Library, and pictures, including the full-length paintings of Marie Antoinette and Louis XVI, which had been presented by that unfortunate monarch to Congress, the whole structure was soon in flames. * * *

The foregoing statement is used for the purpose of showing the destructive methods adopted by the British while in possession of the Capitol and also to show the destruction of probably the only two paintings in the possession of the Government at the Capitol at the time of its invasion by the British, August 24, 1814. It will be noted that heretofore what has been written upon the works of art and the artists of the Capitol has related only to its sculpture, and it may not be amiss at this time to give the history of these two paintings thus destroyed. The writer is aware that there is a wide difference of opinion concerning the possible destruction of these paintings, and it is claimed by some that the paintings were not destroyed as before described, but that they were in the Capitol at a much later date. The complete and full history of these two portraits would occupy far too much space and probably fail to interest those who may read this work. As briefly as possible it may be stated that they were received as gifts from France prior to May, 1784, and that they followed the varying changes of the Capitol of the United States from one place to another until the Capitol was finally located at Washington in 1800. Mrs. William Thornton in her diary notes the presence of these two paintings in the Senate Chamber at the opening of the session of Congress. Just how long they remained in the Senate Chamber is not known. David Bailie Warden, in his statistical description of the District of Columbia, published in Paris in 1816, states that the portraits are in the Senate Chamber. It appears, however, from a careful examination of this volume that, although published in 1816, there is nothing to show that any of the events recorded belonged to a later date than 1811. It is, of course, wholly within the possibilities of the case that these portraits were in the Senate Chamber at the time of the writing of the book and may not have been at the time of its publication. The records of the Senate tend to show that they were not considered as being of great value, for we find that in 1813 a resolution was introduced looking toward their transfer to the Pennsylvania Academy of Fine Arts, there to remain until the further wishes of the Senate should be contrary to their retention in that institution. This resolution failed to pass, and almost immediately afterwards another resolution was adopted by the Senate instructing the Sergeant at Arms of the Senate to remove these paintings from the apartment in which they were then hanging and, after having them thoroughly cleaned and repaired by some skillful person, to have them placed in some one of the offices of the Senate. This resolution was passed only a day or two before the close of the session for the summer of 1813. It has been contended by others that the portraits were in existence and in the Senate Chamber as late as 1817, and this contention is based upon a letter written by John Adams on March 29, 1817, to William Tudor, in which reference is made to the portraits in the Senate Chamber. Careful examination of the tenth volume of the works of John Adams and the correspondence contained therein fails to show that John Adams was in Washington at any time after August 24, 1814, to the time of the writing of the letter referred to. That Mr. Adams had seen at some time these portraits in the Senate Chamber is not doubted, but the records of the Senate show that in 1813 the pictures were not then in the Senate Chamber and that they were to be placed, after being restored, in some office of the Senate. The contention that these paintings were not destroyed by the British is almost wholly based upon information contained in volume 14 of the records of the Columbia Historical Society, in which volume Thomas Forsythe Nelson published a letter from David Cooke, dated Washington, June 20, 1842, written to his wife in Philadelphia and describing very interestingly his trip to Washington, his visit to the Capitol, and the many objects of interest seen by him upon this trip. In the course of this letter the following language occurs:

They have removed the much-admired, full-length likeness of the murdered King and Queen of France. They have removed the large paintings representing many figures of the first white settlers and the ab-originals engaged in desperate rencounters and sanguinary combat, some expiring while the bloody affray was going on at a time when the land here and around was England's hunting ground. * * *

Mr. Nelson, in his annotation, asks this question: "Were these the same portraits which are referred to in the following interesting record gleaned from the secret journals of the acts and proceedings of Congress? * * *" Upon this portion of the letter and the query of Mr. Nelson has been built up a theory that the portraits were not destroyed and that at some time previous to 1842 they had hung in the rotunda of the Capitol. It is possible that a likeness of the King and Queen of France, as well as the other pictures representing warfare between the whites and the Indians, had at some time been in the rotunda, but it should be remembered that from the time of the completion of the central portion of the Capitol the rotunda and other portions of the Capitol were frequently used for the purpose of the exhibition of pictures which the artists or the owners by this public exhibition hoped to sell to the Government. It would not be strange if portraits of the King and Queen of France other than those claimed to be destroyed by the British were on exhibition in the rotunda a short time before the visit of Mr. David Cooke in 1842, as the rotunda was used for the exhibition of paintings not belonging to the Government up to the year 1868, when Congress enacted legislation prohibiting the exhibition of works of art in the Capitol other than those owned by the Government. Having disposed of the only paintings known to have been in the possession of the Government at the time of its invasion by the British, we may now turn our attention to the condition of the other works of art in the Capitol on August 24, 1814.[1]

It should be borne in mind that the Hall of the House of Representatives was the scene of the greatest demonstration of the intent of the enemy to damage our legislative building. Furniture and all other combustible material had been brought into the Hall of the House and set on fire. The sculptural work of Giovanni Andrei and Giuseppe Franzoni was in a very short time destroyed by the flames. That the columns of sand-stone in the Hall of Representatives did not fall seems to have been a surprise to everyone who realized the extent of the fire within this Chamber. It was necessary to pile cordwood around the columns to prevent their falling during the work of removing the damaged portions of the frieze and of the supporting columns. We are indebted to a sketch by Andrei for the best-known appearance of this Hall after the fire. The extent of this disaster was the subject of a proclamation by President Madison on September 1, 1814, addressed to the people of the United States. A special message was issued September 17, 1814, addressed to the President of the Senate, and his sixth annual message addressed to the Senate and House of Representatives was issued September 20, 1814. As soon as it had been determined that the condition of the walls of the north and south wings would permit the restoration of the interiors without razing walls and rebuilding, Latrobe was sent for and the work of restoration commenced.

Giuseppe Franzoni, who came to this country to execute the sculptural decorations in the Capitol, died in Washington April 6, 1815. It had been expected that both Franzoni and Andrei would be returned to Italy, but the condition of the ocean travel, owing to the war with Great Britain, had been such that both sculptors remained in Washington, although Congress had made an appropriation providing the money for their return to Italy and their contract with the Government had terminated. Mr. Franzoni had been a substantial citizen of the city during the period of his residence here and had accumulated considerable property. At his death he was survived by his wife Camilla Franzoni, four daughters, and one son in this country and one daughter in Italy. He died without leaving a will, and his wife and George Blagden were appointed as the administrators of his estate.

The experience of Mr. Latrobe, the architect, with these Italian sculptors had not been entirely satisfactory. Mr. Latrobe seemed to feel the sculptors were too slow in completing work assigned to them, and before severing his connection with the work in 1811 he had intimated that the carving of the Corinthian capitals could be accomplished

---

[1] Another reference to the destruction of the portraits of Marie Antoinette and Louis XVI is found in Philp's "Washington Described," p. 65, published in 1861, in which the following statement is made:

"In the room adjoining the Senate Chamber portraits of Louis XVI and Marie Antoinette, King and Queen of France were cut out of the frames and burned or stolen. The building was fired in several places and soon wrapped in flames."

Further reference to the portraits of King Louis XVI and Marie Antoinette is found in the following legislation as shown by Senate bill 2591, Forty-eighth Congress, second session, introduced January 27, 1885:

"A Bill to authorize the purchase of certain portraits to replace those presented by the French Government and destroyed in the burning of the Capitol in eighteen hundred and fourteen.

"Whereas at the close of the Revolutionary War the Government of France presented through the American minister Robert Morris, portraits of King Louis the Sixteenth and Queen Marie Antoinette, which were placed in the Capitol and were destroyed with that building in 1814: Therefore, Be it enacted by the Senate and House of Representatives of the United States of America in Congress assembled, That in commemoration of the invaluable services rendered to our forefathers by King Louis the Sixteenth and Queen Marie Antoinette their portraits shall be replaced in the Capitol, and that the same shall be obtained through the American minister accredited to France.

"Section 2. That the sum of ———— thousand dollars, or so much thereof as may be necessary, now in the Treasury of the United States is hereby appropriated for said purpose, subject to the order of the Secretary."

Beyond the reference of this bill to the Joint Committee on the Library there appears to be no further action taken. This is referred to in proof of the existence for many years of the tradition that portraits were burned in the Capitol in 1814.

CARLO FRANZONI

Sculptor of the Car of History

Painting presented by Charles H. Franzoni, great-grandson of the sculptor

{ 26 }

with much less cost in Italy than in this country. It seems that this opinion was concurred in by others, and accordingly in August, 1815, Giovanni Andrei was sent to Italy to make arrangements for the carving of the necessary Corinthian capitals for the new Hall of the House of Representatives, which was to take the place of the Chamber destroyed by the British.[2] Mrs. Andrei accompanied him upon this journey, and upon their return in 1816 they brought with them Carlo Franzoni, a brother of Giuseppe Franzoni, and Francisco Iardella. Carlo Franzoni was a sculptor of statuary, Francisco Iardella a decorative sculptor. There is a tradition, and none the less interesting even if only based upon imagination, that Francisco Iardella had been a suitor for the hand of Camilla, now the widow of Giuseppe Franzoni, and that because of the influence of the parents of Camilla the suit of Iardella had been frowned upon on account of the preference for Giuseppe Franzoni. Tradition also has it that Iardella was a cousin of the Franzonis. So much for tradition. The facts are these: Francisco Iardella married Mrs. Giuseppe Franzoni, and the Franzoni children and a large number of Iardella's children formed a happy family, which remained in Washington for many years.

Some interesting history of the conditions existing during the rebuilding of the Capitol is found in the following letter from Latrobe to William Lee, the second auditor, a confidant of President Madison, and evidently a man occupying a place of power in the matter of the administration of the affairs of the Government:

WASHINGTON, *August 13, 1816.*

WILLIAM LEE,
        New York.

MY DEAR SIR: I am sincerely happy to find that you again are on this side of the Atlantic, where you are valued and respected, and are safe from the Anglo Gallican persecution you have lately undergone at Bordeaux. * * * As to Mr. Capellano, we certainly have urgent and immediate occasion for his talents, and yet the organization of the system is such that I fear he will not be employed. Considering my letter to you to be partly confidential I will write you without reserve. * * * At first the commissioners took my advice and sent to Italy for one of whom Carlo Franzoni is arrived and is employed, and his brother [Emanuele Franzoni] is expected, and Mr. Valaperti formerly in the service of the King of Spain came hither and I provided that he should be employed also, but at the end of their reign they acted independently of all advice of anybody—, made daily blunders, and their dismissal gave such general and undisguised satisfaction that the men were really to be pitied.

We certainly have ample employment for Mr. Capellano at the Capitol and nothing would be more serviceable than to obtain the assistance of more able sculptors to restore the figures destroyed by the British. I much fear that with all the aid that we can procure of the two Franzonis,[3] Valaperti and of your Capellano we shall still be behindhand, but I can only recommend, being so situated as to be without the power to employ even a laborer. I will, however, speak to the Commissioner Colonel Lane on the subject and recommend his being sent for, but I can do no more.

        Believe me very truly yours,

B. H. LATROBE.

It has heretofore been stated that the claim has been made by descendants of Giuseppe Franzoni that a cordial friendship existed between the sculptor and President Jefferson. Of course the Washington of 1806 was not the Washington of the present time, and President Jefferson managed in some way to find time to be helpful and friendly in his

---

[2] On July 28, 1816, the following article appeared in the Florence Gazette, as a letter from Carrara, Italy:

"The Duchess Maria Beatrice, while visiting numerous studios in this city, was charmed by the beautiful work being done under the personal direction of Signor Andrei for the Capitol of the United States. The work is being done by Messrs. Franzoni and Casoni. Andrei, an Italian, is at present domiciled in the United States and has returned to Italy for a period of nine months to have created 24 column tops for the main salon of the New Capitol."

[3] The expectation that Emanuele Franzoni would later be employed was not realized.

SMALL ROTUNDA, SUPREME COURT SECTION

The "tobacco" capitals date from 1816 and are the work of Francisco Iardella

relations with the sculptor Franzoni. This is shown by the following copy of a letter from Mr. Jefferson to Giuseppe Franzoni under date of March 5, 1807:

Thomas Jefferson informs Mr. Franzoni that he had inquiry made into the subject of his two statues and he now incloses him the information from the Collector of Baltimore. By this you will perceive that to obtain a more proper appraisement Mr. Franzoni must appoint one appraiser and the Collector another who will estimate them on such evidence as Mr. Franzoni can give of their value, but he will see that there is no time to be lost as they are advertised to be sold on the 12th inst.

If Mr. Franzoni needs further information he had better wait on the Comptroller, Mr. Duvel, with an interpreter. Thomas Jefferson salutes Mr. Franzoni with esteem.

An interesting note upon the conditions attending the restoration of the Capitol, some of the changes made, and some new features introduced is found in a letter from Mr. Latrobe to Thomas Jefferson, written from Washington, November 5, 1816:

THOMAS JEFFERSON, Esq.,
    Monticello, Virg.

DEAR SIR: Your letter of the 27th. of August received. I was confined to my bed by a bilious fever. * * * You have done my capital much honor in making it the support of your dial. The columns and capitals as executed and standing in the north wing of the Capitol on the ground floor were not much injured by the British, so little indeed that I wish some part of the building to remain as they left it. I do not propose to repair them unless the president shall order it to be done.

By the suggestion of the Senate I devised a very material alteration of their accommodations especially a great enlargement of the Chamber itself.

The great staircase must give way to the improvements. You probably recollect that, as a curious and difficult combination of admirably executed stone work, it was one of the most remarkable parts of the Capitol, but it was much injured by the Lanthorn, which being of wood, fell burning through the dome, and resting on the stairs, burnt many of the principal stones.

The staircase has now another situation. It will be less curious but have I think some beauty. The area of the stairs will be occupied by a vestibule, in the center of which a circular colonade will support a dome for the purpose of admitting light. The columns of the rotunda, 16 in number, must be more slender than the Ionic order will admit, and ought not to be of the Corinthian because the chamber itself is of the Ionic order. I have therefore composed a capital of leaves and flowers of the tobacco plant which has an intermediate effect approaching the Corinthian order and retaining the simplicity of the Clepsydra or Temple of the Winds. Below is a very hasty, and imperfect sketch of the capital.

Iardella a sculptor who has just arrived, has made an admirable model for execution in which he has well preserved the botanical character of the plant, although it has been necessary to enlarge the proportion of the flowers to the leaves, and to arrange them in clusters of three. When we have done with the model I will take the liberty of forwarding it to you. I have neglected so long to answer your very kind letter, that I must intreat you to attribute my silence to anything but a diminution of my respect and attachment. Believe me, that it never can cease.

    Yours very respectfully,   B. HENRY LATROBE.

This letter is important for the reason that it fixes definitely the period of the tobacco capitals in the small rotunda just north of the main rotunda of the Capitol and for the further reason that it conclusively proves that the six cornstalk columns in the small vestibule at the entrance of the present law library were in the Capitol at the time of its being burned by the British in 1814, the only instance of decorative sculpture work known to remain after the occupancy of the Capitol by the British.

Although the death of Giuseppe Franzoni had ended the employment of the only statuary sculptor at the Capitol and by some considered the leading sculptor in the United States at that time, there was near at hand a sculptor of considerable merit who was later to appear at the Capitol and assist in the sculptural decorations of the central portion of the Capitol. For the following information we are indebted to the reminiscences of Rembrandt Peale in the January number of The Crayon for the year 1856:

The Battle Monument of Baltimore was designed by Maximilian Godefroy. For the execution of the sculptures designed for it, Sig. Capellano, recently arrived in New York, was recommended, who came

THE OLD HALL OF THE HOUSE OF REPRESENTATIVES
NOW KNOWN AS STATUARY HALL

The plaster model of Liberty above the frieze is by Enrico Causici; the eagle on the frieze
by Giuseppe Valaperti; the ceiling painted in relief by Pietro Bonanni

on to Baltimore; but not finding Mr. Godefroy at home, made his house his domicile, much to the surprise of the black cook who had charge of the house with a limited supply of change.   I was informed of the dilemma, and wrote to Mr. Godefroy, but received no answer, as the artist, in a secluded spot was absorbed in making an elaborate drawing of the Natural Bridge in Virginia and forgot everything connected with the Battle Monument.   The poor sculptor became impatient and talked of returning to New York.   Not to lose the chance of detaining perhaps an excellent artist, an occupation was suggested.   Robert Cary Long, the architect of St. Paul's Church, in anticipation of some future occasion of completing his design had caused two large blocks of freestone to be built in the upper front—one for the figure of Christ breaking bread; the other, Moses holding the tables of the law.

Mr. Capellano was delighted with the idea of getting to work; but it was necessary to decide upon his ability, and I proposed to Mr. Long that I would give forty dollars, if he would contribute an equal amount to pay the sculptor for two small models in clay.   They were executed to my satisfaction, and a subscription of a thousand dollars was soon raised for the Church.   The sculptor was quickly installed on his elevated platform, and one of the figures was nearly completed before Mr. Godefroy returned to bargain for the proposed sculpture for the Battle Monument.   It was not long before he found full employment at the Capitol at Washington, as well as at Baltimore.

He was a most industrious man and so devoted to his marble that he could not spare an hour to learn either French or English; and his wife who had joined him from New York, told me that she believed that he would turn to stone himself.   Fifteen years after this (in 1830) I was surprised one fine afternoon in the Boboli gardens at Florence on being accosted by a well dressed Signor with his gay wife and five fine children.   It was Capellano, who acknowledged my timely service to him, and informed me that having made money enough in America, he had bought "uno piccolo pallazzo" to enjoy the remainder of his days in his native city.

Another sculptor who aided in the restoration of the Hall of the House of Representatives, now known as Statuary Hall, was Valaperti, a sculptor possessed of considerable ability and who left but one example of his work[4] so far as known in this country. Soon after its completion he disappeared. It has been suggested that he may have committed suicide by drowning in the Potomac, but of this nothing definite is known. At about this time the State of North Carolina enacted legislation providing for a statue of Washington to adorn the State Capitol at Raleigh. The authorities in charge of this project placed considerable reliance for advice upon their Representatives in Congress, and these Representatives secured such information as was possible from those best calculated to give advice which would aid in the selection of a sculptor. From a publication entitled "Canova's Statue of Washington," by R. D. W. Connor, we select the following letters which give important information upon the condition of the sculptor's art in this country at that time:

CITY OF WASHINGTON *8th Jany: 1816.*

SIR: I had yesterday the honor of your letter, respecting the very praiseworthy determination of the Legislature of your State to erect a Statue to the great Washington, and it would give me very great satisfaction to be in any manner instrumental in forwarding a work so highly honorable to the State you represent.

I went this morning to see an Italian Artist of great merit, Signor Valaperti, who has had some expectation of being employed in the public works here; but nothing has yet been decided relative to him. I inquired what price would be demanded for a full size Statue of the General executed here in his best manner. He said about five thousand dollars. I enquired how much would be demanded by the great Statuary Canova, an Artist in Rome, whose works equal the best Antiques. He answered about the same sum. We have found Marble in this Country equal to the fine Marble of Carrara. It is to be had in large Blocks near Baltimore as fine and correct likeness. The celebrated Ceracchi executed Waterford in Loudoun County, Virginia, of equal quality, and may be obtained in large blocks. The bust of Washington was taken by Houdon of Paris, and the Casts in this Country are all from that Bust. Houdon took an impression from the Face of the General, and finished his work by a good impression from the Mask; whereby he obtained a very fine and correct likeness. The celebrated Ceracchi executed a grand bust of the General, which was purchased for, and is still in possession of the King of Spain. This marble Bust had great dignity of character, and was considered as a masterpiece. I doubt, however, whether the likeness exceeded or even equalled the one by Houdon. These Busts being done by the first Artists, and Casts being within the command of the European Sculptors a fine Statue could no doubt be executed there. The Statue of Pitt, in New York, cost one thousand Guineas many years ago, and I have heard that it is a capital performance. Flaxman engaged to execute a fine full length Statue of the General for seven hundred and fifty Guineas, and he is the first Artist in England, or in the world, except Canova. Whoever should be employed to execute the Statue should be particularly cautioned against using the full length Painting of the Genl. by our Countryman Stuart; for though he is unequalled in a Head he cannot draw a Figure. The one in possession of the Marquis of Lansdowne is entirely out of proportion; but the proportions by our Countryman Trumbull are correct; yet the head is not to be compared to the Stuart's. Any Statue executed in marble may easily be packed up so safely as to be imported without danger. Any further information in my power will be given at any time with pleasure.

I am, Sir, with the highest respect and esteem yrs. etc.

WILLIAM THORNTON.

Honble. NATHL. MACON,
     Represe. in Congress.

WASHINGTON, *January 9th, 1816.*

The Honble N. MACON,
     Senate U. S.

DEAR SIR: I received your letter yesterday afternoon, and give you with pleasure all the information I possess on the subject of the Statue of General Washington proposed to be erected in the State House of N. Carolina.

The Statue may be very admirably made in this country by Mr. Valaperti. He is an Italian artist who after being long employed in Spain, was engaged before the fall of Napoleon in the decoration of his palace at Malmaison. The distracted state of France induced him to seek his fortune in this country,

[4] The eagle on the frieze of south wall. (Mills's Guide to the Capitol.)

and he has brought with him the most portable of his works,—a few most admirable sculptures in Ivory. He also brought with him letters of recommendation to the President and to other prominent characters in this country. I have likewise received by him letters from France bearing high testimony to his character as an artist and as a Man. But his works bear him the best testimony, and in a few days, I will call upon you with him, and you shall see them. I may therefore answer that the Statue may be as well executed in this country, as in Italy, unless an enormous price is given to Canova, or Thorkeld, men who for many Centuries have had no equal, and whose abilities it is almost impossible to purchase.

I give it now as my opinion, that the Statue would be made by Mr. Valaperti for $1,500. I wished to have had a bust of General Jackson made for the Corporation of this city, but the project ended in an address. On this occasion I made an estimate with Mr. Valaperti, and rating the time necessary to be employed very moderately, we found that it would cost $800 in workmanship. The Marble and putting up would probably have made it $1,000. Now the bust being the most important part of the work, I presume $1,500 would be a just price for a whole length figure. The block, transportation, and putting up, upon a plain and solid pedestal, would cost, I think, $1,000 more; at the outside, say in all $2,500.

We have in America marble very superior in texture to that in Italy which is the kind always used for statues, and I believe, is the best that country affords. The Parian and Penthelic Marbles of antiquity are not inferior to ours, but they are very superior to that of Italy. They are however inaccessible, being in the hands of the Turks. The difficulty here is that our quarries are scarcely opened. An admirable Mass of Statuary Marble has lately been found very near Baltimore, and I have found as good as any in the world in Loudoun county, Virginia. From what I hear of the Baltimore Marble, as to its size it would probably be the source from whence to obtain a proper block. The strata of that of Loudoun County are too thin. Vermont is inexhaustible in good statuary marble, but the transportation of so large a block as is necessary would render it inadvisable to procure it from thence. The only doubt therefore which remains is as to procuring a proper block of Marble. Enquiry will either remove it, or oblige you to resort to Europe. This enquiry I will most cheerfully make, if you wish me to do so.

Of the two sculptors for whom I sent in the year 1804, Franzoni, the sculptor of Statues, is dead. But Andrei is now in Italy directing the Sculpture of the Capitals of the Columns of the House of Representatives, experience having taught us, that they may be procured for about half the price there of Marble, for which they could be made here of Freestone. If therefore the Statue were made in Italy, there would be a certainty that it would be well executed, Mr. Andrei being not only an excellent Sculptor, in his line, himself, but a Man of rare personal virtue, united to first rate talents, and firmness of character. He has also a perfect knowledge of the temper of our country, and would see that no Italian frippery should degrade the dignity of a figure of Washington. He would employ a good artist. But I feel an objection to the Carrara Marble which is subject to black specks in the body of the stone, which sometimes hit upon the nose or under the eye and disfigure the finest Statues. Nor may they be discovered until the work is too far advanced to be thrown away. Mrs. Barlow has a bust of Carrara Marble by Houdon, of her husband. The likeness is strong, but the face has many black spots about it. Our Marble is free from this defect, and is also of much finer grain.

As to the price of the work in Italy, it would be less there, than here. The transportation, freight, duties and charges, would however lessen the difference of price. Mrs. Barlow's bust cost in Paris 600 dollars, including the Material. Mr. Bacon in London 20 years ago, executed the Marble Statue of Lord Rodney, for the Island of Jamaica, with its Marble Pedestal, also decorated with Sculpture, for 1000 Guineas, about $5000 besides the price of the Marble which was 3 Guineas per foot ($15). In Italy it would have been done cheaper, but not so well.

Upon the whole, whether executed in Italy or in America, less than $2,500 to $3000 should not be calculated upon. If, by any endeavors of mine, the price can be diminished, or in any way the object of the Legislature of your State promoted, my anxiety for the advancement of the fine arts would impell me to exert myself on the occasion, without the inducement which I sincerely and warmly feel, to contribute as much as possible to honor the memory of Washington, as well as to show my personal respect for yourself.

Yours very truly,

BN. LATROBE.

Although the only paintings belonging to the Capitol had been burned in the fire of August 24, 1814, and although the opportunities for hanging paintings in the Capitol were limited, still the Congress seems to have turned from the art of the sculptor to the art of the painter and commenced legislation providing for paintings to decorate the central portion of the Capitol, which at that time consisted chiefly of plans upon paper. In

{ 32 }

JOHN TRUMBULL

Represented by four historical paintings in the Rotunda

From a painting by Gilbert Stuart, with the background by Trumbull, while Trumbull was confined in prison in England as a suspicious and dangerous alien

3

the Senate on Monday, January 13, 1817, this being the second session of the Fourteenth Congress, the following resolution was introduced:

"*Resolved by the Senate and House of Representatives of the United States of America, in Congress assembled,* That the President of the United States be and he is hereby authorized to employ John Trumbull, of Connecticut, to compose and execute a painting commemorative of the Declaration of Independence; to be placed when finished in the Capitol of the United States." Wednesday, January 15, 1817, read the second time and on motion of Mr. Goldsborough referred to a select committee with instructions to confer with Colonel John Trumbull for the purpose of selecting two additional scenes from the period of the revolution to be the subjects of paintings which together with the Declaration of Independence, when completed, are to be deposited in the Capitol of the United States. Messrs. Barbour, Goldsborough and King were appointed the committee.

On January 22, 1817, the Senate resolution to employ John Trumbull to compose and execute certain paintings was read twice and referred to Messrs. Calhoun, Hopkinson, Wilde, Randolph, and Pitkin.

On January 25, 1817, the resolution was reported without amendment and committed to a committee of the whole House.

On January 27, 1817, the resolution was voted upon—ayes, 114; noes, 50. Mr. Randolph voted for the resolution.

It may be interesting to note that at the time this legislation was pending a small copy or sketch of the proposed painting, Signing the Declaration of Independence, was on exhibition in the House of Representatives. This is shown incidentally by the remarks of Mr. Wright in the House of Representatives on January 24, 1817, in the discussion of the bill for enforcing neutrality. Mr. Wright said:

He believed it would be found that it had its origin in treason and disaffection and came from some whose devotion to Kingly governments and hostility to Republican principles had induced them to oppose the American Revolution and who would now rejoice to commit to conflagration that constellation of worthies (pointing to Colonel Trumbull's painting of the signature of the Declaration of Independence). The acts of 1794 and 1797 went far enough for any necessary purpose and he, therefore, hoped the bill would be rejected altogether.

An interesting comment upon the debate in the House of Representatives which preceded the passing of the Senate resolution for the employment of Colonel Trumbull to execute paintings of the Revolutionary War is found in the National Intelligencer for Tuesday, January 28, 1817:

The subject which occupied the larger part of the sitting of the House of Representatives yesterday, was the joint resolution which has already passed the Senate for authorizing the President to employ Col. Trumbull, the distinguished American Artist, to execute four paintings commemorative of the principal events of the Revolution. The debate was desultory, but pleasing, and occasionally animated by flashes of eloquence. The resolution was passed by a very large majority, and no doubt will receive the approbation of the President.

The subjects spoken of for these national paintings, are the Declaration of Independence by the Congress; the surrender of Burgoyne at Saratoga; the surrender of Cornwallis at Yorktown, and the resignation of his sword to Congress by General Washington at Annapolis. The size of the pictures is proposed to be 12 x 18 the figures to be as large as life.

Judging from one or two of these paintings on a small scale, now exhibited in the Hall of the Representatives, these great historical paintings, when executed, will do credit to the artist and to his country.

On February 6, 1817, the President approved the legislation of Congress, the approved act reading as follows:

Resolved by the Senate and House of Representatives of the United States of America, in Congress assembled, That the President of the United States be, and he is hereby, authorized to employ John Trumbull of Connecticut, to compose and execute four paintings commemorative of the most important events in the American Revolution, to be placed when finished in the Capitol of the United States.

By this legislation the four historical paintings by John Trumbull, now in the rotunda of the United States Capitol, were bargained for. The execution of the paintings occupied some six years or more, and the amount paid therefore was $32,000. This sum was paid in installments; the first, of $8,000, was evidently paid before the work had been commenced, and the four remaining installments of $6,000 each were paid from appropriations made at different times up to March 3, 1823, when the last appropriation was made. The first painting delivered was that one known as the Signing of the Declaration of Independence, and the interesting history of that painting, delivered at the Capitol in 1819, will appear in the chronological events of that year.

An interesting contribution to the history of the historical paintings in the rotunda and the difficulties which were encountered in arranging for a suitable method for their presentation will be found in the attached letters of July 13, 1817, and October 10, 1817, from B. H. Latrobe to Col. John Trumbull, the painter of Trumbull's historical paintings in the rotunda.

WASHINGTON, *July 13, 1817.*

Colonel TRUMBULL,
    New York.

DEAR SIR: You know how I am obliged to fight my way along in completing the Capitol. I have now arrived, not without a hard struggle at the commencement of the only apartment in this enormous piece of patch work, the center hall, that is to say, in completing the fourth side of the north wing, part of the wall of this grand circular hall is now actually erected, and that in the handsomest manner possible, although even at this moment exertions are made to defeat my ultimate intentions.

In the mean time the circular form of the room, has made me reflect whether after all the intention may be agreeable to you, because it is concaved. The distance between the chord and circumference will be about one foot. The distance between the grand niches of the Hall will be 24 feet, a margin of three feet of plain freestone wall on each side leaves 18 feet clear for the picture including the frame. Now I fear that this space may be too little, for if the frame should be one foot wide there will remain only sixteen feet clear canvas, I am unwilling to diminish the breadth of the freestone margin much below three feet but I would spare 6 inches on each side if you require it, so as to give you 17 feet of canvas and perhaps you could be satisfied with a frame of narrower dimensions making out in depth what you want in breadth. I conceive I shall carry up the margins 3 feet wide and if you must narrow them I will contrive them so as that they may be cut to please you when the picture is to be put up.

As to the frame I would solicit your advice. It appears to me that so small a curvature will not injure the effect of the picture, and the canvas I think can be as easily stretched on a concave frame as upon a flat one after it has been painted upon a flat one, but I am on forbidden ground and succumb entirely to your opinion and directions.

I propose to carry up the back of the recess of the picture in brick and to make it 14 inches deep so as to leave room for a deep frame and at the same time to be able to line the back of the recess with cedar plank and also leave an inch of air between the canvas and the wall lining in order to preserve perfect dryness, but otherwise it would be safer if the canvas touches a lining, if you have heard a Dutch woman at New York poked her finger up to the hilt through the Queen of France's petticoat to try what stuff it was made of, and the hole remained 'till the picture was destroyed in 1814.[5]

The height of the picture may be what you please, and you please and you will much oblige me by letting me know what your intentions are in that respect that I may build accordingly.

I have begun and intend to finish and transmit to you a decent drawing of the whole hall but now at this season I am so wholly occupied that I must ask your indulgence for the present.

Pray present my best respects to Mrs. Trumbull, and be assured of the most sincere esteem and attachment of

    Yours respectfully,

                                  B. H. LATROBE.

---

[5] Evidently referring to the portrait of Marie Antoinette, and its destruction by the British in 1814.

{ 35 }

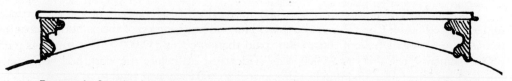

Drawing by Latrobe showing curvature of picture frames for historical paintings in rotunda to fit recessed wall to contain paintings

WASHINGTON, *October 10, 1817.*

COL. TRUMBULL,
    New York.

    DEAR SIR: You will I am sure forgive my delay in answering your two kind letters, when I inform you that the death of my eldest son at New Orleans has so depressed and almost broken my mind that I have not been able for the last fortnight, to attend to business or to friendship. He was perhaps too much the pride of his parents and upon his early eminence the hopes they had built were too sanguine and too confidently cherished. But regrets are now, alas, useless, and it is both necessary and wise to turn away if possible to all that can recall him to our recollection until time shall have softened the grief that never can be extinguished.

    To advert therefore to the situation of your pictures. I have contrived to make the spaces devoted to them 19 feet long by 14 ft. 7½ inches high. Therefore they may be raised to the highth of 5 ft. 7½ inches from the floor which would protect them against the touch and an iron railing in front at three feet distance would protect them even against the reach of a cane. There would in this case remain 6 inches on each side for a wooden frame and a foot may, if required be put upon the surrounding stones. The space of 2 ft. 7½ inches which remains after deducting the height of the picture, may be filled up with an architectural tablet containing the inscription or an index to the portraits of the piece, an index, which it appears to me, will be very properly given, for most of those personages whose features your pencil will immortalize, as history will their attainments, are already dead, and tradition itself will in a few years forget all but their names.

    The springing line of the great niches, is unfortunately also irrevocably fixed in solid stone. It is 22 ft. 6 inches from the floor. If therefore, your pictures could (on account of other obstacles which I will presently mention) be hung above the impost which surrounds the hall, and from which the heads of the niches spring, I should regret to see them at such a distance from the eye, which even if they leaned forward, would require the spectator to be 40 or 50 feet from the wall to prevent the effect of foreshortening the figures on the picture itself by the natural perspective. If again the pictures were considerably elevated, the refraction of the light in the angle nearly in which it would fall upon them from the Dome would give them that glazed appearance, that is so injurious to pictures lighted horizontally. Besides as the wall is circular it would be very difficult to lean them forward. The picture is so large that the chasm between the middle of the frame and the wall below would be very large. The leaning forward of the picture would also hide the sculpture intended above.

    In the situation now prepared no such objections exist provided your two objections can be got out. The first, too great vicinity to the finger, will be removed in the manner above explained; the second the circular surface I think may be made advantageous to the stretching of the canvas, but if it can not then the frame may be laid flat at the back of the recess. The only inconvenience, if it is one, would be that the external ornamental frame would be shallow in the middle and deep at the extremities. You may probably find the above very confusing and unintelligible. I am conscious that my mind wanders perpetually to the sad subject that almost wholly occupies me. But it will serve to explain what I mean generally and especially that our stonework is actually carried up and can not now be changed for I have made your pictures part of the essential character of the design, and, if I could by magic alter the whole arrangement, I should be wholly at a loss how to improve it. The architecture of this vast Dome will in fact owe its merit to your merit.

    I have now to thank you for the pleasure which is mingled with my sorrow, when I look upon the mild countenance of talent and virtue which your bust presents to me at this moment. I have not deserved so much friendly attention at your hands. You might have distinguished older, more eminent, and richer friends, by such a testimony of your esteem; but you never could have bestowed it where it would have been more gratefully received; and where in fact it would have had more of the character of humanity and consolation. The first smile that has shown through the tears of the mother of my lost son, fell on this mark of your kindness. I shall never cease to value it, were it hallowed only by that circumstance, and in truth the only ray of light, from earthly objects that beams through the gloom of our abode at present is shed from your countenance. I thank you sincerely, though I fear incoherently.

As to Cardelli, I know not what to do with him. I have to do with a Commissioner and with a very angry President, to whom I have no access for the law forbids it, and who is surrounded by those who having to justify themselves, naturally lay blame upon the absent.

On his arrival the President misled by I don't know who, expected the Capitol to be finished; of course he was disappointed, and in his first emotion would have ordered my dismissal had he not been prevented by some very disinterested friends. He appointed however, Gen'l Mason, Colonel Bomford, and Mr. Geo. Graham a commission of enquiry into the conduct at the Capitol. These are honorable and good men; but what a system is that which shutting out from the President all direct and professional information, interposes that of men whom neither leisure or knowledge of the subject qualifies to give it, or to explain difficulties or remove the misrepresentations of ignorance or malice. And under such a system it is expected that Genius shall freely act and display itself. I will do for Cardelli what I can, I fear it will be but little.

With the truest and most affectionate respect, believe me very truly yours,

B. Henry Latrobe.

CHAPTER III

CONSTRUCTION OF THE ROTUNDA SECTION OF THE CAPITOL

W E HAVE seen that in the year 1815 Antonio Capellano was employed in Baltimore. Our attention is directed to him again by the following correspondence, which shows the tendency of the time to dispose of sculptors seeking commission in some other way than by paying out real money for their services. From the manuscript files of the Library of Congress we find the following:

[Capellano, Antonio—Letter to James Madison]

SIR: Understanding from Mr. Lee[1] that it was your desire I should go to your Seat to take your bust in the month of September, I have the honor of informing you that I am now at leisure and will set off at any moment you may be pleased to appoint.

The price of a bust the natural size in Italian marble is $800.00. I need not assure you, Sir, that if you do me the honor of permitting me to take your portrait my utmost skill shall be exerted to do justice to the subject.

If you should desire me to go to Montpelier may I request you to have the goodness of indicating the most direct way of reaching it.

I have the honor to be Sir; very respectfully your obedient servant,

ANTONIO CAPELLANO.

PACA STREET, BALTIMORE, *Sept. 5, 1817.*

[Mr. Madison's reply]

SEPT. 8, 1817.

To ANTONIO CAPELLANO.

SIR: I have received your letter of the 5th inst. and thank you for your disposition to accommodate yourself to my conveniency.

Unforeseen engagements will deprive me of the pleasure of seeing you at Montpelier during the present month; and it is probable that the period will be somewhat prolonged. Under these circumstances I can not do better than to leave the favor of a visit from you to be arranged with Mr. Lee to whom I communicate the contents of your letter.

Be pleased to accept my respect.

J. M.

[Extract]

To Mr. LEE, *Auditor.*

DR. SIR: I have just received the enclosed letter from Mr. Capellano, and write him the answer also enclosed. Be so good as to seal and forward it. As it is not presumable that a model in clay without a marble copy would induce him to visit me, and as the expense of the latter is not to be thought of, it will be best to let the object vanish in a manner most delicate towards the artist, and I must apologize for involving on you the task of bringing it about.

In the meanwhile Latrobe was following out the plans for the restoration of the Capitol and the building of a central portion to connect the House and the Senate Chamber. He had found out, however, that the conditions in Washington were not the same as during his previous occupancy of the position of architect. Although Latrobe's journal, from

---

[1] Noted on this letter: "a misapprehension in the case."

which we quote his letter of resignation, does not go into details about the causes which led to his resignation, we find from the Life and Letters of Charles Bulfinch that it had been expected in Washington for some time that either Mr. Latrobe or the commissioner, Colonel Lane, would be obliged to resign. It seemed to be impossible for the two to work in harmony, and conditions were growing worse instead of improving. From letters from William Lee and Hon. Harrison Gray Otis, it appears that their sympathies were with Mr. Latrobe, and it was thought at one time that Colonel Lane would be obliged to vacate his position. The difficulty, which had been pending for several months, was finally settled by the resignation of Mr. Latrobe. We quote the following from the journal of Latrobe:

WASHINGTON, *November 20, 1817.*

The PRESIDENT OF THE UNITED STATES.

SIR: My situation as architect of the Capitol has become such as to leave me no choice between resignation and the sacrifice of all self-respect. Permit me then, sir, to resign into your hands an office in which I fear I have been the cause to you of much vexation while my only object has been to accomplish your wishes. You have known me more than twenty years. You have borne testimony to my professional skill—and my integrity has never been questioned. You will, I am confident, do me justice, and in time know that never the delay nor the expense of the public works are chargeable to me.

I am aware that much inconvenience may arise from my retiring from my office so suddenly. But I pledge myself to furnish drawings and instructions for all the parts of the works that are in hand for a reasonable compensation being made, while my circumstances do not permit me to decline.

I am, very respectfully, your Obdt. servt.

B. H. LATROBE.

The resignation of Latrobe had not been unexpected in Washington. In a confidential letter from William Lee to Charles Bulfinch, under date of September 14, 1817, it was suggested that Latrobe would probably resign and intimated that the place could be acceptably filled by Mr. Bulfinch. It is proper to state in this connection that although Mr. Bulfinch was fully advised of the conditions existing in the office of the architect and of the extent of the friction between the architect and Colonel Lane, Commissioner of Public Buildings, no overtures were made by Mr. Bulfinch toward the acceptance of this office or the possibility of accepting it during the continuance of Mr. Latrobe in the position of architect. The biography of Latrobe is given in a footnote.[2]

---

[2] B. Henry Latrobe was descended from the Boneval family of France, a younger branch of which, John Henry Boneval de la Trobe, emigrated to Holland after the revocation of the edict of Nantz, entered the military service of the Prince of Orange, went with him to England, was severely wounded at the Battle of the Boyne, married and settled in Waterford, and died in Dublin at the age of 96. His son Benjamin Latrobe, born April 19, 1728, joined the Moravian Church, was married, in 1766, to Anna Margaretta Antes, of Pennsylvania, who had been sent to England by her Moravian parents to be educated at a school of "the United Brethren," where Mr. Latrobe met and married her. They had three sons, Christian Ignatius, prominent in the Moravian Church, distinguished for his compositions in sacred music, and known to the literary world by his travels in Africa; Benjamin Henry, the subject of this notice; and Frederick, a physician, who settled at Dorpat, in Livonia. In the history of Manchester, there is an admirable engraving by Bromly of the Rev. Benjamin Latrobe, from a painting by Astley, a distinguished artist, and a memoir showing the high position he held in the regard of his contemporaries.

B. Henry Latrobe was born May 1, 1764, in Yorkshire, England, where his education was carefully attended to by his father; and at 12 years of age was sent to a Moravian Seminary in Saxony, where he remained until prepared to enter the University of Leipsic, where he completed his education. In 1785 he left Leipsic, and with some college friends, in a spirit of adventure and frolic, entered the Prussian Army, as a cornet of hussars; was twice in severe actions, in the last of which he was badly wounded; resigned his commission, and after some time passed in traveling, returned to England in 1786.

On the death of his father, which happened soon after, he entered the office of Mr. Cockerill, as stated in the text, and adopted the profession of an architect.

Here his probation was brief. His acquirements on all subjects, extraordinary for his years, gave him great advantages, and on leaving Mr. Cockerill in 1788, he soon found himself fully occupied, and was made, in the following year, surveyor of the public offices and architect and engineer of the city of London.

In 1790 Mr. Latrobe married Miss Lydia Sellon, sister of the well-known law writer of that name, and by her had two children, a son and a daughter. In 1793 his wife died; and two years afterwards, influenced largely by his political and republican views, and by the same spirit that had carried him into the Prussian Army, he came to America, regardless of the prospect of lucrative employment in England, and declining a surveyorship of the Crown, offered him by Lord Barham, at a salary of £1,000 a year. Embarking at London on the 25th of November, 1795, he landed in Norfolk on the 20th of March, 1796. To

It is worthy of notice that the town of Latrobe—Westmoreland County, Pa.—was named for the architect, B. H. Latrobe.

On the 4th day of December, 1817, Hon. John Quincy Adams, Secretary of State, addressed the following letter to Mr. Bulfinch:

Sir,—I have received your letter of the 26th ult. and am happy to have it in my power to inform you that the office of Architect of the public buildings at this place is offered to your acceptance, with a Salary of 2,500 dollars a year, and the expenses of your removal with your family to this City to be paid. It is the wish of the President and of Col. Lane, the Commissioner of Public Buildings, that you should come on as soon as it may suit your convenience.

I am, with great respect, Sir, your very humble and obedient Servant,

John Quincy Adams.

The formal appointment of Charles Bulfinch as Architect of the Capitol of the United States was made by Samuel Lane, Commissioner of Public Buildings, and dated at Washington, January 8, 1818. Mr. Bulfinch at once proceeded to take up the duties of the office and with his family took up his residence in Washington.

The year of 1817, if Wyeth is correct, marked the completion of the bas-relief in the Supreme Court room of the United States. Wyeth credits this work to Carlo Franzoni, and an inspection of the work upon the west wall of the law library of the Supreme Court, formerly the court room of the Supreme Court, will probably raise a doubt in the mind of the beholder as to whether the same artist who produced that beautiful sculptural work, the Car of History, on the gallery front of Statuary Hall, could ever have produced the bas-relief in the law library of the Supreme Court. Just when Carlo Franzoni commenced his work upon the Car of History is not known. It is claimed by some of the members of the Franzoni family that a daughter of Giuseppe Franzoni posed for the figure of History in this composition. The writer has not found any of the Franzonis contradicting this statement, and it is probably true that a daughter of Giuseppe posed for this celebrated figure. This statuary was completed in 1819 and is signed "C. Franzoni

continue the account of his life would be to make this notice a biography, to do justice to which, a volume would be necessary. Sufficient has been said to supply what seems to be wanting in the brief reference in the text.

Mr. Latrobe died September 3, 1820, in New Orleans, where, at the time of his death, he was engaged in erecting works for supplying the city with water. (Address of John H. B. Latrobe.)

An illustration of the regard of B. H. Latrobe for the sculptor Giovanni Andrei is shown by the following letter by Latrobe to the National Intelligencer. This letter is also a proof of the strong sense of justice existing in the character of Latrobe. He would not permit the character of a worthy man to be called in question without a vigorous protest. The letter referred to follows:

Messrs. Gales and Seaton:

A pamphlet is in circulation, and has been distributed I believe, to the members of Congress, in which the characters of two very worthy men are extremely misrepresented.

Mr. Blagden is one of the most respected citizens of Washington. In the course of thirty years active direction of public works I have never met with his superior as a stone cutter. He has from the establishment of this city, either as foreman, as contractor, or as general superintendent of the work in freestone, conducted himself with such propriety, and exhibited so much skill, activity and honesty, that the author of this pamphlet in question, is the first, perhaps the only one who has called his character in question. A personal dispute, in which both parties were wrong has given occasion to this very unjustifiable attack; and I cannot help regretting that an artist of such great and varied skill as its author, should not have been prevented by respect for himself from making it.

That Mr. Blagden has a secret interest in the quarries of freestone, of which he is appointed to inspect the produce, ought not to be asserted without proof. I do not believe it. But he certainly is innocent of having recommended freestone to be employed where brick would have answered the purpose equally well. The fault, if it exists is mine.

As to Mr. Andrei, as a sculptor of decorations, his superiority speaks for itself, but the trusts which he has faithfully and successfully discharged, independently of his employment as an artist have been very important, and have deserved ample recompense. His average salary, for about 12 years, has exceeded $1200. It is now $1500. If out of this sum he has saved so considerable a fortune as is stated, it proves only that his frugality and good management have equalled his personal virtues and professional skill.

I have no interest *now* in defending these men from an attack upon their characters. But knowing their merits better probably than any one else, a love of justice impels me, without their knowledge to step forward in their behalf. As to the aspersions upon my conduct, they cannot hurt me.

B. H. Latrobe.
Late Surveyor of the Public Buildings, U. S.

(From National Intelligencer, Monday, December 8, 1817.)

CHARLES BULFINCH

Architect of the Capitol (1818–1830)

In Statuary Hall, gallery, front

THE CAR OF HISTORY
Carlo Franzoni, sculptor

faciebat 1819." Unfortunately for the decorative work of the Capitol, Carlo Franzoni died soon after the completion of this memorable composition. From a grandson of the sculptor the writer is indebted for the following information:

Carlo Franzoni was born in Florence, Italy, about 1786. He was a picturesque figure, 6 feet 4 inches in stature, and dressed richly in the prevailing style of his day, wearing knee breeches, silk stockings, and silver buckles on his shoes. His education was of the best. He was a graduate of a school of anatomy before beginning his life work as a sculptor. It is claimed that some of his earliest productions are preserved in the Vatican, Rome, and one piece in the Louvre, Paris. Close application to his work had to some extent impaired his health, and he sought the advice of a physician, who told him that what he needed was regular physical exercise and advised him to get a sawhorse and a saw and spend some time of each day in sawing wood. He used the cellar of his residence for the storage of wood and was working there on the morning of the 12th of May, 1819, when the doorbell was rung violently, startling him to such an extent that he dropped dead from disease of the heart.

We should remember in following the history of the development of the art of the Capitol from year to year that following the burning of the Capitol Congress had to seek other quarters for its legislative assemblies. The first session, following the burning of the Capitol, both Houses of Congress met in the Blodget Building, at that time located at the corner of Seventh and E Streets NW., the site being now occupied by the General Land Office Building. The following session of Congress found both Houses quartered in a building at the corner of First Street and Maryland Avenue NE., known locally for some time as the old Capitol, later as the old Capitol Prison, as it was used for the purposes of a prison for the incarceration of Confederates and suspected Confederate sympathizers during the Civil War. A portion of the building is now occupied as the headquarters of the National Women's Party. In this building Congress remained until the session of December 6, 1819, when the restoration of the Capitol had progressed to such an extent that it was accommodated in its former quarters in that building.

In the meanwhile John Trumbull had been working upon his historical paintings which were designed when completed to be hung in the United States Capitol. Early in 1819 the first painting, The Signing of the Declaration of Independence, was completed and started upon its journey to the Capitol. The painting was exhibited at Philadelphia for some time, where the artist succeeded in taking many subscriptions for engravings of this celebrated painting, which had been engraved probably from one of the smaller sketches. Mr. Trumbull wrote frequent letters to his wife, then residing at 27 Park Place, New York. These letters are admirable examples of letter writing and interesting in the description of a large number of events which formed topics for his ready pen. Among the things he discussed was that always popular and common topic, the weather, and from these letters we have a good description of the condition of the weather from the 8th of January, 1819, to the 3d day of March, 1819, at which time he was ready to return to his home in New York. The letters, 27 in number, are interesting in several particulars. It seems to have been his custom to address his wife as "Dearest and best friend" or "Dearest friend" or "Best friend," and in only 1 of the 27 letters is there anything to show that the person to whom the letters are addressed is his wife. At one time he addresses her as "Dear Sarah." In his letter of February 12, 1819, written from Washington, after complimenting his wife upon her ability to read and define character and stating that one of her predictions had proved to be true, he used the following language:

* * * When the Appropriation Bill was before the House, Mr. Spencer, a New York Member and son of Judge Spencer, one of the Governor's great friends or enemies, as the case may be, made the liberal proposition, that nothing should be appropriated for me because I had exhibited the picture in various cities and made a great deal of money by it. The wise young man persisted in his opposition and found twenty-two or three who voted with him. The bill passed, however, and will soon be before the Senate, where I shall meet either no opposition or a very feeble one. * * *

The letters from Washington relate his experience in making calls at Georgetown during a very stormy night and with the roads in bad condition; of his attending service on Sunday held in the Hall of Representatives, which must, of course, have been in the old Capitol Building; of his calling on Mr. Bulfinch upon Sunday evening and meeting there the clergyman who had preached in the morning, Doctor Kirkland. Of his stay in Baltimore particular reference is made to meeting Judge Pinkney (William Pinkney) and of the messages sent by Mrs. Pinkney to Mrs. Trumbull. It appears that Trumbull called several times upon the Pinkneys and he wrote interestingly of the hope enter-

Washington 19th February 1819 Saturday

My dearest best friend I have just received your sad
Letter of the 16th — I truly regret that you pass your
time so much alone and that you are ill in
addition to the discomforts of Snow Storms & solitude
— be assured dear friend, that I have not lost a
moment here, and will not — it is a strange
place as you know — I have this morning
obtained a Receipt for the picture by order of the
President — and nothing remains but for the
Appropriation to pass — I hope this will be in a
few days, but I really am afraid to leave the
business with any one: for every body is too busy
with their own affairs to pay any attention to me
or mine, unless I worry continually — I am tired
to death, but see no remedy for either of us but patience.
God bless you my dear friend: I will return as soon as possible, and
in the mean time wish you health & what comfort you can find —
Farewele — faithfully ever your T. Trumbull

Letter of John Trumbull to his wife, written from Washington at the time of the delivery of his first
historical painting, The Signing of the Declaration of Independence

tained by Mrs. Pinkney that at last Judge Pinkney would be willing to settle down and remain in his own country, as it seemed she was not at all suited with the life of the wife of a diplomat and with residence in foreign countries. Judge Pinkney afterwards served in the United States Senate, from 1820 to 1822, and died February 25, 1822.

Trumbull remained in Washington watching with eagerness the legislation in his favor which was finally to give him $6,000 in addition to the $8,000 already received. The business was not finally terminated until March 3, 1819, when from a letter written upon that date we find that he intends to sail from Baltimore to New York and by that route he will be able to reach his home much earlier than by traveling by stagecoach. Trumbull continued work upon the remaining three pictures, and on January 27, 1823, he wrote to Charles Bulfinch, the Architect of the Capitol, the following letter:

> DEAR SIR,—May I beg you to inform me the progress which you have made in the great room at the Capitol and when you expect it will be in such a finished state as to be ready to receive the paintings. I am busily employed on the last and should have made great progress but for the loss of time last spring at Washington and subsequently here by the fever. I shall have it ready to deliver early in the next session when I hope the room will be finished so that I may assist in placing them and have the pleasure of seeing them all placed as intended in a good light. I have not received the print which I left for your son to forward to me, nor any letter from you or him since I left you. I conclude that occupation (I hope not ill health) has prevented its being sent and that it is safe in its case at the Capitol.
>
> With kind remembrances to Mrs. Bulfinch, I am, dear Sir, your faithful servant,
>
> J. T.

Among other artists employed in the decoration of the Capitol during the restoration period was one Peter Cardelli. The name of Cardelli brings up another Cardelli who signs his name G. Cardelli, but whose work seems to have been that of a sculptor of portrait busts. Some letters are found of 1819 during the months of August, October, and November, in which he refers to busts which he is forwarding of Jefferson, Madison, Monroe, and J. Q. Adams, and in November, of 1819, he writes concerning a bust of Jefferson and two medals. In this letter he states he is working at the Capitol at carving and that he wishes Madison to recommend him to his friends. In July, 1820, he sends to Madison some busts, which are not described, and states that he leaves soon for a tour to New Orleans. Whether this G. Cardelli and Peter Cardelli are the same is not known. In a sale of autographed letters held in Philadelphia in July, 1923, was a series of letters in Italian by the sculptor, Peter Cardelli, and in a letter of October 3, 1818, he stated:

> I am all the time at work in the Capitol upon the capitals and ornaments, and although it makes me very sad to give up sculpture, I console myself by seeing that I am gaining my living. But the dear Mr. [Bulfinch] does nothing but take away everything which embellishes the Capitol. Mr. Latrobe always knew this, otherwise he would have made the most ordinary store house.

Cardelli seems to have had some very decided opinions upon the general matters of interest; for instance, in one letter he comments upon the ignorance of the commissioners for erecting the Capitol at Washington, but unfortunately he does not give us the benefit of his opinion as to the proper location of the Capitol. He also refers to his reception by Jefferson and Madison in the following language:

> I have been more than well received by Jefferson and Madison; at each house I have been treated as if I were Mr. Adams himself.

So far as the records show there was no further attempt to introduce pictures as a part of the decoration of the Capitol until 1825. In the records of the Eighteenth Congress, second session (vol. 1, p. 624), we find the following:

The Senate next took up the bill making an appropriation of $6,000.00 for the purchase of Mr. Rembrandt Peale's picture (exhibited in the rotundo) embracing an equestrian portrait of General Washington, and equestrian portraits of General Lafayette, General Hamilton and other officers.

Mr. Mills, chairman of the committee, stated to the Senate the reasons which induced the committee to report the bill * * *.

Mr. Holmes of Maine, said that he should be pleased to know what was an adequate compensation for the work in question. "The sum you propose to give is equal to the annual salary of your Secretary of State, superior to that of your Chief Justice of the Supreme Court." He asked whether this work was a year's labor. He thought that the rule adopted by the committee would not have much weight with the Senate, as in his opinion, in the purchase of Trumbull's paintings, they had been abominably taken in. Those paintings, which cost thirty two thousand dollars, were not worth thirty two cents. Mr. Holmes said that he did not pretend to be a critic in painting, but he would say that Trumbull's last painting, commemorative of the resignation of General Washington, was a piece of the most solemn daubing he ever saw. The event it was intended to commemorate was one of the most sublime incidents that ever took place in the country. "But what do you see in the picture? Why, a man, looking like a little ensign, with a roll of paper in his hand, like an old newspaper, appearing as if he were saying 'Here, take it; I don't want to give it up.'" He concluded with moving to strike out $6,000 and insert $4,000.

Mr. Mills replied * * *. He thought it not proper for any gentleman to speak of Colonel Trumbull's paintings as the gentleman from Maine had done, much less so to criticise a work performed by a gentleman who had borne a conspicuous part in the events of those days. * * *

The bill was on motion of Mr. Mills ordered to be laid on the table.

With the death of Carlo Franzoni in 1819 the Capitol was left without a sculptor of statuary. It appears that there had been contemplated considerable statuary for the Senate Chamber. Elliott, in his guidebook, published in 1837, states that it was the purpose of Latrobe to have one of the galleries of the Senate Chamber supported by figures emblematical of the thirteen original States, and that models were actually made by one of the fine Italian artists for this scheme but never completed.

The year of 1824 marks the death of Giovanni Andrei, one of the original sculptors who came to this country in 1806. He was a modeler and carver of decorative sculpture as contradistinguished to a figure sculptor. He was born in Carrara, Italy, in 1770, and died in Washington, D. C., October 21, 1824. His wife survived him and in 1826 was given, through an appropriation of Congress, $400, to enable her to return to Italy.[3] She was the only one of the number of people who had been brought to this country in connection with the sculptural work of the Capitol to return to her native country. It is said by some that Andrei had relatives in Florence, Italy, and that Mrs. Andrei returned to that city in the year 1826. In his report for the year 1824 Charles Bulfinch, the architect, pays a deserving tribute to the memory of Giovanni Andrei.

With the advancement of the construction of the central wing of the Capitol the opportunity for employment increased, and many new artists made their appearance as participators in the decoration of this central building. It is here that we first learn of Luigi Persico, and his previous history has been interestingly related in the reminiscences of Rembrandt Peale, published in The Crayon in 1856.

Although Capellano had been profitably employed in Washington, an artist of superior talents was chosen for more important works—this artist was Persico, who, a few years before obtained a scanty subsistence in Philadelphia by miniature painting and teaching drawing, till an event occurred which brought him forth as a sculptor. On the distribution of medals awarded by the Franklin Institute, there were none for fine arts, but an honorary committee of three was appointed of which I was one, to decide on the merits of two models in plaster—one a portrait from life, by Wm. Rush, our celebrated ship head carver; the other a colossal head from memory, by Persico of Lafayette, who had recently been on a visit

---

[3] Act of May 22, 1826. Stats. L., vol. 4, p. 194.

to Philadelphia. I was late in joining the committee, who had kindly agreed in praise of the work of their fellow citizen; but when I expatiated on the beauty of Persico's classic creation, as the outburst of a genius that had been buried in obscurity, and almost in despair, they agreed with me in voting it the palm of excellence. The language of our decision aroused the torpid ambition of the young sculptor, who proceeded to Washington, to be employed in the costly decorations of the Capitol.

The work of Mr. Persico at the Capitol is represented by the statues occupying niches in the central portico and known as Peace and War. Mr. Persico also executed the large group on the south blocking of the central portico of the Capitol, and known as the Discovery Group. It is stated upon what seems to be reliable authority that the head of Columbus in the Discovery Group was copied from an authentic bust of the explorer in an art museum in Spain. Persico assisted in the decoration of many churches and palaces in Italy, and in the Museum of San Martino in Naples, Italy, is preserved a document showing his employment as a sculptor at the United States Capitol. The sculptural decorations in the pediment of the eastern portico of the Capitol are also the work of Persico. It is claimed by some that the design was furnished by President John Quincy Adams, but if this be true Mr. Bulfinch gives no hint which would furnish an excuse for such a statement, as we can see by reference to a letter from Mr. Bulfinch, dated Washington, June 22, 1825, from which we quote:

* * * Our work at the Capitol proceeds but slowly, owing to delay of contractors in delivering the large blocks for columns. We have received only 4 this season, which are raised into their places, and must have 7 more before the much talked of Pediment can be commenced. With respect to the ornament proposed to decorate this, the artists in general feel much disappointed; about 30 persons presented 36 designs, some well and others badly executed, but none answering the President's idea of a suitable decoration for a legislative building. He disclaimed all wish to exhibit triumphal cars and emblems of Victory, and all allusions to heathen mythology, and thought that the duties of the Nation or its Legislators should be expressed in an obvious and intelligible manner. After several attempts, the following has been agreed upon: a figure of America occupies the centre, her right arm resting on the shield, supported by an altar or pedestal bearing the inscription, July 4, 1776, her left hand pointing to the figure of Justice, who with unveiled face, is viewing the scales, and the right hand presenting an open scroll inscribed Constitution, March 4, 1789; on the left of the principal figure is the eagle, and the figure of Hope resting on her anchor, her face and right hand uplifted,—the whole intended to convey that while we cultivate Justice we may hope for success. The figures are bold, of nine feet in height, and gracefully drawn by Mr. Persico, an Italian artist. It is intended that an appropriate inscription shall explain the meaning and moral to dull comprehensions. I have given you the above, which you may speak of, but I wish it not to be put in print, as the subordinate parts are still subject to alterations.

It would seem, although the records fail to justify the assertion, that the precedent established by the construction of the beautiful ornamental clock known as the Car of History and located upon the gallery front of the Hall of the House of Representatives had created a tendency toward the erection of a clock of an elaborate design for the Chamber of the Senate. Accordingly in 1824 Enrico Causici succeeded in securing a contract for the execution in marble of an allegorical ornament for a clock for the use of the Senate and he received for the model of this projected clock the sum of $2,000. It seems that the expense of the model removed the possibility of any sanction by the Senate of the expense of the execution of this model in marble, and the project was therefore dropped. It seems unfortunate that some engraving or other sketch does not exist to show the design of the proposed ornament.

[From report of Commissioner of the Public Buildings—House Report 106, 18th Cong., 1st sess. (April 13, 1824)]

ENRICO CAUSICI'S CONTRACT FOR A CLOCK FOR THE SENATE

Know all men by these presents that we, Enrico Causici, William W. Seaton, and Joseph Gales Junr. of Washington City, are jointly and severally held, and firmly bound, to Joseph Elgar, Commissioner of Public Buildings, in said City, in the sum of four thousand dollars, to be paid to the said Joseph

THE CENTRAL PORTION OF THE EAST FRONT OF THE CAPITOL

The sculpture in the pediment and the Discovery Group, at the left, together with the statues of Peace and War, under the portico, are by Luigi Persico; the Rescue Group, at the right, is by Horatio Greenough

4

Elgar, his certain attorney, or successor in office; for the which payment, well and truly to be made, we bind ourselves, and each of our heirs, executors, and administrators, firmly by these presents. Sealed with our seals and dated this 21st. day of March, 1823.

Whereas the above Enrico (Causici) hath covenanted, contracted, and agreed to, and with, the above named Commissioner, to execute in marble, an allegorical ornament for a clock, for the use of the Senate, agreeably to a *plaister* model, designed by the said Enrico; to faithfully devote his time, and services, and professional skill, to that object, for and during the term of one entire year, commencing with the date hereof; and to deliver over the said ornament, at the expiration of said term, in its then existing state, to the aforesaid Commissioner, or his successor in office, if required thereto: for, and in consideration of which the said Enrico is to receive the sum of two thousand dollars, to be in full for his professional services, as well as for all expenses incident for the execution of said ornament, for the term aforesaid:

Now, the condition of the above obligation is such, that, if the above-bound Enrico Causici shall well and truly do, execute, and perform, all and singular the covenants, contracts, and agreements above stated, according to the true intent and meaning of these presents, then the obligation to be void, and of no effect; otherwise, to remain in full force and virtue.

ENRICO CAUSICI.
W. W. SEATON.
JO. GALES, Jr.

Signed, sealed, and delivered, in the presence of Thos. Donoho.

I have authorized and directed the Commissioner of Public Buildings to advance to Mr. Causici two thousand dollars, appropriated for an allegorical ornament for a Clock for the use of the Senate on authority of the within obligation.

JAMES MONROE.

WASHINGTON, *March 24, 1823.*

Received, of the Commissioner of Public Buildings, two thousand dollars, it being the consideration within mentioned.

ENRICO CAUSICI.

Witness—GRIFFITH COOMBE.

[Copy of letter from E. Causici to the Commissioner of Public Buildings]

NEW YORK, *16th February, 1824.*

SIR: The model large as life of the allegorical group, intended for the Senate Chamber of the United States, has been completed, some days since. I am only waiting for the new appropriation to begin it in marble.

Accept the sentiments of my perfect esteem, and believe me, sir, your most obedient servant,

ENRICO CAUSICI.

To the COMMISSIONER OF THE PUBLIC BUILDINGS,

Washington City.

NEW YORK, *17th. Feb. 1824.*

I certify, that I have seen, at Mr. Causici's the above mentioned model completed.

J. G. SWIFT.

OFFICE OF COMMISSIONER OF PUBLIC BUILDINGS,
Washington, April 6, 1824.

SIR:—I had the honor to receive your letter of the 3d. instant, requiring information whether the ornament for a clock, for the use of the Senate, was nearly completed, at the time two thousand dollars were paid, on account thereof, to Mr. Causici; or whether he had then executed any considerable portion of the work; and also, whether said ornament is now completed, and if not, when it may be expected to be completed.

During the last session of Congress, Mr. Causici exhibited a plaster model, in miniature, of a group of figures, designed by him, as a time piece for the use of the Senate; and when the bill, making appropriations for the public buildings, came before that body, an amendment was introduced, appropriating

THE PLASTER STATUE OF LIBERTY

Executed for the old Hall of the House of Representatives by Enrico Causici

On the frieze below is shown a fragment of the eagle by Giuseppe Valaperti

{ 51 }

two thousand dollars, for that purpose, as it was understood, of having Mr. Causici's design executed in marble, Mr. Causici had previously estimated, that it would occupy him five years to execute his design, and that the cost would be 10,000 dollars. This statement was made in the House of Representatives, (by the Chairman of the Committee on the Public Buildings) in opposition to the Senate's amendment, but that amendment was finally passed. In consequence of the representations made to the President of the United States, of these circumstances, I received his directions to pay the 2,000 dollars appropriated as above to Mr. Causici, as a salary for one year of his services; and upon his giving satisfactory security, to advance that sum before the work commenced, which was done accordingly. A copy of the contract made with Mr. Causici and his securities, is enclosed. Of the progress made in execution of his contract by Mr. C. I have no information, but what is contained in his letter of the 16th. ultimo, a copy of which is also enclosed.

I have the honor to remain with great respect, Your most ob't. serv't.

J. ELGAR. *Com. P. B.*

Hon. JEREMIAH NELSON,
Chairman of the Committee of Expenditures on the Public Buildings &c. &c.

While contracts were being made for the decoration of the exterior of the central portion of the Capitol, work was also progressing upon the interior of the rotunda. The work as completed does not command commendation from the various critics who have discussed it. To the casual observer it will seem as though the unfavorable criticisms are just, but it should be remembered that a great difference exists between the standards of 1825 and the standards of the present day, and that decorations in high relief in public buildings were rare at that time. It should also be considered that the material (soft sandstone) in which these carvings were executed does not permit of the best of sculptural efforts. The attempt to place in these small spaces a suitable presentation of historical events seems to have been doomed to failure, and perhaps the existing works are as good as could reasonably be expected under the circumstances. The Preservation of Captain Smith by Pocahontas is the work of Antonio Capellano, who has executed much better work in his bas-relief upon the wall of the portico over the Columbus doors. Enrico Causici executed two bas-reliefs in the rotunda, entitled "The Landing of the Pilgrims" and "Conflict between Daniel Boone and the Indians." Another work of Causici is the plaster cast of Liberty which occupies the niche above the frieze in Statuary Hall. His most ambitious work in this country, however, is the colossal statue of Washington which surmounts the Washington Monument in Baltimore. Two other sculptors who were employed upon the work in the rotunda were competitors for the commission for the Washington Statue in Baltimore, but Causici underbid Antonio Capellano and Nicholas Gevelot. The height above the street of this statue is so great that it is not possible to judge whether the likeness of Washington has been retained. The sculptor Causici was a native of Verona, Italy, and is said to have been a pupil of Canova. Causici claims for himself the distinction of having executed the first bronze bust in the United States, that of William Pinkney, which in 1823 he offered to the Baltimore bar for the sum of $700. It would be interesting if this bust could be located, as its claim to being the first one executed in the United States would make it valuable as a record showing the condition of bronze founding in the year 1823.

Over the north door of the rotunda is the bas-relief William Penn's Treaty with the Indians, by Nicholas Gevelot. Wyeth in his monograph upon the rotunda and dome states that this work has been severely criticized, and in his general remarks upon the condition of the works upon the walls of the rotunda quotes from an article by Mr. William Q. Force, entitled "Picture of the City of Washington," as follows:

Many years ago a band of Winnebagos, one of the most savage of the North American Indian tribes, came through the Rotunda. The delegation consisted of about twenty. They were wild, savage, proud, and almost intractable, and had never before permitted themselves to be induced to visit the settlements of the whites. They were all of them noble looking fellows dressed in their own barbaric uniform. Their faces were painted of various colors, and in their belts were their scalping knives and tomahawks, and over their backs their long iron-looking bows and arrows. Their attention was immediately arrested by this group of statuary—Boone killing the Indian. They formed a semicircle, and the head man stepped forward and stood before the rest. They looked intently for some moments, scrutinizing and recognizing every part of the scene, and suddenly, as of one impulse, they raised their dreadful war cry, and ran hurriedly from the hall.

We have something further relating to Nicholas Gevelot from the House Journal (vol. 21, 19th Cong., 2d sess., p. 297), wherein we read that Mr. Verplanck presented a petition of Nicholas Gevelot setting forth that he executed the tablet in sculpture in the rotunda of the Capitol representing the treaty of William Penn made in 1662 with the Indians, without having previously established by contract with the Commissioner of the Public Buildings any price therefor, but with an understanding that it was not to be less than $1,500, that the commissioner now refuses to allow him more than $750, and praying that he may be allowed the $1,500 for executing the said tablet, which memorial was referred to the Committee on the Public Buildings.

It seems to be impossible to determine whether Mr. Gevelot was successful in his petition for additional compensation for his work over the north door of the rotunda. It is true, however, that none of the people employed about the Capitol received what would be considered in these times sufficient compensation. We find in a report of J. Elgar, Commissioner of Public Buildings, a statement showing an abstract of expenditures for the year 1827, and we reproduce his figures so that an idea of the prices paid at that time may be given:

    Charles Bulfinch, architect, for one year.............................. $2,500
    Antonio Capellano, sculptor, salary for one year....................... 1,500
    Luigi Persico, sculptor, salary for one year........................... 1,500
    Francis Iardella, carver, salary for one year.......................... 1,250

From this same document we learn that George Blagden was paid a salary of $1,500 per annum, and that the rent for a modeling room for Mr. Persico was $75, and that the transportation of stonecutters had cost $122.75.

In a report of the Architect of the Capitol, dated December 27, 1827, for the year 1827, he states:

* * * In the interior of the building the sculptures of the rotunda have been finished and the walls painted * * *. In closing this report I ask leave to add that the rotunda cannot be considered complete while the four large panels are suffered to remain vacant; and to suggest a hope, that measures may be taken to supply them with paintings, conformable to the others, on great national subjects. In the meantime, frames might be made at present with more economy than at any time after the workmen are discharged and their appearance would give an air of finish to the room. * * *

In an estimate of the expense of the work on the Capitol for 1828 we find the following relating to the art of the Capitol:

    Four picture frames complete in rotunda............................ $1,200
    Sculptors and carvers.. 3,000

It can be seen by this that the architect considered that the decorative work for the completed Capitol was then drawing to a close. His suggestions of filling the four vacant spaces in the rotunda probably came from the failure of the Nineteenth Congress in its second session to formulate an acceptable plan for providing paintings for the vacancies.

THE SIGNING OF THE DECLARATION OF INDEPENDENCE

John Trumbull, painter

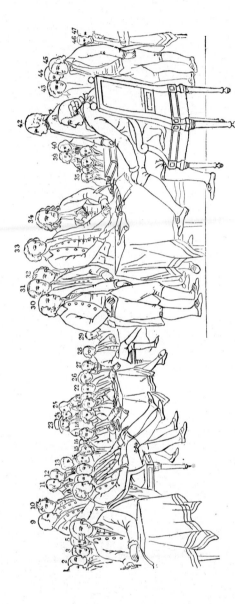

DECLARATION OF INDEPENDENCE

In Congress, at the Independence Hall, Philadelphia, July 4ᵗʰ 1776.

1. George Wythe, Virginia
2. William Whipple, New Hampshire
3. Josiah Bartlett, New Hampshire
4. Benjamin Harrison, Virginia
5. Thomas Lynch, South Carolina
6. Richard Henry Lee, Virginia
7. Samuel Adams, Massachusetts
8. George Clinton, New York
9. William Paca, Maryland
10. Samuel Chase, Maryland
11. Lewis Morris, New York
12. William Floyd, New York
13. Arthur Middleton, South Carolina
14. Thomas Heyward, jr., South Carolina
15. Charles Carroll, Maryland
16. George Walton, Georgia

17. Robert Morris, Pennsylvania
18. Thomas Willing, Pennsylvania
19. Benjamin Rush, Pennsylvania
20. Elbridge Gerry, Massachusetts
21. Robert Treat Paine, Massachusetts
22. Abraham Clark, New Jersey
23. Stephen Hopkins, Rhode Island
24. William Ellery, Rhode Island
25. George Clymer, Pennsylvania
26. William Hooper, North Carolina
27. Joseph Hewes, North Carolina
28. James Willson, Pennsylvania
29. Francis Hopkinson, New Jersey
30. John Adams, Massachusetts
31. Roger Sherman, Connecticut
32. Robert R. Livingston, New York

33. Thomas Jefferson, Virginia
34. Benjamin Franklin, Pennsylvania
35. Richard Stockton, New Jersey
36. Francis Lewis, New York
37. John Witherspoon, New Jersey
38. Samuel Huntington, Connecticut
39. William Williams, Connecticut
40. Oliver Wolcott, Connecticut
41. John Hancock, Massachusetts
42. Charles Thompson (Secretary), Pennsylvania
43. George Read, Delaware
44. John Dickinson, Pennsylvania
45. Edward Rutledge, South Carolina
46. Thomas McKean, Delaware
47. Philip Livingston, New York

THE SURRENDER OF GENERAL BURGOYNE

John Trumbull, painter

In the Rotunda

SURRENDER OF GENERAL BURGOYNE
At Saratoga N Y October 17th 1777

1. *Major Lithcow, Massachusetts*
2. *Colonel Cilly, New Hampshire*
3. *General Stark, New Hampshire*
4. *Captain Seymour, of Shelton's Horse*
5. *Major Hull, Massachusetts*
6. *Colonel Greaton, Massachusetts*
7. *Major Dearborne, New Hampshire*
8. *Colonel Scammell, New Hampshire*
9. *Colonel Lewis, quartermaster general, New Hampshire*
10. *Major General Phillips, British*

11. *Lieutenant General Burgoyne, British*
12. *General Baron Riedesel, German*
13. *Colonel Wilkinson, deputy adjutant general, American*
14. *General Gates*
15. *Colonel Prescott, Massachusetts Volunteers*
16. *Colonel Morgan, Virginia Riflemen*
17. *Brig. Gen. Rufus Putnam, Massachusetts*
18. *Lieut. Col. John Brooks, late Governor of Massachusetts*
19. *Rev. Mr. Hitchcock, chaplain, Rhode Island*

20. *Maj. Rob. Troup, aid-de-camp, New York*
21. *Major Haskell*
22. *Major Armstrong*
23. *Maj. Gen. Philip Schuyler, Albany*
24. *Brigadier General Glover, Massachusetts*
25. *Brigadier General Whipple, New Hampshire Militia*
26. *Maj. M. Clarkson, aid-de-camp, New York*
27. *Maj. Ebenezer Stevens, Massachusetts, Commanding the artillery*

THE SURRENDER OF LORD CORNWALLIS AT YORKTOWN, VA.

John Trumbull, painter

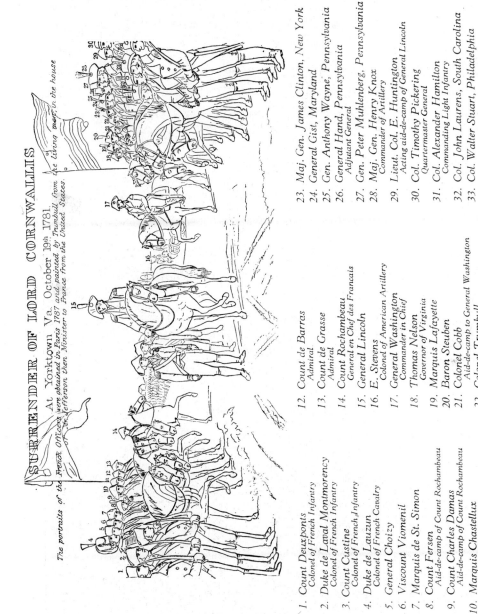

SURRENDER OF LORD CORNWALLIS

At Yorktown Va. October 19th 1781.

The portraits of the French Officers were obtained in Paris 1787 and painted by Trumbull from the living until in the house of Mr. Jefferson then Minister to France from the United States.

1. **Count Deuxponts**
   Colonel of French Infantry
2. **Duke de Laval Montmorency**
   Colonel of French Infantry
3. **Count Custine**
   Colonel of French Infantry
4. **Duke de Lauzun**
   Colonel of French Cavalry
5. **General Choizy**
6. **Viscount Viomenil**
7. **Marquis de St. Simon**
8. **Count Fersen**
   Aid-de-camp of Count Rochambeau
9. **Count Charles Damas**
   Aid-de-camp of Count Rochambeau
10. **Marquis Chastellux**
11. **Baron Viomenil**

12. **Count de Barras**
    Admiral
13. **Count de Grasse**
    Admiral
14. **Count Rochambeau**
    General en Chef des Francais
15. **General Lincoln**
16. **E. Stevens**
    Colonel of American Artillery
17. **General Washington**
    Commander in Chief
18. **Thomas Nelson**
    Governor of Virginia
19. **Marquis Lafayette**
20. **Baron Steuben**
21. **Colonel Cobb**
    Aid-de-camp to General Washington
22. **Colonel Trumbull**
    Secretary to General Washington

23. **Maj. Gen. James Clinton,** New York
24. **General Gist,** Maryland
25. **Gen. Anthony Wayne,** Pennsylvania
26. **General Hand,** Pennsylvania
    Adjuant General
27. **Gen. Peter Muhlenberg,** Pennsylvania
28. **Maj. Gen. Henry Knox**
    Commander of Artillery
29. **Lieut. Col. E. Huntington**
    Acting aid-de-camp of General Lincoln
30. **Col. Timothy Pickering**
    Quartermaster General
31. **Col. Alexander Hamilton**
    Commanding Light Infantry
32. **Col. John Laurens,** South Carolina
33. **Col. Walter Stuart,** Philadelphia
34. **Col. Nicholas Fish,** New York

In the Rotunda

GEORGE WASHINGTON RESIGNING HIS COMMISSION AS COMMANDER IN CHIEF OF THE ARMY

John Trumbull, painter

GEN. WASHINGTON RESIGNING HIS COMMISSION

to Congress at Annapolis Md. Decemb. 23ᵈ 1783

1. Thomas Mifflin, Pennsylvania, President
   Delegate
2. Charles Thompson, Pennsylvania
   Secretary
3. Elbridge Gerry, Massachusetts
   Delegate
4. Hugh Williamson, North Carolina
   Delegate
5. Samuel Osgood, Massachusetts
   Delegate
6. Eleazer McComb, Delaware
   Delegate
7. George Partridge, Massachusetts
   Delegate
8. Edward Lloyd, Maryland
   Delegate
9. Richard D. Spaight, North Carolina
   Delegate
10. Benjamin Hawkins, North Carolina
    Delegate

11. Abiel Foster, New Hampshire
    Delegate
12. Thomas Jefferson, Virginia
    Delegate
13. Arthur Lee, Virginia
    Delegate
14. David Howell, Rhode Island
    Delegate
15. James Monroe, Virginia
    Delegate
16. Jacob Read, South Carolina
    Delegate
17. James Madison, Virginia
    Spectator
18. William Ellery, Rhode Island
    Delegate
19. J. Townley Chase, Maryland
    Delegate
20. Samuel Hardy, Virginia
    Delegate

21. Charles Morris, Pennsylvania
    Delegate
22. General Washington
23. Col. Benjamin Walker
    Aid-de-camp
24. Col. David Humphreys
    Aid-de-camp
25. General Smallwood, Maryland
    Spectator
26. Gen. Otho Holland Williams, Maryland
    Spectator
27. Col. Samuel Smith, Maryland
    Spectator
28. Col. John E. Howard, Maryland
    Spectator
29. Charles Carroll and two daughters, Maryland
30. Mrs. Washington and her three grandchildren
31. Daniel of St. Jennifer, Maryland
    Spectator

[Ho. of Reps., 19th Congress, 2d session.   Rep. No. 8]

DESIGNS OF PAINTINGS

DECEMBER 19, 1826.—Read, and laid upon the the table

Mr. EVERETT, from the Committee of the Library of the House of Representatives, to whom the subject had been referred, made the following report:

The Committee of the Library of the House of Representatives, who, on the 11th of December, 1826, were instructed by the House to inquire into the expediency of offering a suitable premium for each of the best four designs in Painting, to be taken from some of the most interesting and remarkable events of the American Revolution other than those executed by Colonel Trumbull, and now placed in the Rotundo, and to be furnished by native artists before the next session of Congress, have had that subject under consideration, and respectfully report thereon as follows:

The expediency of offering a premium, as indicated by the resolution of the House, appears to depend upon the probability that it would be the means of engaging the ablest and most respectable artists in the country to enter into the competition.   If it be unlikely that artists of this character would enter into the competition, the committee conceives that it would be inexpedient to propose the premium, even though it should be the means of procuring designs of high merit.   It is desirable that the pannels in the Rotundo should be filled with the productions, not merely of respectable artists, but of the very best which the country has produced.

There are some considerations which lead the Committee to fear, that a premium offered for designs, to be furnished in a short time, would not engage artists of this character to enter into the competition. In a large historical painting, the design, though certainly an object of very great importance, is, by no means, the primary merit, which resides in the united result of design and execution.   It is not a matter of course, that the artist able to furnish, in a few months, what would be reputed to be the best design, would be able to produce the best picture.   This remark applies with even greater force to Paintings literally historical—that is, such as borrow their action and personages from history—than to other Paintings, which though technically called historical, impose no restraints on the invention of the artist. In selecting and executing designs of Paintings of scenes of the American Revolution, accident might guide to the choice of a happy subject, and a moderate degree of skill exhibit it, in the form of a very reputable design, without either circumstance furnishing assurance of the talent necessary to the infinitely higher task of executing a historical Painting of the largest size and in the highest style.

The committee have further considered that, in a question touching a liberal profession, respect must be paid to the feelings usually cherished in that profession.   Unless such a mode as that under consideration, of procuring works of art, of the first character, for the decoration of public halls of powerful and prosperous States, be usual, the committee apprehend that the best artists of the country might not regard it with perfect satisfaction.   Without being able to assert the fact positively, as one to which there are few or no exceptions, the committee are nevertheless impressed with a belief, that the offer of a premium for the designs of Paintings is not the accustomed mode of obtaining works of art of the highest character for public halls like those of the Capitol of the United States.

The more usual mode unquestionably has been, at once to engage the services of an artist, who has previously proved himself competent to the trust.   The number of those existing in any one country, at the same time, has not been usually so great, as to make the choice difficult.   The length of time, and the expense of preparations and materials, necessary for the execution of a first rate work of art, on the largest scale, are so great, that nothing but a certain engagement is, in general, an adequate inducement to artists of this character to undertake the execution of a work of the kind in question.   Whenever, therefore, in the opinion of Congress, the time shall have arrived to complete the decorations of the great Hall of the Capitol, the committee are of the opinion that a highly proper course would be, to engage such artist, or artists, as Congress should deem competent to the work, to execute it for an honorable compensation, and under proper directions, as to the choice of subjects.   If it be thought preferable to offer a premium at any stage of the work, the committee apprehend that a premium, equal to the value of the painting should be offered for that which should be accepted as the best.   From the best consideration they have been able to give the subject, they are of the opinion that one of these two courses should be pursued.   They consequently report the following resolution.

Resolved, That it is inexpedient to offer a premium for designs in painting for pictures to fill the vacant spaces in the Rotundo.

Notwithstanding the fact that the movement toward filling four vacant panels in the rotunda with historical paintings, as set forth in the foregoing report (No. 8, 19th Cong., 2d sess.), had met with failure, those in the House of Representatives who seemed disposed to antagonize the expenditure of money for works of art were in the habit of improving every opportunity for the adverse criticism of such works of art as had been installed. In the House proceedings of May 17, 1826, during the debate upon the appropriation bill for completing and furnishing the public buildings, then being considered in Committee of the Whole, Mr. Ingham stated:

He did not rise to oppose the appropriation but said that he had noticed on the walls of the rotunda, certain carvings in stone and among them, the commencement of a design which he understood to be intended to represent the Treaty made by William Penn. He was persuaded that no person could cast his eye on the figure intended for that great and venerable person, and not turn away in disgust. To see a character so eminent for the principles of peace, and so distinguished by his opposition to everything in the shape of military employment, portrayed as himself wearing a sort of military uniform, with a large cocked hat upon his head could produce nothing but surprise and disgust. He had always heard and read that William Penn was a portly figure, with rather commanding and dignified appearance; but the figure here sculptured was a dwarf, and his appearance more ludicrous than anything else. Nor could any descendant of the pilgrims look on the female figure in another compartment of the same room, and be told it was meant to represent one of those who landed at Plymouth, and not feel an emotion of indignation. He wished to know if these pieces of sculpture were to be left in their present state or were to be removed.

Mr. Everett agreed in the opinion expressed by the gentleman from Pennsylvania as to these pieces of carving—he was as much mortified as that gentleman at their appearance, and would be glad to get rid of them—but poor as they would be, he thought that if finished they would not present so great a blemish as if left in their present situation.

It may appear as strange that before the building had been completed grave objection should be raised concerning the acoustic properties of the Hall of the House of Representatives. On the 9th day of February, 1827, there was presented to the House of Representatives a report from a board of inspection appointed by resolution of the House on the 19th of May, 1826, looking toward the employment of William Strickland, of Philadelphia, to act in conjunction with the architect (Mr. Bulfinch) in devising a plan for improving the Hall so far as to render it better suited to the purposes of a deliberative assembly. The report, condensed, indicates that the architects concurred in the opinion that the only effectual remedies of the defects complained of in the Hall were, first, to suspend a flat ceiling of lath and plaster over the whole area of the Hall within the columns and upon a level with the stone cornice or springing line of the same; or, second, to break up the existing smooth surface of the dome by deeply sunk caissons in the manner of the ceiling of the Senate Chamber and of the rotunda. Both architects agreed that the first-mentioned plan would materially impair the symmetry and proportions of the Hall, and Mr. Bulfinch thought it might injuriously diminish the cubic volume of air in the Hall.

This subject, however, should not be dismissed without the statement that this question of acoustics continued to intrude itself upon the attention of the House from time to time until the extension of the Capitol, thereby providing better accommodations for the Senate and House of Representatives.

CHAPTER IV

STATUARY OF THE EAST FRONT OF THE CAPITOL

W HILE the portrait of Lafayette, the gift of the artist Ary Scheffer, had been the property of the House of Representatives for several years, it was not until 1832 that an effort was made to provide a companion portrait of Washington to afford a balance to the decorations of the House of Representatives. On February 17, 1832, the following resolution was reported to the House of Representatives by Mr. Jarvis from the Committee on the Public Buildings:

Resolved, That the clerk of this House be directed to employ John Vanderlyn, of New York, to paint a full length portrait of Washington, to be placed in the Hall of Representatives opposite to the portrait of Lafayette, the head to be a copy of Stuart's Washington, and the accessories to be left to the judgment of the artist, and that the sum of one thousand dollars be appropriated from the contingent fund of the House for the purpose of carrying this resolution into effect. (House Journal, 1st sess. 22d Cong., p. 376.)

Two years later the attention of Congress is again directed to the matter of this full-length portrait of Washington by a second resolution providing for additional compensation for the execution of this portrait commission. This resolution was reported on Friday, June 27, 1834, by Mr. Jarvis from the Committee on the Public Buildings, in the following terms:

Resolved, That the clerk of this House be directed to pay to John Vanderlyn, out of the contingent fund of the House, fifteen hundred dollars as additional compensation for the full-length portrait of Washington, executed by him, to be placed in the Hall of Representatives, in pursuance of a resolution of this House of February 17, 1832. (House Journal, 1st sess. 23d Cong., p. 833.)

Those who have seen the portraits of Washington and Lafayette in the present Hall of Representatives may be interested in the fact that these portraits have always occupied the same relative position—Washington's to the right of the Speaker's chair and Lafayette's to the left. The spaces occupied by these portraits in the old Hall of Representatives, now Statuary Hall, were two panels just north of the screen of columns at the south side of the Hall, these panels now being occupied by ornamental bracket chandeliers.

It was during this same year that definite steps were taken to provide a statue of Washington for the Capitol, and on July 14, 1832, the following legislation was enacted:

To enable the President of the United States to contract with a suitable artist to execute in marble a pedestrian statue of George Washington to be placed in the center of the rotunda of the Capitol the sum of $5000. (Stats. L., vol. 4, p. 581.)

This was the commencement of the legislation providing the means whereby Horatio Greenough was given what was probably the most important commission for a single piece of statuary to any American sculptor. Greenough was but 27 years of age at this time. His life had been one of comparative ease. He was the son of a well-to-do merchant in Boston, Mass., where he was born September 6, 1805. His education was that of the public schools and Harvard University. He had commenced carving figures in chalk while a boy and without any serious study. Solomon Willard, of Boston, gave him some instruction in modeling in clay. Alpheus Cary, a stonecutter, interested him in the carving of marble, while a French sculptor, Binon, then residing in Boston, gave him daily instruction in modeling. He met Thorwaldsen while on a visit to Rome in 1825 and was kindly received by him. Unfortunately, his health was impaired by malaria and he was obliged to return to his native city after an absence of less than a year. Proceeding to Washington, he modeled busts of President Adams and of Chief Justice Marshall. He returned to Italy in 1827 and established himself in Florence on account of its climate and its art advantages. The history of his statue of Washington as erected in the east plaza of the Capitol belongs to a later period, when the further account will be given in its approximate chronological place.

It was early in the year 1834 that Uriah P. Levy, a lieutenant of the United States Navy, presented to the Nation a bronze statue of Jefferson, which for some time occupied a place in the rotunda of the Capitol and was later removed from there to the grounds east of the Executive Mansion, where it remained until the year 1874, 40 years after its gift by Lieutenant Levy. The history of this statue is an interesting one, for the reason that some of its history seems to be clouded in mystery. Lieutenant Levy presented this gift by a letter, one copy of which was sent to the Speaker of the House of Representatives, the other copy to the Vice President. The letter upon being read was in each case referred to the Library Committee for a report. The report was favorable, and it seems to have been the intention of Congress to accept the statue, and the Library Committee practically anticipated the action of Congress and sent to Mr. Levy a letter of thanks for his gift. It appears that a resolution passed the House accepting the statue and requesting the concurrence of the Senate therein and that an almost identical resolution passed the Senate in which the concurrence of the House was asked. For some reason or other it does not appear that final action was taken upon either of these resolutions, although both branches of the Congress had practically voted to accept the gift. Just why it happened that the statue was placed in the rotunda when Congress had voted to place it in the square at the eastern front of the Capitol is not understood. Neither is there any definite record so far as has been found showing the means by which the statue was taken from the rotunda and placed in the grounds of the Executive Mansion. After the lapse of 40 years Mr. Jonas P. Levy addressed a letter to the Committee on Public Buildings and Grounds in relation to this statue and requested that if it was not the purpose of the Government to accept the statue that the statue should be turned over to the heirs of Lieutenant Levy, who had presented it to the Government. The letter was referred to the Committee on Public Buildings and Grounds, and Senator Morrill presented the report of that committee. From this report much information is obtained. It appears that the statue never was placed in the grounds east of the Capitol, the location selected by the Congress at the time of the introduction of the resolution of acceptance. A resolution was introduced February 16, 1835, nearly a year after the statue came into the possession of the Government, which throws some light upon the subject but does not wholly explain how it happened to be located in the grounds of the Executive Mansion. The resolution referred to is as follows:

Resolved, That the Commissioner on the Public Buildings and Public Grounds be directed to remove the bronze statue of Jefferson from the rotunda to some suitable place for its preservation until the final disposition of it be determined by Congress.

There had been from time to time considerable objection to the acceptance of this statue, which, however, never materialized as bearing the support of a majority of the Members of the Congress. One of the objections was based upon the theory that if Congress desired to have a statue of this distinguished man (Jefferson) it would be more consistent with propriety to procure one for themselves than to be indebted to any person

STATUE OF THOMAS JEFFERSON

David d'Angers, sculptor

The first statue placed in the Rotunda

{ 67 }

whatever. At the time that the resolution was introduced providing for its removal from the rotunda one of the Members in discussing the question said that a present ought not be accepted from any but a distinguished source. After being absent from the rotunda for about 40 years the statue was returned to the Capitol and has since been considered a valuable accession to the art works of the Capitol. The work was executed by David d'Angers, and Lieutenant Levy, in the letter in which he tenders the statue to the Government, states that it was executed under his supervision in Paris. The ability of the sculptor has heretofore been referred to in connection with his gift to the Government of a bust in marble of General Lafayette, and further reference will be made in due time to the acquisition by purchase of a replica of the portrait bust of Lafayette and the presentation by the French Government of a bust of Washington, all being the works of this same distinguished sculptor.

So many references have been made to Lafayette on account of the close connection of the works of art with this distinguished person that we feel that it will be in keeping with the purposes of this work to record the fact of his death, which occurred at this period, May 20, 1834. The arrival in this country of the news of his death gave occasion in the House of Representatives on June 21, 1834, for the appointment of a committee to join with a committee of the Senate to "consider and report by what token of respect and affection it may be proper for the Congress to express the deep sensibility of the Nation to the event of the decease of General Lafayette."

President Jackson in his message of June 21, 1834, directed the same honors be rendered on this occasion by the military and naval stations as were observed at the death of Washington.

The Joint Committee on Resolutions reported June 24, 1834—

Resolved, That the President send a copy of these resolutions to George Washington Lafayette and the members of his family, that the members of both houses are directed to wear badges of mourning for thirty days; that the Halls of both houses be dressed in mourning for the remainder of the session, and that John Quincy Adams be invited to deliver an oration upon the life and character of Lafayette at the next session of Congress.

Lafayette was born September 6, 1757, and died May 20, 1834. He had nearly reached the seventy-seventh anniversary of his birth, and his death formed a bond of sorrow between France and the Nation he had served in time of war.

The decoration of the court room of the Supreme Court was continued by giving a commission for a portrait bust of Chief Justice Ellsworth. The legislation referred to is contained in Statutes at Large, Volume IV, page 717, and the act, which was approved June 30, 1834, is as follows:

Be it enacted by the Senate and House of Representatives of the United States of America, in Congress assembled, That the Joint Committee of the two Houses of Congress on the Library be and they are hereby authorized and required to contract with a suitable American artist for the execution in marble and delivery in the room of the Supreme Court of the United States a bust of Chief Justice Ellsworth, and be it further enacted that for the purpose of carrying this act into effect, there be, and hereby is, appropriated $800, to be paid out of any money in the Treasury not otherwise appropriated.

The reader may have noticed the expression "suitable American artist," and it is proper to state in this connection that the busts of the Chief Justices, from the time that the first bust was ordered of John Frazee, with the exception of the bust of Chief Justice White, have been executed by American artists.

Another reference to matters occurring during the year 1834 is found in the diary of Philip Hone, under the date of November 24, which refers to Persico, who had received

DAVID d'ANGERS

*Represented in the Rotunda by the bronze statue of Jefferson, the bronze bust of Washington
and the marble bust of Lafayette*

commissions for statues of Peace and War to be placed in niches of the eastern portico of
the central portion of the Capitol. The reference is as follows:

> The fine old frigate *Constellation* arrived at Norfolk on Thursday, in thirty-eight days from Gibral-
> tar. * * * Has brought over two fine marble statues by Louis [Luigi] Persico emblematical of
> Peace and War intended to ornament the Capitol of the United States accompanied by the artist who has
> also a bust of the hero, General Jackson.

Reference to the records of the Joint Committee on the Library show that on June
21, 1834, the committee voted that H. Auger, of New Haven, Conn., be employed as the
artist for the execution of the bust of Chief Justice Ellsworth, and that the chairman be
authorized to contract with him accordingly. It also appears from the same record that

the Library Committee voted that a joint resolution be reported making an appropriation for the erection of an equestrian statue of Washington in bronze. This action was taken May 30, 1834, and on February 7, 1835, it was voted that an unfavorable report be made on the joint resolution for procuring an equestrian statue of Washington referred by the Senate to the committee on the 3d instant, and on February 14, 1835, Mr. Everett was requested to report facts to the next meeting in relation to the memorial of Nicholas Gevelot, referred by the Senate to the committee, in which he prays compensation for making the model of an equestrian statue of Washington.

The duties of the Joint Committee on the Library extended over a wide field. They were expected not only to attend to matters as related to the equipment and continuance of the Library of Congress, but were also expected to exercise a supervisory power over works of art offered to the Capitol by gift or for purchase, and to have a general charge of such works of art as might be required for the public squares of the city or for the house of the President. At this time there were but very few works of art in the White House, and many efforts were made by those having works of art to dispose of to induce Congress to purchase them either for the Capitol Building or for the White House.

In 1835 Senator Preston offered a resolution to purchase certain paintings in the city on sale by John Brett. The intimation in this resolution is that they might be tastefully arranged in the President's house. In the Senate on February 5, 1835, the joint resolution authorizing the purchase of certain paintings on sale in the city of Washington by John Brett to ornament the President's house was taken up and considered as in Committee of the Whole, and on motion of Mr. Poindexter the blank was filled in with $40,000, the amount to be appropriated for the purchase. The resolution was advocated by Messrs. Preston, Cuthbert, Porter, and Lee and opposed by Mr. Hall, on whose motion the yeas and nays were ordered. On taking the question on ordering the resolution to the third reading, it was negative—yeas, 20; nays, 22.

To the casual observer it may seem that an attempt to involve the Government in an expenditure of $40,000 for the purchase of paintings for the decoration of the presidential mansion was an expense that at that time the country could not well afford. A careful reading, however, of the letter of Mr. Brett, as printed in the National Intelligencer, will show that he was offering not only a large number of works of art, but works of art of exceptional value, and judging from prices obtainable at the present time for paintings of this class the investment would have been a good one for the Government and would have been a great help toward the founding of a national gallery in this city. The letter of Mr. Brett follows:

To the EDITORS.

GENTLEMEN: Do me the favor to insert the following account of the collection of paintings, now under consideration in Congress, to furnish the Presidential Mansion.

I have adopted this plan, desirous of expressing my entire confidence in the value and originality of the paintings comprised in this collection, which, during the long time they have been before the American public, I should imagine to have been seen by the greater part of the artists and amateurs of America, and it was with a view of giving the fullest opportunity for public scrutiny they were exhibited publicly in the Rotunda six months of the last session of Congress.

I would here state of the paintings in this collection, that with one exception, (the denial of Peter by Gherard de laNotte,) they are entire the property of a gentleman of the west of England.

Of these choice works of art, the De Witt Family is an invaluable specimen of portrait painting. Its originality is unquestionable. If not by Rembrandt, by Vanderhelst, who, in some instances is known to have united the grandeur in Chiaroscuro and color of Rembrandt to a superior grace; and for one of whose works, in the Stadt House of Amsterdam, the late Emperor of Russia offered 10,000 guineas.

The Clive family and Dr. John Thomas, by Sir Joshua Reynolds, are not only unquestionable, as to originality, but of the choicest works of this master. Such was the opinion of Sir Thomas Lawrence as to the merits of the Clive Family; and that of Dr. Thomas received the highest encomiums from two of the best judges of the arts, Reynolds and Smith. The Clive Family came from the collection of Lord Morely. Their want of nationality in design in no way detracts from their value or interest, which may be said to be infinitely greater even in America than England, there being no other fine work of Sir Joshua in this country. Their valuation here, however, is assuredly much below their valuation in England.

The Judith and the Ascension (Guidi Reni) are exquisite works of the master. The first was brought from Italy by a gentleman now deceased, and cost him double the sum at which it is now offered. It was pronounced by judges in England as one of the noblest works of the master, and, with one exception, incomparably the finest of his productions in England. And the Ascension was brought from Italy by Barry, the Royal Academician, who considered it a chef-d'œuvre of the master.

The Landscape (by Domenichino) was purchased at the Colonna Palace, by Sir Joshua Reynolds, and sold with his effects after his decease. I know of but one landscape of this great master comparable with it.

The Sea Piece (Calude) the Landscape (Berghem) the Landscape (Van Lint) and the Storm (Backhurpen) are choice specimens, and unquestionable as to originality. The Berghem was purchased from a gallery in Holland by de Blenie; The Van Lint from an amateur of known taste (Col. Hugh Bailey) and the Claude was brought from India by Gen. Moreland who bought it of the Rajah of Bhirtpore.

The St. Jerome, (Leonardo da Vinci,) which is considered the most rare picture in the collection, was a known chef-d'œuvre in the Aldobrandini Palace, and brought to England by Lt. Gen. Maitland, about 23 years ago, who purchased it from the walls of that palace, where it had probably hung from the time of Leonardo. It bears date 1465, with his monogram.

The Herodias and Magdalen (Carlo Dolci) were brought from Italy by an English Nobleman who gave for them three times their present valuation. They are choice works, from the united pencils of Carl and Agnes Dolci.

The pair Game Pieces (by Fyt) the pair Entombment and Descent (Raphael Mengs) The Crucifixion (Tintoretto) and the Gamesters (Recco) were brought to England about 18 years since, from the gallery at Madrid, and received the confirmed guaranty of the Spanish Academy, as known works of the master.

The Garden of Love (Vandyk) The Festival (Jan Steen) and the Calm (Vandervelde) were bought, the first from a gallery in Antwerp, by Reneigale, The Royal Academician—the Jan Steen from an artist in Holland, who preserved it as a chef-d'œuvre for study; and the Vandervelde by Bonelli, an amateur of known taste in Holland.

The Entombment (Titian) The Agony in the Garden (Murillo) and Joseph's Dream (A. Carracci) are undoubted originals of high character; but the time and circumstances of their original importation are unknown.

The Dance of the Seasons, (Nicolo Pousin,) and the Holy Family (Maturino.) The first was purchased in Paris during the revolution, and the latter brought from Italy by Webb, the known critic on the fine arts.

The Landscape, (Gasper Poussin or Oriconati) is an original and beautiful picture. It was purchased from a collector in England.

The Holy Family (Vandyck) is a fine picture of the school. The Landscape, (Teniers,) Flowers, (Van Huysum,) St. John, (LeBrun) and Hunting Season (Vandermeulen,) are unquestionable and fine originals of the masters; and the death of Hyppolitus, (Harlow) and Cottage Grandfather, (Russell,) are good specimens of the English school.

I have only to add, that, from a knowledge of the choice character of this collection (adapted as it is to combine, with suitable and permanent ornament, for the Presidential Mansion, the advantages of a school or gallery) I am confident of the impracticability of procuring works of equal excellence and originality in any degree comparative with the reduced price at which these are offered to Congress.

Respectfully yours,

J. W. BRETT.

(National Intelligencer, Monday, February 23, 1835.)

Concerning the letter of Mr. Brett, the National Intelligencer for February 23, 1835, contains the following:

We insert today in our columns from Mr. Brett, a descriptive catalogue of the splendid collection of Paintings, of which he is proprietor, and for the purchase of which, for the decoration of the President's mansion, a bill is now before the Senate. Mr. B. (who himself is an artist of the first order) has placed in the vestibule of the House of Representatives sketches of all the pictures, showing the proper arrangement of the collection. The effect is very fine and the advantage of thus appropriating them as a permanent ornament to the country and a valuable study for its artists, must be acknowledged by every one. It converts the bare Hall of the Presidential mansion into a splendid gallery, and gives the spacious east room a finished and appropriate elegance.

The year of 1835 was made memorable by the filing of Report No. 5, House of Representatives (24th Cong., 1st sess.), the same being the report upon the petition of Virginia Franzoni, a daughter of Giuseppe Franzoni, who represented not only the Franzoni children but the children of Francisco Iardella. There is so much in this report which relates to the history of the artists connected with the early days of the Capitol that the report is herewith presented in full in order that this valuable history may be preserved:

[Ho. of Reps., 24th Congress, 1st session. Report No. 5]

VIRGINIA FRANZONI, &C.

[To accompany bill H. R. No. 5]

DECEMBER 21, 1835

Mr. E. Whittlesey, from the committee of Claims, made the following report:

The Committee of Claims, to which was referred the petition of Virginia Franzoni, as guardian of the children of Francis Iardella, and also as administratrix of the estate of her father Giuseppe Franzoni, report:

That this case was examined by the committee at the first session of the 23d Congress, and a bill was then reported, accompanied with a report, which this committee refer, and make the same a part of this report. This committee concur in the former report, and report.

FEBRUARY 28, 1834

The Committee of claims, to which was referred the petition of Virginia Franzoni, as guardian of the children of Francis Iardella, and also as administratrix of the estate of her father Giuseppe Franzoni, report:

That the petitioner refers to a claim made by said Francis Iardella, by petition to Congress in 1828, as the foundation of her claim as guardian, and to the facts connected with that claim as the foundation of her claim as administratrix of her father's estate. To understand the grounds of these claims, and how they are connected, the committee have endeavored to trace the history of Giuseppe Franzoni and Francis Iardella, and the character of their contracts with the Government.

Giuseppe Franzoni was engaged with other Italian artists, as early as 1806, to do the carving and statuary for the Capitol and public buildings at Washington. What the precise contract with Franzoni was, does not distinctly appear; but in 1812, after the commencement of the late war, he and Giovanni Andrei, another Italian artist, joined in a letter addressed to Thomas Monroe [Munroe], superintendent of the public buildings, in which they submit certain proposals for executing certain sculpture, agreeably to some verbal conference they had had on the subject, and speak of an act of Congress to which he had drawn their attention, in which an appropriation was made of $1,000 to enable them to return to Italy, in fulfilment of, and to close a contract before entered into &c. (See Laws U. S. vol. 4, page 462, chapter 444.) They go on to speak of their being strangers, and preferring to return home to remaining here, and tender themselves ready to embark whenever it suits the convenience of the Government, in compliance with its part of the original contract. But they say, in consequence of the unexpected state of war, and difficulty in affording them a safe and unmolested conveyance, they are willing to waive or suspend the execution of that part of the contract till a change of circumstances render the performance more convenient to the Government and themselves, provided they are employed in the proposed new contract. It appears that they were employed accordingly, the said Franzoni at the monthly wages of one hundred dollars, and house rent, or to have one hundred and fifty dollars per annum as equivalent to house rent, and this employment to continue till the wishes of either party should put an end to it.

Mr. Franzoni continued in this employ till his death, after the close of the war in 1815. He left a widow, four daughters, and one son here, and one daughter in Italy. No allowance has ever been made to his family to enable them to return to Italy.

{ 72 }

In August, 1815, the Commissioners of public buildings sent said Andrei to Italy, under a new contract, to procure capitals for the columns in the present Hall of Representatives and Senate Chamber, and to engage another artist as a statuary or sculptor of figures, and two inferior artists. In his letter of instructions he was authorized to stipulate to pay the expenses of the passages of these artists and families to this country, and also the expenses for the return of the principal artist or statuary, and family, after he should have served three or four years, and to give him the same salary paid to said Franzoni (equal to $1,350 per annum). To the inferior artist he was to promise them employment for three or four years, and receive allowances adequate to their skill.

Mr. Andrei accordingly engaged Charles Franzoni as statuary or sculptor of figures, and Francis Iardella as one of the inferior artists, and they arrived in 1816. Charles Franzoni brought with him a family. Iardella was unmarried, but after he came to this country, married the widow of Giuseppe Franzoni, and in consequence, probably, the children of G. Franzoni did not return to Italy. On the death of Charles Franzoni, in 1819, his family had an allowance of four hundred dollars to enable them to return to Italy. On the death of said Andrei, in 1824, his family had the same allowance to return to Italy. Andrei had also an allowance for the expenses of his wife's voyage to Italy, when he went there in 1815.

After the death of Andrei, in October, 1824, Iardella was advanced to his place as superintendent of the carving, statuary, and ornamental work of the Capitol, in which employment he remained till the close of the year 1827, and continued occasionally to execute work for the Capitol till his death in 1830. His wife died a year or two previously, leaving, beside the children by G. Franzoni, one daughter and six sons, by Mr. Iardella. These constituted his family at his decease.

Charles Franzoni received $1,350 salary per annum. Mr. Andrei received $1,500 per annum, Mr. Iardella received $1,000 per annum till the 1st of January 1825, and then received $1,250 per annum till December 31, 1827.

In February, 1828, Mr. Iardella petitioned Congress for relief and in his petition set forth that, after his arrival here, under the promise of employment by Mr. Andrei, he was employed on various kinds of work in trial of his skill, for fifteen days, when his compensation was fixed by Mr. Latrobe, the architect, at thirteen hundred dollars per annum, and that he went to work accordingly under what he considered a contract at that compensation; but that afterwards Col. Lane, the Commissioner of public buildings, reduced and fixed his salary at one thousand dollars per annum. That against this he remonstrated, but, after taking counsel, he submitted, with the avowed intention of asking Congress for the difference when he should complete his engagement, and rely on his contract and the justice of his claim for relief.

He further set forth in his petition, that after the death of Mr. Andrei, in 1824, he (Iardella) was advanced to the vacant place for which Andrei had received fifteen hundred dollars salary per annum: yet his own salary was not raised till January, 1825, and then only to $1,250. He asked Congress to make up to him a sum equal to that fixed by Mr. Latrobe, and further, to make to him an allowance to enable him to return to Italy, agreeably to the agreement with Mr. Andrei in Italy, and as had been done for other artists associated with him in the same contract.

The petition was referred to the committee on expenditures on the public buildings, who reported thereon March 4, 1828, unfavorably to the claim. In the report of that committee, they admit it was proved that Mr. Latrobe induced Iardella to believe he was to receive $1,300 salary, and that he was undeceived for one year, when Col. Lane, who alone had the right to fix his compensation, then fixed it at $1,000, and that Iardella, having so long received that sum, and expressed his satisfaction with it, was not entitled to any further compensation. They make no comment on that part of the petitioner's complaint that he was not allowed the same salary as was paid Mr. Andrei, after he was advanced to the same situation. They refer to the instructions given to Mr. Andrei when sent to Italy, to show that he was not authorized to make any agreement with Iardella to make him any allowance to enable him to return to Italy after he ceased to be employed by the Government.

The evidence referred to in the petition of Mr. Iardella to prove Mr. Latrobe had fixed his compensation at $1,300 is not now among the papers nor any other on which the committee on expenditures on the public buildings made their report on that part of the claim. This committee, therefore, adopt the facts admitted in that report to have been proven, and their conclusion also, as far as relates to the compensation of Mr. Iardella, from the time his salary was fixed by Col. Lane to the time he was advanced to the place of Mr. Andrei. It was certainly reprehensible in the agent of the Government here to have so conducted towards a stranger, and one ignorant of our language, as to have induced him to believe his compensation was $1,300, and not to undeceive him for a whole year. He could hardly have been supposed to have known but that the architect had authority to decide on his compensation, as the commissioner had not made known to him the fact to be otherwise for one whole year. On looking into Mr. Andrei's instructions, it will be seen he was authorized to offer the principal artist $1,350 only, and it is not reasonable to suppose he would have held out as encouragement to an inferior artist the probability of receiving so nearly that sum. His disappointment, therefore, did not arise probably from any misrepresentation before he left his native country; but of this there is no evidence one way or the other. This consideration, with the fact reported by the committee when Iardella was alive, that he had expressed his satisfaction with his pay at $1,000, induces this committee to think that no relief to the guardian of his children can be justly required on this part of her claim, except for the first year, when he had been led to believe his compensation was $1,300.

The instructions to Mr. Andrei did not authorize him to provide by contract to pay the expenses of the return of the inferior artists to Italy after they had finished their work here; still he might have misunderstood that part of his instructions, and not have noticed the distinction in that particular between the principal and inferior artist. It does not appear what was Mr. Andrei's representation in that particular to Mr. Iardella. It would be very natural for Mr. Iardella to expect an allowance for that purpose, as the other artists had such made them. In the case of Mr. Bulfinch, without any contract, when he had ceased to be architect, he had an allowance made him by Congress, to enable him to return to Boston, the place of his former residence. However the case might be with Mr. Iardella, the committee are satisfied that the family of G. Franzoni were entitled by contract to such allowance, and have not had it. To this perhaps Iardella was entitled, as he took the charge of the family upon him, but, in return, the care and charge of his young children have been cast on the elder daughter of Franzoni.

The residue of the claim is that arising from the difference between his salary after the death of Mr. Andrei and that received by his predecessor for the same services.

James Young, Richard Holdsworth, and Jeremiah Sullivan, all testify to nearly the same facts, of the skill, industry, modesty, and integrity of Mr. Iardella; that he complained that the superintendent or commissioner did not allow him the same compensation as his predecessor, Mr. Andrei, and that, from necessity, he was compelled to take what was arbitrarily given him, and constantly declared his intention of making a claim for the difference between what he had received, and what had been paid his predecessor, to Congress. It is also stated by the persons employed about the Capitol, and those who had an opportunity of seeing him daily and knowing his habits, that he was very industrious, and not only superintended the work and made the drawings, but continued to perform the manual labor, when not otherwise employed, as constantly as though he had not had any other care or responsibility upon him.

The Committee are of the opinion that Mr. Iardella was well entitled to as high compensation as Mr. Andrei was, while discharging the same duties, and that such was his situation that he was compelled to accept such pay as was offered him, and that he was not bound to be satisfied with what he received as full compensation as under a contract deliberately made.

The committee are of the opinion that the children of Iardella are entitled to $300 for his services for the first year, while he supposed his salary was fixed by Mr. Latrobe at $1,300, and for $1,500 the difference between what he actually received and the rate of compensation paid his predecessor for similar services; and that the heirs of G. Franzoni are entitled to $400, under the contract to return him and family to Italy; and report a bill for that purpose.

The claim of Virginia Franzoni was approved by the Congress, and on February 17, 1836, the following legislation (found in Statutes at Large, vol. 6, pp. 620, 621) was enacted:

Be it enacted * * * That the Secretary of the Treasury pay, out of any money in the Treasury not otherwise appropriated, the sum of four hundred dollars, to Virginia Franzoni, as administratrix of Giuseppe Franzoni, as an allowance to close a contract with him, to return his family to Italy their native country.

SEC. 2. *And be it further enacted,* That the Secretary of the Treasury pay, out of any money in the treasury not otherwise appropriated, the sum of one thousand and fifty dollars, to Virginia Franzoni, as guardian of the children and heirs of Francis Jardella, being the amount due said Iardella for services on the Capitol, in executing the ornamental fine carving and superintending the same, in addition to what he received in his life time.

On January 30, 1836, the Joint Committee on the Library voted in favor of the employment of Hiram Powers as an artist to make a bust of the late Chief Justice Marshall, and on May 9, 1836 (Stats. L., vol. 5, p. 25), an appropriation of $500 was made for the marble bust of Chief Justice Marshall.   It appears that the bust executed by Hezekiah Augur of Chief Justice Ellsworth had been received at the Capitol in the fall of 1837, as the Joint Committee on the Library on October 5 of that year voted that $800 be paid to Mr. Augur for the bust and pediment (bracket) upon condition that he was to put the same up in the court room of the Supreme Court and that the $800 was to be in full payment of all claims and all expenses of every kind and nature.   As this is the only work of this sculptor in the Capitol Building, a brief biography is here given.

Hezekiah Augur was born in New Haven, Conn., in February, 1791.   He was the son of a carpenter and showed at an early age proficiency in wood carving, and his inventive genius found expression in a carving machine, which found much favor among his craft.   His success in carving wood led Professor Morse to advise him to try carving marble.   As a sculptor he seems to have been self-taught and some of his work was carved in marble direct.   His group Jephthah and His Daughter is now in the Art School at Yale.   In 1833 he was made an honorary member of the alumni of Yale College.   His most important commission seems to have been for the portrait bust of Chief Justice Ellsworth in the Supreme Court room.   He died in January, 1858.

In the meanwhile there were four vacant panels in the rotunda of the Capitol. Another effort to complete the series of historical paintings was made in 1837, and a report from Mr. McKeon, known as House Report No. 294 (24th Cong., 2d sess.) is given for the purpose of showing the determination arrived at by the select committee to whom this matter had been intrusted:

[Ho. of Reps., 24th Congress, 2d session.   Rep. No. 294]

PAINTINGS FOR THE ROTUNDA

FEBRUARY 28, 1837.—Read and laid upon the table

Mr. McKeon, from the Select Committee to which the subject had been referred, made the following report:

The select committee to which was referred the resolution of the 23d. June 1836, that a joint committee be appointed to contract with one or more competent artists for the execution of four historical pictures, upon subjects serving to illustrate the discovery of America, the settlement of the United States, the history of the revolution, or the adoption of the constitution, to be placed in the vacant panels of the rotunda, the subject to be left to the choice of the artists, under the control of the committee, report:

They have applied to Messrs. Vanderlyn, Weir, Inman, and Chapman, to undertake the execution of the said paintings.   Two of these gentlemen have agreed to accept the trust, and there is but little doubt that the other two will also undertake.   The committee have agreed that a fair compensation should be allowed to the artists engaged in this national work.   Great labor and some time will be required for a proper execution of the pictures.   Intended, as they are, for monuments as well of the state of the arts in this country at the present period, as for memorials of important events connected with the history of the nation, liberal support ought to be extended to those to be employed by the Government.

The committee have agreed to allow ten thousand dollars for each picture, and recommend that two thousand for each be appropriated at the present session.   This plan of partial payments was practiced in the case of the paintings now in the rotunda; as the artists necessarily will be subjected to some expense, it has been deemed just to give them a portion of the amount to be paid for the several works.

Although Persico had succeeded in securing commissions for the two statues Peace and War and for the group for the south blocking of the east front of the central portion of the Capitol, known as the Discovery Group, he had not entirely disappeared from the notice of the Joint Committee on the Library.   On January 22, 1838, we find this record:

Voted that the consideration of the letter from L. Persico presenting a bust in marble of the Honorable John Q. Adams to the Library of Congress be postponed until the next meeting.

So far as the next meeting is concerned, the question of the acceptance of the bust seems to have entirely disappeared from the mind of the Library Committee, as no reference to this subject is found for several meetings thereafter. It may, however, be one of those matters which are forgotten, for we find in the records of the art works destroyed at the time when the Library was burned, December 24, 1851, that portraits of Washington and John Quincy Adams and a number of old paintings are referred to as having been destroyed, but no reference is made to a marble bust of John Quincy Adams. The bust of John Quincy Adams is in the room of the Clerk of the House of Representatives and is by John Crookshanks King, but the whereabouts of the bust by Persico is not known.

It also appears that in the year 1838 Ferdinand Pettrich presented a claim to the Joint Committee on the Library asking for payment for certain models for statuary prepared by him. Action upon this claim was postponed and the matter referred to Mr. Preston, a member of the committee. The facts in the case are not known except that in the meeting of June 14, 1838, the Library Committee refused to grant any compensation to Mr. Pettrich for the preparation of the models for which payment is asked. Just what these models were and for what purpose they were prepared and whether upon the request of some official of the Government or whether upon the initiative of the sculptor are matters which are not contained in the very brief records of the committee. Mr. Pettrich is not represented in the Capitol by any of his statuary works. Many years later a statue, known as the Dying Tecumseh, was brought to the Capitol and placed upon exhibition for the purpose of sale to the Government. A sale, however, was not consummated, and the work was excluded under the act of 1868, which provided that only works of art the property of the Government could be exhibited in the Capitol. As has been stated, the character or the subject of these models has not been learned, except that the act of July 7, 1838 (Stats. L., vol. 5, p. 267), shows that an appropriation of $600 was made—

for compensation to Ferdinando Pettrich for models of statues for blocking to the western front of the Capitol.

From an old print of the period of 1840 the western front is seen with blockings flanking the steps leading to the western entrance at what is now the terrace level, and the models paid for were probably ordered for the purpose of providing statuary for the western front as a balance to the statuary provided for the eastern front, but the plan evidently ended with the payment to the sculptor Pettrich for the models. Whether the models were excellent or ordinary, this much is proved, that the eastern front continued to be the location of importance, the western front being neglected as though it were the rear of the building, and yet only recently fault has been found because the equestrian statue of General Grant, located in the Botanic Garden, has been erected facing toward the west instead of facing the Capitol.

At the present time our attention is directed to the contract of Luigi Persico by which he was to furnish two statues, War and Peace, to be erected in the niches under the eastern portico of the central portion of the Capitol. These statues were authorized by the act of March 3, 1829 (Stats. L., vol. 4, p. 362)—

To enable the President of the United States to contract with Luigi Persico to execute two statues in front of the Capitol, $4,000.

By the act of May 18, 1830 (Stats. L., vol. 4, p. 382), provision is made for the second payment upon these statues, and the legislation reads as follows:

For the second payment to Luigi Persico for statues for the Capitol, $4,000.

Provision for the third payment was made by act of March 2, 1831 (Stats. L., vol. 4, p. 458), in the following terms:

For the third payment to Luigi Persico for statues for the Capitol, $4,000.

The fourth payment is provided for by the act of May 5, 1832 (Stats. L., vol. 4, p. 512):

For the fourth payment to Luigi Persico for two colossal statues for the Capitol, $4,000.

The fifth and final payment was provided for by act of March 2, 1833 (Stats. L., vol. 4, p. 625), as follows:

For the fifth payment to Luigi Persico for two colossal statues for the Capitol, $4,000.

It is to be presumed that payment was made to the sculptor Persico considerably in advance, the fifth and final payment being made under the act of March 2, 1833, while, by reference to the diary of Philip Hone, it will be seen that the statues did not reach this country until the year 1834 had nearly closed. It will also be remembered that these statues cost the Government $10,000 each, and whether this might be for the time of the contract considered much or little is a matter which will not be discussed at this time. The statues have suffered greatly from their exposure to the varying changes of the climate of Washington and from injudicious attempts in the direction of cleaning and restoring. The last attempt at restoration was made in the year 1921, and at that time portions of hands and portions of the faces of both statues were supplied by the restorer. It was found that the marble had deteriorated to such extent that portions of considerable size could be crushed between the thumb and the finger and reduced to the condition of white sand. This experience and the experience which has attended the deterioration of other statues from Italian marble have conclusively proven that it is unfit for exposed conditions where freezing and thawing can affect the marble.

It was about this time that an opportunity was afforded for the purchase of a bust of Thomas Jefferson, and by the act of May 5, 1832 (Stats. L., vol. 4, p. 513), provision was made as follows:

For the purchase of the bust of Thomas Jefferson, executed by Ceracci, now in the possession of Mr. Jefferson's executor, $4,000, if so much should be deemed necessary by the Committee on the Library.

Unfortunately this bust, with several other works of art, was lost to the Government through the disastrous fire in the Library of Congress in 1851.

We should not forget to mention that occasionally works of art were donated to the Government, and we find by referring to the records of the Joint Committee on the Library, under date of May 28, 1836, that the Library Committee voted that a favorable report should be made on the acceptance of the portrait of the late Judge Johnson, presented to Congress by John S. Coydell, of Charleston, S. C. The Judge Johnson referred to was Justice William Johnson of the Supreme Court, whose death occurred in 1834.

Notwithstanding the previous attempts to provide paintings for the four vacant spaces in the rotunda, those who had been in favor of the continuation of this form of decoration continued their efforts to secure favorable legislation for this purpose. On the 24th of January, 1834, in the House of Representatives, the following resolution was introduced by Mr. Wise:

Resolved, That the Committee on the Public Buildings be instructed to inquire into the propriety and expediency of employing American artists to execute four national paintings appropriate to fill the vacant niches in the rotunda of the Capitol corresponding to those executed by Trumbull.

Upon February 11, 1834, Mr. Jarvis, from the Committee on the Public Buildings, to whom the resolution of January 24 was referred, reported the following joint resolution:

Resolved by the Senate and House of Representatives of the United States of America, in Congress assembled, That a joint committee be appointed to contract with four competent American artists for the execution of four historical paintings on subjects relating to the history of our country to be placed in the vacant panels of the rotunda of the Capitol; the subjects of the paintings to be selected by the artists under the control of the Committee.

On May 7, 1834, in the House of Representatives, the following was ordered:

That the consideration of the Joint Resolution directing contracts to be made for historical paintings for the rotunda be postponed until Tuesday next, the 13th instant.

Without following step by step the progress of the legislation, it will be sufficient to say that the joint resolution was finally enacted June 23, 1836 (Stats. L., vol. 5, p. 133), for the execution of four historical paintings for the vacant panels of the rotunda of the Capitol. This resolution seems to have been enacted for the purpose of fulfilling the contracts made with John Vanderlyn, Henry Inman, Robert W. Weir, and John G. Chapman, and upon March 3, 1837, an appropriation was passed, as contained in Statutes at Large, volume 5, page 173, appropriating $8,000 as a first payment to the artists selected and given commissions for the four paintings referred to. Without going into detail at this time, it will be sufficient to say that Vanderlyn, Weir, and Chapman executed their respective commissions. Henry Inman died during the progress of the work upon which he was engaged, and the panel to have been occupied by the work of Inman was later filled by the painting, Discovery of the Mississippi, by W. H. Powell. Further reference to these four historical paintings will be made at the various periods during which they were delivered to the Government.

While Luigi Persico had been selected as the sculptor for the statues Peace and War and had received payment therefor, he appears to have been successful in securing a contract for two groups of statues to adorn the two blockings on the east front of the Capitol, receiving therefor, under the act of March 3, 1837 (Stats. L., vol. 5, p. 173), the sum of $8,000, of which $4,000 was paid in 1837 and $4,000 in 1838. He also received $4,000 in 1839 and a further payment of $4,000 in 1841. In some manner not disclosed by this brief synopsis of the legislation, in 1840 Persico and Horatio Greenough are mentioned as the sculptors for statues to adorn the two blockings of the east front of the Capitol. It has been previously stated that a commission had been given to Horatio Greenough for his statue of Washington designed for the rotunda of the Capitol, and payments had been made from 1832 to 1840, when we find by the act of July 21, 1840, that an appropriation was made for the cost of preparing suitable foundations for supporting the colossal statue of Washington for the center of the rotunda of the Capitol. It will be seen that approximately at this time Horatio Greenough appears with a commission to execute a statue for one of the east blockings of the Capitol, and inasmuch as the commission for the statue of Washington was the first given it will be far more appropriate for the purpose of this book to relate the facts connected with the making, the transportation, and erection of this statue in the rotunda before taking up the other work of Greenough, that known as the Rescue Group, which occupies the north blocking of the east front of the central portion of the Capitol.

Referring again to the records of the Joint Committee on the Library in so far as they relate to the accessions of works of art, we find that on January 9, 1840, the following appears upon the records of the committee:

Voted that the portrait of Hernan Cortez bequeathed to the United States by the late George G. Barrett, American Consul at Malaga, received from the Department of State be accepted and placed in the Library by the side of the portrait of Columbus agreeable to the desire of the testator.

Again, on January 9, 1840, we find further reference to works of art contained in the following language:

That permission be granted during pleasure for exhibiting in the Library five portraits representing the first five Presidents of the United States, painted by the late Gilbert Stuart and owned by Mr. Phelps of Boston.

We find further reference to these same portraits on March 17, 1840, at which time the records of the committee show

A letter from Mr. Phelps of Boston respecting the five portraits painted by "Steward" (Stuart) was read and ordered, That Mr. Phelps' request to leave them in the Library for a time be granted at his pleasure.

It may be that some who read these records of the Joint Committee on the Library may be curious to know why permission was given for the exhibition of five paintings by Gilbert Stuart in the Library of Congress, and in explanation we must refer to the statement made in the discussion of the portraits of Marie Antoinette and Louis XVI, wherein it was stated that for many years after the completion of the central portion of the Capitol and up to the year 1868 it had been the custom for the Congress to grant permission for the exhibition of works of art in the Capitol to those who hoped by such exhibition to secure the interest of Congress and the possible purchase on the part of Congress of the art works thus exhibited. With this explanation we will proceed with the further explanation that the Joint Committee on the Library for some reason, probably on account of their experience and possibly on account of their willingness, were made the persons through whom works of art were expected to be sold for the adornment of the house of the President. We have heretofore referred to the exhibition of the works of J. W. Brett, who had a collection of paintings on exhibition in the rotunda for quite a period of time and succeeded in having a bill introduced providing for their purchase for the adornment of the President's house. The portraits of the first five Presidents exhibited by Mr. Phelps, of Boston, were placed on exhibition with the hope that Congress might be induced to purchase them for the President's house, which at this time contained only the full-length portrait of Washington by Gilbert Stuart, which had escaped the fate of much of the furniture of the President's house through the foresight of Mrs. Madison in taking this picture from its frame and having it conveyed with her when she made her rapid flight from the city in anticipation of the speedy occupation of the White House by the British. It may not be inappropriate to state at this time that these portraits of the first five Presidents seemed to have been burned during the fire at the Library December 24, 1851, but fortunately Gilbert Stuart had painted several sets of the first five Presidents, and it was not long before another set of portraits of the Presidents were on exhibition at the Capitol in the hope that a sale might be effected. Upon this subject alone—the portraits in the White House and the history of their purchase—an interesting book might be written, but to include it in the present work would be outside of the field intended to be covered.

Much of our information concerning the early days of the art of the Capitol gained from official records fail in the human interpretation, and we are obliged at times to consult the few art books written at about that period in order to understand the impression made upon the writers of these books by the works existing in the Capitol at the various periods.   From Sculpture and Plastic Art, by Pickering Dodge, we obtain the following interesting description:

The capitals of the columns in the Representatives Hall are of the Corinthian order, of white Italian marble, sculptured after the model of those at the Temple of Jupiter Stator at Rome; the colossal figure of Liberty was modeled in plaster by Causici who intended to have executed it in marble; the Eagle sculptured in relief on the stone beneath was copied from nature by Valaperti, an Italian sculptor of high reputation who has left but this single specimen of his talent in our country; and the beautiful Statue of History Recording the Events of the Nation is the work of Franzoni, who died shortly after its completion.   The Goddess is represented upon Winged Car which is in the act of rolling over the globe upon which is figured in bas relief the signs of the zodiac.   Upon the wheel of the car are placed the hours, thus forming the face of the clock in the Hall.   In the Library are two fine marble busts; the one of Jefferson by Cerrachi, and the other that of Lafayette by David of Angers, of colossal and bold proportions presenting simply the head of this noble friend of liberty.   The allegorical representation of Justice and Fame in the Supreme Court Room has neither received nor merited much praise as a high work of art.

Several years had elapsed since Greenough had been given a commission for a statue of Washington.   In 1840 a resolution was adopted placing upon the Navy Department the care for the transportation and the erection in the city of Washington of the statue, which by this time had been completed and was ready for shipment to this country, and accordingly preparations were being made for the reception and installation of this work; a record of such reception and installation is given in the sixth chapter.

CHAPTER V

AILURE attending the efforts of the Joint Committee on the Library to secure favorable action on their plan to provide paintings for the vacant panels in the rotunda through the award of suitable premiums for the best designs submitted, the question of providing additional paintings was permitted to rest until January 8, 1828, when Mr. Hamilton introduced in the House of Representatives the following resolution:

> *Resolved:* That the Committee on the Library be instructed to inquire into the expediency of having an historical picture of the Battle of New Orleans painted and placed in one of the panels of the Rotunda. And that they further inquire into the expediency of engaging Washington Allston to design and finish the work, and if expedient in both contingencies, to ascertain whether, and on what terms he can be so engaged.

As can readily be understood, the fixing in this resolution of a definite artist to design and execute this painting resulted in serious opposition. In the debate which followed Mr. Ingersoll stated that Mr. Trumbull, who had executed the paintings in the rotunda, had not been mentioned as a worthy person for this commission; that he (Ingersoll) did not think Trumbull had been treated fairly; that he well remembered that his paintings had first been placed in a small and obscure room beneath their feet and most unkind and unfeeling strictures had been passed upon them in consequence of this their unfavorable location. The artist and his friends had suffered from this; that he had witnessed the tears of joy in his venerable eyes when they were moved to a situation more worthy of their excellence; therefore he moved to strike out the name of Washington Allston and insert the words "some suitable artist."

Mr. Hamilton said the commission should go to some younger man on account of fatigue attending visiting places to get material for pictures. Mr. Dwight wished to amend to include Battles of Bunker Hill, Monmouth, Princeton, and the attack on Quebec.

Mr. Kremer wished two pictures painted, the Battle of New Orleans and the meeting of the Hartford convention. Mr. Everett, chairman of the Committee on the Library, wished to have the resolution enlarged so that it would provide for the filling of all the panels of the rotunda. Mr. Storrs moved to amend so as to include the words "or such of the victories achieved by the Navy of the United States as in their opinion should be selected for such national commemoration." This was discussed by Representative Hamilton, Representative Barney, of Maryland, and Representatives Storrs, Drayton, Miner, Bassett, Burger, Bartlett, and Everett, and upon vote 80 voted in the affirmative and 99 in the negative. The House then voted on an amendment of Mr. Dwight, "to embrace the Battles of Bunker Hill, Monmouth, and Princeton," and the vote was— yeas, 83; nays, 107. Mr. Hamilton moved the postponement of other business so as to proceed with his resolution; 113 voted in favor of this motion and 80 voted against it, so the discussion proceeded. The resolution was again read. Mr. Everett moved to amend by including the following:

> That the Committee of the House of Representatives on the Library be instructed to inquire into the expediency of taking suitable measures at this time to procure a series of historical paintings for the empty panels of the rotunda.

6

Mr. Randolph said he should vote for the amendment. He added:

Many years ago, when Congress sat in the brick building to the left of this room (probably the old Capitol), a proposition not dissimilar to this was brought forward and referred to a committee of which committee I was one. The result of that proposition is seen now in the rotunda. It ended in that. I should have contented myself with saying nothing if I had not been represented as having expressed a very high opinion; whether of these paintings themselves, or of the original sketches of these paintings I am unable to say which * * * I protest against the whole of these paintings * * *.

He hardly ever passed through that avenue (the rotunda) to this Hall (which was almost every day, the other avenues to it being nearly impossible) without feeling ashamed of the state of the art in this country; and, as the pieces of the great masters of the art have, among the cognoscenti, acquired a sort of nom de guerre, so ought, in his opinion, the picture of the Declaration of Independence to be called the Shin Piece, for surely never was there before such a collection of legs submitted to the eyes of man.

Further amendments were offered, and upon vote the amendments and resolution were defeated.

There is a great deal of traditional history tending to create the impression that Mr. Randolph was enthusiastically in favor of the paintings by John Trumbull at the time of the award of the commission therefor and that in after years he occupied a position of hostility. There can be no doubt that his attitude during this debate was anything but friendly, but the writer has spent considerable time in attempting to find upon what basis the claim of Mr. Randolph's friendliness at the time of the award of the commission has been based, and can find nothing further than has previously been stated in that portion of this work relating to the award, where it is stated that Mr. Randolph voted in favor of the giving of the commission to Mr. Trumbull. Mr. Trumbull, however, seems to take an entirely different view upon this subject, as the following letter to T. Dwight, Esq., of New York, dated at Washington, January 13, 1828, will show:

WASHINGTON, *January 13th, 1828.*

T. DWIGHT, Esq.,
    New York.

DEAR SIR: The newspapers will have shown you that in the memorable battle of the 9th, the mangled bodies of all the painters strewed the bloody field,—Allston, Morse, and myself all fell; but we fell gloriously by the side of the immortal Hero of the Day. You will see that I in particular was most barbarously tomahawked and scalped by the unrelenting hand of the half breed chief of Roanoke and saddest of all to say, by the faithless hand of him who had once been my friend. To speak seriously, it was my fate to be selected on that occasion, by the Hon. John Randolph, of Roanoke, as the butt of his merciless sarcasms.

But, when Mr. Randolph, in his exordium, assigned as the cause of his taking a part in the debate, "the misrepresentations of some obscure annuary published in Philadelphia, in which it was erroneously stated, that he had been partly instrumental in procuring those wretched specimens of the state of the fine arts in this country" he unfortunately for himself gave demonstration of a fact of which the world was not before aware. It is evident that his body is in a state of decay;—but it remained for himself to give the melancholy but irresistible evidence of mental decrepitude; the loss of memory is one of the most unhappy proofs of the rapid approach of that sad hour, "when he will be as if he had not been, and been most witty."

The gentleman had forgotten that the National Intelligencer of the 28th of January, 1817, after stating the arguments on the subject of the Four Paintings, records his name, Mr. Randolph, among those who spoke in favor of the work, as in favor of employing me to perform it.

The gentleman forgot that persons are still living who heard that debate, and who retain a fresh and vivid recollection of the brilliant and beautiful eulogium which he then pronounced upon the small picture of the Declaration of Independence the prototype of that large one which he now so sneeringly abuses.

The gentleman forgot what some others most distinctly recollect—that he then called the attention of the House to the portrait of Richard Henry Lee (whose *shins* are the most conspicuous *shins* in the picture) and pointing to the figure he exclaimed: "Small as this picture is, I seem to see that venerable man sitting in person before me, in all the sober dignity of a senator of ancient Rome, in that elegant attitude so habitual to him, and so well remembered by me; the right hand laid over the left, concealing so happily and so delicately its mutilated remains."

Mr. Randolph forgot, that a copy of the National Intelligencer was at that moment in the library of Congress—where it now lies open to the inspection of every one; convicting him either of loss of memory, or of something incomparably worse;—that human memory should decay as age advances is the decree of Him who formed us, and though we may deplore, we cannot blame;—but the alternative, malignity, is the vile and voluntary production of a wicked heart,—of that I am reluctant to admit the most remote suspicion. When, however, a member of the House of Representatives stoops from his high estate, and forgetting his duty, becomes, not the protector, but the slanderer of individual reputation, he should be reminded that although within these sacred walls, he is privileged to indulge in ample liberty of speech, and may ramble on for hours in all the licentious revellings of wit or of folly, if his colleagues, amused by his wanton eccentricities, are willing to endure him; still there is a limit which it is not wise to pass—for, happily, the Constitution reserves to every individual of us, the sovereign people the same free and equal liberty of speech wherewith to defend our characters out of doors, as any representative can assume to abuse and vilify us within.

Generous minds will also recollect that the professional reputation of an artist, like the fair fame of woman, is a delicate plant, easily blighted by any pestilent breath—and that although it may be sport to some, to indulge in ribald criticisms at our expense—yet, it is death to us.

I make this reply to Mr. Randolph with feelings of deep regret, for I had indulged the hope that his former friendly disposition towards me would have been continued through life;—and that his elegant education, his ample fortune, and his retired mode of life, might have induced him to become an eminent patron and protector of the Fine Arts.

I am, dear sir, your obliged and faithful servant,

JNO. TRUMBULL.

The table showing the scale of wages paid, introduced earlier in this work, showed that Francisco Iardella was paid $1,250 per annum as a carver. The death of Giovanni Andrei left the place of foreman of sculptural decorations vacant, and it appears that this position was filled for some time by Francisco Iardella. It is unquestionably true that he considered his services should be paid for at the same rate formerly received by Giovanni Andrei so long as he was occupying the position made vacant by Mr. Andrei's death. Accordingly, on February 28, a petition in behalf of Iardella was introduced, as follows:

Mr. Van Rensselaer presented a petition of Francis Iardella sculptor at the Capitol, praying to be paid arrearages of salary to which he is entitled by contract, and that provision be made for his return to Italy, at public expense, according to agreement, which petition was referred to the committee on expenditures on the public buildings.

March 4, 1828:

Mr. Swift from the Committee on expenditures on the public buildings, made an unfavorable report on the petition of Francis Iardella, which was read and laid on the table.

May 12, 1828:

Mr. Anderson of Maine, presented a petition of Francisco Iardella, sculptor of the Capitol of the City of Washington, praying that provision be made for the expenses of his return to Italy, according to a contract entered into between him and an officer of the Government of the United States; which petition was referred to the committee of the public buildings.

Francisco Iardella, whose petition has been referred to, was born in Carrara, Italy, in 1793. He was engaged by Giovanni Andrei in 1816 to come to the United States to work upon the sculptural decorations of the Capitol. His first work at the Capitol was the modeling of the tobacco capitals in the small rotunda near the Supreme Court. After the death of Andrei, in 1824, Iardella succeeded to his position as a sculptor in charge of the work at the Capitol and continued in this position to 1827 and was after that time occasionally employed about the Capitol until his death, which occurred in Washington, January 23, 1831. Although unmarried when he came to the United States, he afterwards married Camilla Franzoni, the widow of Giuseppe Franzoni. From the records of the probate court it appears that a stepdaughter of Iardella, Virginia Franzoni, was appointed as guardian of the children of Francisco Iardella on the 23d of April, 1831. These records show the names of the following children: Josephine, Charles, Francis, Nicholas, John, Lawrence, and Joseph. It will be seen that later Virginia Franzoni appears as the petitioner in a claim as the guardian of the children of Francisco Iardella and also as administratrix of the estate of her father, Giuseppe Franzoni. This petition and the report thereon have been previously referred to.

The completion of the original Capitol as first projected by Thornton, that of a central building separating a section devoted to the Senate from a section devoted to the House, was drawing to a close. On the 25th day of June, 1829, the Commissioner of Public Buildings addressed the following letter to Mr. Bulfinch:

SIR: I am directed by the President to inform you that the office of Architect of the Capitol will terminate with the present month.
Respectfully I remain your faithful and obedient servant,
J. ELGAR.

Upon receipt of this communication Mr. Bulfinch addressed a memorial to President Jackson, in which he stated that there were yet several portions of the work in hand and one of particular weight and massiveness which required the superintendence of an architect and suggested that if the President should think proper to recall his order and continue his employment for another quarter it would insure the right execution of the work. It appears that the request was granted and that he was continued in service for a considerable period afterwards. On March 5, 1830, Mr. Bulfinch wrote to Mr. Greenleaf:

Our destination is yet undecided. I may have employment in this city for one more summer but it is uncertain. The Building Committee have unanimously reported in favor of allowing me a sum for extra services and expenses of removal. * * *

On June 3, 1830, Mr. Bulfinch writes his last letter from Washington, in which he states:

I date from this place for the last time; we have taken places in the stage and leave for Baltimore at two o'clock. We have not time to dwell upon regrets at leaving friends who appear sincerely attached to us and a place which has given us a pleasant and respectable home for twelve years and where we leave memorials of us which we hope will long endure. * * *

The departure of Mr. Bulfinch practically closed the completion of the old Capitol Building. It also closed for quite a period the permanent employment of an architect of the Capitol. Thereafter the building was cared for by the Commissioner of Public Buildings with such special services as were required from time to time by an architect temporarily employed. In bringing the history of the Capitol to the year of 1830 we have not by any means carried along the art history so far as that date. While it appears that the actual purchase of works of art had been suspended for a period, although commissions had been given for statuary which were not as yet filled, the purchasing of paintings had been practically frowned upon by the action of the House at the time a proposition had been submitted to fill the vacant panels of the rotunda. In chronological order the next painting to be received was the full-length portrait of the Marquis Lafayette, and this event is connected with history that is interesting irrespective of its connection with the gift of the portrait referred to.

On February 4, 1824, the following resolution was adopted:

The Marquis de Lafayette having expressed his intention to revisit this country—
Resolved by the Senate and House of Representatives of the United States of America, in Congress assembled, That the President be requested to communicate to him the assurances of grateful and affectionate attachment still cherished for him by the Government and people of the United States.

And be it further resolved, That whenever the President shall be informed of the time when the Marquis may be ready to embark, that a national ship, with suitable accommodations be employed to bring him to the United States. (Approved February 4, 1824. Stats. L., vol. 4, p. 78.)

The second session of the Eighteenth Congress met on Monday, the 6th day of December, 1824. Henry Clay was the Speaker of the House at that time. The message of President Monroe was received on December 7, 1824, and in that message a reference to the coming visit of General Lafayette is referred to in the following language:

In conformity with a resolution of Congress of the last Session an invitation was given to General Lafayette to visit the United States with an assurance that a ship of war should attend at any port of France which he might designate to receive and convey him across the Atlantic whenever it might be convenient for him to sail. He declined the offer of the public ship from motives of delicacy, but assured me that he had long intended and would certainly visit our Union in the course of the present year. In August last he arrived at New York where he was received with the warmth of affection and gratitude to which his very important and disinterested services and sacrifices in our revolutionary struggle so eminently entitled him. * * * But the circumstance which was most sensibly felt and which his presence brought forcibly to the recollection of all was the great cause in which we were engaged and the blessings which we have derived from our success in it. * * *

On Friday, December 10, 1824, General Lafayette was publicly received in the Hall of the House of Representatives, the Members of the Senate being present on that occasion. Mr. Mitchell, of Maryland, chairman of the committee on reception, introduced Lafayette, to whom the Speaker made an address of welcome. General Lafayette in his response made use of the following language:

My obligations to the United States, Sir, far exceed any merit I might claim. They date from the time when I have had the happiness to be adopted as a young soldier, a favored son of America. They have been continued to me during almost half a century of constant affection and confidence. And now, Sir, thanks to your most gratifying invitation, I find myself greeted by a series of welcome one hour of which would more than compensate for the public exertions and sufferings of a whole life. * * *

On Tuesday, December 21, 1824, the following bill was presented:

SECTION 1. That in consideration of the services and sacrifices of General Lafayette in the War of the Revolution, the Secretary of the Treasury be and he is hereby authorized to pay to him the sum of $200,000 out of any money in the Treasury not otherwise appropriated.

SECTION 2. That there be granted to General Lafayette and his heirs one township of land to be laid out and located under the authority of the President on any of the unlocated lands of the United States.

On Thursday, December 23, 1824, the Speaker laid before the House the following communication:

PARIS, *October 17, 1824.*

SIR: I sent by the ship *Cadmus* Captain Francis Allyn (who had kindly promised to take it on to Washington) a full-length portrait of General Lafayette [1] painted by me, which I pray you to do me the honor to accept for the Hall of the House of Representatives over which you preside.

As the friend and admirer of General Lafayette and of American liberty, I feel happy to have it in my power to express in this way my grateful feelings for the national honors which the free people of the

---

[1] The Speaker mentioned to the House that the portrait had not been received by him at that time.

ARY SCHEFFER, PAINTER

*Who presented to the House of Representatives his portrait of General Lafayette
now in the Hall of the House*

United States are at this moment bestowing on the friend and companion in arms of your illustrious Washington, on the man who has been so gloriously received by you as the "Nation's guest."

Accept, Sir, with the above testimony of my sentiments for your country and for my venerable friend and sincere assurance of my profound respect.

A. SCHEFFER.

To the Honorable, the Speaker of the House of Representatives, U. S., Washington.

The letter was read and laid on the table

On January 1, 1825, a committee of the House and of the Senate addressed a letter to General Lafayette advising him of the passage and approval of the bill granting to him $200,000 and a township of land. The committee was composed of Samuel Smith, Robert Y. Hayne, and Dominique Bouligny on the part of the Senate, and of William S. Archer, Stephen Van Rensselaer, and Philip S. Markley on the part of the House of

PORTRAIT OF GENERAL LAFAYETTE
Ary Scheffer, painter
Presented by the artist to the Government in 1824

Representatives. The letter of the committee and General Lafayette's answer are contained in the Journal of the Eighteenth Congress, second session, on page 98.

On January 20, 1825, on the motion of Mr. Van Rensselaer, it was—

Ordered, That the Speaker answer the letter of Mr. Scheffer of Paris and make to him suitable acknowledgment for the fine portrait of General Lafayette which he has presented to the House of Representatives.

Ordered, That the Speaker direct where the portrait of General Lafayette be suspended.

This portrait has continued to hang in the Hall of the House of Representatives from the date of this last action until the present time. It has been attributed by some as a gift to the United States from Lafayette, but the error in this can be seen by anyone who has read the foregoing statements relating to the gift and its acceptance. The painter, Ary Scheffer, was an artist of distinction, and the gift of this portrait from an artist of his eminence is one of the pleasant events which have occurred between France and the United States. Scheffer was born in Dordrecht, Holland, February 10, 1797; died at Argenteuil, France, June 15, 1858; history and portrait painter; son of Johann Baptist Scheffer; a pupil of Guerin. Sympathizing neither with the classic school represented by his master nor the romantic led by Gericault and Delacroix, he took up a class of subjects which showed his sympathy with the cause of freedom, such as the Suliote Women, an episode of the Greek war, and the Battle of Morat. Influenced by Ingres, he sought and obtained greater purity of form, and painted subjects from Goethe and Byron. In 1836 he was appointed art instructor to the Orleans family and directed the studies of the Princess Marie in sculpture. The same year he accompanied the Duc d'Orleans and General Baubrand, whose widow he afterwards married, to the siege of Antwerp, and after his return painted several military episodes for Versailles. Between 1835 and 1848 he produced his greatest works, the Christus Consolator and Judex, the Francesca, and the Mignons. When the revolution broke out, Scheffer assisted the King and his family in their escape from Paris, and then went to Holland and England for rest. The coup d'état of 1852, which gave Louis Napoleon the throne, was a blow to his hopes, which finally disgusted him with politics, from which he withdrew altogether. Five years later, after a last visit to England, he lost his friends, Manin and the Duchess d'Orleans, to whom he was much attached. After attending the funeral of the latter he returned, much broken, to France, and shortly after died.

Another gift to the Congress from a distinguished sculptor, Pierre Jean David (David d'Angers), a portrait bust in marble of Lafayette, was received during the year 1829 and unfortunately destroyed by the fire which occurred in the Library of Congress on December 24, 1851. The story or history of this bust is contained in Senate Report No. 2544 (57th Cong., 2d sess.), from which we have quoted a portion:

* * * Shortly after the return of Lafayette to France from his farewell visit to this country his portrait bust in marble, with patriotic inscriptions, was executed by Pierre Jean David, commonly known as David d'Angers, who was not only an eminent sculptor of that period but an ardent republican in French politics and an enthusiastic admirer of the American Republic.

This bust was presented by David, through President John Quincy Adams, to the Congress of the United States, with the request that it "might be set up in the Hall of Congress, near the monument erected to Washington." It was received and placed in the Hall of the House on January 28, 1829. David's letter presenting the bust, together with extracts from the National Intelligencer and the Journals of the Senate and House at the time, are given below:

[From the National Intelligencer, Washington, January 29, 1829]

It will be perceived, from the reading of our report of the proceedings of the House of Representatives of yesterday, that Congress has been presented with a bust of General Lafayette.

The bust is of fine white marble, and is the work of P. J. David, of d'Angers, in France.

It is of a size larger than the life; and exhibits a fine likeness of that distinguished apostle of liberty. On the front is "Au General Lafayette," and the name and residence of the artist, with the year (1828) of its execution. On the left side is an inscription indented in the stone, in the following words:

"Lafayette's speech in the House of Representatives, December 10, 1824: 'What better pledge can be given of a persevering national love of liberty, when those blessings are evidently the result of a virtuous resistance of oppression, and institutions founded on the rights of man, and the republican principle of self-government.' "

On the right side is the following: "Lafayette's last words in his answer to the President's farewell speech, Washington, September 7, 1825: 'God bless you, sir, and all who surround us. God bless the American people, and each of their States, and the Federal Government. Accept this patriotic farewell of an overflowing heart, and such will be its last throb when it ceases to beat.' "

As the bust was unaccompanied by any letter of presentation, we are unadvised to whom the Congress of the United States are indebted for this very handsome and acceptable present.

It was placed by order of the Speaker, at the Clerk's table in the Hall, where it remained at the adjournment of the House yesterday.

[Extract from the Journal of the House of Representatives, January 28, 1829]

The Speaker informed the House that he had received from the Clerk of the House the following letter, viz:

JANUARY 26, 1829.

SIR: I have received a letter from Thomas Turner, esq., collector of the port of Georgetown, in this district, informing me that he had received by a packet, from New York, a box containing a bust of General Lafayette, intended for Congress. He informed me, further, that he had called on the President of the United States, who requested him to state the fact to the Secretary of the Senate and Clerk of the House.

I have thought proper to obtain your orders on the subject.

Your obedient servant,

WM. ST. CLAIR CLARKE,
Clerk of the House of Representatives.

Hon. ANDREW STEVENSON,
Speaker of the House of Representatives.

That he had given immediate directions to have the bust sent for; which had been accordingly done, and had been placed in the Hall, subject to the future disposition of the House.

Ordered, That this communication be referred to the Committee on the Library.

[Extract from the Journal of the Senate, Monday, February 2, 1829]

The Vice-President communicated the following letter from the President of the United States:

WASHINGTON, *January 29, 1829.*

SIR: I transmit herewith a letter which I have received from Mr. David, member of the Institute of France, professor of the School of Painting at Paris, and member of the Legion of Honor, the artist who presents to Congress the bust of General Lafayette, which has been received with it. And I have to request the favor that, after it has been communicated to the Senate, it may be transmitted to the Speaker of the House of Representatives, for similar communication to that body.

JOHN QUINCY ADAMS.

The PRESIDENT OF THE SENATE OF THE UNITED STATES.

[Extract from the Journal of the House of Representatives, Monday, February 9, 1829]

A message from the Senate, by Mr. Lowrie, their Secretary:

"Mr. SPEAKER: I am directed to communicate to the House of Representatives the letter of the President of the United States, transmitting a letter which he had received from Mr. David, of Paris, presenting to Congress a bust of Lafayette, together with the letter of Mr. David."

The letter of Mr. David is as follows:

PARIS, *September 11, 1828.*

The PRESIDENT:

I have executed a bust of Lafayette. I could have wished to have raised a statue to him; not for his benefit, for he does not require it, but for ourselves, who feel so ardently the desire to express the love and admiration with which he inspires us.

The whole youth of France envy both the youth and the old age of him whose resemblance I send you:

{ 89 }

They envy that glory which was acquired on your American soil, by the side of the immortal Washington, in defense of your inestimable rights.

They envy that glory which was acquired on the soil of France, in the midst of the troubles of Paris and Versailles, in those councils where it required more courage to contend in argument than is necessary to combat in arms.

They envy that glory which crowns a head white with age, but still glowing with the fires of liberty and patriotism.

It is in the name of this youth of France, anxious to imitate whatever is generous and great, that I present to you the work on which I have bestowed much time and labor.

I could have wished it had been more worthy of the subject—more worthy of the place I desire it should occupy. Yes, sir, I could wish that the bust of our brave general, of our illustrious deputy, might be set up in the Hall of Congress, near the monument erected to Washington; the son by the side of the father, or, rather, that the two brothers in arms, the two companions in victory, the two men of order and of law, should not be more separated in our admiration than they were in their wishes and in their perils.

Lafayette is one of the ties that connect the two worlds. A few months since he revisited your land, consecrated by justice and equality, and you restored him to us, honored by your hospitality and your homage.

In my turn, I restore him to you; or, rather, I only restore to you his image, for he himself must remain with us, in order to recall frequently to the national councils those eternal principles on which the independence of nations repose and the hopes of mankind are built.

I am, with profound respect, Mr. President,
    Your very humble and obedient servant,

DAVID,
Member of the French Institute and Professor of the School of Painting,
Member of the Legion of Honor.

And then the House adjourned.

Later the bust was removed to the central portion of the Capitol building, then occupied by the Library of Congress, and was destroyed, with a number of other valuable works of art, when the Library was burned, December 24, 1851.

[National Intelligencer, December 25, 1851]

* * * Besides the books, a number of superior paintings hanging around the Library walls and between the alcoves were included in the destruction. Of these, we can call to mind Stuart's paintings of the first five Presidents; an original portrait of Columbus; an original portrait of Peyton Randolph; a portrait of Bolivar; a portrait of Baron Steuben, by Pyne, an English artist of merit; one of Baron De Kalb; one of Cortez, and one of Judge Hanson, of Maryland, presented to the Library by his family. Between 1,100 and 1,200 bronze medals of the Vattemare exchange, some of them more than ten centuries old and exceedingly perfect, are amongst the valuables destroyed. Of the statuary burnt and rendered worthless, we recollect a statue of Jefferson; an Apollo in bronze, by Mills; a very superior bronze likeness of Washington; a bust of General Taylor, by an Italian artist, and a bust of Lafayette, by David.

[Washington Daily Union, December 25, 1851]

The marble busts of Jefferson, Lafayette, Taylor, etc., the portraits of Washington and J. Q. Adams, a number of old paintings—all are gone.

In our anxiety thoroughly to treat the matter of the presentation of the portrait of Lafayette and the presentation of the bust of Lafayette we have, in order to preserve the connection, omitted some intervening events which may now be considered before leaving the period of the completed Capitol in 1830. We have not as yet heard the last of Colonel John Trumbull and his relation to the art of the Capitol. At the time when Trumbull delivered his first painting in 1819, the Signing of the Declaration of Independence, the letters written by the artist show that he had fears of the result of the dampness in the rooms where these paintings were to be located. It appears from subsequent events that his fears were well founded, for in 1828 the four historical paintings were in such condition that Mr. Everett, on the 26th day of May, introduced the following resolution:

Resolved, That the Commissioner of the Public Buildings be, and he is hereby authorized to cause the proper measures to be taken to secure the paintings in the rotunda from the effects of dampness under the direction of John Trumbull and to allow the said John Trumbull a reasonable compensation for the same.

Mr. Haynes moved to amend the resolution by striking out that part of it which directed the work to be done under the superintendence of Mr. Trumbull.

After some conversation between Messrs. Everett, Haynes, Weems, and Silas Wood on the propriety of employing an experienced artist in this operation, the amendment was rejected—ayes, 52; noes, 58.

The resolution as introduced was then adopted. (20th Cong., 1st sess., 1827–28, vol. 4, Pt. II, pp. 27–68.)

It was not until the following December that the work of restoration and protection of the four historical paintings was completed. The steps taken to insure these valuable works from further injury on account of dampness are stated in a letter from John Trumbull, addressed to the Speaker of the House of Representatives, and known as House Document No. 10 (20th Cong., 2d sess.), which was read December 9, 1828, and the facts stated therein are believed to be of such general interest to those desiring information upon the protection of valuable paintings that the letter is given in its entirety:

SIR: On the 30th of May last, I received from the Commissioner of the Public Buildings a copy of the resolution of the honorable the House of Representatives, dated the 26th of May, authorizing him to take the proper measures for securing the paintings in the rotunda from the effect of dampness, under my direction.

I had always regarded the perpetual admission of damp air into the rotunda from the crypt below as the great cause of the evil required to be remedied; and, of course, considered the effectual closing of the aperture which had been left in the centre of the floor [2] as an indispensable part of the remedy. I had communicated my opinion on this subject to the Chairman of the Committee on the Public Buildings, and had been informed that this had been ordered to be done.

So soon, therefore, as I received information from the Commissioner that this work was completed, (as well as an alteration in the skylight, which I had suggested,) and that the workmen and incumbrances were removed out of the room, I came on, and proceeded to take the several measures for the preservation of the paintings, which are stated in detail in the following report, which I beg leave to submit to the House.

1st. All the paintings were taken down, removed from their frames, taken off from the panels over which they are strained, removed to a dry warm room, and there separately and carefully examined. The material which forms the basis of these paintings is a linen cloth, whose strength and texture is very similar to that used in the topgallant-sails of a ship of war. The substances employed in forming a proper surface for the artist, together with the colors, oils, etc. employed by him in his work, form a sufficient protection for the threads of the canvas on this face, but the back remains bare, and, of course, exposed to the deleterious influence of damp air. The effect of this is first seen in the form of mildew; it was this which I dreaded; and the examination showed that mildew was already commenced, and to an extent which rendered it manifest that the continuance of the same exposure, which they had hitherto undergone, for a very few years longer, would have accomplished the complete decomposition or rotting of the canvas, and the consequent destruction of the paintings. The first thing to be done was to dry the canvas perfectly, which was accomplished by laying down each picture successively on its face, upon a clean dry carpet, and exposing the back to the influence of the warmth of a dry and well aired room. The next thing was to devise and apply some substance which would act permanently as a preservative against future possible exposure.

I had learned that, a few years ago, some of the eminent chemists of France had examined with great care several of the ancient mummies of Egypt, with a view to ascertain the nature of the substance employed by the embalmers, which the lapse of so many ages had proved to possess the power of protecting from decay a substance otherwise so perishable as the human body. This examination had proved that, after the application of liquid asphaltum to the cavities of the head and body, the whole had been wrapped carefully in many envelopes, or bandages of linen, prepared with wax. The committee of chemists decided further, after a careful examination and analysis of the hieroglyphic paintings with which the cases, etc. are covered, that the colors employed, and still retaining their vivid brightness, had also been prepared and applied with the same substance.

---

[2] Evidently at this time an opening existed between the rotunda and crypt.

I also knew that, towards the close of the last century, the Antiquarian Society of England had been permitted to open and examine the stone coffin deposited in one of the vaults of Westminster Abbey, and said to contain the body of King Edward I., who died in July, 1307. On removing the stone lid of the coffin, its contents were found to be closely enveloped in a strong linen cloth, waxed. Within this envelope were found splendid robes of silk, enriched with various ornaments covering the body, which was found to be entire, and to have been wrapped carefully in all its parts, even to each separate finger, in bandages of fine linen, which had been dipped in melted wax; and not only was the body not decomposed, but the various parts of the dress, such as a scarlet satin mantle, and a scarlet piece of sarsnet which was placed over the face, were in perfect preservation, even to their colors. The knowledge of these facts persuaded me that wax, applied to the back of the paintings, would form the best defense, hitherto known to exist, against the destructive effects of damp and stagnant air; and therefore,

2dly. Common beeswax was melted over the fire with an equal quantity (in bulk) of oil of turpentine; and this mixture, by the help of large brushes, was applied hot to the back of each cloth, and was afterwards rubbed in with hot irons, until the cloths were perfectly saturated.

3dly. In the meantime, the niches in the solid wall, in which the paintings are placed, were carefully plaistered with hydraulic cement, to prevent any possible exudation of moisture from the wall; and as there is a space of from 2 to 8 inches deep between the surface of the wall and the back of the panels on which the cloths are strained, I caused small openings to be cut in the wall, above and under the edge of the frames, and communicating with those vacant spaces, for the purpose of admitting the air of the room behind the paintings, and thus keeping up a constant ventilation, by means of which the same temperature of air will be maintained at the back of the paintings as on their face.

4thly. The cloths were finally strained upon panels, for the purpose of guarding against injury from careless or intentional blows of sticks, canes, etc., or children's missiles. These panels are perforated with many holes, to admit the air freely to the back of the cloths; and being perfectly dried, were carefully painted, to prevent the wood from absorbing or transmitting any humidity. The whole were then restored to their places, and finally cleaned with care, and slightly revarnished.

5thly. As the accumulation of dust arising from sweeping so large a room, and, what is much worse, the filth of flies, (the most destructive enemies of painting,) if not carefully guarded against, renders necessary the frequent washing and cleaning of the surface of pictures, every repetition of which is injurious. I have directed curtains to be placed, which can be drawn in front of the whole, whenever the room is to be swept, as well as in the recess of the Legislature during the Summer, when flies are most pernicious.

6thly. As nothing is more obvious than the impossibility of keeping a room warm and dry by means of fire, so long as doors are left open for the admission of the external air, I have further directed self-closing baize doors to be prepared and placed, so that they will unavoidably close behind every one who shall either enter or leave the room.

When the doors are kept closed, and fires lighted in the furnaces below, to supply warm air, I find the temperature of this vast apartment is easily maintained at about 63 degrees of Fahrenheit; and the simple precaution of closed doors being observed, in addition to the others which I have employed, I entertain no doubt that these paintings are now perfectly and permanently secured against the deleterious effects of dampness.

I regret that I was not authorized to provide against the danger of damage by violence, whether intended or accidental. Curiosity naturally leads men to touch, as well as to look at, objects of this kind; and, placed low as they are, not only the gilded frames and curtains, but the surface of the paintings are within the reach of spectators: repeated handling, even by the best intentioned and most careful, will, in the course of a few years, produce essential damage. But one of the paintings testifies to the possibility of their being approached, for the very purpose of doing injury: the right foot of General Morgan, in the picture of Saratoga, was cut off with a sharp instrument, apparently a penknife. I have repaired the wound, but the scar remains visible. If I had possessed the authority, I would have placed in front, and at the distance of not less than ten feet from the wall, an iron railing, of such strength and elevation as should form a complete guard against external injury by ill-disposed persons; unless they employed missiles of some force.

I beg leave to commend to the attention of the House this further precaution.

All which is most respectfully submitted to the House, by

JNO. TRUMBULL.

Before closing the period of the completion of the Capitol in 1830, let us try and visualize the condition of its interior so far as art works are concerned.

PORTRAIT OF GEORGE WASHINGTON

Rembrandt Peale, painter

In the Supreme Court section, in the then court room of the Supreme Court, now the law library, there was upon its west wall a bas-relief of Justice, whose authorship is uncertain, but probably the work of Giuseppe Franzoni. In the vestibule leading to this law library or Supreme Court room were the six cornstalk columns modeled by Giuseppe Franzoni in 1809. On the floor above in the small rotunda, there were the tobacco capitals executed by Francisco Iardella in 1816. In the rotunda, which was then surmounted by a low dome, there were the four historical paintings, the work of Col. John Trumbull, also the four groups in high relief over the four doors of the rotunda, and also upon the walls of the rotunda were four portraits in high relief and some ornamental sculpture. The portraits were those of Columbus, Raleigh, Cabot, and La Salle and are attributed to Antonio Capellano and Enrico Causici, and are said to have cost with their wreath-work adornment the sum of $9,500. The date of their execution is fixed as that of 1827.

In the old Hall of the House of Representatives, now known as Statuary Hall, there was upon the frieze the sculptured eagle with outstretched wings, the work of Valaperti. The date has heretofore been fixed as about that of 1817; others have fixed it as 1829, but the authority for the latter date is not stated. There was also upon the gallery front of the north wall the Car of History, by Carlo Franzoni, and hanging probably at one side of the chair of the Speaker was the full-length portrait of General Lafayette. At this time the floor of the Hall of Representatives was much lower than at the present time, and its proper level at that time can be readily ascertained by going into the House document room or into the corridor leading to the offices of the Clerk of the House of Representatives.

There was also in the Library of Congress a marble bust of Lafayette by David d'Angers and a portrait of Columbus, which had been presented to the Nation by G. G. Barrell, United States consul at Malaga, Spain, the receipt of which is shown by a joint resolution approved May 26, 1824, and contained in Statutes at Large, volume 4, page 78.

We are now entering upon the period of 20 years during which time, from 1830 to 1850, the legislative home of the Nation was contained in what has since been styled the old Capitol. As has been stated before, the building during this period was under the charge of the Commissioner of Public Buildings, and without doubt that official failed to find much rest or pleasure in his office for the reason that the question of acoustics was continually agitating the Members of the House and remained unsettled during the remainder of the period of its occupancy as a legislative chamber, or until December, 1857. During all of this period various reports of architects supposed to be masters of the principles governing acoustics were presented to the House of Representatives and at times the recommendations contained in these reports were acted upon. To go into details to such an extent as to summarize all of the reports made and to describe such alterations as were attempted to improve the acoustics of this legislative chamber would hardly be within the scope of a work intended to describe the art and the artists of the Capitol. Enough, however, has been said to give a suggestion of the disadvantages experienced in the old Hall of the House of Representatives, which even now is celebrated as a famous whispering gallery.

In taking up the art belonging to the period of 1830, we find that the record books of the Joint Committee on the Library give many suggestions as to probable material related to the art history of the Capitol. In the records of the meeting for January 9, 1830, we find the following:

Resolved, That all the letters, accounts, etc., of the Committee be filed by the Librarian and that he record the minutes of the Committee in a book which he is authorized to purchase for that purpose.

REMBRANDT PEALE

Self-portrait

Represented by a portrait of Washington in the room of the Vice President and by a portrait of
Chief Justice Marshall in the robing room of the Supreme Court

{ 95 }

[Letter from Rembrandt Peale relating to his portrait of Washington owned by the Government, and to his portrait of Marshall, which he offers for sale]

Philad.ª Dec.ʳ 13. 1858

Dear Sir

I perceive by the papers there is some prospect that the new Senate Chamber may be ready for occupation this Session. In this Case my Portrait of Washington will be removed from its dark & unsatisfactory situation to one, no doubt infinitely better, in the New Chamber. Besides this it has occurred to me, that in assigning it a situation, you might find it desireable to have a Companion for it. With such a view, many years ago, I painted a Portrait of Chief Justice Marshall, with the intention of offering it to the Senate — but was deterred by the total unfitness of the Chamber. The Picture is now temporarily in the State Library at Richmond. It is composed expressly as a Companion picture, with an Oval of similar Stones

{ 96 }

=work — Washington having the Oak
Wreath & Head of Jupiter — Marshall's
the Olive & palm Wreath. And Head of Solon.
Washingtons inscription "Patria Pater"
Marshalls' "Fiat Justicia".

I thought you would not take it amiss,
nor find it too great an intrusion on your
time, to make these statements, & perhaps
to to give me a few lines in reply — hoping
also a favorable word for my Painting
of "Washington before Yorktown," which
I trust you may think worthy of
preservation in some part of your
noble Edifice.

The Senatorial Portrait probably
wants cleaning & revarnishing.

Respectfully Yours
Rembrandt Peale

Captain Meigs.

It can be surmised that much valuable information could be obtained if the "letters, accounts, etc.," could be located and their contents interwoven with the story of the art of the Capitol from year to year.

We find that in March, 1831, the following legislation was enacted:

For rebuilding and removing the monument erected in the Navy Yard at Washington by the officers of the American Navy to the memory of those who fell in the Tripolitan War, a sum not exceeding $2,100, to be expended under the order of the Secretary of the Navy. (Stats. L., vol. 4, p. 462.)

The year 1831 marked the commencement of the commemoration of the Chief Justices of the United States by the placing of busts in the Supreme Court room:

For employing John Frazee to execute a bust of John Jay for the Supreme Court room, $400. (Approved March 2, 1831, Stats. L., vol. 4, p. 474.)

The Senate wing continued to provide for works of art to take the place of the severity which must have existed there as compared with the Hall of the House of Representatives, as appears by the following:

[In the Senate, June 23, 1832]

Mr. Frelinghuysen from the Committee on the Library presented the following resolution:

Resolved: That the Secretary of the Senate be, and he is hereby authorized to purchase from Mr. R. Peale of New York, his original portrait of George Washington, for the Senate Chamber: *Provided*, That the cost of the same does not exceed the sum of ——— dollars to be paid out of the contingent fund of the Senate. (Senate Journal, 22d Cong., 1st sess., vol. 22, p. 365.)

[In the Senate, July 2, 1832]

The resolution directing the purchase of Peale's original portrait of Washington, having been reported by the committee correctly engrossed was read the third time; and

Resolved, That it pass. (Senate Journal, 22d Cong., 1st sess., vol. 32, p. 382.)

The records of the disbursing office of the Senate for the year 1832 show that the sum of $2,000 was paid for this portrait.

CHAPTER VI

GREENOUGH'S STATUE OF WASHINGTON AND PRE-REVOLUTION PAINTINGS IN THE ROTUNDA

T HAS heretofore been stated that, with the termination of the services of Charles Bulfinch, the architect who completed the central portion of the Capitol, for many years thereafter such architectural services as were required were obtained from sources which seemed to be the most convenient or the best qualified for the occasion. For the proper preparation of the rotunda for the reception of that immense work, the statue of Washington, Robert Mills was selected to consider the conditions existing for the purpose of reporting a plan. His report was made to the Committee on Public Buildings of the House of Representatives and by that committee presented through Mr. Levi Lincoln to the House of Representatives on March 5, 1840. Robert Mills, at that time Architect of Public Buildings, was an architect of distinction and in his professional capacity had completed and remodeled some of the Government department buildings. The report follows:

[Ho. of Reps., 26th Cong., 1st session   Doc. No. 124]

FOUNDATION FOR STATUE OF WASHINGTON

[To accompany bill H. R. No. 244]

MARCH 5, 1840

Mr. LINCOLN, from the Committee on Public Buildings, submitted the following documents:

CITY OF WASHINGTON, *February 10, 1840.*

SIR: The cost of preparing suitable foundations for supporting the colossal statue of Washington, in the centre of the rotunda of the Capitol, need not exceed two thousand dollars. These foundations will have to be cased with cut stone, as they are exposed and rise the whole height of the crypt to the top of the floor of the rotunda. The sub-foundations (being those enclosing the vault prepared to receive the remains of General Washington) are considered sufficient to bear those for the statue.

In connection with this location of the statue, I would suggest the plan of isolating it, by laying open the floor of the rotunda to a suitable extent, and having a grand flight of steps ascending from the crypt, and winding around the pedestal of the statue. By this plan a fine light will be thrown into the crypt; and thus the beauty and grandeur of this second rotunda be brought into view—now lost for the want of light.

The plan of locating the statue near the west entrance will be attended with many inconveniences, and present an awkward aspect to the eye. The only cause for giving it this location, is to be traced to the supposed unfavorable position of the light in the apex of the dome; but this is yet to be proved; and if the evil should be serious, I shall be able to present a plan to remedy it. The proper position for the statue being, as designated in the act, "the centre of the rotunda," another location in the room should not be substituted, except no plan could be shown to remedy the evil that may make the centre objectionable.

Respectfully submitted.

ROBERT MILLS,
Architect of Public Buildings.

The COMMISSIONER OF PUBLIC BUILDINGS.

From an old print

THE UNITED STATES CAPITOL ABOUT 1840

OFFICE OF THE ARCHITECT OF PUBLIC BUILDINGS,
February 26, 1840.

SIR: On the subject referred to me, and contained in Mr. Greenough's letter, relative to the foundation, position, etc., of the statue of Washington to be placed in the rotunda of the Capitol, I have the honor to report as follows:

1. *Foundations.*—The estimate rendered by me to you will, I think suffice to meet the expenses incident to this work. As the foundation will be in a conspicuous place in the crypt, its facing must necessarily correspond with the architecture around it and hence its cost will be greater than it would be independent of these circumstances. Though Mr. Greenough does give the weight of his statue, with its pedestal, I should judge it to be not less than thirty tons, which will require a corresponding strength of foundation to support it. As there is a probability that the statue will be here in July next, a natural anxiety is expressed by Mr. Greenough that no time may be lost in preparing the foundations. This might be necessary if common mortar was used in cementing the materials; but as the hydraulic lime can be used, which sets in a few weeks, the immediate construction of the foundations may not be absolutely required; but still, for so heavy a weight coming suddenly upon it, prudence may dictate its early preparation.

2. *Position of the statue.*—The act of Congress designates the centre of the rotunda as the location of the statue. Mr. Greenough objects to this position, upon the ground that the light would strike the figure too vertically, and thus destroy its effect. He observes, that the angle of light should not be steeper than 45°; but, unfortunately, very little advantage is gained, even by placing the statue in the position marked by Mr. G., the angle here varying not more than 27° from the vertical line. The position of the present aperture for light in the rotunda is fatal to the effect of the figure, wherever it may be placed in it; the question, therefore, presents itself, How may this evil be remedied, and a true angle of light obtained for the figure? I answer, that from the construction of the dome of the rotunda, it is practicable to introduce such a light from any, or all, of the cardinal points—still preserving the figure in the centre of the rotunda. The diagram accompanying this letter will tend to explain this plan further, and show, at the same time, the two positions of the figure, and the angle or flow of the light, both from the present aperture at the apex of the dome, and that proposed on the sides.

With reference to the central position of the statue, I would respectfully suggest an improvement which may be associated with it, which, while it would add to the effect of the figure by presenting it under new views, would give what has long been wanting, and complained of, namely, a grand ascent to the magnificent hall above. The improvement consists in opening up the floor of the rotunda around the pedestal of the statue, and filling it up with a grand double flight of stairs. The beauty of the crypt below, for the want of light, is now lost sight of; and, instead of proving a useful room may be almost said to be the reverse. The fine light which would flow down through this stairway would light up this second rotunda and add to its interest as a promenade, and to that of the statue seated on its lofty pedestal, rising over the vaulted tomb prepared to receive the mortal remains of the immortal Washington.

3. *Inscription.*—If I may be allowed to express an opinion on this subject, I would say that no inscription should be admitted on the pedestal. If the artist has succeeded in stamping the features of the Father "of his country" on the stone, it requires no word to identify the man; and, again, what statue but that of Washington would be found to occupy the centre of the Capitol of the Union?

Respectfully submitted.

ROBERT MILLS,
Architect of Public Buildings.

Hon. LEVI LINCOLN,
Chairman of the Committee on Public Buildings.

———

CITY OF WASHINGTON, *Feb. 22, 1840.*

DEAR SIR: Annexed is presented a detailed estimate for the foundations of the statue of Washington, proposed to be placed in the rotunda. If we are to have any reference in the exterior finish of this sub-base to the surrounding architecture, it will require the sum stated. The cut stone work is valued low for circular work.

Respectfully submitted.

ROBERT MILLS,
Architect Public Buildings.

Hon. LEVI LINCOLN,
Chairman, Committee on Public Buildings.

———

Estimate for sub-pedestal, or foundations for the statue of Washington, in the rotunda of the Capitol

800 sq. feet of circular cut stone	$1,000
200 sq. ft. of sunk and moulded work	400
100 perches of filling behind cut stone	400
Extra work connecting new and old work	35
150 yds. of painting	45
Superintendence, scaffolding, &c	120
	2,000

It has been stated previously that this commission was the largest which had ever up to that time been given to an American for a single piece of statuary, and in the course of its construction the necessary expenses incurred by the artist, and for which he presented a bill which was transmitted to the Congress with a message from the President on August 4, 1841, were included in the cost of the statue. (House Doc. No. 45, 27th Cong., 1st sess.). The document consists of 16 pages and contains a fairly concise record of the steps which accompanied the completion of the statue and its transportation to Washington. The statement of expense submitted by the artist amounts to $8,311.90 in all and includes a variety of items exclusive of any compensation to the sculptor for the completion of the work. Among these are the lease of the studio, repairs and enlarging of the same, wages to foreman, wages to servants, cost of packing, damage done to trees on the road from Florence to Leghorn, and for a large variety of articles necessary in the construction of a statue of this large size. It should be remembered that the statue was 10 feet 6 inches in length and 10 feet 6 inches in height, 6 feet in width, and weighed nearly 20 tons. It was expected at the time that Congress passed the resolution directing that the Secretary of the Navy be authorized and instructed to take measures for the importation and erection of the statue of Washington that there might be some Government vessel of sufficient capacity to bring this immense statue to this country. At that time Commodore Hull was in command of the Mediterranean station, and through him an agreement was entered into for the transportation of the statue to the United States. The ship *Sea* was selected for this duty, and the United States sloop of war *Preble* also visited Leghorn, the port from which the statue was shipped, and the commander of the sloop was instructed to oversee and assist in the shipment. There were, of course, many delays occasioned in getting the statue on board the ship, and Captain Delano, in charge of the ship *Sea*, submits a bill of $100 per day demurrage for his detention at Leghorn over and above the 15 days specified in the charter. So that $1,400 in demurrage was due at the time when the ship sailed from Leghorn to Washington. The statue arrived in Washington on the 31st of July, 1841, and demurrage was claimed for the 13 days required to transfer the statue from the ship. This expense was increased by the cost of removing the statue from the navy yard to the Capitol and for the expense of a pedestal to place the statue upon in the rotunda. Captain Delano, as appears by the records in this case, received as transportation and demurrage for detention of the ship at the port of embarkation and at the navy yard the sum of $7,700. To this should be added the sum of $5,000, probably expended in moving the statue from the navy yard, erecting it in the rotunda, and for the cost of the pedestal for the same. So that in additional expense the statue at the time of its erection in the rotunda had cost, exclusive of the sum paid to the sculptor, over $21,000. The exact date of the erection of the statue does not seem to be shown by the papers in the case, but the position of the statue in the rotunda was not satisfactory to the sculptor, and in January, 1843, less than three years after its erection, the sculptor presented a memorial to Congress praying for the removal of the statue from its position to the ground in front of the western façade of the Capitol. This memorial is known as Senate Document No. 57 (27th Cong., 3d sess.) and contains fully four pages of printed matter. In this document the sculptor discusses not only the position of the statue but also many art conditions which seem to have entered into the criticism of the statue as completed and erected. A few extracts are given:

It is apparent, however, that the point so indicated and actually occupied by the statue, though it is the best which a proper regard for the uses of the Hall and a due observance of architectural symmetry will allow, is still wholly unfit for it since the descent of the light upon the work is so nearly vertical as to throw all the lower portions of the face into shade and to give a false and constrained effect to the whole monument. * * *

The sculptor then proceeds to present an argument as to the best location for the statue outside of the rotunda and advances the opinion that the west side of the Capitol is a better location than the east side on account of the natural conformation of the ground as it then existed. He then discusses at some length the question of the form of the composition which has been given to his work and as to the costume or lack of costume employed to carry out his artistic expression. Concerning this we wish to make a further quotation from the document referred to:

It has been hinted to your memorialist that being aware of the prejudice which existed in this country against naked statuary and in favor of a literal copy of the dress of the time it was his duty blindly to renounce his own views upon the subject and conform to those believed to be of the majority. The proper mode of treating modern statues, however, having been of late years repeatedly discussed, and yet those authorized to contract with him having left him entirely free on this head, your memorialist deems that the responsibility of the decision fell upon him and therefore consulted only his own conscience and the comparative results of the different models and methods which had fallen under his observation. Having already outlived the sneer with which it was intended to crush his first effort to make a bust of a distinguished fellow citizen "without a shirt" he trusts that the prejudice which has yielded in these few years the neck and shoulders not unfit to be looked upon will continue to decline before the efforts of high art until his successors in sculpture shall be enabled to show that the inspired writer meant not merely the face when he declared that God had made men after his own image.

As a part of an appropriation asked for the civil and diplomatic expenses of the Government for the fiscal year of 1844, the following relates to the Greenough statue of Washington:

For the removal of the statue of Washington from its present position and permanently placing the same on a proper pedestal and covering it temporarily in the enclosed and cultivated public grounds, east of the Capitol directly in front of the main entrance and steps of the east front of the Capitol as suggested by the report of the Joint Committee on the Library and in the letter of Mr. Greenough, dated February 3, 1843, referred to and reported by said Committee in connection with the memorial of Horatio Greenough, under the direction and supervision of the said Greenough, the sum of $5,000. (Stats. L., vol. 5, p. 642.)

For many years this statue was located on the grounds east of the Capitol, approximately in the location described in the foregoing act. In the earlier years there seems to have been a temporary building erected over the statue to protect it from the weather, but in 1847 we find this legislation:

For removal of the building over the statue of Washington and erecting an iron fence around the same, $1,000. (Stats. L., vol. 9, p. 93.)

It had been the desire of the sculptor to have this statue placed in a building where it might be protected from possible injury owing to changes of temperature and the severity of the climate as compared with the climate of the country where the stone was quarried, but it does not appear that after 1847 this statue was so protected, except at times during the winter a temporary building was erected over the statue, which was removed as soon as the freezing weather had terminated. This idea of winter housing was continued for many years, and in the meanwhile the statue was becoming more and more damaged by its exposure to the weather. It was therefore considered by the Congress that it would be advisable to remove the statue entirely, and accordingly in 1908 Public Resolution No. 26 (60th Cong., 1st sess.) provided for its removal and transfer to the custody of the Smithsonian Institution, and in the deficiency act approved May 30, 1908, we find this legislation:

Washington Statue: For transfer of the marble statue of Washington by Greenough from the plaza in front of the Capitol to the Smithsonian Institution under the direction of the Secretary of the Smithsonian Institution and the Superintendent of the Capitol Building and Grounds, including the construction of a foundation and a marble base, $5,000. (Stats. L., vol. 35, p. 492.)

In this manner the history of this commission, so important in the days when it was granted, was finally terminated, the actual removal being completed November 21, 1908. It is probable that but few statues have ever received as much adverse criticism as the statue whose history has been given. There can be no doubt but that the sculptor and his friends, and they were many, felt severely that the criticism to which this statue was subjected was unjust. Concerning this it is proper to say that whoever presents in a new or unusual form any work of art places himself in a position where criticism is inevitable.

Whether the criticism is just or unjust depends largely upon the point of view of the critic. It seems, however, that Charles Bulfinch, the architect, from his home in Boston, was measuring accurately the condition of public sentiment in Washington at this time. We find in the Life and Letters of Bulfinch the following reference:

From the mention of Greenough's Washington both by you and Charles I fear that it will cause much disappointment. It may be an exquisite piece of work, but our people will hardly be satisfied with looking on well developed muscles when they wish to see the great man as their imagination has painted him. I send you a sort of defense of this statue from Everett, but am not convinced that the sculpture is suited for modern subjects. The dress presents insuperable difficulties. The first statue of Washington was made by Houdon who was sent for by the State of Virginia. His work is in the Capitol at Richmond and a more unpleasant figure was never seen. It is represented in an old-fashioned coat, etc., with stiff ear curls and a heavy club behind. The next statue was by Chantrey in our State House, clothed as a Roman Senator. It was highly commended at first, but is now seen with perfect indifference. It, in fact, wants interest. And now I fear that this with you will only give the idea of entering or leaving a bath,—but I will hope that when raised on its pedestal it will be improved and that it will do credit to the artist and satisfy the public, but my fears prevail.

I mention another instance of unsuccessful modern statuary. It is the statue of the Duke of Wellington near Hyde Park, London. It is represented as a Achilles, naked a la Greque,—and has even been complained of by the Society for Improving Public Morals.

Mr. Bulfinch, although separated from the place of his former activities in Washington, seems to be able to keep in touch with current events, and soon after the presentation of the memorial by Greenough, suggesting a removal of the statue from the rotunda to the grounds outside, writes the following under date of January 31, 1843:

* * * I observe by the papers that Mr. Greenough wishes to have something built in the Capitol grounds to contain his statue. I cannot think that Congress will consent to this expense; they are not so much pleased with it as to be ready to lay out much more money upon it and any temple or room of any kind built for this purpose must be large to view the statue at a proper distance and must show some architectual magnificence or it will look only like a work-shop now dignified by the name of studio. I would propose, and wish you would mention it to him, that the statue be placed on the middle of the upper platform of the east portico; there is, I think, sufficient room for it without hindering convenient access to the door; it would be a principal object to meet the eye of members and visitors immediately upon ascending the steps and surrounded by a rich display of columns and between Peace and War, would be a very appropriate situation for it; at least, the experiment might be tried at little expense.

Mr. Bulfinch, in a letter of April 10, 1843, says:

In a letter from T. B. to Mrs. Hall about three weeks since, I added a postscript asking D. A. Hall to send me any printed account of debates upon the resolution respecting the removal of the statue and for plans of a new Congress Hall. Not having heard from him I fear that the letter has not reached him; it was sent under cover to Mr. Elsworth. Will you inquire about it? Between both of you notwithstanding the old saying of two stools, etc., I hope to receive the papers, reports or debates. I think such subjects could not have been acted upon sub silentio. I have no motive for wishing for these papers but to gratify my inquisitive curiosity; but if I should give my advice it would be to send the statue to Athens, a present to King Otho, to be placed in the Parthenon with other naked great men; and before they commence a new hall let a flat ceiling be formed over the present one to try its effect upon the voice. I find that the ablest advisers upon building the new Houses of Parliament in London recommend avoiding all concave surfaces.

At about this period Watterston, at one time Librarian of Congress, in his Guidebook, gives some interesting facts concerning art works at the Capitol during the period prior to 1850. Concerning the rooms occupied at the Capitol by the Library of Congress, he states that marble busts of Washington, Jefferson, Lafayette, Judge Marshall, John Quincy Adams, Van Buren, and plaster busts of Jackson and Moultrie, and a medallion of

Madison, most of the busts standing on pedestals, are placed in different parts of the room. Concerning the Supreme Court room he describes the bas-relief on the west wall of the court room, now the law library, in the following words:

On a wall in a recess in front of the bench is sculptured in bold relief the figures of Justice holding the scales and that of Fame crowned with the rising sun pointing to the Constitution of the United States.

Referring to other art works in the Supreme Court room Mr. Watterston states:

On a stone attached to the pier of one of the arches on the left of the fire-place is a fine bust in marble of Chief Justice Ellsworth and a similar bracket on the right is a marble bust of Chief Justice Marshall.

Mr. Watterston fails to mention the location of other busts of Chief Justices. It may be that this Guidebook was a reprint of an earlier work and had not been corrected so as to show what changes had occurred from later accessions. The date given for this Guidebook seems to be that of 1847 and 1848, and yet in referring to the Greenough statue of Washington it is stated that it is about 12 feet high, weighs 14 tons, and is elevated on a pedestal 12 feet high in the center of the rotunda. If this Guidebook was up to date, it would seem that the statue of Washington had not been removed from the rotunda, as provided by the act referred to as forming a part of the appropriation act for the fiscal year 1844. Some peculiar and conflicting historical references are sometimes found when different authorities are compared.

It may not be inappropriate at this time to make a closing reference to the distinguished architect Charles Bulfinch, whose activities connected with the construction of the central portion of the Capitol closed many years ago. By some architects he has been given a place of equality with the architects Thornton and Latrobe, his predecessors. By some it is claimed that the west front of the central portion of the Capitol is the only portion in which his individuality is seen and that the remainder of the work follows the plans of Latrobe. Be this as it may, at the time of his death, April 15, 1844, there were standing to his credit as his creations four courthouses, five churches, six banks, four insurance offices, two school buildings, the statehouse at Boston, several other buildings of a public character devoted to miscellaneous purposes, and the work upon the Capitol of the United States, a record of achievements of which any architect might well be proud.

In turning to the records of the Joint Committee on the Library, we find under date of January 24, 1846, the following record:

The petition of sundry artists, citizens of Boston, and of George P. Healy, artist, praying Congress to purchase the portraits of the first five Presidents of the United States, painted by the late Gilbert Stuart, now in the Library of Congress, was referred to the Honorable Mr. Chalmers.

We also find in the records of the committee for March 10, 1846, the following record:

The resolution from the Senate and the House of Representatives in relation to a painting for the vacant panel in the rotunda and a piece of sculpture by Powers to be placed in the Capitol, was again considered and laid over until the next meeting of the Committee.

It will be remembered that steps had already been taken to secure paintings for the four vacant panels in the rotunda and that it had been expected that Henry Inman would provide one of the paintings desired. His death, however, after he had received a portion of the compensation for painting the picture, left a vacancy to be filled by a commission for this panel, and the friends of Prof. Samuel F. B. Morse used all possible efforts to secure for him the commission formerly given to Mr. Inman. A petition was prepared and presented to Congress in the first session of the Twenty-ninth Congress which explains fully the reasons for the request of the selection of Professor Morse.

[Senate 280, 29th Cong., 1st session]

PETITION OF A. B. DURAND AND OTHERS, PRAYING THAT PROFESSOR MORSE MAY BE EMPLOYED TO EXECUTE THE PAINTING TO FILL THE PANEL IN THE ROTUNDA OF THE CAPITOL SET APART FOR MR. INMAN, SINCE DECEASED

MAY 26, 1846.—Referred to the Committee on the Library. JUNE 8, 1846.—Ordered to be printed

To the Honorable the Senate of the United States.

The undersigned, the friends of Professor Samuel F. B. Morse, beg leave respectfully to represent:

That Professor Morse, whose early life for thirty years was devoted to the cultivation of the art of painting, studied for four years in the Royal Academy of London, then under the presidency of that distinguished painter, Benjamin West; but Mr. Morse was more especially, while in England, under the tuition, in historical painting, of the late Washington Allston, and was a fellow pupil under the same master with Leslie, so well known as one of the first painters in England; when he returned to this country, and practiced painting with distinguished success.

In the year 1826, Professor Morse was the principal instrument, aided by other artists, in founding and establishing, at great personal sacrifices, The National Academy of Design, one of the most flourishing of the institutions of the city or State of New York. From its foundation, for nineteen years he was annually unanimously chosen to preside over the academy, and then declined a reelection, from causes which will be presently explained.

In 1829, he again visited Europe to perfect himself in historical painting, having in view to offer himself as a candidate for the commission to paint one of the great historical paintings to be placed in the rotunda of the Capitol, and pursued his studies for three years in Rome, Naples, Florence, Venice, and Paris; and with the common consent of the artists and connoisseurs of this country, it was conceded that this honor would unquestionably be conferred upon him, and for this purpose he had made all the requisite preparation for a painting to represent the germ of the republic. That the committee of Congress, then appointed, (contrary to the universal expectation of those best qualified to judge of the merits of the several candidates,) set aside the claims of Professor Morse, and as an evidence of the sense of injustice which was felt among the profession, we can state that the late eminent and excellent artist, Mr. Inman, wrote President Van Buren a letter, in which he offered to resign the panel which had been assigned to him, expressing the hope that Professor Morse might be appointed to supply his place—a generous offer, which the committee to whom this letter was referred did not think proper to accept. That as a further expression of the sense of the injustice done to Professor Morse, in rejecting his application to be employed as one of the painters, an association was voluntarily formed, of twenty-nine artists and amateurs of New York and Philadelphia, (among whom we note the names of three out of the four successful candidates for these pictures,) who subscribed a sum of money, and appointed a committee of their body to request Professor Morse to paint for them, in small, the picture he had intended to paint for the rotunda, had Congress seen fit to grant him the commission. Although the money was subscribed, the neglect to pay promptly the quarterly installments embarrassed Professor Morse in the progress of painting the picture, and after every effort to proceed, he was reluctantly compelled to abandon the enterprise. He consequently laid aside his pencil, determining to devote himself for a while to pursuits which would furnish him with the means of resuming his picture at a future day; to which determination the country is indebted for the successful establishment of his magnetic telegraph—an invention destined to associate his name in our country's annals with that of Franklin—an invention of which the country may justly be proud—the benefits of which are but beginning to be appreciated and understood.

The death of Mr. Inman now presents an opportunity of securing to the country a painting, which we have no doubt, will form one of the chief ornaments of the Capitol, and also of retrieving the error which refused the commission to an artist to whom the arts of design in our country are so much indebted for his self sacrificing devotion to their interests for so many years.

As the friends of Professor Morse, we beg leave to present to the due consideration of your honorable body his claims for executing the painting of the panel now vacated by the decease of Mr. Inman; claims which we are sure the great body of those whom he has benefited as an artist would sanction.

While Professor Morse will, very probably, (under the circumstances,) not request the commission by any personal solicitation for himself, we are assured that he will accept the commission, if offered to him by Congress.

That the commission may be so conferred your petitioners will ever pray.

A. B. Durand, Pres't. N. A. of Design; Thomas S. Cummings; John G. Chapman; John L. Morton; F. W. Edmonds; C. C. Verplanck; J. F. E. Prudhomme; Jon. Goodhue; P. Perit; Philip Hone; Frederick R. Spencer; Alfred Jones; James Harper; Chas. C. Ingham, V. P. N. A.; S. DeWitt Bloodgood; R. Watts, jr., M. D., Prof. of Anatomy; Regis Gignoux; Jasper F. Cropsey; Chas. L. Elliott; Jas. J. Mapes; Jas. Renwick; Clinton Roosevelt; Geo. P. Morris; Henry C. Shumway.

(Doc. Hist. Cap., pp. 340, 341.)

This petition, heretofore referred to, had received the sanction of the Joint Committee on the Library on June 30, 1846, when the records of this committee show the following:

A memorial requesting that Professor Morse might be engaged to paint a picture for the vacant panel in the rotunda was referred to the Honorable Mr. Campbell.

Notwithstanding the fact that the leading artists of the country had petitioned Congress for the selection of Professor Morse as the artist to provide a painting for the vacant panel in the rotunda we find that the appeals of his friends were unsuccessful and that other applicants for this commission were pressing their claims. On January 9, 1847, there was before the Joint Committee on the Library for their consideration a memorial from Charles D. Drake and others, citizens of the city of St. Louis, Mo., in relation to a painting for the vacant panel in the rotunda of the Capitol and recommending Charles Deas, a western artist, to execute for this purpose a design prepared by him and then exhibited by him in the Library of Congress.

We also find with reference to the memorial of Charles D. Drake that at the meeting of the Library Committee on January 16, 1847, this action was taken, "laid over for the present," and that similar action was taken at the meeting of January 23, 1847.

The custody of the Joint Committee on the Library over works of art in the Capitol Building was recognized at a very early date, and an instance in which they exercised the right to grant permission for copying works of art belonging to the Government and located in the Capitol is shown by the following extract from their minutes for the meeting of January 9, 1847:

Ordered that permission be granted to Thomas Blanchard to make casts in plaster from the busts in the Library of Congress and that he be permitted to remove the busts from the Library for that purpose. Ordered that permission be granted to Plumbe to make daguerreotype copies of the paintings in the Library belonging to Congress.

It will be noted that this permission did not give to Mr. Plumbe authority to make daguerreotypes of the paintings of the first five Presidents of the United States by Gilbert Stuart, which were then being exhibited in the Library of Congress.

The vacant panel in the rotunda, still under consideration, was finally settled, as indicated by the action of the Joint Committee on the Library, January 14, 1848. We give herewith the following memorandum:

A contract to be made with Mr. Powell for a painting ordered by Congress, to be executed by him, to fill the vacant panel in the rotunda of the Capitol, was under consideration; and Mr. Powell having been consulted in relation to its terms it was on motion voted that the Chairman of the Library Committee on the part of the Senate, and the Chairman of the Library Committee on the part of the House of Representatives, be requested to complete the contract with Mr. Powell on the condition agreed upon in the Joint Committee.

South blocking, east entrance steps, central portion

THE DISCOVERY GROUP

Luigi Persico, sculptor

The head of Columbus is said to be a copy from an
original bust in Spain

The coming importance of Gen. Zachary Taylor is indicated by the following record found upon the books of the Joint Committee on the Library for April 7, 1848:

A letter was received from William G. Brown offering to sell to Congress a full-length portrait of General Zachary Taylor for $1,000.

It occasionally happened that gifts of works of art were made to the Government, and in these early days a custom existed which has since been sanctioned by an enactment of Congress, that of placing in the hands of the Library Committee the right and privilege of passing upon such works of art as were offered as gifts or for purchase. An instance of a gift is found in their records of June 2, 1848:

A letter was received from William Brent, Esquire, of the city of Washington, stating that he had received, addressed to his care, from Robert Walsh, Esquire, Consul of the United States at Paris, a portrait of Major General Baron de Kalb, to be presented to Congress as an offering from the surviving family of de Kalb, persons of great consideration and worth. Voted that the portrait be received and that a joint resolution be reported for placing it in the Library of Congress.

We have followed for a little time the effort to provide works of art for the interior of the Capitol Building, and we must now turn our attention to the work of Persico, who since the completion of his two statues, Peace and War, had been engaged upon a group for the southern blocking of the east portico of the central portion of the Capitol. This group is known as the Discovery Group, and it is alleged that Persico obtained his material from which to model the head of Columbus from an original bust of Columbus found in Spain. The date of the erection of this group is not at this time definitely known, but we find in the civil and diplomatic act, approved June 17, 1844, the following provision relating to the final payment for the Discovery Group by Luigi Persico:

For removing Persico's statues from the Navy Yard to the Capitol, preparing the pedestal, erecting the statues and enclosing the same with an iron railing, $1,350. (Stats. L., vol. 5, p. 682.)

It seems that this group had not been favorably received, or that the changes in the personnel of Congress had resulted in a membership which did not look so kindly upon the works of this artist as did the Members of earlier Congresses. A resolution had been referred to the Joint Committee on the Library in which it is evident that a change of the location of this group had been suggested, as the following extract from the records of this committee, under date of September 23, 1850, seems to show:

Voted, That the further consideration of the resolution referred to the Committee by the Senate to inquire into the propriety of removing the group containing the statue of Columbus from its present position on the east portico of the Capitol to a suitable place in some one of the public squares, be postponed until the next meeting.

The purpose of the consideration of this resolution referred to the committee by the Senate seems to have been fully satisfied by the placing of this record in the minute book, as subsequent records fail to show that this subject was ever again considered by the committee.

During the year 1850 other business considered by the committee of interest, on account of its relation to the art of the Capitol, is shown by the following entries:

August 28, 1850. Voted, That the Committee decline to recommend the purchase by Congress of the apotheosis of George Washington painted by R. Burns and temporarily exhibited in the rotunda of the Capitol.

August 28, 1850. A resolution from the Senate which was referred to the Committee in relation to a medal in memory of General Z. Taylor, late President of the United States, to be made by Mr. Gevelot, was received and considered. Voted, That the proposition of Mr. Gevelot to make a medal in memorial of the late General Z. Taylor, President of the United States, be laid on the table.

BUST OF ZACHARY TAYLOR
Sculptor unknown

February 20, 1850. A proposition was received from the executors of the estate of the late A. Phelps, of Boston, to sell to Congress the portraits of the first five Presidents of the United States painted by Gilbert Stuart at the price of $1,000. each portrait. The subject was considered and laid over for the present.

It may be interesting in this connection to state that the writer has recently been informed that portraits of Washington by Gilbert Stuart have been sold within a short time for the sum of $41,000. When we consider that it is claimed by some contemporaries of Stuart that he painted 40 copies of his atheneum portrait of Washington, we may readily conclude that investments in works of art are sometimes well worth while.

We are now approaching the period when conditions seemed to demand an enlargement or extension of the Capitol Building. The growth of the country had resulted in a larger representation in the Halls of Congress, and the accommodations which in 1830 were considered ample had now become inadequate. In addition to this crowded condition there had been for many years a feeling that the Hall of the House of Representatives and also the Senate Chamber were not well adapted for the "purposes of deliberative assemblies." Several reports had been made outlining methods by which the acoustics of the Hall of the House of Representatives could be improved, and one report had been made tending to establish the possibility of a removal of the assembly Chamber of the Hall of Representatives to a location then occupied by the Library of Congress. This plan, however, had met with but little support. The report seems to have been made for the purpose of establishing the possibility of the change without much expectation that the change would be made. Early in the year 1850 Congress had taken upon itself, through an advertisement offering prizes for plans for extension to the Capitol, the solution of the problem of securing more comfortable quarters. Congress seemed to have forgotten that the Capitol had from the earliest times been under the direct charge and supervision of the President of the United States. Reference to this care and supervision on the part of the President has been previously made, and at the time of its writing it was felt that perhaps some explanatory statement should be made, and it is possible that this explanation should not be delayed longer. Lest it be thought that the duties and responsibilities and special care of the President have been overstated, it may be well to consult in this connection The National Capitol, its Architecture, Art, and History, by George Hazelton, jr., where the following quotation may be found on page 43:

In its construction and rebuilding the Capitol was never without the direct supervision of the President. Washington, Adams, Jefferson, Madison, Monroe and John Quincy Adams, each in turn, presided over its destiny and often descended to the consideration of the most minute details with a grace rather startling to the ideas of dignity commensurate with the office in the minds of some later Presidents. During the work of restoration, in the spring of 1817, President Monroe guarded its rebuilding with a fatherly concern almost equal to that displayed by Washington in its building. He gave directions as to the Potomac marble to be used in the columns for the chambers of the House of Representatives and Senate and as to the quarrying of the same, not forgetting instructions for the workmen. He ordered that the dome of the Senate wing be built of brick and the corresponding one above the House of Representatives, of wood, adding specific directions as to where and how materials for each should be obtained. He urged, beyond everything, the necessity of so far completing the building as to have it in readiness for the meeting of Congress the following fall. The President considered even the "tools, lumber, nails, spikes and provisions" for the Capitol, and ordered "sheds to be erected for the workmen, for cooking and as store houses without delay." At the same time, he gave directions for the distribution of provisions to the employes, the keeping of accounts and receipts, and for a report to be made to the Executive each Monday regarding the progress on the work.

THOMAS U. WALTER
Architect of the Capitol Extension (1851–1865)

The right of the President in place of that of the Congress to take charge of the extension of the Capitol seems to be clearly set forth in the following legislation contained in the civil and diplomatic act of the Thirty-first Congress, first session, approved September 30, 1850, as follows:

For the extension of the Capitol, according to such plans as may be approved by the President, $100,000; to be expended under his direction by such architects as he may appoint to execute the same. (Stats. L., vol. 9, p. 538.)

It does not seem necessary nor within the scope of this work to state in detail the history of the competition of architects for the position created by the law quoted. Without doubt there were some disappointments, but the President certainly acted within his rights, and subsequent events have proved that he acted wisely in the appointment of Thomas U. Walter, who took the oath of office on the 11th day of June, A. D. 1851. The commencement of the work known as the extension of the Capitol, which included the erection and the addition to the original building of the wing now containing the Hall of the House of Representatives and the wing now containing the Senate Chamber, and also included the reconstruction of the dome of the Capitol, marked a new period in the art history of the Capitol. It may be well for us to consider the condition of the art of the Capitol during the year 1850, when the act was passed providing for its extension. Considering first the works of art outside of the Capitol, we must remember that at the west front there was standing a monument erected to the memory of the naval officers who fell at Tripoli in the year 1804. At the east front of the Capitol the statue of Washington, by Greenough, had then been located; on the south blocking of the east portico of the central portion of the Capitol Persico's Discovery Group had been erected; in the niches on either side of the east entrance to the Capitol were placed Persico's statues of Peace and War; and in the central pediment the group by Persico. Capellano's bas-relief over the east entrance of the rotunda was then in place, and these works constituted all of the art outside of the Capitol in the year 1850.

Considering the condition of art in the interior of the Capitol we must remember that in the Senate wing there was hanging in the Senate Chamber a portrait of Washington by Rembrandt Peale—the same portrait now hanging in the room of the Vice President—and in the Supreme Court room busts in marble of Chief Justice Oliver Ellsworth, Chief Justice John Jay, and Chief Justice John Marshall. It will be seen, therefore, that the number of works of art in the Senate section of the Capitol was very small.

In the Library of Congress there was a much larger collection of art work. Of course it will be remembered that all of the art works in the Library were destroyed by fire December 24, 1851, but we are at present writing of an earlier period. The authorities consulted differ somewhat as to the number of works existing in the Library at the time of the fire, but all authorities agree that the entire collection was destroyed. It is probably safe to say that the following sculpture existed in the Library during the year 1850, of which we are now writing: Marble bust of Lafayette by David d'Angers, marble bust of General Taylor by an Italian artist, busts of Columbus, Vespucci, George Washington, and Thomas Jefferson. These busts were all by Giuseppe Ceracci. There were also a bust of John Quincy Adams by Luigi Persico, and a bust of Ferdinand R. Hassler, presented by his children. It would be interesting if there could be found some drawings or reproductions of these busts which were destroyed. This would be especially valuable for the reason that the Government is now in possession of a bust of General Taylor by an unknown artist,

THE LANDING OF COLUMBUS

John Vanderlyn, painter

LANDING OF COLUMBUS

At the Island of Guanahani, West-Indies. October 12th 1492.

1. Columbus
2. Martin Alonzo Pinzon
3. Vincent Yannez Pinzon
4. Rodrigo des Escobedo or Escobar, notary of the armament
5. Roderigo Sanchez, inspector of armament
6. Mutineer in a suppliant attitude
7. Alonzo de Ojeda
8. Cabin boy in kneeling posture

9. Soldier whose attention is partly diverted from the ceremony by the appearance of the awe-stricken natives in the forest
10. Sailor in attitude of veneration for the admiral
11. Friar bearing a crucifix

In the distance, groups express joy and hilarity on their landing. Two figures somewhat nearer are contending for glittering particles in the sand. The three vessels—Santa Maria, Pinta, and Nina—are seen in the distance

In the Rotunda

THE DISCOVERY OF THE MISSISSIPPI RIVER BY DE SOTO

William H. Powell, painter

DE SOTO'S DISCOVERY OF THE MISSISSIPPI
A.D. 1541

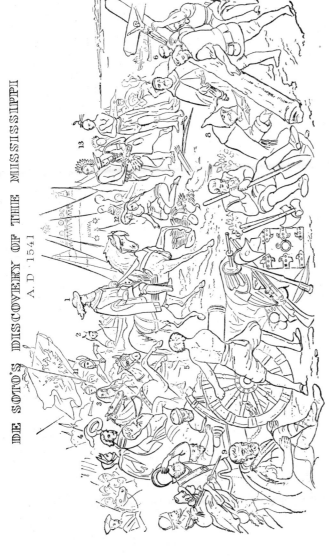

1. De Soto
2. Moorish servant
3. Confessor
4. Young Spanish cavalier
5. Cannon dragged up by artillerymen
6. Company of stalwart men planting a cross
7. Ecclesiastic bearing the censer
8. Old priest blessing the cross
9. Soldier dressing his wounded leg
10. Camp chest with arms, helmets, and other imple-
    ments of war
11. Group of standard bearers and helmeted men
12. Two young Indian maidens
13. Indian chiefs bearing the pipe of peace
    In the distance is seen the Mississippi. Its waters
    are broken by glancing canoes, magical islands,
    and purple shores

THE BAPTISM OF POCAHONTAS

John G. Chapman, painter

BAPTISM OF POCAHONTAS
At Jamestown Va. 1613

1. Pocahontas
2. John Rolfe
3. Alexander Whiteaker
4. Sir Thomas Dale
5. Sister of Pocahontas
6. Nantequaus, brother of Pocahontas
7. Opechancanough
8. Opachisco, uncle of Pocahontas
9. Richard Wyffin
10. Standard bearer
11. Mr. and Mrs. Forrest, the lady being the first gen-
    tlewoman to arrive in the colony
12. Henry Spilman
13. John and Anne Laydon, the first persons married
    in the colony
14. The page

THE EMBARKATION OF THE PILGRIMS
Robert W. Weir, painter

In the Rotunda

EMBARKATION OF THE PILGRIMS

At Delft Haven, Holland. July 22nd 1620.

1. Mr. Robinson, pastor of the congregation
2. Elder William Brewster
3. Mrs. Brewster and sick child
4. Governor Carver
5. William Bradford
6. Mr. and Mrs. White
7. Mr. and Mrs. Winslow
8. Mr. and Mrs. Fuller
9. Miles Standish and his wife Rose
10. Mrs. Bradford; she fell overboard the day the
    vessel came to anchor
11. Mrs. Carver and child
12. Captain Reynolds and sailor
13. Boy belonging to Carver and family
14. Boy in charge of Mr. Winslow
15. Boy belonging to Mrs. Winslow's family
16. A nurse and child

WILLIAM H. POWELL

Represented by the paintings, The Battle of Lake Erie and The Discovery of the Mississippi

and the best information obtainable seems to point to the fact that this bust was purchased in Italy. It may be possible that this second bust was from the same artist who executed the bust destroyed in the Library fire. In addition to the loss of the busts before referred to there were several paintings (portraits) lost in the same fire, among them two portraits of Columbus, a portrait of John Hanson, and a portrait of Baron de Kalb, and there appears to be no information identifying the artists by whom these portraits were painted. There were burned also portraits of the first five Presidents, the work of Gilbert Stuart, which were not the property of the Government and had been placed on exhibition in the Library with the prospect of a sale to the Government for the Executive Mansion. Portraits of Peyton Randolph, Bolivar, and of Baron von Steuben were among the works of art destroyed by the fire referred to.

JOHN G. CHAPMAN

Self-portrait

Represented by the painting, The Baptism of Pocahontas, in the Rotunda

{ 123 }

JOHN·VANDERLYN
Self-portrait

*Represented by the painting, The Landing of Columbus, in the Rotunda, and the portrait of Washington
in the Hall of the House of Representatives*

PORTRAIT OF ROBERT W. WEIR
Daniel Huntington, Painter

Weir is represented by the painting, The Embarkation of the Pilgrims, in the Rotunda

In the rotunda of the Capitol there were the four historical paintings by Trumbull, The Embarkation of the Pilgrims, by Robert Walter Weir, and The Baptism of Pocahontas, by John G. Chapman. The dates of the installation of these paintings are not definitely settled. The authorities consulted seem to indicate that at the period of which we are writing seven of the historical paintings were installed in the rotunda and that The Discovery of the Mississippi, by Powell, was not placed there until some years later. Wyeth fixes the date of the installation of the painting The Landing of Columbus, by Vanderlyn, as 1846, and the records of the appropriations and payments for this and the paintings by Weir and Chapman show the date of 1847, so it is presumed that the last of the paintings referred to were installed in 1846 or 1847. It may be interesting to know that John Vanderlyn, the painter of The Landing of Columbus, was a descendant of a portrait painter of considerable ability for the period in which he worked, as his grandfather, Pieter Vanderlyn, was a painter of portraits, some 30 or more of which have been identified as having been painted in Kingston, Albany, and Poughkeepsie, N. Y., during the period from 1719 to 1732. (See article by Charles X. Harris, New York Historical Society, Quarterly Bulletin for October, 1921.)

As Vanderlyn had also furnished for the Capitol a full-length portrait of Washington as a companion portrait for the portrait of Lafayette for the House of Representatives, it may be proper at this time to give some brief biographical notes of this painter. He was born in Kingston, Ulster County, N. Y., in 1776, and died there September 23, 1852. He was a pupil of Gilbert Stuart and a friend and protégé of Aaron Burr. He studied in Paris from 1796 to 1801 and occupied a studio in that city from 1803 to 1815. He was awarded a medal in 1808 for his painting entitled "Marius among the Ruins of Carthage," exhibited in Paris. Among his portraits may be included those of Washington, Burr, Monroe, Madison, Calhoun, Clinton, Zachary Taylor, and many other men of distinction. His Ariadne in Naxos is owned by the Pennsylvania Academy of Fine arts. A self-portrait of the artist is owned by the Metropolitan Museum of New York. In later life Vanderlyn was unfortunate in business affairs and died penniless and alone in a hotel in his native town.

As The Embarkation of the Pilgrims is the only painting by Robert Walter Weir in the Capitol, and as it belongs to the period of which we are now writing, the following biographical notes are included: Mr. Weir was born in New Rochelle, N. Y., June 18, 1803, and died in New York, 1889. His art education consisted of his studies under Jarvis; also at Florence, Italy, under Benvenuti. He also studied in Rome, Italy. He became a professional painter at the age of 20 and in 1829 became a member of the National Academy of Design. In 1832 he was made professor of drawing in the United States Military Academy at West Point, a position which he occupied over 40 years. It was at West Point where he became the instructor of James McNeill Whistler, who at that time was showing marked evidences of the eccentricities which followed his artistic career through life. One of Whistler's West Point accomplishments in drawing was to draw the ·shadow before drawing the object from which the shadow was cast. Among the works of Mr. Weir are: The Bourbons' Last March; Landing of Henry Hudson; Indian Captives; Christ and Nicodemus; Taking the Veil; Child's Evening Prayer; The Portico of the Palace of Octavia, Rome; Our Lord on the Mount of Olives; and Last Communion of Henry Clay. The Embarkation of the Pilgrims, in the rotunda of the Capitol, remained upon the wall, as did the other historical paintings, during the building of the new dome, at which time a falling beam rebounded and damaged the canvas. Professor Weir repaired the injury in 1861, having a special detail from the War Department for this purpose.

The remaining picture, The Baptism of Pocahontas, the work of John G. Chapman, is a picture which has probably been criticized on account of alleged defects in drawing far more extensively than the circumstances would warrant. Mr. Chapman was born in Alexandria, Va., in 1808. He studied for some time in Italy, afterwards painted in New York, and was one of the founders of the Century Club. He was elected a full member of the Academy of Design in 1836. He was also interested in wood engraving and became a teacher of this art. He was also an etcher of note and produced many etchings from original designs, among them being Return from the Vintage; A Monk Asking Alms; Italian Goatherds; The Gleaner; A View on the Campagna; and Maswaddox Creek, Eastern Shore, Maryland. Mr. Chapman furnished the illustrations for Harper's Bible and was the author of a drawing book, said to be the best of its kind in the English language and which passed through many editions in this country and Great Britain. Among his paintings are Sunset on the Campagna; Etruscan Girl; Vintage Scene; Last Arrow; and Valley of Mexico. In 1848 he went to Italy a second time and resided there from that time to 1890. He died in Brooklyn, N. Y., July 6, 1890.

THE CORRIDOR OF COLUMNS

CHAPTER VII

EXTENSION OF THE CAPITOL

I N THIS review of the works of art belonging in the Capitol in the year 1850 we have thus far included the entire Capitol with the exception of the Hall of the House of Representatives. This Hall was at that time and still remains the most interesting section of the old Capitol Building. Its works of art included the full-length portraits of Washington and Lafayette; the heroic-size statue in plaster of Liberty, by Enrico Causici, occupying a place above the frieze; the bas-relief of an American eagle upon the frieze, the work of Giuseppe Valaperti; and the Car of History, by Carlo Franzoni.

Inasmuch as reference has been made to the plans for the extension of the Capitol, we should not omit at this time to call attention to the fact that it was in the minds of many legislators, when the new Hall of the House of Representatives had been completed, that the old Hall of the House should then become a storehouse for art works, an exhibition room for paintings and statuary, and a general assembly place for the people. This plan, however, was not consummated until many years after the occupancy of the new Hall of the House, but the record should be made that there were those who had the vision to see the possibilities of making this beautiful hall a place where the arts might be given a more appropriate setting than they had theretofore received in other portions of the Capitol.

On the 4th day of July, 1851, the corner stone of the Capitol extension was laid with elaborate civic and Masonic ceremonies.[1] These ceremonies were attended by the President of the United States, Millard Fillmore, and Mayor of Washington Walter Lenox, George Washington Parke Custis, the heads of departments, Army and Navy officers, Masonic orders, and civil organizations. The organizations formed at the city hall and marched to the Capitol. Architect Thomas U. Walter deposited in the corner stone a sealed jar containing historical documents, coins of the United States, a copy of the oration of Daniel Webster, then Secretary of State, copies of newspapers, and other memorials. President Millard Fillmore laid the corner stone and the customary Masonic ceremony followed. Benjamin B. French, grand master of the Masonic fraternity, made a short opening address and was followed by the orator of the day, Daniel Webster. From this address it seems appropriate that the following extract should be given in order that the patriotic sentiments therein contained may be more widely disseminated:

* * * If, therefore, it shall hereafter be the will of God that this structure shall fall from its base, that its foundation be upturned and this deposit brought to the eyes of men, be it known that on this day

---

[1] The authorities upon the location of this corner stone seem to be in conflict. Edward Clark, Architect of the Capitol, in an article found on page 116 of the book entitled "Celebration of the One Hundredth Anniversary of the Laying of the Corner Stone of the Capitol of the United States," uses the following language: "The work was commenced by laying the corner stone of the south wing July 4th, 1851." From a manuscript of August Schoenborn it is learned that the corner stone was laid in the northeast corner of the House wing. Mr. Schoenborn was head draftsman during the building of the extension of the Capitol and remained in the service of the Capitol until his death, in 1902.

On page 133 of the same book an illustration shows that the corner stone was laid at the northeast corner, north wing of the Capitol. As Edward Clark was probably present at the laying of the corner stone of the extension, or came to this city soon afterwards, his statement should be accepted as final upon the location of this corner stone.

9

PORTRAIT OF DANIEL WEBSTER
John Neagle, painter

the Union of the United States of America stands firm; that their Constitution still exists unimpaired and with all its original usefulness and glory, growing every day stronger and stronger in the affections of the great body of the American people, and attracting more and more the admiration of the world.   *   *   *

It has heretofore been stated that the plans for the extension of the Capitol included new uses for that section now known as Statuary Hall.   Suggestions that the Hall of the House of Representatives could be used for the display of works of art are found in Senate Report No. 145 (31st Cong., 1st sess.), dated May 28, 1850.

The question of the purchase of portraits for the Executive Mansion, particularly with reference to the purchase of the portraits by Stuart of the first five Presidents, was again brought to the attention of the Joint Committee on the Library on January 22, 1851.   It will be remembered that in the review of the art works in the Capitol for the year 1850 these paintings were referred to as being burned December 24, 1851.   The recommendation at this present time came from G. P. A. Healy, a portrait painter of distinction, who, for some reason not shown in the record, recommended at this time the purchase by Congress of these paintings.   The recommendation was considered and laid over.   At this same meeting of the committee a resolution was presented from the Senate referring to the committee the proceedings of a meeting of American citizens in Liverpool, England, favoring the erection by Congress of a suitable monument to the memory of Zachary Taylor, late President of the United States.   This resolution was considered by the committee and laid over for the present.

The next item relating to works of art is found in the records of the meeting of the Joint Committee on the Library for June 14, 1852, when the following resolution was considered:

Resolved, That the portrait of Henry Clay, painted by Giuseppe Fagnani, a resident of New York, for the Library of Congress be accepted and that a joint resolution to this effect be presented to the House of Representatives.

The next action in this matter occurred in the House of Representatives on Tuesday, June 22, 1852:

Mr. CHANDLER. I ask the unanimous consent of the House to offer a resolution authorizing the Library Committee to receive and place in the Library a likeness of Henry Clay presented by an artist in New York. The resolution was read as follows:
"Resolved, That the portrait of Henry Clay presented to the Nation by Giuseppe Fagnani, a resident in New York, be placed in the Library of Congress. There being no objection to the resolution it was considered as agreed to." (Congressional Globe, vol. 24, part 2, p. 1595.)

The final action on the part of the Senate occurred on June 23, 1852:

Portrait of Mr. Clay.
The message from the House of Representatives also announced that it had passed the following joint resolution:
"Resolved by the House of Representatives, in Congress assembled, That the portrait of Henry Clay, presented to the Nation by Giuseppe Fagnani, a resident of New York, be placed in the Library of Congress."
The resolution was read a first and second time by its title and considered as in Committee of the Whole; no amendment being offered it was read a third time and passed. (Congressional Globe, vol. 24, pt. 2, p. 1602.)

In the Speaker's lobby

PORTRAIT OF HENRY CLAY

Giuseppe Fagnani, painter

The first portrait of a Speaker owned by the Government
Presented by the artist in 1852

GIUSEPPE FAGNANI (1819–1873)

Represented by the portrait of Henry Clay, in the Speaker's lobby

The first portrait in oil of a Speaker owned by the Government

So far as known, this was the first work of art to be presented to the Government after the disastrous fire in the Library of December 24, 1851. It should be noted that this was offered to the Library of Congress, but that in the action of the House of Representatives and also of the Senate it is described as a gift to the Nation to be placed in the Library of Congress. It is singular that this tender of a portrait should be made at a time when the earthly career of Henry Clay was nearing its close. The last action in the Senate occurred June 23, 1852. Henry Clay died June 29, 1852, and the resolution was approved July 3, 1852. The painter of this portrait, Giuseppe Fagnani, was born in Naples, Italy, December 24, 1819, and died in New York May 22, 1873. His ability for painting at the age of 13 attracted the Queen of the two Sicilies, Marie Isabelle, who granted him a pension for five years. He resided successively in Vienna, Paris, Madrid, and London, painting portraits of the most prominent people in the world of society and politics. In 1849 he came to Washington, D. C., with his friend the English ambassador, Sir Henry Bulwer. While a resident of Washington he painted portraits of Henry Clay, Daniel Webster, General Cass, President Fillmore, and others. In 1851 he married Harriet Emma Everett Goodwin, of Charlestown, Mass., became an American citizen, and took up his residence in New York. The general public will remember him best by his painting entitled "Nine Muses," types of American beauty. This painting is now in the Metropolitan Museum in New York. In the manuscript division of the Library of Congress a letter is found relating to his art work, and a copy is herewith introduced, in the belief

EMANUEL LEUTZE

*Represented by the mural decoration, Westward the Course of
Empire Takes Its Way, on the wall of the
west staircase, House wing*

it may be of interest to those who have seen his portrait of Henry Clay, now in the Speaker's lobby of the Hall of the House of Representatives:

NEW YORK, *May 15, 1852.*

Hon. DANIEL WEBSTER:

MY DEAR SIR: I have just received a letter from Sir Henry Bulwer begging me to paint your portrait to add to his collection, and as you may remember, you promised him when in Washington to sit to me. He is very anxious to close the fulfilment of that promise—and if in passing through New York you could make it convenient to give me one sitting, you will greatly oblige both Sir Henry and myself.

I remain, my dear Sir, with sentiments of the most respectful consideration,

Your very obedient servant,

GIUSEPPE FAGNANI.

The possibility of additional space being provided by the extensions to the Capitol Building aroused considerable interest upon the part of artists who desired to be represented in the decoration of the new buildings to be erected. Long before any actual space was ready for decoration applications were received, some of them of a very indefinite character, so far as the records show, as the following extract from the records of the Library Committee will explain:

July 29, 1852. Petitions from artists and others in relation to historical paintings for the Capitol referred to the Committee by the Senate and House of Representatives were considered and laid upon the table.

The Library Committee in some instances proved to be a resting place for the hopes of many ambitious artists. It is not probable that this was done with any feeling of hostility toward the painters or their friends, but this committee without doubt felt that its responsibility to the public would not permit of favorable consideration of a large number of petitions and applications which to them seemed inappropriate for the purposes of decoration for a building of this character. It was not, however, possible at all times to quiet the ambitions of certain artists, for the reason that some of them were fortunate enough to have influential friends in Congress who were sufficiently interested to press their claims in such a manner that they were at least known about if they were not successful in securing commissions. An illustration of this character is found in the proceedings of the United States Senate of April 8, 1852, when Senator Cooper spoke in behalf of Emanuel Leutze, an artist of marked ability and whose reputation has been greatly aided by his well-known painting, Washington Crossing the Delaware.

Mr. Leutze was born in Gmund, Wurttemberg, Germany, May 24, 1816. He came to the United States while quite young and was educated in Virginia and Philadelphia. He studied art in the latter city and later in Dusseldorf, Prussia; also in Rome. His specialty was historical painting, and he executed many pictures connected with American history. While the effort of Senator Cooper in his behalf did not result immediately in securing for Mr. Leutze a commission, he was afterwards awarded the important commission of placing upon the wall of the west staircase of the House of Representatives the large mural decoration entitled "Westward the Course of Empire Takes Its Way," a painting which has been severely criticized by some, but by many competent critics declared to be a very notable example of the best of historical paintings adapted to the purposes of a mural decoration. Mr. Leutze was also a notable painter of portraits, and his portraits of Mr. and Mrs. Thomas U. Walter are well worth a place in any collection of portraits. Mr. Leutze died in Washington, D. C., July 18, 1868. The remarks of Senator Cooper concerning the granting of a commission to Mr. Leutze as found in the Congressional Globe (vol. 24, pt. 2, p. 1004) follow:

[U. S. Senate, April 8, 1852. Cong. Globe, vol. 24, pt. 2, pp. 1004–1005]

"Mr. COOPER. Mr. President, I hold in my hand an application from Mr. Leutze, the distinguished American artist, author of the painting representing 'Washington Crossing the Delaware,' exhibited for the last two or three weeks in the rotunda of the Capitol, and which, I presume, you and most of the Members of this body have seen and admired. The application of Mr. Leutze is addressed to Congress, and proposes to repeat, with such emendations as experience may suggest, the beautiful painting to which I have just referred, together with a fellow to it the subject of which is to be likewise drawn from that portion of American history which represents Washington rallying our retreating troops at the Battle of Monmouth.

"I need not state, Mr. President, that subjects better calculated to inspire the genius of the artist, or awaken the patriotism of the American spectator, can hardly be selected. Of the truth of this there is evidence in the painting which the memorial proposes to repeat. Who that has looked upon that admirable picture, and contemplated that majestic form, and composed, yet inflexible, determination which beams from the countenance of the heroic chief, working his perilous way through the ice of the Delaware to reach the enemy and strike a decisive blow for freedom, then almost expiring, has not felt his patriotism stimulated, and the blood flowing in warmer and quicker currents through his veins? And who, in addition to this, has not experienced a just pride in learning that this fine stirring representation of one of the great acts of the drama of our Revolution, was the production of American talent? No one, I am sure, could contemplate this noble picture without experiencing the glow of both of these emotions of patriotism and pride. With the true tact of genius, the artist has seized the turning point in the great struggle for independence—the moment when hope was attending with despair, to present the leader of our armies, upon whom all hopes were concentrated and all eyes turned, in the attitude of striking a great and decisive blow, calculated, if successful, to revive the drooping courage and cheer the fainting hearts of his almost desponding countrymen. It was the critical moment, pregnant with the result of the impending contest, with the hopes of humanity, with the destiny, perhaps of the world. All these hung suspended on the events of the night, and the success of the morning which was to follow it. The event of the crossing of the Delaware was an event more justly memorable than the crossing of the Rubicon. The spirit of all this the artist has caught, and transferred to the canvas with a fidelity and truthfulness which must have struck every beholder.

"The other event which the artist is to commemorate, when embellished by his fine imagination, and graceful, but vigorous touch, can scarcely fail to result in a beautiful soul-stirring picture. The subject is one of the most striking in the history of our Revolutionary War. General Lee has been sent forward to bring on the action, and keep the enemy employed until Washington with the main body of the Army, should come up; but instead of doing so, he retreated in disorder at the approach of the enemy. Washington, arriving on the ground, vexed and disappointed at the conduct of Lee, and losing for a moment the lofty and habitual composure, which, until then, had never forsaken him, even in the most trying situation of his life, rebuked the retreating general with asperity. Then, turning to his troops, upon whom the enemy were pressing, asked them if they could fight and ordered them to face about and charge. The subject is a fine one and well calculated to develop the highest powers of the artist. I hope, however, that the matter will not end with the presentation of the memorial; but that the Committee on the Library, to whom I design to refer it, will give it an attentive and favorable consideration. Liberality, intended to adorn and beautify the Capitol, at the same time that it operates to encourage the development of American talent, will never be disowned by the American people.

"Since the application of Mr. Leutze was placed in my hands, Mr. Healy, an artist of equal eminence and merit, has expressed his wish to execute for Congress, from subjects connected with our Revolutionary history, two paintings—the subject of one to be 'Throwing Overboard of the Tea in Boston Harbor,' the other 'The Battle of Bunker Hill.'

"In the first of these events was contained the germ of the American Revolution. The second will represent the first of the great battles in which our untried troops measured their strength with veterans of England. Both are subjects of deep and lasting interest, well calculated to draw out and develop the highest powers of the artist.

"Mr. President, I pretend to no very refined judgment in matters of art; but if I were permitted to express an opinion on the subject, it would be to state that Healy's 'Webster Replying to Hayne in the Senate' and Leutze's 'Washington Crossing the Delaware' are amongst the finest modern historical paintings which I have anywhere seen. Of such artists the country may well entertain a just pride, and if her representatives would but echo her sentiments, they would receive encouragement.

"Allow me, sir, one word more. It seems to me that it is the duty, as well as the privilege, of Congress to do something to encourage the development of native talent, in this most attractive and refining branch of art. We have evidence in the pictures of Leutze and Healy, exhibited in this city during the present session of Congress, to prove that American genius, in this branch of the fine arts, needs but scope and encouragement to give it a commanding and enviable reputation. But in this country public taste in this direction has not been sufficiently educated and developed. Congress should, in my judgment, take the initiative and lend its aid. Private fortunes possessed by men of refined taste and judicious liberality are still too rare amongst us to afford either constant or certain encouragement to the artist. There is one individual in this District to whom the friends of art are indebted of an intelligent dispensation of his ample means in collecting a gallery of pictures; and it is to be hoped his example will be followed elsewhere, and by others in similar circumstances. Let others, like him, thus dispose of their abundant means, and they will thereby acquire, as he has done, a just title to the gratitude of the artist and the friends of art wherever they are found.

"In other countries the fine arts are objects of the patronage of the Government. They are encouraged, not only for their refining influences, but likewise with a view to the perfection of the useful arts. Schools of painting and design have done much to perfect various branches of manufactures, furnishing patterns for tapestry, brocades, laces, carpets and various kinds of damask and figured fabrics. Heretofore we have been obliged to resort to Europe for designs for all these kinds of articles which are produced by our artisans. But, by encouraging painting and the kindred art of design we would soon cease to be dependent upon Europe for our patterns."

The memorials were referred to the Committee on the Library. Mr. Cooper presented the following resolution for consideration:

"*Resolved*, That the Committee on the Library be, and it is hereby instructed to inquire into the expediency of employing Mr. Leutze to repeat for Congress his painting 'Washington Crossing the

From a photograph in the collection of Hon. Nicholas Longworth

WEST FRONT OF THE CAPITOL IN 1858

Showing canal and greenhouse in foreground

Delaware` together with a fellow to it representing `Washington Rallying the American Troops at the Battle of Monmouth,` also of employing Mr. Healy to paint two pictures, one representing `The Throwing Overboard of the Tea in Boston Harbor,` the other `The Battle of Bunker Hill.`"

The consideration of the resolution submitted by Mr. Cooper and the result of the same is found in the Congressional Globe (vol. 24, pt. 2, 1st sess., 32d Cong. (1852), p. 1533).

HISTORICAL PAINTINGS

The Senate proceeded to consider the resolution submitted by Mr. Cooper, on the 8th of April, respecting the employment of Leutze and Healy to execute certain paintings for Congress; and, having been amended, it was agreed to as follows:

"*Resolved,* That the Committee on the Library be and it is hereby instructed to inquire into the expediency of employing Mr. Leutze to repaint for Congress his painting representing Washington crossing the Delaware, together with a fellow to it representing Washington rallying the American troops at the Battle of Monmouth; also of employing Mr. Healy to paint two pictures, one representing the throwing overboard of the tea in Boston Harbor, the other the Battle of Bunker Hill; also Mr. Rothermel to execute two paintings, the subjects likewise to be drawn from American Revolutionary history."

(Cong. Globe, vol. 24, pt. 2, 32d Cong. 1st sess. (1852) p. 1533.)

An opportunity to purchase a collection of paintings known as Catlin's Indian Scenes was offered to the Senate at about this same period. The record is as follows:

CATLIN'S INDIAN SCENES

In the Senate on June 10, 1852, the following resolution previously offered was taken up:

"*Resolved,* That the Committee on the Library be requested to inquire into the expediency of reporting a bill for the purchase of Mr. George Catlin's Indian scenes and portraits, which are in danger of being sold and lost to this country."

Mr. Seward moved to amend by striking out the words "Committee on the Library" and inserting "Committee on Indian Affairs."

This amendment was discussed by several; in the course of the discussion Mr. Borland said: " * * * we have now in the rotunda a painting in which Indians are delineated, and in which there are figures representing anything in the world but Indians. Any one who knows what an Indian looks like could not select from that painting a single figure representing an Indian at all * * *."

After further discussion Mr. Borland made the statement that Capt. Eastman was willing to paint pictures for no greater compensation than he now receives as an officer of the Army, that he had never seen Capt. Eastman, but had seen his illustrations in Mr. Schoolcraft's book.

Mr. Hale asked that the committee be instructed to inquire into the expediency of removing "that thing in the east yard called `Greenough's Washington` and also those matters which so disfigure the eastern portico where strangers from all parts of the country assemble on Inauguration Day. I hope that before next Inauguration Day shall come, let which party may succeed, those dreadful looking images which deface what would otherwise be a beautiful building and mar the prospect, may be removed * * *."

In the meantime the Library Committee had arrived at that portion of their deliberations where they were considering the petitions and resolutions referred to them by the Senate during the preceding year and relating to the artists Healy, Leutze, and Rothermel. In the records of the meeting of February 10, 1853, we find the following:

A resolution from the Senate instructing the Committee to inquire into the expediency of Commissioning Messrs. Healy, Leutze and Rothermel or such other eminent native artists as they may think proper to paint with a view to the encouragement of American artists and the decoration of the chambers now being built for the use of the Senate and the House of Representatives two pictures each, representing scenes in our revolutionary or ante-revolutionary history was considered and laid over for the present.

Again on February 23, 1853, there is further reference to the same subject:

The resolution from the Senate directing the Committee to inquire into the expediency of commissioning certain artists to paint four pictures representing revolutionary and ante-revolutionary history was further considered.

Meanwhile conditions relating to the work on the extension of the Capitol were becoming somewhat complicated. It will be remembered that the initiative looking toward the erection of a new Senate wing and House wing was taken by the Congress, that a competition was instituted, and before any decision had resulted Congress passed an act of authorization which included an initial appropriation and constituted the President as the authority to select an architect who was to take charge of the proposed additions to the Capitol. This course was from the start destined to produce trouble, and trouble soon followed. Charges were instituted against the architect; investigations were ordered which seemed to prove nothing except that the work had been exceptionally well performed, but in the meantime President Millard Fillmore was succeeded by President Franklin Pierce. One of the early official acts of President Pierce was to issue the following order:

EXECUTIVE OFFICE, *March 23, 1853.*

Believing that the public interest involved in the erection of the wings of the United States Capitol will be promoted by the exercise of the general supervision and control of the whole works by a skilful and competent officer of the Corps of Engineers or of the Topographical Corps, and as these Corps are more amenable to the Secretary of War, I hereby direct that the jurisdiction heretofore exercised over the said work by the Department of the Interior be transferred to the War Department and request that the Secretary of War will designate to the President a suitable officer to take charge of the same.

FRANKLIN PIERCE.

In accordance with this suggestion of President Pierce contained in the foregoing order, the Secretary of War, Jefferson Davis, on March 29 detailed Capt. Montgomery C. Meigs to act as superintendent. Captain Meigs was evidently well fitted for this position. His education at West Point and his wide experience in engineering work since his graduation from the Military Academy had tended to make him valuable and efficient under the conditions then existing. His faults, if he had any, and he probably had, seem to the writer to be those occasioned by overzealousness, and in the zeal manifested in the work in which he was engaged he seemed, Atlaslike, to be carrying the whole Government, including the construction of the Capitol, upon his shoulders. It is possible that in his zeal to demonstrate his ability in this important position he was not always as considerate of the architect, Mr. Walter, as he should have been. At all events their relations soon became strained, and Mr. Walter, who, by the way, was a lineal architectural descendant of Latrobe, soon found himself in a position where he was treated more as a draftsman than as an architect. These strained relations continued for many years and charges and countercharges were made by both parties to the controversy. It finally resulted, however, in Captain Meigs being relieved from the position of superintendent of the construction of the Capitol and being assigned to another position in active Army service. Aside from the controversy with Walter, there is very much to admire and approve in the conduct of Captain Meigs. He was a hard-working, well-informed, and loyal official, and his efforts to assist in the completion of the Capitol upon such a scale as the dignity of the Nation demanded were ably seconded by those with whom he was in official relations in the War Department.

We have now reached the period of the completion of the Rescue Group by Horatio Greenough. From the appropriation bills it appears that the commission for the statuary for the north and south blockings of the east central portion of the Capitol were originally awarded to Luigi Persico and finally separated into two commissions, one of which was awarded to Persico, the other to Greenough. The commission awarded to Persico had been completed several years earlier, and in the appropriation act of August 31, 1852, for the fiscal year of 1853, we find the following:

> For freight and transportation of the group of statuary contracted for with Horatio Greenough from Leghorn to Washington, and for placing it on a pedestal in front of the eastern portico of the Capitol a sum not exceeding $7,000. (Stats. L., vol. 10, p. 95.)

The exact date of the erection of this Rescue Group does not seem to be stated in any of the authorities consulted.[2] The date of its erection is immaterial. The thing that seems to be of the greatest importance is that it is claimed by the friends of the sculptor that the group was not properly assembled and that the mother and child instead of being upon the right side of the Indian should have been immediately in front. This information is contained in letters on file in the office of the Architect of the Capitol, and from measurements made of the base area of the group it is apparent that the mother and child could have been placed directly in front of the Indian, and thus give to the group the interpretation desired by the sculptor. It is said that the statuary was erected by Clark Mills, the sculptor of the Jackson Statue and of the Washington Statue in this city, but it is supposed that no plan was sent with the statuary to show the manner in which it should be assembled. The sculptor Greenough died in Somerville, Mass., December 18, 1852, and as the appropriation for the bringing of the group to Washington did not become available until July 1, 1853, it is fair to presume that the sculptor died without leaving any instructions to guide those who were to place the group in position. It was a matter of regret to the sculptor's friends who survived him and who knew of the plan of this composition that some memorandum was not furnished which would have prevented the commission of this error in the erection of the work.

Some of the important art matters with which Capt. Montgomery C. Meigs was intimately associated was the granting of a commission for the statuary for the Senate pediment of the Capitol, the commission for the bronze doors for the main eastern entrances of the Senate and House wings, the group of statuary over the main Senate entrance, and for the figure of Freedom which surmounts the dome. All of these commissions were given to Thomas Crawford, a sculptor of marked ability of his period, a man of tremendous energy, and who was unfortunate in not living to see any of these commissions completed. Mr. Crawford was born in New York City March 22, 1814. He studied in New York with Robert E. Launitz and John Frazee. Frazee was a sculptor of some ability. Launitz seems to have been a skillful marble worker, but regarding his ability to design or to model there seems to be no record of any work of this class having been produced by him. Launitz, however, occupied a position of considerable importance in New York City, and nearly all the foreigners who had known Mr. Crawford in Rome upon coming to New York always called upon Mr. Launitz to secure his influence and cooperation in finding them positions in this country.

The correspondence between Captain Meigs and Mr. Crawford is of itself of sufficient interest to require its publication in a separate book. It is important because it traces clearly the conditions of art in this country in the early fifties and the care and painstaking method adopted by Captain Meigs in carrying out the plans which he had formulated for the art works of the Capitol. It appears from the correspondence that in August, 1853,

---

[2] John S. Meehan, Librarian of Congress, in a letter dated Sept. 7, 1853, and addressed to J. A. Pearce, chairman of the Joint Committee on the Library, states: "* * * The group of statuary by Greenough is on the blocking opposite to Persico's group but is not yet ready for public inspection. Those who have seen all the figures and have had the grouping explained to them speak warmly in favor. So they did of Persico's. It is said that Mr. Greenough's group will all be in place and exposed to public view in the course of a fortnight. * * *"

BUST OF THOMAS CRAWFORD
Tommaso Gagliardi, sculptor

Crawford is represented by the Crawford bronze doors, the statue of Freedom, and the Senate pediment

THE SENATE PEDIMENT

Statuary by Thomas Crawford

Captain Meigs sent to Thomas Crawford tracings of the eastern doorway of the south wing and of the pediment over the eastern portico. He also stated that he had sent similar tracings relating to the north wing to Mr. Powers (Hiram Powers), and that he had consulted with Mr. Jefferson Davis, Secretary of War, who had authorized him (Meigs) to communicate with some American sculptors and request them to submit designs accompanied with an estimated cost. In explanation he stated that it was not possible for Congress to decide upon designs, that the construction of the building was in the hands of the President, and provided such a design was submitted as might meet with the President's approval there could be no question concerning his authority for ordering its construction, provided the cost was within reasonable limits. Captain Meigs also stated in this same letter:

The pediments and doorways should be a part of the original construction of the building, and I do not see why a republic so much richer than the Athenian should not rival the Parthenon in the front of its first public edifice. Permit me to say that the sculpture sent here by our artists is not altogether adapted to the taste of our people. We are not able to appreciate too refined and intricate allegorical representations, and while the naked Washington of Greenough is the theme of admiration to the few scholars, it is unsparingly denounced by the less refined multitude.

* * * In our history of the struggle between civilized man and the savage, between the cultivated and the wild nature are certainly to be found themes worthy of the artist and capable of appealing to the feeling of all classes.

The immense popularity of the Greek Slave is probably due to its meaning being within the comprehension of all. Its eminent beauty would not alone have gained it such success.

In a letter of August 23, 1853, which Captain Meigs marked "Private," he suggested that it would be advisable to forward sketches as soon as possible and not to give too much publicity to the matter until his designs were adopted. The reason for this advice is shown by the following quotation:

I have no hesitation in asking first the assistance of yourself and Mr. Powers, as I am well aware that you are at the head of your profession, but if it gets abroad too soon we may have jarring interests and claims urged by personal influence to make members of Congress interfere. The whole construction of the building is expressly committed to the President by law, by him placed in the hands of the Secretary of War, under whose order I am in charge.

In a letter from Thomas Crawford from Rome October 13, 1853, in which he thanked Captain Meigs for his consideration and stated that he would give immediate and earnest attention to the composition of a suitable design for the pediment of the eastern portico of our great national structure, he also used the following language:

I fully agree with you regarding the necessity of producing a work intelligible to our entire population. The darkness of allegory must give place to common sense. I have faith enough to believe that poetry and grandeur are inseparately connected with the history of our country's past and future and that the dignity of sculpture may well be devoted to the perpetuation of what the people love and understand. As yet I have not had the honor of being employed by our national Government, but the Washington monument I am now engaged upon for the state of Virginia will serve as a practical exponent of my desire to illustrate American history without having recourse to sculpture as practiced in the age of Pericles. * * *

In reply to an inquiry of Captain Meigs, Mr. Crawford stated that Mr. Clevenger died of consumption off Gibraltar on his way to Rome in 1843, and that he was greatly lamented by his brother artists. It may be that from reading what has preceded relating to Captain Meigs the impression has been gained that he started about his work without proper preparation. If this impression exists, it should be corrected. So far as careful examination has shown it appears that Captain Meigs used every possible means to inform himself upon all questions liable to come under his supervision in the position which he occupied. His letters to Thomas Crawford may create the feeling that he was acting without authority and without a thorough acquaintance with the subject. In order that his position may appear in its proper relationship, the following letter, which appears to be an answer to a letter of Captain Meigs, is quoted to establish the fact that he was eager to fortify himself in every possible way for the efficient performance of the tasks assigned to him:

BOSTON, *July 12, 1853.*

DEAR SIR: I have duly received yours of the 7th requesting me to designate the distinguished American artists whom I think most capable of designing and executing the works in sculpture contemplated for the enrichment of the pediments to the Capitol extension buildings. I have no hesitation in expressing the opinion that Mr. Hiram Powers, of Ohio, now at Florence, and Mr. Crawford, of New York, I believe now at Rome, are at the head of the artists of this country; and perfectly competent to design and execute the proposed works in a manner to do honor to the country I consider Mr. Powers in some respects the first living artist; he is the author, as you are aware, of several first-rate works. He has lately been selected by the Committee of Mr. Webster's friends in this region to execute a statue of our great statesman. Mr. Crawford, now engaged in a great monumental work for Richmond, is also a first-rate artist and quite competent to design and execute a work like that proposed.

I am, dear Sir, with great respect, faithfully yours,
EDWARD EVERETT.

HIRAM POWERS (1805–1873)
Represented by full-length statues of Franklin and Jefferson, and in the Supreme Court room by portrait bust of Chief Justice Marshall

Referring to that portion of the letter heretofore quoted from Captain Meigs to Thomas Crawford, wherein it is stated that he had also sent to Hiram Powers a copy of the letter, with drawings and other information, it seems proper at this time to introduce the following letter from Hiram Powers to show the manner in which the request of Captain Meigs for a proposal for statuary for the extension of the Capitol was received:

FLORENCE, *September 22, 1853.*

M. C. MEIGS, Esquire,
    Captain of Engineers,
        In Charge of the Capitol Extension and Washington Aqueduct.

MY DEAR SIR: I have received your welcome and most interesting letter of August 18, 1853, but not the tracings which I suppose have been accidently left out.

I fully coincide with your views which seem both natural and just and I thank you much for the frank and kind spirit in which you have written to me. But I have not the time to prepare designs for the decoration of our Capitol Buildings even if it were a desirable object with me *to propose* for a commission from the Government of my country.

With sincere regards, I beg you to believe me, my Dear Sir,
    Most respectfully your obedient servant,

HIRAM POWERS.

Allowing for the time which must elapse in the transmission of mail across the Atlantic in the year 1853, it appears that Mr. Crawford acted very promptly in placing in the hands of the superintendent, Captain Meigs, designs for the pediment, which were presented through the medium of photographs and mailed October 31, 1853. An acknowledgment from Captain Meigs contains the following:

I have this moment received your letter of the 31st of October with photographs of your design for the pediment. * * * I am myself very much pleased with the design which is appropriate and intelligible, and if wrought out in large with the same skill displayed in the making of the design cannot fail to be a noble ornament to our Capitol and a worthy monument to the youthful and vigorous artistic power of our country.

On the same day of the writing of the foregoing letter (November 29, 1853) Captain Meigs wrote a letter to Hon. Jefferson Davis, Secretary of War, in which, referring to Crawford's designs, he stated:

* * * The time which he estimates necessary for the completion of the life-size models in plaster ready for the marble is thirty months. The price $20,000.

There are fourteen figures and numerous accessories and I think that the price is reasonable and respectfully request authority to give him the order for the execution of the models should the design meet the approval of yourself and the President.

It is evident that both the Secretary of War and the President gave immediate attention to the letter of Captain Meigs submitting designs for the proposed pediment. It may be that these officials in those days did not have as much to occupy their time as officials have at the present time. On the 30th of November, 1853, Captain Meigs informed Mr. Crawford of the acceptance of his design and of his terms. In this letter the following language occurs:

We accept your terms and conditions and you will please consider this as the order for the execution of the models; much will remain to be settled as to the mode of executing the sculpture and on this I will write at leisure.

The next letter in this chain of correspondence is from Thomas Crawford, dated Rome, January 17, 1854. From this the following extracts are given:

* * * In a conversation with Mr. Powers during my visit to Florence I learnt from him with great surprise that he had positively refused to be employed upon the second pediment. I mention this subject in connection with a proposition I shall now make to you of my desire to offer my services where those of Mr. Powers have been withheld. The result at least will be the consequence of their acceptance and that result is of considerable importance as you are aware of the general effect of the entire front of the Capitol. I allude to the harmony of light and shadow to be obtained by the grouping of the statuary in both pediments. * * *

* * * With regard to carving the models into marble, I have, after much reflection, concluded this can be better accomplished and with more economy at Carrara or Rome than in the United States. The first quality of statuary marble is thus insured and the convenience of obtaining the required number of good workmen united with the advantage of having the work personally attended to by myself are reasons which I doubt not will induce you to take this information into consideration. * * *

It seems very fortunate that Captain Meigs, or those with whom he consulted, formed other plans for the carving of the statuary than those proposed by Thomas Crawford. It is possible that there were those who remembered the caution of Horatio Greenough concerning the placing out of doors of statuary carved from Carrara marble, and those who have seen the condition of the statues Peace and War by Luigi Persico, installed probably in 1835, can readily imagine the extent to which the Crawford pediment would have been damaged if it had been executed from Carrara marble.

In addition to a general correct information upon the properties of marble to resist the weather of Washington, Captain Meigs possessed some art ideas, and he was not at all afraid to advise Mr. Crawford in art matters, as the following quotation will show:

DECEMBER 27, 1853.

THOMAS CRAWFORD, Esquire,
        Rome.

DEAR SIR: In my last letter which was hurriedly written I said that I would write further on some minor points of the design. It seems to me that in making the figure of the soldier bear a certain

10

From a portrait by Charles Loring Elliott in the Corcoran Gallery of Art

HORATIO STONE

*Represented by the statues of John Hancock, Alexander Hamilton, and
Edward Dickinson Baker*

STATUE OF JOHN HANCOCK
Horatio Stone, sculptor

resemblance to Washington you incur the danger of being misapprehended; the many will say that you have attempted a portrait and failed. The few persons to whom I have shown the photograph have told me that this was their impression. Artists would appreciate your allusion, but I think you will find it better either to make a portrait, or divest the figure of all resemblance to the Father of his Country.

For the accessories of Indian life I hope to be able to send you the work upon the manner and customs of our Indian Tribes now in course of publication by the Government. If it be true that a shoemaker can criticize a shoe tie, will it not be as well for the artist to disarm his criticism by making the shoe tie correctly? If it is all that he is able to appreciate, let him too be gratified.

It should not be considered that the entire art interests were centered in the sculptural work of Thomas Crawford, for we find in the records of the Joint Committee on the Library for January 19, 1854, the following:

A letter was received from Charles Fisher in relation to his picture of the Battle of New Orleans; laid on the table.

And on February 16, 1854, the following:

Mr. Fisher's application to sell to the United States his picture of the Battle of New Orleans was considered and rejected.

On the same date we find the following record:

On application of the Honorable Justice Wayne,
Ordered, That the bust of Chief Justice Taney by Horatio Stone be placed on exhibition a short time in the Library.

It is probable that the bust referred to is the same bust now in the Supreme Court conference room. This is our first introduction to the sculptor Horatio Stone, or, as he was familiarly known in Washington, Doctor Stone, and whose influence in the art matters of Washington was a few years later to be widely recognized all over the country. Doctor Stone was born in Jackson, Washington County, N. Y., December 25, 1808. He was the second child of Reuben and Nancy Fairchild Stone. At an early age he attempted wood carving, but his father, a serious farmer, did not discover in these attempts any evidence of genius and emphasized the fact that it was more important to work on the farm than to attempt to carve wood. Accordingly the young artist, as is sometimes customary with young people, differed with his father in his estimate of the value of wood carving and abruptly left home without consultation or conference with his parents and was not heard of by them for many years. In the meanwhile he had studied medicine, and his studies in anatomy had awakened the longing of his boyhood days for sculpture. While a practicing physician with probably a fair degree of success awaiting him, he abandoned the practice of medicine and in 1848 came to Washington. His instrumentality in the organization of the Washington Union Art Association and his activities in connection with other artists in memorializing Congress requesting recognition of American artists will be referred to in a later chronological sequence. During the residence of Doctor Stone in Washington he maintained studios in the northwestern part of the city; at the navy yard; and later in a room in the subbasement of the Capitol. He visited Italy twice in the study of his work as a sculptor. His busts of Benton and Taney were awarded the medal of the Maryland Institute in 1857, and he exhibited in the National Academy of Design in 1849 and 1869. He is credited with models for the statues of Professor Morse, Admiral Farragut, and Doctor Harvey, the discoverer of the circulation of the blood. He died in Carrara, Italy, August 25, 1875.

CHAPTER VIII

 LITTLE earlier in this work reference has been made to the purpose expressed by some of transforming the old Hall of the House of Representatives when it should be abandoned for legislative purposes by the completion of the new Hall of the House of Representatives into a room devoted to the exhibition of such works of art belonging to the Government as might be more suitably shown in this room than in other parts of the old Capitol Building. In support of this proposed use of the room we now know as Statuary Hall, some letters bearing on this subject from Capt. M. C. Meigs to Gouverneur Kemble, of Cold Spring, N. Y., are herewith introduced. It is true that the subject would be more attractively presented if we were able also to publish the letters from Gouverneur Kemble to Captain Meigs, but from the completeness of these letters used a fair understanding of both sides of the correspondence may be obtained.

Gouverneur Kemble was an enthusiastic lover of art and was well versed in current art matters. He had served as a Representative from the State of New York in the Twenty-fifth and Twenty-sixth Congresses (1837–1841), and from such service was well acquainted with the legislative Chamber in which Congress was meeting at the time of the writing of the letters which follow.

8TH FEBRUARY 1854.

G. KEMBLE, Esq.,
    Cold Spring, N. Y.

MY DEAR SIR: I have read with much interest your note of the 3d inst., and thank you for the information it contains in regard to our painters. The result of your remarks is, I think that unless Weir be excepted, we have as yet no artist fully qualified to undertake the decoration of our staircases.

Weir probably could do it if he could determine to use his rich style of coloring. The sad tone of his Embarcation would never do for these light and airy structures.

I suppose that the proper course will be what I proposed, to finish them with surfaces proper for the reception of pictures but decorated in our architectural forms in color for the present. When the artist arrives the commission will be given. Perhaps we can get one picture placed on our stair as a seed from which others should grow, perhaps Weir might present it, but all the others are either portrait or landscape artists. Rothermel's Patrick Henry seemed to me a sketch, as though he had not the industry or skill to paint a finished picture. Healy's Webster is smudgy. His portrait of Soult in Gen. Cass' house at Detroit is fine.

Young Deas showed a better talent than Glass I thought at western scenes, but I believe he has ceased to paint. The last I heard of him I think was that he was insane, but none of them has shown himself equal to a great historical picture Weir perhaps excepted. In without being pleasing (which all pictures should be) his Embarcation is a very noble production.

I thought Leutze's Image Breaker, and Sacking of a Cavalier's House by Puritans very good, the fellow hewing the altar piece in the latter showed some fine painting about him.

I have proposed from the first to make the Hall of the House of Representatives a place for the public to congregate, and for the display of Works of Art. As it is not suited for painting at least for any great collection of them, I hope that in time it will be furnished with statues, and I think that whenever the time may come to renovate it if it be committed to my charge, I will contrive to include in the appropriation for the purpose a sum to place proper pedestals between the columns and they will soon be occupied. It is on this principle that I have put so many niches in the wings.

I have been to look at the drop scene. I recognized the design as a familiar wood-cut, the color is pretty but it is not a heroic treatment of the subject. This only is a landscape and do you notice the perspective? The figures are all on the beach at the ocean level. The horizontal line runs through the head of the oarsman, and the waists of the distant Indians, and the legs of Columbus, consequently the spectator must be seated at the water's edge to bring his eye to the proper position. The near group of standing Indians, some height above the water's edge have their heads in the horizon. This fault in this picture is very offensive to me. I have seen an engraving of a picture by a celebrated English artist where the horizon passed through the ankles of figures standing on a plain. He must have sat at a table on which they stood while he studied the figures and put in the distant landscape as he then saw it. I suppose a desire to save the trouble of painting and carelessness or ignorance of perspective led to this error. A skillful, one of our best marine painters once told me that a knowledge of perspective was an embarrassment to a painter.

I have written you a long epistle, but I take a great interest in this subject and I wish to see the same interest extended. I hope to see the day when these new portions of the Capitol will contain the germs of a collection worthy the most powerful and the most wealthy nation of the earth. The only one that can point to a prosperous people and an overflowing treasury.

Very truly your obt.

M. C. MEIGS.

———

APRIL 24, 1854.

GOUVERNEUR KEMBLE, Esq.,
    Cold Spring, opposite West Point, N. Y.

DEAR SIR: I have delayed this long answering your letter in the expectation of being able to inclose to you the letter of Chapman. After reading it I sent it to Senator Pearce requesting him to return it to me as you wished it. He has left the city to attend to some business and I must write lest you think me careless. I will send it as soon as I can procure it from him.

Mr. Chapman's letter is a delightful one and is full of the true feeling of an artist and of information valuable to me at this time; he writes too like a man of common sense. The observations that he makes about fresco I do not doubt are just. I have never seen a fresco except a monochromatic painting on the ceiling of the Philadelphia Exchange, and from this no idea of fresco proper can be obtained. I have read much at various times on the processes, and upon the results produced by the great masters in Fresco., and while I found much upon the freedom and boldness, etc., and upon the scope given in fresco for the genius of the master, it has always seemed to me that the superiority of execution necessary upon the wet plaster, and the very fact that the work must be completed piece meal, each days work being separate and finished, and being incapable of being retouched, precluded all effects except the more strik-ing and coarse ones such as we see in scene painting. The work can not be completed as a whole as an oil painting where the accidental effects produced by the drying and sinking in of the colors requires the toning down of other parts, and makes it impossible that the finished picture should represent the sketch. The changes must be much greater in fresco, and yet the artist is confined to making each day as exact a copy as possible of the portion of the cartoon for which his plaster is prepared.

Mr. Chapman remarks upon the thinness and weakness of the effects of fresco. I was aware that Raphael had painted part of the Stanze, a few figures only in one large picture in oil, and wondered why it was done, and why the same material was not used to complete the picture. Chapman's explanation is probably correct.

There still remains however, Michael Angelo's celebrated speech, that fresco alone was worthy of a man, and oil painting was only fit for women and children, and that speech has doubtless done much to keep the repute of fresco at height, to which perhaps it has no right.

Of the encaustic I know nothing: I fear that it is one of the specialities which we so often see announced, a quackery perhaps, but has the great advantage of being capable of finishing in the studio and afterwards being placed in the building.

I regret that I have not been able to see the N. Y. exhibition. I perceive that the date of its close has arrived, and I have not been able to go to New York. I had the satisfaction last Saturday of walking through a short piece of the Washington aqueduct, in which the brick arch was completed and fit to transmit the Potomac water for the inhabitants of this city. I hope that as it rivals the aqueducts of Rome in quantity, it may also in duration. I am,

Very truly and respectfully,

M. C. MEIGS.

{ 150 }

WASHINGTON, D. C., *Dec. 7, 1854.*

GOUV. KEMBLE, Esq.,
    Cold Spring, N. Y.

DEAR SIR: I return Chapman's letter which I have just received again from Mr. Pearce, who says that he had read it with much interest.

I am much obliged to you for the opportunity of reading it.

Mr. Chapman is evidently a scholar as well as an artist, and the opinions of such a man upon the subject which has been the object of his life could hardly fail to be interesting and valuable to any one connected in any way with art.

I am glad that he takes the same view as myself that the places being provided the works of art will follow. By quietly pursuing this course I do not doubt that art and artists will receive much more benefit than by striving now to engage Congress in any large appropriation for decoration. We have full authority and shall have ample funds for all purely architectural decorations, and will I trust make a building so beautiful in itself as to inspire a desire for something beyond mere architectural beauty.

I hope to leave spaces in the wall which will be so arranged as to need no inscription on them crying out for a picture as plainly as the niches will call for inhabitants.

I am glad to hear that you will be here this winter.

I shall have a busy winter for we are working now some 1000 hands, most of them marble carvers. I am building a roof which I think will do me credit as a worker of iron.

Very truly and respy. yours,

M. C. MEIGS.

Those who have remembered the story of the early sculptural work of the Capitol will recall that in the year 1815 Giovanni Andrei was sent to Italy to make arrangements for the carving of the Corinthian capitals and also was instructed to secure sculptors to carry on the work in the rebuilding of the Capitol after it was burned by the British in 1814. It seems fair to presume that this commission had been handed down as a tradition connected with the Capitol and in pursuance of the theory that history repeats itself it appears that Francis Vincenti had planned to secure a trip to Italy or to some place where workmen could be secured and thereby possibly gain a higher compensation than he was then receiving. This subject was disposed of by Captain Meigs with the following letter:

OCTOBER 17, 1854.

SIGNOR VINCENTI.

MY DEAR SIR: Looking over your project again I notice that you proposed in case it was adopted to bring the workmen out at your expense. You to receive a certain sum as reimbursement.

I write now to caution you in writing for workmen not to engage the United States for their employment, or for their expenses in crossing the ocean. Let them understand that skilful workmen get from $2.50 to $2.75 per day of ten hours work, and that this is to be the inducement, but they must bear their own expenses, and when here they will be in the employment of the contractor for the marble work, and not in the direct or immediate employment of the United States.

I am very respectfully,

M. C. MEIGS,
Capt. Engineers,
In charge of Ex. U. S. C. & Wash. Aqueduct.

Notwithstanding the emphatic refusal of Hiram Powers to compete for sculptural work for the Capitol, this was not considered by his friends to be a final refusal to furnish sculpture if it could be executed as an order and not in competition with other artists. A resolution had been introduced in the House of Representatives looking toward securing examples of the sculptural work of Hiram Powers, and the records of the Joint Committee on the Library for April 27, 1854, show the following:

A resolution from the House of Representatives instructing the Committee to inquire into the expediency of purchasing from Hiram Powers some work of art commemorative of American genius and history that may be an appropriate embellishment of the Capitol of the United States was considered and laid over.

{ 151 }

This evidently was not a favorable day for the art of the Capitol, as is shown by further record of April 27, 1854:

Several applications were received from artists requesting permission to place in the Library for exhibition statuettes of Daniel Webster, J. C. Calhoun and "Psyche" were considered and not allowed.

The burning of the five portraits of Presidents by Gilbert Stuart in the disastrous fire in the Library December 24, 1851, had not disposed of all the original portraits by this artist. Under date of April 6, 1854, we find the following:

A proposition from Mrs. Gibbs to sell to Congress original portraits of the first five Presidents of the United States by Gilbert Stuart which was referred to the Committee by the Senate was considered and on motion voted that a bill be reported to the Senate to authorize the purchase of them.

It can readily be understood that in the commencement of the extension of the Capitol the change made soon after the inauguration of President Pierce in taking the charge of the construction of the Capitol from the Office of the Secretary of the Interior and placing it under the charge of the Secretary of War had not met with the universal approval of both of the political parties. It was not very long after this change had been made that an investigation was ordered and the work already commenced examined by the partisans on each side of the subject—those in favor of the work being done under the Interior Department and those in favor of the work being done under the War Department. A great deal of time was wasted and widespread animosity engendered in the discussions upon the merits of the two sides of the question. It is not the purpose of this work to determine where the right and where the wrong was located, and this condition is only referred to for the purpose of laying the foundation of what followed a few years later. Just at this place we will include some quotations from the House proceedings of June 14, 1854 (Congressional Globe, vol. 33, pp. 1392 to 1492). Mr. Stanton, of Kentucky, was engaged upon a lengthy criticism of the military management then directing the building of the Capitol. In the course of his remarks he used the following language, referring to Captain Meigs:

He makes contracts with whom he pleases; he purchases materials when and where he chooses; he employs mechanics and laborers, and pays for all them by his own check or order. I cannot see the authority for all this. I look in vain for the law of Congress which authorizes it; and if I say that Captain Meigs occupied his position against the expressed enactment of this body I give utterance only to what any candid man will believe who examines the subject.

After commenting in somewhat severe terms upon what he claimed to be unnecessary expenditures in providing for the execution of the work contemplated under the law, he finally arrived at the point where he criticized the expenditures for art purposes, and we again quote from the same authority which we have cited above:

When the last appropriation was made for continuing the work on the Capitol, I offered an amendment to it proposing to apply $20,000 of the sum to employ Hiram Powers, an eminent American artist, to execute a piece of statuary for the adornment of the wings of the Capitol. The House refused to sanction it. The honorable gentleman from North Carolina (Mr. Clingman) changed the amendment and offered it again; but it met with no better fate. The same amendment or a similar one was twice offered in the Senate and twice voted down so here were the two Houses of Congress twice refusing to divert any portion of the money intended for building the wings of the Capitol to the procurement of statuary. And would it be believed that after these emphatic expressions of both Houses of Congress against such an application of the appropriation, $20,000 of it have been sent to Italy by the engineer to procure not the statuary, but the mere designs and plaster models. The Secretary of War says to the Committee:

"Mr. Thomas Crawford, a distinguished American artist, now in Rome, has been commissioned at a cost of $20,000. to prepare designs and plaster models for fourteen statues and their accessories to fill the tympanum of one of the eastern porticos and to decorate one of the eastern doors. These it is intended to have sculptured in this city and of American marble." I need not comment upon this act further than to say that no matter on whose direction it was done, it shows but little respect for the will of Congress. * * *

Notwithstanding the severe criticisms which had attended the management by Captain Meigs of the construction of the wings of the Capitol, he was not at all dismayed and possibly may have enjoyed the spirit of criticism and antagonism which seemed to be opposing his efforts. We find that as early as 1855 he had opened negotiations with Mr. Randolph Rogers for further art works of a sculptural nature for the Capitol. Randolph Rogers was born in Waterloo, Seneca County, N. Y., in 1825, but lived during his boyhood in Ann Arbor, Mich., where he commenced his study of sculpture, being self-taught. In 1848 he went to Rome, Italy, where he studied for two years under Bartolini. With this preparation he returned to New York and practiced the art of a sculptor for five years. He secured the commission for the Columbus Doors of the United States Capitol in 1855 and worked upon these doors at intervals until 1859. These doors were cast in Munich at the Royal Bavarian Foundry by Ferdinand von Miller, a bronze founder of world-wide reputation. The original models are supposed to be still in the possession of the Royal Bavarian Foundry. A duplicate set of the models were presented by the sculptor to the University of Michigan at Ann Arbor. These models became injured during the quartering of troops at the university during the World War and casts were made of portions of the doors at the Capitol in order that the models might be repaired. The doors were originally intended for and at first erected at the southern entrance of Statuary Hall opening upon the corridor leading to the Hall of the House of Representatives, but it was soon discovered that they could hardly be appreciated and that they were of such great importance that they were better adapted to the east entrance to the rotunda— their present location—than to the position for which they had been primarily designed. Other works of this sculptor are "Angel of the Resurrection"; Colt Monument, Hartford, Conn.; ideal figure in bronze, entitled "Michigan," for the military monument in Detroit; "Genius of Connecticut," capitol at Hartford; bronze statue of President Lincoln, Fairmount Park, Philadelphia; "Nydia," Chicago Art Institute; and a kneeling figure of Ruth, in the Metropolitan Museum of New York. Mr. Rogers was honored in Rome by election to a chair in the Academia di St. Luca, the oldest art academy in the world and the academy in which Constantino Brumidi and Filippo Costaggini were pupils, both having been employed in the decorative work of the Capitol. Mr. Rogers died in Rome January 15, 1892.

So far as is shown by the records of the Office of the Architect of the Capitol, it appears that Mr. Randolph Rogers had called upon Captain Meigs and had left photographs of work already executed. The receipt of this work and the estimate of the same by Captain Meigs is shown in a letter from Captain Meigs to Randolph Rogers, February 16, 1855. Mr. Rogers at that time was addressed at the National Hotel in Washington.

I have examined with much pleasure the photographs of your work which you were so kind to leave with me and I now return them as you will doubtless find other persons who will be glad to see them. They are beautiful examples of both arts, those of photography and of sculpture. I wish you every success in the continued practice of your art and hope that Congress will before long provide the means of placing a specimen of your work in some of the niches of this building. * * *

From a photograph made in Munich in 1860

RANDOLPH ROGERS
Represented by the bronze doors, east portico of the Capitol

{ 154 }

BRONZE DOORS, EAST ENTRANCE, ROTUNDA

Randolph Rogers, sculptor

{ 155 }

It appears from the memorandum left by Captain Meigs that he was far more impressed with the work of Mr. Rogers or with his personality than the letter from which we have quoted would seem to indicate. It is evident that, without making any direct statement or promises, he had in mind the employment of Mr. Rogers in sculptural work at the time when the foregoing letter was written. It was only a short time afterwards when the following letter was sent by Captain Meigs to Mr. Rogers:

WASHINGTON, D. C., *March 8, 1855.*

RANDOLPH ROGERS, Esq.,
    Care of L. Edgerton & Doane, 58 Broadway, New York, New York.

MY DEAR SIR: Pressing other occupations have prevented the earlier preparation of the enclosed tracing of the doors.

The doors in order to operate the arch wing must terminate with the spring of the arch.

The filling up of the space above is a thing which may enter into the province of either sculptor or architect. Let your sketch show what you propose to do.

All I have at present from Crawford in regard to the subjects of his front doors is the following:

"It is difficult to compress the thrilling events of our Revolutionary History, merely because a few feet and inches cannot be given to the artist in the Capitol of our Nation."

Little as this is it will be sufficient to enable you to guard against the danger of repeating his subjects.

The new dome of the Capitol will offer a fine field for sculpture, on which I would like to talk with you about.

I shall be very much disappointed if it is not placed under my direction. I know from inquiries in the Senate and House that such was their intention, and I know that my own exertions were mainly instrumental in procuring the appropriation.

The figure upon the top of the lantern is colossal.

What is your idea for it? I know that statues at such impossible heights are not looked upon very favorably by artists, and there is to me something beautiful and poetical in this colossal figure presiding over the whole and viewing the first rays of the rising, and the last rays of the setting sun.

We shall have plenty of room for reliefs in the interior which will be designed with special reference to such decorations. When the superintendence is decided I wish to see you about these subjects. I shall be in New York after a few days at the Metropolitan.

Respectfully, yours in haste,

M. C. MEIGS,
Capt. Engrs.

To the foregoing letter Mr. Rogers replied on the 17th of March, 1855, and announced that he proposed to make a history of Columbus, and this story was to be portrayed in the designs of the doors. The suggestion was approved by Captain Meigs, and the sculptor was encouraged to complete his designs. Other letters followed, and as a result Mr. Rogers came to Washington in the latter part of April, 1855, and evidently remained in Washington some time, as we find by quoting the following extract from a letter of Captain Meigs to Thomas Crawford, May 11, 1855:

* * * Young Mr. Randolph Rogers is here. He is making a sketch for a bronze door for an interior. Has taken the life of Columbus as his subject. If the sketch shows ability he will probably receive a commission for executing it. I wish it was not so incumbent upon our sculptors to live abroad. * * *

In the meanwhile it appears that the sketch had become satisfactory, and Mr. Rogers, who was still in Washington on May 24, 1855, submitted the following proposal:

The undersigned offers to make for the United States Government, and deliver in the city of Washington within two years from this date, the models in Plaster of Paris for a bronze door for the United States Capitol; the subject to be the life of Columbus, which will be illustrated by eleven alto-reliefs, which will contain in all about one hundred and fifty figures, besides twelve portrait statuettes and twelve heads of the distinguished contemporaries of Columbus, together with suitable ornamental work for the rails and stiles of said door, such as animals, fruit, foliage, etc., etc. The sum demanded for the above work is eight thousand dollars, payable on the completion and delivery of the work.

Yours truly,

RANDOLPH ROGERS.

There can be no doubt but that Captain Meigs showed great efficiency in the promptness with which he advocated action on any of the projects in which he was interested. On the same day, May 24, 1855, on which the proposal was submitted by Mr. Rogers, Captain Meigs sent a long letter to Jefferson Davis, Secretary of War, explanatory of the proposal and estimating the expense, as follows:

Supposing the bronze and the casting to cost $2,000, in addition to the design, this would make the whole cost of the gates $10,000.   *   *   *

It is also evident that Captain Meigs was not half-hearted in his desire to have Mr. Rogers secure the commission indicated by his proposal. A further quotation from the letter addressed to Secretary Davis illustrates Captain Meigs's personal interest in the matter:

Mr. Rogers is young, full of ambition, self-reliant, not younger than Ghiberti when his designs secured him the preference over all competitors for the gates of Florence Baptistry. If he can succeed as well with these as with his Ruth, of which you have a photograph, it will be well enough. I confess that the hasty sketch which he has made has not so much spirit as I had hoped to see, but I believe that with careful study from the life he has the ability to make a great work. This opinion is based upon the photographs now in your hands.

It would seem that less formality was made use of in that day in the office of the Secretary of War in dealing with matters of this kind than would probably obtain at the present time. The proposal of Randolph Rogers was definite enough for all practical purposes, even though it might be lacking in legal phrases and sentences usually included in a formal proposal upon which a contract is based. The main essential of a contract is that the wish of the contracting parties be definitely stated. The proposal, as has been said, was definite; the action of Jefferson Davis was equally definite and is a fine illustration of brevity in Government transaction. The letter of Captain Meigs bears this indorsement:

Approved, Jefferson Davis, Secretary of War, War Department, May 25, 1855.

In this brief manner the contract, based upon the approval of the proposal of the sculptor, was awarded.

Other art events connected with the art of the Capitol in the year 1855 are found in the act approved March 3, 1855, which is section 28 of an appropriation act, and which reads as follows:

And be it further enacted, To enable the President of the United States to contract with Hiram Powers for some work of art executed or to be executed by him and suitable for the ornament of the Capitol, a sum not exceeding $25,000. (Stats. L., vol. 10, p. 674.)

In this manner it seems that the effort of the friends of Mr. Powers in the House of Representatives, to which reference has been previously made, was not barren of results and that finally, whether upon merit or upon a gentleman's compromise, they had succeeded in obtaining the recognition for Mr. Powers which they had been working for so earnestly for quite a period of time, as the letter of July 27, 1855, from Captain Meigs to Jefferson Davis tends to show.[1]   In justice, however, it might be said that, although this thought does not appear in the records of the debate upon this question, it is quite possible that Mr. Powers's refusal to furnish designs for one of the pediments of the Capitol may have resulted as a handicap in securing his further recognition and the appropriation therefor.

Let us for a moment review the condition of the art work which had been contracted for since the commencement of the wings or extensions to the Capitol.   Briefly stated, there had been contracted for two bronze doors for the House and Senate wings and sculptural decorations for the Senate pediment, and overtures had been made toward the submitting of a design for a statue to surmount the dome.   These were exterior adornments. For the interior the bronze doors by Randolph Rogers had been contracted for, and all of this in the period between the commencement of work upon the extension and July 1, 1855.   We should remember also that there were other art matters under consideration. The painting for the vacant panel in the rotunda, for which the commission had been given to William H. Powell on account of the death of Mr. Inman, to whom it had originally

---

[1] JULY 27TH, 1855.

Hon. JEFFERSON DAVIS,
    Secretary of War.

My DEAR SIR: In consequence of a reference in a late conversation with you to a letter which you had seen in relation to the sculpture of the Capitol, I desire to place in your hands the accompanying extracts from the correspondence with Mr. Everett, Mr. Powers and Mr. Crawford in regard to that subject.

By these letters it will be shown that when seeking for artists properly qualified for this work, I wrote to Mr. Everett to ask his advice. This I did because he had lately returned from Europe, was regarded as a man of eminent taste and was known to have paid particular attention to the works of our sculptors in Italy.

His reply, No. 2 of the enclosed names Mr. Powers and Mr. Crawford as the first two American sculptors.

With your approbation I wrote to them the letters No. 3 and 3a which, except in the addresses and in the fact that one of them invited a design for the North Wing of the Capitol Extension and the other for the South Wing, are identical.   I accompanied these letters by others in which I gave more fully my own views in regard to the sculpture and its execution.   These letters are marked 4 and 4a.   They differ in no important particular and are merely copies of each other.

The invitation thus extended to these two artists was promptly accepted by Mr. Crawford and as promptly rejected by Mr. Powers.

Mr. Crawford prepared designs which were approved and accepted by the President and he has completed some of the figures which have arrived in this city.   Upon the others he is now engaged.

Mr. Powers in his letter of September 22nd, assigns as his reason for refusing that he had not the time to prepare designs even if it were a desirable object with him to propose for a commission from the Government of his country.   This letter was handed to me by a friend of Mr. Powers, Mr. S. G. Asher who seemed to regret the refusal and undertook to write to Mr. Powers and endeavor to induce him to reconsider the subject.

I received at a later date a letter from Mr. Powers in which while thanking me for the manner in which I have written to him, he positively declined making any design for the Capitol Extension in consequence of engagements which left him "no time to make designs much less to execute so extensive a work."

Sometime after this I called upon Mr. Everett and told him of this correspondence requesting him, as he seemed to take a deep interest in Mr. Powers, to use his influence towards persuading him to make designs.

Mr. Everett requested me to leave the matter open until he could communicate with Mr. Powers.

The matter was thus left open and remains so at this day.   No other artist has been invited to prepare designs for this pediment, and I should be very much gratified now to receive from Mr. Powers an intimation that he was willing to put his talent at the disposal of his country for this purpose.

Surely no objection can be made by Mr. Powers or by his friends to the request that he would submit designs and estimates for the approval of the President in so great and important a work.   It would not be proper to request any artist to fill a pediment with sculpture leaving to him the design and the price without any understanding in regard to it before the execution of the work.   No individual, no country is rich enough to give such an order.

In writing the above I wish only to prevent any impression which might lead you to suppose that I had been guided by prejudice or favor in any action on this matter.   I know neither of the artists and I sought designs from both.   It is not my fault if unsuccessful with Mr. Powers.

There will be ample room for his statue of America in the niches of the Extension of the Capitol and judging from his reputation and the description I have read of his work I should rejoice to see it adorning the building.

I had hoped to see many other figures from his chisel in the more honorable places upon two Pediments.

    I am, very respectfully, your obedient servant,

                                        M. C. MEIGS,
                            Capt. of Engineers, in charge Capitol Extension.

    I enclose a list of the letters and extracts herewith.

been given, was now nearly, if not quite, complete.[2] In fact, it seems to have been completed to such an extent that it was being exhibited in different sections of the country, and this had been referred to in some of the art magazines of that period. The matter was also brought to the attention of the Joint Committee on the Library, whose record for the meeting of January 17, 1855, is as follows:

> A letter was received from Peter C. Washington, Assistant Secretary of the Treasury, in relation to the picture painted by William Powell of Ohio by order of Congress, to be placed in one of the panels of the rotunda in the Capitol, and which Mr. Powell is now exhibiting for money in different parts of the United States; and on consideration of the subject, voted that the Chairman write to Mr. Powell and request that the picture be delivered and placed in the panel as early as practicable.

This subject is also continued at the next meeting of the Joint Committee on the Library, held February 26, 1855:

> The memorial of William H. Powell praying further compensation for his services in executing the historical painting of the discovery of the Mississippi by De Soto for Congress, which was referred to the Committee by the Senate, was considered and on motion voted, that the Chairman move as an amendment to the appropriation bill of $2000 to enable the Committee to pay Mr. Powell in full for the picture painted by him in addition to the sums heretofore appropriated by law.

The statement of the appropriations connected with the commission for this painting and for other paintings ordered at the time when the commissions were granted to Weir, Vanderlyn, Chapman, and Inman is somewhat perplexing on account of the payments made to Mr. Inman, which do not seem to have been returned to the Government. According to information concerning the payment to Mr. Powell, it appears that the resolution, which was referred to the Joint Committee on the Library, was considered favorably when the appropriations were made, and that on March 3, 1855, there was a balance paid to William H. Powell of $2,000, making the cost to the Government of the painting, the Discovery of the Mississippi, $12,000.

From the annual report of Captain Meigs, under date of October 14, 1855, we find the following reference to the sculpture of the Capitol:

> The original models of several of the figures designed by Mr. Crawford for the eastern pediment have been received and workmen are now engaged in carving in marble the figures of the mechanic and the groups of Commerce and Instruction. The marble has not yet been received for the other group. These figures are being carved in American marble which is believed to be more durable than Italian statuary marble when exposed to our climate. It is, though not of so delicate a texture, quite as white and though not so well suited for parlor statues, it is better adapted to the situation in which this sculpture will be placed. We have received the models of the mechanic, the groups of Instruction, Youth, Commerce, and War. I am informed by Mr. Crawford that he has completed the models of America for the center of the pediment and the figures of the woodman and Indian boy and is now engaged upon that of the Indian. A small figure for the decoration of one of the principal stairs has been nearly completed in the studio at the Capitol by the artist there employed. A skilful worker in bronze is engaged in casting the bronze decorations for the gallery doors of the House of Representatives. As Congress appropriated $20,000. at its last session for the purchase by the President of a work of art from Mr. Powers, it is hoped that his statue of America will be one of the decorations from his hand for the new Halls of Legislature. One of the rooms of the basement of the south wing is now being painted in fresco. This will enable Congress to see a specimen of this, the highest style of architectural decoration. It is the most appropriate and beautiful mode of finishing the building, and it will afford a field for the talent of artists never before offered in this country. It is not necessary that it be done rapidly as the designs and cartoons being made and approved, the painting can be done after the completion of the building during the annual recesses of Congress.

---

[2] Mr. Inman had selected as the subject for his painting "The Emigration of Daniel Boone to Kentucky," but the work had not proceeded further than a sketch.

From a photograph by Brady

CONSTANTINO BRUMIDI, PAINTER

The reference to the decoration in the basement floor of the House of Representatives wing in fresco relates to the work then being executed by Constantino Brumidi. The artist Brumidi had a varied career. He was born in Rome, Italy, July 26, 1805. He was a pupil of the Academy of Fine Arts and the Academia di San Luca, Rome, studying modeling under Thorwaldsen and Canova and painting under Baron Camuccini. He was also a soldier and captain of the national guard, and during the pontificate of Pius IX was commissioned by him to restore the loggia of Raphael in the Vatican. As captain of the guards he refused to order his command to fire on the people and was arrested and thrown into prison, where he was confined for 14 months without any charges being preferred against him. On account of his friendship with Pius X, he was released from prison without a trial and counseled by the Pope to leave Italy because he had not the power to again protect him against the enmity of Cardinal Antonelli, the Minister of State.[3]   He

[3] It has been learned since the above was written that Monsignor John Norris, at that time attached to the Vatican, was instrumental in securing the release of Brumidi and inducing him to come to the United States.

concluded to come to America and journeyed to the City of Mexico by way of New York, where important commissions were given to him. At the request of a prominent Senator that he, Brumidi, should make a personal statement of his coming to Washington and his employment at the Capitol, he filed with the Architect of the Capitol the following:

The French occupation of Rome in the year 1849 for the suppression of republican institutions determined the artist C. Brumidi to emigrate to America, where a great Republic was already established. He landed in New York City in 1852 and soon thereafter declared his intention to become a citizen of the United States, obtaining his naturalization papers in the city of Washington two years later. The rapid progress of the Capitol extension under the superintendency of Capt. Meigs suggested to him the idea that the solid construction of this national building required a superior style of decoration in real fresco, like the palaces of Augustus and Nero, the Baths of Titus and Livia at Rome, and the admired relics of the paintings at Herculaneum and Pompeii. At the first meeting with the said superintendent, who was always in earnest to emulate the example of majestic Roman grandeur, he accepted the service of Brumidi.

The Committee room on Agriculture, in the south wing of the Capitol, was painted in 1855 as the first specimen of real fresco introduced in America.

The work of Constantino Brumidi forms an important part of the art history of the mural decorations in the Capitol. Commencing, as it did, in 1855, it extended over 25 years, and further reference will be made from time to time as different important works were completed by this artist. It should be remembered at this time that this decoration in the room of the Committee on Agriculture was probably the first completed work of art executed for the wings of the Capitol.

In order to keep a connected idea of the progress of the art work in the Capitol before the reader, we are obliged now to refer to the records of the Joint Committee on the Library, and in the minutes of their meeting for June 27, 1856, we find the following:

A resolution of the Senate directing the Committee to inquire into the propriety of procuring a bust in marble of the late Chief Justice John Rutledge, to be executed by an American artist of merit and reputation, and to be placed in the Room of the Supreme Court of the United States, was considered, and on motion voted that the Chairman be requested to report in favor of the resolution and a bill to procure the bust.

On this same date we find that the committee considered other matters relating to sculptured designs for the interior decoration of the Capitol Building, as the following record shows:

A proposition by Horatio Stone, sculptor, to execute a statue with accessories representing the Republic be erected within the Capitol, which was referred to the Committee by the Senate, was considered and on motion voted, that the application be referred to the Honorable Mr. Tyson and that he be requested to ask the opinion of eminent artists and connoisseurs as to the merits of Dr. Stone and Mr. Saunders as artists, and as to the merits of the design submitted by the former.

An interesting bit of history is attached to this application or this reference to the artist Saunders, or, as he was properly known, Henry Dmochowski, who was at this time probably living in Philadelphia. Whether because he was a Polish refugee he adopted the name of H. D. Saunders, or whether he thought that the name Dmochowski would be a handicap to his employment, is not known. He was a sculptor of marked ability for his period and was a student of the University at Wilno, Poland. He was born in Poland in 1810 and in 1830 sought refuge in France on account of political conditions. In 1846 he studied sculpture in Paris under the ablest teachers, after which he resided for some time in London and then came to America and resided in Philadelphia. This application, as referred to by the Joint Committee on the Library, is our first official reference to

{ 161 }

Dmochowski, or Saunders, in connection with the Capitol. He resided for some time in Washington and in 1857 exhibited in the rotunda of the Capitol a bust in plaster of Thomas Jefferson and also offered to the Joint Committee on the Library his bust of Pulaski, which is signed Dmochowski, and his bust of Kosciuszko, which is signed H. D. Saunders. These busts were afterwards acquired by the Government and are now located in the Senate lobby, gallery floor. The sculptor returned to Poland and executed a statue of Queen Barbara Radziwillowna, wife of King Sigismund of Poland, and a bust of the Polish poet Wladyslaw Syrokomla. His return to Poland offered another opportunity for his engagement in military service, and he died fighting for Poland's liberty near Wilno in 1863.

On August 26, 1856, it appears that the "eminent artists and connoisseurs" who had been approached by Mr. Tyson concerning the artistic ability of Horatio Stone must have indorsed that sculptor to such an extent that he was considered worthy of commissions, for in their records of August 26, 1856, we find the following:

> *Resolved,* That Horatio Stone, sculptor, be authorized to make a model 7 ft. high of John Hancock, President of Congress, for which the Committee will pay him $500.; and if approved they will, upon agreeing to terms, employ him to execute a statue in marble after the model; and the Chairman of the Committee is authorized as the work on the model advances to pay the artist in his discretion for the work on said model.

We are now approaching one of the events in the art history of the Capitol which produced consequences which neither the Joint Committee on the Library nor the people who were interested in art could have expected. In order to explain fully this matter, we are obliged to combine the reports of two meetings, as they both relate to the same subject, and to take them up separately, as other events intervening might lessen the purpose of the committee in their attempt to award this commission. The meeting of August 26, 1856, transacted the following business:

> On motion, voted that the Chairman of the Committee be requested to open a correspondence with Horace Vernet, of Paris, and ascertain whether and for what price he would execute a battle scene for one of the grand staircases of the addition to the Capitol.

On January 30, 1857, the final action in this matter was reached:

> On motion, voted the Chairman is authorized to inform Mr. Vernet that the Committee will advance $1,000. to defray the expenses of his visit to the United States in addition to the sum heretofore named, $10,000 as their offer for a battle scene by Mr. Vernet. If that be not sufficient they do not doubt that Congress will enlarge the sum.

It will be remembered that the expression "American artists" and "American sculptors" had been frequently used with the description of commissions to be granted. The artists of this country had for a long time been making somewhat ineffectual efforts to secure commissions, but few commissions had been granted with the exception of the historical paintings for the rotunda and some busts for the Supreme Court room. The commissions to Crawford, Rogers, and Powers had all been given to American artists, and the fact of their American citizenship had been referred to frequently in the conversations and correspondence relating to these commissions. Just why this effort was made to secure the service of Horace Vernet to decorate one of the staircases of the new additions to the Capitol is not understood unless it had been determined after careful consideration that the United States had not as yet produced a landscape painter whose ability was equal to such a task. We have referred to this at some length at this time because later in the history we shall take up the concerted action of the artists of this country against

THE BATTLE OF LAKE ERIE
William H. Powell, painter

the employment of any but American artists in the decoration of the Capitol. This protest of the artists led to the action of Congress in curtailing the expenditure of money for decoration and the appointment of an art commission to act in connection with the Joint Committee on the Library in the selection of works of art for the Capitol. A more detailed statement concerning the protest of the artists will follow in its chronological order.

The Library Committee on January 3, 1857, had before them for consideration the following:

The memorial of William R. Barbee asking Congress to order a figure of the young Republican to be placed in the Capitol was referred by the House of Representatives to the Committee, also the memorial of John M. Stanley praying Congress to purchase his gallery of Indian paintings now deposited in the Smithsonian Institute. Referred to the Committee by the Senate.

The interests of Horatio Stone and the John Hancock statue are again before the Joint Committee on the Library on January 23, 1857, when the following record was made:

The Committee had under consideration a statue of John Hancock proposed to be made by H. Stone, sculptor, and after some time spent therein postponed the subject to the next meeting.

And again on January 30, 1857, the same subject is under consideration:

The Chairman of the Committee was authorized to propose $5,500 to Dr. Stone for his statue and pay him from time to time, and the Chair was requested to report the results to the Committee.

After the consideration of sculpture, the art of painting is brought to the attention of the committee by the following record of February 27, 1857:

On motion of Mr. Tyson, resolved that General Cass be authorized by the Committee to ask for $10,000. for a picture by Mr. Powell illustrating the battle of Lake Erie according to his sketch.

It may be interesting to know that, although a commission several years later was given to Mr. Powell for a painting—the Battle of Lake Erie, which now occupies the east stairway of the Senate wing of the Capitol—this painting is not the first from that subject by Mr. Powell, and it is probable that the lack of interest at this particular time in the completion of this painting, of which he had already presented a sketch to the committee, led to his painting the same subject and disposing of it to the State capitol of Ohio, where it was placed on view a long time before the one now in the Capitol was executed.

CHAPTER IX

THOMAS CRAWFORD'S SCULPTURAL WORKS

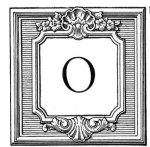O UR REFERENCE to the bust of Kosciuszko would have prepared the reader for the following record of the Joint Committee on the Library under date of February 27, 1857:

Resolved, That the Committee agree to take the bust of Kosciuszko at $500. from Mr. Saunders provided so much money be at the command of the Committee or be obtained by appropriations at the present session.

Another action of the committee which occurred earlier than the previous action (January 30, 1857) tends to show that the committee did not contemplate giving commissions to every sculptor for no other reason than that they had given a commission to Doctor Stone:

The applications of Dr. Stone, W. R. Barbee, Thomas Ball and other sculptors who desire to be employed for statuary for the north and south extensions of the Capitol, were received and on motion postponed for the present except as to Dr. Stone.

In the meanwhile Congress seems to have had a continual contention over the conditions surrounding the construction of the wings of the Capitol and particularly in relation to the employment of Captain Meigs as the superintendent of the work. On May 26, 1856, Mr. Ball, in the House of Representatives, used the following language:

* * * If the Government desired to build a fortress to be made as impregnable as Cronstadt is represented to be, I doubt if a man in the nation could be found better qualified to take charge of such a work than Captain Meigs, but gentlemen schooled in the military service learn a great deal more about constructing public works with strength than with economy and seem to have no idea of the value of money. Such must be the conclusion of all who examine into the cost of the various structures placed under their direction. * * *

Another item of these Capitol expenditures demands our particular attention. Are gentlemen aware that this Government has become an extensive manufacturer of statuary? It is even so. Just around the corner may be found two shops filled with Italian and German sculptors busily engaged in manufacturing statuary to be placed in the east pediment of the two wings. This too is with no authority of law that I can find unless under the general authority to construct the two wings to the main building. * * *

The statuary in question does not seem designed to commemorate any historical events or personages connected with this country. It seems to be a mere amateur collection and therefore deserves no place in the national Capitol. The graven images have the likeness to nothing in the Heaven above or the earth beneath—I beg pardon, however—one was pointed out to me as the wife of one of the foreign workmen. Yes, Sir, we are to have this copy of a living original to adorn our Capitol.

On the 28th of July, 1856, under a resolution of the House of Representatives of July 17, 1856, calling for a variety of information relating to the marble work and the sculptural adornment of the Capitol, Captain Meigs makes a detailed report of every branch of the work under his charge. As most of these matters have been referred to, we make this explanation and introduce the facts of the report in order to place upon record some facts concerning the Post Office Building which was then under construction and under the charge of Captain Meigs. The principal gateway into the Post Office Building is an arch located on the west side of the building and therefore opening upon Eighth Street NW. This is in the ordinary form of triumphal arches and the spandrels are decorated with winged figures representing steam and electricity. The keystone of the arch is decorated

EIGHTH STREET ENTRANCE TO THE OLD POST OFFICE DEPARTMENT BUILDING

With sculptural decorations by Guido Butti, one of the sculptors at the Capitol
during the building of the Capitol extensions

{ 166 }

with a mask of Fidelity. The composition is the work of Guido Butti, and is probably the best recognized example of his work in Washington. The plaster models for this arch are on deposit in the Pennsylvania Academy of Fine Arts. The work of Mr. Butti at the Capitol was largely that of a modeler. He had reached that degree of proficiency where he modeled so that others might reproduce his work in marble. Very many of his works doubtless exist about the Capitol, but as the carving was done by different sculptors there is very little in the matter of record to identify his work. He may be referred to again in this history, but little is known about the man, and his biography was not included in the publication of 1913 known as Works of Art in the United States Capitol Building, Including Biographies of the Artists. (S. Doc. No. 169, 63d Cong., 1st sess.) Some of the carvers employed have failed to furnish any material from which a biography of Mr. Butti could be prepared, while their recollections seem to be very definite concerning others employed during the same period.

It will be necessary, in order that we may form a connected story establishing by periods the accession of different works of art, that we should go back for a little while to the year 1855. If we refer to the correspondence between Captain Meigs and Thomas Crawford, we will find the suggestion of Captain Meigs concerning the treatment by Crawford of his models for the Indian to be used in the pediment and the suggestion of a work which would give him information on this subject which would be sent him. It is quite probable that Captain Meigs knew of the interest shown by Capt. Seth Eastman in paintings of portraits of Indians, and it may be that he had stated to Captain Eastman his desire to have some of the Indians who were occasionally visiting Washington as members of treaty delegations act as models for some of the sculptors then engaged in the work at the Capitol. At all events, the records show that on February 17, 1855, Captain Eastman wrote to Captain Meigs that the Chippewa Indians were here in the city and that as soon as they complete their treaty they will sit to be modeled in clay. He also states that there were 12 Winnebago chiefs here. From this slight reference there comes one of the interesting art stories of the Capitol.

Several years ago the architect's office was advised that there was a marble bust of an Indian in one of the committee rooms in the Senate wing of the Capitol. It was not known at that time whom this bust was intended to represent. Inquiry in the office where it was then placed resulted in the information being given that it was a bust of Tecumseh, but subsequent investigation revealed the fact that there were no valid grounds upon which to make the claim that it was a bust of this celebrated warrior. For many years this bust had been carried upon the records of the Senate wing of the Capitol as being private property and that the owner was unknown. As a matter of decoration it was considered of enough importance so that it had found a place in one of the committee rooms. It was felt that possibly some information might be secured through the Bureau of Ethnology, and accordingly an expert from that bureau called and examined the bust and gave it as his opinion that it could not possibly be a bust of Tecumseh and that it belonged to some of the Indians whose tribal homes were in the northern part of the Middle Western States. In the quest for information a photograph of the bust was published in several papers, with the result that an elderly man, who had been a Senate page at the time when the Senate met in the present Supreme Court room, came and identified this bust as one that had formerly been in the Senate lobby and that it had been called by one of the Senators "Billy Bowlegs," a famous Seminole chief. This identification seemed to be of value, and the Bureau of Ethnology was again called upon for an opinion.

Notwithstanding this seemingly positive identification, the Bureau of Ethnology stated that "Billy Bowlegs" had never been in Washington and that the cranial development of the bust was not that of a Seminole. At about this time Lot Flannery, a local sculptor, who was an apprentice sculptor at the Capitol in the fifties, came and identified the bust as the work of Francis Vincenti and stated that he had seen Vincenti modeling in clay from the Indian whose bust had been reproduced in marble. Mr. Flannery, however, was unable to give the name of the Indian or his tribal relation. It seemed at this time almost a hopeless quest to determine the name of the Indian who served as the model for this bust, and at last an attempt was made through the Indian Office to devise some means by which this work might be identified. Acting upon the suggestion of the Indian Office, several photographs of the bust were supplied and the office assumed the task of sending a photograph around to different Indian agents occupying the territory indicated by the Bureau of Ethnology as the probable location of the home of the tribe of Indians to which this Indian belonged. One identification was made, but it did not seem either to the architect's office or to the Bureau of Ethnology sufficient to warrant the belief that the bust had been properly identified. A second identification from another source on information produced through the Indian agents identified this bust as that of "Flat-mouth," known by the Indian name of Aysh-ke-bah-ke-ko-zhay, a Chippewa chief who was known to have been in Washington at the period to which the letter from Captain Eastman refers. This has been corroborated by the Bureau of Ethnology upon a comparison of the records of the treaty Indians in Washington at the time referred to. It was then considered that the identification was complete, and the proof that the clay model had been made by Francis Vincenti and that it had been reproduced in marble by the same sculptor settled the question of ownership and showed conclusively that it was the property of the Government. For this reason it was considered best to remove this bust from the committee room where it had been for many years and place it on the gallery floor of the Senate in the east corridor. At the time that the bust was removed it happened that Senator Clapp, of Minnesota, occupied the room in which the bust was located. He showed much interest and was very anxious to find out who the Indian might be who had posed for this bust, and upon being informed that it was "Flat-mouth," or Aysh-ke-bah-ke-ko-zhay, looked at it steadily for a moment and said, "I knew him. It is a good portrait." He then requested to be given all the facts concerning the identification and after going over all the papers in the case expressed himself as well satisfied with the proof of identification. A record was therefore made in the case of the examination of papers by Senator Clapp and his agreement upon the completeness of the identification. This was done not so much for the satisfaction of those who at this time were in possession of these facts, but for those who might ask for this information in later years. While not a part of the art history of the Capitol, it may be that some have become interested in "Flat-mouth" and will find further interest in having it brought to their attention that "Flat-mouth" was made one of the chief characters of a story "Gentlemen of the North," by Hugh Pendexter, who has not only used this Indian as one of his characters but has shown in the development of his book a large amount of research in the records of the Indian tribes of the period prior to 1860. The sculptor of this bust, Francis Vincenti, an Italian sculptor of marked ability, was employed upon the work of the Capitol from 1853 to 1858. From his time reports and letters written during the early part of his employment it is observed that his knowledge of the English language was quite limited, as most of his reports were written in the French language. In his ability he seems to have ranked with Butti and was clever as a modeler and furnished anatomical models for the sculptors engaged upon the Senate pediment. He was permitted to carry the names of the models who posed for him in blank, so that the pay rolls might not show by whom these services had been performed. Vincenti also modeled and carved a portrait bust of the "Buffalo," Be-sheck-kee. This bust is also located in the Senate gallery lobby, east side of the Capitol. After concluding his services Mr. Vincenti was employed for a short time by Mr. E. V. Valentine, a sculptor of Richmond, Va., and some years later Mr. Valentine met Vincenti upon the streets of Paris. The biography of this artist is limited to what has heretofore been stated.

In a copy of The Crayon for the month of February, 1857, we find a reference to the works of Thomas Crawford, in which it is stated that he was engaged in the execution of two figures for the decoration of the cap of the Senate doorway. These figures, Justice and History, were executed in Italy and are the only part of the work which Crawford was commissioned to execute for the Capitol which was completed in that country. In the case of his other works the models were executed in Italy and sent to this country to be reproduced in marble or bronze as the work required.

In this same year (1857) we find from The Crayon (vol. 4, p. 107) that Mr. W. H. Powell had been appointed by the Ohio Legislature to paint a representation of Perry's Victory on Lake Erie; the price was stated to be $5,000, and the painting when completed was to be placed in the rotunda of the new statehouse. It is probable that Mr. Powell, after having painted the Discovery of the Mississippi by De Soto and not being encouraged for the immediate completion of a painting of the Battle of Lake Erie for one of the staircases of the Senate, painted this smaller picture for the statehouse of Ohio and later reproduced the same picture for the United States Capitol. Further reference to the picture in the Capitol will be given in the proper period.

While Crawford had completed his work for the pediment so far as the execution of the models was concerned and had also made sketches for the bronze doors for the Senate and House wings, his next work in order of completion was the model for the statue of Freedom for the dome of the Capitol. In a letter from Captain Meigs to Jefferson Davis, Secretary of War, under date of January 11, 1856, Captain Meigs referred to the inclosure of two photographs as sketches for the statue under consideration and that the price for the model was to be $5,000. At this time Captain Meigs reported the shipment of many of the models for the pediment and that the remaining models were well advanced toward completion. Secretary Davis, with his customary promptness, disposed of the question of the statue for the dome of the Capitol by a letter which is interesting on account of the manner in which this art subject is considered:

WAR DEPARTMENT, *Washington, January 15, 1856.*

SIR: The second photograph of the statue with which it is proposed to crown the Dome of the Capitol impresses me most favorably. Its general grace and power, striking at first view, has grown on me as I studied its details.

As to the Cap, I can only say, without intending to press the objection previously made, that it seems to me its history renders it inappropriate to a people who were born free and would not be enslaved.

The language of art, like all living tongues, is subject to change; thus the bundle of rods if no longer employed to suggest the functions of the Roman Lictor, may lose the symbolic character derived therefrom, and be confined to the single signification drawn from its other source, the fable teaching the instructive lesson that in Union there is strength. But the Liberty Cap has an established origin in its use, as the badge of the freed slave; and though it should have another emblematic meaning today, a recurrence to that origin may give to it in the future the same popular acceptance which it had in the past.

PROFILE VIEW OF STATUE OF FREEDOM, ON DOME OF CAPITOL
Thomas Crawford, sculptor

Why should not armed Liberty wear a helmet? Her conflict being over, her cause triumphant, as shown by the other emblems of the statue, the visor would be so as to permit, as in the photograph, the display of a circle of stars, expressive of endless existence, and of a heavenly birth.

With these remarks I leave the matter to the judgment of Mr. Crawford, and I need hardly say to you, who knowing my high appreciation of him, that I certainly would not venture, on a question of art, to array my opinion against his.

Very respectfully, your obt. servt.,

JEFFN. DAVIS,
Secretary of War.

Capt. M. C. MEIGS,
In charge of Capitol Exn., Washington City.

While Mr. Crawford was busily engaged upon the commissions he had received from the Government, Randolph Rogers was completing his model for the door which was to serve as an entrance from Statuary Hall to the House wing of the Capitol. In a letter dated Rome, May 15, 1857, in which he refers to the progress being made upon the model for the door, he writes concerning the expense of having it cast in bronze as follows:

I almost despair of having the doors cast here or in Munich for I fear the price they ask will frighten you. A few months ago I got Hopfgarten, a German, who was one of the best workers in bronze in Rome, to make an estimate from my sketch of the probable cost of casting and finishing the work. He then thought it could be done for $16,000. Since that time he has seen the elaborate manner in which I am doing the work and now says it cannot be done for less than $18,000. A few days since I called Signor Derossi, the Government founder, who is very capable and anxious to do the work. This morning his estimate was brought me which was $21,000. * * * I am willing you should put this photograph by the side of any of the panels in the Ghiberti Gate and have no fear for the comparison. This may seem to you like vanity, but to me it is only common sense, for I am not willing to acknowledge that an American of the nineteenth century cannot produce a work equal to that of any Florentine of any period. I feel and believe I can and will, but let me beg of you once more not to make me feel that I am short of time, for my whole attention is given to this work and you may be assured there will be no unnecessary delay.

On the 17th day of July, 1857, Captain Meigs wrote to Randolph Rogers as follows:

The caster and founder in bronze, whom I expected to make the doors, died on Saturday last. I shall be pleased, therefore, to have some definite offer from Munich and from Rome for its casting and completion in bronze.

Having shown the condition of the work under the charge of Randolph Rogers, we must again turn to the work of Mr. Crawford, and in order to give an adequate idea we quote entire the following letter. This is done for the reason that this seems to be the last official communication from Mr. Crawford.

PARIS, *April 1, 1857.*

Capt. MEIGS,
Washington.

DEAR SIR: In a recent interview held with Mr. Miller, Director of the Royal Foundry at Munich, the question of the transportation of the colossal statue of America from Rome to that city was discussed, and I hasten to make known to you Mr. Miller's willingness to include the expense of transportation in the sum named for the bronze casting $14,000. Finding that the statue does not measure more than 20 feet, he is enabled to undertake the whole expense for this amount first mentioned as the price of casting alone. His hesitation in acceding to this before, arose from his misapprehension as to the height of the figure, but being certified that it measures precisely 20 ft. from the base to the top of the helmet, he considers that he can without loss to himself, bear all these incidental expenses.

Will you therefore, dear Sir, at your earliest convenience, let me know if you accept or reject Mr. Miller's proposal to convey from Rome to Munich, cast in bronze and deliver at Bremen or Amsterdam the colossal statue of "America" for the sum of $14,000?

I cannot but express a strong hope that your answer may be favorable. The greatest justice would thus be done to my work, and our Capitol will be surmounted with a masterpiece of art, as far as the bronze casting is concerned.

BRONZE DOORS, EAST ENTRANCE, SENATE WING

Thomas Crawford, sculptor

BRONZE DOORS, EAST ENTRANCE, HOUSE WING

Design by Thomas Crawford; completed by W. H. Rinehart, sculptor

I regret extremely that the money needed for the purchase of the marble for the statues of Justice and History cannot be advanced.   I have been put to very serious inconvenience by the long delay in forwarding my equestrian work to Richmond, inasmuch as the last payment by the terms of the contract can only be made when the horse arrives.   My payment to Mr. Miller on the contrary had to be made when the casting was completed; so that for one year I have been deprived of the use of the $8,500 actually due to me by the Virginia Govt.   I cannot, therefore at present incur the fresh expense of so large a block of marble as would be necessary for these two figures, and so the work must just now stand still.

You will be glad to know that I am suffering somewhat less than a month ago, and have a hope of ultimate recovery of health and strength, if not of the use of my afflicted eye.

I am dear Sir, with great respect, very truly and sincerely yours,

THOS. CRAWFORD.

My address is Messrs. Munroe & Co., 5 rue de la Paix, Paris.

The hopes expressed by Mr. Crawford of a recovery of health and strength seemed to have been based upon a very insecure foundation.   The trouble with which he was suffering terminated in his death in London, England, September 10, 1857.   Much of his work was in an incomplete state, and the burden of the completion of the contract was taken up by his wife.   The work was carried on under her supervision for a time until her remarriage, when W. H. Rinehart in 1858 received from the widow of Thomas Crawford a commission to complete the work upon the Crawford models for the bronze doors of the Capitol.   Rinehart has been credited by some with having designed one of the doors for the House wing of the Capitol, but the photograph of the original clay model for the same is signed by Crawford.   Mr. Rinehart is represented in the art works of the Capitol by the bronze fountain in the office of the architect and by the figures of an Indian and a hunter supporting the clock in the Hall of the House of Representatives.   Mr. Rinehart was born in Carroll County, Md., in 1825, and died in Rome, Italy, October 28, 1874. He was a farmer's son and reared upon a farm.   In 1846 he found employment as a stonecutter and attended the night schools of the American Institute.   In 1855 he went to Rome and remaining there a short time returned to Baltimore and opened a studio in that city.   Among the works of Rinehart other than those referred to as being in the Capitol are bronze seated statue of Chief Justice Roger Brooke Taney, Annapolis, Md., and a replica of this statue in Mount Vernon Square, Baltimore; Latona and Her Children, Metropolitan Museum; Pensoroso, Corcoran Gallery of Art; and Clytie, Peabody Institute, of Baltimore, Md.

The delay in coming to a conclusion concerning the installation of a bust for Chief Justice John Rutledge, which was referred to by the Library Committee on June 27, 1856, finally terminated in the following enactment:

Be it enacted by the Senate and House of Representatives of the United States of America in Congress assembled, That the Joint Committee of the two Houses of Congress on the Library be and they are hereby authorized to contract with a suitable artist for the execution in marble and the delivery in the room of the Supreme Court of the United States a bust of the late Chief Justice John Rutledge.

SECTION II. *And be it further enacted,* That for the purpose of carrying this act into effect, there be and hereby is appropriated $800. to be paid out of any money in the Treasury not otherwise appropriated.   Approved January 21, 1857.   (Stats. L., vol. 11, p. 155.)

The sculptor selected for this commission was Alexander Galt, a Virginian, born in Norfolk, Va., June 26, 1827.   He was the sixth child and third son of Alexander Galt and Mary Silvester Jeffery Galt.   His art education was received in Florence, Italy, where in after years he located his studio.   He returned to the United States in 1854, and while on a visit in his home country he received a number of commissions, among which was the commission for a bust of Chief Justice Rutledge, now in the Supreme Court room.

He also received from the State of Virginia a commission for a statue of Jefferson. His ideal bust, the Bacchante, is in the Corcoran Gallery of Art, Washington, D. C. He returned to Virginia in 1860 and allied himself with the cause of the South and served on the staff of the governor. He also made valuable drawings for the Confederate engineers. He died of smallpox in Richmond, Va., January 19, 1863. This disease was incurred in the camp of Gen. Stonewall Jackson, where he had gone to make sketches of a bust of that officer. Among his works are the busts of many prominent public men. His bust of Jefferson Davis, made from actual measurements, was the only one made of him while he was President of the Confederacy.

While outside of its chronological order and not particularly related to the art of the Capitol, yet, inasmuch as we have referred several times to the attempt made through the Library Committee and by enactment of Congress to procure an equestrian statue in bronze of General Washington, it is proper to state that on the 25th of January, 1853, the following statute was approved:

Be it enacted by the Senate and House of Representatives of the United States of America in Congress assembled, That the sum of Fifty thousand Dollars is hereby appropriated to enable the President of the United States to employ Clark Mills to erect at the city of Washington a colossal equestrian statue of George Washington at such place on the public grounds in said city as shall be designated by the President of the United States. (Stats. L., vol. 10, p. 153.)

We are aware that the question of a statue to Washington had been many times before the Congress and that the references that we give do not by any means include all of the references that might be made to attempts to provide such a statue. This matter was before the Library Committee May 30, 1834; February 7, 1835; February 14, 1835; January 29, 1845; February 12, 1845, and doubtless at other times not noted in this work. The matter is referred to in this manner for the purpose of illustrating the length of time that seems necessarily to elapse before definite action can be secured in the direction of procuring a work of art in memory of any distinguished citizen of the United States. This time, however, the plans culminated in an effort which resulted in the erection of a statue at Twenty-fifth Street and Pennsylvania Avenue. The statue is the work of Clark Mills, a sculptor of considerable prominence during the period of the fifties and sixties. His equestrian statue of General Jackson, in Lafayette Park, Washington, D. C., unveiled February 8, 1853, is said by some to have been the first equestrian statue erected in this country. This was followed by the equestrian statue of Washington above referred to. Mr. Mills was born in the State of New York in 1816. His opportunities as a boy were exceedingly limited, and his first employment on his own account was at driving oxen and hauling logs to a charcoal pit. He afterwards worked as an apprentice at building mills. While residing in Charleston, S. C., he took up the work of a plasterer and in the ornamental stucco works developed a desire to be a sculptor. He commenced this work without instruction. His first work in marble was the bust of John C. Calhoun, for which he was awarded a gold medal by the City Council of Charleston, S. C. Following this his work received the approval of many public men. The bronze statue of Freedom surmounting the dome of the Capitol was cast at Mills's foundry on the Bladensburg Road, some 3 miles from the Capitol. The plaster model of this statue is the work of the sculptor Thomas Crawford. This model is now preserved in the National Museum. Mr. Mills died in Washington, D. C., January 12, 1883.

We have now approached the period when the House of Representatives was about to move from its old quarters in that section of the Capitol known as Statuary Hall to its new quarters in the House wing of the Capitol. The completion of the Hall was announced through a letter from the Secretary of War, as follows:

WAR DEPARTMENT,
Washington, December 9, 1857.

SIR: I have the honor to state that the engineer now in charge of the work has reported to me that the Hall of the House of Representatives and the room for the office of the Clerk of the House in the extension of the Capitol of the United States are ready for occupation.

In communicating this information I beg leave to say that the rooms aforesaid are now at the disposal of the House.

Very respectfully, your obedient servant

JOHN D. FLOYD,
Secretary of War.

Honorable JAMES L. ORR,
Speaker of the House of Representatives.

According to Hazelton's National Capitol, Its Architecture, Art and History, the first occupancy of the House is described as follows:

The House met for the first time in the new Hall of the House of Representatives, in the South extension at 12 o'clock December 16, 1857.

It is probable that at this time the only works of art in the House wing of the Capitol which had been completed were the decorations by Brumidi in the room of the House Committee on Agriculture, at the present time used as one of the committee rooms of the House Committee on Appropriations. We should, however, make one exception to this statement, and that is the fresco on the wall in the southwest corner of the Hall of the House of Representatives entitled "Cornwallis Sues for Cessation of Hostilities Under a Flag of Truce." Those who have followed carefully the letters from Captain Meigs to Gouverneur Kemble will remember that he stated therein that he planned to leave spaces throughout the portions of the new buildings which should be naturally adapted for decorations. In this instance Captain Meigs does not seem to have been willing to leave spaces to suggest the need of paintings so far as the southwest corner was concerned, and while the fresco has remained upon the wall, it has been severely criticized, and perhaps justly so, although it is possible that if the critics knew the circumstances and the purpose for which this fresco was placed upon the wall they might be less caustic in their criticism.

It has been stated that the occupancy of the new Hall of the House of Representatives commenced on December 16, 1857. On December 14, 1857, an anonymous letter was received by Captain Meigs as follows:

DEAR SIR: It will be no news to you, I dare say, to learn that there is a party organizing to effect your removal from the Superintendent of the Capitol extension and I take leave to say to you that the wall painting, "The Surrender of Cornwallis" is universally condemned. The subject is considered inappropriate and the execution execrable, in view of all of which I suggest to you to have the painting wiped out.

Your friend and supporter

OFFICIOUS.

Of course we are unable to record just what Captain Meigs's language was at the time of the receipt of this letter. Upon the whole we are of the opinion that he enjoyed having things stirred up generally. We can, however, state what he did. Captain Meigs, although not a legible writer, was a capable office man, and with great care he preserved all correspondence received and suitably indorsed thereon such replies as were made. Of course in this case no reply could be made because the name and address of the writer were not stated. He therefore made upon this letter the following indorsement:

One of many indications. The picture is as good as could be painted in six weeks. It serves to show what the effect of painting on the panels will be which is all I intended. It cost little, and I have not the least objections to a better painting being by Congress put over it, but it is the best that could be done at the time and no more time was at my disposal.

M. C. M.

Whether fortunately or unfortunately, the attention of Congress has not been very favorably turned toward the filling of the vacant panels of the side walls of the House of Representatives with paintings. There were at one time, in addition to the portraits of Washington and Lafayette, which were brought to the new Hall of the House of Representatives from Statuary Hall, where they had occupied spaces upon the side wall next to the gallery front of the south gallery, on the walls of the new Hall of the House of Representatives two landscapes, the work of Albert Bierstadt, entitled "Entrance into Monterey" and "Discovery of the Hudson River." These paintings are shown by illustrations in books published about 1900 as then occupying spaces at the right and left of the Speaker's desk. For many years thereafter they occupied positions at the east and west end of the room used as a retiring room and connected with the Speaker's lobby, but have recently been moved to the walls of the staircases leading from the Speaker's lobby to the floor below.

Courtesy of the Macbeth Galleries

ALBERT BIERSTADT

Represented by the landscapes, Discovery of the Hudson River and Entrance into Monterey, in the Speaker's lobby

The painter, Albert Bierstadt, was born in Dusseldorf, Germany, January 7, 1830. He was brought to America at an early age, but returned to Dusseldorf in 1853 and entered the academy, afterwards studying in Italy and Germany. He was elected national academician in 1860, chevalier of the Legion of Honor of France in 1867, and received medals and various orders from Austria, Germany, Bavaria, and Belgium. He was at one time a pupil of Emanuel Leutze. He died in New York, February 18, 1902.

We have noted how an anonymous friend and supporter of Captain Meigs had suggested that a party was organizing to effect his removal. These may have been merely idle words. They may have been used for the purpose of securing the removal of the fresco upon the wall and for no other purpose, but at all events a great deal of opposition had arisen and the removal into the new quarters had not cured the dissension; possibly the removal into the new quarters may have hastened some of the unfavorable criticism manifested at that time. During the consideration of the sundry civil bill for 1859 Mr. Lovejoy said:

* * * Now, Sir, these military men are to be found everywhere. The Superintendent for constructing this Capitol must be a military man; and if you ask for their monuments I would reply in the language of the epitaph of Sir Christopher Wren in St. Paul's; "Si monumentum quaeris circumspice." If you want a monument of military architecture look at the meretricious and garish gilding of these walls and the splendid specimen of fresco paintings in these panels. And then go down into the Agricultural Committee room, at one end is a representation of Old Put. leaving his plow, and at the other end is Cincinnatus also leaving his plow.

Now, Sir, the proper idea is in my view to have given some paintings that would represent the agriculture at the present time of 1858, so that one or three hundred years hence those who see them could learn what was the condition of agriculture of the present year. There is one exception, that of a reaper. This is as it should be. That is one side of the middle of a field of wheat and looks very well, except that it ought to have been at the side of the field, as that is where cutting begins. Overhead we have pictures of Bacchus, Ceres, and so on surrounded with cupids, cherubs &c. to the end of heathen mythology. All this we have, but not a single specimen of the valuable breeds of cattle, horses, sheep, etc., which are now found in the country. In another panel we have a company of harvesters with the sickle which is well enough only a quarter of a century too late. * * *

The picture of Putnam would have been very well in the Committee Room of Revolutionary Claims, but has no significance where it is as it is a revolutionary reminiscence. In the place of this should have been the picture of a western plow with its polished steel mold-board, with the hardy yeoman, with one hand resting on the plow handle and with the other holding a span of bays, with arched neck and neatly trimmed harness. Pictures are symbols of ideas and this would have told to the future the present mode of culture of free labor. At the opposite end, in the place of Cincinnatus and his plow (the plow of two thousand years ago) there should have been a negro slave with untidy clothing, with a slouching gait, shuffling along by the side of a mule team, with ragged harness and rope traces, drawing a barrel of water on the forks of a tree. This would represent the idea of slave labor. Thus we should have a symbol of the two systems of labor now struggling for the ascendancy.

On this same date (House proceedings of May 19, 1858) while the sundry civil bill was under discussion, Mr. Marshall, of Kentucky, offered the following amendment:

Provided, That this appropriation shall not be expended, in whole or in part, upon the embellishment or decoration of the Capitol extension, either by painting or sculpture in the panels or niches of the Senate or House, or in the pediments of the porticoes, or in the finish of the halls, committee rooms, or passages, unless the designs for such embellishment and decoration shall have been first submitted to and accepted by a committee, to be selected by the President, composed of three distinguished artists, citizens of the United States, which committee shall be employed by the President for the purpose of examining and determining upon such designs as shall be adopted for the embellishment of the Capitol extension: *And Provided Further,* Said Committee of artists shall act in connection with and subordinate to the Joint Committee on the Library of Congress, and shall not be authorized to conclude any contract for the execution of such design without the direction of said committee.

In the United States Senate upon May 28, 1858, the Senate as in Committee of the Whole having under consideration the sundry civil bill for 1859 considered this amendment:

For United States Capitol Extension $750,000: *Provided,* That this appropriation shall not be expended in whole or in part upon the embellishment or decoration of the Capitol Extension either by painting or by sculpture, in the panels or niches of the Senate or House, unless the designs for such embellishment and decoration shall have been first submitted to and approved by the Joint Committee of the Library of Congress.

This amendment was of such a drastic nature that it resulted in a long debate in the Senate. After a prolonged discussion, in which Mr. Jefferson Davis took a prominent part, a new amendment was inserted in lieu of the one quoted above. The amendment offered by Mr. Davis is as follows:

To enable the Library Committee to contract with distinguished artists for historical paintings and sculpture for the panels and niches of the legislative halls and of the great stairway of the Capitol Extension, $50,000. in addition to the funds already in their hands for this purpose.

In the House of Representatives on the 7th day of June, 1858, the House as in Committee of the Whole on the state of the Union, having under consideration the Senate amendment to the sundry civil bill for 1859 Mr. Taylor, of New York, offered the following as an amendment to the amendment:

Provided, That no portion of this appropriation shall be expended for painting or decorating the interior of the Capitol unless the same be made under the direction of three American artists to be appointed by the President of the United States nor shall any contract be made for such painting or decoration except by the Joint Committee on the Library.

The Chair, in ruling upon a question of order, ruled that the foregoing amendment was out of order. Mr. Taylor, of New York, then added the following amendment:

Provided, That no portion of this appropriation shall be expended on the interior painting and decoration of the Capitol.

This amendment was held to be out of order, and the decision of the Chair was overruled by a vote of the House. Mr. Maynard then offered the following amendment:

Provided, That no part of the same shall be expended for paintings or statuary.

Enough has perhaps been quoted from the proceedings of the House and the Senate to show that there existed a strong hostility toward using any of the appropriation expended for the construction of the wings of the Capitol for decorative purposes. The idea of a formation of an art commission was still being strongly urged by some of the Members of the House of Representatives. The act as finally passed and approved by the President, was as follows:

JAMES WALKER

Represented by the painting of The Battle of Chapultepec, in the Senate wing, west grand staircase

For United States Capitol Extension, $750,000: *Provided*, That none of this appropriation shall be expended in embellishing any part of the Capitol extension with sculpture or paintings unless the designs for the same shall have undergone the examination of a committee of distinguished artists not to exceed three in number, to be selected by the President and that the design which said committee shall accept shall also receive the subsequent approbation of the Joint Committee on the Library of Congress, but this provision shall not be so construed as to apply to the execution of the designs heretofore made and accepted from Crawford and Rogers.

This act was approved June 12, 1858. (Stats. L., vol. 11, p. 323.)

THE BATTLE OF CHAPULTEPEC

James Walker, painter

On the 15th of November, 1858, Capt. M. C. Meigs filed his annual report. In this report the first use of the Hall upon the 16th of December is stated, but the first public use of the Hall occurred on the 13th of December, Sunday, when services were held in the Hall, the Rev. G. D. Cummins officiating. Captain Meigs in his report referred to the appropriation act providing for a committee of distinguished artists and for their recommendations to be subsequently approved by the Joint Committee on the Library of Congress. Concerning this commission, Captain Meigs made the following statement:

Mr. Walker, who was employed in painting a picture of the storming of Chapultepec for the Military Committee Room of the south wing, has been stopped in this work by this proviso. This picture was perhaps half finished at the time. It is to be hoped that it may be found possible to authorize him to complete it. In regard to a permanent committee of artists, I venture to suggest here that there are some difficulties. It would be difficult to select three distinguished American artists whose reputation should be such as to entitle them to sit without appeal in judgment on the work of their brother artists and whose pencils or chisels could at the same time be spared from the decoration of the building. * * * The most liberal and it seems to me most judicious mode of granting commissions for works of art would be to constitute somebody with the power to give to such artists as may have established a sufficient reputation, commissions at a fixed price for pictures to fill certain panels; or to grant to one artist a commission to decorate one of the great staircases leaving the subject and the mode of treatment to the artist, subject only to the revision of the committee granting the commission. * * * It is a matter of course that an artist honored by a liberal commission from the country for a picture to be placed in the Capitol to be seen and criticized by all would do his best. * * *

Notwithstanding the fact that the appropriation bill for the fiscal year 1859 implied the appointment of a committee of distinguished artists by the President, no committee was appointed. The movement for the selection of an art commission was again presented to the Congress and renewed efforts were made to secure action. This subject will be taken up after reference to some other art matters which chronologically belong to this section of the art history.

CHAPTER X

E MUST now direct our attention for a short time to the contract for the statue of Freedom awarded to Thomas Crawford. The model had not been delivered at the time of the death of the sculptor and was packed and loaded upon the bark *Emily Taylor* for shipment to this country. The bark containing the plaster model of the statue of Freedom sailed from Leghorn, Italy, April 19, 1858, bound for New York. On the 22d, having sprung a leak which continued with more or less force until the 19th of May, it was decided to put into Gibraltar to make the necessary repairs before proceeding farther on the voyage. Upon arrival the cargo, excepting the model, was landed and stored, and the vessel was calked. Upon the completion of the repairs, the vessel sailed thence on the 26th day of June for the port of destination, New York. Having encountered much stormy weather with heavy gales from the northwest from the date of leaving Gibraltar, the vessel was found on the 1st of July to be leaking badly. The leak gradually increased until the 12th, when, finding the vessel to be making water at the rate of 12 inches per hour, it was resolved to lighten her by throwing overboard a part of the cargo. One hundred and seventeen bales of rags and 48 cases of citron were jettisoned. On the following day 133 bales of rags were thrown overboard. Finally, on the 27th of July, the leak having increased to 16 inches per hour, it was determined for safety to put into Bermuda, at which port they arrived on the 29th of July. Upon surveys held the vessel was condemned and sold. The cargo, which had been landed and stored, was finally forwarded to destination by a vessel which had been chartered and sent to Bermuda for that purpose.

On December 27, 1858, Tappan and Starbuck, of New York, who acted as general agents for the United States in the receipt and forwarding of the statuary received from abroad, notified Captain Meigs that the bark *G. W. Horton*, from Bermuda, had arrived with some of the statuary on board. It was not possible to bring all of the statuary, and as late as March 30, 1859, the last of the statuary, or portions of the model, were shipped from New York to Washington by the schooner *Statesman*. It also appears that the special charges of transshipment, salvage, etc., including freight, amounted to $1,974.05, but it is probable that the Orient National Insurance Co. of New York assumed the charge of this expenditure, as seems to be indicated by correspondence found in the papers relating to this case. It seems, therefore, that from the first there had been a great variety of mishaps attending the completion and delivery of this model. The sculptor had died, the work had been taken up by another, and shipwreck followed upon the attempted delivery, so that by piecemeal the model reached Washington some time in April, 1859. A long time had elapsed since the commission had been given, and much more time was to elapse and other hindrances occur before the completed statue in bronze was finally placed upon the dome of the Capitol.

The final order for the casting of the bronze doors designed by Randolph Rogers was given by Captain Meigs April 17, 1858. His letter is as follows:

RANDOLPH ROGERS,
                Sculptor,
                        Care Packenham, Hooker & Company,
                                Rome, Italy.

DEAR SIR: Your letter of this 21st inst. just received. I think you had better send the doors at once to Munich for the price offered, 10,000 scudi, paid in Munich. They will not be made more cheaply or better anywhere else. Bronze tone I prefer to bronze gilt.
        Respectfully,
                                M. C. MEIGS, Captain, Engineers.

The next letter in the correspondence between Captain Meigs and Randolph Rogers occurred nearly a year later and is as follows:

                                                ROME, Jan. 1st, 1859.
Capt. M. C. MEIGS,
        Superintendent of the U. S. Capitol Extension,
                Washington, D. C.

DEAR SIR: You will see by the enclosed certificate of the U. S. Consul at Rome, that the models for the bronze doors which you were kind enough to order me to execute for the Capitol are finished and have been forwarded to Munich. A large portion of the door left Rome on the 31st. day of July last and Mr. Miller informs me that immediately on their arrival they commenced work upon them. The last shipment of the remaining portions left Rome on the 8th. inst.

I send you photograph of the rest of the panels and only hope they will be as satisfactory to yourself as they have been to all who have seen them in my studio. You will find in the photograph that some of the statuettes have been repeated as they were photographed some time ago and before the statuettes were all completed. I am now putting together the duplicate model of the entire door and when finished I shall have a large photograph taken of the entire work and will send you a copy as soon as possible.

As far as possible I have fulfilled my contract with you. Sending the doors to Munich has cost me more than it would have done to send them to Washington, as I was obliged to send them all the way by wagon. My transportation bill to Verona has amounted to 352 scudi and 11 cents. Had the doors been sent to America I would have insured them for the actual cost of repeating them from the wax models, which would be about $1,500.00. The insurance would be 1½%; deducting this from 352.11 leaves 329.61 which is much more than the cost of sending the models to Washington. I have this day made a draft on you through Messrs. L. Edgerton & Dunning of New York for $8,000.00 which I have no doubt will be honored at once. I shall go to Munich next summer to look after the bronze casting.
        Yours truly,
                                RANDOLPH ROGERS.

We find further reference to the completion and payment for the models for the bronze doors in the letter from Captain Meigs to Randolph Rogers dated May 11, 1859, in which he stated:

I have paid a draft for $8,000, dated Rome, January 1, 1859, and drawn by you at three days after sight in favor of L. Edgerton & Dunning, but I doubt whether this, which is not the usual form of vouchers or receipts, will be sufficient to pass the payment to my credit. I, therefore, ask your signature to these vouchers in the usual form. Upon receipt of these signed by you, I will cause them to be placed with the draft as additional evidence of payment.

On June 20, 1859, Randolph Rogers wrote to Captain Meigs, and from this letter we give the following extract:

I received a letter a few days since from Miller of Munich informing me that he was advancing rapidly with the doors and expects to have the whole cast by the 1st of October. He says that a large portion of it is entirely complete. In regard to the payment on the casting of this work, he desired me to say to you that it is the rule of the foundry to receive half when the work was entirely and successfully cast in bronze and the balance on completion.

From a photograph by Remillard

HENRY KIRKE BROWN

President of the Art Commission appointed by President Buchanan

*Represented by the statues of Nathanael Greene, Richard Stockton,
Philip Kearny, and George Clinton, in Statuary Hall*

As a correspondent Captain Meigs was accustomed to write items of general interest and information as well as business details. In his letter to Randolph Rogers of July 23, 1859, he gives the following information about art conditions at the Capitol. As we have given the view of the legislators as expressed and enacted into appropriation bills, we will give the personal views of Captain Meigs as stated in his letter to Randolph Rogers:

  *   *   *   I am glad to see that the notices of your work in the correspondence of our press are favorable, and it is gratifying to know that President Pierce under whose authority I was able to order the work is pleased with the result.

  As for the other work, the artists have as you know, looked with some jealousy upon what has been done for the Capitol Extension in art, and they succeeded in getting such provisions attached to the appropriation bills during the past two years as prevent my giving orders for more sculpture or painting.

  Messrs. H. K. Brown, J. R. Lambdin and J. F. Kensett, have under the law been appointed a "Commission of three distinguished American Artists" to whom all designs for sculpture or painting must be submitted before being executed. The designs after passing this ordeal must be approved also by the Library Committee, of Congress, which is prohibited contracting for the execution of any others. So if you look with ambition to the frieze of the Rotunda, 300 feet long, by 9 feet high, it will be proper for you to submit your ideas to this committee of one sculptor, one portrait painter, and one landscape painter.

So also of the other pediment. There is no provision for paying for designs. These gentlemen seem to hold only a veto power, or powers of approval like that of the President in legislation.

Crawford had proposed to me to make the frieze in plaster, which he said he could do for $50,000.00 and he advised that it should be put up in plaster which would last under cover, and at this height, sixty feet above the floor be quite as effective as any other material, and would have the advantage of bearing the very original touches of the artist's hands and not as in marble or bronze be the handiwork of others in finishing.

Had I been left with the same authority as when I ordered the doors, and had Mr. Crawford lived, this frieze would have been partly up in place by this time, serving to teach our people the value and beauty of art in public buildings. Now with the commission of artists, and various other obstructions, I do not know when, if ever in my life time it will be accomplished. I shall be pleased however to hear that you intend trying your future with the commission.

Recalling for a moment the action of the Joint Committee on the Library in offering to Horace Vernet a commission for a battle piece for one of the grand staircases of the Capitol, the culmination of which was the heated discussion in the Senate and House of Representatives and the final restrictions of all art matters to be passed upon by a committee of distinguished artists, whose opinion, however, was subject to the approval of the Joint Committee on the Library, we now come to the memorial presented by the artists themselves in which they requested the appointment of an art commission to select and control the future decoration of the Capitol Building. This memorial was signed by 127 prominent artists of New York, Philadelphia, Washington, and Boston, and several from localities other than those given. Among the names were those of Rembrandt Peale, J. R. Lambdin, H. K. Brown, Johannes Oertel, Horatio Stone, William H. Rinehart, Henry D. Saunders, Albert Bierstadt, S. R. Gifford, T. Addison Richards, George Innes, William H. Furness, jr., Samuel Sartain, William T. Richards, Frederick D. Williams, Joseph Ames, and a large number of well-known artists, from the list of which the foregoing have been selected. Space will not permit the inclusion of the memorial or of the report of the special committee to whom it was referred. From the memorial we only quote the last paragraph:

Your memorialists believe that the appointment of such a commission would be hailed throughout the country as an evidence of a just and generous appreciation by your honorable body of the claims and the interests of art and would secure for it a future commensurate with the exalted character of the history and the time which it is its purpose to commemorate.

It is proper to state as a good and sufficient reason for the lack of the inclusion of the memorial and the report that it occupies 21 pages of space as a public document and is known as Report No. 198 (H. R., 35th Cong., 2d sess.). It was read March 3, 1859, laid on the table, and ordered to be printed. This report is of the select committee. It had been appointed on the 1st day of June, 1858, in pursuance of the following resolution:

Resolved, That the memorial of the artists of the United States be, and the same is hereby referred to a select committee of five to be appointed by the Speaker with instructions to report upon the expediency of granting the petition of the memorialists and with power to report by bill or otherwise.

If an opinion may be given concerning the report of this special committee, it seems to be evident that the report was prepared with great care and with the object in view to say a great many pleasing things without committing the Government to any fixed policy. In fact, the committee said:

This special committee not finding themselves clothed with instructions to present any general plan or design for the completion of the work have not entered upon the consideration of any specific proposition and have none therefore to be submitted to Congress at this time. * * *

The appointment of the commission was in the following form:

In conformity with the provisions of the Acts of 12th June, 1858, and 3d March, 1859, requiring that all designs for sculpture or paintings for the decoration and embellishment of the United States Capitol Extension shall undergo the examination of a committee of distinguished artists, not to exceed three in number to be selected by the President, I do hereby appoint Henry K. Brown, of the city of Washington, James R. Lambdin, of the city of Philadelphia, and John F. Kensett, of the city of New York, to compose the said Art Commission.

JAMES BUCHANAN.

WASHINGTON, *May 18, 1859*.

It may not be out of place in this connection to give an extract from The Crayon (vol. 6, p. 220) in order that a clear understanding may be had by those who are reading this story of the art development of the Capitol of the favor with which the appointment of H. K. Brown, J. R. Lambdin, and J. F. Kensett was received by the artists of the country; of course we must understand that The Crayon was looking at the subject from motives that were not wholly disinterested:

WASHINGTON.—The Century contains, in a late number, a summary of the qualifications of the members of the commission lately appointed by the President, Messrs. H. K. Brown, J. R. Lambdin, and J. F. Kensett. We reprint it with emphatic indorsement.

"Brown is in the prime of life, full of knowledge and experience as well as inspiration, and no man in America is so well fitted to head this commission and lead in this national enterprise. His manly devotion to character and fact is the element most needed, not only at Washington, but through all our artistic and literary endeavor.

"Mr. Lambdin occupies a high position. His standing as a portrait painter is one of assured respectability, while his judgment and generosity, his knowledge of Art and artists, and his well recognized ability in the management of all business connected with the interests of Art, and his personal integrity, give him eminent fitness for his place in the commission.

"Mr. Kensett enjoys a popularity well earned and fully deserved. He stands very nearly, if not quite, at the head of our landscape art. He has abundant strength of representation; his color is, we think, unrivalled in our landscape practice, for truth, purity and luminousness; he has emerged from the struggle with materials into mastery over them; his composition is simple and dignified; he is never misled into mere imitation, into genre or object painting and exaggeration of detail, or exhibition of skill in dealing with it; his feeling is large and cheerful, sometimes rising into solemnity, never trivial and seldom broken or disturbed. In personal as well as artistic character, Mr. Kensett is in every way worthy of his new position, and the happy selection of these gentlemen to fill a post of so much responsibility will be matter for congratulation among all artists and lovers of Art in America."

We understand that the commission met in Washington last month.

The Art Commission, having been duly appointed by the President of the United States, proceeded very soon to take up the duties belonging to that office, and after calling upon the Architect of the Capitol for blue prints showing different portions of the extension of the Capitol they proceeded to discuss the art regulations or art principles which should govern the decoration of the Capitol. The report is inclined to be academic in its position, and possibly it should be viewed with charity, for the commission was standing upon a rather unsatisfactory basis and no doubt had fears that it would be short lived no matter in which way it might turn. They commenced to consider what was already embraced in the art of the Capitol, and in the course of their report the following occurs:

Are portrait statues in which the Greek or Roman costume has been substituted for that worn by the individuals represented satisfactory? Do they not rather convey a feeling of shame for the paucity of invention on the part of the artists and an acknowledgment that we have sought refuge in stuffs and draperies to conceal our want of power in this special character? We want nothing thrown in between us and the facts of our history to estrange us from it. We want to be brought near it, to realize it as an existence, not as a myth. True genius presents us no nightmares, no vagaries; but is clear-seeing and by its subtleness of perception and power of expression renders truth palpable to duller senses.

The foregoing may have been pleasing to the people of 1860, at the time this report was made, but it may be that some may consider it equally as reprehensible or as an evidence of poor taste to have art works showing the vagaries of fashions as they are changed from year to year as to adhere to classic costumes which are recognized as belonging to a period and not to be a representation of anything that could be called modern. The commission also commented upon a room in the style of the "Loggia of Raphael"; another was that of Pompeii; a third after the manner of the Baths of Titus, and even in the rooms where American subjects have been attempted the commission stated that they were so foreign in treatment, so overlaid and subordinated by symbols and impertinent ornaments, that they were hardly recognized. The commission further stated that its chief delight in this survey was in a few nicely painted animals and American birds and plants in some of the lower halls. It is evident that the commission examined and approved of the decorations in the basement floor of the Senate wing of the Capitol, and if their "chief delight" was in the decorations there found one may perhaps remark that this commission was easily delighted. In the rotunda they recommended that below the frieze, which at that time had not been commenced, there should be given space for the representation of the colonial history of the country, followed by that of the Revolution. For the Senate Chamber they recommended the introduction on either side of the desk of the Vice President of an appropriate statue or bust of the first Vice Presidents, Adams and Jefferson, and in corresponding spaces in the House of Representatives busts of James Madison and Fisher Ames. Concerning the four great stairways, the commission stated:

It is not thought advisable to recommend their permanent decoration at this time, but merely to paint them in simple colors. None but pictures of the highest order should be admitted to places of such prominence. To acquire these not only time, but the utmost care and deliberation are requisite. There can be no doubt of the ability of our artists to perform this work, but time should be given them for preparation both in fresco and in oil. Heretofore they had been engaged with few exceptions on easel pictures, and it is impossible at once for them to adopt the style required in works of such magnitude. It is said that Horace Vernet has been offered one of these spaces to fill, and it is readily conceded how valuable would be the acquisition of a work from such a master for a national gallery or the Executive Mansion. * * * Vernet's studies have been from French life and manners and his works consequently are thoroughly imbued with his nationality, which constitutes in fact one of their great merits. It is morally impossible that he should wholly adapt his style or form of expression to ours. The expediency, therefore, of inviting even the most distinguished foreign artist to paint on the walls of the Capitol may well be questioned.

While the report as a whole is interesting on account of the difficulties which were being avoided by the commission, they finally rendered it as their opinion that their "functions and powers" were not sufficiently defined by the acts of Congress to enable them to perform the duties contemplated in their appointment. The report concludes with an estimate, which is interesting to such an extent that we quote it in its entirety:

For eight pictures to fill four panels in each of the halls of Congress...................... $40, 000
For four statues for Senate retiring room.. 20, 000
For two statues for eastern front door of south wing.................................. 5, 400
For two colossal busts for Senate Chamber...................................... 3, 000
For two statues for House of Representatives..................................... 10, 000
For painting Speaker's room.. 2, 000
For painting private stairways and passages behind Speaker's chair..................... 7, 500
For painting room east of Speaker's room....................................... 2, 000
For painting post office, south wing... 4, 000
For modeling valves for two eastern doorways..................................... 12, 000
For casting and chasing the same in bronze (original estimate)......................... 16, 000
For commencing the decoration of lobbies and halls of both wings of Capitol extension and
    designs for same.. 20, 000
For casting statue of Freedom for new dome...................................... 15, 000
For painting anteroom of Senate.. 10, 000

                                                166, 900

      The Art Commission, upon consideration of its report by the Senate and the House of Representatives, failed to receive such indorsement as would seem to justify its continuance. The conditions in Congress are best explained by the following extract from the House proceedings of June 20, 1860:

[Congressional Globe, 36–1, p. 3199]

      Mr. SHERMAN. I desire to report from the committee of conference on the bill No. 501, making appropriations for sundry civil expenses of the Government for the year ending 30th June, 1861. There was a very large number of disagreeing votes on this bill, and, as a matter of course, a great variety of questions have been brought before the committee of conference. * * * The Senate agree to the House Amendment limiting the appropriation for the completion of the Capitol to the work necessary to complete the building, excluding painting and sculpture. In connection with that amendment the House is recommended to concur with the Senate amendment abolishing the art commission. This was done by a majority of the committee; one of the members of the committee (Mr. Bingham) dissenting from the abolition of the art commission. The effect of the amendment is to confine the expenditure of the $300,000 for the Capitol extension simply to complete the building, and excluding the expenditure of any money for painting or sculpture. As, therefore, there will be no employment for the art commission next year, it is suspended or abolished.

      Thus passed the first and the only Art Commission which has been permitted to interfere in the art matters pertaining to the Capitol. To many it seemed a great mistake that Congress did not continue this commission in force, and The Crayon, in volume 7 (p. 231), is particularly sad. We quote from this issue some extracts:

      We regret to record the repeal of the law by which the country had the benefit of the counsel and judgment of the art commissioners. We are not surprised at it, the act being in keeping with the usual course of the Government to the arts. * * * The causes of the repeal of the law providing for the Art Commission are characterized with the coarseness, ignorance and cunning which are always brought into play in all matters when Government aid and protection are sought. They are due both to the craft of politicians and to the impassive state of opinion in relation to the art that prevails throughout the country. * * *

      From the same issue of The Crayon we take some extracts copied from the Macon Republic:

      * * * The gentlemen of the Art Commission evidently did not understand Congress or they would not have proposed to undo so much or demanded so large a sum to do what they (the Congressmen) had not taste to appreciate, especially as the space to be covered was so much smaller than their

notions of what such an amount of money ought to cover. * * * Congressmen estimate paintings by the yard and are willing to give liberally of the public money if only a corresponding amount of space be covered. * * *

It is quite evident that the Macon Republic was, for some reason which is not disclosed in the article from which we quote, strongly incensed against the Congress for the failure to continue the Art Commission in power. Looking back over more than half a century, some of the expressions of opinion that were put in public print in those days cause us sometimes to wonder if people are becoming sweeter tempered as the years go by.

Capt. W. B. Franklin, who succeeded Capt. M. C. Meigs in charge of the Capitol extension, stated in his report dated November 6, 1860, some interesting items showing the progress of work at that time. Captain Franklin stated that work was suspended upon the building from December 1, 1859, until July 1, 1860, and that some men were employed at the marble sawmill, but no work was done on the building except some painting in the corridors. The report also stated:

The bronze door ordered from Mr. Randolph Rogers I have been informed by him is three-fourths completed and will soon be entirely finished. He reports the work as done entirely to his satisfaction.

Arrangements have been made with Mrs. Crawford for the completion of the two bronze doors ordered from the late Mr. Thomas Crawford, sculptor, her husband. Studies and sketches of these doors in clay were complete when Mr. Crawford died and it is a subject of congratulation that Mrs. Crawford had undertaken to superintend their construction.

During the past winter two marble statues of Justice and History intended to be placed above the main door of one of the eastern porticoes were received at the Capitol. They are by Crawford and are beautiful figures. They have been deposited in the old Hall of Representatives for storage until the portico is ready to receive them.

It will be seen by this reference to the statues of Justice and History that the section of the Capitol now known as Statuary Hall was made a resting place or a storage place for works of art much earlier than had been contemplated. Those who remember the correspondence between Captain Meigs and Gouverneur Kemble will recall the earnestness with which the possibilities of Statuary Hall for an art museum were urged by both these writers. It must indeed have been a barren and an unsightly place to those who had known this hall when it was the meeting place of the Representatives in Congress, but at this time, divested of its furniture and with the only art objects which it had formerly contained removed with the exception of the Car of History, it must have been somewhat of a relief to even use it as a temporary abiding place for the statues of Justice and History, which, it is probable, but few of the visitors to the Capitol ever discover.

In this same report there is an incidental reference showing that "sundry skylights of ornamental glass were received and set." It is possible that this refers to the work in the skylight of the Hall of the House of Representatives, where the seals or coats of arms of different States have been painted upon glass and form a part of the decoration of the skylight. If we are correct in this supposition, it will be proper for us to turn back somewhat in this history of the art of the Capitol in order to record the work of Johannes Adam Oertel, by whom the ceiling decorations in the skylight of the House of Representatives were designed. Mr. Oertel was born in Furth, Nuremburg, Germany, November 3, 1823. At an early age he commenced to study for the ministry, but was persuaded to abandon it for the study of art. It seems that throughout his long life he filled several positions as minister and teacher, but his love for art persisted and it became with him a favorite medium of expression of religious feeling. Mr. Oertel was employed by Captain Meigs early in 1857 to come to the Capitol to assist in the decorative work in that building, but was persuaded to give up the idea of his employment at mural decorations for the purpose of designing the coats of arms in the ceiling of the House of Representatives before referred to. It seems unfortunate that this artist is not more adequately represented in the Capitol. He attempted to plan decorations for one of the rooms of the Capitol, but found that he was superseded by Brumidi in this work. The resentment shown by Oertel and the hostility thereby engendered upon the part of Brumidi precluded the possibility of further employment in the Capitol in the direction of mural decorations. Mr. Oertel is well and favorably known throughout the country for his religious pictures, which have formed important parts in the decoration of many churches. He will probably be better remembered by one picture, Rock of Ages, than by any of his other works. This picture has been reproduced in almost all possible forms of reproduction and in various sizes, and the failure of the artist properly to protect his interests through copyrights unquestionably deprived him of a large source of income. Mr. Oertel died in Vienna, Va., December 9, 1909. The story of his life has been attractively presented in a book entitled "A Vision Realized." This book contains reproductions of many of the most notable works of this artist, and its romance makes it a volume of great interest.

In our attempt to follow along certain lines of art development of the Capitol it has been necessary to allow some matters of interest to go unreferred to in their proper chronological setting. This will be understood by any who consider for a moment that if it were attempted to carry the history along with a close attention to the different years it must necessarily result in taking away much of the interest of the work as a whole.

Those who remember the attitude of Hiram Powers and his refusal to submit a plan for the Senate pediment, which it was originally intended he should fill, and the subsequent substitution of the design of Crawford for the Senate pediment will understand that this arrangement left the House pediment unprovided for. It should not be imagined that there was a lack of applications for filling with sculpture this unassigned space, and in 1856 H. K. Brown, a sculptor of distinction and who afterwards became a member of the Art Commission, completed a design for the House pediment and in a letter dated Brooklyn, February 12, 1856, explained the design he submitted as follows:

Captain M. C. Meigs.

Dear Sir: I have been most vexatiously delayed for the last three weeks in consequence of the failure of my photographer and the very bad weather we have had for printing and am at last compelled to send you very poor impressions of the work, though they may be sufficient to show you the general intention of my design and for you to judge of its capabilities.

You will see by it that my country is no myth in my eyes and that I have had recourse to no unfamiliar symbols to express my idea of it, but have sought the America of today surrounded with the material interests which stimulate her children to action. America occupies the central position in the group extending her blessing and protection alike to all, not merely to her own citizens, but to the poor and distressed foreigner who kneels at her feet on the left. On her right are the anvil, wheel and hammer representative of the mechanic arts. The first standing figure to the left of America represents a citizen depositing his vote in the ballot box, a very distinguishing feature of our country and the symbol of equal rights. Next to him is the farmer cultivator of the soil, ingenuous and simple resting on his plow with the products of his labor at his feet. Next comes the fisherman seated upon his upturned boat mending his nets. Lastly upon that side is the brave and athletic hunter combating the wild animals. I have placed him upon the outskirt of civilization showing him to be hero of all border strife and hardship.

Upon the other extremity is the Indian trapper in whom I have desired to express that stillness and wariness peculiar to his race. Beside him are his dog, trap and the dead object of his pursuit. He stands for the interests of the fur trade.

Next to him I have introduced the miner, or gold seeker of California with his pick, shovel and pan. Next the American boy, frank and brave, with his little boat which he evidently intends to launch upon the first convenient sheet of water. He is the promise of commerce and navigation, the perpetual renewal of the hope of all. Next the old weather-beaten navigator and discoverer demonstrating with globe and maps the characteristics and resources of the countries he has found and exhibiting a specimen of mineral ore to the statesman, who stands attentively considering his propositions.

My feeling is that all art to become of any national importance or interest must grow out of the feelings and the habits of the people and that we have no need of the symbols or conventionalities of other nations to express ourselves. Our country has a rich and beautiful history to illustrate, full of manliness and grandeur and every American artist should endeavor to infuse into his works all the vitality and national policy in his power that when future generations shall look back upon his work they may see that he has expressed himself with truthfulness and honesty.

I have sought in the general composition of the work in question to produce a fullness and harmony of effect [which] should not be destroyed or rendered little by the massiveness of the building and have avoided all staring projections of arms or of other objects, but have sought the same serious simplicity which characterizes the sculpture itself. In this specific idea of America I have represented my country as showing favoritism to no class, she holds out no prizes to any, but distributes equal blessing to all trades and professions. Further than this the design will show for itself its merits and demerits you will discover. I would be judged by them.

I have sought the true dignity of my country and my art and if you find in what I offer that which is worthy a place in her Capitol I shall be happy with the hope of soon hearing from you.

I remain with great esteem,

H. K. BROWN.

The succeeding step in the history of this design furnished by H. K. Brown is shown by the letter of Capt. M. C. Meigs, dated March 20, 1856, and sent to the Secretary of War. The letter follows:

Honorable JEFFERSON DAVIS,
Secretary of War.

MY DEAR SIR: I send herewith the photograph of a design submitted for your judgment by Mr. H. K. Brown, of Brooklyn. Mr. Brown is the sculptor who is engaged in making the large bronze equestrian statue of Washington to be placed in Union Square. With the photograph I send the description which accompanied it.

Mr. Brown some months since when on a visit to Washington desired to know whether the second pediment was open for designs. I informed him of the manner in which Mr. Powers had been invited to offer designs for it and that his friends had during the past winter been again informed that it was still open to him, but that I did not think Mr. Powers would propose a design for it.

He then desired to know whether if he presented a suitable design it would have a chance of success. I said that I could not invite him to submit one; but, I might say to him, that if any American sculptor presented a design of *pre-eminent* merit I thought it would be likely to be adopted. With this understanding Mr. Brown has prepared and submitted the enclosed.

I regret to say that I do not think it is of such pre-eminent merit that I can advise its execution in marble, but in fulfilment of the promise made to Mr. Brown I respectfully submit it to you and ask your instructions as to the answer to be given to his letter.

I have the honor to be: Very respectfully, your ob't servant,

M. C. MEIGS,
Captain of Engineers in Charge.

It could hardly be expected from the nature of the letters of transmission by which the design and the communication of Mr. Brown were forwarded to the Secretary of War that the Secretary would consider it advisable to approve of a design which Captain Meigs had referred to in such terms as " I regret to say that I do not think it is of such preeminent merit that I can advise its execution in marble." The Secretary did, under the circumstances, probably what Captain Meigs had anticipated he would do, and so upon the letter of Captain Meigs the Secretary of War placed the following indorsement:

Captain Meigs will answer Mr. Brown's letter declining his proposition in terms the most acceptable to this artist.

JEFFERSON DAVIS, *Secretary of War.*

MARCH 26th, 1856.

This concluded the episode of the application of Mr. H. K. Brown for a commission for the House pediment. The absence of a photograph of the sketch sent with his description does not give us an opportunity to judge whether Captain Meigs treated the application of Mr. Brown as cordially as it may have deserved. On the other hand, it may have been entirely inadequate to meet the popular idea of the necessary qualifications for the pediment at that time. Mr. Brown was a sculptor of far more than ordinary merit and distinction. He was born in Leyden, Mass., February 24, 1814. He was reared upon a farm. Educated at an academy, he studied art and portrait painting under Chester Harding and began his career as an artist in Cincinnati, Ohio, in 1836, depending also upon surveying to furnish him with the means of support. He moved to Albany, N. Y., where for several years he devoted most of his time to sculpture. In 1842 he went to Rome and remained there five years. After this period he returned to the United States, making his home in New York and Brooklyn until 1857. It was during this period he modeled the equestrian statue of General Washington in Union Square, New York, and the statue of De Witt Clinton in Greenwood Cemetery, Brooklyn, N. Y. From 1857 to 1861 he was at work on a large pediment for the capitol of South Carolina, which with other work there was destroyed during the War between the States. From 1861 to the time of his death he resided in Newburgh, N. Y., where he made the equestrian statues of Generals Scott and Greene, and the statues of General Greene, Governor Clinton, Gen. Philip Kearny, and Richard Stockton in Statuary Hall of the United States Capitol. Mr. Brown died in Newburgh, N. Y., July 10, 1886.

It was at this period or a little later that Erastus Dow Palmer, a sculptor of New York, became interested in the prospect of a commission for the House pediment of the Capitol. It seems, although the facts have not been fully proved by the records and correspondence examined, that through a personal conference with Mr. Palmer some promise had been held out to him of the possibility of the acceptance of his works for the remaining pediment. Mr. Palmer seems to have been fortunate, or possibly unfortunate, in having a host of friends who very zealously pressed his claims for recognition as a sculptor upon the authorities at Washington. We find in relation to this the following letters:

AURORA, NEW YORK, *April 13, 1857.*

DEAR SIR: I find in the Albany Journal of the 10th inst. the enclosed article of his recent work.

A friend well qualified to judge, who visited Palmer's studio a few days since, informs me that he never saw a man who more truly appeared inspired. His whole soul is in his work, scarcely leaving it day or night, and that he did not, could not doubt that it would be approved by every lover of art. The visit of Palmer to Washington, his conversations with yourself and others, particularly with Governor Seward and Fish, whom he values as friends, and they in return admire him as a man and artist, appeared to open to him a new world, a new train of thought, and he will, I am entirely confident, produce a work that will be an honor not only to himself, but the country if permitted to execute it.

Very truly yours,

EDWIN B. MORGAN.

Captain M. C. MEIGS,
   U. S. A., Washington, D. C.

The following quotation from the Albany Journal is probably from the issue of that paper referred to by Edwin B. Morgan as being of the 10th inst. (April, 1857):

PALMER'S LANDING OF THE PILGRIMS

Our gifted townsman, Palmer, has completed his design for the east pediment of one of the wings of the Capitol Extension at Washington.

The design represents the Landing of the Pilgrims at Plymouth, or, more strictly speaking, it represents a scene supposed to occur just subsequent to the debarkation. A group of them have gathered

13   { 193 }

ERASTUS DOW PALMER

From a crayon portrait by Samuel W. Rowse

Palmer is represented by the bronze statue of Chancellor Livingston, in Statuary Hall

round their pastor in various devotional attitudes, while he is standing with uplifted hands, in the act of returning thanks for their safe passage through the perils of the voyage, and imploring Divine aid and guidance in the trials to come. The sculptor has seized the moment when all are wrapt in prayer to transfer the motionless group to marble.

The central figure is that of the venerable Elder Brewster. He is dressed in the simple Puritan garb, while a long cloak hangs loosely from his shoulders. He stands with his face turned towards Heaven, and his arms outstretched in devotion. Next to him kneels Rose Standish—her hands clasped and her upturned face glowing with a woman's trust and religious fervor. In strong contrast, by her side, stands Captain Miles Standish, with his head reverentially bent, but his body erect, rigid and soldierly, and his arms folded on his breast. Just behind him sits upon a chest a more youthful soldier. He leans partially on his gun, his hands resting on the muzzle, while his eyes and his thoughts wander from the religious exercise before him toward the forest around, and the adventure that lurks there. A mother holding upon her knees a babe born on shipboard during the voyage, divides her attention between the pastor and her child. On the right of the central figure kneels a man habited like Standish, and next him an athletic, sturdy Puritan is leaning on the axe that is to hew out a home for him in the wilderness. Behind him are a young girl and two children, and behind them sits Mr. Clifton upon a fragment of rock, his head bowed over the open Bible that rests upon his knees, to whose assurances of a still watchful Providence he clings, on this new and untried shore. The savage winter character of the surrounding scene is evinced by the rocks and leafless trees in the background. Behind one of the latter crouches an Indian, listening, and silencing by a motion of his hand the dog that crouches beside him. Behind the rocks upon the left of the group two wolves, half in surprise, half in fear, peer cautiously out. In the distance the mast of the *Mayflower* is seen against the sky.

This impressive and happily chosen scene is not disfigured by any of the so-called "classical" adjuncts often resorted to by modern sculpture. The accessories all befit the time and place. The costume of the figures is such as the Puritans wore. The chests, barrels, boxes, &c., are just such as a party of emigrants, at that day, would be likely to carry first ashore.

The form of the pediment of course renders it necessary that the figures near the ends should be lower than those in the centre. But this, instead of being a defect, is happily turned into an advantage. While it gives unity and expression to the group, it permits the artist to symbolically arrange his figures in the ascending scale of intellectual development. Lowest of all is the savage life, typified by the Indian and his dog. Then the domestic affections of civilized life are indicated by the mother and child. Then the restless spirit of American enterprise, by the young man looking eagerly around him. Then the stern energy of early Colonial times, by the figure of Miles Standish. Lastly, the kneeling form of Rose, and the Elder absorbed in prayer typify Religion, the crowning glory of our civilization. So, too, on the left of the group, the figures are each expressive of some phase of American life and growth. The energetic, hardy worker grasping his axe, and the old man with open Bible, need no explanation.

This beautiful design is not to be a mere bas relief, but each of the principal figures (Brewster, Clifton, Miles and Rose Standish, &c.,) is a complete and perfect statue, of colossal size. The trees, wolves, Indian, &c., are to be depicted upon the marble background, so that the whole group will stand out much more than they appear to in the photograph. The labor will of course be great and tedious. Upwards of three years will probably be required before it will be complete in marble. But when so completed, it will be at once an enduring monument of Palmer's genius, and a fitting memorial for the National Capitol, of an event which determined the character of our National Existence and history. Americans at Washington will hereafter point to it with patriotic pride, as evidence that American art no longer owns inferiority, even to that of Europe.

It was later in this year of 1857, in the month of August, when a concerted effort was made in behalf of Palmer by distinguished citizens of the State in which he was a resident. Several letters were written in his behalf to President Buchanan, and the many years which have elapsed seem to warrant the use of these letters at this time. The names of the writers are those of men well known in the political history of the Empire State.

UTICA, NEW YORK, *August 22, 1857.*

MY DEAR SIR: The Honorable Thomas W. Olcott, in behalf of many of our own citizens, wishes to get an order from you for statuary to be executed by E. D. Palmer for the National Capitol. We think Mr. Palmer is not excelled by any living artist and we are confident he will soon be known in this country and in Europe as a man of great genius. Mr. Olcott, who will lay this matter before you, is a gentleman of ample fortune and of high social position, who has been prominent among our citizens in promoting science, literature and the fine arts. His views are entitled to great consideration and I hope it will be in your power to accede to his request with regard to Mr. Palmer.

Very truly yours,

HORATIO SEYMOUR.

To His Excellency, JAMES BUCHANAN.

In reference to the same matter there is also a letter from Greene C. Bronson, as follows:

NEW YORK, *August 25, 1857.*

DEAR SIR: I learn that the name of Mr. E. D. Palmer, a distinguished American sculptor, has been mentioned to you for a work of art to adorn the Capitol at Washington, and it gives me great pleasure to say that he is a most excellent artist and every way worthy of public patronage. Should he be employed I feel the fullest confidence that he will produce a work which will do credit to our age and country.

I am very respectfully and truly yours,

GREENE C. BRONSON.

To his Excellency, JAMES BUCHANAN.

The letter from Thomas W. Olcott, who seems to have been the chief representative of the friends of Mr. Palmer, is as follows:

MECHANICS' & FARMERS' BANK,
Albany, August 26, 1857.

His Excellency, JAMES BUCHANAN.

SIR: In addition to the personal assurances which I had the pleasure to give your Excellency some days ago concerning Mr. Palmer, the American sculptor, allow me to present the accompanying letters to you to your address from Governor Seymour, Senator Dickinson, and Judge Greene C. Bronson. I would reiterate my unbounded confidence in the genius and skill of Mr. Palmer and my belief that he will, if favored with a commission, come up to the utmost limit of your expectation. I believe that of the many and beautiful decorations of the Capitol, the illustration of the Landing of the Pilgrims will be an object of paramount attraction and one which may be pointed to as among the durable and gratifying achievements of the present administration.

I have the honor to be, Your Excellency's most obedient,

THOMAS W. OLCOTT.

The letters as quoted were referred by President Buchanan to the War Department, where they met with unfavorable action for reasons which will appear in the following letter from the sculptor, Mr. Palmer, dated Albany, November 12, 1857. The letter is as follows:

DEAR SIR: Before returning home from Washington, I called to take my leave of you, but finding you were engaged I left without seeing you. Since my return I received the following note, dated the same day of my departure from Washington.

"WAR DEPARTMENT, *Washington, November 6, 1857.*

"DEAR SIR: On returning from Cabinet Meeting today the Secretary of War directed me to inform you that your matter was before Cabinet and it was decided to examine the law closely and if it did not specifically authorize the purchase of ornaments, such as you propose, if indeed they are regarded by the law as ornaments, that nothing could be done until the meeting of Congress.

"Very respectfully, your obedient servant,

"W. R. DRINKARD.

"To E. D. PALMER, *Albany.*"

Thinking that six months or more may elapse (judging from the past in my state) before you would be advised of the action of the President and Secretary in the matter of my pediment, I take the liberty of sending the above copy as this seems to bring the case to a close so far as I am concerned, and as my affairs are in every way hindered by my application to and the long delay by the circumstances attending this work, I hope you will pardon what might be thought great haste on my part to make a finish of it in every particular. You proposed for the execution of the models, $500. or more if you thought proper. Now since I began this work I could have modeled one of the statues I have orders for which would have profited me at least $2,500., and had I not expected daily (and I think reasonably) a decision in the case, it would have been done. Seven months of my time, the expenses of my trip to Washington, the time and expenses of my friends, (which I cannot allow them to sustain) in going to Washington to ask only a duty of the President and Secretary, I do not expect to be fully remunerated for, but I cannot think it unreasonable on my part to expect at least $1,000., especially inasmuch as my design was not rejected for one of merit or suitableness as the following remarks of the Secretary to me induces me to believe. He said, "I am much pleased with your pediment. I like the whole character and spirit of it. I think it far superior to Crawford's."

On seeing in the possession of Mr. Olcott nicely mounted and framed one of your fine photographs of my pediment, I find that somebody had taken the wind from my sails by sending it here before my arrival with mine. However, the gratification was far greater than the disappointment. By your favor I am daily and nightly in the enjoyment of much pleasure with my friends in showing and explaining, so far as I can, the photographs at the Capitol and its appurtenances which you gave me while in Washington, and I can assure you they have elicited much genuine appreciation of the high ability evinced in everything pertaining to this great work.

I regret not having gone with you to the Falls as I am sure I would have seen much to instruct and interest. I hope at some future day to accompany you there.

I am now preparing for hard work upon one of my statue orders which I hope to finish in model by May or June next. My head of Moses will be at the Art Exposition in Washington. Will you go and see it?

I cannot close without thanking you for the uniform kindness to me and for the genuine interest you have manifested in behalf of my success in the pediment undertaken. Be assured I fully appreciate it and shall ever remember with a grateful heart.

Faithfully your friend,

ERASTUS D. PALMER.

To Captain MONTGOMERY C. MEIGS,
    Washington, D. C.

In this manner ended the proposal of Erastus D. Palmer for his pediment for the House wing of the Capitol. Although it may seem to some that the act of the officials of the Government in rejecting his work upon the ground that the appropriation did not provide for the sculptural adornment of the Capitol was hardly warranted under the circumstances, in view of the fact that a commission had been given for the pediment of the Senate wing of the Capitol, yet it may be that this seemingly unfavorable act had a larger value than was appreciated at that time. Without in any manner attempting to estimate the value of the composition of Mr. Palmer it must be considered that the subject, The Landing of the Pilgrims, was a matter which might have been of greater local than of national interest. We do not mean by this to minimize the importance of the landing and the colonization by the Pilgrims at Plymouth, but in the greater interest of the Nation it might have seemed as though the pediment of the House should be filled with statuary which would tell a story of wider national importance than the subject proposed by Mr. Palmer for this work. Be this as it may, more than half a century passed away before the sculptural adornment of the House pediment was contracted for, and many more years elapsed before the statuary under this contract was erected in place. To this we shall refer at greater length later in this history.

It should be stated, however, that the request of Mr. Palmer for expenses incurred by him in the preparation and preliminary work of his model for the House pediment was paid by voucher and that he received the $1,000 as requested.

[216]

NOTHER matter should be referred to at this time, although we have written before of matters of a later date. It will be remembered that Crawford's models for the Senate pediment had been brought to this country and that the carving in marble had been done in the sculptor's shop upon the Capitol Grounds. After the work of carving in marble had been completed, Captain Meigs upon advice considered it to be for the best interest of the Government to transfer these models to the United States Military Academy at West Point, N. Y., and from his letter dated Washington, September 27, 1859, we quote as follows:

Colonel RICHARD DELAFIELD,
    Superintendent, United States Military Academy,
                    West Point, New York.

DEAR SIR: I enclose bill of lading for seventeen boxes containing the original models of Crawford's figures for the pediment of the Capitol extension, and four boxes containing other models executed by an Italian artist for the Capitol extension, intended to be placed in the public corridors as drinking fountains.[1] The pediment by Crawford of which the original figures in plaster are now shipped, is the most extensive and the greatest work of American sculpture.

The artist received for the design and modeling of the pediment and for other figures, which were included to surmount one of the eastern doors of the Capitol, (the figures of Justice and History), the sum of $20,000.

These plaster models were brought from Rome to this city at great expense, and having now been carved in marble I have obtained the consent of the War Department by Acting Secretary W. R. Drinkard to send them to the Military Academy to be deposited for preservation and for the art adornment of the institution.

They remain the property of the United States and subject, of course, to the future order of the Government. These are the original plaster casts, the first cast taken from the molds made on the clay models which receive the final touches of the master's skill and as such they have with artists a value greater than the duplicates carved from them in marble which are to adorn the Capitol.

Mr. Crawford when he last visited this country spoke with me of the disposition to be made of them and very clearly expressed his wish that they should be deposited in an institution which would not fail to set them up as the marbles will be arranged upon the pediment of the building. * * *

Unquestionably Captain Meigs, a military man, felt that he was doing a great favor for the Military Academy at West Point, and he was probably as certain as one could be that these models would be cared for as Government property and as the original work of an artist whose designs had been accepted and used in the adornment of the Capitol. Unfortunately, however, the fate of these models seems to be veiled in the obscurity of the many activities of this military institution. Inquiries made a few years since did not result in any satisfactory explanation concerning the whereabouts of these models, but it is presumed that they have been destroyed, for what reason and by whose orders the replies do not indicate.

For some time we have paid but little attention to the condition of Congress and have failed to mention that the Senate had moved into its new quarters on the 4th day of

---

[1] References to the models for these fountains have been found in reports or other documents relating to the progress of the work, but it seems unfortunate that no specific description of the subject employed as designs for these fountains is known.

ERECTING A COLUMN, SENATE CONNECTION OF THE CAPITOL

At the right of the column being hoisted and nearest to it is Jefferson Davis; beside him is Thomas U. Walter, Architect of the Capitol

January, 1859. This event seems to have been one of greater importance than the moving of the House of Representatives from Statuary Hall to the present Hall of the House in the south wing. On the part of the Senate a dignified procession was formed, headed by the Vice President, the Secretary and Sergeant at Arms, the Senators, and clerks of the Senate, and even the pages were included in this short but triumphal march into the larger and more commodious quarters.

After the removal of the Senate to its new quarters arrangements were made and appropriations asked for to provide for remodeling the Supreme Court section of the Capitol, so that the former Senate Chamber might be fitted for the use of the Supreme Court, and the old Supreme Court room, now the law library, made ready for the purpose for which it is now used.

The period immediately preceding the breaking out of the Civil War was not marked by any particular activity in art matters. It may be that even at that time the shadow of the impending conflict seemed to hover over and stifle such activities as might otherwise have been entered into. We have before referred to the arrival in this country of the model for the statue of Freedom, which surmounts the dome of the Capitol. Negotiations for the casting of this statue by Clark Mills had been entered into and some correspondence occurred on the 3d of April, 1860, between the Secretary of War and Capt. W. B. Franklin, who had temporarily superseded Captain Meigs in the management of the construction of the extension of the Capitol. On May 24, 1860, the Secretary of War, in a statement concerning the casting of this statue of Freedom, states that it will be cast by Clark Mills at his foundry near Bladensburg, under the direction of Capt. W. B. Franklin, and that Clark Mills will be paid for his services and for the rent of his foundry and necessary expenses at the rate of $400 per month and that the materials, fuel, labor, etc., will be paid for by the Government. This arrangement had been entered into and the work had progressed to quite an extent when Captain Meigs, who had been returned to duty at the Capitol, issued a formal statement of the existence of war, in which the following language was used:

By direction of the Secretary of War, work upon the Capitol Extension and the new dome is suspended. This order is given in consequence of the condition of the country. The Government has no money to spend except in self-defence, and all good citizens will cheerfully submit to their necessary share of the sacrifices imposed upon them by the Government assailed by widespread conspiracy and rebellion.

M. C. MEIGS, *Captain of Engineers.*

15TH OF MAY, 1861.

On May 17, 1861, Captain Meigs issued orders to get a car from the Government agent of railroads and bring in (from Mills's foundry) everything that had been paid for and to stop work. It was not long after this before Captain Meigs was considering the advisability of proceeding with some of the work in the Capitol. It will be remembered that at a much earlier period there had been a strong effort made through public speeches and resolutions of Congress to have works of art, such as paintings, executed for the Capitol Building by the artists Emanuel Leutze and G. P. A. Healy. Mr. Leutze in the meanwhile had been studying and painting in Dusseldorf and had kept in touch with Captain Meigs and had at times proposed commissions. He had not, however, been able to convince Captain Meigs of the details of such schemes of decoration as he had in mind, and the years had slipped by without any definite conclusion being arrived at. Early in 1861 he seems to have presented his sketches for the painting for the west staircase of the House of Representatives, and the scheme of decoration having been approved by Captain Meigs, it was felt that the time was not opportune for having this work done. With reference to these sketches Captain Meigs, on the 20th of June, 1861, submits with the sketches the following memorandum to the Secretary of War:

The design of Mr. Leutze for the western staircase of the Capitol typical of emigration to the Pacific, was submitted to the Secretary of War at a time when the Capitol itself was hardly out of danger.

The Government was exerting itself to create and move an army to its defence and putting a stop to all expenditures not absolutely necessary for that defence.

The Secretary did not permit the work to be then commenced.

The people of the country have so responded to the call of their Government that danger to the Capitol has now passed away, and it is a question worthy of consideration whether the Government by pursuing in some degree the project of completing its Capitol would not give to the people a welcome assurance of its confidence in its own strength and in its patriotism of its people.

The people do not intend to permit rebellious hands to deface the Capitol and they probably would hail with joy such evidence of the determination and confidence of the Government.

For myself as Superintendent of this great building it was with great regret that I saw the intended decoration of its stairway delayed and I would be gratified, all other expenditures upon the building having been stopped, to see in this time of rebellion one artist at least employed in illustrating our western conquest.

M. C. MEIGS,
Superintendent, U. S. Capitol Extension.

This letter in due course received the attention of the Secretary of War and the following action was indorsed thereon:

Approved. Simon Cameron, Secretary of War, 2d of July, 1861.

The agreement was entered into as follows:

It is agreed this 9th day of July, 1861, at Washington, D. C., between E. Leutze, artist of the first part, and General M. C. Meigs, Superintendent of the Capitol Extension for the United States, of the second part, that Mr. Leutze shall paint upon the western wall of the western stairs of the Capitol extension a picture of emigration, size including the ornamental border to be twenty by thirty feet, to be finished within two years from date, and that for this work Mr. Leutze shall be paid by the United States, a total sum of $20,000., deducting any sums he may have already received towards paying for the design. Said sums to be paid in installments, as follows: For completing the design, deducting the sum already received, $3,500. In equal installments during the progress of the study and execution of this work at the end of each month, $500. until the total sum paid amounts to $15,000. The remaining sum of $5,000. to be paid upon the completion of the painting.

(Signed)   E. LEUTZE,
(Signed)   M. C. MEIGS, *Brig. Gen.,*
Supt., Capitol Extension.

By this instrument the commission for the painting of the picture now known as Westward the Course of Empire Takes Its Way was given. It may have been emphasized by other writers that work was progressing upon the Capitol during all the period of the Civil War, but it will be observed that at the time when this contract was entered into this was the only work then in contemplation of execution. It is probable that not long after this such a feeling of security prevailed that work was resumed at Mills's foundry upon the casting of the statue of Freedom, which was to surmount the dome. The contract with Leutze called for its completion within two years from the date of its execution, and it appears that the work was executed within the specified time. As a mural decoration it is one of the well and favorably known works of this country, and possibly the best example of the process by which it was placed upon the wall. The artist, although born in Germany, was distinctively an American and an enthusiastic believer in American principles. By his correspondence it is shown that his desire was to place upon the walls

WESTWARD THE COURSE OF EMPIRE TAKES ITS WAY

Emanuel Leutze, painter

In the House wing, west staircase

of the Capitol a view illustrative of American history rather than to spend his time in a matter of mere decoration. He preferred to teach and instruct rather than to entertain.

It seems, however, that this production was not received favorably by some of the art critics of that early period. In fact, it seems to have been the fate of any who may have left the beaten path recognized as a thoroughfare by artists to be assailed in severe terms by the critics, who were strong adherents to the principle that nothing new could be produced in art which showed a variance with well-recognized compositions which had preceded it. We include one of the criticisms referred to, not because we feel that its line of reasoning is correct or just, but in order that our readers may understand the conditions of this period and the severity with which this work of Mr. Leutze was criticized. We quote from Art Thoughts, by James Jackson Jarves, published by Hurd & Houghton (1869, p. 297):

America has at last a class of painters of realistic tendency, eclectic and scientific in practice, as sincere and chaste in motive as the English school, though not its equal in execution, nor on the level of the best style of the French, to which it seemingly aspires. This class is represented by Eastman Johnson, Elihu Vedder, Winslow Homer, and others of their stamp. These already contest with the landscapists the popular favor. If they have not as yet succeeded in notably raising the standard of idea in art, considerable has been accomplished in elevating its execution. But the principal service is the reproof they offer to the slop-work of the melodramatists, of whom Leutze was chief. Of all his frantic compositions, the fresco of Westward Ho! in the glass method, painted in the Capitol at Washington, is the maddest. A more vicious example in composition and coloring, with some cleverness of details, could not be presented to young painters. Confusion reigns paramount, as if an earthquake had made chaos of his reckless design, hot, glaring coloring, and but ill comprehended theme.

It may be of interest to turn our attention for a few moments to conditions existing during this period or shortly preceding it. On February 24, 1860, an act was approved (Stats. L., vol. 12, p. 114) as follows:

Be it resolved by the Senate and House of Representatives of the United States of America in Congress assembled, That the sum of $10,000 be and the same is hereby appropriated out of any money in the Treasury not otherwise appropriated to be expended by the Secretary of the Interior in transporting and placing Mills' statue of Washington on the pedestal designated by the proper authorities and in the ceremonies appropriate to the occasion.

On the 15th day of June, 1860 (see Stats. L., vol. 12, pp. 35, 36), a National Gallery and School of Arts for the purpose of promoting the improvement of the fine arts and their application to patriotic purposes by means of exhibitions, libraries, museums, instruction, and other practicable operations was incorporated by the following incorporators, who acted as trustees of this institution: Horatio Stone, John Cranch, J. M. Stanley, J. G. Bruff, Robert Boyle, W. W. Corcoran, A. F. Cunningham, T. G. Clemsen, J. G. Berret, F. B. Stanton, A. Thomas Smith, H. G. Fant, Charles Eames, B. Ogle Taylor, George W. Riggs, Charles Haskins, Seth Eastman, Samuel F. Vinton, and L. B. Gale.

Our earlier references to the work of Constantino Brumidi recorded his completion of the decorations in the committee room of the House Committee on Agriculture and also his painting of a fresco in one of the panels in the southwest corner of the Hall of the House of Representatives. Mr. Brumidi was also almost constantly employed in decorations in different portions of the Capitol, the exact nature of which are not clearly defined from the statement made by him and incorporated in the vouchers issued in payment for his services. We know that in addition to the decorations of rooms and corridors in the Senate wing principally he had in view the painting of the canopy in what is known as the "eye of the dome." (This designation is frequently used by the people discussing this work at the time of its execution.) His employment seems

From a fresco by Constantino Brumidi

PORTRAIT OF JOHN FITCH
Steamboat inventor

In the Senate wing, basement floor

PORTRAIT OF WILLIAM BREWSTER

From a ceiling fresco by Constantino Brumidi

{ 206 }

MURAL PAINTING, THE DEATH OF GENERAL WOOSTER

From a fresco by Constantino Brumidi

In the room of the Senate Committee on Appropriations

to have been almost continuous, notwithstanding the announcement of the commencement of hostilities and the suspension of work in consequence thereof made by Captain Meigs, of which a copy has already been quoted.

It will be remembered that when the work upon the extension of the Capitol first commenced the supervision of the erection of the Capitol was under the direction of the Department of the Interior and that not long after the actual commencement of work the building was taken from under the charge of the Interior Department and placed under the charge of the War Department. We have now reached the place where the retransfer of the charge of this work occurs, as is shown by the following joint resolution:

Resolved by the Senate and House of Representatives of the United States of America in Congress assembled, That the supervision of the Capitol extension and the erection of the new dome be and the same is hereby transferred from the War Department to the Department of the Interior. And all unexpended money which has heretofore been appropriated and all money which may hereafter be appropriated for either of the improvements heretofore mentioned shall be expended under the direction and the supervision of the Secretary of the Interior: *Provided,* That no money heretofore appropriated shall be expended upon the Capitol until authorized by Congress, except so much as is necessary to protect the building from injury by the elements and to complete the dome. (Approved April 16, 1862.) (Stats. L., vol. 12, p. 617.)

The legislation above quoted seems to have placed in the discretion of the Congress the selection of specific purposes for which money could be used, namely, the protection of the building from injury and the erection of the dome. All other enterprises were thus immediately checked, except that Congress could designate purposes of expenditure. It is sometimes easier to enact a law than it is to enact a law that is just in its provisions, and consequently in the legislation known as the Army appropriation bill, approved July 5, 1862, we find the following:

SECTION 11. And be it further enacted that the restriction or limitation contained in the proviso to the Joint Resolution approved April 16, 1862, transferring the superintendency of the Capitol Extension from the War Department to the Department of the Interior shall not be so construed or applied as to prevent the completion of and the payment for the painting now in progress on the wall over the stairway on the western side of the south wing agreeably to the terms of the contract made between General M. C. Meigs on behalf of the Government and E. Leutze, the artist, on the 9th day of July, 1861. (Stats. L., vol. 12, p. 510.)

The section above quoted remedied one defect, but it did not provide for the continuation of the work upon the canopy of the dome under Brumidi, but there are few laws which are, when considered according to their intent, not subject to a different interpretation than the strict reading of the actual text of the legislation would imply. For instance, it was decided later on, and wisely so, that the decoration by Brumidi of the canopy in the "eye of the dome" was in reality a part of the dome itself as contemplated by the architect when the plans for the dome were completed, and therefore it was proper that this work should be continued without any further action by Congress of an explanatory character.

The year of 1863 was an important one in that it marked the period of the erection of the statue of Freedom upon the dome and the reception of the bronze doors, known as the Rogers bronze doors, which had been cast at the Royal Bavarian Foundry in Munich, and after many delays were transported to this country. However, we should not forget to quote a letter from the architect, Thomas U. Walter, at that time in charge of the construction of the extension of the Capitol and the erection of the new dome. For many years he had been handicapped by an animosity which had grown up between himself and the military superintendent of the work, which followed the transfer from the Interior Department to the War Department. This retransfer, to which we have referred in quoting the act of April 16, 1862, seems to have placed Thomas U. Walter in full charge not only of the architectural plans but also of the construction of the building in accordance with the plans already completed. By this change he also became closely associated with the art of the Capitol, an association formerly held by Capt. (now Gen.) Montgomery C. Meigs. Accordingly, on December 2, 1862, he writes to Emanuel Leutze as follows:

DEAR SIR: There is now due you upon your picture entitled "Immigration to the West" a balance of $8,500. which I would be very glad if it were in our power now to pay you. We have, however, several large bills due the contractors which we have promised out of the draft on the Treasury now in process of being passed and which will too far exhaust it to admit of your account being settled until another draft is made. This will require some two or three weeks. You may, therefore, not receive the balance due you before the beginning of the year. I think you may depend upon it at least by that time.

Very respectfully yours,

THOMAS U. WALTER,
Architect in Charge, U. S. Capitol Extension.

We find another interesting letter relating to the Rogers bronze doors written by Thomas U. Walter in his capacity as Architect of the Capitol to Hon. J. P. Usher, Secretary of the Interior, on January 12, 1863, as follows:

SIR: I herewith transmit to you a letter from the Assistant Secretary of State inclosing a communication from the United States Consul at Munich in reference to the bronze doors modeled by Mr. Randolph Rogers and cast by Mr. F. von Miller at Munich for the United States Capitol.

The door was finished more than a year ago and it appears from the correspondence referred to that Mr. Rogers directed Mr. Miller to put the whole work permanently together and pack it in one piece; thus requiring a box eighteen feet six inches long, ten feet nine inches wide, and four feet six inches deep, which with its contents weighs 16,000 pounds.

The immense size of this box seems to have been the chief cause of its not having been delivered according to the agreement. Mr. Miller stipulated to send it to Amsterdam, Rotterdam, Hamburg, or Bremen as Mr. Rogers might thereafter designate; but it was too large to pass through the various gates on the road either to Hamburg or Bremen, leaving Amsterdam and Rotterdam as the only ports to which it was possible to convey it. It will be observed that Mr. Miller offered to deliver it at Amsterdam where a vessel was in waiting to receive it, having offered to take it to the United States for $6,000., but Mr. Ten Brook, the former Consul, and Mr. Rogers both refused to consummate the arrangement and asked time to communicate with the Government at Washington; being, no doubt, influenced to take this course by the large sum demanded for transportation; so that the great magnitude and weight of this box has been the chief impediment to its delivery.

Mr. Rogers directed the door to be thus packed in one piece in order that it might be put up on its arrival without further work upon it, as he feared that some injury or defacement might be caused by unskillful handling in putting it together. Of this, however, there need have been no apprehension. Should it be taken to pieces and repacked as suggested by the communication of Mr. Webster, I have no hesitation in saying that we have skilled workmen here who can put it together again as perfectly as it ever was; and I am certain that it will be less liable to receive injury if it is put up in pieces, than it would if it were put up whole, should that indeed be practicable. Besides, to transport such a mass as this either to Amsterdam or Rotterdam; to stow it in a vessel, which would have to be altered to receive it; to bring it across the ocean; and then to deliver it at the Capitol would involve great risk, as well as a very heavy and unnecessary expense. I am therefore of the opinion that the box should be unpacked by Mr. Miller, the door taken to pieces by boring out the screws, and the whole repacked in six boxes.

There still remains due to Mr. Miller $6,429, or one half the price of casting and finishing the entire work, which sum he was to receive on its delivery at either of the aforementioned ports which Mr. Rogers might designate. To this will be added the cost of taking the work to pieces, repacking it, and furnishing new screws to put it together again with, which, it is stated by Mr. Webster, will amount to 200 or 250 dollars; there will also be some expense for storage, etc., to all of which will be added the premium on exchange at the time the remittance is made.

As it is important that the contract with Mr. Miller should be faithfully carried out, and as it is also desirable that the Government should be put in possession of the work in question, upon which so much has already been expended, I respectfully recommend:—

First, that the United States Consul at Munich be authorized to enter into an agreement with Mr. F. von Miller, to take the bronze door to pieces by boring out the screws, to have it packed in six cases, furnishing such new screws as may be necessary to put it together again; and to send it to whichever of the ports stipulated in the agreement, that he, the said United States Consul, may find to afford the best facilities for shipment to the United States.

Second, that the said United States Consul be authorized to receive the said door, on the part of the Government, and to act on its behalf in coming to an understanding with Mr. Miller as to the aggregate amount of his claim against the United States on account of the same, and as soon as it is delivered to authorize Mr. Miller to draw for the sum thus determined upon, at 20 days sight, on "B. B. French, Disbursing Agent of the Capitol Extension" at Washington, D. C., payable in coin at Munich. The draft to be accompanied by a bill, and vouchers in duplicate, duly certified to, by the said Consul.

Third, that Mr. Webster, the Consul aforesaid, be authorized to ship the said door to the United States by any conveyance that yourself, or the Honorable Secretary of State may designate; and he be likewise authorized to draw, in the same manner on the aforesaid disbursing agent for whatever expenses may be incurred after the receipt of the door from Mr. Miller.

I have the honor to remain, Sir, very respectfully, your obt. servt.,

THOS. U. WALTER,
Architect of the U. S. Capitol Extension.

This subject was continued by the following letter, which we quote in its entirety:

ARCHITECT'S OFFICE, U. S. CAPITOL,
Washington, D. C., May 4, 1863.

Hon. J. P. USHER,
Secretary of the Interior.

SIR: I have read, and carefully considered the communication of the Hon. F. Webster, United States Consul at Munich, with its inclosures, respecting the claim of Mr. F. von Miller, referred to me by your endorsement of the 29th. ult., and find that instead of the United States Government being indebted to the said Mr. von Miller the sum of $6,429, as stated in my letter to the Department under date of Jan. 12, 1863, he sums up the indebtedness at about $6,825, being a difference of about $400, assuming a guilder to be equal to 40 cents, as stated by Mr. Webster, on the first page of his dispatch. Mr. Webster has also given the sum of 41.174 cents, indicated in brackets, with a note of interrogation, which I understand to imply a doubt as to the exact value of the guilder, in comparison with United States coin. Were the latter sum adopted as the basis of the calculation, it would add $200 to the aggregate. The following is a summary of the charges of Mr. von Miller, as contained in paper No. 2:

Balance due on contract . . . . 15, 000 guilders.
Cost of protest and interest from Oct. 10 to Dec. 12, 1861, @ 4% 876   "
Interest from Dec. 12, 1861, say 18 mos., at 66 guilders per month . . . . 1, 188   "
_____
17, 064 guilders.
40¢
_____
6, 825. 60

To this will be added the cost of taking the door to pieces and repacking it, and the difference of exchange between New York and Munich.

My impression is, from the correspondence submitted to me, that Mr. von Miller has not been enough at fault in these transactions to affect the validity of his claim,—He seems to have relied upon Mr. Rogers and the United States consul, Mr. Ten Brook, to make the document satisfactory to the Government, and as he remarks, the second draft being made in the same manner as the first, he had no reason to doubt that it would be honored.

As the difference claimed by Mr. von Miller over and above our own estimate, is but about $400, or at most $600, and inasmuch as it is desirable, under the present circumstances of the country, to act with liberality and promptness in the liquidation of its foreign debts, I consider it inexpedient to make any formal objection to this claim. I therefore respectfully recommend that Mr. Webster be authorized to settle with Mr. von Miller on his own terms.

As to the propriety of taking the door to pieces and repacking it in *six* boxes, I agree with Mr. von Miller that it would be preferable to send it in one piece, if it were possible to do so without involving an expense that would not be warranted by any advantage that might be gained by it, and without incurring great risk in transporting it. I can therefore see no reason to change the opinion I expressed on the subject, in my letter before alluded to.

I herewith return the papers submitted to me, and have the honor to remain

With great respect, your obt. servt.

Thos. U. Walter,
Architect U. S. Capitol Extension and New Dome.

It is apparent that interest in the execution of these doors by Randolph Rogers had become a matter of common knowledge throughout the country and that there were those who had remembered that other works belonging to the Government, such as some of the Trumbull pictures and pictures by other artists, had been exhibited throughout the country before being permanently installed in the Capitol. We therefore refer to a letter from the Governor of the State of Indiana, in which a request is contained for the public exhibition of the Rogers bronze doors throughout the country:

Architect's Office, U. S. Capitol,
Washington, D. C., June 12, 1863.

Hon. J. P. Usher,
Secretary of the Interior.

Sir: The letter of his Excellency O. P. Morton, Governor of the State of Indiana, asking that the bronze doors for the United States Capitol, executed from the models of Mr. Randolph Rogers, may "be placed on exhibition, for the benefit of the artist, at least for a limited time, in the larger cities of the United States," having been referred to me by the Department, for the purpose of obtaining my opinion as to the practicability, and expediency of complying with the said request, I have respectfully to say, that however desirous we may be to promote the interest of the estimable artist who designed the door, I am of the opinion that it would be impracticable to carry out the suggestions of Gov. Morton. The door in question was originally put together permanently in Munich, by Mr. von Miller, the manufacturer, by direction of Mr. Rogers, and it was packed in a box measuring 18' 6" long, 10' 9" wide, and 4' 6" high, which with its contents weighed 16,000 pounds. The immense size and weight of this box rendered it impossible to transport it to this country at any reasonable cost; and, after a delay of more than a year, Mr. von Miller was directed by the Department to take it to pieces by boring out the screws, (which was his own suggestion) and to pack it in *six* cases instead of one; it can not be exhibited, therefore, without being put together and taken to pieces again, at each place of exhibition.

This would involve a very heavy expense, which of course, could not be paid out of the appropriation for the Capitol Extension, as we have no authority to divert any of that appropriation to such a purpose.

In addition to this, the handling and moving of a work, so heavy, and so delicately finished, in order to prepare it for the proposed exhibitions, would deface it if not absolutely mutilate it and ruin it. Each time it is taken to pieces, the screws would require to be bored out, (as was done by Mr. von Miller,) for the purpose of repacking it; and it would be necessary to procure new screws, probably from Munich.

The putting of the door together again, so as to be as perfect as it was when put together originally by Mr. von Miller, will require the best skill we have in the country; and the greatest care will have to be exercised in handling. I think it inexpedient, therefore, to run any unnecessary risks, even though it could be demonstrated to be practicable, which I very much doubt.

I hope therefore that the packages will not be permitted to be opened until they reach the Capitol, which is certainly the proper place for this great work first to see the light in America.

I have the honor to be, Sir, with great respect, your obt. servt.,

Thos. U. Walter,
Architect of U. S. Capitol Extension, etc.

With the appointment of the Art Commission reference was made by Capt. M. C. Meigs to the injustice that such restrictions as would be imposed by the selection of designs and the approval of the same by the Art Commission and the Joint Committee on the Library would work upon the contract which was then in force with James Walker, who was at that time engaged in the painting of the Battle of Chapultepec. Reference to this painting is found in the following letter:

DEPARTMENT OF THE INTERIOR,
Washington, July 18, 1862.

SIR: I herewith send you the bill of Mr. James Walker for the painting representing the Battle of Chapultepec executed by him under a commission from Captain Meigs and designed for the Military Committee Room of the House of Representatives, amounting to $6,000. with a credit of $2,120. advanced to him at sundry times. Under the peculiar circumstances of the case I feel constrained to pay the balance due Mr. Walker and secure the painting to the United States. You will, therefore, ascertain the exact sum of the advances which have been made to Mr. Walker, cause the painting to be carefully removed to the Capitol and pay him the balance due him; that is, the difference between the sum of the advances made to him and $6,000.

I am respectfully, your obedient servant,

CALEB B. SMITH,
Secretary of the Interior.

BENJAMIN B. FRENCH, Esquire,
Disbursing Agent, Capitol Extension, etc.

The painting above referred to now hangs in the west staircase of the Senate wing of the Capitol, and it is probable that not long after it was secured by the Government it was placed in its present position. This inference is based upon the fact that upon taking down the painting in the summer of 1923 it was discovered that the wall space covered by this painting had been painted a dark maroon color and that upon inquiry of those who had been employed in the Capitol for a very long period of time it seems to be established that very early in the history of the Senate wing of the Capitol the staircases were painted that color. It was probably too large for the committee room of the House Committte on Military Affairs, and it is also probable that even at an earlier date than the period of the commencement of the painting of the Battle of Chapultepec (1857) there was in the mind of some of the legislators the purpose to secure for the decoration of the room of the Committee on Military Affairs the services of Lieut. Col. Seth Eastman, by whom the decorations for this committee room were eventually made.

The artist James Walker was born in England June 3, 1819, and was brought to New York City as a child, where he resided at intervals during the larger portion of his life. When a young man, he resided for one winter in the city of New Orleans. He was a resident of the City of Mexico at the breaking out of the Mexican War; and although the Mexican commander had issued an edict banishing all American residents to a distance of 300 miles in the interior, he remained hidden for six weeks in the city. After a while an opportunity afforded itself for his escape to the lines of the American Army, which he joined as an interpreter and afterwards returned with the Army to the city from which he had so recently fled. He was with the Army during the battles of the valley and remained during its occupation of the Mexican capital. After an absence of eight years he returned to New York in 1848. He subsequently visited South America and in 1850 established a studio in New York, continuing to reside in that city until 1884, with exceptions of brief intervals spent in other cities. In 1857 and 1858 he was in Washington, during which time he painted his Battle of Chapultepec. His art work consisted principally of large battle paintings, and in addition to this painting owned by the Government he received a commission from General Hooker for the Battle of Lookout Mountain, and also painted a mammoth canvas, the Battle of Gettysburg. His work is largely reminiscent of the period of the early sixties and is probably more distinctly marked by the closeness of his technique than by his ability to compose. He died in Watsonville, Calif., in September, 1889.

Some time has elapsed since reference has been made to the work of Thomas Craw-ford, who died in 1857, leaving in an incomplete condition sketches for his bronze doors, and probably the figures of Justice and History to be placed over the door of the main entrance of the Senate wing. Mrs. Crawford contemplated the completion of the work of her husband and received from the Government at Washington permission to do so. The work was afterwards intrusted to William H. Rinehart for completion, and at this period we introduce a letter in which the conditions existing with relation to the completion of the work of Thomas Crawford are discussed in detail.

ARCHITECT'S OFFICE, U. S. CAPITOL,
Hon. J. P. USHER, *Washington, D. C., June 22, 1863.*
    Secretary of the Interior.

SIR: In compliance with the request contained in your letter of the 11th. ult., I have examined the correspondence of the military engineers heretofore in charge of the United States Capitol Extension, on the subject of the plaster casts of the two bronze doors, ordered of the late Thomas Crawford, together with the records on file in this office relating to the same; also the draft of Wm. H. Rinehart in favor of Messrs. Ward & Co., New York, dated at Rome April 8, 1862, for $6,000, and I have the honor to submit, as my opinion, that the conditions of the agreement, as far as it relates to one of the aforesaid doors, have been complied with, and that the holders of the draft are entitled to payment.

In connection with this subject, I deem it proper to suggest that these models be brought directly to this country, to be put in bronze by American artists instead of sending them to Munich to have the doors cast from them by Mr. von Miller, as was originally intended, and, as will certainly be done, unless immediate directions are given to the contrary. Mr. Rinehart says, in his last letter, "as soon as my draft is paid, I will send the door to Munich: I would have sent it immediately but have not the money." It therefore becomes necessary to take action on this subject simultaneously with the payment of the draft. I consider it by no means a settled question that a work in bronze, equal in every respect to that of the Munich foundry, cannot be produced in the United States. But even admitting that our work-men are inferior to those of the Bavarian workshops, it is but just and appropriate, that our National Capitol, at the date of its construction, should be an exposition of the state of the arts in our own country, and not a museum of foreign art.

I find, from the correspondence referred to, that the plaster models for both of these doors were definitely ordered from Mr. Crawford on the 11th. of October, 1855, at $6,000, for each door; that Mr. Crawford died in 1857, leaving the models incomplete; and that, on the 9th. of June, 1860, nearly five years after the first order was given, it was definitely confirmed to Mrs. Crawford by the military engineer then in charge of the work, under the sanction of the Secretary of War. The following extracts from the letter of the aforesaid engineer to Mrs. Crawford will show the nature of the order.—" It gives me great pleasure to transmit to you a copy of a letter to the Secretary of War, from myself, written by his direction, after a careful examination of the photographs of the studies of the doors designed by your lamented husband, for the U. S. Capitol Extension, with his endorsement upon it, approving my recom-mendations. You are therefore authorized to have these models finished in plaster at once." * * * " It is hardly necessary to say to you that on account of the long delay in settling this business, it is very desirable that the doors should be delivered as soon as possible." A copy of the letter alluded to, with the endorsement of the Secretary of War, also a copy of the letter from which the foregoing is an extract, are hereto appended, marked A and B.[2]

In view of these facts there can be no doubt that Mrs. Crawford was duly authorized by the Gov-ernment to execute the models for *both* of the doors in question, at $6,000. for each door—only one of them has however been completed, and I am informed that, notwithstanding more than *three* years have elapsed since the renewal of the order, nothing has been done to the other, except the original sketches remain as Mr. Crawford left them. Should this be the case, I am of the opinion that it would be proper to withdraw the order, and have the second door modeled in this country.

It appears, from the correspondence, that a definite order was given by the military engineer in charge of the work, on the 23d. of October, 1860, to Mrs. Crawford to employ Mr. von Miller to cast both of these doors in bronze, in Munich, at a cost of 5,000 Roman scudi per piece (the Roman scudi being understood to be equivalent to the American dollar); a copy of the letter containing this order is hereto annexed, marked C.[2] I find, however, no response from Mr. von Miller, and no information from

---

[2] Not printed.

STATUE OF BENJAMIN FRANKLIN

Hiram Powers, sculptor

which the inference can be drawn that the bargain was ever consummated. In view of this fact, and the great length of time that has elapsed since Mrs. Crawford was authorized to enter into the arrangement referred to, I do not anticipate any objections on the part of Mr. von Miller to the withdrawal of the order.

The building is now ready for these doors; but fortunately, they are not absolutely necessary to its completion. Wooden doors will answer the same purpose, and by bold and tasteful panelling will produce an architectural *ensemble* as effective as can be derived from any minutely sculptured details— doors of this description are now being made with a view to the completion of these entrances, prior to the next meeting of Congress.

I respectfully suggest that the door to be cast from the model now completed, which it will require in all probability a year or more to execute in bronze, be used for the north wing, and thus finish the sculptural decorations of this part of the work. This wing will then be embellished by the group of statues in the pediment, representing "The Progress of Civilization," the group consisting of "Justice and History," which forms the crowning feature of the front door, and the bronze valves in question; all of which are the work of Crawford.

No sculptural decorations have yet been ordered for the pediment of the south wing, nor for the group over the front door; it seems proper therefore to omit the decorations for the valves of the door also, and thus leave the entire sculptural ornamentation of this wing to be designed and executed by artists in our own country.

I do not suppose that Mrs. Crawford will insist, at this late day, on modelling the second door; nor do I believe that Mr. von Miller will be anxious to cast either of the doors upon the terms formerly stated. I think, however, that it will be proper to communicate with the United States Consul at Rome, on both these points, before taking any final action.

In conclusion I respectfully recommend:—First, that the draft of Wm. H. Rinehart in favor of Messrs. Ward & Co., No. 54 Wall St., New York, dated at Rome, April 8, 1862, for six thousand dollars, be paid; all of the conditions of the agreement with Mrs. Crawford having, on her part, been fully complied with. Second, that the United States consul at Rome be requested to ascertain whether anything has been done to the second door, beyond the original sketches of Mr. Crawford; what the nature and condition of said sketches are; and whether there would be any objections on the part of Mrs. Crawford to the withdrawal of the order for the aforesaid second door. Third, that the said United States Consul be requested to ascertain whether any definite bargain was ever made with Mr. von Miller, at Munich; and if there was, whether he would consent to the withdrawal of the order.

Fourth, that the models be safely packed, and forwarded to this country without delay, in case it shall be found that the Government is not under obligation to Mr. von Miller to employ him to execute the castings in bronze;—or in case such an obligation is found really to exist, and he consent to the withdrawal of the order.

I have the honor to remain, Sir, very respectfully, your obt. servt.,

THOS. U. WALTER,
Architect of the U. S. Capitol Extension, etc.

P. S.—I herewith return the papers you transmitted to me.

The year 1863, notwithstanding that the Civil War was in progress, was filled with activities in art direction. It was in this year that the statue of Franklin, located at the foot of the east grand staircase of the Senate wing, was received and during this same year that the statue of Thomas Jefferson, located at the foot of the east grand staircase of the House wing, was placed in position. These statues were the work of Hiram Powers, and, with the exception of the bust of Chief Justice John Marshall, in the Supreme Court room, are the only works of this celebrated sculptor in the Capitol Building. Ample opportunity had been given to Mr. Powers to submit a proposal for the pediment of the House wing or of the Senate wing of the Capitol; in fact, the opportunity to choose which pediment he would decorate seems to have been offered to him, but for reasons known to himself he states plainly, but extremely courteously, that he did not care to submit any proposition for sculptural work for the Capitol. It will be noted that he does not by this positively decline, but gives one the right to infer that he did not consider himself in the light of a competitor. The commission must seek the sculptor and not the sculptor the commission. As this may be the last opportunity to refer to the work of Hiram Powers, it may be well to give in this connection some biographical information. He was born in Woodstock, Vt., June 27, 1805. He began life in Cincinnati, Ohio, as an errand boy, later was employed in Watson & Clark's factory, and finally as a wax modeler in D'Operille's Museum, and was the originator of the famous show called the Infernal Regions. After this he began modeling in clay and making portraits. He then went to Washington, D. C., where he modeled portraits of Calhoun, Webster, John Marshall, and other distinguished men. Through the financial aid of Nicholas Longworth, of Cincinnati, Ohio, and William C. Preston, of South Carolina, he was enabled to go to Florence, Italy, in 1837, to pursue his studies in art. He was the sculptor of many statues, both ideal and portrait, being unsurpassed in the latter. His most celebrated work is the statue of a Greek Slave, exhibited at the Crystal Palace Exposition in London in 1851. This statue was also exhibited in many places in the United States. The original is owned in England by the Duke of Cleveland; the second is in the possession of the Corcoran Gallery of Art, Washington, D. C.; four other copies are in different portions of the United States. He died in Florence, Italy, June 27, 1873, and is buried in the Protestant cemetery in that city. A son, Preston Powers, also a sculptor, was his only pupil.

In the meanwhile the work, largely preliminary in its character, being done by Brumidi toward the fresco in the "eye of the dome" had received the official sanction of the Interior Department. The work of Mr. Brumidi was greatly diversified, so that he was not continuously employed upon the preliminary work, such as the preparation of his cartoons for the decorative features for the "eye of the dome." At times, as shown by his vouchers, he was performing services of a decorative nature in other sections of the Capitol, so that during any cessation of his work in one direction his time could be employed in another. On July 7, 1863, the Secretary of the Interior addressed a letter to Clement L. West, Esq., who seemingly at that time acted in some supervisory capacity in relation to the work at the Capitol. The letter is as follows:

SIR: In reply to your oral inquiry of yesterday, I have to inform you that in view of the explanations made by the Architect of the Capitol Extension and new dome in reference to the agreement between himself and Mr. Brumidi for the painting in fresco of the canopy over the "eye of the dome," I have concluded that it is a part of the original plan and that it is the will of Congress that it should be executed. Mr. Walter has, therefore, been authorized to cause the work to be resumed.

I am, Sir, very respectfully, your obt. servant,

J. P. USHER, *Secretary of the Interior.*

The question of the financial arrangements for the payment for services of Brumidi are called to the attention of Mr. West, the general superintendent and disbursing agent, by a letter from the Department of the Interior under date of November 6, 1863, as follows:

SIR: In March last an agreement was entered into with Mr. C. Brumidi for painting the canopy over the eye of the new dome of the Capitol, in real fresco at an entire cost, including the cartoons and every other expense, of not over $40,000., payment to be made in monthly bills as the work progressed, not to exceed $2,000. each; $10,000, one-fourth the entire cost of the work, has already been paid to Mr. Brumidi. I am of the opinion that the progress which has been made does not justify any further payments at present. You will therefore suspend any advances to Mr. Brumidi until further orders.

I am, Sir, very respectfully, your obt. servant,

J. P. USHER, *Secretary.*

It will be necessary, in order to continue what seems to be a connected history of this frescoing of the canopy over the "eye of the dome," to submit a letter from Thomas U.

Walter, the Architect of the Capitol extension, to the Secretary of the Interior under date of December 3, 1864. More than a year had elapsed since the Secretary of the Interior had caused a suspension to be made in the advances to the artist. The letter is as follows:

Honorable J. P. Usher,
> *Secretary of the Interior.*

Sir: As the canopy for the picture over the eye of the new dome is ready for Mr. Brumidi and as he is now about to commence to work, I deem it proper to say that he has not received any payment on account of his contract since November 6, 1863, and that in the interim he has been occupied in perfecting the full-size cartoons, which are now ready for the work. I, therefore, respectfully recommend that payments to him be resumed in accordance with his contract and that they be continued as the work progresses until he shall have received the aggregate sum of $30,000, after which no further payments to be made until the work is completed and approved.

I have the honor to be, Sir, with great respect, your ob. serv.

Thos. U. Walter,
Architect U. S. Capitol Extension, etc.

In the meanwhile we must understand that sculptural work which had been intended for the decoration of the Capitol had in many instances been placed in the Grounds of the Capitol or at convenient points in the interior of the Capitol in order that the Congress and those generally interested might have the opportunity of inspecting these new accessions. The statue of Freedom had finally been completed and preparations were being made for its erection. The completion of this statue was important not only as an event in the progress of the work upon the new dome but also because of its art qualities, which probably excelled those of any object designed for such a lofty situation. It also served to inform the people throughout the country of the fact that the Government was still actively engaged in the completion of the Capitol, notwithstanding it was greatly handicapped on account of war conditions then existing.

CHAPTER XII

STATUE OF FREEDOM PLACED ON THE DOME
THE FUNERAL OF PRESIDENT LINCOLN

A T THE time of the completion of the statue of Freedom the city of Washington was encircled by forts, known as the defenses of Washington. The thousands of soldiers then quartered in these forts were greatly interested in the hoisting of a flag from the dome which should signalize the completion of the dome and the erection of this heroic bronze statue of Freedom. Accordingly plans were made that this event should be one befitting the completion of this important enterprise, and the Architect of the Capitol, by virtue of his office, made all necessary preparations, the details of which are contained in the following letter, which is quoted in its entirety:

Capt. C. F. THOMAS,   DEC. 2, 1863.
        Superintendent of the work of the Dome.

    SIR: It is the wish of the Department that no demonstrations whatever be made, on our part, on the placing of the head on the statue of the Dome; and this expression of desire agrees precisely with my own taste; I have therefore to request that the head be put on as a matter of every day work, that none of the persons on the Dome be permitted to make any noise whatever, or to wave their hats, and also that no attempt be made by anyone at speech making. And you are further directed to permit no one to get on the head after it is up. It is always dignified, when we do a good or great thing to appear to be unconscious of it ourselves; the raising of the American flag will be all that we shall have to do; the War Department will do the rest.

    I will not be on the Dome at that time, as I do not desire to render myself conspicuous. I have ordered Mr. Schoenborn to be there in my place, as he has been engaged on the work from the beginning.

    You are requested to be on the Dome yourself at 12 o'clock and I will start the head from below precisely at that hour. It is also ordered that no person whatever be permitted to go up on the head, and that no flags, or emblems of any kind be displayed on any part of the work.

    I have promised General Augur that the American flag shall go up at 15 minutes past 12 o'clock, and I have to request you to see that there be no delay; it will not be necessary to put in the screws to fasten the head to the statue, until after the salute is fired.

    I shall send a copy of these instructions to the Department, in order that they may become a matter of record.

        Very respectfully, your obt., servt.

                                            THOS. U. WALTER,
                                 Architect of U. S. Capitol Extension, etc.

The importance attached to the unveiling of this statue is shown by the following order from the War Department, known as Special Order No. 248, Headquarters, Department of Washington, Twenty-second Army Corps, December 1, 1863:

    *   *   *   *   *   *   *

    SEC. 3. At 12 m. on the 2d inst. the Statue of Freedom which crowns the dome of the National Capitol will be inaugurated. In commemoration of this event and as an expression due from the Department of respect for this material symbol of the principle from which our Government is based, it is ordered—

    First, at the moment at which a flag is displayed from the statue a national salute of 35 guns will be fired from a field battery on Capitol Hill.

THE WEST TERRACE OF THE CAPITOL

Photograph by Charles E. Fairman

From an early photograph by R. G. Searle

THE CAPITOL, SHOWING THE NORTH AND WEST FRONTS

Second, that last gun from the salute will be answered by a similar salute from Fort Stanton, which will be followed in succession from right to left by salutes from Forts Davis, Mahan, Lincoln, Bunker Hill, Totton, De Russy, Reno, Cameron, Corcoran, Albany and Scott.

*   *   *   *   *   *   *

Fourth, Brigadier General W. F. Barry will make the necessary arrangement for and superintend the firing from Capitol Hill, Brigadier General De Russy from the works south and Lieut. Colonel J. A. Haskin from those north of the Potomac.

By command of Major-General Augur:

CARROLL H. POTTER,

Assistant Adjutant General.

The question as to who actually raised the flag over the statue at the time of its erection has given rise to considerable controversy, and the honor of raising the flag has been claimed by different people who were at that time stationed in the city as soldiers. It seems from the letter of Thomas U. Walter to Capt. C. F. Thomas that it is quite probable that Captain Thomas had in charge this signaling to the forts by the raising of the flag; that if he did not himself raise the flag, the person who did was undoubtedly acting under his instructions.

Those who have followed closely the correspondence between Capt. M. C. Meigs and Gouverneur Kemble will remember that at that early date, before Statuary Hall had been vacated as the meeting place of the House of Representatives, the thought had found expression that at some time the old Hall of the House of Representatives would be made a place where works of art could be assembled. It is quite probable that it may have seemed desirable to make some use of this vacant space, and it is possibly true that, as at an earlier date the rotunda of the Capitol had become a lounging place for those with nothing better to do than to congregate in such public places, the same condition existed in the old Hall of the House. In the House of Representatives on January 6, 1864, Mr. Morrill, of Vermont, submitted the following resolution:

Resolved, That the Committee on Public Buildings be requested to examine and report as to the expediency of setting apart the old hall of the House of Representatives as a hall for statuary; and also as to the cost of a new flooring and bronze railing on each side of the passage-way through the hall preparatory to the reception of such works of art. (Read, considered and agreed to.) (House Journal, 38th Cong., 1st sess., p. 108.)

This resolution resulted in a joint resolution being reported from the Committee on Public Buildings and Grounds by Mr. Rice, of Maine, on April 19, 1864:

JOINT RESOLUTION SETTING APART THE OLD HALL OF THE HOUSE OF REPRESENTATIVES AS A HALL OF STATUARY

Whereas the old Hall of the House of Representatives being now worse than uselessly occupied as a place of storage and traffic, and as it must of necessity remain a thoroughfare between the two wings of the Capitol: Therefore

Resolved by the Senate and House of Representatives of the United States of America in Congress assembled, That the President be, and he is hereby, authorized to invite each and all the States to provide and furnish statues in marble or bronze, not exceeding two in number for each State, of men who have been citizens thereof and illustrious for their historic renown or from distinguished civic or military services, such as each State shall determine to be worthy of this national commemoration; and that they be placed in the old Hall of the House of Representatives, in the Capitol of the United States, which is hereby set apart, or so much thereof as may be necessary, as a national statuary hall, for the purposes herein indicated, and the same shall be under the care and supervision of the Commissioner of Public Buildings.

SEC. 2. *And be it further enacted,* That a marble floor, similar to that of the Congressional Library or the Senate vestibule, shall be constructed in said old Hall of the House of Representatives, using such marble as may be now on hand and not otherwise required, and that suitable structures and railings shall be therein erected for the reception and protection of statuary, and the same shall be under the

PORTRAIT OF SENATOR JUSTIN S. MORRILL

Eastman Johnson, painter

supervision and direction of the Commissioner of Public Buildings; and so much of the moneys now or hereafter appropriated for the Capitol extension as may be necessary, not exceeding the sum of twenty-four thousand dollars, is hereby set apart and shall be disbursed for the purposes hereinbefore mentioned.

The joint resolution was debated and passed the House. On January 13, 1864, Thomas U. Walter, Architect of the Capitol, stated in a letter that the estimated cost of taking up the existing floor, removing the flagstone pavement, laying a new floor similar to that of the Congressional Library or the Senate vestibule, and the putting up of an iron railing 6 feet high to form a passage through the Hall, would cost $24,000. During the debate upon the resolution Mr. Morrill said:

* * * The old Senate Chamber has been already fittingly devoted to the use of the Supreme Court. The old hall of the House of Representatives empty and deserted, remains an unappropriated waste and as it now appears—draped in cobwebs and carpeted with dust, tobacco, and apple pomace— a conspicuous nuisance. Congress is the guardian of this fine old hall, surpassing in beauty all the rooms of this vast pile, and should protect it from desecration. Its noble columns from a quarry exhausted and incapable of reproduction—

"Nature formed but one,
And broke the die in molding"—

its democratic simplicity and grandeur of style; and its wealth of association with many earnest and eloquent chapters in the history of our country, deserve perpetuity at the hands of an American Congress. * * *

Will not all the States with generous emulation proudly respond, and thus furnish a new evidence that the Union will clasp and hold forever all its jewels—the glories of the past, civil, military, and judicial—in one hallowed spot where those who will be here to aid in carrying on the Government may daily receive fresh inspirations and new incentives—

"To scorn delights and live laborious days"—

and where pilgrims from all parts of the Union, as well as from foreign lands, may come and behold a gallery filled with such American manhood as succeeding generations will delight to honor, and see also the actual form and mold of those who have inerasably fixed their names on the pages of history.

The suffrages of no State will fail to be honestly and fairly bestowed, for no local shams will be intruded where the judgment of the world is sure to be challenged, and where partisanship loses its current value. We may reasonably expect that the State contributions, without charge to the National Government, will speedily furnish here in the Capitol of the nation a collection of statuary that will reflect honor upon the illustrious dead, upon the republic found to be neither ungrateful to its distinguished sons nor unmindful of its obligations; and incidentally, it may be hoped, there will be brought forth worthy monuments to the genius of the artists of the country who will vie with each other for distinction in the execution of the various works which may be required. * * *

The resolution, after discussion both in the House and the Senate and in its amended form, was referred to a committee of conference and finally resulted in the law known as the act of July 2, 1864 (Stats. L., vol. 13, p. 347), as it appears in the Revised Statutes of the United States (edition of 1878, p. 321), as follows:

SEC. 1814. Suitable structures and railings shall be erected in the old Hall of Representatives for the reception and protection of statuary, and the same shall be under the supervision and direction of the Chief of Engineers in charge of public buildings and grounds. And the President is authorized to invite all the States to provide and furnish statues, in marble or bronze, not exceeding two in number for each State, of deceased persons who have been citizens thereof, and illustrious for their historic renown or for distinguished civic or military services, such as each State may deem to be worthy of this national commemoration; and when so furnished the same shall be placed in the old Hall of the House of Representatives, in the Capitol of the United States, which is set apart, or so much thereof as may be necessary, as a national statuary hall for the purpose herein indicated.

The former condition of this old Hall of the House of Representatives must indeed have been deplorable. We have learned from the remarks of Justin S. Morrill upon the subject that the dignity of the hall had suffered greatly from the uses to which it had been put during the time immediately preceding the legislation converting it into a national Statuary Hall. Mr. Schenck, in the course of the debate, stated that the condition of the Hall was a disgrace and a reproach; that in entering it from the present Hall of the House of Representatives one passes through an expensive bronze door—the Rogers door was at that time at the southern exit from the old Hall of the House—and finds in the old hall apple stands and hucksters. In his remarks he used the following language:

I never pass through the old hall of the House of Representatives without feeling myself reproached by the spirits that haunt that place. I look around to see where the venerable John Quincy Adams trembled in his seat and voted and I see a huckster woman selling ginger bread. I look to see where Calhoun sat—for there was a time when we might speak with reverence even of him—I look to see where he sat and where Clay sat and I find a woman selling oranges and root beer. I look around the floor where these men stood and uttered their patriotic sentiments in the day when patriotic sentiments were heard with reverence everywhere and by every man and I see a floor rotting and trembling under my tread.

So far as the necessary legislation is concerned, all had been done that could be done to inaugurate the National Statuary Hall. It may not at this time be out of place to make some comments upon the interpretation of the law by which this Statuary Hall had been created. Many seem to think that, notwithstanding the fact that the duty of inviting the States to a representation in this hall had been placed upon the President and that all that remained to complete this action was the acceptance by the States, there still remained in Congress the right of supervision and of selection. To many it seems that it is necessary that a statue sent from a State to the Statuary Hall under the provision of the act above quoted still required the approval or the acceptance of Congress to complete the gift and ratify its acceptance. Upon the occasion of the presentation of the first statue, that of Nathanael Greene, of Rhode Island, a resolution was offered in the Senate providing for its acceptance and proper recognition through sending a copy of that resolution to the governor of the State. On that occasion, January 20, 1870, Mr. Wilson, of Massachusetts, said:

I rise simply to say one word. The law as it now stands is complete in itself. I shall not oppose, however, the passage of this resolution as the matter has been inaugurated, and I hope, as it has been introduced, it will be put in proper form and passed. I repeat, however, the law in itself is complete and requires no legislation whatever and I trust that hereafter it will be so regarded.

It might be stated, although in advance of the actual installation of statues in Statuary Hall, that several statues representing three or four different States have been installed in Statuary Hall without any public acknowledgment on the part of the Congress of their receipt or of their acceptance. While the exercises arising from the presentation of resolutions of acceptance and the speeches in relation to the same have always been of interest, as Senator Wilson said in 1870, the law is complete as it stands and no action on the part of the Congress is necessary.

At last Statuary Hall had been set apart for the purpose contemplated by a great many people, particularly those to whom we have previously referred, Capt. Montgomery C. Meigs and the Hon. Gouverneur Kemble, of New York. They were by no means the only ones and probably not the first to offer the suggestion; in fact, the need of a room of this character had been brought to the attention of the public at a very early day through a small and seemingly unimportant weekly newspaper known as the National Register and published in Washington by Joel K. Mead, and in its issue of Saturday, October 4, 1817, we find the following:

EDITOR'S CABINET

A Hint to Congress.—A writer in the New York Columbian recommends that Congress pass an act to authorize the erecting in this city of a spacious building suitable for the reception of marble busts of all the general officers of the revolutionary and late war—The Presidents of the United States; and other patriots of distinction who had rendered important services to the republic either in the field or the cabinet, and to be called the American or Columbian Repository.

Whilst we applaud the liberal motives of this writer, we beg leave to differ with him as to the policy of erecting, at present, a building for the purpose he has suggested. We would much prefer to see the capitol finished; where, it is presumed, ample room will be found for all the marble busts that will be made in this country for a half century to come.[1] Besides, we think the inauguration hall, which will be quite as appropriate a place for the reception of the busts of the Presidents as a separate building. This would afford to strangers, visiting this metropolis, an opportunity to gratify their curiosity without taxing their liberality.

We would humbly recommend to the consideration of Congress to authorize by law, whilst the opportunity lasts, a full length portrait, the size of life, to be taken of each of the late Presidents of the United States, by the best American artists; or what would be better, perhaps, to offer a premium, for

---

[1] At this date the central portion of the Capitol had not been completed.

the best likeness and painting, of a sum adequate to call forth the ablest pencils and genius—none but native born American citizens to be admitted as candidates for preference. When these portraits are finished, to be placed upon the walls in the Senate chamber of the United States or such other place as Congress may designate. To each might be attached the name of the original, the place and time of his birth—his age at and the year of his entering upon his official duties—the time he remained in office, and whether he retired voluntarily or otherwise, or died whilst in office. There now exists more than one painting of General Washington, by Stewart [Gilbert Stuart], taken from life. The subsequent Presidents are yet alive and their likenesses may yet be taken, but the opportunity may not long exist. Mr. Adams is now more than eighty-one years of age—Mr. Jefferson approximates very near to it—Mr. Madison is far advanced in life, and Mr. Monroe by the time he quits official life, will have lived more years than are allotted to many of our species. The present time should therefore be embraced before the opportunity be lost. It would have a powerful tendency to promote the liberal arts in this country, and contribute much to the forming a national character. It would operate as a stimulant to candidates for the honor of Chief Magistrate to emulate their illustrious predecessors, in virtue and patriotism. By being, as it were, in the presence of those who contributed to the establishment of our government, and those who have sustained it, they would be continually admonished to use their endeavors to preserve it. With due deference to the Pennsylvanian, who figured in the columns of the National Intelligencer last spring, recommending the policy of giving the ex-president a seat for life in the Senate, and a yearly salary of five thousand dollars—we think the above would have a better effect and would not be liable to the same objections.

We must now leave the question of Statuary Hall and take up the matter of some very spirited criticisms which occurred on account of the statue of Freedom, which had been erected only a short time. It is regrettable that we have not the complete correspondence, but the letter from the Architect of the Capitol under date of April 20, 1864, covers so clearly the letter to which it was a reply that the subject matter may be understood. The architect's letter follows:

ARCHITECT'S OFFICE U. S. CAPITOL,
April 20, 1864.

Hon. JOHN H. RICE,
Chairman of committee on Public Buildings and Grounds, H. R.

SIR: In compliance with the request contained in your note of the 14th., inst., I have the honor to submit the following;—

First;—you inquire whether the crest on the Statue of Freedom, on the Dome of the U. S. Capitol, is in accordance with the original design, to which I respectfully reply, that it conforms, in every particular, to what is understood to be the original design;—viz. the design of Mr. Thomas Crawford, approved by Jefferson Davis, who at that time held the office of Secretary of War. The considerations which led the artist to adopt this particular form of crest, or helmet, are stated in the annexed correspondence, which embraces all that I can find on the subject, on the files of this office.

The plaster model, from which this statue was cast, was made in Rome by Mr. Crawford, and shipped to this country; the bronze casting was executed from it by Mr. Clark Mills, without the slightest alteration, so that it is precisely what Mr. Crawford intended that it should be. The annexed photograph marked "B" exhibits this design. I have caused the original plaster model to be preserved, with the view of having it put up in the old Hall of Representatives, where it was formerly placed for exhibition;—or in the Rotunda, as may hereafter be deemed most expedient.

Your inquiry secondly "whether, and in what manner, and at what cost the said crest can be removed." To these interrogatories I have to say, that the mere removal of the crest would not cost more than about $300, provided it was done before the scaffolding which now remains, is removed;—the chief expense would be incurred in constructing proper apparatus, on the present scaffolding, to lower it after it is detached from the figure. The annexed photograph of the upper part of the statue, marked "C" which was taken from the plaster model while it stood in the old Hall of representatives, will show the manner in which the crest is united to the head. It will be observed that the connection is so small that it may be cut off without difficulty.

In the third place you ask whether in my judgment "it is advisable to remove this crest." To this inquiry I may be permitted to say, that I have always considered it a very objectionable feature of the figure; but that the removal of it alone would leave the statue imperfect as a work of art; the idea of leaving the head bare could not be entertained for a moment; the figure is so formed, and so draped,

Photograph by Elmer E. Richards   CAPITOL IN WINTER, SOUTHWEST VIEW

and so armed, that some kind of a head ornament is absolutely necessary;—to omit it would subject us to the severest criticism.

If therefore the crest were removed, it would be necessary to substitute one of a different design, or a wreath, as in Mr. Crawford's first design, or some other crowning feature consistent with the character of the statue. This can only be done by remodelling the head, with its crowning ornament, and recasting the whole upper section of the figure. This would protract the work many months, and cost several thousand dollars—these are considerations which should not be overlooked.

What I would most regret in changing the present head would be the opening again of the statue after it has been so securely, and so perfectly put together. The weight of the upper section, which embraces the head is 2,700 lbs.; it would therefore be necessary, in order to remove it, to re-construct the original scaffolding, and to replace the hoisting apparatus with which the statue was raised.

All this, however, can readily be accomplished if the object to be attained should be deemed worth the expense that would be incurred, and the delay it would occasion.

In view of all the considerations suggested by a thorough examination of the subject, I am decidedly of the opinion that the crest on the statue should be suffered to remain without alterations, it is now precisely as it came from the hands of one of the most distinguished artists our country has ever produced, and he is no more among the living. I would, therefore, be inclined to let it remain as it is, even though there were less difficulties in the way of effecting a change in the design.

I have the honor to remain, Sir, with great respect your obt. servt.,

THOS. U. WALTER,
Architect of the U. S. Capitol Extension etc.

We can but admire the diplomacy of Mr. Walter as shown by his answer, and he cleverly hid his own feelings through the thread of his correspondence. It should be remembered that he probably had but very little to do with the selection of the sculptor or with the acceptance of the design, and now that the statue seems lacking in popular favor he is too wise to say "I told you so" or "I expected this."

While the statue of Freedom had been in place but a few months when the correspondence between Representative John H. Rice, of Maine, and the Architect of the Capitol occurred, it seems that Mr. Rice was not the originator of the plan to change or modernize the headdress of the statue of Freedom. The credit of being the originator of the objection may belong to Representative Robert McKnight, of Pennsylvania, who served during the Thirty-sixth and Thirty-seventh Congresses. Mr. McKnight on February 8, 1863, introduced as an amendment to a bill then under discussion the following proviso:

Provided, That the Architect of the Capitol be, and he is hereby authorized and directed to have the nondescript ornament removed, under the direction of the sculptor from the head of the bronze statue Liberty before the same is elevated to its position on the apex of the Capitol Dome.

It is probable that the reference "under the direction of the sculptor" was intended to refer to Clark Mills, who was the bronze founder of the statue. It will also be noticed that the statue is referred to as the bronze statue of "Liberty," as the work has often been incorrectly called.

In the meanwhile nearly a year had passed before any definite movement toward inviting States to send statues to Statuary Hall had been taken by the President. It must not be imagined that Justin S. Morrill was a man who slept upon his rights, and having succeeded in securing legislation establishing Statuary Hall he did not intend that the matter should be forgotten and the purposes for which the hall had been set aside left unnoticed. He, therefore, on the 25th of January, 1865, addressed a letter to the President in which he called attention to the act of Congress of July 2, 1864, and in the course of the communication used the following language:

That you approve of the high purposes of this law I have no doubt, and in view of the fact that several of the State Legislatures are now in session but soon may adjourn, may I ask you to take such action at once as you shall deem appropriate in order to notify and give the invitation provided for to the Governors of the several states so that they can take early steps to carry the purpose of Congress into full effect.

The letter from Representative Morrill seems to have produced the desired results, for on the 3d day of February, 1865, the following circular letter was sent to the governors of each of the 36 States:

DEPARTMENT OF STATE,
Washington, February 3, 1865.

His Excellency GOVERNOR OF THE STATE OF ———.

    SIR: I have the honor to transmit to your Excellency, a copy of a letter of the 25th ultimo, addressed to the President by the Honorable Justin S. Morrill of the House of Representatives, inviting his attention to the 2d Section of the Act of Congress of the 2d July, 1864, on the subject of statues for the old Hall of the House of Representatives. The President has directed this Department to request through your Excellency that the State of   may take the matter into consideration.

    I have the honor to be, Your Excellency's most obedient servant,

F. W. SEWARD, *Acting Secretary.*

NOTE.—The blank spaces in the circular were left that the name of the State might be inserted.

The progress of work upon Statuary Hall in the course of its adaptation to its new purposes is referred to in the annual report of B. B. French, Commissioner of Public Buildings, November 8, 1864, in which he states:

In the course of the past season some very prominent improvements have been made. Congress appropriated $15,000. out of the appropriation for the Capitol extension for constructing a marble floor and making other improvements in the old hall of the House of Representatives. This was a very limited sum for doing the large amount of work required, even when the provision of the act making the appropriation that "such marble as may now be on hand and not otherwise required" should be used in tiling is taken into consideration. The work was however, commenced in the most economical manner possible and has gone on and we expect by the time Congress assembles to have the passage-way from the main entrance from the rotundo to the bronze doors at the south side of the Hall, finished and closed in with a proper railing. It is hoped that by employing men engaged on the Capitol extension, and using the waste material, that the entire job may be completed for the sum appropriated, but it is very doubtful whether it can be.

The same officer in his report as Commissioner of Public Buildings under date of October 12, 1865, in referring to the work in Statuary Hall stated that the appropriation of $15,000 and a further appropriation of $3,875 made at the last session was used in its completion. He also referred to the work as having been completed for some time and that circulars had been sent to the governors of all the States, but that no statuary had yet been sent from any State. It will be noted that in the legislation creating Statuary Hall was incorporated a provision for a bronze railing to inclose a passage-way from the rotunda to the new Hall of the House of Representatives. This railing was erected in accordance with the expressed provisions of the act, but for some reason it lacked the approval of the House of Representatives, and in the Fortieth Congress, second session, a resolution was adopted directing the Speaker to require the Architect of the Capitol to remove forthwith the unsightly railing, so that the provision for compelling people to walk directly from the rotunda to the House of Representatives was nullified, and from that time to the present the entire hall has been open.

In 1865 W. H. Powell was given a commission to paint a large picture for the east stairway of the Senate wing of the Capitol, depicting the Battle of Lake Erie, or Perry's victory at Lake Erie. An earlier picture of the same subject but of a smaller size was painted by this artist for the State capitol of Ohio. It is probable that it was the intention of Powell to have delivered this earlier picture to the Capitol, but owing to lack of what he considered proper encouragement it was sold to the State of Ohio and the larger picture painted for the space it now occupies. Capt. Howard F. Kennedy, for many years chief guide of the Capitol, knew the painter in New York and has filed in the office of the Architect of the Capitol an interesting statement of his recollections of the artist Powell and of his acquaintance with facts concerning his work while in New York City. Mr. Kennedy in his statement names some of the models who were employed about the Capitol and served the painter during the completion of this work. A careful comparison of this work—the painting owned by the Government—with the reproduction of the smaller painting owned by the State of Ohio does not disclose any changes in the arrangement or composition of the picture, and while people employed about the Capitol may have posed for this later work it is quite evident that the artist followed closely the portraits of those introduced in his earlier picture. Mr. Powell was born in Ohio in 1824 and is represented in the Capitol by his Discovery of the Mississippi in addition to the Battle of Lake Erie. His principal work was that of a portrait and historical painter. His portraits of General McClellan and Major Anderson are in the city hall of New York and his Landing of the Pilgrims was purchased by Marshall O. Roberts. His death occurred in New York in 1879.

We have noted from the discussion which occurred in the House of Representatives prior to the enactment of the legislation creating National Statuary Hall that the bronze doors ordered of Randolph Rogers had been received and installed. The work of installation was under the charge of Mr. Ames, of Chicopee, Mass., in whose foundry the Senate bronze doors were cast. The location selected for these expensive and beautiful doors at the south entrance to Statuary Hall was not considered appropriate by the Architect of the Capitol, and in his report of November 1, 1863, he suggested that they would be far better located in some other position. They remained, however, as they were until 1870, when Mr. Schenck, by unanimous consent, on the 13th day of January submitted the following resolution, which was read and agreed to:

Resolved, That the Architect of the Capitol be requested to make an immediate examination and report to this House whether the great bronze doors closing one of the passages leading from the rotunda to the Hall of the House of Representatives may not be removed and put up either at the principal entrance in the east front of the south wing of the Capitol or at some other entrance or doorway where they will be more eligibly placed for ornamentation and convenience.

The report of the architect, dated January 14, 1870, locates the most eligible place either at the principal doorway of the central building leading into the rotunda or at the doorway leading from the Congressional Library to the western portico. The selection of the eastern entrance to the rotunda seems to have been extremely fortunate, and one upon observing the doors in their present location would naturally conclude that they were designed for this location and erected in place during the construction of the building. It may be hard for many to understand how it could have been possible to have imagined that these doors would be appropriate for the south doorway of National Statuary Hall and yet upon due consideration it seems to have been in the mind of the officials in charge of the construction of the Capitol to make Statuary Hall in every particular the most impressive portion of the entire Capitol. The north doorway is crowned by the Franzoni clock, the Car of History, and with the south doorway closed by these bronze doors executed by Randolph Rogers both of the doorways would possess in sculptural adornment a decorative quality not to be found elsewhere in the Capitol Building. Most of the gallery, or a large portion of it, of Statuary Hall has been taken away, but we can imagine that with the gallery complete and with the use of the hall for legislative purposes and

PORTRAIT OF ABRAHAM LINCOLN

Freeman Thorp, painter

with the furnishings belonging to that period it must have been unequaled as a legislative chamber by any then existing throughout the world.

We ought not to pass over the period of 1865 without reference to the funeral of President Lincoln, which occurred in the rotunda of the Capitol and which was the first funeral held in that place after the erection of the new dome. It will, of course, be remembered that much of the new dome was but an enlargement of the dome which existed at the time of the completion of the central portion of the Capitol by Bulfinch, and in the old rotunda on the 1st of July, 1852, the remains of Henry Clay laid in state previous to the commencement of the journey of the funeral train to Mr. Clay's former home. From that time until the funeral of President Lincoln it does not seem that any funeral services had been held in the rotunda. The remains of President Lincoln were brought from the White House on Wednesday, April 19, 1865; services were held at the White House and at the conclusion thereof a military escort was formed and the casket taken to the east central portico steps and from there conveyed into the rotunda by 12 members of the Veteran Reserve Corps to whom this honor had been assigned. The casket was placed on a catafalque which since that time has been used upon several occasions. At 3.30 the burial service was read by the Rev. P. D. Gurley, the service commencing with the words "It is appointed unto men once to die." After the service the assemblage left the rotunda and the remains were placed in charge of a guard of honor consisting of the Capitol police, Captain Newman, and a detail of the Twenty-fourth Veteran Reserve Corps. On Thursday during the entire day the public was admitted to the rotunda to view the body of the former President. On Friday at an early hour the body was taken from the rotunda to the Baltimore & Ohio Railroad station and the funeral train departed for Baltimore, where the first stop was made. Several cities were visited en route to Springfield, Ill., the final resting place of President Lincoln.

The foregoing information has been taken from the Evening Star (Washington) of April 20, 1865. It has been given for the purpose of locating and identifying an important event in the history of the rotunda of the Capitol and for the further purpose of showing the respect paid to the President, in that all of the works of art in the rotunda, paintings as well as statuary, were covered with black, with the exception of the statue of Washington, and this was draped with a black scarf. Just what works of art in addition to the eight historical paintings were located in the rotunda at this time it is very difficult to determine. If the statues of Franklin and of Jefferson, the work of Hiram Powers, had been placed in position, their present locations would eliminate the possibility of their presence in the rotunda. The only other statue so far as known which at this time was in the possession of the Government was the statue of John Hancock, now located at the foot of the west grand staircase of the Senate wing. It may be, however, that this had not been placed in its present position. It is known by a reference contained in the newspaper from which this information has been secured that the statue of the Dying Tecumseh was then in the rotunda, as the newspaper article in question mentions the covering of this statue with black material. This work, however, never belonged to the Government and was removed from the Capitol some years later to the Corcoran Gallery of Art in order to comply with an act of Congress which prohibited the exhibition of works of art in the Capitol which were not the property of the Government. The statue of Washington, however, referred to as being draped with a black scarf is the plaster model of the statue of Washington by Houdon which was at that time and still is located in the rotunda. This statue, however, was

PORTRAIT OF JEAN ANTOINE HOUDON, SCULPTOR

Rembrandt Peale, painter

The plaster model of George Washington in the Rotunda and the bronze statue of Washington in Statuary Hall were
copied from the marble statue by Houdon now in the State capitol, Richmond, Va.

{ 233 }

not in 1865 the property of the Government, and some uncertainty exists as to the exact time when this plaster cast reached the Capitol. Wyeth, in his Rotunda and Dome of the United States Capitol, published in 1869, states:

A plaster cast of Houdon's Washington was placed in the Capitol March 16, 1854, and has remained there ever since. It is the property of the Mr. Hubard, of Richmond, before alluded to, and he proposed to furnish copies in bronze to the different States.

Capt. Howard F. Kennedy, for many years the chief of guides of the Capitol Building, has stated that he was informed by an aged colored man who was employed about the Capitol at the time of the funeral of Henry Clay that this statue was then in the rotunda and that it was necessary to move it on account of the funeral exercises. This fixes the date some two years earlier than the date fixed by Wyeth. Both of these statements are at variance with the statement of Joseph Segar, who in a letter addressed to The Crayon fixes the date of the casting of Hubard's bronze replicas February 23, 1856.

The connection of the sculptor William James Hubard with the works of art at the Capitol Building is confined to this copy of Houdon's Washington, and it is on account of his very artistic acquirements that it seems proper to include his biography in this work. Mr. Hubard was born in Warwick, England, in 1810. At an early age he showed marked art tendencies, and when but a lad he joined himself to a man who offered him the opportunity of travel and study. At 14 years of age he visited Edinburgh and Glasgow, cutting silhouettes and painting landscapes. While at Glasgow he was presented with a silver palette inscribed "William James Hubard, by the admirers of his genius in Glasgow, Scotland." Under his contract with the man referred to he traveled in Germany, France, and Italy, coming to the United States when 19 years of age. Here he was abandoned by his traveling companion after the proceeds of the young artist's work had netted him some $10,000. This desertion left young Hubard almost penniless in a strange land. He was, however, soon able to provide for himself by his talent in cutting silhouettes and painting. By the advice of Sully and others he was induced to return to Europe for further study in painting and sculpture. He again came to the United States and opened a studio in Philadelphia, where several of his paintings are now preserved. Taking up his residence in Virginia, he met and afterwards married Maria Mason Todd. Soon after his marriage he made a second trip to Europe, studying in the life schools of Paris, Florence, and Rome. He was a personal friend of Powers and Greenough, and his studio was near the studios of these well-known sculptors. Mrs. Hubard posed as the model for the foot of Powers's famous statue, The Greek Slave. On his return from his second trip to Europe he opened a studio near Richmond, Va. One of his ambitions was to reproduce in bronze the statue of Washington from the marble by Houdon in the State capitol at Richmond, Va. Under an act of the Legislature of Virginia Hubard was commissioned to copy this statue. A large foundry was erected near Richmond and six copies in bronze were cast. The plaster model of the statue by Hubard is in the rotunda of the Capitol. Many portraits and paintings by Hubard are owned in Virginia, among these being the portraits of Daniel Webster, Ole Bull, and John Marshall, the latter owned by descendants of Marshall. While engaged in making powder for the Confederate Government an explosion occurred which resulted in the death of Mr. Hubard on February 17, 1862.

It was at about this time that a commission for a full-length statue of President Abraham Lincoln was given to Vinnie Ream, a young sculptress then about 18 years of age. Miss Ream had had unusual opportunities for studying and observing President

Lincoln. Her faculty for modeling in clay and her marked art ability had interested in her behalf one of the Members of the Congress, who was anxious that she should have an opportunity to study President Lincoln. He accordingly called upon President Lincoln and made the request that Miss Ream be permitted to come to the Executive Mansion for the purpose of making studies in order to develop her art ability, and in the course of the conversation, as related to the writer by the sculptress, the following statement was made to President Lincoln:

Now this young lady will just come and sit down where she can observe you at work and record her impressions. She will not talk with you or annoy you or do anything to disturb you in your usual routine. I wish that you would grant this request for she is a young woman of marked ability and I would like to help her. Beside this, she is young and a poor girl and this opportunity will mean much to her.

Mr. Lincoln quickly dropped into the vernacular and replied:

So she's young and poor, is she? Well, that's nothing agin her. You may tell her she can come.

Miss Ream, afterwards Mrs. Hoxie, completed the full-length statue of Lincoln, which was her first important commission. The statue was unveiled in the rotunda at night, January 25, 1871, and speeches were made on that occasion by Senator Cullom, Senator Carpenter, Justice Davis, and other men of distinction. After her marriage she executed the bronze statue of Admiral Farragut, in Farragut Square, Washington, D. C., the statue of Governor Kirkwood, one of the contributions of the State of Iowa to Statuary Hall, and had completed a full-size model of the statue of Sequoyah at the time of her death, which occurred in Washington November 20, 1914. In addition to the work above referred to Mrs. Hoxie executed the ideal statues of Miriam and the Young West, portrait busts of Senator Sherman, Ezra Cornell, General Custer, Abraham Lincoln, and E. B. Hay.

In an earlier portion of this work, during a discussion in Congress upon the merits of different painters and the advisability of securing their services in the decoration of the Capitol, a very strong indorsement was made in favor of Seth Eastman, who has been referred to before as assisting Captain Meigs in securing some Indian models for the sculptors at the Capitol to model in clay. It was Captain Eastman who secured for the sculptor Vincenti, Aysh-ke-bah-ke-ko-zhay (Flat-mouth) as a model for the bust which was referred to during the period of its execution. Interest in Captain Eastman, who had since become brevet Brig. Gen. Seth Eastman, United States Army, retired, had not lessened, and on March 26, 1867, in the House of Representatives, Mr. Schenck made the following remarks:

Mr. SCHENCK. I ask unanimous consent to offer a joint resolution agreed to unanimously by the Committee on Military Affairs of the last Congress, but which was objected to when we endeavored to get it in by the gentleman from Pennsylvania (Mr. Boyer) who since then has become satisfied that it ought to pass. If there be no objection I will make a brief explanation.

There was no objection.

The Clerk then read a resolution authorizing the employment of Brevet Brigadier General Seth Eastman of the United States Army, now on the retired list, to duty so as to entitle him to the full pay, emoluments and allowances of his lineal rank, that it shall be competent to have such duty consist in the employment of the said officer in the execution under the supervision of the Architect of the Capitol, of paintings from his own designs for the decorations of the rooms of the Committee on Indian Affairs and on Military Affairs of the Senate and House of Representatives, and other parts of the Capitol; and no additional compensation for such service is to be paid to said Eastman beyond his pay, allowances and emoluments as aforesaid.

Mr. CULLOM. I believe I was one of the persons who objected to that resolution when it was up before. I have since learned it is important it should pass, and I withdraw any objection on my part.

STATUE OF ABRAHAM LINCOLN   *In the Rotunda*
Vinnie Ream, sculptress

Mr. SCHENCK. We have been paying for decorations, some displaying good taste and others of a tawdry character, a great deal of money to Italian artists and others, while we have American talent much more competent for the work. Among others possessing native talent, is General Eastman, who is now a Lieut. Colonel in the Regular Army and a Brevet Brigadier General. He is more of an artist, in all that relates to the Indians, except possibly Catlin and Stanley than anyone we have had in the country. He is disabled from doing full duty now and is on the retired list suffering from rheumatism occasioned by exposure in the field on active duty. The General of the Army is perfectly willing to have Congress, if it thinks proper, provide for detailing General Eastman for the duty of executing for the Capitol some of his magnificent paintings. It is not military duty and it is thought better the General should be authorized to assign him to this duty. If assigned to this duty, General Eastman will draw his full pay as Lieut. Colonel instead of as on the retired list, making a difference of about $1200. or $1500. a year. For at the most $1500. a year we will secure services for which we have been paying tens of thousands of dollars to foreign artists and we will get better work done. I think under the circumstances a gallant American officer, who has taste and artistic ability, should be permitted to be assigned to this duty. I invite Members to look at a book I have here of engravings from his paintings, which display everything that is elegant and tasteful in art.

The joint resolution was ordered to be engrossed and read a third time; and being engrossed, it was accordingly read the third time and passed.

Mr. Schenck moved to reconsider the vote by which the joint resolution was passed; and also moved that the motion to reconsider be laid on the table.

The latter motion was agreed to. (Congressional Globe, 40th Cong., 1st sess., proceedings for Mar. 26, 1867, pp. 361, 362.)

Under Special Order 427, Headquarters of the Army, Adjutant General's Office, Washington, D. C., August 28, 1867, Lieutenant Colonel Eastman was placed upon the active list and assigned to duty under the Secretary of the Interior. At this time the Capitol Building was under the Interior Department, and the assignment to the Interior Department really meant assignment to the Capitol for the purpose of decorative work therein. It seems that the Architect of the Capitol was not certain that it would be permissible for him to pay to General Eastman commutation of fuel and quarters to which he was entitled as a lieutenant colonel upon the active list. On October 5, 1867, Captain Eastman requested of the Interior Department that instruction be given to the Architect of the Capitol to govern his action in this particular case. In accordance with the request of General Eastman the following communication was sent to the Architect of the Capitol:

EDWD. CLARK, Esq.,
    Architect of the Capitol Extension.

SIR: Brevet Brigadier Genl. Seth Eastman, Lieut. Col., U. S. Army (retired), was by direction of the President detailed by Special orders of the War Dept. No. 427, dated August 28″, 1867, for duty in this Department. He is and has been on duty in the Department, in connection with the Capitol Extension, and is entitled to commutation of fuel and quarters, agreeably to Army regulations from the 1st September 1857. (1867.)

I am, Sir, very respectfully, your obt. servant

W. T. OTTO,
    Acting Secretary.

Under the commission as outlined above Lieutenant Colonel Eastman executed nine paintings of Indian life. There may be some misconception connected with the idea of decorations which may lead many to conclude that they are painted upon the walls of the rooms for which they were executed. On the contrary, these paintings are upon canvas, properly framed, and hang about the walls of the rooms of the House Committee on Indian Affairs. As works of art they are creditable examples of the best of that period, but their art value is overshadowed by their historical value, as they admirably illustrate various incidents of Indian life. These examples could not be obtained at this

THE RICE GATHERERS

Brig. Gen. Seth Eastman, painter

In the room of the House Committee on Indian Affairs

time, as the present mode of savage life is far removed from the conditions which Colonel Eastman has so well portrayed. In addition to these nine paintings illustrating Indian life, Colonel Eastman painted 17 pictures of United States forts for the rooms of the House Committee on Military Affairs.

It is learned from the correspondence relating to the work of Colonel Eastman that on the 23d of June, 1870, the Architect of the Capitol advised the Secretary of the Interior that the artist proposed to proceed with the pictures for the decoration of the rooms of the House Committee on Military Affairs at a compensation of $100 per month in addition to his pay as a retired officer of the Army. It also appears from correspondence in relation to this work that Colonel Eastman had discussed the matter with the chairman of the Committee on Military Affairs, Hon. J. A. Logan, and that as a result of this conference the plan of decoration was approved provided that it only included views of the principal forts and West Point, but there was no inclination on the part of Mr. Logan to have battle scenes used as subjects for the decoration of this room.

The paintings representing the 17 forts of the United States are probably more valuable as examples of historical accuracy and as illustrations of the conditions of the fortifications existing at that period than for purely decorative purposes. The Committee on Military Affairs, however, is not supposed to be a committee particularly solicitous in art direction. It was important that knowledge concerning the fortifications of the Government should be easily accessible, and these medium-size framed pictures contain desired information and also relieve acceptably what might otherwise be blank spaces upon an uninteresting wall. The acquaintance of the artist with military life as well as with Indian life was the natural result of his long-time service in the Army, much of which had been spent upon the then frontier of the country in close contact with Indian tribes.

BRIG. GEN. SETH EASTMAN

Represented by 17 paintings of forts in the rooms of the House Committee on Military Affairs and by 9 paintings of Indian life in the rooms of the House Committee on Indian Affairs

Colonel Eastman was born in Brunswick, Me., January 24, 1808. He was the eldest child of Robert and Sarah (Lee) Eastman. He was of pure New England stock and was of the sixth generation from Roger, the first of the name in this country, who settled in Salisbury, Mass., soon after landing in Salem in 1638. He graduated at the Military Academy at West Point in 1831, passed through the several grades from second lieutenant to lieutenant colonel of Infantry, and was placed on the retired list December 3, 1863. He was brevetted brigadier general August 9, 1866. Lieutenant Eastman was teacher of drawing at the Military Academy 1833 to 1840. He published a treatise on topographical drawings in 1837, and soon after 1850 a history of Indian tribes. He was stationed with part of his regiment for several years at Fort Snelling, Minn., and there became greatly interested in the history and customs of the Sioux and Chippewa Indians. During that period he made many drawings and paintings of the Indians and their various tribal ceremonials. His death occurred in Washington, D. C., August 31, 1875.

CHAPTER XIII

THOMAS U. WALTER, ARCHITECT OF THE CAPITOL, RESIGNS
EDWARD CLARK APPOINTED ARCHITECT

OUR ATTENTION should at this time be invited to the consideration of further facts concerning the decoration over the "eye" of the Capitol dome. We are indebted to the report of the Architect of the Capitol, dated November 1, 1865, for the following reference to this work of art:

> The picture over the eye of the dome is all painted in, but the artist is unwilling to have the scaffolding removed until the plastering is thoroughly dried and the picture toned. As it will be at times viewed by gas light, he wishes to have the opportunity of trying it by this light before dismissing it from his hand.

The reference to the trying of the picture under gas light brings to mind another reference in this same report which relates to a proposed scheme for illumination of the dome. The reference is as follows:

> The arrangements for lighting the dome by means of Gardiner's electro-magneto apparatus is now in progress and will probably be finished early in the session.

This fixes the time relatively of the change in the method of igniting the gas for the illumination of the dome of the Capitol.

It appears that there had arisen some question in the mind of the Architect of the Capitol concerning the art merit of the fresco before referred to, and the result of his inquiries is shown by the following letter from A. R. Spofford, Librarian of Congress, who occupied relations with the Joint Committee on the Library which gave him an opportunity of discovering the opinion of this committee upon art topics. The letter is as follows:

LIBRARY OF CONGRESS,
Washington, May 10, 1866.

EDWARD CLARK, Esquire,
   Architect of Capitol Extension.

SIR: In regard to the matter of Mr. Brumidi's fresco painting in the eye of the Capitol dome upon which you desired me to procure the opinion of the two chairmen of the Joint Committee on the Library I have to report, that Senator Howe, Chairman on the part of the Senate, expresses his opinion that the Library Committee have no concern with matters not referred to them by either House of Congress; and that Honorable R. B. Hayes, Chairman on the part of the House, concurring officially in this opinion and doubtful whether his personal opinion is of any value, expresses his judgment as highly favorable to the painting as a work of art.

   With high respect, your obt. servant,

A. R. SPOFFORD, *Librarian.*

The letter is really self-explanatory. It would seem, however, that the Architect of the Capitol did not care to be placed in a position where it would seem that he acted upon his own judgment in art matters relating to the Capitol without attempting to secure the opinion of those who as members of the Joint Committee on the Library were at least supposed to be conversant with the art values of decorations.

It will probably be noted that the Architect of the Capitol is addressed and signs his name as Architect of the Capitol extension. It may also be noticed that there has been no reference made to the fact that Thomas U. Walter was no longer Architect of the Capitol.

PORTRAIT OF THOMAS U. WALTER

Francisco Pausas, painter

His connection with the construction of the extension and with the Capitol in general ended in the year 1865, when Edward Clark, upon the resignation of Mr. Walter,[1] was appointed as architect. It will be noted that the term "Capitol extension" is a literal description of the office, for at this time a portion of the building, particularly such portions as belonged to the old Capitol, were under the control of the Commissioner of Public Buildings and Grounds. In this manner there existed a divided authority, and it is generally understood that in the control of the affairs of the Capitol this divided authority became so unpleasant to Mr. Walter that he felt that for his own peace of mind resignation was the only course left for him.[1] Those who have followed closely the development of the construction of the old portion of the Capitol will remember that Latrobe, in 1817, was practically driven out of his position by the interference of the Commissioner of Public Buildings and Grounds and that there was also a disposition on the part of the occupant of that office to restrict and hamper the usefulness of Mr. Bulfinch near the close of his occupancy of the position as architect. This divided authority continued until the legislative appropriation act of August 15, 1876, at which time all the duties relative to the Capitol Building previously performed by the Commissioner of Public Buildings and Grounds were transferred to the Architect of the Capitol. Another peculiar condition exists in the Capitol Building. When the law for the establishment of a National Statuary Hall was enacted this phraseology was used:

* * * and the same shall be under the supervision and direction of the Chief of Engineers in Charge of Public Buildings and Grounds. * * *

While the Secretary of the Interior could not appoint or dismiss the Architect of the Capitol, as the position was one of presidential appointment, and while it may be doubtful, under the circumstances, whether the Secretary of the Interior had the legal authority to place work which the President had placed in the care of the architect under the charge of the Commissioner of Public Buildings and Grounds, nevertheless the object in view, that of getting rid of Architect Walter, was accomplished by means which many will fail to commend.

By the appointment of Edward Clark as Architect of the Capitol, August 30, 1865, the completion of the Capitol after the plans of Architect Walter was assured, as Mr. Clark had been in the employ of Mr. Walter at the time of the preparation of the plans for the extension of the Capitol, served as superintendent of construction of the building for the Post Office Department, and continued in office as architect until the time of his death, which occurred February 6, 1902, a service under the Government of 51 years. His successor, Elliott Woods, was appointed February 19, 1902. Mr. Woods had been in the office of Mr. Clark for 17 years and had served as chief clerk and assistant architect.

---

[1] The resignation of Mr. Walter was contained in a letter addressed by him to the Secretary of the Interior dated May 26, 1865, from which the following extracts are made:

"* * * I have likewise received a letter from the Commissioner of Public Buildings and Grounds, inclosing a copy of a communication received by him from the Department of the Interior, under date of the 23rd instant, in which you direct him to take immediate charge of all work on public buildings in the District of Columbia in course of construction, extension or repair, and now in progress, that are legally subject to the control of the Secretary of the Interior! This, of course, places me in a position subordinate to the aforesaid Commissioner of Public Buildings and Grounds.

"These changes, particularly the stoppage of the enlargement of the Library of Congress, suggest the present as the proper time for me to retire altogether from the charge of the public works. I therefore respectfully request you to accept this as my resignation as Architect of the United States Capitol Extension, the new Dome, the continuation of the Patent Office Building, the enlargement of the Library of Congress, and the extension of the Government Printing Office. In order that time may be afforded for the proper arrangement of the drawings and papers in my office, I respectfully suggest that this resignation shall take effect on the 31st instant.

"In taking this step I am moved by considerations of self-respect as well as by the fact that the public buildings heretofore under my charge have so far approached completion as to render the services of an architect no longer absolutely necessary * * *."

EDWARD CLARK

Architect of the Capitol (1865–1902)

Mr. Woods continued in office until his death, May 22, 1923. His successor, David Lynn, who had served under Mr. Woods for more than 20 years, was appointed Architect of the Capitol by President Coolidge, August 22, 1923.

Under the act of August 15, 1876, the supervision and direction of the Chief of Engineers, or Commissioner of Public Buildings and Grounds, as far as related to the Capitol, was transferred to the Architect of the Capitol, and it has been held in debates in Congress that neither the Senate nor the House nor the two bodies acting concurrently have any jurisdiction over Statuary Hall, but that the same is under the direct supervision of the Architect of the Capitol, and this condition through the peculiar legislation by which Statuary Hall was created. It is proper to state, however, that there has never been any clashing of authority over the supervision of Statuary Hall, nor has the question of jurisdiction of that section of the Capitol ever arisen so far as known.

Up to this time, with the exception of the findings and report of the Art Commission appointed in 1859, there had never been any extensive tabulation or criticism of the entire art works of the Capitol. Of course it will be understood that many books had been published, such as guidebooks and general books of travel, in which the Capitol and its contents had been discussed at such length as the writers seemed to consider the subjects warranted. But some time in the later sixties or early seventies a somewhat ambitious effort was made by the Bureau of Education to compile and present in the form of a report a lengthy treatise upon the art of the Capitol, which also included a discussion of general art conditions in Washington. The report was not wholly confined to art conditions. A general survey was made upon educational topics and lengthy reports upon both the white and the colored schools in the District and also an interesting statement of the steps that were taken which led to the establishment of the seat of government in Washington. Whether the Commissioner of Education had a blanket authority to report upon everything that could be thought of that was related to the District of Columbia we do not know, but little seemed to escape his notice. The document is known as House of Representatives Executive Document No. 315 (41st Cong., 2d sess.) and is entitled "Special Report of the Commissioner of Education," submitted to the Senate June —, 1868, and to the House with additions June 13, 1870. We are indebted to this report for a large amount of information, though much of it seems to have been compiled upon very insufficient authority.

In the introduction to this report, or so much thereof as is entitled "Art in the District of Columbia," the following language is used, and from this we may learn the mental attitude of the writer toward art matters in general. We quote the following:

* * * The same may be said of the statues of the great men who, by their wisdom, courage, and foresight, gave us the form of government under which we have enjoyed freedom and prosperity equaled only by our greatness as a nation. The people always find in these subjects matter to interest and instruct them; and in selecting works of art to decorate the Capitol our effort should not only be directed to their entertainment and improvement but to giving them what they can readily understand and appreciate. * * *

The writer then discusses in general terms some of the events which had preceded the ordering of works of art for the Capitol, refers to the commissions given for the four historical paintings by John Trumbull and to the Weir, Chapman, and Vanderlyn pictures, which were ordered in June, 1836, and criticizes adversely the Landing of Columbus, by Vanderlyn, and the Baptism of Pocahontas, by Chapman, and in referring to this picture we quote a few words from the criticism thereon:

* * * It has been several times suggested that this picture be removed, and its place filled by something that more correctly represents the art taste of the country and less violently outrages the truth of history. The suggestion is well worthy the consideration of Congress. * * *

The real point of this criticism, we are afraid, will be lost upon the average reader. If actual truth of history must be placed upon canvas in order to give to that canvas a superlative quality as a work of art, then it is feared that if this rule were to be applied to all of the works of art in the Capitol none would be found to conform to such a standard. In this same report the writer refers to the painting of the Battle of Chapultepec as being "generally set down as a failure." Whether this criticism be just or unjust, we must hasten along to other matters in order to give our readers the opportunity to form their own estimate of the value of this treatise as an art document.

The writer then discusses the pictures of Washington and Lafayette. This is of such an informing nature that we will again quote:

The full-length portraits in the new House of Representatives on the right and left of the Speaker's desk are works of considerable merit, especially that of Lafayette. Considerable controversy has taken place as to who painted the Washington and not a few persons have credited it to Stuart. No name appears on it. It has none of Stuart's color, however, and a close examination will convince any one familiar with the subject that the flesh tints are not such as that artist was famous for. Mr. Clark, the present Architect of the Capitol, says it is by Sulley [Sully], of Philadelphia, and that he has the authority of Mr. Peter Richings for his assertion, that gentleman informing him that he stood for the figure. This is undoubtedly correct; but the statement will seem strange considering how much has been written to prove it the work of some other artist. That of Lafayette was by the celebrated French artist, Ary Sheffer [Scheffer], a personal friend of Lafayette's and was a present from the artist to our Government. What the portrait of Washington cost the Government we have not been able to learn nor can we get the desired information from any one of the Departments.

We do not wish to be placed in the position of being unkind, and possibly it may have been better to have left this report entirely unreferred to. There would, however, exist the danger that some investigator might happen to come across this report and wonder why no reference had been made to it in the present work and conclude from this lack of reference that the work was superficial and did not entail any great amount of research. It is for the reason principally that the readers may know that this report was within our knowledge and for the further reason that we do not wish to have statements contained in the matter above quoted left unexplained that we have given this amount of space to its discussion. It is only proper to state that if, as the critic has assumed, the picture was the work of Thomas Sully it would have been comparatively easy to inquire of Sully, who was then living, whether he painted or did not paint this picture. What to us seems the worst part of this criticism is that the attribution to Sully of this portrait of Washington is claimed to be based upon a statement made by Edward Clark, at that time the Architect of the Capitol. That is the most improbable part of the whole reference to this picture. It is very difficult after the lapse of so many years to determine whether or not Mr. Clark ever made the statement attributed to him, but the facts are largely against such a probability. Mr. Clark was not only an architect of distinction, but a citizen well beloved in the city of Washington, where he made his home for something like half a century. He was a man of wide information and of culture and refinement. He was interested in art matters in addition to the ordinary interests which an architect would have in other fields. He was for many years a trustee of the Corcoran Gallery of Art and generally well informed upon art matters, and the examination of a large number of letters found in the letter-press copy book of the office, written as replies to people who were asking information upon art subjects, fails to disclose any such careless statements as that attributed to him by the critic from whom we have quoted. In order that it may be definitely known, although it has already been stated in this work, by whom this portrait was painted, it is again stated that the work was ordered in 1834 by a resolution of the House of Representatives and that the commission was given to John Vanderlyn and that he received therefor the sum of $2,500. Why the critic should have inquired of "all the departments" and failed in finding any information about this work is not easily explained.

In discussing the decorations throughout the Capitol the report contains the following reference:

The error was first committed by those in power adopting a style of decoration in which Americans were not proficient and at once bad, expensive and unsuitable to such a building and a libel on our taste as a people. It does not seem to have occurred to those in power that however suitable this style of decoration might be for a theatre, music or banqueting hall, something more subdued and impressive was required for a great national building where a grave and deliberative body of men met to discuss the affairs of the nation. No one would think of decorating a court room in bright shiny colors; why should the halls of Congress and committee rooms where subjects are discussed requiring study and deep thought be exposed to such aggression against correct taste. Another error was in permitting those men to go outside of their duties as ornamental painters and try their skill in the loftier sphere of the fine arts. What they did in that line, however, turned out a lamentable failure. The two or three pictures they gave us would pass perhaps for good bits of ornamental sign painting; but their claim to ranking as works of art is low indeed. * * *

It is possible that the critic is taking himself entirely too seriously upon the probable effect of these decorations—which, he estimates, might be "good for ornamental sign painting"—on the public at large. It has been laid down as a general principle and used by artists of ability that the best art is that which has given to the largest number of people the greatest amount of satisfaction for the longest period of time. Is it true that the general effect upon the thousands who visit our Capitol every year is only that of ornamental sign painting? If it is not true, our critic is at fault, and his worry and mental anxiety are all in vain. The report contains some passages which are encouraging in that the writer states:

England, however, had expended ten times the amount of money we had on art, as the report of her art commission will show, and yet her failures so far as they apply to her public buildings were so transparent as to cause a general outcry against them. * * *

So long as our mistakes have not been worse than those of England we may take courage and proceed. It seems, however, that this report is not content with this mere reference to the extravagant mistakes of England, but states that for its public buildings, which include its national gallery, national portrait gallery, the Houses of Parliament, and for the purchase of works of art and maintenance and care of the same, England expended in the year of 1867–68 more than six million and a half of dollars, or to be exact in the figures quoted, £1,359,400 2s. 4d., and with this expenditure he contrasts the appropriation or the estimates for the Capitol for the year 1867–68 at $450,500, so that in matters of expenditures, whether wisely or unwisely, the comparison is in our favor. From the date of this report we might expect that it contains the very latest items of information upon art matters in the Capitol. We do not, of course, know at what time the report was prepared, although the time of its presentation is fixed from the fact that the writer refers to estimated expenditures for 1867–68; we would naturally conclude that the report must have been completed subsequent to the preparation of these estimates, and yet in discussing the old Hall of the House of Representatives he states:

The hall of the old House of Representatives, as it is called, might be advantageously converted into a gallery for statues and portraits. The means of lighting from above can very easily be so improved and enlarged as to furnish a good and strong light over all parts of it. Upper and lower galleries could be built and fitted with panels and niches, one for pictures, the other for statues. In this way it might be made an interesting instructive and attractive feature of the Capitol.

It would seem from the foregoing quotation that the critic was entirely uninformed as to the action taken by the Congress in the setting apart by means of the act of July 2, 1864, of this room as a National Statuary Hall. Why this has been omitted we can not understand except upon the explanation that the critic had never heard of such action.

There is one more statement contained in this report which ought not to go unnoticed. A table was prepared showing the number of paintings, their cost, when they were painted, and the name of the artist. The value of the paintings thus tabulated amounts to $200,620. Following this tabulation is the following statement:

In addition to this we have discovered that nearly $20,000. has been voted for work we have been unable to find in the building, and which we infer were such utter failures that they are hidden away from the public. This would make a sum total exclusive of incidental charges of $220,620.

Notwithstanding this evident insinuation that much had been wasted in the purchase of works of art which were hidden away from the public, an insinuation which hardly seems warranted by the fact, the writer of this report is inclined to admire and commend some of the art work found in the Capitol. In speaking of the figure of Liberty in plaster above the frieze in the old Hall of the House of Representatives he uses this language:

The design is bold and strong and the execution exceedingly delicate; in short, the whole work is a proof that Cusici [Causici], the artist, could do something really good when confined within the limit of the work he had been accustomed to do.

In referring to the Eagle in bas-relief, by Valaperti, he also in this finds something to commend and states:

It is an exceedingly fine piece of work and was copied from nature, the artist having procured one of the finest specimens of the bird ever seen in this country for a model. This is the only specimen of his work the artist has left in this country. Valaperti was an acknowledged genius, but a man of eccentric habits and misanthropic. He came to Washington poor but with the hope of finding a new field for the exercise of his genius and bettering his condition. He had been led to believe that he would get important orders from Congress for works to decorate the public buildings. In this he was mistaken; and being of too sensitive a nature to push his own claim did not succeed. After finishing this one work he suddenly disappeared from Washington and nothing more was heard of him. It is very generally believed that he committed suicide by drowning in the Potomac and in that way put an end to his troubles. * * *

The writer of this article also seems to have found something worth while in the statue known by some as the Car of History and by others as the Franzoni clock, and expresses himself as follows:

There is something exquisitely chaste about the conception and execution of this work, and few persons, as they pass to and fro, casting a hurried glance at it, appreciate its rare merits. History stands in a winged car, also of white marble, elaborately worked, with a book open and recording the events of the nation as she rolled around the globe. All this beautiful piece of art is merely an accessory to the House clock. The wheel of the car is made the dial on which the hands record time. The artist who designed and executed this clever work was an Italian of the name of Franzoni, who died in this city a short time after this work was finished and put up. * * *

In preparing this report the compiler has gone outside of the Capitol Building; in fact, his report is intended to include all art conditions in the District of Columbia. He refers to the bronze statue of Jefferson as being in front of the President's house, records the fact of its being a gift from Captain Levy of the Navy, an admirer of Jefferson, and in concluding his remarks uses the following language:

No one has yet been able to find out how much was paid for it or who the artist was who executed the work. It is reported and believed by many that the work was done in Genoa by an Italian artist.

One can not help thinking that the writer of this report had a greater gift for expression of his ideas in words than for the finding of facts upon which to base his statements. If it were not for the fact that this stature is plainly marked with the name of the artist, David d'Angers, and has the name of the bronze founders also engraved thereon, there might be some reasonable excuse for the statement that no one has been able to find out the name of the artist who executed the work. We hope, however, that greater care was used generally in securing the material upon which his report was based than is evident by some of the cases to which we have called attention.

From this report we find a statement showing that from an appropriation known as a lump-sum appropriation, placed in the charge of the Joint Committee on the Library for the purpose of the purchase of works of art with which to decorate the Capitol, there had been purchased a marble bust of Kosciuszko, by H. D. Saunders, an American, for $500; the statue of Hancock, by Dr. Horatio Stone, an American, $5,500; a bust of President Lincoln, by Mrs. S. F. Ames, an American, $1,500; a portrait of Joshua R. Giddings, by Miss C. L. Ransom, an American, $1,000; a statue of Hamilton, by Dr. Horatio Stone, American, $10,000. These works of art have been referred to for the purpose of establishing their existence in the Capitol Building at the time of the making of this report. The bust of Kosciuszko and the statue of Hancock have been heretofore referred to, but this is our first reference to the bust of President Lincoln, by Mrs. S. F. Ames, or to the portrait of Joshua R. Giddings, by Miss C. L. Ransom. Concerning these last two works of art it may be well at this time to make some further reference and also give biographical information concerning the artists by whom these works were executed.

The bust of Lincoln is now located in the Senate gallery, east lobby, and stands upon a pedestal of Scotch granite donated and forwarded to this country from Scotland by admirers of President Lincoln. The bust is the work of Sarah Fisher Ames, who was born in Lewes, Del., August 13, 1817. She studied art in Boston, Mass., and in Rome, Italy. As Miss Clampitt she was married to Joseph Ames, a portrait painter and member of the National Academy of Design. During the Civil War she went as a nurse with the sanitary commission to the hospitals of the battle fields and at one time had charge of the hospital in the Capitol. She was personally acquainted with President Lincoln and many of the antislavery leaders, as well as with the leading literary and artistic people of her times. Among her works are busts of President Lincoln, of which a replica was furnished the State capitol of Massachusetts; Anson Burlingame, Ross Winans, and General Grant, the latter winning an award at the Paris Exposition of 1900. There is no complete list of her sculptural work. Mrs. Ames died in Washington, D. C., March 8, 1901.

The portrait of Joshua R. Giddings, referred to, illustrates a peculiar condition in the purchase of art works for the Capitol Building. Just what reasons impelled the Joint Committee on the Library to its purchase it is difficult at this time to determine. It is not meant that it should be inferred from this statement that the portrait is in any sense unworthy of a place in the Capitol Building, but rather that it appears to be in a class by itself and that the precedent for its purchase does not seem to have been established. There are, of course, other portraits in the Capitol concerning which the same conjecture might arise, but in the other instances there seems possibly to have been stronger reasons for the inclusion of these works in the Capitol Building than existed in the case of the purchase of the Giddings portrait. The subject of the portrait, Joshua Reed Giddings, was born at Tioga Point (now Athens), Pa., October 6, 1795; moved to Ohio and located in Ashtabula County; served in the War of 1812; admitted to the bar in 1821; State representative in 1826; elected a Representative from Ohio to the Twenty-fifth Congress as an antislavery Whig; reelected to the Twenty-sixth and Twenty-seventh Congresses; resigned March 22, 1842, after a vote of censure had been passed on him by the House; subsequently reelected to the Twenty-seventh Congress, and to the Twenty-eighth, Twenty-ninth, Thirtieth, Thirty-first, Thirty-second, Thirty-third, Thirty-fourth, and Thirty-fifth Congresses; appointed consul general to

PORTRAIT OF GUNNING BEDFORD, Jr.
Charles Willson Peale, painter

Canada by President Lincoln, and died at Montreal May 27, 1864. This portrait was for some time in the National Statuary Hall, but in later years has been in the office of the Architect of the Capitol. The artist, Miss Caroline L. Ormes Ransom, was born in Newark, Ohio, in 1838. She graduated with high honors from Oberlin College, where she afterwards occupied the positions of principal of the women's department and professor of Greek and Latin for two years. Her mother taught her drawing and painting in water colors, and she also received some help from an itinerant portrait painter who visited her father's home and painted portraits of the family. Afterwards she visited New York and studied landscape painting under A. B. Durand and portrait painting under Thomas Hicks and Daniel Huntington; visited Europe later and was for some time a pupil of Kaulbach at Munich. During some of her stay abroad, which lasted for two years, she made copies of the works of many of the old masters found in art galleries that she visited. After her return to this country she had a studio in Cleveland, Ohio; also in New York. She later came to Washington, D. C., where she occupied a studio at 915 F Street NW. for many years. Miss Ransom founded the Classical Club of Washington, D. C., was one of the founders of the Daughters of the American Revolution, being No. 7 of the first list of charter members, and in July, 1876, was elected as a member of the Society of the Cumberland. The large portrait of Gen. George H. Thomas was her gift to the United States Capitol, but unfortunately its size has rendered it impossible thus far to assign it a suitable location. She is also represented in the Speaker's lobby of the House of Representatives by her portrait of former Speaker John W. Taylor. Other works by this artist are portraits of Major General McPherson, Salmon P. Chase, Senator Benjamin F. Wade, Alexander Hamilton, John A. Dix, James A. Garfield, Thomas Jefferson, and Judge C. C. Baldwin of Cleveland, and Judge Rufus P. Ranney of the same city. The artist died in Washington, D. C., February 12, 1910.

Another work, the portrait of Gunning Bedford, jr., at one time was exhibited in what is now known as Statuary Hall of the Capitol. At that time, however, but few statues had been received from the States in response to the circular letter of invitation from the State Department issued in 1865. It was necessary therefore that some effort should be made toward the furnishing with works of art of this large room, which now seems somewhat overcrowded by the number of statues which it contains. This portrait of Gunning Bedford, jr., is attributed to Charles Willson Peale, and the attribution seems to be a proper one. It came into the possession of the Government as a bequest contained in the will of Henrietta Bedford, filed in Wilmington, Del., August 21, 1871, and which contained the following provision:

Eleventh. It is my will that my executor have the portrait of my father (one of the framers of the Constitution of the United States and a room-mate of James Madison of Princeton College) placed in the Capitol at Washington City near that of Madison as one of the framers of the Constitution and if that can not be done, then to be handed over to the Historical Society of Delaware.

It seems to be somewhat singular that there is no portrait in the Capitol of President Madison. This of itself, it would seem, should have rendered this section of the will inoperative, but it may be that the executor, William McCaulley, upon consideration of the conditions contained in this will, was given the assurance that if this portrait was presented to the Capitol a portrait of Madison would be obtained, so that they might hang near to each other. If such a promise was made, it has never been complied with. The picture for some time, as has been stated, hung in Statuary Hall. The guidebooks state that it was received in 1872, but there has not as yet been found any correspondence with either of the Library Committees or with any of the officials of the Capitol which relates to this picture. So far as the records show, the picture has never been officially accepted by either body, or if accepted such acceptance has not been properly indexed. The year of 1872, as fixed by the guidebook as the year of the receipt of this portrait, is probably correct and is corroborated to some extent by the account of the executor filed with the court among other papers in the case. In the executor's account is found the following entry:

June 11, 1872. Cash paid William H. Foulk for box and expenses to United States—$3.75.

Of course the absence of a suitable record has nothing to do with the value of the picture, nor does it affect in any way the interest which the picture may have to those who may care to inspect it, but it would seem as though in the ordinary transactions of affairs connected with a matter so important as the presentation of a portrait of one of the framers of the Constitution, and by such a distinguished artist as Charles Willson Peale, it would have been the duty of some one, for the benefit of those who might search for this information, to have made a record which would have been acceptable to all concerning the receipt of this work of art.

In the development of the art work of the Capitol it seems that the time has arrived at which something should be said in relation to the historical frieze of the rotunda. While this frieze was not commenced as early as the date of the history to which we have before referred, still it had been in contemplation for a long time. The letters of Captain Meigs to Randolph Rogers and to Thomas Crawford show that he had it in mind at the time (the late fifties) that this recess panel, 9 feet in height, should be filled with sculpture, so that there might be a continuous frieze 300 feet in length of figures in alto-relievo. The correspondence with Crawford shows that this project was fully discussed and that Crawford had advised as a finality that the figures should be executed in plaster and that, on account of their elevation above the floor of the rotunda and in view of the fact that they would be protected from the weather, plaster would answer for the purpose equally as well as marble, that the weight would be much less, and the expense trifling as compared with marble. The death of Crawford in 1857 rendered his participation in the matter out of the question. Randolph Rogers does not seem to have been very enthusiastic. On the contrary, his great enthusiasm seemed to be in the direction of the completion of his bronze doors and securing the payments therefor. The occurrence of the Civil War resulted in a transfer of Captain Meigs to the Quartermaster General's Department, and it was not long thereafter before the care of the extension of the Capitol and the new dome were transferred to the Department of the Interior. Thomas U. Walter, who had been the Architect of the Capitol since 1851, was now in charge of the completion of the work in accordance with his plans. It is not known whether Mr. Walter felt that it was necessary to carry out such plans as had been simply dreams of Captain Meigs. We mean by this that the plans of Captain Meigs probably had never been reduced to the form of sketches and specifications. At all events there were some who understood the intention of filling this space—9 feet high by 300 feet in length—with statuary. Whether the information was received from Captain Meigs or from the architect, Thomas U. Walter, is not known, but we find in a guidebook entitled "Philp's Washington Described" (1861) the following reference to the proposed decoration of the frieze under the subtitle of "Rotunda":

* * * Above this cornice a vertical wall will be raised with a deep recessed panel 9 ft. in height, to be filled with sculpture, forming a continuous frieze 300 ft. in length of figures in alto relievo. The

FRANKLIN SIMMONS

Represented by the statue of Gen. Ulysses S. Grant, in the Rotunda; by the statues of Roger Williams,
William King, and Francis H. Pierpont, in Statuary Hall; and by the
busts of Vice Presidents Hamlin, Stevenson, and
Fairbanks, in the Senate wing

subject to be the history of America.   The gradual progress of a continent from the depths of barbarism to the heights of civilization; the rude and primitive civilization of some of the ante-Columbian tribes; the contest of the Aztecs with their less civilized predecessors; their own conquest by the Spanish race; the wilder state of the hunter tribe of our own regions; the discovery, settlement and wars of America; the advance of the white and retreat of the red races; our own Revolutionary and other struggles with an illustration of the higher achievement of our present civilization will afford a richness and variety of costume, character and incident which may worthily employ our best sculptors in its execution and which will form for future ages a monument of the present state of the arts in this country.   *   *   *

The plan is quite comprehensive and seems so much in its general scope like that of Captain Meigs that one is led to believe it may be possible the person who prepared this guidebook either had been favored with a personal interview with Captain Meigs or had been given an opportunity to read some of the letters which he had addressed to sculptors upon this subject.   While the frieze was not commenced for many years subsequent to the publication of this general outline in the guidebook referred to, and while Captain Meigs had nothing whatever to do with the painted frieze which was to

STATUE OF ROGER WILLIAMS (RHODE ISLAND)

Franklin Simmons, sculptor

give the effect of high relief to the composition occupying this space, still in the mind of Captain Meigs there was ever present the idea of a sculptured frieze as a suitable belt course for a building of this public character, and accordingly while he was in charge of the construction of the Pension Office his desire for a sculptural frieze found expression in the terra-cotta frieze which encircles the exterior of that plain brick structure. Whether this Pension Office frieze is really worth while or not we shall not attempt to determine. We have stated this as an illustration of the fact that if a person starts with an objective in view and never loses sight of such formulated plans they usually materialize.

Having laid the foundation for future reference to the historical frieze, it will be proper at this time to retrace our steps somewhat and note the progress which had been made in securing statues from the States for Statuary Hall. While it is true that invitations were extended to all of the States early in the year 1865, it is also true that the States were recovering from the effects of the Civil War and that some of the States invited to send statues of distinguished men were not in a position, owing to the recently terminated war, to give much attention to art matters, particularly to those of a national character. Some six years elapsed after the passage of the act and five years after the invitation had been extended before any practical response was made to the invitation extended, and this response, strange as it may seem, came from one of the smaller of the Eastern States— Rhode Island. The first statue received was that of Gen. Nathanael Greene, and public exercises were held in the Senate in relation to the acceptance of this statue on the 20th day of January, 1870. The House took action upon the resolution of acceptance on January 31, 1870. The sculptor for this statue was Henry Kirke Brown, whose autobiography will be found on page 193. The second statue received was also from the State of Rhode Island, the statue being that of Roger Williams, the celebrated champion of religious liberty. Public exercises relating to the acceptance of this statue were held in the Senate on January 9, 1872, and a concurrent resolution was passed in the House on January 11, 1872. This statue is the work of the sculptor Franklin Simmons, who has been credited with several sculptural works both in the Senate and House sides of the Capitol, as well as in the rotunda, where his statue of Gen. U. S. Grant is located. Mr. Simmons was born in Webster, Me., January 11, 1839. His ancestry dates back to the earliest settlers of New England. After leaving college he devoted himself to sculpture and produced several works before establishing a studio in Rome in 1868, where he continued to reside, with the exception of visits to the United States, until his death, which occurred in Rome, Italy, December 8, 1913. He is represented in the city of Washington by his equestrian monument to Gen. John A. Logan and the Naval or Peace Monument at the western boundary of the Capitol Grounds. In the Capitol Building he is represented in Statuary Hall by the statues of Roger Williams, William King, and Governor Pierpont, and in the Senate wing by the portrait busts of Vice Presidents Hamlin, Stevenson, and Fairbanks. In addition to the works referred to he has executed for other cities statues of Longfellow, Alexander Hamilton, and Gov. O. P. Morton. Among his ideal sculpture may be mentioned Penelope, Medusa, the Mother of Moses, Galatea, the Woman of Endor, and Hercules and Alcestis. He was decorated several times by the King of Italy, the latest decoration being that of commendatore.

The next State to send her quota of two statues, as invited, was the State of Connecticut. The first statue sent was that of Jonathan Trumbull. Connecticut also sent in the same year, 1872, the statue of Roger Sherman. Both statues are the work of the sculptor Chauncey Bradley Ives, who was born at Hamden, near New Haven,

STATUE OF ROGER SHERMAN (CONNECTICUT)

Chauncey B. Ives, sculptor

STATUE OF ROBERT R. LIVINGSTON (NEW YORK)

Erastus Dow Palmer, sculptor

STATUE OF GEORGE CLINTON (NEW YORK)

Henry Kirke Brown, sculptor

{ 258 }

Conn., December 14, 1810. He was the son of a farmer and one of seven children. As a boy he evidenced ability in wood carving and at the age of 16 was apprenticed to E. R. Northrop, a wood carver. From carving wood he commenced to carve portrait busts direct from the marble without the intermediary step of a model in clay or in plaster. One of these busts, that of a young boy, William Hoppin, was exhibited in the window of a jeweler of Boston, and from this exhibition commissions resulted. He also studied for a time with Hezekiah Augur and later opened a studio in New York. Being threatened with tuberculosis and ordered south, he obtained financial assistance from a friend and instead of going south sailed for Florence, Italy, where he resided for seven years and earned by the practice of his art the money to repay the friend who had made his trip possible. He then in 1851 moved to Rome, Italy, and from that city made several visits to the United States to exhibit and dispose of his works. On October 4, 1860, he was married to Maria Louisa Davis, daughter of Benjamin Wilson Davis, of Brooklyn, N. Y., and returned with his bride to Rome, where all of their married life was spent. Seven children were born of this marriage, six of whom were born in Rome. A long residence in Rome resulted in many friendships among the Americans in that city, including Randolph Rogers and Elihu Vedder. Among his works are statues of Rebecca, Sans Souci, Cupid with his Net, Shepherd Boy, Pandora, Bacchante Nursing the Infant Bacchus; busts of General Scott and William H. Seward, sent to the Centennial Exposition at Philadelphia; and a marble statue of Trumbull in front of the statehouse at Hartford, Conn. His only sculptural work in the Capitol Building is that of the statues of Roger Sherman and Jonathan Trumbull. He died at Rome, Italy, August 2, 1894.

The next State to contribute to the collection of statuary was the State of New York, from which was received in 1873 the statue of George Clinton in bronze, the work of Henry Kirke Brown. In 1874 the statue of Robert R. Livingston, popularly known as Chancellor Livingston, who administered the oath of office to George Washington upon his accession to the Presidency, was received. No action has been taken by the Senate or House of Representatives toward the acceptance of either of these statues, and such action is not in any manner necessary, for the reason that the State, having been invited to send statues and having accepted the invitation, by sending the statues complied with all of the conditions. Senator Wilson, of Massachusetts, in speaking upon the acceptance of the statue of Nathanael Greene stated:

* * * The law in itself is complete and requires no legislation whatever, and I trust that hereafter it will be so regarded.

The statue of Livingston is the work of Erastus Dow Palmer, a self-taught sculptor who had never studied abroad or visited Italy until he went there to attend to the commission received from the State of New York for the bronze statue of Livingston. This statue is considered by sculptors whose opinions are valuable to be one of the choice compositions in Statuary Hall. Mr. Palmer was born in Pompey, Onondaga County, N. Y., April 2, 1817. He began life as a carpenter and was engaged in various forms of woodworking until 1846, when he, without any instruction, commenced the making of cameo portraits at Utica, N. Y. In 1849 he moved to Albany, N. Y., where he resided during the remainder of his life. Soon after his removal to Albany he began the production of works in sculpture, the first being Infant Ceres, exhibited at the Academy of Design in New York in 1850, achieving a great success. Ideal works and portraits followed through many years of steady application and widespread recognition. The Indian Girl, White Captive, Morning and Evening, Peace in Bondage, and Angel at the Sepulcher are among his best known creations. The originality and Americanism of his art will probably be considered its most valuable qualities. The Indian Girl and the White Captive are in the Metropolitan Museum in New York. The Albany Historical and Art Society possesses an almost complete collection of his original models in plaster. The statue of Robert R. Livingston was the last important work of this sculptor, although his health and faculties were unimpaired until within a few weeks of his death, which occurred in Albany, N. Y., March 9, 1904.

CHAPTER XIV

I N CHRONOLOGICAL sequence it is proper at this time to mention the official acceptance of the statue of Thomas Jefferson, the work in bronze of the celebrated French sculptor, David d'Angers. The reception of this statue in 1834, its temporary position in the rotunda, and its subsequent location in the grounds of the Executive Mansion have heretofore been referred to, and it appears that the question of the lack of a proper acceptance of this statue or a disclaimer of any title therein was brought to the attention of Congress by a letter from the brother of the donor, and after its discussion in Congress the following resolution was passed:

Whereas it appears that the late Commodore Uriah P. Levy while a lieutenant of the United States Navy in 1834, procured in Paris a bronze statue of Jefferson by the celebrated sculptor, David, which was presented by him through Congress to his fellow citizens of the United States, and to which attention is now called by his brother Jonas P. Levy, who requests that the statue, if not accepted by Congress, shall be returned to the heirs of the late Commodore Levy:

Therefore, *Resolved by the Senate and House of Representatives of the United States of America, in Congress assembled,* that the bronze statue of Jefferson presented in 1834 by Lieutenant Uriah P. Levy of the United States Navy, be accepted with grateful appreciation, and that the officer in charge of Public Buildings and Grounds be directed to properly prepare and place the same in the National Statuary Hall of the Capitol. (Approved March 18, 1874.) (Stats. L., vol. 18, pp. 285–286.)

We have spoken of the seeming lack of interest shown by the States in sending statues for Statuary Hall, and from the records it appears that there were in 1874 six statues, two from Rhode Island, two from Connecticut, and two from New York. In 1880, according to a guidebook known as Roose's Companion and Guide to Washington and Vicinity, published in 1880, there had been received in addition to the six statues heretofore mentioned the statues of John Winthrop, by Richard S. Greenough, and Samuel Adams, by Miss Anne Whitney, both statues from the State of Massachusetts, and from the State of Vermont the statue of Ethan Allen, by Larkin G. Mead, and the statue of Gov. William King, sent by the State of Maine, the work of Franklin Simmons, so that in the year 1880 there were but 10 statues contributed by the States in Statuary Hall. There were, however, other works of art being exhibited in Statuary Hall at this time. It may be well before naming works of art in Statuary Hall which were not contributed by the States to give the biographies of the sculptors represented by the four statues which had been contributed during the period from 1874 to the date of the publication of the guidebook referred to in 1880.

The statue of Gov. John Winthrop, of Massachusetts, as has been stated, was the work of Richard S. Greenough, a younger brother of Horatio Greenough, whose colossal statue of Washington and group The Rescue have been referred to earlier in this work. Richard S. Greenough was born in Jamaica Plain, Mass., in 1819. His early professional life was spent in Paris. For several years he resided in Newport, R. I. Among his works are statues of Franklin, City Hall Square, Boston; Governor Winthrop, Scollay Square, Boston; Boy and Eagle, in the Boston Athenæum; Carthaginian Girl,

Boston Museum of Fine Arts; Psyche (erected as a monument to his wife), in the cemetery in Rome, Italy. He died in Rome, Italy, April 23, 1904, aged 85 years. From 1874 until the time of his death he resided in Italy the greater portion of the time. The other statue from Massachusetts, that of Samuel Adams, is the work of Miss Anne Whitney. It was the first statue by a sculptress to be admitted to Statuary Hall. Miss Whitney was born in Watertown, Mass., in 1821. She was the youngest of seven children of Nathaniel Ruggles Whitney and Sarah Stone, descendants of the earliest English settlers in New England. Her education was that common to young women of her period. She showed no manifest tendency toward the study of art or inherited ability and waited until far beyond the period in which many commence their art studies before doing anything which might be considered in the direction of art expression. She spent from four to five years in Europe in study and work, following the customary routine of students under similar circumstances. In 1870, immediately after the death of Charles Sumner, there was a call to raise some fitting tribute to his memory. The committee appointed decided upon a colossal seated statue of Sumner. Twenty-eight sculptors were represented in the competition. Prizes were to be awarded, and the author's name was not to be known until the choice was made. The unanimous choice of the committee was, however, set aside upon the ground that the successful competitor (Miss Whitney) being a woman could not be supposed to understand and delineate the features of a man. After this Miss Whitney declined to enter further competitions. Her recognition, however, came when there was erected in front of the law school in Cambridge a seated statue of Charles Sumner enlarged from the very sketch rejected by the Boston committee in 1870 and with the high approval of the surviving members of that committee. Miss Whitney died in Boston, Mass., January 23, 1915.

The statue of Ethan Allen, the first statue contributed by the State of Vermont, the work of Larkin G. Mead, is an interesting addition to the collection of statuary on account of the colossal size of the statue and the interesting life of the sculptor. Mr. Mead was born in Chesterfield, N. H., January 3, 1835, but his early life was spent in Brattleboro, Vt., where his father was a prominent lawyer. It is related that the artistic talent of young Mead first found expression in modeling statues in snow and that a colossal snow figure of an angel was considered such a notable production that it was mentioned in the papers, thereby attracting the attention of Mr. Longworth, of Cincinnati, Ohio, who through the medium of the Brattleboro postmaster was able to learn something of the young snow sculptor and encouraged him in the development of his artistic talent, with the result that he became a student in the studio of Henry Kirke Brown, where he remained during the years 1853 to 1855. At the breaking out of the Civil War Mr. Mead represented an illustrated paper at the front as sketch artist. In 1862 he went to Italy, where he was encouraged by Hiram Powers. He returned to the United States in 1865, bringing with him a sketch for a memorial monument to Abraham Lincoln, which found favor and acceptance with his countrymen, and he was awarded the commission at a price of $200,000, the largest at that time ever given to an American sculptor. This monument, located at Springfield, Ill., was not completed until 1883. Other works by this sculptor are a statue of Ethan Allen, State capitol, Montpelier, Vt.; a similar statue in Statuary Hall; the Father of Waters, a heroic marble half-reclining statue; the Battle Story; the Thought of Freedom; and Echo, the latter in the Corcoran Gallery of Art. During the summer of 1878 Mr. Mead resided for some months in the city of Washington, when he submitted to the Washington Monument Commission suggestions relating to the completion of the Washington Monument. He died in Florence, Italy, October 15, 1910.

In Statuary Hall

STATUE OF ETHAN ALLEN (VERMONT)

Larkin G. Mead, sculptor

STATUE OF JOHN WINTHROP (MASSACHUSETTS)

Richard S. Greenough, *sculptor*

STATUE OF WILLIAM KING (MAINE)

Franklin Simmons, sculptor

The last statue from the States received prior to the publication of the guidebook was that of Gov. William King, contributed to the collection by the State of Maine. This statue was received, so far as the records tend to show, in January, 1878, and on the 22d day of January the Senate agreed to the customary resolution of acceptance. Action was taken in the House of Representatives on the same date. This statue is the work of Franklin Simmons, whose biography has been given in connection with the installation in Statuary Hall of the statue of Roger Williams.

There was also in Statuary Hall a collection of statuary not contributed by the States—for example, the plaster cast of Washington, a copy of the marble, by Houdon, in Richmond; a bust of Kosciuszko, by Dmochowski, otherwise known as Saunders; the statue of Lincoln, by Vinnie Ream, which seems to have been removed from the rotunda after the exercises of acceptance referred to earlier in this work; also the bust of Lincoln, by Mrs. Sarah Fisher Ames; the bust of Crawford, by Gagliardi; the statue of Alexander Hamilton, by Doctor Stone, which had been in the Capitol Building since 1868; and the bronze statue of Thomas Jefferson, by David d'Angers. There were also other works of art on exhibition in Statuary Hall, such as the mosaic portrait of Lincoln, by Salviati; the portrait of Joshua R. Giddings, by Miss C. L. Ransom, before referred to; the portrait of Charles Carroll of Carrollton, painted by Chester Harding; the portrait of Gunning Bedford, jr., to which reference has also been made; a portrait of Thomas Jefferson, by Sully; a self-portrait of Benjamin West, which had been added to the collection only a short time before 1880; and, as though this were not enough, there was also upon exhibition in Statuary Hall at the time of the publication of this guidebook a safe, commonly known as the centennial safe, which had been filled with mementoes of the first 100 years of independence and then closed to remain closed for 100 years. This safe is now located underneath the central portico and is an inconspicuous object whose location is known to but few.

It may be interesting to state the location of some of these works of art at the present time. Of course it will be understood that the statues presented by the States have remained in Statuary Hall during all of the years which have intervened. The plaster cast of Houdon's Washington, the statue of Lincoln, the statue of Alexander Hamilton, and the bronze statue of Thomas Jefferson are now located in the rotunda. The bust of Kosciuszko, the bust of Lincoln, and the mosaic portrait of Lincoln are now in the Senate lobby, gallery floor, on the east side of the Senate wing of the Capitol. The bust of Crawford is in the small north lobby connected with the Senate lobby referred to and in the same room with the two landscapes by Thomas Moran and the painting of Niagara by Regis Gignoux. The statue of Col. E. D. Baker, the last work of Horatio Stone and which was at the time referred to included in the collection in Statuary Hall, has also been removed to the rotunda. The portrait of Joshua R. Giddings is in the office of the Architect of the Capitol. The portrait of Gunning Bedford, jr., and Charles Carroll of Carrollton are hanging upon the wall facing the east staircase of the House of Representatives. The portrait of Thomas Jefferson by Sully is in the main corridor of the Senate at the west end, and the self-portrait of Benjamin West is now temporarily loaned to the collection of the National Gallery. The portrait bust of Thomas Crawford, by Tommaso Gagliardi, is interesting on account of the historical connection which it bears to the sculptor who produced it. Gagliardi was one of the many Italian sculptors who found employment at the Capitol during the period of the construction of the extension of the Capitol. He had been employed by Crawford in Rome, and when he came to this country he called at the place of business of Robert E. Launitz, a place usually sought out by most of the Italian sculptors upon coming to this country. From New York he came to Washington and secured employment at the Capitol. By those who were upon the Capitol extension with him he is described as being a wonderful carver of marble and a tireless worker. It appears, however, by the correspondence between Captain Meigs and Thomas Crawford that Mr. Crawford was not altogether pleased with some of the representations made by Gagliardi concerning his (Gagliardi's) ability as a scupltor. Whether this was professional jealousy or not we shall not attempt to decide. It ought, however, to be sufficient proof of the ability of this sculptor that he seems to have been able to perform all of the work intrusted to him, and it was through Gagliardi that we have this bust of Crawford. The bust came into possession of the Government by purchase from people who had rented to Gagliardi and other sculptors a shop or studio situated on Maryland Avenue near the Capitol. Whether upon leaving the city the bust was left in payment for rent or left because of no further use for it is not known.

There were other people, however, in Rome who were interested in Gagliardi besides Thomas Crawford. On the 24th of March, 1855, L. B. Binsse, consul general of the Pontifical State, addressed a letter to Captain Meigs and inquires—

If T. Gagliardi has been engaged to do some sculpture on the frontice piece of the Capitol and requests that the party named be not informed of the inquiry.

Captain Meigs appears to have been somewhat diplomatic in his reply to the letter referred to, for on March 28, 1855, he states:

I do not know whether Tommaso Gagliardi is employed here or no. I might ascertain by inquiry, but I do not feel at liberty to make such inquiry while restrained from informing him of them unless it be shown to me that there are good reasons of police or family for doing so.

It may be that some have imagined from the inquiry and the reply as quoted above that there was something radically wrong with Gagliardi, but little was known about him so far as the official records of the architect's office show other than the information given above and the additional fact that there were several proposals and acceptances relating to sculptural work performed by him upon the Crawford pediment. It was many years after the publication of Works of Art in the Capitol Building and Biographies of the Artists when conversation was had with one of the Piccirilli brothers concerning the difficulty attending the securing of information of a biographical nature relating to Tommaso Gagliardi. Very much to the surprise of the writer Mr. Piccirilli replied, "Tommaso Gagliardi was my godfather," and from him was obtained the material from which the following biography was compiled.

Tommaso Gagliardi was born in Rome, Italy, in 1820. He was an apprentice in the studio of Tenerani, a pupil of Canova, and was for some time employed in the studio of Thomas Crawford in Rome. His early life and liberal ideas and his antagonism to the papal authorities led to his emigration with comrades from Rome and Carrara to the United States early in 1855 and on coming to Washington he secured contracts to carve in marble some of the statuary for the Senate pediment, this work continuing during the years 1855 to 1858. In some of these contracts he was associated with Vincenzo Casoni, and it was during his stay in Washington that he executed the bust of Thomas Crawford. An ardent admirer of Garibaldi, he returned to Italy and participated in the campaign which resulted in the capture of Venice, September 7, 1860, also serving under Garibaldi at the time of his defeat at Mentana in November, 1867. In the early seventies he went to Japan and founded a school of sculpture in the Royal Academy at Tokyo. His discovery of marble quarries in Japan resulted in the conferring of honors upon him by

In the House wing, east side, facing the painting of the Reading of the Emancipation Proclamation

PORTRAIT OF CHARLES CARROLL OF CARROLLTON

Chester Harding, painter

the government of that country. He visited India in later years, and through his acquaintance with General Roberts was able to secure many commissions for portrait busts from the dignitaries of that country, the models for this work being sent to his friend Piccirilli for execution in marble. He was an extensive traveler, a brilliant conversationalist, and formed many close friendships with influential people whom he met in his travels. Amassing a competence, he was able to spend his last years in his villa near Lucca, Tuscany, in a life of ample ease. His death occurred at his villa in 1895.

Concerning the portrait of Charles Carroll of Carrollton by Chester Harding, some interesting events occurred in the work of identifying and establishing the author of this work. It appears that in 1880 this portrait was known to be the work of Chester Harding, but that in later years, in some manner which is not clearly explained, it was credited to Thomas Sully and exhibited in its present location with the name of Sully as the artist upon the name plate. It was believed by some that this attribution was incorrect, and upon an examination of the records relating to the purchase of this portrait it was learned that it was first offered to the Joint Committee on the Library as being the work of Thomas Sully. The picture, however, was not at that time purchased, but the offer to sell had probably created the impression that Sully was the painter, and it may be that in this way the mistake occurred. A further examination of the records of the Joint Committee on the Library disclosed the fact that the picture was again offered for sale as being the work of Chester Harding, and after some delay its purchase was directed by that committee. An examination of the record in the office of the Auditor for the Treasury Department showed that the voucher drawn in payment described the picture as being the work of Chester Harding, but as it was considered necessary to have this information corroborated a careful study of all of the known portraits of Charles Carroll of Carrollton was made, and, so far as these portraits had been made the subject of illustrations, the illustrations were also examined. This search led to the information that the portrait painted by Chester Harding had been engraved by Asher B. Durand, and a copy of the engraving was obtained and compared with the picture, and it was the unanimous opinion of those to whom this subject was submitted that the engraving was clearly from the portrait owned by the Government and hanging facing the east staircase in the House wing of the Capitol. This identification has been stated at some length in order that it may be definitely known what investigations were made so that this question might be authoritatively settled.

The painter of this portrait, Chester Harding, illustrates by his biography the great changes which may come to a person who follows steadfastly an ideal whether that ideal leads in the direction of business or in the direction of art. Mr. Harding was born September 1, 1792. His parents were poor and he went to work at an early age. At 14 he helped his father clear an unbroken wilderness in northern New York and build a log house. In the War of 1812 he enlisted as a drummer boy, afterwards becoming a peddler, working in a cabinet and chair manufactory, and keeping a tavern. He began his career as an artist by painting signs, and finally, although entirely self-taught, turned his attention to portrait painting, in which branch of art he became both popular and successful. He resided and practiced his art in St. Louis, Philadelphia, and Boston; going to London in 1824 at the height of his fame he painted several members of the royal family and the nobility of England—the Dukes of Sussex, Hamilton, and Norfolk, and Mr. Coke and his daughter, Lady Anson. In August, 1846, he made a second trip to England, where he painted Rogers, the poet, and Allison, the historian. Among his American portraits are those of Daniel Boone and General Sherman (one of his latest works). His portrait of Washington Allston, belonging to S. Batchelder, was exhibited at the Centennial Exposition of 1876; his portrait of Daniel Webster, painted for Hon. George Ashman, of Springfield, Mass., is now in the possession of the Bar Association of New York; his portrait of John Randolph is in the Corcoran Gallery of Art; and his portrait of Henry Clay is in the courthouse, Washington, D. C. Mr. Harding died April 1, 1866.

For some time our attention has been directed almost entirely to the art works on exhibition in Statuary Hall during the period of its being set apart for works of art up to the year 1880. We should not forget that during this period—from 1864 to 1880—there were other art interests worthy of reference which should not be neglected. In the House of Representatives, on the 21st of January, 1867, Mr. Banks, by unanimous consent, submitted the following resolution, which was read and referred to the Committee on the Library:

Resolved, That the Committee on the Library be authorized to contract with Albert Bierstadt for two paintings thoroughly American in character, representing some prominent feature of scenery or important event in the discovery or history of America to fill 2 unoccupied panels in the chamber of the House of Representatives.

This resolution was duly taken up at a meeting of the Joint Committee on the Library, held February 12, 1867, at which time it was voted that Mr. Bierstadt be requested to submit his views to the committee in writing, with specification and plans for covering two or more subjects, and communicating his price for the same.

We again hear of the progress of this matter from the meeting of the Joint Committee on the Library held on March 13, 1867, at which time a communication was read from Mr. Bierstadt proposing to execute his historical paintings for the panels in the Hall of the House of Representatives at the price of $40,000 each, and upon the reading of this communication it was voted:

That the Librarian be instructed to inform Mr. Bierstadt that no appropriation having been made to carry out the purpose of the House resolution respecting the panels in their Hall the Committee deemed it inexpedient in the present state of our finances to recommend an appropriation for the object in question.

It does not seem, however, that Mr. Bierstadt was discouraged by the action of the committee to which reference has been made. He seems to have disappeared from public view for some years, and on March 3, 1875, we find that the following action was taken by the Joint Committee on the Library:

The Chairman was authorized to purchase of Mr. A. Bierstadt his painting of the landing of Hendrik Hudson now on exhibition in the hall of the House of Representatives at a price not exceeding $10,000.

Some one has reasoned that Mr. Bierstadt's original price of $40,000 is only what might have been expected under the circumstances and has stated that he probably felt that if the Government would pay Leutze $20,000 for Westward the Course of Empire Takes Its Way, and Powell $25,000 for the Battle of Lake Erie, there would probably be no difficulty, inasmuch as a resolution in his behalf had been introduced in Congress, in obtaining for such works as he might produce for the Government the sum of $40,000. It may be, however, that this price was asked so that the opportunity might be afforded of making a reduction if the price was considered too high; that the reduction was made is quite evident. It seems that as late as 1878 the second panel in the Hall of the House of Representatives had not been filled. We find by reference to the records of the Joint

Committee on the Library for the 25th of January, 1878, the following, which relates not only to Mr. Bierstadt but to Thomas Moran:

Communications were read from Albert Bierstadt and Thomas Moran both wishing to fill the panel in the hall of the House of Representatives at the right hand of the Speaker; on motion of Mr. Edmunds it was voted that the Chairman of the House Committee be authorized to add to the appropriation bill an appropriation for the purpose of filling the panel at the right hand of the Speaker's desk. * * *

The appropriation bill for that year carried the following items:

To enable the Joint Committee on the Library to purchase works of art for the Capitol Building, $15,000.

To purchase portraits of the Presidents, $3,000. (Stats. L., vol. 20, p. 239.) (Act approved June 20, 1878.)

For many years the Joint Committee on the Library exercised almost unlimited authority in the direction of the purchase of works of art. Sometime in the sixties they had established a rule that it was not the province of the Joint Committee on the Library to take any action in relation to any work of art unless the matter had been referred to them by the Congress, and that rule has been followed to a greater or lesser extent ever since that time. In the purchase of works of art it has been in many instances the practice for those who desired to sell works of art to the Government to obtain some action upon the part of the Library Committee through the reference of the subject by one of the branches of Congress to the committee for consideration. The committee, however, has usually understood whether the work of art offered for sale was of such a standard or of such a subject that its acquisition by the Government would be desirable, and in this way has protected itself from the purchase of many works of art which had been offered and through a resolution of Congress placed before the committee for action. In former years lump-sum appropriations were made from time to time to enable the committee to purchase such works of art as seemed necessary for the purposes of a public building like the Capitol, and this committee for many years had the entire charge of the purchase of portraits of the Presidents to be placed in the Executive Mansion. The Congress has usually considered that a favorable report advocating the purchase of a specific work of art or of any particular line of decoration of such importance that the necessary appropriation has been granted. In later years it has been the rule to make specific appropriations, naming therein the character of the work to be acquired. This is particularly true in the instance of the purchase of portraits or busts of Chief Justices of the United States. The purchase of portraits for the collection in the Speaker's lobby has always been considered a matter to be determined by the House Committee on the Library, and action of the Joint Committee is not expected in such instances.

It will be noted that the collection of works of art in Statuary Hall consisted of a miscellaneous gathering of different art objects which have now been distributed in various portions of the Capitol Building. The one thing then contained in Statuary Hall which seemed rather out of place among the works of art there collected was the centennial safe and the centennial album, to which some reference has heretofore been made. This matter was called up by a news item printed in the New York Tribune of February 25, 1879. This item from Washington contains the following:

The centennial safe which was closed at the Capitol on Saturday to be opened again in 1976 and which contains the autographs of the President, his Cabinet, and members of Congress, turns out to have a curious history. The prime mover in the undertaking was Mrs. C. F. Deihm. She charged each Senator and Representative, who was allowed to insert his name in the album which was put into the safe, the sum of $5. This aggregated $1,840. She now comes forward with a bill requiring Congress to pay an additional $1,500. for the safe, making a total of $3,340.

In reply to this article Mrs. Deihm, on the 26th of February, 1879, sends the following reply:

To the Editor of the Tribune:

Sir: A Washington dispatch appeared in your issue of yesterday in relation to the century safe that was closed on Washington's birthday at the Capitol containing statements that are both untrue and unjust. It states that I received $5. from each Senator and Representative, that inscribed his name in the album and that I have asked an appropriation of $1500. for the safe. These statements are wholly without foundation and I deny them most emphatically. I never received a dollar from anyone for the privilege of signing the book and have never asked Congress for a dollar. Several Representatives are subscribers to my paper, Our Second Century, for which they pay me $2.50 per year, but this has nothing to do with the safe. My enterprise cost me $15,000. but my services, the safe and its contents I have given gratuitously and I feel it a great injustice to me to see such charges reflecting such discredit while I am trying to make an honest living out of my paper. I know of no malicious feeling that could prompt it and do not understand its origin.

Mrs. C. M. Deihm,
27 Union Square, New York.

Concerning this communication the editor of the Tribune comments as follows (it will be noted that his effort to sustain what appeared in the Tribune is rather remarkable):

On inquiry we learn from Washington that the dispatch in question was based upon the statement of a Congressman who said he had seen Mrs. Deihm's bill. Unless other evidence is brought forward her card above must be accepted as conclusive; but it is obvious that there is an unpleasant impression about her work prevalent in Washington, for Senator Morrill has offered a resolution in the Senate the object of which is to cause her safe to be removed from the Capitol.

There is much in this editorial statement which seems calculated to give a wrong impression. The resolution referred to was undoubtedly a resolution submitted by Mr. Morrill in the Senate on February 22, 1879, where under the subtitle "Use of National Statuary Hall" we find the following record:

Mr. Morrill submitted the following resolution; which was considered by unanimous consent, and agreed to. *Resolved,* That the Committee on Public Buildings and Grounds be instructed to inquire by what authority the National Statuary Hall set apart by law exclusively for statues has been permitted to be used for any other exhibitions. (Senate proceedings, February 22, 1879, Congressional Record, vol. 8, pt. 2, pp. 1749–1750, 45th Cong., 3d sess.)

It seems only fair to suggest that this resolution is not wholly in line with the law which existed governing Statuary Hall. The intent of the law was doubtless as construed by Senator Morrill in his resolution, but the actual letter of the law seems hardly to justify such a conclusion. This resolution was referred to the Committee on Public Buildings and Grounds, but no report on the subject from said committee has been found. It is quite probable, however, that this resolution, although there seems to have been no discussion on it in the Senate, had its effect through the Committee on Public Buildings and Grounds in the framing of the following legislation, which appeared in the sundry civil act of March 3, 1879 (Stats. L., vol. 20, p. 391):

No work of art or manufacture other than the property of the United States shall be exhibited in the National Statuary Hall, the rotunda, or the corridors of the Capitol.

During the period between 1870 and 1880 there was added to the art collection of the Capitol a bust portrait of Washington, the work of Gilbert Stuart, and known as the Thomas Chestnut portrait. This purchase was authorized by the Joint Committee on the Library on June 7, 1876, and was purchased of W. W. Corcoran on the 16th of June, 1876, for the sum of $1,200. It has been claimed by those who are supposed to be authorities upon the value of portraits of Washington by Gilbert Stuart that this portrait is now worth more than $40,000. It is now hanging in the main corridor of the Senate.

PORTRAIT OF GILBERT STUART

John Neagle, painter

Stuart is represented by two bust portraits of George Washington, in the Senate wing

Another portrait of Washington by Gilbert Stuart, known as the Edward Pennington portrait, was purchased 10 years later of Mrs. C. W. Harris, February 24, 1886, for $1,200, and by connoisseurs this portrait is considered to be the best of the two portraits by Gilbert Stuart in the Capitol. It is rarely seen, however, by the general public, as it is hanging in the committee room of the Senate Committee on Post Offices and Post Roads. There is also hanging in the same room a notable portrait of Henry Laurens, purchased in 1886 for the sum of $1,200, the work of John Singleton Copley, and is, therefore, one of the rare pictures in the Capitol, as examples of the work of Copley are not at all common in this country, many notable museums being without a single example of his work. The purchase of this picture was materially aided by the kind offices of the officials of the Corcoran Gallery of Art. As this is the only instance in the Capitol of a work of Copley, his biography properly follows at this time.

In the Senate wing

PORTRAIT OF GEORGE WASHINGTON
Gilbert Stuart, painter

{ 274 }

The artist was born in Boston in 1737. By some he was considered self-taught; by others it is believed his talent was developed by his stepfather, Peter Pelham, a painter and engraver who died in 1751. The portrait of his half brother, Henry Pelham, was sent to England in 1760 and exhibited at Somerset House, receiving high commendation from West and other good judges. In 1774 he went to London and began a career of uninterrupted success; was patronized by the royal family and nobility; in 1777 became an associate of the Royal Academy and in 1779 a Royal Academician. Lord Chancellor Lyndhurst, Copley's son, collected many of his works. The subject of this work, Henry Laurens, was born in Charleston, S. C., in 1724. He was a Delegate from South Carolina in the Continental Congress, and its President, 1777 and 1778; elected a minister to Holland by the Continental Congress October 21, 1779; captured on the voyage and held a prisoner in the Tower of London for 15 months; appointed one of the peace commissioners and signed the preliminary treaty of Paris November 30, 1782; returned to farming in South Carolina, and died at Charleston, S. C., December 8, 1792. His portrait, according to the accessories contained in the painting, seems to have been painted while a prisoner in the Tower of London. The portrait is in good condition and an excellent example of the best work of Copley.

Reference has recently been made to the two portraits in the Capitol of Washington by Gilbert Stuart. Just what reason impelled the Joint Committee on the Library to purchase these two almost identical portraits is not definitely known, but as one is used as a decoration in a committee room, it was probably as inexpensive a method of securing decorations for that room as could be found.

While the work of Gilbert Stuart is well known and his Washington portraits are easily recognized by all, it may not be out of place at this time to give some brief biographical notes concerning this artist, whose career was unusual and whose fame increases as the years go by. He was born in Narragansett, R. I., December 3, 1755, and attempted his art expression unaided, but later received some instruction from Cosmo Alexander, a Scotch portrait painter, whom he accompanied to Scotland in 1772. The death of his master left Stuart friendless, and after a short course of study at the University of Glasgow he returned home. In 1775 he went to England and entered the studio of Benjamin West, to whom he afterwards became an assistant. Opening a studio in London in 1785, he became popular and financially successful. During a visit to Ireland in 1788 he painted the portraits of many distinguished persons, and during his residence abroad he painted portraits of three Kings, Louis XVI, George III, and George IV while Prince of Wales. He returned to this country in 1792 and while here painted portraits of six Presidents of the United States from personal sittings, viz, George Washington, John Adams, Thomas Jefferson, James Madison, James Monroe, and John Quincy Adams. After painting in New York, Philadelphia, and Washington, D. C., where at one time he occupied a studio on F Street NW., he settled in Boston and resided there until his death, which occurred July 27, 1828. For some little time preceding his death Mr. Stuart seemed envious of the success of Chester Harding and is credited with having made some dissatisfied remarks concerning Harding's popularity. Mr. Stuart, however, had many friends and admirers in Boston, and after his death a collection of his works was exhibited in the Boston Athenæum. At this exhibition 215 of his works were collected.

In the schoolbooks of over a half century past, especially those books edited by Salem Town, LL. D., there was contained an interesting anecdote concerning Stuart which gives us a fair idea of the natural wit of this celebrated artist. This article, as it appeared in the school readers, seems to have been an abridged version of the anecdote as contained in the Life and Works of Gilbert Stuart, by George C. Mason. The anecdote is given in full, as it is apparently well worth reading by those who have never read it and a rereading by those who have before had an opportunity of becoming acquainted with this example of Stuart's personal qualities:

STUART DEFINES HIS PROFESSION

The following anecdote was related by Dr. Waterhouse, who probably had it from Stuart:

"The artist was traveling by stage in England. His fellow passengers were a number of gentlemen who were strangers to him and who, finding him very amusing, ventured to ask him who he was and what was his calling.

"Mr. Stuart answered with a grave face and a serious tone that he sometimes dressed gentlemen's and ladies' hair, (at that time the high-craped pomatumed hair was all the fashion). 'You are a hair dresser, then?' 'What?' said he, 'do you take me for a barber?'

"'I beg your pardon, sir, but I inferred it from what you said. If I mistook you, may I take the liberty to ask what you are then?'

"'Why I sometimes brush a gentleman's coat or hat, and sometimes adjust a cravat.'

"'Oh you are a valet then to some nobleman?'

"'A valet! Indeed, sir, I am not. I am not a servant—to be sure I make coats and waistcoats for gentlemen.'

"'Oh you are a tailor?'

"'Tailor, do I look like a tailor? I assure you, I never handled a goose, other than a roasted one.'

"By this time they were all in a roar. 'What the devil are you then,' said one.

"'I'll tell you' said Stuart. 'Be assured all I have said is literally true. I dress hair, brush hats and coats, adjust a cravat and make coats, waistcoats and breeches, and likewise boots and shoes, at your service.'

"'Oh, a boot and shoe maker after all!'

"'Guess again, gentlemen; I never handle boots or shoes, but for my own feet and legs, yet all I have told you is true.'

"'We may as well give up guessing.'

"After checking his laughter, and pumping up a fresh flow of spirits by a large pinch of snuff he said to them very gravely: 'Now, gentlemen, I will not play the fool with you any longer, but will tell you upon my honor as a gentleman my bona fide profession. I get my bread by making faces.'

"He then screwed his countenance, and twisted the lineaments of his visage in a manner such as Samuel Foote or Charles Matthews might have envied. When his companions, after loud peals of laughter had composed themselves, each took credit to himself for having all the while suspected that the gentleman belonged to the theater and they all knew that he must be a comedian by profession; when to their utter surprise, he assured them that he was never on the stage, and very rarely saw the inside of a playhouse, or any similar place of amusement. They now all looked at each other in blank astonishment.

"Before parting, Stuart said to his companions: 'Gentlemen, you will find that all I have said of my various employments is comprised in these words: I am a portrait painter. If you will call at John Palmer's York Building, London, where I shall be ready and willing to brush you a coat or hat, dress your hair á la mode, supply you, if need be, with a wig of any fashion or dimension, accommodate you with boots or shoes, give you ruffler or cravats, and make faces for you.'

"While taking a parting glass at the inn, they begged leave to inquire of their pleasant companion in what part of England he was born. He told them he was not born in England, Wales, Ireland or Scotland. Here was another puzzle for John Bull.

"'Where then?'

"'I was born in Narragansett.'

"'Where's that?'

"'Six miles from Pottawoone, and ten miles from Poppasquash, and about four miles from Conanicut, and not far from where the famous battle with the warlike Pequote was fought.'

"'In what part of the East Indies is that sir?'

"'East Indies, my dear sir, it is in the State of Rhode Island, between Massachusetts and the Connecticut River.'"

(From Life and Works of Gilbert Stuart, by George C. Mason.)

CHAPTER XV

SPEAKERS OF THE HOUSE OF REPRESENTATIVES
COLLECTION OF THEIR PORTRAITS COMMENCED

N THAT section of the House wing of the Capitol usually referred to as the Speaker's lobby a collection of 37 portraits of former Speakers is to be found. Definite information concerning the reasons for this collection is not readily obtainable, if possible. It seems, however, that it had its origin in a collection of engravings and photographs of former Speakers once contained in the room occupied by the Speaker as an office. In Keim's Illustrated Handbook of Washington (1875) we find the following, which perhaps will explain something of the conditions existing at the time of the publication of that book:

On the left of the south corridor is the member's retiring room now used by the official reporters. * * * On the right the doors open into the hall and on the left is the Sergeant at Arms room, in which the mace is kept when the House of Representatives is not in session. The Speaker's room, next on the left, is entirely finished in iron enriched with gilt. The furniture and fittings are extremely fine. On the walls are engravings or photographs of the Speakers.

It is probably from this small collection of pictures, which were of quite a small size and contained in oval frames, that the present collection of 37 portraits had its origin. It will be remembered that in 1852 there was presented to the Nation and accepted to be placed in the Library of Congress a portrait of Henry Clay, by Giuseppe Fagnani. This portrait is now in the collection in the Speaker's lobby and is probably one of the earliest painted portraits in that collection. It presumably, however, was retained in the Library of Congress until a businesslike method of collecting portraits of former Speakers had been inaugurated. Just when this movement commenced is not at this time known, but it probably followed soon after the three rooms described in Keim's guidebook as the room occupied by the Official Reporters, the Sergeant at Arms' room, and the Speaker's room were converted into one large room now used as the Members' retiring room. This change in the original plan arose from a desire on the part of the Members of the House of Representatives for an improved condition of ventilation, a question which was constantly recurring in the history of the proceedings of the House. It did not even seem to be confined to regular cycles, but was liable to be introduced upon almost any occasion. During the period of the seventies there happened to be in the House a large number of Members who believed in such methods of ventilation as are usually obtained by the opening of a window, and the often repeated controversy concerning the advisability of having the Chamber of the House of Representatives moved to the southwest corner of the House wing of the Capitol came up for its usual discussion. This had been agitated on many previous occasions and it had usually been decided that the scheme was impracticable. The desire for the "open window," "God's sunlight," and the "free air of heaven" existed at this time as it had on many previous occasions, and as a compromise it was decided to combine the three rooms named into one room and to increase the openings from the lobby into this converted room, so that when the doors leading from the lobby into the Hall of the House were kept open and the windows of this retiring room were opened a better ventilation could be obtained. The changes sought were made possible through the following legislation:

For making the necessary changes and alterations for the proper heating, lighting and ventilation of the hall of the House of Representatives, according to the plans and specifications made by the Architect of the Capitol Extensions to be expended under the commission appointed by resolution of the House, $30,000. (Act March 3, 1879; Stats. L., vol. 20, p. 402.)

According to the report of the Architect of the Capitol for the fiscal year ended June 30, 1880, these changes secured the desired improvement in the heating, lighting, and ventilating system of the Capitol. The report states:

* * * The improvements to the Hall of Representatives which were ordered by the commission of which the Honorable Abram S. Hewitt is Chairman, have been completed. These consist mainly in connecting the rooms at the south of the Hall with the lobby, by which a large retiring room for members was made; constructing air-duct and shaft, opening some distance from the building on the west front, so as to prevent the introduction of air into the hall charged with coal gas from chimneys and other impurities from the building, as has been the case formerly; and by greatly increasing the openings in the floor of the hall for the admission of fresh air.

These changes have added largely to the comfort of the occupants of the hall, and have afforded an ample supply of pure air for respiration. Fire-places have also been placed in the hall. These changes and improvements seem to have given general satisfaction. * * *

It is safe to conclude that with the changes made the small photographs and engravings of Speakers seemed out of place in the retiring room and were finally placed in the Speaker's lobby. In fact, the writer was informed by a former employee of the House, John Chancey, whose period of service extended over a time antedating the changes made by which the retiring room was formed, that these small oval pictures referred to were at one time all of the portraits representing the Speakers hanging in the Speaker's lobby. It is very easy to assume that with the introduction of some full-sized portraits in oil the smaller portraits seemed out of place, and the collection of portraits in oil naturally followed. During the past 15 years nearly two-thirds of the present number of portraits have been placed in the Speaker's lobby. It should not be understood that all of this number (two-thirds) are original or newly acquired portraits, for the reason that prior to 1911 there were hanging in the Speaker's lobby a large number of portraits in crayon, in highly ornamented gilt frames, which were properly considered as being out of harmony with some of the really fine portraits in oil then in the lobby, so that by the resolution of March 3, 1911, which provided for 19 portraits for the Speaker's lobby, it was the intention to replace all of the crayon portraits by portraits in oil. Previous to this time, however, there had been several notable portraits in oil furnished by the States or individuals for the Speaker's lobby, the most celebrated of which was probably the portrait of Thomas B. Reed, by John S. Sargent. This was presented by several Members of the Fifty-first Congress to the National House of Representatives. The Members engaged in this presentation were: Belden, of New York; Lodge, of Massachusetts; Randall, of Massachusetts; Wallace, of New York; Sanford, of New York; Bayne, of Pennyslvania; Dalzell, of Pennsylvania; Neidringhaus, of Missouri; Walker, of Massachusetts; Adams, of Illinois; Hitt, of Illinois; Dorsey, of Nebraska; Van Schaick, of Wisconsin; Scranton, of Pennsylvania; Bingham, of Pennsylvania; Reyburn, of Pennsylvania; Wallace, of Massachusetts; Ketcham, of New York; Culbertson, of Pennsylvania; Darlington, of Pennsylvania; and Bliss, of Michigan. The presence in such a collection of a portrait by Sargent is sufficient to give a certain distinction to the entire collection. There were, however, other portraits of note. Massachusetts, about 1885, had presented to this collection the portrait of Robert C. Winthrop, painted by Daniel Huntington, one of the

BRONZE TABLET IN THE SPEAKER'S LOBBY
Design by Paul W. Bartlett, sculptor; text by Charles E. Fairman

most celebrated portrait painters of his period, and in April, 1886, the Legislature of Massachusetts authorized the furnishing for the National Capitol at Washington of "worthy portraits" of former Speakers Sedgwick, Varnum, and Banks. These portraits were by the following artists: Theodore Sedgwick was painted by Edgar Parker and a copy from a work by Gilbert Stuart; Joseph B. Varnum was painted by Charles L. Elliott; and Nathaniel P. Banks was painted by Robert W. Vonnoh. These portraits were presented January 19, 1888, at which time public exercises were held in the House of Representatives and speeches were made by Mr. Long, Mr. Rockwell, Mr. Allen, Mr. Collins, Mr. Hayden, and Mr. Lodge, all of Massachusetts. Mr. Randall, of Pennsylvania, presented the following resolution:

Resolved, That this House has received with great satisfaction the portraits of Honorable Theodore Sedgwick, Speaker of the 6th Congress; Honorable Joseph B. Varnum, Speaker of the 10th and 11th Congresses; and Honorable Nathaniel P. Banks, Speaker of the 34th Congress, presented by the Commonwealth of Massachusetts and will cause them to be placed and preserved among those of the other distinguished men who in times past have presided over the House of Representatives.

The motion was seconded by Mr. Breckinridge, of Kentucky, who also made an address of acceptance.

Concerning the four portraits presented by the State of Massachusetts, inasmuch as the artists who executed these paintings, with the exception of Elliott, are not otherwise represented by works of art in the Capitol Building, their biographies should appear at this time.

Edgar Parker, who painted the portrait of Theodore Sedgwick, was born in Framingham, Mass., in 1840. He was self-taught. He is represented in Faneuil Hall, Boston, by portraits of Charles Sumner, Henry Wilson, and Rear Admiral John A. Winslow. Other works by this artist are Hon. Charles Hudson, ex-governor; Onslow Stearns, of New Hampshire; and Nathaniel Hawthorne. In 1875 the poet Whittier gave him sittings. This is the only original portrait of Whittier, with the exception of one painted when he was a young man, by Hoyt.

Robert William Vonnoh, who painted the portrait of Nathaniel P. Banks, was born in Hartford, Conn., September 17, 1858. His art education was received in the Massachusetts Normal Art School of Boston and at Julien's Academy, Paris. He was the principal instructor in portrait and figure painting in the Museum of Fine Arts, Boston, 1885 to 1887, and in the Pennsylvania Academy of Fine Arts, Philadelphia, Pa., 1891 to 1896; member of the National Academy of Design, New York; practiced portrait painting in Boston, Mass., New York City, Philadelphia, Pa., and Chicago, Ill. He painted the portraits of many people of note in these cities.

Daniel Huntington, the painter of the portrait of Robert C. Winthrop, was born in New York in 1816; educated at Hamilton College; pupil of Prof. S. F. B. Morse and of G. P. Ferrero in Rome; exhibited first in 1836 at the National Academy of Design, New York; elected associate in 1838 and academician in 1840; president, 1862 to 1869 and 1877 to 1891; painter of portraits and genre subjects. His painting Mercy's Dream is owned by the Corcoran Gallery of Art, and his portrait of Abraham Lincoln is the property of the Union League Club, New York. Many of his portraits of eminent men are to be found in the collection of the New York Chamber of Commerce and in other public buildings in New York. He died in New York in 1906.

Charles Loring Elliott, the painter of the portrait of Joseph B. Varnum, was born in Scipio, N. Y., in 1812. He was the son of an architect; pupil of Col. John Trumbull and Quidor; painted portraits in the western part of the State while a young man and

ROBERT WILLIAM VONNOH

Self-portrait

Represented by a portrait of Nathaniel P. Banks, in the Speaker's lobby

{ 281 }

DANIEL HUNTINGTON
Self-portrait

Represented by the portrait of Robert C. Winthrop, in the Speaker's lobby

In the Speaker's lobby

PORTRAIT OF THOMAS B. REED
John S. Sargent (1856–1925), painter

{ 283 }

Courtesy of Ruel P. Tolman

JOHN S. SARGENT

Early photograph (1884) in his Paris studio. The full-length portrait on the easel is that of Madame Gautreau Sargent is represented in the Speaker's lobby by a portrait of former Speaker Thomas B. Reed

afterwards opened a studio in New York; elected as an associate of the National Academy of Design in 1845 and academician in 1846; is credited with having painted more than 700 portraits of eminent people. His portrait of W. W. Corcoran, in the Corcoran Gallery of Art, is a conspicuous example of his work. Other portraits are those of Fletcher Harper, Fitz-Greene Halleck, J. Fenimore Cooper, Governor Seymour, and Erastus Corning. Mr. Elliott is also represented by a portrait of Chief Justice Oliver Ellsworth in the Supreme Court robing room. He died in Albany, N. Y., in 1868.

Inasmuch as the portrait of Thomas B. Reed is the only example of the work of the celebrated painter John S. Sargent in the Capitol, his biography should follow at this time. He was born in Florence, Italy, of American parents in 1856; studied with Carolus Duran in Paris; member of Society of American Artists and of Société Nationale des Beaux Arts; honorable mention, Paris Salon, 1878; medal of the second class, Paris Salon, 1881; grand prize, Exposition Universelle, Paris, 1889; chevalier of the Legion of Honor, 1889; medal, World's Columbian Exposition, 1893; Temple gold medal, Pennsylvania Academy of Fine Arts, 1894; medal of honor, Paris Exposition, 1900; gold medal, Pan American Exposition, Buffalo, 1901; gold medal of honor, Pennsylvania Academy, 1903. The portraits by Mr. Sargent are to be found in many of the public art museums of the United States and usually form a feature of the prominent art exhibitions in this country and abroad. Mr. Sargent died in London, England, April 15, 1925.

Other portraits in the collection to be found in the Speaker's lobby, placed there prior to 1911, were those of Frederick Muhlenberg, Jonathan Trumbull, John W. Taylor,

Samuel J. Randall, James G. Blaine, Charles F. Crisp, Galusha A. Grow, and David B. Henderson, of Iowa. The last-named portrait is by Freeman Thorp, who also painted the portrait of James G. Blaine. Mr. Thorp was born in Geneva, Ohio, June 16, 1844. His boyhood was spent on a farm. He became a stationary engineer at 15 years of age; served as a volunteer in the Second Ohio Cavalry during the Civil War; at the age of 20 commenced the study of art, applying himself to portrait painting. At the age of 27 he was installed in a studio built for his use on the roof of the Capitol. In this studio President Grant sat for his portrait, the work being later completed in the White House. While in Washington he painted portraits of many eminent people, among them being President Grant, Chief Justice Chase, Horace Greeley, Robert E. Lee, Charles Sumner, and Generals Sherman, Sheridan, and Gordon. Among his many portraits of prominent Americans are counted those of five Presidents, Grant, Garfield, McKinley, Cleveland, and Lincoln, the latter portrait being painted from a pencil sketch made by the artist and from vivid recollections of the martyred President. Mr. Thorp is also represented in the Speaker's lobby by the portrait of Schuyler Colfax and in the room of the House Committee on Appropriations by the portraits of Joseph G. Cannon and James A. Tawney; in the room of the House Committee on Ways and Means by the portraits of William McKinley and Claude Kitchen; and in the Senate main corridor by the portrait of President Lincoln, the last work executed by Mr. Thorp for the Capitol. He died in Brainerd, Minn., October 20, 1922.

The portrait of Frederick Muhlenberg, by Samuel B. Waugh, is one of the most interesting of the early portraits in the collection in the Speaker's lobby. It is a copy of an earlier portrait by Joseph Wright, painted at a period prior to 1800 by that celebrated artist. Mr. Waugh was born in 1814 and died in 1885. He studied in Philadelphia and abroad, and while abroad painted a number of portraits of distinguished foreigners, among them Thorwaldsen. He was for many years a prominent portrait painter of Philadelphia. His portrait of Hon. Joseph Reed Ingersoll, Member of Congress, minister to England, and president of the Pennsylvania Academy of Fine Arts, is the property of that institution.

The portraits of Galusha A. Grow and Samuel J. Randall are the work of W. A. Greaves, who was born in Watertown, N. Y., March 12, 1847; educated in and a graduate of the public schools of his birthplace, he was made an instructor of drawing when but 14 years of age. His art instruction was received under the well-known artist Thomas LeClear, and he was also a student at the Cooper Institute, New York City. He resided for several years at Utica, N. Y., removing to Warren, Pa., in 1873, where he continued to reside until his death. Among the most notable of his works, in addition to the portraits in the Speaker's lobby, are the portraits of Hon. M. S. Quay, Governor Fenton, of New York, and Gov. James A. Beaver, of Pennsylvania. He died in Warren, Pa., May 9, 1900.

The portrait of John W. Taylor is the work of Miss Caroline L. Ormes Ransom, whose biography appears in connection with the portrait of Joshua R. Giddings (p. 249).

The portrait of Jonathan Trumbull is by Harry I. Thompson, who was born in Westhaven, Conn., January 31, 1840. His business career commenced as a clerk in a country grocery in his native town. He first painted under the instruction of Benjamin Coe, a water colorist of local reputation in New Haven, Conn., whom he finally succeeded as an instructor in the drawing school. While his landscape and figure work was well received, his best work was that of a portrait painter. At the fifty-second annual exhibition of the

PORTRAIT OF FREDERICK MUHLENBERG

Samuel B. Waugh, painter

Mr. Muhlenberg was the first Speaker of the House of Representatives

National Academy of Design he exhibited a large portrait of Dr. Leonard Bacon, of Yale. He painted many portraits of governors of Connecticut now found in the library of the State capitol. He died in Westhaven, Conn., April 23, 1906.

Robert Hinckley, the painter of the portrait of Charles F. Crisp, was born in Boston, Mass., April 3, 1853; studied art in Paris from 1868 until 1884; founded in 1872 the School of Carolus Duran, where Sargent, Low, Beckwith, Fowler, and other Americans received their art education; has had a studio in Washington, D. C., since 1884, where he has painted 350 portraits of eminent Americans. He painted The First Operation with Ether for the Boston Medical Museum, and Alexander's Feast for the Arlington Hotel, Washington, D. C. He was instructor of the portrait class, Corcoran Art School, for six years; and author of the Utopian Romance, Geyserland. Another portrait by Mr. Hinckley, that of Chief Justice John Rutledge, is in the Supreme Court robing room.

This concludes the list of the portraits contained in the Speaker's lobby at the time of the passage of the resolution of March 3, 1911, which provided for 19 portraits in oil to be added to this collection. Reference to these portraits added since 1911 will be made after other art events belonging to an earlier period have been related.

In the attention given to the collection of portraits in the Speaker's lobby we have neglected for some time to refer to the progress of the different art works executed by Constantino Brumidi. His work is of such a nature that it is difficult to give a description of it in chronological sequence. In the report of the Architect of the Capitol for 1870 reference is made to the decorations of the lunettes of the walls of the reception room of the Senate. In the report of the architect dated November 1, 1871, the architect states:

The decorations of the room of the Committee on Military Affairs of the Senate have been completed by three pictures in fresco from subjects chosen by the chairman of that Committee. The decoration of the Senate reception room is progressing, leaving places to be filled in with portraits.

In the report of the architect dated November 1, 1872, we find the following reference to the work of Brumidi:

The large panel on the wall of the Senate Reception Room is being embellished by a picture of Washington, Jefferson and Hamilton, and portraits in medallion are being painted in one of the committee rooms of the Senate.

In the report of the architect dated November 1, 1874, the work of Brumidi is given the following reference:

The wall in front of the room of the Committee on Foreign Affairs of the Senate has been enriched by a picture in fresco representing the signing of the first treaty with Great Britain from a sketch by Benjamin West.

November 1, 1875, the architect in his report stated:

The following frescoes in the Senate wing have been completed: The First Treaty with Great Britain at the entrance to committee room on Foreign Affairs; the Negotiation for the Acquisition of Louisiana at the entrance to the room formerly occupied by the committee on Territories; and Belona at room on Military Affairs. Also Science, Architecture, Painting and Sculpture on the ceiling of the room of the committee on the Library, besides several figures and emblems in small lunettes in the corridor.

No further reference is given to work by Brumidi until the year 1877, when the architect in his report dated October 1 used the following language:

The belt of the rotunda intended to be enriched with basso relievos is being embellished in real fresco representing in light and shadow events in our history, arranged in chronological order, beginning with the landing of Columbus and ending with a period of our revolutionary history.

No further reference to the work of Mr. Brumidi appears in subsequent reports of the Architect of the Capitol. The pay rolls show that he was employed at a compensation of $10 per day during the years 1877, 1878, and 1879, and the work presumably was all upon the decoration of the belt of the rotunda. As Mr. Brumidi was born in 1805, he was at this time suffering from disability incident to his period of life; and while his work in actual development of the decorations may not have been continuous, it seems from correspondence in the files that at times when he was not upon the scaffold engaged in frescoing he was at work upon the cartoons necessary for the completion of the work. One letter addressed to the Architect of the Capitol, dated September 29, 1879, will probably show the condition of Mr. Brumidi's health better than in any other manner. The letter is as follows:

DEAR SIR: I received the visit of Dr. Taylor, and I hope to obtain much benefit from his prescription; but my illness is more mental than physical weakness, because my mind is much worried by the terrible future prospect of starvation as soon as my bad health prevents me from doing my daily work. I have saved nothing in the past when Fortune provided me with very profitable work.

Probably you know that when Superintendent Meigs was promoted to Quartermaster General, that Senator Foot, President pro tempore of the Senate, placed my name on the roll of the Senate employees, and while I was continuing the decoration of the basement corridor of the Senate I was continued on the pay-roll.

Now sickly and old, with 26 years service as an artist in the Capitol, I ask the comfort of being reinstated on the roll as a reward for my work, and thereby regain the tranquility of my mind.

Very respectfully,

C. BRUMIDI.

This letter seems to be the latest expression from Mr. Brumidi concerning his personal affairs, and it is very easy for those who read to understand that there is much truth in his statement that his mental troubles were greater than his physical ones. It may be that his mental troubles had pictured to him a degree of poverty which never could have existed.

Mr. Brumidi died in Washington February 19, 1880. The work which he had commenced was left in an unfinished condition, but was soon taken up by Filippo Costaggini, who was born in Rome August 13, 1837. He was a pupil at the Accademia di San Luca, Rome, the same art institute in which Brumidi had been educated, and in which Randolph Rogers was honored by election to the chair of a professorship, the oldest art academy in the world. Mr. Costaggini, however, did not know Brumidi so far as his connection with this art institute was concerned. In 1881 in the report of the architect we find the following in relation to the work upon the belt of the rotunda:

* * * Mr. Costaggini has painted in fresco on the belt of the rotunda The Settlement of New England, Oglethorp and the Indians, and Lexington. He has also completed Penn and the Indians left unfinished by Mr. Brumidi and is now engaged on the Reading of the Declaration of Independence.

It is proper to state here that Mr. Brumidi made the designs for these sections only in small size and Mr. Costaggini has had to make the full size cartoons.

While Mr. Costaggini continued his work upon this historical frieze, he did not live to complete it. It is estimated that he painted about two-thirds of the frieze as it now exists. The frieze in its incomplete condition exists in part because no satisfactory subjects have been found to complete the historical circle and for the further reason that there seems to have been a lack of interest concerning its completion. It is claimed by some that the work is better to be left as it is; by others that it is out of harmony with the architectural features of the interior of the dome. Some claim that as a work of art it has but little, if any, value. Others claim it to be one of the most interesting deco-

In the House wing, facing east grand staircase

PORTRAIT OF HENRY CLAY

John Neagle, painter

rative features of the Capitol. There are possibly as many differing opinions as there are people who care to express one, and with all these conflicting views it is probably safe to say that if this belt of the rotunda had been left undecorated until this time it is unlikely that the form of decoration used would be adopted. Mr. Costaggini, in addition to his work upon the frieze in the rotunda, painted many historical and religious pictures and was also a painter of portraits. It is claimed that one of his notable portraits is that of the late Senator Justin S. Morrill, of Vermont. Many of his decorations are said to be in cathedrals and churches of the United States, especially in New York, Philadelphia, and Baltimore. He died at his summer home, Upper Falls, Baltimore County, Md., April 13, 1907.

There are some portraits in the House wing of the Capitol other than in the Speaker's lobby which should be referred to at this time. In 1871 there was purchased a notable portrait of Henry Clay, the work of John Neagle. This portrait now hangs facing the east staircase of the House wing and it is of such large size that it would be conspicuous in any collection. Before being hung in its present location it was exhibited in Statuary Hall and probably remained there for some years after its purchase. The price paid was $1,500, and the purchase was made of Garrett C. Neagle, a son of John Neagle and a grandson of Thomas Sully. In one of his letters relating to this portrait and requesting a commission for furnishing a frame therefor, he gives an interesting reference to his grandfather, as follows:

My grandfather [Mr. Thomas Sully] met with a very serious accident some three weeks since which has compelled him to keep his bed ever since. He fell while exercising in his garden and received a compound fracture of the knee cap. His surgeon informs us a day or two since that the fracture appears to be knitting and hopes to have him out of bed in a week or ten days. This at the age of 89 seems to be impossible, but such is the fact. He is very cheerful and has been so during his entire confinement and hopes to be able to be about once more.

Mr. Sully, to whom this reference was made, is represented in the Capitol by two portraits, one of Thomas Jefferson, hanging in the Senate main corridor, and one of Andrew Jackson, also hanging in the same corridor. It may be interesting to know that the portrait of Andrew Jackson was offered to the Government in 1873 and declined and was finally purchased in 1921 at a much higher price than when first offered. The portrait of Thomas Jefferson is a very interesting example of the work of this artist. It is painted with a freedom and ease which is not noted in some of his other works. It seems to have all of the qualities of a fine portrait and less of the laborious method as exhibited in the portrait of Andrew Jackson. Mr. Sully was born in Horncastle, Lincolnshire, England, in 1783. He was taken to Charleston, S. C., by his parents; was first instructed by M. Belzons, French miniature painter, in Richmond, Va., and painted there and in Norfolk until his brother's death in 1804. He married his brother's widow and in 1806 moved to New York and lived there until 1808, except during a visit to Boston for instruction from Gilbert Stuart. He moved to Philadelphia in 1808; went to London in 1809 and studied under Benjamin West, returning in 1810; visited England in 1837, and in 1838 painted from life a portrait of Queen Victoria, from which he painted a full-length portrait of the Queen arrayed in robes of state, which now belongs to the Society of the Sons of St. George in Philadelphia. Between 1820 and 1840 he exhibited 10 portraits at the Royal Academy. A comprehensive catalogue of his work has been compiled from his diary. His death occurred in Philadelphia in 1872, the same year in which reference is made to his condition in the letter of Garrett C. Neagle.

John Neagle, the painter of the portrait of Henry Clay, was born in Boston, November 4, 1796, during a visit of his parents, who were Philadelphians. His art instruction was received from Bass Otis and Gilbert Stuart; married a stepdaughter and niece of Thomas Sully and devoted his time to portrait painting. He was a director of the Pennsylvania Academy of Fine Arts in 1830–31. He is represented in the Senate main corridor of the Capitol by a portrait of Daniel Webster. Mr. Neagle died in Philadelphia, Pa., September 17, 1865. This portrait and the portrait of Henry Clay, by Henry F. Darby, and a portrait of John C. Calhoun, by the same artist, were at one time the property

PORTRAIT OF ANDREW JACKSON

Thomas Sully, painter

THOMAS SULLY
Self-portrait

Represented by portraits of Thomas Jefferson and Andrew Jackson

PORTRAIT OF JOHN NEAGLE
I. L. Williams, painter
Neagle is represented by portraits of Henry Clay and Daniel Webster

{ 293 }

of M. B. Brady, the celebrated photographer, who sold these portraits to the Government. At one time one of these portraits was erroneously marked as a portrait by Brady. At the time of the sale of these portraits Mr. Brady furnished a statement to the Joint Committee on the Library in which he claimed that the painters of these portraits made their sketches in his studio while he was making daguerreotypes of these distinguished patrons. Those acquainted with the work of John Neagle and Henry F. Darby do not feel at all inclined to the belief that they were aided in their work by recourse to photography.

Earlier in this work reference has been made to the portrait of Henry Laurens, by John Singleton Copley. At that time it was stated that this work was secured through the kind offices of the Corcoran Gallery of Art. Upon consideration it is thought that a portrait of so much importance deserves a more detailed statement relating to its purchase. Its sale was offered by Henry Stevens & Son, of 4 Trafalgar Square, Charing Cross, W. C., London, by a letter dated December 3, 1885, and addressed to Anthony Hyde, secretary of the Corcoran Gallery of Art, Washington. In this letter, after giving historical facts relating to Mr. Laurens, which are well known and which have heretofore been stated, the following points are included in the summary:

> The chief points of interest about the picture are,
> I—Portrait of a President of Congress.
> II—Painted while in the Tower as a prisoner.
> III—Painted by Copley, the distinguished American artist.
> IV—Pedigree of the picture perfectly satisfactory.

> It was painted by Copley for Hollis one of the benefactors of Harvard College. It was hung for more than 100 years in the hall of the family mansion of the Hollises "The Hyde near Ingalstone Essex." Thomas Hollis bequeathed his estate and property to Thomas Brand Hollis, and he in his turn left the estate and possessions to his friend John Disney in whose family the "Hyde" has continued to date. This old establishment long in the family has just been broken up and the contents of the house sold by auction.

> Copley's intimacy with the Hollis family may be inferred by there being now preserved in the Gallery of Harvard College portraits of more than one member of the family painted by Copley and presented by the family to the college. Copley also painted another John Adams when in London and Adams was very intimate with Hollis. (See Disney's Memoirs of Thomas Brand Hollis.)

> This portrait of Laurens does not appear to be known while another portrait by the same artist appears to have been engraved, though we are unable to ascertain for the moment where the original of the engraved portrait is.

> The portrait is in capital condition and the frame bears the name of Copley. The inscriptions on the portrait and the view of the Tower in the background add to its interest.

> We should esteem it as a favour if you will kindly give us a decision by cable as soon as possible, whether you would care to have the picture sent for inspection. Our registered address is Muller, London, and words or Decline} Send }Laurens will be quite sufficient instruction to us.

> The price is two thousand guineas (Pounds 210) and we give you the definite refusal of it till we hear from you.

> We are Sir, your obedient Servants,
>   (Signed)   HENRY STEVENS & SON.

We wish to invite attention to a paragraph above:

> This portrait of Laurens does not appear to be known while another portrait by the same artist appears to have been engraved, though we are unable to ascertain for the moment where the original of the engraved portrait is.

This paragraph becomes important owing to the fact that there was imported to this country early in the year 1920 a portrait of Laurens, by Copley, which had been engraved and of which engravings were in existence, although it was supposed that the original painting had been burned. The appearance of this portrait after a space of some 60 years created quite an excitement in art circles, and the letter above referred to was considered to be an important factor in clearing up the mystery surrounding this portrait which made its appearance in 1920. The portrait of Laurens in the Capitol was referred to and cited as a well-known example of the style of Copley and his particular form of expression in the portrait painting of Henry Laurens. How the controversy ended we have never learned.

During the period from 1870 to 1880 we have given some little attention to the sculptural work in the Capitol in so far as it relates to the statues in Statuary Hall. It will be remembered that the south pediment of the Capitol was still vacant and that many of the sculptors of the country considered this as a suitable field in which to display their ability. We find in the records of the office of the Architect of the Capitol the following letter, which will serve to show that interest in the House pediment had not subsided with the ineffectual attempts of Henry Kirke Brown and Erastus Dow Palmer:

PORTRAIT OF HENRY LAURENS
John Singleton Copley, painter
This portrait was painted while Mr. Laurens was a prisoner in the Tower of London. Now in the room of the Senate Committee on Post Offices and Post Roads

ARCHITECT'S OFFICE,
U. S. CAPITOL EXTENSION,
Washington, D. C., April 16, 1870.

L. THOMPSON, Esq.
Studio Bldg. 4th St.
New York.

DEAR SIR: Captain Adams has favored me with your description for a group for the South Pediment of the Capitol. I freely say that I like your design— Peace and Abundance—better than any that has been offered.

It would be well to make a sketch or small model, to submit to the committee. This could be done at your convenience, as I do not believe Congress will take any action on the subject this session. The right time in my judgment to press this will be early next session. In case the Committee desire to consider the subject this session I will inform you.

My reason for saying that nothing will be done by Congress this session is based on their action in the case of young Mills, whose design was, by resolution of the House, referred to the committee on Public Buildings and Grounds, and they decided not to act on the subject of enriching the pediment in question this session.

Very respectfully, your obt. servant,

EDWARD CLARK, *Architect.*

It does not appear that the sculptors referred to were able to convince Congress of the necessity of providing statuary for the House pediment, for it was 39 years after the above correspondence before a commission was given for the statuary for the pediment of the south wing. The completion of this commission really marked the completion of the House wing of the Capitol, but the Capitol as yet has not been completed in accordance with the plan prepared by Thomas U. Walter, who had provided for an extension of the east front of the central portion of the Capitol to such an extent that the dome would be located equidistant between the east and west fronts of the Capitol.

When the first statues were received from the States under the invitation from the President to furnish two statues from each State for Statuary Hall, this invitation was evidently construed to refer simply to statues and not to the pedestals upon which the statues were located. It appears from correspondence between the office of the Architect of the Capitol and the Governor of the State of Connecticut that there was an implied promise upon the part of the Government to provide pedestals for such statues as were received from the States. Just how this implication gained ground we do not know. We find in a letter of October 26, 1871, to Hon. Marshall Jewell, Governor of the State of Connecticut, the following statement:

The statues will be on temporary pedestals for the present, it being the intention of Congress to provide proper ones for all statues. * * *

That temporary pedestals were used there can be no doubt, for references to temporary pedestals are found for some years subsequent to the installation of the first statues furnished by the States, but at length the rule seemed to be firmly established that the Government would not provide permanent pedestals, and so far as any record has been found all of the pedestals in Statuary Hall have been furnished by the States from which the statues were received.

A further reference to statuary, that belonging to a much earlier period of the Capitol, is found in the report of the architect for 1871. This also contains a reference to the preparation which was made for the relocation of the Rogers bronze doors:

* * * The statuary of the central portico has been cleaned by means of the chisel, all other methods tried proving ineffectual owing, I believe, to the injudicious use of acids in former cleanings.

There can be no doubt but that the marble of the two statues referred to, War and Peace, by Luigi Persico, is in a very bad and unsafe condition. In 1921 it became necessary to make some repairs and restoration of these two statues, and it was then found that portions of the marble, cut away in order that missing parts might be supplied, were in such a damaged and softened condition that small pieces of the marble rubbed between the finger and thumb were easily reduced to the condition of white sand. The report further continues:

The old doorway at the central entrance of the east front has been cut away to make space for the bronze doors and a new doorway supplied. * * *

Another portrait of prominence which at one time hung in Statuary Hall is the full-length portrait of Washington, by Charles Willson Peale, now hanging on the west gallery front of the Senate and facing the Battle of Chapultepec. That it was first hung in Statuary Hall is shown by a letter of W. A. Smith, librarian of the House of Representatives, under date of May 16, 1882, and addressed to Hon. Anson G. McCook, chairman of the Joint Committee on the Library. In this letter complaint is made that the picture is so hung "that it shuts off the light from the window." He also states that Members have complained about the lack of light in the library and have requested that the painting be removed. The letter was referred by Mr. McCook to Mr. Spofford for suggestion or action. In the catalogue of the National Gallery of Art, edition of 1909, it is stated that in 1882 Congress appropriated $5,000 in settlement of the claim of Titian R. Peale, by whom it was claimed that the Peale family had never been properly paid for this picture; that Congress acquired this picture in 1882 seems evident from the letter of the librarian of the House of Representatives before referred to.

This portrait has an interesting history. It bears date of 1779 and is signed by the artist, Charles Willson Peale. Its early history has never been satisfactorily explained, but it was evidently sent to Europe to be sold, probably about the time it was painted.

In the Senate wing, gallery floor, facing west staircase

PORTRAIT OF GEORGE WASHINGTON

Charles Willson Peale, painter

{ 297 }

It was brought back to this country from France by Julius, Count de Menou, from whom it was purchased in October, 1841, by Mr. Charles B. Calvert, of Prince Georges County, Md., for the sum of $200. The latter placed it with the National Institute in Washington, and in 1862 it was turned over to the Smithsonian Institution. It was sent to Philadelphia in 1876 for exhibition in connection with the Centennial Exposition and afterwards remained at the Pennsylvania Academy of Fine Arts until 1881, when it was recalled by the Smithsonian and loaned to the Corcoran Gallery of Art. A claim to ownership of the picture by Titian R. Peale, a son of Charles Willson Peale, was decided adversely by the Board of Regents of the Smithsonian Institution in 1873 on the ground that sufficient proof had not been presented, but in 1882 Congress appropriated $5,000 in settlement of the claim, and the portrait was transferred to the Capitol, where it now hangs. It has been stated by Charles Henry Hart that this picture is but one of many duplications by Mr. Peale of a portrait painted in the first part of 1778. Concerning this allegation we wish to submit material found in The Crayon (vol. 2, pp. 388, 389), in which the following language appears:

The earliest original of the Pater Patriæ is the portrait of Col. Washington painted by Charles Wilson [Willson] Peale in 1772, and now in fine preservation at Arlington House. * * * Next in order of succession we have a full length of the Commander-in-Chief, painted by Peale in 1779, during the revolution, * * * In 1790 appeared the equestrian portrait of the chief by Colonel Trumbull. * * * In 1789 the First President lost his teeth and the artificial ones with which he was furnished answering very imperfectly the purposes for which they were intended, a marked change occurred in the appearance of his face, more especially in the projection of the under lip which forms so distinguishing a feature in the works of Stuart and others who painted portraits of the great man subsequent to 1789.

The above article is from George W. P. Custis, a member of the family of Washington. Is it not reasonable to presume that his opportunities for correct information upon the subject of the dates of the various portraits of Washington is as worthy of belief as even so great an authority as Charles Henry Hart?

This portrait is remarkable for several reasons, one being the fact that it is stated by what is considered unquestioned authority to be the only painting of its period in which a correct representation of the American flag as it then existed is shown; aside from this, the work being that of the pioneer painter of the Peale family, Charles Willson Peale, and an excellent example of his work, is an added reason for its attractiveness. Again, and notwithstanding the time which has elapsed since it was painted, the fact of its having been carried twice across the ocean and moved from one place to another a number of times and it still remaining in such a fine state of preservation, gives it a value which is possessed by but few portraits of that day.

The biography of Charles Willson Peale is of special interest, as he belonged to the class of painters who were self-reliant and obtained a foothold by being self-taught. He was born in Chestertown, Md., April 15, 1741; began his life as a saddler; pursued portrait painting without regular instruction until 1768; then went to England and resided in the household of Benjamin West; returned to this country in 1770; painted at Mount Vernon the earliest authentic portrait of Washington, May, 1772. He is said to have painted Washington from life fourteen times. Was one of the founders of the Pennsylvania Academy of the Fine Arts, in 1805, and a director until 1810. He died in Philadelphia February 2, 1827.

CHAPTER XVI

WORKS OF ART IN SENATE WING, GALLERY FLOOR

ON THE gallery floor of the Senate wing, in that portion of the lobby which extends to the north side of the building, may be seen two notable landscapes, the work of Thomas Moran. One is entitled "The Grand Canyon of the Yellowstone," the other "The Chasm of the Colorado." These paintings, as well as the paintings of Bierstadt in the House wing of the Capitol, referred to earlier in this work, belong to the best class of works of the landscape painters of the period of the production of these paintings. While the paintings of Bierstadt represent historical epochs relating to discoveries of portions of this country and are, therefore, to a certain extent dependent upon the imagination of the painter, the paintings of Moran are accurate topographical illustrations of the scenery of the western country, probably approaching in accuracy the work of the camera without any of the finicky sharpness or faulty perspective of the lens. Moran in his coloring, as well as in his draftsmanship, leaves but little to be desired, and these paintings are full of beauty and give to those who are unable to behold these far distant examples of natural beauty an admirable idea of the charm of the western country. A brother of Thomas Moran, Edward Moran, was a notable marine painter. His technic was entirely different from that of Thomas Moran. He painted with a breadth that was somewhat unusual except to the close adherents of the Barbizon school. Another member of the Moran family, John Moran, was quite celebrated as a photographer. Thomas Moran was born in Bolton, Lancashire, England, January 12, 1837, of Irish-English parents, and died at Santa Barbara, Calif., August 26, 1926. He was brought to this country at the age of 7 and after a fair education in the public schools of Philadelphia was apprenticed to a wood engraver, as the youth had shown an unmistakable aptitude for drawing. After two years at engraving he left it to begin the practice of art without a master and had the skill to succeed. He picked up instruction from the painters of his acquaintance in Philadelphia, especially from James Hamilton, who well suited the boy's imaginative temperament. In 1856 he exhibited his first picture in oil. In 1861 he went to London and studied and copied the works of the great artist, Turner. In 1867 he traveled in France, Germany, and Italy, studying the old masters. He accompanied the expedition under Professor Hayden to the Yellowstone country in 1871, and on his return painted the Grand Canyon of the Yellowstone, which was purchased by the Government and is now in the Capitol. In 1873 he accompanied Maj. J. W. Powell to the chasm of the Colorado in Arizona. The picture bearing this title was also purchased by the Government. An extensive traveler in the western part of this country, he was deeply impressed with its wild and majestic scenery; and although he had traveled extensively in Europe, the most of his paintings are of American subjects, he holding the belief that the true artist can produce the best work from the subjects of his own country. The two pictures referred to are the only illustrations of the work of Mr. Moran in the Capitol Building.

Another notable example of historical painting in the Senate wing of the Capitol is that known as the Recall of Columbus, by Augustus George Heaton. While this painting was acquired at a later date than the Moran paintings, it is thought best at this

Photograph by the Glendhills

THOMAS MORAN, N. A. (1837–1926)

Represented by the paintings, Grand Canyon of the Yellowstone and Chasm of the Colorado

{ 300 }

THE GRAND CANYON OF THE YELLOWSTONE

Thomas Moran, painter

In the Senate wing, north lobby, gallery floor

THE RECALL OF COLUMBUS
A. G. Heaton, painter

In the Senate wing, gallery floor, facing the painting The Battle of Lake Erie

time to refer to it in order that the prominent paintings in the Senate wing of the Capitol be discussed before turning our attention to art works in other portions of the building. This painting was completed in 1883 from studies made in Spain and represents, as the title shows, the turning point in the life of Columbus, who had left what had first seemed to him a possible chance of assistance in his voyage of discovery, feeling that the last chance had failed. The painting was exhibited at the exposition in Chicago, and the 50-cent postage stamp of the Columbian series had its origin in this painting. The painting hangs facing The Battle of Lake Erie, by Powell, and occupies the same position with reference to this battle scene that the portrait of Washington on the west gallery front occupies to The Battle of Chapultepec. The painter, Augustus George Heaton, was born in Philadelphia, Pa., April 28, 1844. From 1860 he studied at the Pennsylvania Academy of Fine Arts and under P. F. Rothermel; exhibited his first picture at the Academy of Fine Arts in 1863; and in the fall of that year went to Paris, where he was the first American to enter the École des Beaux Arts, then first opened to Americans, studying in this school for two years in the class of Cabanel. In 1866 he became art professor and lecturer at the School of Design for Women in Philadelphia and an associate of the Pennsylvania Academy of Fine Arts in 1868; moved to New York, where he resided for several years, and in 1878 went to Paris for the second time and studied under Bonnat; exhibited in the Paris Salon four times, his most notable exhibit being The Bathing Hour, Trouville. He returned to the United States late in 1884 and resided in Washington, D. C., until 1908, when he removed to New York. Among his works are Washington's First Mission, owned by the Union League Club, Philadelphia; portrait of Bishop Bowman for Cornell College, Iowa; portrait group of Mr. Tulane and Senator Gibson for Tulane University, New Orleans; Promoters of the Library of Congress, a group containing 18 prominent statesmen and others, now in the Young Men's Christian Association, Washington, D. C.; Graduation Day; The Day Spring from on High; Grave of Lafayette; and many portraits and other small pictures. As an author he has published the epic poem, The Heart of David, and Fancies and Thought in Verse, also Mint Marks, which is considered an authority on that subject. He is a member of several clubs, and notwithstanding his advanced years he is still interested in painting and publishes for the entertainment of his friends a quarterly publication known as The Nut Shell.

Hanging in the same room or corridor where the two paintings by Thomas Moran are located is a small painting entitled "Table Rock, Niagara." The painting is hanging in a light which is exceedingly flat and unsatisfactory for the exhibition of this work, but in color it is far above the average, although some may consider the point of view of the composition poorly selected. However, it gives us an excellent idea of Niagara in the wintertime, a subject exploited frequently by the photographic art, but to which the painters have given but little attention. This work was presented to the Government in 1899 by Miss Alice Louisa Thompson in fulfillment of a request made by her sister, Mrs. Charles Carroll, of Doughoregan Manor, Md., who wished to donate it in memory of her husband, Charles Carroll. The painter of this work, F. Regis Gignoux, was born in Lyons, France, in 1816. He was educated at Fribourg and at the Academy of St. Pierre in Lyons, where he received an annual premium. Subsequently he entered the School of Fine Arts in Paris and was also a pupil of Delaroche; emigrated to the United States in 1844; was elected a member of the Academy of Design in 1851; was the first president of the Brooklyn Art Academy; returned to France in 1870 and resided there until his death. Among his best known works are Virginia in Indian Summer, Niagara in Winter, Bernese Alps by Sunrise, the Four Seasons in America, the Dismal Swamp, and Moonlight on the Saguenay. The painter died in France in 1882.

AUGUSTUS G. HEATON

Represented by the painting, The Recall of Columbus

{ 304 }

REGIS GIGNOUX, N. A. (1814–1882)

Represented by the painting, Table Rock, Niagara, in the Senate wing, gallery
floor, north lobby

A notable painting hanging in the east staircase of the House wing of the Capitol is the Emancipation Proclamation, or, as stated by its full title, "The First Reading of the Emancipation Proclamation Before the Cabinet by President Lincoln." This picture is of especial interest on account of its historical significance, its inclusion of the portraits of President Lincoln and his Cabinet, and the additional fact that it was painted in the White House and that during the progress of the work it was frequently inspected and commented upon by President Lincoln. The picture after its completion was placed on exhibition in various cities of the United States. It may be of interest to know

THE FIRST READING OF THE EMANCIPATION PROCLAMATION

Francis Bicknell Carpenter, painter

In the House wing, east staircase

KEY TO THE FIRST READING OF THE EMANCIPATION PROCLAMATION

1. Abraham Lincoln
   President
2. William H. Seward
   Secretary of State
3. Salmon P. Chase
   Secretary of the Treasury
4. Edwin M. Stanton
   Secretary of War

5. Gideon Welles
   Secretary of the Navy
6. Edward Bates
   Attorney General
7. Montgomery Blair
   Postmaster General
8. Caleb B. Smith
   Secretary of the Interior

how such a large canvas could be safely transported about the country, the size of the canvas being 14 feet 6 inches long by 9 feet in height. To facilitate its transportation, joints were placed in the frame which allowed the picture to fold over upon itself from each end, thus reducing it within convenient size. Creasing was prevented by laying a light and softly covered roller within the canvas at each folding place, and the whole, being firmly screwed together and boxed, could be transported in perfect security. An interesting story not heretofore published concerning the zeal of the painter, F. B. Carpenter, while engaged upon this work was told to the writer only a few years since. It seems that during the time while the picture was being painted Mr. Carpenter, with his wife, resided at one of the Washington hotels where Members of Congress were also making their home. One morning at the breakfast table Mrs. Carpenter stated that her husband had been gone the entire night and that she was greatly worried for fear some harm might have occurred. Some one at the table, who evidently knew of Mr. Carpenter's complete absorption in the work on which he was engaged, suggested that he was probably at the White House working upon the painting, and accordingly one of the guests at the table immediately started for the White House and found Mr. Carpenter at work entirely oblivious of the fact that the daylight had come, and lights were unnecessary, that it was breakfast time, and that he had a wife who might be anxious to know what had become of him.

As has been stated, the picture was exhibited in various cities of the United States and finally, in 1878, was presented to the Government by Mrs. Elizabeth Thompson. This presentation was a matter of more than ordinary importance. So far as known it was the first occasion when a painting of such great value had been given to the Government by a private individual. Its acceptance was made the subject of Public Resolution No. 6 of the Forty-fifth Congress, as follows:

Whereas, Mrs. Elizabeth Thompson of New York City, has tendered to Congress Carpenter's painting of President Lincoln and his Cabinet at the time of his first reading of the Proclamation of Emancipation: Therefore,

Resolved by the Senate and House of Representatives of the United States of America in Congress assembled, That said painting is hereby accepted in the name of the people of the United States; and the thanks of Congress are tendered to the donor for her generous and patriotic gift.

And be it further resolved, That the Joint Committee on the Library are hereby instructed to make arrangements for the formal presentation of said painting to Congress, on Tuesday, the twelfth of February next; and said committee shall cause said painting to be placed in an appropriate and conspicuous place in the Capitol, and shall carefully provide for its preservation.

And be it further resolved, That the President is requested to cause a copy of these resolutions to be forwarded to Mrs. Thompson. (Approved, February 1, 1878.) (Public Resolution No. 6, 45th Cong., 2d sess.)

As has been indicated by the resolution, the arrangements for the presentation of the painting to Congress were in charge of the Joint Committee on the Library. A joint session of both Houses of Congress was arranged for and resolutions were passed providing for the admission to the floor of the House of relatives of President Lincoln and of the members of the Cabinet at the time when the events portrayed in this painting occurred. Upon the day appointed the House, after it transacted some routine business, recessed until the time selected for the presentation exercises. As the time for the joint session approached the Members of the Senate, headed by the Vice President and the Sergeant at Arms, entered the Hall of the House and were given seats on the floor of the House. Vice President William A. Wheeler presided, and the presentation speech was delivered by James A. Garfield, later a President of the United States. Mr. Garfield in his remarks spoke upon the great value of the painting on account of its preservation of a historical event which would not be kept in mind with all of the circumstances surrounding it but for this picture made at the White House before the room used for Cabinet meetings had been altered and adapted to other purposes. He also referred to the correspondence which had occurred between Horace Greeley and President Lincoln concerning the liberation of the slaves, and of President Lincoln's reply that his chief duty and main object was to save the Union. After the remarks by General Garfield, Alexander H. Stephens, a Representative from Georgia and at one time the Vice President of the Confederacy, spoke upon the presentation and acceptance of the picture. It happened that Mr. Stephens had known Abraham Lincoln, as they had both served as Members of the House of Representatives during the Thirtieth Congress. It also happened that Mr. Stephens was born on February 11 and that Abraham Lincoln was born on February 12,

although Mr. Lincoln was three years his senior. He spoke feelingly upon his acquaintance with Mr. Lincoln and said that probably but one other Member of the Thirtieth Congress (Mr. Toombs) was better acquainted with Mr. Lincoln than himself. He spoke of the rare qualities which placed him intellectually as much above other men as he was physically taller than others. Referring to the emancipation proclamation, he emphasized strongly what had been referred to by Mr. Garfield—that is, the desire of Mr. Lincoln to save the Union rather than to destroy slavery—and directed attention to the fact that the emancipation proclamation only emancipated such slaves as were found in States which were then under insurrection to the General Government, and also to the fact that the final liberty of the slaves was due to

FRANCIS BICKNELL CARPENTER

Represented by the painting, The First Reading of the Emancipation Proclamation (Lincoln and his Cabinet)

legislative enactment in which all of the States joined. The address of Mr. Stephens was marked by high patriotic sentiment, and there was lacking any attempt at apologies or any regrets over changed conditions.

Turning from the consideration of paintings, it may be well at this time to refer to the statue of Edward Dickinson Baker. This statue, the work of Horatio Stone, is now and has been for many years—in fact, since the necessity arose for taking out of Statuary Hall statues which were not presented by the States—located in the rotunda. It has a somewhat peculiar history in that it was purchased by an act of Congress which followed shortly after an unfavorable report from the Committee on the Library. While the Committee on the Library always has been considered to be an efficient body and well equipped to assist the Congress in the selection of works of art, still at times Congress has preferred to do its own thinking, and upon this occasion acted contrary to the advice of the Joint Committee on the Library. The report to which reference has

STATUE OF EDWARD DICKINSON BAKER

Horatio Stone, sculptor

The first statue to be erected in the Rotunda in honor of a soldier of the Civil War

{ 310 }

been made is known as Senate Report No. 331, Forty-second Congress, third session, and was presented on the 24th of January, 1873. The report is as follows:

The Joint Committee on the Library, to whom was referred House bill No. 2762, entitled "An Act providing for a life size marble statue of the late Senator Edward Dickinson Baker," have attentively considered the same and report that—

The proposition is that the Congress of the United States shall provide a marble statue of one of its late members, to be placed in the National Capitol.

The hesitation to recommend a favorable consideration of the measure, the committee desire to state, arises from no lack of appreciation of the character and services, the eloquence and patriotism, of the distinguished man, the subject of it.

The instances are believed to be rare and exceptional where a legislative body has sought to commemorate its associates, living or dead, by the production of their effigies in sculpture or painting, to be displayed in the theater of their common action. The novelty of such a proceeding could not fail to elicit remark were the propriety and expediency less questionable.

If this were not so, an embarrassment quite insurmountable must needs be encountered in any attempt to perpetuate such a practice. The obvious difficulty of determining where to begin would only be less than where to end, as the latter would devolve upon those who come after.

Once entered upon, it is not perceived that the limitations could well be prescribed or enforced; and so the work of multiplying images of departed members must go on, defying alike all distinction or preeminence, and ending only with the capacity of the Capitol to contain more.

Notwithstanding this unfavorable report, in which the reasoning seems justly entitled to due consideration, Congress a little later enacted the following statute:

* * * And of the $15,000 appropriated by act of June 10, 1872, to enable said Committee to purchase works of art, the sum of $10,000. is hereby declared to have been appropriated for the purpose of providing for a statue of the late Edward Dickinson Baker. (Stats. L., vol. 17, p. 513.) (Approved March 3, 1873.)

In this instance the Congress seemed inclined to issue explicit instructions concerning some of the funds which at an earlier date had been placed wholly within the discretion of the Joint Committee on the Library for disbursement. It is difficult indeed to say whether such a course is preferable under all circumstances, but of late years it has been the custom to make specific appropriations, setting forth in the enactment the purpose for which the money intended for works of art is to be expended. While it may be questioned whether the Congress or the Joint Committee on the Library is the better judge as to what works of art should be purchased for the Capitol, there is much truth contained in the report above quoted. If an indiscriminate purchase of works of art should be continued, it would be indeed difficult to determine wisely what should or should not be added to the collection already existing.

Perhaps one of the most popular pictures to the average tourist through the Capitol, among the paintings in the Senate wing, is the painting of the Electoral Commission, the work of Cornelia Adele Fassett. The work is popular for the reason that it contains such a large number of well-painted portraits of Senators, Justices of the Supreme Court, and Members of the House of Representatives who were conspicuous in the history of the country during the period of the late seventies. This commission held its meetings in the Supreme Court room, and the view shown in the picture is the interior of that celebrated room. It is unfortunate that it hangs in such a light that the explanatory key can not be referred to by those who are interested in identifying the many portraits contained in this picture. Some have said that the picture lacks a degree of composition which is required in all works of this kind, and to this the reply might be made that it was not painted for the purpose of demonstrating a rule of composition, but for the purpose of bringing to the beholder a vivid message of the conditions existing while this

THE FLORIDA ELECTORAL COMMISSION

Cornelia A. Fassett, painter

THE ELECTORAL COMMISSION

IN THE CITIES

ON THE MAIN FLOOR

THE ELECTORAL COMMISSION

IN THE GALLERY

(THE PRESS)

1. W. H. Roberts......New Orleans Times.
2. John M. Carson......New York Times.
3. Ben. Perley Poore......Boston Journal.
4. George W. Adams......New York World.
5. T. C. Crawford......Chicago Times.
6. A. M. Gibson......New York Sun.
7. W. Scott Smith......New York Evening Post.
8. C. W. Fitch......Pittsburgh Chronicle.
9. H. V. Boynton......Cincinnati Gazette.
10. Wilson J. Vance......Cincinnati Commercial.
11. Mrs. Jane G. Swisshelm......N. Y. Associated Press.
12. L. A. Gobright......("Grace Greenwood"), N. Y. Times.
13. Mrs. S. J. Lippincott......("Miss Grundy"), N. Y. Graphic.
14. Miss Austine Snead......Toledo Blade, &c.
15. Miss Emma Janes......Home Journal.
16. Mrs. Mary E. Nealy......New York Tribune.
17. Mrs. M. D. Lincoln......("Bessie Beech") Cleveland Plaindealer.
18. Miss Sallie Woodbury......("Ruby Wood") National Union.
19. Mrs. Fannie B. Ward......New Orleans Picayune.
20. Miss Adele M. Garrigues......Courier, East Saginaw, Mich.
21. W. M. Olin......Boston Advertiser.
22. W. O. Fishback......St. Louis Republican.
23. DeB. R. Keim......Philadelphia Press.
24. Crosby S. Noyes......New York Evening Post.
25. James R. Young......Ed. Evening Star, Washington, D. C.
26. W. E. Curtis......Philadelphia Evening Star.
27. E. B. Wight......Chicago Tribune.
28. E. H. Luther......Boston Post.
29. Charles Nordhoff......New York Herald.
30. Clifford Warden......Pittsburgh Telegraph.
31. F. A. Richardson......Baltimore Sun.
32. E. V. Smalley......New York Tribune.
33. L. Q. Washington......Louisville Courier-Journal.
34. Mrs. E. S. Cromwell......Chicago Herald.
35. Mrs. Nellie S. Stowell......Kansas City Journal.
36. Mrs. Fayetta C. Snead......("Fay") Louisville Courier-Journal.
37. Mrs. A. J. Rowland......Oxford (Pa.) Press.
38. Frank Hatton......Ed. Burlington Hawkeye.
39. E. Stoddarth Johnson......Ed. Frankfort Yeoman.
40. A. C. Buell......The Capitol.
41. Mrs. A. D. Johnston......Rochester Democrat and Chronicle.
42. Miss Mary E. Mann......Troy Daily Times.
43. Charles L. Flanagan......Philadelphia North American.
44. Mrs. Elvira Bliss Sheldon......("Aunt True") Grand Rapids Eagle.
45. W. Harry Clarke......National Associated Press.
46. I. N. Burritt......Ed. Washington Herald.
47. C. Cathcart Taylor......Philadelphia Times.
48. Wm. P. Copeland......New York Commercial Bulletin.
49. E. F. Waters......Prop. Boston Advertiser.
50. J. Edwards Clarke......New York Mail.
51. Jno. C. Burch......Ed. Nashville American.
52. Wm. Goddard......Ed. Boston Advertiser.
53. Howard Carroll......New York Times.
54. S. H. Kauffmann......Evening Star.
55. Wm. C. MacBride......Cincinnati Enquirer.
56. Z. L. White......New York Tribune.
57. Edwin Fleming......N. Y. Journal of Commerce.
58. L. W. Kennedy......Daily Chronicle, Washington, D. C.
59. M. J. Dee......Detroit Evening News.
60. George Douglas......Washington Capital.
61. Mr. Parr......Pittsburgh Post.
62. Mrs. G. W. Thomson......Journal.

ON THE MAIN FLOOR

17. William Windom......Senator, Minnesota.
18. W. W. Corcoran......
19. J. C. S. Blackburn......Member of Congress, Kentucky.
20. J. J. Ingalls......Senator, Kansas.
21. John D. Reagan......Member of Congress, Texas.
22. B. E. Catlin......Assistant Secretary Electoral Com.
23. George A. Howard......Assistant Secretary Electoral Com.
24. James H. McKenny......Secretary Electoral Commission.
25. John Sherman......Senator, Ohio.
26. Samuel Shellabarger......Counsel for Hayes.
27. William F. Cooper......Page to Electoral Commission.
28. D. F. Murphy......Stenographer Electoral Commission.
29. George W. McCrary......M. C., Iowa, and counsel for Hayes.
30. Morrison R. Waite......Chief Justice, U. S. S. C.
31. John G. Thompson......Sergeant at Arms, H. R.
32. John J. Nicolay......Marshal, U. S. S. C.
33. W. H. Reardon......Marshal Electoral Commission.
34. E. P. Cornizier......Messenger, U. S. Senate.
35. Mrs. Z. Chandler......
36. Miss G. A. Boutwell......
37. John R. French......Sergeant at Arms, U. S. Senate.
38. Miss G. F. Tucker......
39. Mrs. Charles E. Hooker......
40. Miss Caroline Bradley......
41.
42. Miss Lida Miller......
43. Miss Julia D. Strong......
44. Prof. Joseph Henry......Smithsonian Institution.
45. Charles G. Williams......Member of Congress, Wisconsin.
46. Mrs. S. Virginia Fidd......
47. Mrs. Mary A. Matthews......
48. Mrs. Ruth A. Hoar......
49. Mrs. Chapman Coleman......
50. Hamilton Fish......Secretary of State.
51. Mrs. Julia K. Fish......
52. Mrs. Myra Clark Gabions......
53. Mrs. Julia G. Tyler......(Widow of Ex-President Tyler.)
54. Mrs. I. V. Swearingen......
55. Mrs. Virginia M. Wilson......
56. Mrs. Rachael H. Strong......
57. Charles Gordon......
58. Mrs. Imogen R. Morrill......
59. Mrs. Jean M. Lander......
60. Miss Katharine Lee Bayard......
61. John J. Patterson......Senator, South Carolina.
62. Mrs. Catherine Hardenbergh......
63. John H. Flagg......Legislative Clerk, U. S. Senate.
64. John Hitz......Consul General of Switzerland.
65. Charles Page Bryan......
66. George M. Adams......Clark, House of Representatives.
67. Horatio King......
68. S. W. Dorsey......Senator, Arkansas.
69. M. B. Brady......
70. Ambrose E. Burnside......Senator, Rhode Island.
71. George C. Gorham......Secretary, U. S. Senate.
72. Samuel J. Randall......Speaker, House of Representatives.
73. F. M. Cockrell......Senator, Missouri.
74. J. Proctor Knott......Member of Congress, Kentucky.
75. John B. Clark, Jr......Member of Congress, Missouri.
76. H. B. Anthony......Senator, Rhode Island.
77. Bainbridge Wadleigh......Senator, New Hampshire.
78. Benjamin H. Hill......Senator, Georgia.
79. Fernando Wood......Member of Congress, New York.
80. A. C. Harmer......Member of Congress, Pennsylvania.
81. Amanias Herbert......Doorkeeper, U. S. Supreme Court.
82. G. A. Clark......Member of Congress, New Jersey.
83. Augustus W. Cutler......
84. A. R. Shepherd......
85. S. L. Phelps......Commissioner, District of Columbia.
86. J. W. Powell......United States Survey.
87. S. A. Hurlburt......M. C., Illinois, and counsel for Hayes.
88. John A. Kasson......M. C., Iowa, and counsel for Hayes.
89. George W. Chittle......
90. James L. Andrm......Reporter for N. Y. Associated Press.
91. Stanley Matthews......Counsel for Hayes.
92. Mrs. J. A. Garfield......
93. George M. Robeson......Secretary of Navy.
94. Alphonso M. Taft......Secretary of War.
95. Belva M. Lockwood......
96. George S. Boutwell......Senator, Massachusetts.
97. Aaron A. Sargent......Senator, California.
98. Dr. Peter Parker......
99. James O. Woodruff......Scientific Expedition.
100. Eugene Hale......Member of Congress, Maine.
101. Charles Foster......Member of Congress, Ohio.
102. John H. Mitchell......Senator, Oregon.
103. W. P. Lynde......Member of Congress, Wisconsin.
104. John D. C. Atkins......Member of Congress, Tennessee.
105. A. A. Hardenbergh......Member of Congress, New Jersey.
106. Thomas Ewing......Member of Congress, Ohio.
107. William E. Chandler......Counsel for Hayes.
108. James P. Root......Counsel for Hayes.
109. James N. Tyner......Postmaster-General.
110. William Lawrence......M. C., Ohio, counsel for Hayes.
111. D. T. Corbin......
112. C. D. Drake......Chief Justice, U. S. Court of Claims.
113. Charles W. Jones......Senator, Florida.
114. P. Phillips......
115. Saunders W. Johnston......Member of Congress, Mass.
116. N. P. Banks......
117. J. G. Cannon......Member of Congress, Illinois.
118. Elizabeth B. Johnston......
119. Flora Fassett......
120. W. A. J. Sparks......Member of Congress, Illinois.
121. Frederick Douglass......
122. William M. Evarts......Counsel for Hayes.
123. Edwin W. Stoughton......Counsel for Hayes.
124. Zachariah Chandler......Secretary of the Interior.
125. Abram S. Hewitt......Member of Congress, New York.
126. America V. Rice......Member of Congress, Ohio.
127. Mrs. Celia S. Sherman......
128. Mrs. Jennie B. Bryan......
129. Mrs. Susan M. Edmunds......
130. W. E. V. Miller......
131. William D. Kelley......Member of Congress, Pa.
132. Mrs. Mary Clemmer......
133. Charles O'Conor......Counsel for Tilden.
134. Richard T. Merrick......Counsel for Tilden.
135. George A. Jenks......M. C., Pa., and counsel for Tilden.
136. W. H. Forney......Member of Congress, Alabama.
137. J. Randolph Tucker......M. C., Va., and counsel for Tilden.
138. Timothy O. Howe......Sen., Wis., and counsel for Hayes.
139. Henry Watterson......Member of Congress, Kentucky.
140. Mrs. Ellen F. Windom......
141. Thomas B. Bryan......
142. Hiram P. Bell......Member of Congress, Georgia.
143. L. Q. C. Lamar......Member of Congress, Mississippi.
144. Hannibal Hamlin......Senator, Maine.
145. George Bancroft......Historian.
146. Justin S. Morrill......Senator, Vermont.
147. John A. Campbell......Counsel for Tilden.
148. Roscoe Conkling......Senator, New York.
149. Montgomery Blair......Counsel for Tilden.
150. Matt N. Ransom......Senator, North Carolina.
151. David Dudley Field......M. C., N. Y., counsel for Tilden.
152. William C. Whitney......Counsel for Tilden.
153. Thomas W. Ferry......President pro tempore of the Senate.
154. James H. Blount......Member of Congress, Georgia.
155. J. D. Cameron......Senator, Pennsylvania.
156. Martin I. Townshend......Member of Congress, New York.
157. William M. Springer......Member of Congress, Illinois.
158. Lyman Trumbull......Counsel for Tilden.
159. Matt H. Carpenter......Counsel for Tilden.
160. Jeremiah S. Black......Counsel for Tilden.
161. George Hoadly......Counsel for Tilden.
162. Ashabel Green......
163. Matthew G. Emery......
164. Alex. Porter Morse......Counsel for Tilden.
165. H. B. Banning......Member of Congress, Ohio.
166. Mrs. Nannie Merrick......
167. Blanche K. Bruce......Senator, Mississippi.
168. Henry W. Blair......Member of Congress, New Hampshire.
169. Miss M. Y. Fretinghuysen......
170. Mrs. Christina Tyner......
171. Sir Edward Thornton......British Minister.
172. Hester Clymer......Member of Congress, Pennsylvania.
173. Mrs. Laura B. Tucker......
174. Mrs. Fannie H. Gordon......
175. John B. Gordon......Senator, Georgia.
176. John A. Logan......Senator, Illinois.
177. S. S. Cox......Member of Congress, New York.
178. Mary F. Waite......
179. Mrs. Helen M. Dorsey......
180. Thomas Swan......Member of Congress, Maryland.
181. Mrs. Mary Cameron......
182. Mrs. Adele Fassett......
183. Mrs. Mary A. Rice......
184. James G. Blaine......Senator, Maine.
185. Mrs. Sallie R. Knott......
186. Carlile P. Patterson......Superintendent U. S. Coast Survey.
187. Mrs. C. P. Patterson......
188. Mrs. Mary M. Gibson......
189. W. B. Allison......Senator, Iowa.
190. Randall Lee Gibson......Member of Congress, Louisiana.
191. Mrs. Lillie E. Willis......
192. Charles W. Hoffman......Librarian of Law Library, U. S. S. C.
193. C. H. McCall......Page, Supreme Court, U. S.
194. Robert Brown......Page, Supreme Court, U. S.
195. Fred. M. Matterson......Page, Supreme Court, U. S.
196. H. J. Lauck......Messenger, Electoral Commission.

THE COMMISSIONERS

celebrated commission was determining to whom the electoral votes in disputed States belonged. The membership of the commission consisted of the following Senators: George F. Edmunds, Oliver P. Morton, Frederick T. Frelinghuysen, Allen G. Thurman, and Thomas F. Bayard. The following Members of the House of Representatives were included in this commission: Henry B. Payne, Eppa Hunton, Josiah G. Abbott, George F. Hoar, and James A. Garfield. On the Supreme Court representation were Justices Joseph P. Bradley, Nathan Clifford, Samuel F. Miller, Stephen J. Field, and William Strong. Half a century has passed since the events recorded in this painting transpired. Irrespective of its value as a work of art, it is of vast historical value in thus establishing a permanent record of the principal participants in an event which formed so conspicuous a place in the history of our country. Amid all the dispute and contention arising over the election of 1876, those in charge of the affairs of the Government managed to create a plan by which the disputes were settled without trouble and with probably a minimum of resentment.

Mrs. Cornelia Adele Fassett was born in Owasco, N. Y., November 9, 1831. Her early life was devoted to music, and her first art work was in painting upon ivory. She traveled abroad and studied there for three years, and under the instruction of Meissonier formed the foundation for her successes in later years. She moved to Washington, D. C., in 1875, and her studio entertainments were considered among the most enjoyable features of the social side of Washington life. Her large portrait of the Supreme Court Justices of 1876 was exhibited at the Centennial Exposition at Philadelphia and now hangs in the conference room of the United States Supreme Court. Her familiarity with portrait painting made the creation of the painting of the Electoral Commission a work of more than ordinary interest. Mrs. Fassett established her studio at the Capitol for two summers during the vacation of the Supreme Court in order to give a faithful representation of the room, as well as the scene and its attendants. The individual portraits were painted from life at the artist's home studio. Mrs. Fassett was the mother of eight children at the time the picture was completed, seven of whom were living at the time of her death, which occurred in Washington, D. C., January 4, 1898. In addition to the pictures above referred to, this artist executed the portrait of Morrison R. Waite, former Chief Justice of the United States. This portrait is in the robing room of the Supreme Court. Her portrait of James A. Garfield is in the room of the House Committee on Appropriations.

Another painting in the east lobby of the gallery floor of the Senate is the portrait of Gen. J. A. Dix, sometime Governor of the State of New York and whose name will always be associated with his memorable order promulgated during the Civil War: "If any man attempts to haul down the American flag, shoot him on the spot." This portrait, the work of Imogene Robinson Morrell, seems to belong to the class of portraits in which we have already noted the portrait of Joshua R. Giddings. It seems that at times, whether from the association of some of the members of the committee with the subject of these portraits or whether from some strong demand from political sources, an occasional portrait has found its place in the Capitol collection when the person forming the subject of the work seemed to have no immediate connection with our national history. While it is true that both Joshua R. Giddings and John A. Dix were staunch supporters of the Union, still if all who supported the Union should have their portraits placed in the Capitol the difficulty in finding suitable space would have presented itself long ago. The portrait in question is well painted, and a portion of the flag is seen in the background of the composition. The painter, Mrs. Morrell, lived for many years in Washington. She was born in Attleboro, Mass., and studied art under Camphausen and in Paris under Couture. During her residence in Paris for several years she enjoyed the friendship of Meissonier, Bouguereau, and other prominent artists of France. On her second visit to Paris she was accompanied by Elizabeth Jane Gardner, who became a pupil and later the wife of W. A. Bouguereau. Mrs. Morrell's work was recognized by medals at the Mechanics' Institute in Boston and at the Centennial Exposition in Philadelphia. Among her important pictures are First Battle Between the Puritans and the Indians, Washington and His Staff Welcoming a Provision Train, and David before Saul. During her earlier residence in Washington her studio teas, at which large numbers attended, were among the features of the art life of Washington. She was unfortunate in the loss of her pictures in the disastrous fire at the Knox storage rooms. In her advanced years she was unable to teach or to find purchasers for her work and was subjected to all the discomforts of extreme poverty. She died in Washington, D. C., November 21, 1908.

In the same lobby which contains the portrait of Governor Dix by Mrs. Morrell may be found two historical paintings, the work of John Blake White, which were presented to the Congress February 17, 1899. (See Record, p. 1968.) Continuing around the corridor until we reach the south corridor of the gallery floor, we find two more paintings by the same artist. One of these paintings, the Battle of Fort Moultrie, was painted in 1815. This last-named painting was presented to the Senate on January 12, 1901. The paintings as a whole are interesting on account of the historical character of the scenes depicted. The titles describe the paintings as far as possible and are as follows: Miss Mott Directing Marion and Lee to Burn Her Mansion to Dislodge the British; General Marion Inviting a British Officer to Share His Meal; Sergeants Jasper and Newton Rescuing American Officers from the British; Battle of Fort Moultrie. It will be noticed by the titles that the scenes, with the exception of the Battle of Fort Moultrie, are of such a character that they may not easily be understood. The background in all instances is that of a wood interior, and the paintings are therefore so dark that in the light in which they are seen it is difficult to understand properly the really fine technical skill exhibited in the execution of these works. The artist, John Blake White, was born in South Carolina in 1781. He studied art for four years in the early part of the century in London, England, under Benjamin West and then returned to Charleston, S. C., where he studied and practiced law, following painting only as an amateur. While still a young man he was awarded a medal for a historical painting in oils by the South Carolina Institute. The most of his works are owned in his native State. Mr. White was also distinguished as an author and dramatist and is considered by some as a pioneer of southern literature and art. All of these paintings were presented through Hon. Benjamin R. Tillman and were given to the Congress by Dr. Octavius A. White, of New York City. Upon the occasion of the three paintings being presented in 1899 a resolution was adopted by the Senate accepting the paintings and tendering the thanks of the Senate to the donor of these works. On the occasion of the presentation of the Battle of Fort Moultrie the following resolution was adopted:

Resolved, That the Committee on the Library be and it is hereby authorized to accept on behalf of the Senate and caused to be suitably placed in the Senate wing of the Capitol the historical painting known as the Battle of Fort Moultrie executed by John Blake White in 1815 and presented by Dr. Octavius A. White of New York City in a communication to Honorable Benjamin R. Tillman, dated January 12, 1901.

Resolved, That the thanks of the Senate are hereby tendered to the donor. (Senate proceedings, January 22, 1901, pp. 1287–1288.)

THE BATTLE OF FORT MOULTRIE

John Blake White, painter

There are also to be found on the east wall of the east lobby of the Senate gallery floor portraits in mosaic of Presidents Lincoln and Garfield. These are the only portraits in mosaic in the Capitol Building and were presented to Congress by Antonio Salviati. The one of President Lincoln was at one time on exhibition in Statuary Hall, as appears from a guidebook (Roose's) for 1880. At this time Statuary Hall contained a miscellaneous collection of works of art consisting of portrait busts, full-length statues, and a few paintings. With the larger representation of statues by the States the works of art formerly in Statuary Hall were moved to other portions of the Capitol, so that this mosaic portrait of President Lincoln, with its companion portrait of President Garfield, seem now to be permanently located, although the lighting of this section of the Capitol is not of the best, and it is doubtful if the ordinary visitor ever notices these two examples in mosaic. The artist, Antonio Salviati, was born in Vicenza, Italy, 1816, and died in Venice, Italy, January 25, 1890. As an artist he revived the making of Venetian glass at Murano and was deeply interested in the success of its revival about the year 1860, but little is known of the personal history of Mr. Salviati. The works by which he is represented in the Capitol Building were tendered through Tiffany Bros., of New York, who seemed to have business relations with Mr. Salviati, and on this account were made the medium of the tender of these gifts. The work of Mr. Salviati so far as these examples show seems to be of a high order, although the number of mosaics in this country are so few that judgment by comparison is almost entirely out of the question. Of the two pictures, that of President Garfield seems to be the better, but in this work the background is entirely different from that of the portrait of President Lincoln, so that the basis of comparison may not after all be a wise one.

As has been stated, Statuary Hall in the variety of its collection of works of art has changed considerably since the time of the early seventies. At that time, according to Keim's Illustrated Handbook of Washington and Its Environs, there was located in Statuary Hall a full-length marble statue known as Il Penseroso, which was afterwards moved to the Senate side of the Capitol on the gallery floor and placed in the same room where the Moran paintings are now hung. The statue is the work of Joseph Mozier[1] and found its way to the Capitol at a date when there seems to have been permission given to many artists to exhibit their works within the Capitol Building, presumably for the purpose of bringing them to the attention of Congress in the hope of thereby effecting a sale. This work remained in the Capitol for many years, and after the death of the artist a sale was made by the widow through the Joint Committee on the Library, who at that time were provided with funds through a lump-sum appropriation for the purchase of works of art for the Capitol Building. It seems that as the years passed and the artist was to some measure forgotten, and possibly those members of the committee through whom the sale was effected were not in Congress, the Joint Committee on the Library concluded that the statue was more appropriate for the Smithsonian Institution, and on May 17, 1888, the Library Committee instructed the Architect of the Capitol to remove the same to the National Museum, where this statue is now on exhibition.

At about the same time that the statue Il Penseroso was being exhibited in the Senate wing of the Capitol there was also upon exhibition, probably in the east lobby of the gallery floor of the Senate, an equestrian portrait of General Scott. This portrait,

---

[1] Mozier, Joseph; born in Burlington, Vt., Aug. 22, 1812; died in Faido, Switzerland, October, 1870; first entered mercantile business in New York, but retired from that in 1845 in order to study art; studied sculpture for several years in Florence, Italy, and then went to Rome, where he spent the greater portion of his professional life. Among his best works are Esther, The Wept of Wish-ton-Wish, Tacite, Truth, The White Lady of Avenel, The Peri, Pocahontas, The Prodigal Son, and Rizpah.

PORTRAIT OF GENERAL WINFIELD SCOTT

Edward Troye (1808–1874), painter

as we are informed by the guidebooks of that period, had been painted at West Point, where a special studio had been erected for the use of the artist, Edward Troye. It is a peculiar thing that there are two equestrian portraits of General Scott, both by Edward Troye, so closely resembling each other that they are sometimes confused, and statements are made of one portrait that should be applied to the other. The earlier of these portraits, or supposedly so, is referred to in a guidebook by S. D. Wyeth, known as the Federal City, and on page 81 of this publication, in speaking of the eastern staircase of the House of Representatives, Mr. Wyeth used the following description:

A large picture of General Scott on horseback now hangs on the wall that faces the ascent of the stairs. It does not belong to the Government, but was placed in the Capitol by the artist with the hope it would be purchased by the country. It is painted by Mr. Edward Troye and ordered of him by the Virginia Legislature, but the rebellion breaking out the picture was thrown on his hands. The price that was to have been paid for it was $6,000.

We presume, and the presumption seems to be well founded, that this is the same portrait executed at West Point and on the 28th day of November, 1863, sold to Robert McMurdy for 10 acres of land in Keokuk, Iowa. This picture, however, remained in the Capitol and at the time it was claimed by the heirs of the McMurdy estate was not fastened to a stretcher, but was rolled and in a box. This was the condition described in a letter written in the early part of 1894, at which time inquiry was being made by the executors of the McMurdy estate concerning the whereabouts of this picture. At that time the executors stated that there were two pictures, counterparts of each other, and that the one belonging to the estate was the one in which the canvas was rolled and packed in a box. This picture was shipped to Chicago on March 20, 1894, and was at one time on exhibition in an armory in that city. The other picture was purchased by the Government by act approved March 3, 1891, some three years before the picture belonging to McMurdy was shipped to Chicago, and the compensation, $3,000, was paid to the widow of the artist, Mrs. Cornelia A. Troye. It is known that the picture purchased by the Government was for some time on exhibition at the National Museum and at the Corcoran Gallery of Art, and whether the picture purchased by the Government or the McMurdy picture was the one on exhibition at one time in the Senate wing of the Capitol is not known. The description furnished by Mr. Wyeth is contained in a book published in 1865. At this time, according to the records, McMurdy had for some time owned the equestrian portrait supposed to have been painted for the State of Virginia. Whether it was left upon exhibition after its sale to Robert McMurdy or whether the picture purchased by the Government in 1891 was the picture described by Mr. Wyeth is not known. The two pictures have been confused to a considerable degree, but the solution does not seem to be important. The picture owned by the Government has been in storage for years, its size being such that it is impossible to find a suitable space in the Capitol Building where it may be exhibited.

The artist Edward Troye was born near Geneva, Switzerland, in 1808. His parents were French and the family name was de Troy. His grandfather, a French nobleman, was an exile from France for political reasons. His father, J. Baptist de Troy, was an eminent painter and is represented in the Louvre by the Plague at Marseille. The children were well educated in the fine arts. Charles, a brother of Edward, was a noted historical painter. A sister, Esperance Paligi, was a musician and linguist of note, the first woman admitted to the Paris Conservatory of Music. Another sister, Marie Thirion, residing in Verona, was celebrated as a sculptor. Edward Troye, in company with his father, resided for some years in England, where at the age of 14 his sketches of Windsor Castle attracted marked attention. His father became financially involved in some vast engineering scheme and Edward at the age of 20 sought his fortune in the New World. After some time in the West Indies, occupied in sketching and painting, his health became impaired and he left for the United States. Landing at Philadelphia, he soon found professional employment in the art department of Sartain's Magazine. In the discharge of his duties he made sketching trips through Virginia and South Carolina and finally visited Kentucky, where he painted Bertrand and other noted horses. As an animal painter, and especially as a painter of famous horses, he became very popular, and there were few race horses of note that were not at some period painted by Troye. In the bluegrass section of Kentucky he found many subjects for his brush, and by some he was styled the "Landseer of America, one of the important few who painted equines and bovines with equal success." At one time he filled the position of professor of French and drawing at Spring Hill College, Mobile, Ala. Among his acquaintances in Kentucky was Mr. Keene Richards, of Georgetown, Ky., a distinguished patron of art. In the fifties Mr. Troye, in company with Mr. Richards, visited Arabia and the Holy Land. Industrious during this trip, he produced many pictures of note, among them Bazaar at Damascus, The Assyrian Ploughman, The Dead Sea, Sea of Tiberius or Galilee, and Jordan Bethabara. These were painted at the places represented and were afterwards taken to his brother's studio at Antwerp. Here Troye painted duplicates of these pictures, which were presented by Mr. Richards to Bethany College, of Virginia, and are now in the possession of that institution. The original pictures were made for Mr. Richards, who permitted the artist to exhibit them in this country and Canada prior to the breaking out of the Civil War. While Mr. Troye was widely known as a painter of animals, he was also celebrated for his portraits of many of the leading preachers of his day, among them the Rev. Joseph C. Stiles. Of a refined, cultivated nature, he was deeply religious, and it was an ambition again to visit the Holy Land and devote himself to painting pictures illustrating Bible history. He died in Georgetown, Ky., July 25, 1874.

CHAPTER XVII

BUSTS OF VICE PRESIDENTS IN THE SENATE WING

I N THE main corridor of the Senate are three paintings, a portrait of Daniel Webster, by John Neagle, a portrait of John C. Calhoun, by Henry F. Darby, and a portrait of Henry Clay, by the same artist. These portraits were purchased of Matthew B. Brady, a celebrated photographer, by the Joint Committee on the Library, February 23, 1881, and at the time of the purchase Mr. Brady submitted a statement in writing concerning these three pictures which is interesting for the purpose of fixing the time when the sketches were made from which these portraits were completed:

Clay's picture was taken in the City of New York during the winter of 1849. He was accompanied by Mr. William V. Brady, ex-Mayor of New York, on this occasion and by Simeon Draper, Collector of the Port of New York. I made five different sittings on this occasion. In Washington in 1850 I made another sitting and Darby made his study at the same time for the oil painting. Calhoun visited my gallery in Washington in the year 1849 during the months of March and April in company with his daughter, Mrs. Clemson, and the same artist, Darby, made his study for the painting. Webster visited my gallery in June, 1849, accompanied by Mr. Charles Stetson of the Astor House. Five different sittings were made on this occasion. Neagle, the New York artist, made his study for the painting at the same time. The material no longer exists to produce these portraits with such life-like fidelity and accuracy as to facts.

Respectfully,   M. B. BRADY.

For these three paintings Mr. Brady was paid $4,000. The price for the portrait of Webster was $1,900; for the portraits of Clay and Calhoun a voucher was prepared to include both paintings for the sum of $2,100. Biographical data relating to John Neagle have heretofore been given. The artist Henry L. Darby was but little known, and such facts as are herewith presented were obtained from his studio companion, Samuel Colman, who occupied a studio with Mr. Darby during the late fifties. According to Mr. Colman the artist Darby was born about 1831. From 1853 to 1859 he resided in New York and Brooklyn and was represented chiefly by portraits in the annual exhibitions of the National Academy of Design. By his acquaintances he is represented as being a man of high ideals and of a deeply grounded religious temperament. His grief at the loss of his wife some two years after his marriage led him to abandon his profession as a portrait painter, and in 1859 he went to England and became a rector of the Church of England. In 1878 he visited his former studio partner, Samuel Colman, in New York, since which time nothing is known of his whereabouts. So far as known there is no published list of his paintings. His portraits of Henry Clay and of John C. Calhoun are considered fine examples of portraiture, and it is to be regretted that he did not continue his work in a direction in which he had shown such marked ability.

In the south corridor of the Senate and hanging almost opposite the portrait of Daniel Webster, by John Neagle, is a portrait of Charles Sumner, by Walter Ingalls. This portrait hangs in a very unfavorable light, and it is probable that but few people have ever determined whether it is a work of merit or not. The artist Ingalls was accustomed to spend some portion of the year in Washington, where he made many acquaintances, and other portions of the year in New Orleans and other cities of the South and Southwest. But little was known of the artist except what has been stated above until a few years since, when the writer during a summer vacation became acquainted with Colonel Ingalls and learned that he was a cousin of the artist and through this acquaintance was able to secure memoranda for a biography. Walter Ingalls was born in Canterbury, N. H., February 16, 1805, and although as an artist he was self-taught he held an enviable position among the portrait painters of his period. An extensive traveler, he had a wide range of patrons and was given many commissions both in this country and abroad. Among his celebrated portraits is that of Pope Pius IX, painted from sittings given him by this celebrity. His full-length portrait of Washington is in the State capitol at Concord, N. H. His genial personality made him a favorite with people in official life, and at one time he exhibited in Washington a collection of portraits of prominent officials. His portraits of Louis Agassiz and Joseph Henry are in the National Gallery of Art, and his portrait of Thomas Ewing is in the collection of Secretaries in the Interior Department. He died in Oakland, Calif., July 21, 1874.

On the north wall of the south corridor of the Senate hangs a portrait of Senator William B. Allison. This portrait is a comparatively recent acquisition, and it is on account of its proximity to other portraits referred to that it is mentioned at this time without reference to the period of its purchase. At the time of his death it was claimed that Senator Allison had the record of the longest continuous service in the United States Senate. The purchase of this portrait, while not unusual, was somewhat of a departure from the customary practice. Senator Allison died in 1908. On the 26th of January, 1909, Senator Teller spoke as follows:

I have a very brief resolution which I desire to offer and to which I call the attention of the Senate. I am sure it is a resolution which the Senate will be glad to pass. I send it to the desk and ask for its present consideration.

The resolution (S. Res. 264) was read, considered by unanimous consent, and unanimously agreed to, as follows:

Resolved, That the Senate Committee on the Library is hereby authorized to purchase from Wilbur A. Reaser his oil portrait of the late Senator William B. Allison at a cost not to exceed $1,500, the same to be paid from the contingent fund of the Senate. (Senate proceedings, January 26, 1909, p. 1401, Cong. Record, 60th Cong., 2d sess.)

The artist referred to in this resolution, Willbur Aaron Reaser, was born in Hicksville, Ohio, December 25, 1860; moved to Iowa when a child; at the age of 21 went to San Francisco and began life as a musician and illustrator; in the spring of 1888 went to Paris, France, and entered the Académie Julien as a pupil of Lefebvre and Constant, studying there during three periods, about six years; settled in New York in 1896; for last 24 years has devoted himself to portraiture, painting portraits of many public men, including Senator Allison, Senator Dolliver, Senator Scott, and Secretary Wilson; is represented by portraits in Skibo Castle (Scotland), Hursley House (England), Carnegie Institute, United States Capitol, and in the State capitols of Iowa, West Virginia, and Vermont; awarded first Hallgarten prize at National Academy; gold and silver medal, California Exposition, 1894; member San Francisco Art Association and Salmagundi Club, New York.

Another interesting portrait also recently acquired, and which belongs to the same section of the Senate corridor as the portraits above referred to, is that of Senator Justin S. Morrill, who served in the House of Representatives from 1855 until 1867 and in the United States Senate from 1867 until his death in 1898. This portrait, the work of

JOHN ADAMS, MASSACHUSETTS
1789–1797
Daniel Chester French, sculptor

THOMAS JEFFERSON, VIRGINIA
1797–1801
Sir Moses Ezekiel, sculptor

AARON BURR, NEW YORK
1801–1805
Jacques Jouvenal, sculptor

GEORGE CLINTON, NEW YORK
1805–April 20, 1812
Vittorio A. Ciani, sculptor

BUSTS OF VICE PRESIDENTS OF THE UNITED STATES

Eastman Johnson, was a gift to the United States through the will of Miss Louise S. Swan. The portion of the will referring to this bequest is as follows:

And I further give to the United States to be hung in the Capitol at Washington, D. C., the painting of Senator Justin S. Morrill made by Eastman Johnson.

This portrait was accepted by the Joint Committee on the Library acting under authority conferred by section 1831 of the Revised Statutes of the United States, and with its acceptance is shown upon the records the poll vote of the members of the Joint Committee on the Library who acted upon this bequest. The portrait was received at the Capitol in April, 1920, and placed upon the wall soon afterwards. This is the only example of the work of Eastman Johnson in the Capitol Building. The artist was born in Lovell, Me., July 29, 1824. As a young man he exhibited marked ability in portraits in black and white. In 1849 he went abroad and shared the studio of Emanuel Leutze in Dusseldorf, Prussia. For four years he studied painting at The Hague, supplementing this work by studying at Paris. He returned to the United States in 1856 and opened a studio in New York. His characterization of domestic negro life placed him in the front rank of genre painters. His serious portrait work gave him a prominent place with the best portrait painters of his period. In 1860 he was made a member of the National Academy of Design and for 50 years he exerted a powerful influence in the formation of the ideals of American art. He died in New York April 5, 1906.

Those who have kept in mind the correspondence between Captain Meigs and Gouverneur Kemble will recall the thought suggested by Captain Meigs—that if opportunity were given in the construction of the Capitol Building for works of art by providing niches and panels, these niches and panels would sometime demand art objects to complete the decorative scheme of the Capitol. It was not until May 13, 1886, however that any disposition was shown to take advantage of the many niches in the gallery of the Senate Chamber. On that date the following resolution was passed:

Resolved, That marble busts of those who have been Vice Presidents of the United States shall be placed in the vacant niches of the Senate Chamber from time to time; that the Architect of the Capitol is authorized subject to the advice and approval of the Senate Committee on the Library to carry into execution the object of this resolution and the expenses incurred in doing so shall be paid out of the contingent fund of the Senate.

Some 12 years later it was found that the vacant niches of the Senate Chamber were not sufficient in number to furnish locations for the busts of those who had been Vice Presidents, and on January 6, 1898, the resolution of May 13, 1886, was amended by striking out the words "vacant niches of the Senate Chamber" and inserting "Senate wing of the Capitol." By this original resolution and the amendment thereto it became possible to locate busts of Vice Presidents in such places in the Senate wing of the Capitol as seemed desirable to the Committee on the Library.

It will be noted that some 26 years elapsed after the first occupancy of the Senate Chamber before steps were taken to provide busts in memory of those who had been Vice Presidents of the United States. This method of honoring our great men differs from the commemoration of them by statues in Statuary Hall in this, that in Statuary Hall the statues are only those of the deceased, while in the Senate wing of the Capitol a bust of a living Vice President may be placed. These busts have become so numerous that the best sites are now occupied, thus for those who are hereafter honored as contemplated the locations remaining are less desirable. It will be noted by reading the resolution of May 13, 1886, that the Architect of the Capitol was selected as the execu-

PORTRAIT OF HENRY CLAY

Henry F. Darby, painter

tive officer of the Senate Committee on the Library, and on May 20, 1886, seven days after the enactment of the resolution, the Library Committee issued instruction to Edward Clark, then Architect of the Capitol, to proceed to secure busts of the first two Vice Presidents, Adams and Jefferson, to be uniform in size and not to exceed in cost $800 each. The compensation mentioned was not sufficient to arouse any great amount of competition, and yet there were at that time many sculptors of merit who for the sake of the prestige afforded by being represented in the United States Capitol were willing to furnish busts for this very modest price.

In addition to the stipulation relating to the cost of the busts other requirements were considered, although they seem to have been in the form of verbal instructions to the architect. This is shown by a letter dated December 8, 1886, addressed by the Architect of the Capitol to Preston Powers, as follows:

DEAR SIR: In reply to yours relating to the busts for the Vice Presidents, Senate Chamber, I will say that while the Senate has passed a resolution ordering them, yet it was restricted at the present, to five, viz; the three living Vice Presidents, and Adams and Jefferson. The living Vice Presidents were permitted to select their sculptors and it is the desire of the Committee that the work should be given to the sculptors, natives of the States from which they came, therefore, that of Adams was given to French of Massachusetts and that of Jefferson to Ezekiel of Virginia. When others are ordered I will bring your name before the Committee and will be pleased if you will procure a commission for one.

Very truly yours,

EDWARD CLARK,
Architect, U. S. Capitol.

At the time of the passage of the resolution providing for busts for the Vice Presidents the following Vice Presidents were living: Hannibal Hamlin, born 1809, died July 4, 1891. Mr. Hamlin selected as his sculptor Franklin Simmons, whose biography has appeared earlier in this work. Another Vice President, William A. Wheeler, born June 19, 1819, died June 4, 1887. Mr. Wheeler selected as his sculptor E. C. Potter, who is represented in the Capitol by this single bust. Mr. Potter was born in New London, Conn. His education was received at Amherst College. He studied sculpture in Paris under Mercel and Fremo during 1888 and 1889; collaborated with Daniel Chester French in sculpture for the World's Fair at Chicago. Among his works are, equestrian statues of Grant, at Philadelphia; Washington, at Paris; Hooker, at Boston; Derens, at Worcester; Slocum, at Gettysburg; and De Soto, at St. Louis Exposition; statues of Fulton, in the Library of Congress; and Governor Blair, at the State capitol, Lansing, Mich.

The third Vice President living at the time of the passage of this resolution was Chester A. Arthur, who was born October 5, 1830, and died November 18, 1886. He was the first of the three living Vice Presidents referred to in the letter by Architect Clark to pass away, but he had expressed a desire that his bust should be executed by Augustus Saint-Gaudens. Mr. Saint-Gaudens, however, when first approached upon this subject declined the commission, but some time later he concluded to accept, although it was not necessary that he should execute this work in order to be represented in the Capitol Building, as at that time he was represented in the rooms of the Supreme Court.

The other sculptors represented in the first five commissions awarded under the Senate resolution of May 13, 1886, Daniel Chester French and Sir Moses Ezekiel, had, according to the letter of Architect Clark, been given these commissions on account of being natives of the State from which the Vice Presidents came. We suppose that Daniel Chester French was considered a native of the State of Massachusetts, and for this reason was awarded the commission for the bust of John Adams. As a matter of fact, this sculptor

PORTRAIT OF AUGUSTUS SAINT-GAUDENS

Kenyon Cox, painter

Saint-Gaudens is represented by the busts of Vice President Arthur
and Chief Justices Taney and Waite

DANIEL CHESTER FRENCH

Represented by the statue of Lewis Cass in Statuary Hall, by the bust of John Adams in the Senate gallery, and by the bust of Henry Wilson in the room of the Vice President

{ 328 }

was born in Exeter, N. H., April 20, 1850; educated in public schools, with one year at the Massachusetts Institute of Technology; began study of sculpture in 1867 under Dr. William Rimmer of Boston; later (1870) studied with J. Q. A. Ward in New York and again with Doctor Rimmer. His first important commission, The Minute Man of Concord, was erected in 1875 at Concord, Mass. In 1874–1876 studied with Thomas Ball in his studio in Florence, Italy; returned to the United States in 1876 and executed four groups for public buildings in St. Louis, Philadelphia, and Boston; moved to New York in 1887 and has since resided in that city, with a summer home in Stockbridge, Mass.; married in 1888 to Mary French, of Washington, D. C. Among his works are statues of John Harvard at Cambridge, Mass.; Lewis Cass, Statuary Hall, Capitol; Gallaudet and First Deaf-Mute Pupil, Washington, D. C.; George Frisbie Hoar, Worcester, Mass.; Angel of Death and the Sculptor, Boston; and Rufus Choate, Boston; also bronze doors, public library, Boston. The most celebrated work of this sculptor is his seated statue of Lincoln in the Lincoln Memorial, Washington, D. C.

The sculptor of the bust of Thomas Jefferson, Sir Moses Ezekiel, was born in Richmond, Va., in 1844; received a military education and afterwards applied himself to the study of anatomy; studied art at the Royal Academy, Berlin, where his colossal bust of Washington, a copy of which is in the Cincinnati Museum of Fine Arts, gained his admission to the Society of Artists at Berlin; his Apollo and Mercury are also to be found in that city. For many years he resided in Italy. Among his works are Religious Liberty, Fairmont Park, Philadelphia; monument to Thomas Jefferson, Louisville, Ky.; Judith, Cincinnati Museum of Fine Arts; head of Christ, Peabody Institute, Baltimore, and a nude figure entitled "Faith" in the same institution; portrait bust of Thomas Jefferson, Senate gallery, Capitol; and a fountain of Neptune, Nettuno, Italy. One of his most celebrated works is the memorial to the women of the Confederacy in the National Cemetery at Arlington. He died in Rome, Italy, March 27, 1917.

The sculptor Franklin Simmons is also represented by the busts of Vice President A. E. Stevenson and Vice President C. W. Fairbanks, these last-mentioned busts being located in the Senate corridor, main floor of the Senate.

The bust of Aaron Burr is the work of the sculptor Jacques Jouvenal, who for many years lived in Washington and died in that city on the 8th day of March, 1905. Mr. Jouvenal was of old Huguenot stock and was born in Pinache, Germany, March 18, 1829. His parents were obliged to flee from the south of France on account of religious principles. At the age of 16 he commenced his art study under the instruction of Klamner of Stuttgart, Germany. Emigrating to the United States in 1853, he remained in New York until 1855, when he moved to Washington and commenced work on the capitals of the columns of the Capitol, where he was employed for five years. His services terminated at the commencement of the War of the Rebellion. His first work as a portrait sculptor was the bust of Von Steuben at the German Orphan Asylum. His statue of Benjamin Franklin is at the intersection of Tenth Street and Pennsylvania Avenue, Washington, D. C.

The commission for the bust of George Clinton, a Vice President from the State of New York, was awarded to Vittorio A. Ciani, who was born in Florence, Italy, February 4, 1858. As a schoolboy he showed marked ability in the direction of wood carving and upon the advice of his teacher entered the Academy of Fine Arts at Florence. At the age of 12 his family moved to Rome, where he entered the Royal Academy of Art, studying under Professor Mazzini. He was fortunate in winning several prizes, graduating with the privilege of entering the studio of the celebrated Monteverdi. Having attained his

{ 329 }

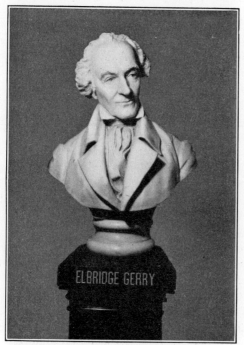

ELBRIDGE GERRY, MASSACHUSETTS
1813–November 23, 1814
Herbert Adams, sculptor

DANIEL D. TOMPKINS, NEW YORK
1817–1825
Charles H. Niehaus, sculptor

JOHN C. CALHOUN, SOUTH CAROLINA
1825–December 28, 1832
Theodore A. Mills, sculptor

MARTIN VAN BUREN, NEW YORK
1833–1837
U. S. J. Dunbar, sculptor

BUSTS OF VICE PRESIDENTS OF THE UNITED STATES

majority, he was compelled to enter the Italian Army and served for the period of three years. After completing his military service he opened a studio in Rome and later decided to come to the United States. In 1889 he married an American and soon thereafter opened a studio in New York. In addition to this bust of George Clinton his other works are panels and fireplace for the Breakers, the Newport home of the Vanderbilts; group, Apollo, Tragedy and Comedy, proscenium arch, Pabst's Theater, Milwaukee, Wis.; reredos, the Lord's Supper, St. Bartholomew's Church, New York; Langdon memorial, Grace Church, New York; Landing of the Pilgrims, Earle Hall, Columbia College, New York; and portrait bust of Austin Corbin. One of his last works was that of an electrolier on the isle of safety presented by the Municipal Art Society of New York. In this work his design was selected in a sealed competition with 48 sculptors. In 1897 King Humbert of Italy awarded the cross of the Crown of Italy in recognition of his artistic merit. He died in Perth Amboy, N. J., March 5, 1908.

It appears that the practice of selecting sculptors from the same State which had furnished the Vice President was not always adhered to. For instance, the bust of John Tyler, of Virginia, and of Andrew Johnson, of Tennessee, were executed by William C. McCauslen, a sculptor of Washington, D. C., who also executed the bust of William R. King, of Alabama. The sculptor William C. McCauslen was born at Steubenville, Ohio, November 9, 1860. He was educated in the high school of Steubenville. His art training commenced with the study of painting in 1884 with a teacher named Boris, and afterwards he took up modeling, and as a sculptor was self-taught. His busts of Andrew Johnson, William R. King, and John Tyler are his only works occupying places of public importance. The commissions for the Johnson and Tyler busts were given subject to the approval of relatives of these Vice Presidents, and the correspondence on file shows that these busts were properly approved. Other busts executed by this sculptor are those of Byron and Apollo. In later years his attention has been given entirely to painting, and for some time he has not produced any works in sculpture.

Another Washington sculptor, U. S. J. Dunbar, was awarded the commissions for the busts of Martin Van Buren, of New York, and T. A. Hendricks, of Indiana, and although born in London, Ontario, Canada, January 31, 1862, he was given the name of Ulric Stonewall Jackson Dunbar. Mr. Dunbar was educated in the common schools of Canada and Rockwood Academy and has been professionally engaged as a sculptor since 1880. Among his works are figures for the Atlanta, Buffalo, and St. Louis Expositions, where he received medals and diplomas; executed more than 100 portrait busts, principally of prominent men, some of which are to be found in the Capitol; the Corcoran Gallery of Art; State capitol, St. Paul, Minn.; Union League Club, New York, etc.; executed bronze statue of Gov. Alexander R. Shepherd, located in the park fronting the municipal building, Washington, D. C.; also executed several monuments; served Canada three years in the volunteer service; was a member of National Art Association, Society of Washington Artists, and National Society of Fine Arts. Mr. Dunbar died in Washington, D. C., May 7, 1927.

James Paxton Voorhees was awarded the commission for the busts of Richard M. Johnson, of Kentucky, and J. C. Breckinridge, of Kentucky. Mr. Voorhees was born in Covington, Ind., October 1, 1855; son of Daniel Wolsey Voorhees and Anna Hardesty Voorhees; educated in the public schools of Terre Haute, Ind., and Georgetown College, Washington, D. C.; began life at the age of 16 in newspaper work, which to some extent he has continued ever since; also read law in the office of his father and followed for some time the theatrical profession; served as private secretary to his father, Senator Daniel W. Voorhees; has written several novels. Among his works of sculpture are portrait busts of J. C. Breckinridge, Richard M. Johnson, and Daniel W. Voorhees; studies of Jefferson and Napoleon for the St. Louis Exposition; ideal head of the Savior; and model for statue of Robert Dale Owen.

The commission for the bust of Elbridge Gerry, of Massachusetts, was awarded to Herbert Adams, who was born in Concord, Vt., in 1858; educated in public schools in Fitchburg, Mass., Institute of Technology, Worcester, Mass., Massachusetts Normal Art School, and at art schools in Paris, where he was a pupil of Mercié; member of the Art Commission of New York, the Architectural League of New York, and the Century and Players' Clubs. Awards: World's Columbian Exposition, 1893; Paris Exposition, 1900; and the Louisiana Purchase Exposition, 1904. Among his works are the Fitchburg fountain, Fitchburg, Mass.; statue of William Ellery Channing, Boston, Mass.; statue of Jerome Wheeler, Grafton, Mass.; Jonathan Edwards memorial, Northampton, Mass.; Welch memorial, Auburn, N. Y.; bronze doors in tympanum, St. Bartholomew's Church, New York; Hoyt memorial, Judson Memorial Church, New York; Pratt memorial, Emanuel Baptist Church, Brooklyn, N. Y.; statues of Joseph Smith and Mathias Baldwin, Philadelphia, Pa.; and bust of James R. Mann, in the connection to the House wing of the United States Capitol.

The commission for the bust of Daniel D. Tompkins, of New York, was awarded to C. H. Niehaus, who, although he has been favored with many commissions for statues in Statuary Hall, has executed only one bust for the Senate wing of the Capitol. Charles Henry Niehaus was born in Cincinnati, Ohio, January 24, 1855. In early life he followed wood engraving, stonecutting, and carving in marble; studied art in the McMicken School of Design, Cincinnati, Ohio, and in the Royal Academy of Munich, receiving conspicuous awards in both institutions; lived for some time in Rome; is a member of the Council of the National Sculpture Society, of the Architectural League of America, the National Art Club, the Players' Club, and fellow of L'Associazione della Artistica Internazionale di Roma. Since 1885 he has resided in the city of New York and its vicinity. Among his works are statues of Hooker and Davenport, statehouse, Connecticut; Astor historical doors, Old Trinity, New York; carved wood tympanums, Library of Congress; statues of Moses and Gibbon, Library of Congress; Hahnemann memorial and statue of John Paul Jones, Washington, D. C.; and statues of Lincoln and Farragut, Muskegon, Mich. One of his latest notable works is the Francis Scott Key Monument, Fort McHenry, Baltimore. Mr. Niehaus is represented in Statuary Hall by the statues of James A. Garfield, Oliver P. Morton, John J. Ingalls, Governor Glick, William Allen, and Zachariah Chandler.

The commission for the bust of John C. Calhoun, of South Carolina, was awarded to Theodore A. Mills, the eldest son of Clark Mills, the sculptor of the equestrian statues of Jackson and Washington in the city of Washington. The sculptor Theodore Augustus Mills was born in Charleston, S. C., April 24, 1839. During his boyhood he pursued modeling as an amusement without regular instruction until 1860, when he became a pupil in the Royal Art Academy at Munich, where he received a prize for his composition Penelope Presenting the Bow of Ulysses to the Suitors. This is said to be the only instance where a prize was conferred by this academy upon an American. Returned to the United States after an absence of five years and commenced work in the studio of his father,

RICHARD M. JOHNSON, KENTUCKY
1837–1841
James P. Voorhees, sculptor

JOHN TYLER, VIRGINIA
March 4, 1841–April 4, 1841
William C. McCauslen, sculptor

GEORGE M. DALLAS, PENNSYLVANIA
1845–1849
Henry J. Ellicott, sculptor

MILLARD FILLMORE, NEW YORK
1849–July 9, 1850
Robert Cushing, sculptor

BUSTS OF VICE PRESIDENTS OF THE UNITED STATES

CHARLES HENRY NIEHAUS

Represented in Statuary Hall by the statues of Garfield, Morton, Ingalls, Allen, Chandler and Glick, and in the Senate gallery by the portrait bust of Daniel Tompkins

Clark Mills, then engaged in making a model for a proposed memorial in Washington to President Lincoln; was afterwards employed by the National Museum, Washington, and later at the Carnegie Institute, Pittsburgh. He died in Pittsburgh, December 16, 1916.

Of the busts of Vice Presidents in the Senate wing of the Capitol two have been executed by women. One of these busts is located in a niche in the Senate gallery, the other in the Senate corridor, main floor. Inasmuch as the busts heretofore referred to have been located in niches in the Senate gallery, we will now refer to the bust of Schuyler Colfax, of Indiana, executed by Miss Frances M. Goodwin, who was born in Newcastle, Ind.; commenced her art study at Indianapolis, Ind., and studied later at the Chicago Art Institute, where she became interested in modeling and abandoned her intention of becoming a painter for the study of sculpture; studied at the Arts Students League, New York, with D. C. French as instructor. Among her works are a statue representing Indiana for Columbian Exposition; bronze bust of Captain Everett, Riverhead Cemetery, New York; and bust of Robert Dale Owen for the statehouse at Indianapolis.

Other busts in the Senate gallery are those of George M. Dallas, of Pennsylvania, and Millard Fillmore, of New York. The commission for the bust of George M. Dallas was awarded to Henry Jackson Ellicott, who was born in Anne Arundel County, Md., June 23, 1847. He studied drawing at the National Academy of Design and also studied under Brumidi, Powell, and Leutze. He died at Washington, D. C., February 11, 1901.

Robert Cushing was awarded the commission for the bust of Millard Fillmore, of New York. Robert Cushing was born in Ireland in 1841; died in New York City March 11, 1896. He was employed for some time in the studio of J. Q. A. Ward, of whom he was a pupil; he also studied under Randolph Rogers; one of the founders of the National Sculpture Society. Among his most important works are portrait busts of John Kelly, in Tammany Hall; Cardinal McCloskey, in St. Patrick's Cathedral, New York City; President Fillmore, United States Senate Chamber; and statue of Rev. John C. Drumgoole, Great Jones Street and Lafayette Place, New York City.

In addition to the busts which have been mentioned and all of which are located in niches of the Senate gallery, there are also in the Senate corridor, main floor of the Senate, busts of A. E. Stevenson, of Illinois, and C. W. Fairbanks, of Indiana, the work of Franklin Simmons, whose biography has been given earlier in this work.

There is also in this corridor the bust of Levi P. Morton, of New York, by F. Edwin Elwell, and the bust of Garret A. Hobart, of New Jersey, by the same sculptor. Mr. Elwell was born in Concord, Mass., June 15, 1858; educated in the public schools of Concord and studied at the École des Beaux Arts, Paris, France, and Royal School of Art, Ghent, Belgium. Among his works are Death of Strength, Edam, Holland, the first statue modeled in America by an American sculptor to be erected in Europe; Dickens and Little Nell, Philadelphia, Pa.; equestrian statue of Gen. Winfield S. Hancock, Gettysburg, Pa.; Awakening of Egypt (ideal), purchased from Paris Salon, 1896, and owned in Paris, France; New Life, Lowell Cemetery, Lowell, Mass.; Greece and Rome, New York Customhouse; Dispatch Rider, Orange, N. J.; the Flag, Vicksburg, Miss.; Lincoln, East Orange, N. J.; Admiral Davis National Naval Monument; busts of Elihu Yale, Yale Club, New York City; S. B. Chittenden, Yale Library, Yale University; Col. Van Horn, Kansas City, Mo.; R. M. Walmsley, New Orleans, La.; F. B. Sanborn, Topeka, Kans.; and Miss L. M. Olcott, Concord Library. Mr. Elwell was awarded highest medal, Chicago Exposition, 1893; two gold medals from Philadelphia Art Club; medal, Pan-American Exposition, 1901; and medal decoration from the King of Belgium. He died in Darien, Conn., January 23, 1922.

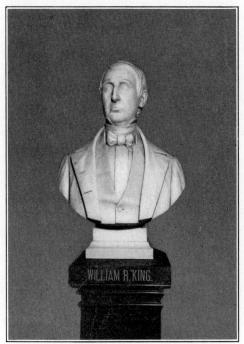

WILLIAM R. KING, ALABAMA
March 4, 1853–April 18, 1853
William C. McCauslen, sculptor

JOHN C. BRECKINRIDGE, KENTUCKY
1857–1861
James P. Voorhees, sculptor

HANNIBAL HAMLIN, MAINE
1861–1865
Franklin Simmons, sculptor

ANDREW JOHNSON, TENNESSEE
March 4, 1865–April 15, 1865
William C. McCauslen, sculptor

BUSTS OF VICE PRESIDENTS OF THE UNITED STATES

SCHUYLER COLFAX, INDIANA
1869–1873
Frances M. Goodwin, sculptress

HENRY WILSON, MASSACHUSETTS
1873–November 22, 1875
Daniel Chester French, sculptor

WILLIAM A. WHEELER, NEW YORK
1877–1881
Edward C. Potter, sculptor

CHESTER A. ARTHUR, NEW YORK
March 4, 1881–September 19, 1881
Augustus Saint-Gaudens, sculptor

BUSTS OF VICE PRESIDENTS OF THE UNITED STATES

The commission for the bust of Theodore Roosevelt was awarded to James E. Fraser, who was born in Winona, Minn., November 4, 1876. He studied at the Chicago Art Institute and at École des Beaux Arts, Académie Julien, Paris; won first prize for best work in sculpture offered by American Art Association of Paris, 1898; medal competition offered by same, 1898; Edison medal competition, 1906; executed first bust made from life of ex-President Roosevelt, 1908, now in Senate corridor, Washington, D. C., and bust of Colonel Roosevelt, 1910, to be placed in public library, Oshkosh, Wis.; group of medals exhibited at the International Exposition, Brussels, 1910, bought same year by Belgium Government for the Musee at Gand, Belgium; represented in Metropolitan Art Museum, New York City; instructor in sculpture, Art Students League, New York City. Important works: Monument to John Hay, Cleveland, Ohio; relief portrait of Morris K. Jessup, Museum of Natural History, New York City; fountain, country residence of the late E. H. Harriman, Arden, N. Y.

The remaining bust in the Senate corridor, that of James S. Sherman, New York, is the work of Bessie Potter Vonnoh (Mrs. Robert William Vonnoh). This sculptress was born in St. Louis, Mo., August 17, 1872; studied sculpture in the Art Institute of Chicago for three years under Lorado Taft; otherwise is self-taught. Her specialty is statuettes of women and children. Received bronze medal of Paris Exposition of 1900; gold medal, St. Louis World Fair, 1904; member National Sculpture Society and associate member of the National Academy of Design; represented by sculptural work in Metropolitan Museum of Art, New York, and other museums; married Robert W. Vonnoh, portrait painter, in 1899.

The last bust of a Vice President purchased under the resolution adopted May 13, 1886, as amended January 6, 1898, is the bust of Thomas Riley Marshall. All of the niches in the Senate gallery having been occupied and all of the most desirable spaces in the Senate corridor having been filled, it was necessary to place the bust of Vice President Marshall in the east Senate corridor, and it is probable that the busts of other Vice Presidents will be placed in this corridor unless some other arrangement is made or some new plan devised for their location.

The sculptor for the bust of Vice President Marshall, Moses A. Wainer-Dykaar, was born in Trab (government of Wilno, Russia) August 15, 1886; educated in the seminary school; at the age of 16 commenced his art studies by carving with a knife on soft stone. At this time he had never seen or heard of modeling clay and in his first efforts was self-taught. He was able later to attend a school of drawing in Wilno and studied in this school until able to go to Paris in 1904, where he became a pupil in the Acadèmie Julien. It was at this academy that he was found by Raul Varlet, who took him under his care and gave him instruction for four or five years. He came to the United States in February, 1916, and has practiced his art in this country since that time. His work while in Paris is comprised of the following: An ideal figure, The First Flower; a group entitled "The Dance of the Shadows"; and an ideal figure entitled "Twilight." His work in the United States includes the following busts: Vice President Marshall, in the Senate wing of the Capitol; bust of the late Speaker Champ Clark; bust of Hudson Maxim; bust of Alexander Graham Bell; bust of W. H. Holmes, curator of the National Gallery of Art; bust of Rabbi Stephen S. Wise, of New York; bust of Eugene V. Debs; bust of Judge Senders, of New York; bust of Abraham Kahn, editor of the Jewish daily paper Forward; bust of Gen. George Owen Squires; bust of Charles D. Walcott, former secretary of the Smithsonian Institution; bust of Justice Wendell Phillips Stafford; busts of President

THOMAS A. HENDRICKS, INDIANA
March 4, 1885–November 25, 1885
U. S. J. Dunbar, sculptor

LEVI P. MORTON, NEW YORK
1889–1893
F. Edwin Elwell, sculptor

ADLAI E. STEVENSON, ILLINOIS
1893–1897
Franklin Simmons, sculptor

GARRET A. HOBART, NEW JERSEY
1897–November 21, 1899
F. Edwin Elwell, sculptor

BUSTS OF VICE PRESIDENTS OF THE UNITED STATES

From a portrait by Robert W. Vonnoh

BESSIE POTTER VONNOH

Represented by the bust of Vice President James S. Sherman

and Mrs. Coolidge; an ideal group of a mother and child entitled "Once upon a Time"; and an ideal bust entitled "Modern Woman."

Although we have concluded the list of the busts of Vice Presidents selected under the resolution of May 13, 1886, it is a somewhat singular circumstance that none of the Vice Presidents referred to was the first to be honored by a bust in the Senate wing of the Capitol. In fact, Vice President Henry Wilson was given that distinction through a sequence of legislation commencing January 16, 1885, Forty-eighth Congress, second session, when Mr. Hoar offered the following resolution, on which he made a few remarks, after which it was unanimously agreed to:

Resolved, That the Architect of the Capitol under the direction of the Committee on the Library place a neat marble tablet in the room in the Senate wing of the Capitol where Vice President Henry Wilson died, properly recording the fact and date.

It will be observed by the foregoing resolution that at this time it seemed to be intended that the memory of Mr. Wilson should be honored by the placing of a marble tablet in the room of the Vice President, in which room Mr. Wilson died.

[Extract from the minutes of the Joint Committee on the Library, January 23, 1885]

Mr. Hoar asked the informal approval by the Committee of a proposition to be submitted to the Senate by Mr. Dawes to request the Committee to purchase of Mr. French [Daniel C. French], sculptor, a bust of Honorable Henry Wilson for $1,000. and have it placed above the tablet to his memory in the room in which he died, which was unanimously agreed to.

[In the Senate of the United States, January 27, 1885, 48th Cong., 2d sess.]

Mr. Dawes offered the following resolution, concerning which he briefly addressed the Senate, after which it was unanimously passed:

"*Resolved*, That the Joint Committee on the Library be requested to cause a bust of the late Vice President Henry Wilson to be placed over the tablet lately ordered to be placed in the room where he died."

[Extract from the minutes of the Joint Committee on the Library, January 30, 1885]

The resolution of the Senate of January 27, 1885, that the Committee be requested to cause a bust of the late Vice President Wilson to be placed over the tablet in the room in which he died was read and on motion of Mr. Hoar it was unanimously agreed that the chairman be requested to contract with Mr. French, sculptor, for said bust at a cost not exceeding $1,000. when placed in position.

In the course of time the bust executed by Daniel Chester French was received and placed upon a bracket in the Vice President's room, but at this time there was no tablet stating the fact of the death of Vice President Wilson in the room in which his bust had been installed. So that the original idea of marking the room with a tablet seems to have been set aside, unless it may have been supposed that the bracket supporting the bust would furnish sufficient space upon which to place the inscription contemplated by the resolution directing the Architect of the Capitol to "place a neat marble tablet in the room in the Senate wing of the Capitol where Vice President Henry Wilson died, properly recording the fact and date." So that from the time of the installation of the bust until 1902, a matter of some 17 years, the original purpose seems to have been lost sight of. On April 26, 1902, Mr. Hansbrough, from the Committee on the Library, reported a resolution which was referred to the Committee to Audit and Control the Contingent Expenses of the Senate and ordered to be printed. The resolution (S. Res. 205, 57th Cong., 1st sess.) is as follows:

Resolved, That the expense incurred by the Superintendent of the Capitol Building and Grounds authorized by Senate Resolution of January 16, 1885, in procuring and placing a commemorative tablet in the Senate wing of the Capitol where Vice President Henry Wilson died be paid from the contingent fund of the Senate.

ELLIOTT WOODS
Architect of the Capitol (1902–1923)

{ 342 }

SOUTHWEST CORNER OF PRESIDENT'S ROOM

Showing bust of President William McKinley; Emma Cadwalader-Guild, sculptress

THEODORE ROOSEVELT, NEW YORK
March 4, 1901–September 14, 1901
James E. Fraser, sculptor

CHARLES W. FAIRBANKS, INDIANA
1905–1909
Franklin Simmons, sculptor

JAMES S. SHERMAN, NEW YORK
1909–October 30, 1912
Bessie Potter Vonnoh, sculptress

THOMAS R. MARSHALL, INDIANA
1913–1921
Moses A. Wainer-Dykaar, sculptor

BUSTS OF VICE PRESIDENTS OF THE UNITED STATES

By this time the marble tablet authorized had been changed to a bronze tablet and its cost provided for out of the contingent fund of the Senate. The tablet was designed by the Henry-Bonnard Bronze Co., the copy for which is said to have been furnished by Senator George F. Hoar:

In this room Henry Wilson, Vice President of the United States and a Senator for eighteen years, died November 22, 1875. The son of a farm laborer, never at school more than twelve months, in youth a journeyman shoemaker, he raised himself to the high places of fame, honor and power, and by unwearied study made himself an authority in the history of his country and of liberty and an eloquent public speaker to whom Senate and people eagerly listened. He dealt with and controlled vast public expenditure during a great civil war, yet lived and died poor, and left to his grateful countrymen the memory of an honorable public service, and a good name far better than riches.

The inscription upon this tablet should prove an inspiration to those whose ambition has been lulled by the to them apparent lack of opportunity. In the same room there may be found another marble bust, that of Lafayette S. Foster, sometime a President pro tempore of the Senate. The recognition by a bust in marble of a President pro tempore is not a common one. This seems to be the only instance where such honor has been shown. This bust, also placed upon a bracket, is the work of Charles Calverly, who was born in Albany, N. Y., November 1, 1833; educated in Albany, N. Y.; became associate, National Academy of Design, in 1872 and a full member in 1875; executed many groups and figures; is especially known by his portrait busts in bronze of Horace Greeley, John Brown, Peter Cooper, and Elias Howe. Mr. Calverly died in Essex Falls, N. J., February 24, 1914.

In the President's room there has been placed a bronze bust of President William McKinley, one of the two Presidents who have been distinguished by the installation in the Capitol of bronze busts. This bust was purchased under the act approved March 3, 1903 (Stats. L., vol. 32, p. 1144):

For the purchase by the Joint Committee on the Library of a bronze portrait bust of the late President McKinley, executed by Mrs. Emma Cadwalader-Guild, to be placed in the Senate wing of the Capitol, $2,000.

The sculptress, Mrs. Emma Cadwalader-Guild, was for many years a resident of Berlin, Germany. Prior to the commission for this bust and for some time subsequent to the St. Louis Exposition she maintained a studio in the city of New York and exhibited in St. Louis a bust of the English painter Watts, bust of Von Joachim, bust of Abraham Lincoln, and two other examples of her work. At this exposition she was the recipient of a bronze medal. From other sources of information it is learned that at an exhibition in Boston she showed both bronze and marble busts of President McKinley, bronze and marble busts of President Lincoln, and a statuette of a negro, "Free." From some of the letters of the artist it is learned that she had secured a commission and was engaged in 1905 upon a bronze bust of Andrew Carnegie.

CHAPTER XVIII

OTHER WORKS OF ART IN THE SENATE WING

ANGING upon either side of the door opening into the Senate document room from the gallery floor are the portraits of Henry Latimer and James Latimer, acquired by gift through Mary R. Latimer in 1916. The first named served as surgeon general in one of the divisions of the Continental Army. He was a Delegate in the Continental Congress, a Representative in Congress from the State of Delaware, and a Senator from that State for many years. James Latimer was a lieutenant in the Continental Army, a distinguished lawyer, and presided December 7, 1787, over the Delaware convention, the first convention to ratify the Constitution of the United States.

The history of the presentation of these portraits is somewhat peculiar. Resolutions of acceptance had been prepared and favorable reports made by the Library Committee on the part of both the Senate and House of Representatives, but for some reason action was not obtained by the Congress before the closing of the session. As both portraits had been brought to the Capitol and had received the favorable commendation of members of the Library Committee and connoisseurs, it seemed best under the circumstances for the Joint Committee on the Library to accept these portraits and designate their location under the provisions of section 1831 of the Revised Statutes of the United States, which provides:

> The Joint Committee on the Library, whenever, in their judgment, it is expedient, are authorized to accept any work of the fine arts, on behalf of Congress, which may be offered and to assign the same such place in the Capitol as they may deem suitable, and shall have the supervision of all works of art that may be placed in the Capitol.

The portraits referred to are the work of Clawson Shakespeare Hammitt, who was born in Wilmington, Del., November 7, 1857, third child of Edmund Marshall Hammitt and Letitia (Harris) Hammitt. Relationship is traced upon the side of the father to the poet Shakespeare; upon the mother's side to Barney Harris, builder of the ship *Nancy*, the first ship to hoist the American flag in a foreign port. He showed decided artistic tendencies at an early age but was discouraged by his parents. His only funds for his art education were earned by his own efforts. Pupil of the Pennsylvania Academy of Fine Arts, studying in this institution under Anshutz, Eakins, and Uhle; was later a pupil of William M. Chase, and in Paris a student under Lefebvre and Benjamin Constant; founded the first school of art in Delaware in 1882 and the first society of artists in that State in 1884, continuing his work in the art school for 30 years; is represented in the statehouse at Dover, Del., by 17 portraits of prominent citizens of that State; fellowship member, Academy of Fine Arts, Philadelphia, and member of National Federation of Arts.

In the Senate corridor, main floor of the Senate, are found two portraits by Thomas Sully, one, the portrait of Thomas Jefferson, which has been the property of the Government since 1874, the other, the portrait of Andrew Jackson, which was purchased by the

Joint Committee on the Library upon a specified appropriation for this purpose in March, 1922. Without stating in detail the price of either portrait, it may be interesting to know that the portrait of Thomas Jefferson purchased in 1874 cost only one-fourth the amount paid for the portrait of Andrew Jackson purchased in 1922. This may suggest that if a wise selection can be made it is profitable to purchase portraits when first offered and not wait until the intervening years have quadrupled the value of the work of art. It appears from the correspondence in the office of the architect that the portraits of Andrew Jackson and Thomas Jefferson were sent to the Capitol for the consideration of the Joint Committee on the Library in June, 1872, and that in May, 1874, the portrait of Andrew Jackson and another portrait, that of General Dearborn, which had been subsequently sent for the consideration of the committee, were returned to the owner, Garrett C. Neagle. After many years and following the death of Garrett C. Neagle his effects were sold at auction in Philadelphia, and this and other portraits, the work of his grandfather, Thomas Sully, were disposed of. Eventually, after the lapse of some 50 years, the portrait of Andrew Jackson was again brought to the attention of the Joint Committee on the Library and a sale effected.

The presentation of the bust of Lafayette S. Foster, sometime a President pro tempore of the Senate, seems to have created a precedent for the recognition of another President pro tempore, John Langdon, who was the first President pro tempore to preside over the Senate. His portrait hangs on the south wall of the main corridor of the Senate and presents an interesting problem in the color scheme selected by the artist. It was acquired under Senate Resolution 118 (64th Cong., 1st sess.), which provided for the purchase of this portrait and limited the cost thereof. The painter, Miss Hattie E. Burdette, is a Washington artist who has been educated in the art schools of that city. She has painted portraits of several notable people, among them being the portrait of Cæsar Augustus Rodney, for Delaware College, Delaware; Robert Treat Paine, for Cambridge Theological Seminary; John Campbell, for Washington and Lee University; Mrs. Ricks, for Ricks Memorial Library, Mississippi; Charles J. Bonaparte, for the Navy Department; and a portrait of Senator John Sharp Williams, of Mississippi.

On the south side of the Senate corridor is a bust portrait of John Adams, a copy from Stuart by Eliphalet Frazer Andrews. Mr. Andrews was for many years the director of the Corcoran School of Art and a pupil under Ludwig Knaus and also of the Dusseldorf Academy. He established the Corcoran School of Art in 1877. His principal distinction is that of a portrait painter, and he is represented by portraits of Martha Washington, Jefferson, Jackson, Taylor, Johnson, Garfield, and Harrison in the White House. He has also painted many other portraits for public and private collections in the United States and Europe. Mr. Andrews was born in Steubenville, Ohio, June 11, 1835, and died in Washington, D. C., March 19, 1915.

Another portrait in the Senate wing is that of Patrick Henry, which hangs at the west end of the corridor. This portrait has an interesting history in that material for a portrait of Patrick Henry was very hard to obtain. There is a tradition that a French painter painted a miniature of Patrick Henry at an early period of his life. The miniature seems to have disappeared, and the portrait in the Capitol and one in the Historical Society's collection in Richmond, Va., both by Mr. Matthews, seem to be at present the best available portraits of the distinguished patriot. The artist, George B. Matthews, was born in Tappahannock, Essex County, Va., in June, 1857, son of James M. Matthews, a gifted jurist and author. He studied painting in Paris 1880–1883 under the

BUST OF LAFAYETTE S. FOSTER

Charles Calverly, sculptor

The only bust to a President pro tempore of the Senate in the Capital

PORTRAIT OF PATRICK HENRY

George B. Matthews, painter

celebrated French portrait painter, Carolus Duran. Among his works are The Crucifixion; Cathedral Church, Mount Clemens, Mich.; Jefferson Davis, Beauvoir, Miss.; Stonewall Jackson, State capitol, Virginia; Lee and His Generals, Memphis, Tenn., also in the Virginia Historical Society; Last of the Wooden Navy, State capitol, Virginia; and many portraits of distinguished men in the various governmental departments. Mr. Matthews is also the painter of the portrait of John Paul Jones, in the room of the Senate Committee on Naval Affairs.

Having discussed the portraits in the Senate corridor, it is proper at this time, on account of the nearness to this collection, to make further reference to the statue of John Hancock, by Horatio Stone, standing at the foot of the grand staircase on the west side of the Senate wing. This statue was one of the early commissions given to Doctor Stone at a time when he seemed to have a certain vogue with the art interests of the Capitol. It was completed in February, 1861, as is evidenced by a letter from Hon. J. A. Pearce, the chairman of the Joint Committee on the Library, to Capt. W. B. Franklin, at that time the superintendent in charge of the construction of the House and Senate wings and the new dome of the Capitol. So far as has been learned, from the time that this statue was acquired by the Government it has always been exhibited in the Senate wing. It should be remembered that with the first introduction of statues in the Capitol Building they were frequently placed upon temporary pedestals, also that several years elapsed before it was determined whether the Government or the States from which the statues were donated would provide the pedestals. It appears that this statue of John Hancock had been placed upon a temporary pedestal and that a permanent pedestal was not secured until 1883, more than 20 years after its completion. It is possible that in this instance it was worth while to wait, for the permanent pedestal came from a granite rock from the Hancock farm in Lexington, Mass. Concerning this pedestal there is quite a bit of interesting history. It appears that the Committee on the Library had in mind some native stone from the Hancock farm for the purpose of a pedestal which had been wanting for so many years, and the services of Rev. Edward G. Porter, the pastor of the Hancock church and a man of considerable reputation as a historical investigator, was secured. Through him was learned the location of the Hancock farm, and orders were given that a pedestal of the dimensions required should be secured for this statue. For some reason, which the correspondence does not divulge, it seems that this work of procuring the pedestal was postponed until the depth of winter, when the fields were snow covered and the ground deeply frozen. It was not at all easy under these conditions to select a stone suitable for the purpose, as this granite was not found in ledges, but in bowlders sometimes half covered by the frozen ground. The item of expenditures in this matter shows that 24 days were spent in the selection and the uncovering of the stone from which the pedestal was finally cut; that 54½ days were occupied in cutting the stone after it had been hauled to the yard of the granite workers at West Medford, Mass.; that it required a six-horse team to haul the stone; and that the polishing cost $150. The whole expense of this pedestal f. o. b. cars West Medford, Mass., was $586.45, and the difficulties are set forth in a letter from Mr. R. K. Stevenson, the granite worker, which accompanied the bill for the expenses incurred:

* * * The stone was taken from the woods at Lexington at midwinter, buried in the frozen ground. It was round and required hard work to bring it into even a movable shape, and cost three times as much as nice granite would have done of which I had plenty at my yard and not frozen solid in the ground. But it is a historical stone which I judge is what you were after. * * *

After all, the color and the form of the pedestal seem to be admirably adapted to this statue and the fact of its coming from the Hancock farm gives it a sentimental value not easily determinable in dollars and cents. Best of all, however, is the inscription on the pedestal, attributed to Senator George F. Hoar:

He wrote his name where all the nations could behold it, and where all Time should not efface it.

From different portions of the Capitol, and principally from the collection which existed in Statuary Hall when but few statues from the States had been donated, the busts on the gallery floor of the Senate, east corridor, have been gathered. The collection is a somewhat peculiar one, as it is practically without classification. It has been said that this section of the Capitol has become an international shrine, for here are gathered representatives from different countries and also two unquestioned Americans, Chippewa Indians, known as Be-sheek-kee and Aysh-ke-bah-ke-ko-zhay, who is probably known by the shorter name of "Flat-mouth." These works are by Francis Vincenti and have been referred to before. Here are also the busts of Kosciuszko and Pulaski, the first signed H. D. Saunders and the latter signed H. Dmochowski. Also the portrait bust of Abraham Lincoln by Mrs. S. F. Ames with its pedestal of Scotch granite, a donation from admirers of Abraham Lincoln in Scotland. In this same collection is a bust of Zachary Taylor by an unknown artist, concerning which there is a vague tradition that it was purchased by a relative of President Taylor while visiting a foreign port as an officer. It would be, indeed, interesting to know if this portrait is the work of the same Italian artist from whom a portrait bust had been supplied to the Library of Congress and was located in the library at the time of the fire of December 24, 1851. Concerning this bust it should be stated that all possible effort has been made to identify the artist by whom it was executed, and wherever the location of a bust of Zachary Taylor has been ascertained inquiry has been made to determine whether such a bust might not be a copy of the bust now in the Capitol. This bust was purchased by the Government from Mrs. Lola Wood, widow and sole executrix of John Taylor Wood, a grandson of President Zachary Taylor, but at the time of its purchase no definite history could be obtained. The resolution authorizing its purchase is as follows:

To enable the Joint Committee on the Library to purchase of Mistress Lola Wood, widow and sole executrix of John Taylor Wood esquire, (who was a grandson of President Zachary Taylor,) a bust of President Zachary Taylor, in her possession, to be placed in the Capitol Building, Two Thousand Dollars, or so much as may be necessary. (Approved March 4, 1909.) (Stats. L., vol. 35, p. 1019.)

The marble bust of the celebrated Italian patriot, Giuseppe Garibaldi, was presented to the Congress of the United States by the members of an Italian society for which Doctor Verdi, then of Washington, D. C., acted as the representative and secretary. This bust was accepted by the Library Committee for the Congress under section 1831, Revised Statutes of the United States. In the correspondence relating to its tender it was stated that the bust was the work of Giuseppe Martegani, a distinguished Italian sculptor then residing in Paris. Efforts to learn such facts concerning this sculptor as would be necessary for a biographical sketch have been fruitless.

Notwithstanding the different nationalities and the different types of sculptors represented in this section of the Capitol, it is by no means a mediocre collection of sculpture. The examples in each instance are notable specimens of the period and represent the practice of the art at the time. There are some examples, however, worthy of any location and of any period. In this collection is found the bust of Charles Sumner, for some time a distinguished member of the United States Senate. The fact that Mr. Sumner is represented by a portrait in oil and a portrait bust in the Senate wing of the Capitol evidences the esteem in which he was held by his countrymen. This bust is the work of Martin Milmore, who was born in Sligo, Ireland, 1844, and who died in Boston, Mass., July 21, 1883. As a boy while in the public schools he occupied his leisure time in the study of wood carving under the instruction of his elder brother, Joseph. This was followed by experiments in modeling. From 1860 to 1864 he was a pupil in the studio of Thomas Ball. In 1864 he was given a commission to execute in granite three large decorative figures, Ceres, Flora, and Pomona, for the Boston Horticultural Hall, an important commission for a sculptor 20 years of age. Among his works are Soldiers' and Sailors' Monument, Boston Common; Soldiers' Monument, Keene, N. H.; monuments at Charleston and Fitchburg, Mass.; statue of Gen. Sylvanus Thayer, West Point, N. Y.; portrait busts of Pope Pius IX, Wendell Phillips, and Emerson, executed while residing in Rome; portrait bust of George Ticknor, Boston Public Library; and busts of Cardinal McCloskey, General Grant, Lincoln, and Webster. The grave of Mr. Milmore in Forest Hills Cemetery, Boston, is marked by one of the most celebrated works of Daniel Chester French, Death and the Young Sculptor.

The latest addition to the collection of busts in this section of the Capitol is the bust of Viscount James Bryce, a gift to the American people by Sir Charles Cheers Wakefield for the Sulgrave Institution of Great Britain through the Sulgrave Institution of the United States. The ceremonies of presentation and acceptance occurred at the United States Capitol in the section of the building where the bust is now located on October 12, 1922. The bust, in bronze, is the work of the English sculptor, Reid Dick, who has recently been made an associate of the Royal Society of British Sculptors and whose biography follows: Born in Glasgow, Scotland, 1879; educated in Glasgow School of Art and at the City and Guilds Technical Institute, London; member of Royal Society of British Sculptors; associate Royal Academy, 1921; exhibitor at exhibitions of Royal Academy since 1908 and at Paris Salon and International Society; on active service in France and Palestine, 1915–1919; principal works, Boy with Catapult, purchased by Bradford Art Gallery; Femina Victrix, purchased by New South Wales Gallery; Androdus (bronze mask), purchased by Chantry trustees; war memorials, Rickmansworth and Bushey, Kitchener Memorial Chapel for St. Paul's Cathedral; large bronze eagle on Royal Air Force Memorial Embankment, London; bronze bust of Viscount Bryce for Senate gallery, east lobby, United States Capitol; and Earl of Chatham, for Pittsburgh, Pa.

In addition to the sculptural work and paintings heretofore referred to as belonging to the Senate wing of the Capitol, there is in the room of the Committee on the Judiciary a portrait of Allen G. Thurman, by John H. Witt, a painter of distinction, who was born in Dublin, Wayne County, Ind., May 18, 1840, and died in New York City October 23, 1900. He began life as a machinist and wagon painter in a small agricultural-implement factory owned by his uncles. He commenced portrait painting, in which he was entirely self-taught, at an early age and finally adopted it as a profession about 1863. While a resident of Ohio, from 1863 until 1879, he painted portraits of many governors and other prominent public men of Ohio. He resided in New York City from 1879 until the time of his death; was associate member of the National Academy of Design and member of various clubs of men of his profession.

BUST OF VISCOUNT JAMES BRYCE

Reid Dick, sculptor

{ 354 }

In the room of the Senate Committee on Rules are portraits of President Ulysess S. Grant, by W. Cogswell, and Pocahontas, a copy of a portrait by an unknown artist. This portrait of Pocahontas was loaned to the Columbian Exposition as a part of the Government exhibit. The artist, William Cogswell, is also represented in the Capitol by his portrait of Salmon P. Chase in the Supreme Court robing room. This painter is also represented in the White House by his portrait of President Lincoln, which for some time previous to its being acquired by the Government was exhibited in the Capitol. Mr. Cogswell was born in Fabius, N. Y., July 19, 1819, a descendant of John Cogswell, of Westburg, Leigh, county of Wilts, England, who settled in Ipswich, Mass., in 1633. At an early age he evidenced ability in art directions and was practically self-taught as a portrait painter. About 1834 he was for a short time in the studio of a portrait painter in Buffalo, N. Y., where his duties were largely those of a helper in grinding colors in oil. After a short time he started in business as a portrait painter on his own account, a work which he continued until within some two weeks of his death. He resided at periods in New York, Philadelphia, Chicago, St. Louis, Cincinnati, Louisville, San Francisco, and Los Angeles; made his first visit to San Francisco in 1850, remaining about one year; returning by way of Panama to New York, he walked across the Isthmus accompanied by a native carrying his baggage. From sketches made in California during the gold excitement and while on his trip across the Isthmus he painted a panorama covering a canvas of 40,000 square feet, which was exhibited throughout the Eastern States. His list of portraits includes the names of many prominent people, among them being Presidents Lincoln, Grant, and McKinley. His painting of President Grant and family, now in the National Gallery, has been reproduced in a steel engraving and thousands of copies sold. Other protraits are those of H. T. Blow, Joseph Charles, Jay Cooke, General Sheridan, Mr. and Mrs. Mark Hopkins, Professor Agassiz, Gov. Leland Stanford and Mrs. Stanford; also the following Governors of California: Burnett, Booth, Downie, Law, Haight, and Latha. In addition to extensive travels in the United States in the execution of commissions, he visited Australia and the Hawaiian Islands, and in Honolulu he painted the portrait of King Kalakaua and Queen Liliuokalani. Mr. Cogswell died in Pasadena, Calif., December 24, 1903, and this extensive and interesting biography was obtained in answer to the request of one of the committees of the Senate, which asked the question, "What do you know or what can you find out about Cogswell?" After many failures, with but little information in addition to a newspaper's notice of the death of this artist, members of his family were located, and from them the material for this biography was obtained.

Inasmuch as reference has been made to the transfer to the National Gallery of the statue Il Penseroso, by Mozier, it will not be out of place to refer to some other works of art which have formerly occupied places in the Senate wing of the Capitol, probably the most prominent of which was the First Fight of Ironclads, by William Formby Halsall, a distinguished painter of marine subjects. This painting for a long time hung in one of the eastern corridors of the Senate, but upon the introduction of elevators in that section of the building it became necessary to remove this notable work, and for some time this picture has been stored. It is unfortunate that there are no vacant spaces in the Capitol Building large enough to accommodate this work, and this is especially true for the reason that the painters of marine battle pictures are rare in this country. The artist was born in Kirkdale, England, March 20, 1841. At the age of 12 he went to sea in the ship *Ocean Rover*, of Portsmouth, N. H., and followed the sea for seven years; was in the United

States Navy during a part of the Civil War and afterwards learned the trade of fresco painting; was a student in the Massachusetts Institute of Technology, class of 1874; since 1877 he has painted the following marine pictures: First Fight of Ironclads, Monitor and Merrimac; The Mayflower, Memorial Hall, Plymouth, Mass.; Niagara Falls; Sheeted Ghost; The Winter Passage; When Sleep Falleth on Men; and Our Glory, the Battleship Oregon. This latter painting is now in the National Gallery. He died November 7, 1919, at Winthrop, Mass.

For many years the portrait of Prof. Joseph Henry occupied a prominent position in the office of the Sergeant at Arms of the Senate. The reason for the purchase of this portrait is not apparent, although it should not be understood that a portrait of Prof. Joseph Henry is not worthy of a place in any of the buildings of the Government, but so few portraits are contained in the Capitol other than those intimately connected with the political history of this country that it seems a little out of the ordinary that the portrait of Joseph Henry should have been purchased. The National Gallery, however, became interested in this portrait and the necessary legislation was enacted to transfer this work to the National Museum. The resolution of transfer (S. Res. 334, 64th Cong., 2d sess.) was read, considered by unanimous consent, and agreed to February 5, 1917 (Congressional Record, 64th Cong., 2d sess., p. 2910).

The painter of this portrait, Henry Ulke, was born in Frankenstein, Germany, January 29, 1821. He died in Washington, D. C., February 17, 1910. His education was received in Berlin as a pupil of Professor Wach, court painter at Berlin; he became associated with the revolutionary party and enlisted in the revolutionary army; was wounded, captured, and for a time held as a prisoner in the fortress of Spandau. Upon his release he decided to emigrate to the United States, and reached New York in 1849, where he found employment as an illustrator and designer, later coming to Washington, D. C., where he continued to reside during the remainder of his life. As a painter of portraits he counted among his patrons many distinguished people, some of whom were Charles Sumner, Salmon P. Chase, Chief Justice Taney, James G. Blaine, John Sherman, W. W. Corcoran, Carl Schurz, A. R. Shepherd, Secretary Stanton, Robert G. Ingersoll, and Mrs. Jefferson Davis. His portraits of different Secretaries of War are in the War Department, and his portraits of the Secretaries of the Treasury are in the Treasury Department. His portrait of General Grant is in the collection of portraits in the White House. Over 100 portraits were produced by this artist while in Washington. As a naturalist he was equally celebrated and is credited with gathering the largest known collection of American beetles, now on exhibition in the Museum of Natural History of the Carnegie Institute, Pittsburgh, Pa.

There is also in the Senate wing of the Capitol, in the room occupied by the Senate Committee on Foreign Relations, a portrait in oil of former Senator Shelby M. Cullom, the work of August Benziger, an artist who, it is claimed, has painted from life the portraits of seven Presidents of Republics and two Popes. This artist is a Swiss by birth and an American by adoption, his father being at the head of a famous publishing house in Einsiedeln, established there in the fifteenth century, which has been publisher to the Pope for 400 years. In 1852 his father went to New York, where he established a branch of the firm. Mr. Benziger studied art in Munich and Vienna, but his father was opposed to his becoming an artist and induced him to take up chemistry. He took French leave of the paternal roof and went to Paris, where he found refuge in the house of a friend of his father's. A few days after his arrival he painted a portrait of his host, which shortly after was exhibited at the Salon. He then studied under Bouguereau and afterwards became a pupil of Bonnat at the École des Beaux Arts. The portrait of Leo XIII, which he painted when he was 26, attracted great attention, and since that time his career has been one of uninterrupted success. Among his portraits are President Forrer, President of Switzerland; Porfirio Diaz, former President of Mexico; President McKinley, President Roosevelt, President Taft, Cardinal Gibbons, Gen. Luke E. Wright, Senator James O'Gorman, Charles M. Schwab, J. P. Morgan, and Curtis Guild, three times Governor of Massachusetts and ambassador to Russia.

Earlier in this work the portrait busts of some of the Chief Justices of the United States have been referred to; in fact, the legislation providing for the erection in the Supreme Court room of portrait busts of Chief Justices began at an early date. Prior to 1860, when the Supreme Court held its sessions in the room occupied at present by the law library, it is shown by some of the guidebooks of that period that the busts of Chief Justices were placed upon brackets attached to some of the columns of the court room. The use of brackets as supports for the busts was continued after the court commenced to hold its sessions in the present court room, so that at present there are now upon the walls the busts of John Jay, John Rutledge, Oliver Ellsworth, John Marshall, Roger B. Taney, Salmon P. Chase, Morrison R. Waite, Melville W. Fuller, and Edward D. White. It will be observed that the first four of the Chief Justices were without middle names, that all of the last five Chief Justices had middle names. Reference having been heretofore made to the legislation providing for busts of John Jay, John Rutledge, Oliver Ellsworth, and John Marshall, we will now refer to the busts of Chief Justice Roger Brooke Taney and to the portrait bust of Salmon Portland Chase. It should be understood that these busts were intended to be approximately of the same dimensions, so that in the Supreme Court room, mounted as they are upon brackets set into the wall and forming in reality a part of the architecture of this room, they should not be at variance so far as size and the manner of their presentation is concerned.

The legislation providing for the busts of Chief Justice Taney and Chief Justice Chase is in the following terms:

Be it enacted by the Senate and House of Representatives of the United States of America in Congress assembled, That the Joint Committee of the two Houses of Congress on the Library be and they are hereby authorized to procure and place in the room of the Supreme Court of the United States busts of the late Chief Justice Roger Brooke Taney and the late Salmon Portland Chase.

That for the purpose of carrying this act into effect the sum of $2,500, or so much thereof as may be necessary be and the same is hereby appropriated out of any money in the Treasury, not otherwise appropriated. (Approved January 29, 1874.) (Stats. L., vol. 18, p. 6.)

At the time of the passage of this act there was in Annapolis, Md., a seated bronze statue of Chief Justice Taney by Rinehart, and from the minutes of the Joint Committee on the Library it may be supposed that it was intended that Mr. Rinehart should have the commission for executing the bust of Chief Justice Taney. A curious mistake was made in connection with this bust, for in United States Reports, volume 173, pages 454–455, the following note made by the reporter is found:

* * * The fifth (appropriation) made January 29, 1874, authorized the Joint Committee on the Library to procure and place in the room of the Supreme Court busts of the late Chief Justice Roger Brooke Taney and of the late Salmon Portland Chase, and appropriated $2,500, for the purpose. The bust of Taney is by Rinehart, and that of Chase by Jones. * * *

While it is true that at the time of the passage of this act the artist William H. Rinehart was living, he seems to have passed away before definite action was taken concerning this bust. Mr. Rinehart died in Rome, Italy, October 28, 1874. The Committee on the Library finally acted upon the matter on the 19th of January, 1876, nearly two years after the passage of the legislation authorizing the procuring of the busts referred to. At the meeting of January 19, 1876, on the motion of Mr. Clymer, it was resolved:

> That the Chairman of the Committee be authorized to contract with some competent artist for a bust of the late Chief Justice Taney, the head of the same to be modeled after that of the Chief Justice at Annapolis. The cost of the same not to exceed $1,000.

The foregoing quotation seems to have been the last action taken by the committee upon this subject. From other minutes it appears that this matter was under consideration for some time and that a visit to Annapolis was made by the committee to see the statue of Chief Justice Taney by Rinehart. It is possible that at the time when the chairman of the committee was authorized to contract with some competent artist the artist had not been selected and for this reason the name of Saint-Gaudens does not appear in the records previous to the awarding of the commission. The following letter from Augustus Saint-Gaudens is sufficient to identify him as the sculptor of the bust of Chief Justice Taney, although by some authorities credit has been given to William H. Rinehart for this work. The letter is as follows:

153 FOURTH AVENUE, NEW YORK, *July 31, 1876.*

EDWARD CLARK, Esquire,
  Architect, U. S. Capitol.

SIR: Senator Howe has communicated to me your request in regard to the turning to the left of the head of Chief Justice Taney that I am to execute. This will be done.

I find it necessary to have the size of the largest as well as the smallest bust that there is in the Supreme Court room. To obtain this I would have to go to Washington. Might I ask you to spare me this trip by sending me the measurements as follows: the height from the top of the head to the lowest part of the bust, not including the base, the width from shoulder to shoulder, and the extreme thickness through the widest part of the body from back to front. I should consider this a great favor if you could do this for me. Hoping that I am not troubling you too much, I am

  Respectfully yours,

AUG. ST.-GAUDENS.

An examination of the audit of this account in the office of the Treasurer of the United States shows that the voucher was prepared February 26, 1877, and that it was audited May 19, 1877, and that it provided for the payment to A. Saint-Gaudens for a marble bust of Chief Justice Taney for the Supreme Court room, under contract with the Joint Library Committee of Congress, the sum of $700.

Inasmuch as the act of January 29, 1874, provided funds to the extent of $2,500 for the two busts included in the appropriation, it would seem that the committee was capable of securing valuable services at a reasonable compensation, as only $1,700 was expended out of this appropriation, of which $700 was paid to Saint-Gaudens and $1,000 to Thomas D. Jones. It is fair to conclude that at this time the artistic importance of Augustus Saint-Gaudens was not appreciated by the committee.

While the bust of Chief Justice Taney is mentioned first in the appropriation act, and for this reason we have discussed this bust before considering the bust of Salmon P. Chase, the bust of Chief Justice Chase was placed in the court room some time in the latter part of the year 1875, as appears from the audit account in the Treasury Department. The sculptor of this work, Thomas D. Jones, was probably selected on account of his being a resident at one time of the State of Ohio. He was born in Oneida County, N. Y., in 1808, of Welsh parentage. His parents moved from Oneida County to Granville,

Ohio, in 1837. Thomas was the eldest of ten children. His education was that of the common schools of that period. Upon arriving at manhood he went to Newark, N. J., to learn the trade of a tanner, but soon abandoned this trade on account of failing health. Returning to Ohio in 1837, he found employment as a stonemason upon the Ohio canals for some three or four years. During the winter months he taught school. In 1841 he moved to Cincinnati, Ohio, and became a marble cutter, and soon thereafter, without instruction, commenced the execution of busts, working first in wood, then in coarse stone, and finally in marble. His first serious work commenced in 1842, and he continued his sculptural work for some 37 years. During this time he resided in the cities of Cincinnati, New York, Boston, Nashville, and Detroit. A list of his works includes 34 busts, 6 statues, 10 medallions, and 3 groups. His patrons include President Zachary Taylor, Gen. Winfield Scott, Henry Clay, Daniel Webster, and John C. Breckinridge. Mr. Jones died at Columbus, Ohio, February 28, 1881.

In a footnote (vol. 173, U. S. Reports, p. 465) it is also stated:

The latest appropriation made March 2, 1889, was to procure and place in the room of the Supreme Court of the United States a bust of the late Chief Justice Morrison Remick Waite, $1,500. The bust is by St. Gaudens of New York.

This reference includes the third bust executed by Saint-Gaudens to be found in the United States Capitol Building. It will be observed that the price, $1,500, is a larger consideration than was paid for the bust of Chief Justice Taney or for the bust of Vice President Arthur. It seems almost incredible that a sculptor of the ability of Mr. Saint-Gaudens would consent to execute an example of his work for even the larger sum received by him for the bust of Chief Justice Waite; much, however, is probably due to the advice of friends and their entreaties that he should execute the various works which have been referred to. The bust of Chief Justice Waite is considered a fine example of the work of this renowned sculptor, and during the Saint-Gaudens Memorial Exhibition, held in Washington at the Corcoran Gallery of Art, this bust was one of the conspicuous objects.

The sculptor Augustus Saint-Gaudens was born in Dublin, Ireland, March 1, 1848, son of Bernard Paul Ernest Saint-Gaudens and Mary McGuiness; came to this country with his parents in 1848, an infant 6 months of age. The father was a shoemaker, and the conditions surrounding his boyhood made it necessary that Augustus, the third of five sons, should as soon as possible aid in the family support. At the age of 13 he was apprenticed to a stone-cameo cutter named Avet, and at the same time he entered the night classes in drawing of the Cooper Institute. In 1864 he revolted at the ill nature of his employer and left him for employment with Jules LeBrethon and changed his art school from the Cooper Institute to the National Academy of Design, where he commenced to model from life. In 1867 he was assisted by his father to go to Paris to study. His living was earned by cutting cameos, while he pursued a course of study at the Petite École and later at the École des Beaux Arts under Jouffroy. During the Franco-Prussian War he was strongly in favor of joining the French Army, but was persuaded by a letter from his mother to abandon the idea, and instead of entering the army he went to Rome for further study, where for about four years his life was a series of struggles with poverty. In 1873 Saint-Gaudens was located in New York City, and in a letter dated May 12, 1873, addressed to A. B. Mullett, then Supervising Architect of the Treasury, he expressed a desire to know whether the competition for the Farragut Statue had been annulled and if another competition would be held. He was at that time anxious to compete for the Farragut Statue and stated that he soon expected to return to Italy. In 1876 he was engaged on his portrait bust of Chief Justice Taney for the Supreme Court room. His letter of July 31, 1876, gives us a glimpse of a young sculptor deferring to the wishes of others and meekly taking orders for commissions to be executed in accordance with the suggestions of his patrons. In 1885 Saint-Gaudens, in a letter to Edward Clark, then Architect of the Capitol, thanked the commission having in charge the proposed Lafayette Monument for the honor conferred by the invitation to furnish a model for the Lafayette Statue, but stated that if the same proposal had been made to other sculptors he must decline the honor. A complete list of Saint-Gaudens's work would include many of the leading examples of sculpture in this country. His prominent works are the Shaw memorial, Boston; the Lincoln Statue, Chicago; the Adams memorial, Rock Creek Cemetery, Washington, D. C.; and the Sherman Statue, New York City. Celebrated as his statues are throughout the country, to many his most attractive works are his charming portraits in low relief. Saint-Gaudens died in Cornish, N. H., August 3, 1907.

CHAPTER XIX

STATUARY AND PAINTINGS IN THE SUPREME COURT SECTION

HILE the Supreme Court room has by the custom of many years been the place for the location of busts of former Chief Justices, the robing room of the Supreme Court has for many years been decorated with portraits in oil of former Chief Justices. The first official legislative enactment providing for the purchase of portraits of the Chief Justices was the act of October 2, 1888, at which time an appropriation of $1,500 was made for portraits of Chief Justices Rutledge, Ellsworth, and Waite. This appropriation also specified that they were to be hung in the robing room of the Supreme Court with those of other Chief Justices already there. The portrait of the first Chief Justice, John Jay, appears by the record to have been presented to the court by the members of the Jay family. It has been carried in lists heretofore made as being a copy from Gilbert Stuart's, by Gray. Just who this artist Gray is does not seem to be shown by any of the references found relating to this picture. The portrait of Chief Justice Roger B. Taney was painted by G. P. A. Healy, and such information as has been received concerning it shows that it was purchased through a subscription by friends of the Chief Justice, who procured the portrait from the artist. The artist, George Peter Alexander Healy, was born in Boston, Mass., July 15, 1813; studied in Paris from 1836; went to Chicago about 1858 and painted portraits; revisited Europe in 1869 and for a long time resided in Rome; was celebrated for his portraits of distinguished people, among whom are E. B. Washburne, General Grant (1878), Webster, Clay, Calhoun, Guizot, Presidents John Tyler, John Quincy Adams, Andrew Jackson, Martin Van Buren, Zachary Taylor, Millard Fillmore, James K. Polk, Franklin Pierce, James Buchanan, and Abraham Lincoln. Many of the foregoing portraits are the official presidential portraits of the Executive Mansion. It is claimed that he had a commission from Louis Philippe to paint portraits of Clay, Calhoun, Webster, and Richard Mentor Johnson. The only examples of the work of this artist in the Capitol Building are the portraits of Chief Justice Taney and Justice Story in the robing room of the Supreme Court. Mr. Healy died in Chicago, Ill., June 24, 1894.

In the robing room is a large portrait of Chief Justice Marshall, by Rembrandt Peale. This is a companion picture to the portrait of Washington, by the same artist, and now hanging in the room of the Vice President. The artist had contemplated these two portraits as decorations for one of the large rooms of the Capitol where they might hang near each other, but was unable to effect the sale of the Marshall portrait to the Government. Years went by and the Marshall portrait was finally purchased by friends of Chief Justice Chase, who bequeathed this portrait to the Supreme Court.

Reference has heretofore been made, in connection with the portrait of General Grant, occupying a place in the room of the Senate Committee on Rules, to the artist, William Cogswell, and in connection with that portrait the biography of Cogswell was given. Mr. Cogswell also painted the portrait of Chief Justice Chase, which was purchased from an old Washington family and placed in the Supreme Court room, where it now hangs. In connection with what has heretofore been said about the artist Cogswell it may be

Copy by Gray from an original painted by Gilbert Stuart   In the robing room of the Supreme Court

PORTRAIT OF JOHN JAY
First Chief Justice of the United States

stated that in a book, Behind the Scenes in Washington, by E. W. Martin (1873), this reference is found:

At the west end (south Senate corridor) is a fine portrait of Lincoln by Cogswell. A bust of Chief Justice Taney stands at the eastern end. * * *

This portrait of Lincoln, referred to in the foregoing quotation, is the portrait now in the White House. The portrait bust of Chief Justice Taney, also referred to, is by the sculptor Horatio Stone. There seems to be no record of its having been purchased, and the supposition exists that it was a subscription bust and presented to the court either by friends of the Chief Justice or friends of the sculptor. This bust is now in the conference room of the Supreme Court.

The act of 1888, providing for the purchase of three portraits, was complied with by the purchase of W. R. Wheeler of a portrait of Chief Justice Ellsworth, copied by C. L. Elliott from a portrait by R. Earle. Charles L. Elliott is also represented in the Capitol Building by his portrait of Joseph B. Varnum, a Speaker from the State of Massachusetts. This portrait has been referred to in that portion of the work which gave the condition of the Speaker's lobby and reference to the portraits therein very soon after that lobby was set apart as a place for hanging portraits of former Speakers.

Another portrait included in the list selected for purchase was that of Chief Justice Rutledge. This portrait was painted by Robert Hinckley, who used as his material a miniature of Chief Justice Rutledge, by John Trumbull. Mr. Hinckley's biography has been given in connection with his portrait of former Speaker Charles F. Crisp in the Speaker's lobby, House of Representatives.

Mrs. Cornelia Adele Fassett, who has been referred to in connection with her large painting, The Florida Case, furnished the portrait of Chief Justice Waite to complete the list of three portraits appropriated for under the act of 1888. Since that time, however, other portraits have been added to this collection in the robing room. Among those added during later years is another portrait of Chief Justice Marshall, which was purchased under the provisions of the act of August 30, 1890 (vol. 26, p. 410, U. S. Stats. L.). This act is as follows:

To enable the marshal of the Supreme Court of the United States, under the direction of the court, to obtain the oil portrait of Chief Justice Marshall, to be hung in the robing room with those of the other deceased Chief Justices already there, $1,000., or so much thereof as may be necessary.

This portrait, which by some is considered a very excellent if not the best portrait of Chief Justice Marshall, was brought to the attention of the court through Justice Bradley, who was able to procure it from a relative of Chief Justice Marshall, such relative furnishing the information that it was considered by the family to be the best known portrait of Mr. Marshall. The only information given at the time of its purchase was that it was painted by Martin, and in some manner in some of the publications relating to the Capitol it has been referred to as "painted by Martin in 1814." The source of such information has never been determined. For many years the identity of the painter was in doubt, and many well versed in methods of search for the authorship of works of art had tried to locate and identify the painter Martin without any degree of success. In a recent reprint of the Arts of Design, by Dunlap, there has been included a supplementary index of painters, sculptors, etchers, and engravers not contained in the original work. In this index there is contained the statement that John B. Martin was an engraver who resided in Richmond in 1822. From this scanty information a trace was discovered which led to the conclusion that the John B. Martin referred to was not

PORTRAIT OF CHIEF JUSTICE JOHN MARSHALL

John B. Martin, painter

JOHN B. MARTIN

Self-portrait

Represented by the portrait of Chief Justice Marshall in the robing room
of the Supreme Court

only an engraver but also a portrait painter, and after long search his identity as the painter of the portrait of John Marshall, purchased under the act of August 30, 1890, was satisfactorily determined.   In this connection the following biography is given:

John B. Martin was born in Bandon, county of Cork, Ireland, September 5, 1797. His ancestry was distinguished; a branch of the O'Neills, monarchs of Ireland, princes of Ulster, earls of Tyrone.   As a child his art tendencies were shown by his drawings on the sands.   He came to the United States soon after the close of the War of 1812; studied engraving in New York; moved to Richmond about 1817, where he followed his occupation as an engraver.   Among portraits known to have been engraved by Martin are those of John Randolph of Roanoke, Robert Bailey, John D. Blair, and Charles I.   As a painter

{ 365 }

ALBERT ROSENTHAL

Self-portrait

Represented in the Supreme Court section by portraits of Chief Justices Melville W. Fuller and Edward D. White
and by portraits of E. B. Caldwell, James H. McKenney, and James D. Maher
clerks of the Supreme Court

In the Supreme Court room

BUST OF CHIEF JUSTICE MELVILLE W. FULLER

William Ordway Partridge, sculptor

{ 367 }

he was self-taught. Mr. E. V. Valentine, the sculptor, who knew Martin, states that his ability to grasp and express the essentials of a portrait was greater than his skill in handling the medium of his expression. No detailed list of his portraits is known. He painted four different portraits of Chief Justice Marshall; also portraits of Thomas A. Rust, Rev. Moses Drury Hoge, and Dr. John B. Brockenborough.

As a citizen of Richmond, Va., Mr. Martin was highly esteemed. For many years he was an elder of the Second Presbyterian Church, and four of his sons became Presbyterian ministers. His knowledge of the Bible, according to his pastor, was greater than that of any except the graduates of theological seminaries. He cared far more for being of service to those about him than for praise of his work as an artist. He died in Richmond, Va., October 22, 1857.

Another portrait occupying a position in the robing room is that of Melville W. Fuller. This portrait is the work of Albert Rosenthal, who has painted portraits of a large number of the Chief Justices of the United States and whose specialty is the painting of portraits. Mr. Rosenthal was born in Philadelphia, Pa., January 30, 1863. His art education was received at the Pennsylvania Academy of Fine Arts and at the École des Beaux Arts in Paris, where he was a pupil of Gérôme. In 1908 he exhibited at the Corcoran Gallery of Art a notable collection of portraits of the Chief Justices and Associate Justices of the Supreme Court of the United States, and his ability as a portrait painter was at that time prominently brought before the public. He was awarded a bronze medal at the St. Louis Exposition, 1904, and the gold medal of the American Art Society at Philadelphia, Pa., 1907. In addition to the portraits of Chief Justice Fuller and Chief Justice White he is represented in the Supreme Court section of the Capitol by the portraits of the following clerks of the Supreme Court: E. B. Caldwell, James H. McKenney, and James D. Maher.

If there has existed an unwritten rule that only the portraits of those who have served as Chief Justices of the United States should be honored by having their portraits placed in the robing room of the Supreme Court, this rule has been set aside by the placing in the robing room of a portrait of Justice Story, painted by G. P. A. Healy, and presented to the court by the widow of Chief Justice White. This portrait was at one time owned by J. B. Bryan and later by an attorney, John Selden; from Mr. Selden it passed to the possession of Mr. C. C. Glover, who presented it to Chief Justice White. As a portrait it is fully worthy of a place in any collection of portraits of distinction, and when it is remembered that it is doubtless through the wise counsel of Justice Joseph Story that the official acts of Chief Justice Marshall have been received with such high favor by those competent to judge of the value of the decisions of the Supreme Court the portrait has an added value in that it is a portrait of a man upon whose wisdom Chief Justice Marshall willingly relied.

One of the attractive busts in the court room of the Supreme Court is the bust of Chief Justice Melville W. Fuller, the work of William Ordway Partridge. At the present time all of the available spaces in the Supreme Court room, or at least the best of them, are occupied by brackets upon which have been placed busts of the Chief Justices. The architectural possibilities of the room would seem to preclude the possibility of the addition of more busts without destroying the symmetrical arrangement which now exists, and yet an appropriation was made (deficiency act, approved March 4, 1923) for the purpose of procuring a bust of Chief Justice Edward Douglass White.

The sculptor of the bust of Chief Justice Fuller, William Ordway Partridge, was born in Paris, France, April 11, 1861. His education was received in the schools of New York

BUST OF CHIEF JUSTICE EDWARD D. WHITE

Bryant Baker, sculptor

BRYANT BAKER

Represented by the bust of Chief Justice Edward D. White
in the Supreme Court room

and in Columbia College. He studied art in Paris, Florence, and Rome; received the degree of M. A. from Adelphi College, Brooklyn, N. Y. Among his best known sculptural works are equestrian statue of General Grant, Union League Club, Brooklyn; bronze statue of Alexander Hamilton, Brooklyn; group, Christ and St. John, Brooklyn Museum of Fine Art; Hamilton Statue, Columbia University; Schermerhorn memorial, Columbia University; statue of Shakespeare, Lincoln Park, Chicago; bust of Edward Everett Hale, Union League Club, Chicago; Kauffman memorial, Washington, D. C.; baptismal font, St. Peter and St. Paul's Cathedral, Washington, D. C.; bust of Whittier, Boston Public Library; statue of Poçahontas, Jamestown, Va.; statue of Horace Greeley, Chappaqua, N. Y.; statue of Nathan Hale, St. Paul, Minn.; statue of Thomas Jefferson, New York City; busts of Van Amringe and Schermerhorn, Columbia University. Has exhibited works in Paris Salon and in Royal Academy, London; member of Authors' Club, Architectural League, City Club, and Psi Upsilon of New York City, and of Cosmos Club and National Geographic Society, Washington, D. C.; author of Art for America, The Song Life of a Sculptor, The Technique of Sculpture, The Angel of Clay (novel), Nathan Hale, The Ideal Patriot, and The Czar's Gift (novel).

When the deficiency act of March 4, 1923, previously referred to, was enacted, it made provision for a marble bust with a pedestal and an oil portrait of Chief Justice Edward Douglass White, the bust to be placed in the court room of the Supreme Court and the portrait in the robing room. Mr. Rosenthal having painted a portrait from life of the Chief Justice, produced under this act a satisfactory portrait which was purchased and placed in the robing room. The commission for the bust was awarded to the sculptor P. Bryant Baker, who was at this time well known in Washington by his many notable sculptures produced in the period following the World War, during which he served with the American forces. In his bust of Chief Justice White he has produced a work comparing favorably with the high achievements of the sculptors represented in the court room. Mr. Baker was born in London, England, July 8, 1881. His father, John Baker, was also a sculptor. His education was completed at the Royal Academy of Arts, London; received first medal for design in sculpture in 1910; executed a bust of King Edward VII, also a heroic statue of King Edward VII, for Huddlesfield, Yorkshire, unveiled by King George in 1912. Many replicas of the bust of King Edward have been furnished to members of the royal family. In the United States Mr. Baker has executed busts of Ex-President Woodrow Wilson, President Calvin Coolidge, Chief Justice William Howard Taft, Gen. John J. Pershing, Secretary Herbert Hoover, Surg. Gen. Merritt W. Ireland, George Harvey, former ambassador to the Court of St. James, John Hays Hammond, Ambassador Sir Auckland Geddes, David Lloyd-George, former Senator Henry Cabot Lodge, and the late Col. John C. Coolidge. He has been an exhibitor at the Royal Academy, the Paris Salon, and the principal galleries of Europe. New Orleans in April, 1926, unveiled a colossal statue of Chief Justice White, the work of Mr. Baker.

In connection with the art of the Supreme Court we should not forget to mention a marble bust of Associate Justice John McLean. This bust was for some time on exhibition in the robing room, but was finally removed to a location in one of the rooms near the conference room on the floor below. This work is that of the sculptor Benjamin Paul Akers, who was born in Westbrook, Cumberland County, Me., in 1825. He was for some time a resident of Portland, Me., where he studied painting. In Boston (1849) he was given lessons in plaster casting by Carew. After making several busts of a prominent character he made his first visit to Europe, visiting Florence, Italy, where he remained during the year 1852 and is said to have studied under Powers at that time. His second visit abroad was made in 1854. This visit, with the exception of a brief return to this country, comprised six years' study abroad, during which time he worked in Rome and Venice, also in England and Switzerland. It is probable that on his return to the United States about 1859 he executed in Washington the portrait bust of Justice John McLean, now the property of the Supreme Court. Among his works are Peace, Una and the Lion, Girl Pressing Grapes, Isaiah, Schiller's Diver, Reindeer, The Lost Pearl Diver, St. Elizabeth of Hungary, Milton, Diana and Endymion; portrait busts of Tilton, Longfellow, Samuel Appleton, Edward Everett, Professor Cleveland, Garrett Smith, and Sam Houston. According to some biographers he was called Paul on account of his serious religious characteristics. He was also a frequent contributor on art subjects to the leading periodicals. He died in Philadelphia, Pa., in 1861.

In the robing room may be seen the mural decorations by Max F. Friederang. While the decorations are small and not attractive, on account of the size, the most noticeable portions of the decorations being in the ceiling, there is to be seen in the row of small vignette heads an example of that branch of fresco work known as sgraffito, a method of fresco in which different shades of color are obtained in relief produced by cutting away portions of the overlaying color in order that the necessary combination of color may be obtained. Mr. Friederang has also decorated another room in the Capitol which is now occupied as a committee room by the Joint Committee on Printing. This artist was born in Storkach, Baden, Germany, October 8, 1856, and graduated at the Normal School of Meersburg in 1876. His art education was received in a course in the art school of Basel and at the Polytechnic School of Zurich; was for some time a teacher in the schools of Germany. His art interest led him to abandon teaching and for some time he traveled in Italy, Spain, Greece, Egypt, and Palestine, finally locating in Rome, Italy, for an extended study of the works of Raphael, Michaelangelo, and other masters of the Italian renaissance. His studies of the art of fresco resulted in important discoveries of the ancient art, his chemical and artistic education greatly facilitating this research. Returning to Germany, he accepted a position under the Government at Baden, but finding that climatic changes were required for his work in fresco he came to the United States in 1889. He furnished illustrations for many publications and was successful in the illustrations for the Prince Henry program and the souvenir book of his tour of the United States in 1902; in 1904 he opened a studio for the introduction of his favorite work in fresco buono. Among his works are St. Patrick Converting the King of Tara, St. Theresa's Catholic Church, Brooklyn; The Grotto of Our Lady of Lourdes, Brooklyn, a mural painting covering an area of 6,687 square feet; decorations, St. Mary's Church, Norwalk, Conn.; exterior of Buckingham Music Hall, Waterbury, Conn. (the last work of Stanford White); the Day of '49; 18 historical frescoes for The Bivouac, the home of Gen. Harrison Gray Otis, Los Angeles, Calif.; history of the face of Christ, 40 frescoes in St. Thomas' Protestant Episcopal Church, Fifth Avenue and Forty-third Street, New York; and the mural decorations for the dome of St. Joseph's Church, Babylon, Long Island. While the work of Mr. Friederang is principally that of a mural decorator, he has also executed several portraits.

Reference has heretofore been made to the marble bust of Chief Justice Taney, by Horatio Stone, in the conference room. There is also in the conference room a portrait group of the Justices of the Supreme Court, the work of Cornelia Adele Fassett. This group is interesting, as it contains the problem in composition of arranging the distinguished members of the Supreme Court in such a manner that an acceptable work of art could be produced. So far as known this is the only instance in the Capitol of a group of this kind being produced by any medium other than photography. There are in different portions of that section of the Capitol occupied by the Supreme Court a number of pictures of the Justices of the Supreme Court made by photography, and they furnish an interesting record of the personnel of this distinguished body of men from time to time. The most of these examples are to be found in the law library, formerly the court room of the Supreme Court. In some of the early guidebooks are found references to brackets attached to the columns of the law library and used to support busts of Chief Justices. We suppose that this reference is reliable, but no traces showing where the brackets had been placed have been found. There is, however, a portrait bust of Associate Justice Story, the work of W. W. Story, and a bas-relief group on the western wall of the law library, attributed to Carlo Franzoni and by some thought possibly to be the work of his older brother, Giuseppe Franzoni. It may not be important whether the work is rightfully attributed to Carlo Franzoni, as it does not appear to be in keeping with that notable example of the work of Carlo Franzoni known as the Car of History, in Statuary Hall, and which has previously been referred to. It may be, however, that the medium in which this work was executed was so entirely different from the marble of Carrara, with which Carlo Franzoni was perfectly familiar, that he was unable to express himself with his customary ease in this coarser medium. This group occupies the lunette on the west wall of the law library. It is rather difficult to describe, for the reason that the emblematology or symbology seems somewhat obscure. The figure of Justice seated in a Roman chair holding the scales in her left hand, with her right hand resting upon a sword, is of itself pleasing and complete, but the additional seated figure at the right, holding a tablet upon which is displayed the words "The Constitution of the U. S.," is somewhat mystical on account of the wings and the sun, which is probably intended as a rising sun on account of its nearness to the horizon. At the other extremity of the lunette are four volumes guarded by an eagle. The whole space is occupied, but the harmony of the composition, if there may be harmony found therein, does not appeal to many who have seen it. Those who have noticed the low relief work upon the Car of History and who have seen the decorations of the mantels in the Supreme Court room may readily conclude that the same artist who executed the Car of History could have executed the mantel decorations without showing any marked deviation from his pronounced ability, but to conclude that the bas-relief group upon the wall of the law library is also the work of Carlo Franzoni seems to be a conclusion which may be possible but not probable.

The reference to the beautiful low relief carving upon the mantel ornamentations of the fireplaces in the passageway formed by the screen immediately back of the seats of the Justices in the Supreme Court room should not be left without some further explanation. It will be remembered from what has heretofore been said of Carlo Franzoni that many of his descendants are now residing in the city of Washington. These descendants are mainly great-grandchildren of this sculptor, and among them are interesting traditions relating to Carlo Franzoni. There is a tradition that while residing in his home on Four-and-a-half Street he carved these mantel ornamentations or panels for his own entertainment and not for the purpose of offering them for sale to the Government. Just how these ornaments came into the possession of the Government is not known, nor does the tradition furnish any explanation of the manner in which the Government obtained possession of them. This much, however, is true, that the mantels are very old and that there seems to be no written history among the records relating to the rebuilding of the Capitol showing their construction.

William Wetmore Story, the sculptor whose portrait bust of Justice Story has been referred to as being located in the law library, was born in Salem, Mass., February 12, 1819. He graduated from Harvard in 1838, with the degree of A. B. and from Harvard Law School in 1840, with the degree of LL. B. He was educated as a lawyer, but never followed that profession; published legal books, two volumes of poems, and a life of his father, Justice Story, prior to 1851. In that year he selected sculpture as a profession and opened a studio in Rome. In the Metropolitan Museum he is represented by statues of Cleopatra, Semiramis, Salome, Media, and Polyxenia; his statues of George Peabody are in London and Baltimore; in Boston are his statues of Edward Everett and William Prescott; and in Washington his statues of Prof. Joseph Henry and Chief Justice Marshall, the latter statue occupying a location upon the west plaza between the stairways of the Capitol Grounds. He died in Vallambrosa, Italy, October 7, 1895.

Before leaving that section of the Capitol known as the Supreme Court section we should not omit reference to the collection of portraits of former clerks of the Supreme Court. These portraits are in one of the rooms attached to the office of the clerk of the Supreme Court and seem to have been gifts to that office. Here may be found a portrait of John Tucker, a copy after Gilbert Stuart by Charles Armor, a painter of Washington, D. C., who is well known as an expert in copying oil paintings; in fact, some have said that his copies are great improvements upon the original paintings.

The portrait of another clerk, Samuel Bayard, is by an unknown artist.

The portrait of E. B. Caldwell is the work of Albert Rosenthal, whose biography has been given in connection with his portrait of Chief Justice Fuller.

The portrait of William Griffith is the work of Harold L. MacDonald, who was born in Manitowoc, Wis., May 13, 1861; pupil of Boulanger and Lefebvre in Paris. For many years he resided in Washington, where he maintained a high standard as a portrait painter. He died in Washington, D. C., January 31, 1923.

The portrait of William T. Carroll is the work of Rufus Wright, who was born near Cleveland, Ohio, in 1832; received his art education from the schools of the National Academy, New York, and was also a pupil for some time of George A. Baker; occupied the position of instructor in the school of the Brooklyn Academy of Design for five years or more; exhibited at the Academy of Design in 1876 the Morning Bouquet, and in 1877 The Inventor and The Banker. In addition to this portrait of William T. Carroll he has painted portraits of Secretary Stanton, Secretary Seward, Chief Justice Taney, and Father McGinn.

The portrait of Daniel Wesley Middleton is the work of Thomas Hicks, who was born in Newtown, Bucks County, Pa., October 18, 1823; began painting at the age of 15; studied in the Pennsylvania Academy of Fine Arts, Philadelphia, Pa., and the Academy of Design, New York. His first important picture, The Death of Abel, was exhibited in 1841. In 1845 he sailed for Europe and painted in London, Florence, Rome, and Paris. In Paris he was a pupil of Couture. In 1849 he returned to New York and entered upon a successful career as a portrait painter. Among his works are portraits of Doctor Kane, Henry Ward Beecher, William C. Bryant, T. Addison Richards, Bayard Taylor, Oliver Wendell Holmes, Henry W. Longfellow, Harriet Beecher Stowe, and William M. Evarts. He died November 8, 1890.

The portraits of James H. McKenney and of James D. Maher are the work of Albert Rosenthal, whose biography has been given earlier in this work.

In former publications relating to the history and the art of the Capitol there has been no reference made to the collection of portraits of the reporters of the Supreme Court. This collection, belonging to the office occupied by the reporters, is a collection by donation or subscription as contradistinguished from such portraits as have been referred to which have been acquired by gift or by purchase. It may not be out of place at this time to give a list of these portraits, with mention of the artist by whom they were executed.

In order to enter the room of the reporter of the Supreme Court we pass through a corridor opening from a door at our left as we enter the Supreme Court section of the Capitol from the north. As the Supreme Court room is semicircular in shape and occupies that portion of the Capitol east of the central corridor running north and south, from necessity at the northeast and southeast corners there must be considerable space, owing to the circular form of the room, so that this door entering into the corridor running east and west really opens into a small room 15 feet in length by 12 feet in width, which has been subdivided for use as a library and for other purposes, leaving the corridor at the north side of this space. This corridor extends 40 feet to the east on the north line of the Supreme Court section, and it is from this corridor that the Justices enter and leave the court room. At the extreme end of the corridor a right-angle turn is made to the south, giving a room 14 feet long by 6 feet in width, with a window near the south end looking toward the east. There is but little in the room in the way of furniture except a desk and a chair. On the east and west walls of the room and in the space on the south wall immediately over the desk can be found portraits of those who have served the Supreme Court in the capacity of reporter. The first reporter was Alexander James Dallas, who served from the February term, 1790, to the August term of 1800. His portrait was copied from a portrait by Gilbert Stuart, painted about 1795 and at one time in the possession of his granddaughter, Mrs. Emory, of Washington. Mr. Dallas was followed by William Cranch, who served from the August term of 1801 until the February term of 1815. The portrait of Mr. Cranch is a copy from an original portrait painted in 1846 by Christopher Pearse Cranch, a son of the reporter, and the original portrait was the property of the Supreme Court of the District of Columbia. Henry Wheaton, the next to occupy this office, served from the February term, 1816, to the February term, 1827. His portrait is in reality a third copy. The original was by Jarvis and painted about 1815. This was copied by Healy and the portrait in the room of the reporter is a copy of the Healy portrait referred to. Richard Peters succeeded Mr. Wheaton and served from the January term, 1828, to the January term, 1842. His portrait is from an original by Rembrandt Peale, painted in 1806; the copy now in the reporter's room was from this original portrait, which at that time was in the possession of Mrs. John Peale, of Albany, N. Y., a daughter of Mr. Peters. Following in the line of succession was Benjamin Chew Howard, who served from the January term, 1843, to the December term, 1860. The portrait in this case was painted from a photograph furnished by members of his family. Mr. Howard was succeeded by Jeremiah Sullivan Black, who served from the December term, 1861, to the December term, 1862. Mr. Black is represented by a portrait painted from a photograph furnished by his daughter, Mrs. Hornsby. Mr. Black was followed in office by John William Wallace, who served from the December term, 1863, to the October term, 1874. The portrait in this case is from a photograph and an oil sketch furnished by his daughter, Mrs. Spencer, of Philadelphia. Next in order was William Todd Otto, who served from the October term, 1875, to the October term, 1882. This portrait was painted from a photograph in the Department of the Interior. The last reporter to be commemorated with a portrait was John C. Bancroft Davis, who served from the November term, 1883, to September 11, 1902. His portrait hangs over the desk and was painted from life by Robert Hinckley, the artist who painted the other eight portraits previously referred to in this connection, and from the material given with each portrait mentioned. Concerning the portraits as a whole, they are of varying quality. The portrait of Mr. Davis, painted from life, is far better than any of the other works. It may be, however, that some injudicious restoration or cleaning has been done to these works and that the artist should not be blamed for the present condition of some of them. Since the termination of the service of John C. Bancroft Davis two other reporters have served. Charles Henry Butler, who was appointed December 4, 1902, and served until the appointment of Ernest Knaebel, the present incumbent, who was appointed October 10, 1916.

CHAPTER XX

STATUES IN THE ROTUNDA AND STATUARY HALL

 N THE period of time which elapsed since reference has been made to the works of art in the rotunda of the Capitol several art works had been acquired and placed in the rotunda. Among these art works is the marble bust of Lafayette, known as the Manigault bust, a replica of the bust presented by David d'Angers, which was burned during the fire in the Library of Congress November 24, 1851. The original bust was presented by David through President John Quincy Adams to the Congress of the United States with the request that it might be set up in the Hall of Congress near the monument erected to Washington. It was received and placed in the Hall of the House on January 28, 1829. The history of the bust by David is covered on pages 88–90.

It may be interesting to those whose sentimental qualities are largely developed to know that this bust is not only the work of a distinguished French sculptor but that it is also made from marble quarried in France. The bust was executed in 1830 for Mr. Charles Manigault, of Charleston, S. C., and the following extract from his diary may be of interest:

Elizabeth and myself left Charleston in May, 1828, for a two and a half years' visit to Europe. The distinguished Col. Frank Huger, of our State, who in his early manhood made the gallant but unsuccessful attempt to rescue General Lafayette from the dungeon of Olmuts, in Germany, where he (Lafayette) was so long imprisoned, hearing of our departure for La Belle France, gave us a letter of introduction to General Lafayette and his interesting family, whom we saw much of in Paris, which resulted in a special invitation to visit them at their chateau, La Grance, about 20 miles from Paris, which is an ancient feudal and in early days a strongly fortified castle. But now we only behold its turrets, moat, and drawbridge.

General Lafayette, among other things of interest shown us here, placed in our hands the ponderous key of the Bastile. * * *

A bust of Lafayette engrossed our interest, having inscriptions on it relating to our country (which inscriptions I will copy below), as seen also on my bust of the general. On inquiring of whom, respecting the artist, he informed us that it was the work of a distinguished young sculptor of Paris named David, and that he, the general, "sent the original of this bust as a present to the United States Government," and that it is now in Washington.

On taking leave of our kind friends at La Grance, General Lafayette gave me a letter to David, and I engaged him to make a similar bust for me. From patriotic feelings the old general and the sculptor had these busts made of French marble from the quarry near Bordeaux, though it be not of so fine and bright a grain as the marble of Italy.

This bust was purchased upon the recommendation of the Joint Committee on the Library contained in Senate Report No. 2544 (57th Cong., 2d sess.), and the legislation enacted for the purchase of this bust is as follows:

For the purchase by the Joint Committee on the Library of a marble bust of General Lafayette by David d'Angers to replace the one destroyed by fire in eighteen hundred and fifty-one, two thousand dollars. (Stats. L., vol. 33, p. 511.) (Approved April 28, 1904.)

It seems to have been very fortunate that the Government was able to purchase this bust of Lafayette. At the time of the fire in the Library there was also destroyed a bronze bust of Washington by some sculptor whose identity is not well established, but in some manner it became attributed to David d'Angers. The French nation, however,

VIEW IN THE ROTUNDA

From the right are the statues of General Baker, General Grant, and Alexander Hamilton
The statues of Baker and Hamilton are by Horatio Stone; the statue
of General Grant is the work of Franklin Simmons

BUST OF GEORGE WASHINGTON

David d'Angers, sculptor

{ 379 }

remembering that a bust of Washington had been destroyed by the fire in the library in 1851,[1] after many years had elapsed presented a bust in bronze from an original model by David d'Angers to the Government through the French ambassador, J. J. Jusserand, February 22, 1905, at which time exercises of unveiling were held in the rotunda, and addresses of presentation and acceptance were made in the room of the President in the Senate wing. The presentation was made by the French ambassador, and addresses of acceptance were made by Senator George Peabody Wetmore, chairman of the Joint Committee on the Library, and by Representative McCleary, of Minnesota.

It is significant that Senator Wetmore in his address, referring to the destruction of the works of art in the Library of Congress in 1851, uses the following language:

> The records of Congress afford no information in regard to the first of these gifts [Washington bust], nor have examination of the records of the customhouses of Georgetown, in this District, or at New York, or of books or newspapers in the Library of Congress yielded better results. It is not even certain whether this bust was of bronze or marble.   *   *   *

It seems certain that Senator Wetmore had never seen the letter from John S. Meehan, quoted below, in which it is stated that the bronze bust of Washington as well as other works of art were privately owned. This private ownership explains the absence of public governmental records relating to the bust destroyed in 1851.

The bust presented by the French ambassador was subscribed for by members of the French nation, the three names heading the list being those of Lafayette, Rochambeau, and de Grasse, descendants of valued allies of the United States in the struggle for independence.

Guarding the western exit of the rotunda are the statues of President Lincoln and Gen. U. S. Grant. In the earlier pages of this book some space was given to the ceremonies connected with the acceptance of the statue of Abraham Lincoln. It was not, however, until the year 1900 that the statue of General Grant was publicly received. It may not be generally known that this statue was the second one of General Grant

---

[1] The attention of the writer has been invited to the fact that it is claimed that a marble bust of Washington was *not* destroyed as alleged, but that it was probably thrown out after the fire or sold to some one as junk, believing that this work was ruined. It is claimed that many years ago it was taken to New York and for years stored in a back yard of one of the homes in that city and finally it was given to a servant. The servant sold it to a marble dealer, thinking that a portion of the work might have some value as marble, when upon a careful examination it was determined that the bust had been but little damaged, and upon being carefully cleaned it was discovered to be the bust by David d'Angers. Athough this bust was on sale in the early summer of 1924, the writer is of the opinion that there are some details which must be explained before it can be believed that this bust was given away or sold as junk and that it was many years before its excellent condition was discovered and it was learned that instead of being an injured block of marble it was really a fine example of the work of the distinguished sculptor, David d'Angers. In fact, the attached copy of a portion of an official report tends to show that there was no marble bust of Washington in the Capitol at the time of the fire of 1851.

[Extract from a letter of John S. Meehan, Librarian of Congress, to Senator James Alfred Pearce, chairman of the Joint Committee on the Library, giving detailed account of the fire in the Library December 24, 1851]

WASHINGTON, *Jan. 7th, 1852.*

SIR: By the fire that occurred in the Library on the 24th ultimo, about 35,000 volumes were destroyed, including nearly all our collection of Parliamentary Debates, and all the Parliamentary Reports and Papers; a complete set of Congressional Reports, from the adoption of the Constitution; the Journals and Reports of the New York Legislature, from 1820 to 1848; nearly all that we had received from Mr. Vattemore, on the principle of international exchange, including the extensive collection of French Medals; a collection of the Napoleon Medals, that were presented to Congress by G. W. Erving, Minister Plenipotentiary of the U. S. to Spain, in the year 1821; a small collection of American Medals; nearly all our extensive collection of Maps; two Portraits of Columbus; Portraits of John Hanson, President of Congress in the year 1782; of Baron DeKalb, of Bolivar, and of Cortes; busts, in marble, of Thomas Jefferson, J. Q. Adams, and Gen. Lafayette; busts, in plaster, of Chief Justice Marshall, L. Woodbury, Gov. Moultrie, Gen. Jackson, and F. Hapler; the volumes of the Exploring Expedition, that were deposited in the Library; many of the Documents that were in charge of the Committee for International Exchanges; and the Furniture of the Library, that was in the principal Saloon.

A bust, in bronze, of Gen. Washington, and a bust in bronze of Apollo; a bust, in marble, of Gen. Taylor; two busts in plaster; and portraits of Presidents Washington, Adams, and Jefferson, by Stuart; a portrait of President J. Q. Adams, by J. Cranch; and a portrait of Baron Steuben, by Pyne; all belonging to private individuals, were in the Library at the time of the fire, and were all destroyed.

*   *   *   *   *   *

prepared for the rotunda of the Capitol. Both statues were by the sculptor Franklin Simmons, to whom reference has heretofore been made and biographical notes given in relation to other works. This statue was presented by the Grand Army of the Republic, its purchase being made possible through contributions raised among the soldiers who had served under General Grant. The design of the statue appears to have been passed upon by the Joint Committee on the Library and accepted. Its acceptance by Congress was provided for by a joint resolution approved August 14, 1890. It will be observed from the date of this joint resolution that nearly 10 years elapsed before its unveiling, which occurred on May 19, 1900. The resolution referred to is as follows:

Whereas the members of the posts of the Grand Army of the Republic, desirous of testifying their affectionate and patriotic regard for their late comrade General Ulysses S. Grant, have contributed a sum of money sufficient for the erection of a statue to his memory; and

Whereas it is their wish and purpose to present such statue to the Congress of the United States to be placed in the Capitol at Washington: Therefore

Resolved by the Senate and House of Representatives of the United States of America in Congress assembled, That a statue in marble, with a proper pedestal, of the late General Ulysses S. Grant tendered by the national encampment of the Grand Army of the Republic shall be received and erected in the Capitol of the United States, and shall thereupon become the property of the United States: *Provided,* That the design of such statue and pedestal shall first be submitted to and receive the approval of the Joint Committee on the Library.

The unveiling of the statue occurred in the rotunda and the exercises were exceedingly simple. Miss Sartoris, a granddaughter of General Grant, officiated at the unveiling by drawing the lanyard which caused the separation of the flags with which the statue had been covered for the unveiling ceremonies. The assemblage then proceeded to the Hall of the House, where the ceremonies of acceptance began shortly after noon. The ceremonies in the Senate took place at 4 o'clock the same afternoon. During these exercises the officers of the Grand Army of the Republic were admitted to the floor of the House, and, through the courtesy of Speaker Henderson, Mrs. Grant and her family occupied that section of the gallery usually set apart for the use of the Speaker. The exercises in the House of Representatives, in addition to the ordinary routine connected with such an occasion, included a report from the chairman of the committee acting for the Grand Army of the Republic in the procuring and presentation of the statue of General Grant. The report, while interesting as a whole, contained one paragraph which is worthy of insertion here:

The fund contributed for the announced purpose represents the offerings of more than 70,000 of his comrades, most of whom had hailed him as a comrade in the later day of peace.

In the House of Representatives addresses of acceptance were made by Mr. McCleary, of Minnesota; Mr. Richardson, of Tennessee (an ex-Confederate soldier); Mr. Warner, of Illinois; Mr. Cummings, of New York; Mr. Berry, of Kentucky (an ex-Confederate soldier); Mr. Grosvenor, of Ohio; Mr. Linney, of North Carolina (an ex-Confederate soldier); Mr. Gardner, of Michigan; Mr. Brosius, of Pennsylvania; and Mr. Dolliver, of Iowa. In the Senate addresses of acceptance were made by the following Senators: Mr. Hawley, of Connecticut; Mr. Harris, of Kansas; Mr. Turley, of Tennessee; Mr. Perkins, of California; Mr. Turner, of Washington; Mr. Carter, of Montana; and Mr. Allen, of Nebraska.

The report of the Grant memorial committee to the thirty-fourth national encampment gives the information that the statue as first made, while entirely satisfactory to the committee, was not satisfactory to the Joint Committee on the Library and that

BUST OF ABRAHAM LINCOLN
Gutzon Borglum, sculptor

the sculptor made a second statue which met with the universal approval of the committee representing the Grand Army of the Republic and of the Joint Committee on the Library.

So far as the statue now in the rotunda is concerned, and notwithstanding it has met with the approval of all who are intimately concerned in its erection, it is doubtful whether any military commander, no matter how distinguished may have been his military service or how prepossessing his personality as a man, could be attractively presented in the conventional uniform of his period and with that military bearing which is supposed to be a soldierly quality in the commander in chief who is reviewing the troops as they pass. It has always seemed as though it were hardly possible to show in one statue the qualities both of a man and of a commander in chief.

Another work of art which is of recent location in the rotunda is the portrait head in marble of Abraham Lincoln, the work of Gutzon Borglum, which was tendered to Congress by Eugene Meyer, jr., by a letter dated April 16, 1908. In this case, it being a matter of gift, congressional action was not taken, and the consideration of the letter of Mr. Meyer and final action thereon was taken by the Joint Committee on the Library on May 7, 1908, at which time the bust was accepted under section 1831, Revised Statutes of the United States, which grants to the Library Committee the authority to accept such works of art as may be considered worthy and to assign such accepted works to locations in the Capitol Building.

The gift of this head of Lincoln was a notable addition to the works of art in the rotunda; in fact, the rotunda is the only appropriate place for a work of this kind. President Lincoln belonged to the whole country, and although there then existed in the rotunda a full-length statue of Lincoln by Vinnie Ream, this fact did not create an objection to accepting and placing in a near-by location this work of Gutzon Borglum. While the head of Lincoln is not completely separated from the mass of rock, enough has been done to create an art object which has met with the approval of thousands of visitors who have passed before this unique specimen of the art of Mr. Borglum.

The sculptor Gutzon Borglum was born in Idaho March 25, 1867, son of Dr. James de la Mothe Borglum and Ida (Michelson) Borglum; educated in the public schools of Fremont and Omaha, Nebr., and at St. Mary's College, Kansas; studied art in San Francisco, and went to Paris in 1890, working and studying in Académie Julien and École des Beaux Arts; exhibited as painter and sculptor in Paris Salon, in Spain in 1892, and in California 1893 and 1894; returned East and went to London in 1896, remaining there and in Paris until 1901; exhibited in Paris in 1896 and 1901; held successful "one-man" exhibit in London; received gold medal for sculpture at Louisiana Purchase Exposition; was sculptor for work on cathedral of St. John the Divine, New York; Sheridan Equestrian Monument in Washington, D. C.; figure of America on American Republics Building; Mares of Diomedes (bronze), Metropolitan Museum, New York; Atlas (marble), New York, etc. Mr. Borglum is a member of the Royal Society of British Artists, Société National des Beaux Arts, and Architectural League. He is also represented in Statuary Hall by the bronze statue of Zebulon B. Vance, presented by the State of North Carolina.

In the crypt of the Capitol may be found a group of portrait busts representing the pioneers in the suffrage movement—Lucretia Mott, Susan B. Anthony, and Elizabeth Cady Stanton—the work of Mrs. Adelaide Johnson and presented to the Congress by

In the Crypt

PORTRAIT MONUMENT TO LUCRETIA MOTT, ELIZABETH
CADY STANTON, AND SUSAN B. ANTHONY

Adelaide Johnson, sculptress

{ 384 }

ADELAIDE JOHNSON

Represented by the monument to great leaders of women

the women of the United States on the 15th day of February, 1921. This memorial to the leaders of the suffrage movement was presented in the rotunda of the Capitol, and under the terms of its acceptance it was stipulated that after the ceremonies of presentation and acceptance had been concluded it should be placed in the crypt of the Capitol as its permanent location. The location of this work in a section of the building which has not as yet been set apart for works of art has been criticized by many who feel that it is entitled to a more conspicuous place. It is, however, proper to state that the possibilities are that before long many other works of art will be placed in the crypt of the Capitol, and if this should be the case this group will have the distinction of being first to be placed in this new location for works of art. The workmanship so far as the carving of the busts is concerned is of the best; the composition is not so easily understood. While the block of marble from which these busts are carved is probably as fine a specimen of Carrara marble as ever found place in the Capitol, the great weight, estimated at between 7 and 8 tons, and the architectural form of the pedestal renders the placing of this work in the rotunda inadvisable. At the time of the presentation this block was placed upon timbers, so that the weight might be distributed over as large an area as was considered necessary to relieve the floor of undue strain. The gathering in the rotunda upon the night of the presentation of this work was conspicuous for its numbers, hundreds being unable to obtain admission. The exercises of presentation included a speech of acceptance by the Speaker of the House of Representatives, Hon. Frederick H. Gillett, and upon the exercises of presentation being completed a pageant representing different sections of women's organizations marched around the outer border of the rotunda carrying banners of their organizations. The record of the acceptance of this work by the Joint Committee on the Library at a meeting held February 10, 1921, is as follows:

* * * That the marble portrait busts of Susan B. Anthony, Lucretia Mott and Elizabeth Cady Stanton, tendered by American women are hereby accepted; that they be temporarily placed in the Rotunda of the Capitol for the purpose of the appropriate ceremonies of tender and reception to be conducted on February 15th and that immediately at the conclusion of the ceremonies, the said sculpture be placed on the first floor of the Capitol, beneath the dome.

The sculptress of this group is represented in the Capitol by this one work of art, and her biography follows.

Adelaide Johnson was born in Plymouth, Hancock County, Ill. Her early life was chiefly passed upon a farm; pupil of St. Louis School of Design, where she studied in all departments as a preparation to her future profession—sculpture; in 1877 awarded first prize, including diploma, for design, and second prize with medal at a State exposition in competition with professional wood carvers; in 1883 studied painting in Dresden; went to Rome in January, 1884, and in the spring of that year was admitted as a pupil to the studio of Giulio Monteverde, a sculptor whose distinction placed him in Italy in the prominence occupied by Rodin in France. With this sculptor she remained for 11 years. During the year 1885, in the absence of Monteverde from Rome, she was a pupil under Fabj Altini, at that time president of the Academia di San Luca, the oldest art academy in the world. So far as known she was the only pupil of Monteverde. For more than a quarter of a century she has maintained a studio in Rome, to which she has taken all of her models for execution in marble, except the monument in the Capitol, executed in her studio at Carrara. In the course of her work she has also had studios in Chicago, Washington, New York, and London. Some of her important works in public places and private homes are bust of H. W. Thomas, Historical Society, Chicago; bust of Susan B. Anthony, Metropolitan Museum, New York; busts of Mrs. O. H. P. Belmont; Mr. William Tebb,

JAMES A. GARFIELD (OHIO)

Charles H. Niehaus, sculptor

{ 387 }

London; Miss M. A. R. Tucker, writer, London and Rome; John Burroughs; Isabella Beecher Hooker; Ellen Hardin Walworth; Emma Thursby; Gen. John A. and Mrs. Logan; May Wright Sewall; Rev. Cora L. V. Richmond; John W. Hutchinson; Dr. Helen Densmore; Lillian Whiting; Ella Wheeler Wilcox; Harold M. Duncan, London, and of Charles L. Johnson, brother of the sculptress. Member of Lyceum Club, International, London, since its foundation in 1904; patroness of International Council of Women, 1888; holds a "veteran's certificate" in National Woman's Suffrage Association, and honorary membership and vice presidencies in other clubs and organizations.

It has been some time since we have referred to the statues in Statuary Hall, and at the time of the last reference to the statues presented by the States we had included only those presented prior to the year 1880, so that from that time until the time referred to in this writing 44 years have elapsed, during which time many statues have been added to the small collection then existing.

The first statue of this new period to be placed in Statuary Hall was that of Jacob Collamer, furnished by the State of Vermont, and the congressional proceedings in regard to its acceptance show that it was referred to in the Senate on January 31, 1881, by Mr. Morrill, of Vermont, who submitted the following concurrent resolution:

Resolved by the Senate (the House of Representatives concurring), That the thanks of this Congress be presented to the governor, and through him to the people, of the State of Vermont for the statue by Preston Powers of Jacob Collamer as an eminent American statesman; that this work of art is accepted and assigned a place in the National Statuary Hall, set apart by Congress for the statues of distinguished citizens from the several States; that a copy of this resolution, signed by the President of the Senate and the Speaker of the House of Representatives, be transmitted to the governor of the State of Vermont.

Action was taken upon this resolution in the House of Representatives on February 15, 1881, at which time addresses were made by Mr. Tyler, of Vermont; Mr. Loring, of Massachusetts; and Mr. Stephens, of Georgia. This statue for quite a period of time after its erection remained upon a temporary pedestal provided by the Architect of the Capitol, and some years elapsed before a marble pedestal was furnished by the State of Vermont to accompany the gift of the statue.

The sculptor, Preston Powers, while born in Florence, Italy, April 3, 1843, was in reality a son of Vermont, as his father, Hiram Powers, was born in Woodstock, Vt. Mr. Preston Powers began life as a mechanical draftsman in railroad repair shops in Florence, Italy, and was employed in the Grant Locomotive Works in Paris, France, and in New Jersey; was two years in the United States Navy as captain's clerk and interpreter on the U. S. S. *Canandaigua,* Captain Strong, European Fleet; became a pupil of his father, Hiram Powers, in 1868, being his only pupil; spent several years at various times in the United States practicing his profession in Boston, Mass.; Washington, D. C.; Portland, Me., and in Denver, Colo., where several of his works are to be found. His principal works have been in portraiture. His most important work is the Closing Era, now in the capitol grounds at Denver, Colo.; also exhibited at the Columbian Exposition in Chicago in 1893. Mr. Preston Powers has for several years been a resident of Florence, Italy.

In the year 1886 the statue of James A. Garfield, presented by the State of Ohio, was received in Statuary Hall. The concurrent resolution of acceptance was presented in the Senate January 5, 1886, by Mr. Sherman, of Ohio. This resolution was presented in the House January 19, 1886, at which time addresses were made by Mr. Ezra B. Taylor, Mr. McKinley, Mr. Geddes, Mr. Butterworth, all of Ohio; and Mr. Pettibone, of Tennessee.

PRESTON POWERS

Represented by the statue of Jacob Collamer (Vermont) in Statuary Hall

The statue of William Allen, of Ohio, was placed in the national Statuary Hall in 1888. No action was taken by the Senate or House of Representatives in the direction of the acceptance of this statue.

Both of the statues from the State of Ohio are the work of the sculptor Charles H. Niehaus, whose biography has heretofore been given in connection with the bust of Daniel D. Tompkins, a Vice President of the United States.

New Jersey followed Ohio with a marble statue of Richard Stockton and a bronze statue of Philip Kearny. Both statues are the work of the sculptor Henry Kirke Brown, whose biography has been given in connection with the statue of Nathanael Greene, the first statue to be presented to Statuary Hall. The statues from New Jersey were received in the year 1888, and the concurrent resolution of acceptance was presented in the House

STATUE OF RICHARD STOCKTON (NEW JERSEY)

Henry Kirke Brown, sculptor

of Representatives August 3, 1888, and in the Senate on August 8, 1888. The concurrent resolution was agreed to in the Senate August 21, 1888, and in the House on the same date.

Michigan was the next State to furnish a statue for Statuary Hall. The contribution of this State was the statue of Lewis Cass. Resolutions of acceptance were presented in the Senate on February 18, 1889, at which time addresses were made by Mr. Palmer, of Michigan; Mr. Morrill, of Vermont; Mr. Chandler, of New Hampshire; Mr. Morgan, of Alabama; and Mr. Hoar, of Massachusetts. The resolutions were agreed to unanimously. On February 10, 1889, the concurrent resolutions passed by the Senate were laid before the House. Objection was made to fixing a time for their consideration, and they were referred to the Committee on the Library. The resolutions were again brought before the House on February 21, 1889, when objection was made to fixing a date for their consideration and they were, therefore, not considered. On February 28, 1889, the concurrent resolution passed by the Senate on February 18, 1889, was again before the House for consideration, and as at this time there was no objection addresses were made by Mr. Chipman, of Michigan; Mr. Randall, of Pennsylvania; Mr. O'Donnell, of Michigan; Mr. Seymour, of Michigan; Mr. Burrows, of Michigan; Mr. Whiting, of Michigan; Mr. Cutcheon, of Michigan; and Mr. Allen, of Michigan, and after these addresses the resolution was unanimously adopted.

The statue of Lewis Cass is considered by many one of the celebrated statues in marble in the collection in Statuary Hall. The work is that of Daniel Chester French, who is also represented by the bust of Vice President Henry Wilson and the bust of Vice President John Adams. His biography has been given earlier in this work.

In connection with this statue it may be of interest to state that the seal of the State of Michigan, attached to its pedestal, has been changed since the statue was erected. This change occurred because of the fact that the bronze seal placed at the time of the erection of the statue was found to be incorrect. As a matter of fact, there had been several semmingly unauthorized changes in the seal, and through the perseverance of one of the members of the Daughters of 1812 the irregularities which had crept in in the formation of the seal were brought to the attention of the State officials, the proper corrections made, and a new seal cast in bronze to supply the place of the incorrect seal formerly upon the pedestal of this statue. The amount of work necessary to bring about the correction referred to seems hardly possible, but the result is a matter of historical accuracy, and when later on the statue of former Senator Chandler was contributed by Michigan the correct seal was then available as a part of the decoration of the pedestal of the Chandler statue.

The Commonwealth of Pennsylvania was the next to tender statues to Statuary Hall. Her contribution consisted of the statues of J. P. G. Muhlenberg and Robert Fulton. Proceedings in the House of Representatives were commenced by Mr. Ermentrout, of Pennsylvania, who on February 28, 1889, offered a resolution of acceptance. The resolution was agreed to as of that date, and on March 1, 1889, the concurrent resolution passed by the House of Representatives was laid before the Senate and read and ordered to lie on the table. No further action was taken in the Senate, so that so far as the acceptance of these statues by the Congress is concerned it is as yet incomplete.

The statue of Muhlenberg is the work of Blanche Nevin, and in this work she has portrayed Muhlenberg at a dramatic period of his history. He was a clergyman, but strongly devoted to the cause of independence, and at the close of an emphatic patriotic sermon he threw aside his clerical vestments and revealed himself in the uniform of an

STATUE OF JOHN PETER GABRIEL MUHLENBERG (PENNSYLVANIA)

Blanche Nevin, sculptress

STATUE OF LEWIS CASS (MICHIGAN)

Daniel Chester French, sculptor

officer of the Continental Army. Immediately following his sermon many of his congregation joined the ranks and fought for the cause of independence in the Revolutionary War. As this is the only work of Miss Nevin in the Capitol, her biography follows appropriately at this time.

Blanche Nevin was the daughter of John Williamson Nevin and Martha Jenkins Nevin; born in Mercersburg, Pa., September 25, 1841, and died in Lancaster, Pa., April 20, 1925. Both her parents were native Pennsylvanians. Her art education was received principally in Italy, at the Royal Art Academy of Venice, where she studied under Ferrari, and was also a student at Carrara. Miss Nevin practiced the sculptors' art but little so far as public exhibits are concerned, not caring to undertake the strain of business connected with such commissions. She executed many works of a private character, some of them being for her own home, others being models for sculptural work. Her home, known as Windsor Forges, located in Churchtown, Lancaster County, in the Welsh Mountain section of Pennsylvania, was the colonial home of her mother and had been the family residence for six generations; a lover of nature, she enjoyed the quiet of this historic home. Nevertheless, much of her time was spent abroad, usually living six months of each year in a milder climate. She resided for a period in China and Japan, and was familiar with oriental life. Miss Nevin spoke several languages fluently. Possessed of ample means, she beautified her home with examples of art. In addition to her accomplishments as a sculptress Miss Nevin was a painter and a writer; much of her poetry has been published. She was a member of the Royal Art Society of England and the numismatic and geographical societies of New York.

CHAPTER XXI

STATUES IN STATUARY HALL

ENNSYLVANIA has the distinction of furnishing the first and only seated statue, that of Robert Fulton, for Statuary Hall. This seated statue represents Fulton as the inventor keenly interested in the contemplation of a model of a boat which he holds in his hands. It may be of interest to state that Fulton, celebrated for his invention of steam navigation, was an artist and a painter of miniatures, although his art abilities are very seldom mentioned when the name of Fulton is referred to.

The sculptor of this statue, Howard Roberts, was born in Philadelphia, Pa., 1843. He studied art in Philadelphia at the Pennsylvania Academy of Fine Arts and under the sculptor J. A. Bailly. He first went to Paris in 1866 and studied for several years in the École des Beaux Arts and in the studios of Dumont and Gumery. Among his works are a bust, Eleanor, in the Pennsylvania Academy of Fine Arts; La Premier Pose, medaled at the Centennial Exposition; Hypatia; Lot's Wife; Hester Prynne; and a number of portraits and ideal busts. He died in Paris, France, April 19, 1900.

The State of Illinois contributed to the collection in Statuary Hall in 1893 the bronze statue of James Shields. Proceedings in connection with this statue were first instituted in the Senate on the 4th of December, 1893, at which time the communication from the Governor of Illinois stating that the statue of James Shields had been placed in Statuary Hall and would be unveiled December 6, at 2 o'clock p. m., was laid before the Senate. Mr. Cullom, of Illinois, moved that the communication lie on the table and gave notice that on the following day he would introduce a resolution regarding the statue. A similar communication was brought to the attention of the House of Representatives, on December 5, 1893, and on the same day Mr. Springer, of Illinois, offered a resolution fixing the 6th day of December at 1.30 in the afternoon as the time for the consideration of the resolution of acceptance. On the 6th of December, 1893, Mr. Cullom, of Illinois, introduced in the Senate concurrent resolutions of acceptance, after which addresses were made by Mr. Cullom, of Illinois; Mr. Vest, of Missouri; Mr. Davis, of Minnesota; and Mr. Palmer, of Illinois. The resolution was unanimously agreed to. On the same day, in the House of Representatives, addresses were made by Mr. Springer, of Illinois; Mr. Cannon, of Illinois; Mr. Bland, of Missouri; Mr. Black, of Illinois; Mr. Hall, of Minnesota; and Mr. Oates, of Alabama. Mr. Henderson, of Iowa, who was ill, was given permission to print his remarks in the Congressional Record. During these proceedings a message from the Senate announcing the passage of the resolution relative to the statue of James Shields was received and Mr. Springer, of Illinois, moved that his resolution be laid on the table and the resolution of the Senate be substituted. It was so ordered, and the resolution of the Senate was concurred in.

The statue referred to is the work of Leonard W. Volk, who was born in Wellstown, N. Y., November 7, 1828. He had but few educational advantages, learning the trade of marble cutting with his father. Choosing sculpture as a profession, he moved to St. Louis and opened a studio. Among his first productions was a bust in marble of

STATUE OF GEN. JAMES SHIELDS (ILLINOIS)

Leonard W. Volk, sculptor

STATUE OF ROBERT FULTON (PENNSYLVANIA)

Howard Roberts, sculptor

Henry Clay, a copy from Hart's bust. Stephen A. Douglas recognized his talent to such an extent that he offered to defray his expenses for a course of study in Rome, where he studied for a year and a half. In June, 1857, he opened a studio in Clark Street, Chicago. For some time he was the only sculptor in that city and was a prime mover in the first exhibition of fine arts held in Chicago, in 1859; was one of the founders of the Academy of Design of Chicago. His important works are the Douglas Monument in Chicago and the statues of Lincoln and Douglas in the statehouse at Springfield, Ill. He is also represented by soldiers' monuments at Erie, Pa.; Rochester, N. Y.; and Rock Island, Ill., and is said to have been the only sculptor privileged to make a life mask of President Lincoln. His last work was the statue of Gen. James Shields, in Statuary Hall. He died in August, 1895.

In the year 1894 New Hampshire presented to Statuary Hall the marble statues of John Stark and Daniel Webster. Proceedings in the Senate were commenced on December 3, 1894, at which time Mr. Chandler, of New Hampshire, submitted a resolution fixing the 20th day of December as a date for the exercises in connection with the reception of the statues of John Stark and Daniel Webster. This resolution was considered by unanimous consent and agreed to. In the House on December 12, 1894, Mr. Baker, of New Hampshire, offered a resolution providing that the exercises relating to the acceptance of statues of John Stark and Daniel Webster be made a special order for Thursday, December 20, at 2 o'clock p. m., and, as objection was made, the resolution was referred to the Committee on Rules. On the same day Mr. Baker offered a resolution in substance the same as the one before referred to, which was agreed to. On the 17th of December, 1894, the Speaker laid before the House a communication from the Governor of New Hampshire, presenting the statues of John Stark and Daniel Webster to the Congress. The communication was ordered to be laid on the table. On the 20th day of December, 1894, a resolution of acceptance of the statue of John Stark was presented in the Senate and addresses were made by Mr. Gallinger, of New Hampshire; Mr. Proctor, of Vernont; Mr. Dubois, of Idaho; and Mr. Chandler, of New Hampshire. The resolution was unanimously agreed to. Mr. Hoar, of Massachusetts, then offered a concurrent resolution of acceptance relating to the statue of Daniel Webster, and upon this resolution addresses were made by Mr. Chandler, of New Hampshire; Mr. Hoar, of Massachusetts; Mr. Morgan, of Alabama; Mr. Morrill, of Vermont; Mr. Davis, of Minnesota; Mr. Platt, of Connecticut; Mr. Cullom, of Illinois; Mr. Mitchell, of Oregon; Mr. Lodge, of Massachusetts; and Mr. Gallinger, of New Hampshire. Following these addresses the resolution of acceptance of the statue of Daniel Webster was unanimously agreed to. In the House of Representatives on December 20 separate resolutions of acceptance were presented regarding the statue of John Stark and the statue of Daniel Webster. In relation to the statue of John Stark addresses were made by Mr. Baker, of New Hampshire; Mr. Powers, of Vermont; and Mr. Grout, of Vermont. In relation to the statue of Daniel Webster addresses were made by Mr. Blair, of New Hampshire; Mr. Everett, of Massachusetts; Mr. Curtis, of New York; Mr. Morse, of Massachusetts; and Mr. Baker, of New Hampshire. The House upon the same day concurred in the Senate resolution relating to the statue of John Stark and on the 21st of December, 1894, concurred in the action of the Senate in relation to the statue of Daniel Webster.

Both of these statues were executed by Carl H. Conrads, who was born in Breisig on the Rhine, Germany, February 26, 1839. He began life as a carver in wood; studied modeling at Munich until 1860, when he came to the United States; worked a short time in New York; enlisted May 3, 1862, in Company G, Twentieth New York Infantry, for two

STATUE OF THOMAS H. BENTON (MISSOURI)

Alexander Doyle, sculptor

years, and after serving for a time in that organization was transferred to Battery F, Third United States Artillery, and remained with the battery until the expiration of his term of enlistment. Among his works are statues of Alexander Hamilton, for Central Park, New York; General Thayer, for West Point; General Halleck, for the public park in San Francisco, Calif.; and various works of statuary for cemeteries and public monuments.

It should be stated in this connection that the statue of Daniel Webster is a copy from the bronze statue at Concord, N. H., by Thomas Ball.

In chronological order it appears that the statues of Thomas H. Benton and Francis P. Blair, from the State of Missouri, were the next to be tendered to the collection in Statuary Hall. Proceedings were first instituted in the House of Representatives on February 4, 1899, at which time a resolution of acceptance and thanks was introduced and addresses made by Mr. Dockery, of Missouri; Mr. Carmack, of Tennessee; and Mr. Clark and Mr. Lloyd, of Missouri. More than a year elapsed before action was taken by the Senate in the direction of the concurrence with the action of the House upon the resolution agreed to in the House of Representatives February 4, 1899. At this time addresses were made by Mr. Vest, of Missouri; Mr. Cockrell, of Missouri; Mr. Hoar, of Massachusetts; and Mr. Elkins, of West Virginia; and upon this occasion the resolution of the House of Representatives was unanimously concurred in.

Both of these statues were executed by Alexander Doyle, who was born in Steubenville, Ohio, January 28, 1857; went to Italy with his family to reside when 9 years of age; studied sculpture in the Government academy at Carrara, and also at Florence and Rome. He returned to the United States in 1878. Among his works are a bronze equestrian statue of Gen. Albert Sidney Johnston, bronze statue of Gen. Robert E. Lee, and marble statues of Margaret Haugherty (known as the "Bread Giver"), for New Orleans, La.; the New Haven (Conn.) soldiers' monument; granite statue, Peace, a heroic alto-relief or drum of the thirteen original States, and National Revolutionary Monument, Yorktown, Va.; bronze statue of Gen. Philip Schuyler, Saratoga, N. Y.; marble statue of General Garfield, Cleveland, Ohio; bronze statue of Gen. James R. Steedman, Toledo, Ohio; marble statue of Senator Benjamin H. Hill, Atlanta, Ga.; bronze statue of Horace Greeley, New York; bronze statue and monument to Henry W. Grady, Atlanta, Ga.; and in addition to the statue of Francis P. Blair and Thomas H. Benton, Mr. Doyle is also represented in Statuary Hall by the statue of John E. Kenna, of West Virginia. He died in Boston, Mass., December 21, 1922.

The statue of John E. Kenna, of West Virginia, was placed in Statuary Hall in 1901 and no action of acceptance was taken by either the Senate or House with reference to this statue.

Another statue from West Virginia, that of Francis H. Pierpont, was placed in Statuary Hall in 1903. This is the work of Franklin Simmons, whose biography has been given earlier in this work. Although it has been stated that the statue of Francis H. Pierpont, a gift from the State of West Virginia, was placed in Statuary Hall in 1903, it was not until 1910 that exercises in commemoration of the gift of this statue occurred.[1] On April 30, 1910, at 10 o'clock a. m. in Statuary Hall formal exercises, including the presentation of the statue to the State of West Virginia on behalf of the statue com-

---

[1] * * * Work on the model and the statue progressed satisfactorily, and it was completed and placed where it now stands in December, 1904. * * * For various reasons the presentation of the statue has been delayed till this hour. The principal cause has been the inability of the governor's only daughter, Mrs. W. H. Siviter, on account of feeble health, earlier to attend the ceremonies which she to-day witnesses with gratitude and thanks to all who have had any part in thus honoring her father. * * * (From the address of Hon. Thomas C. Miller, of the Pierpont statue commission, at the ceremonies in Statuary Hall Apr. 30, 1910.)

STATUE OF FRANCIS H. PIERPONT (WEST VIRGINIA)

Franklin Simmons, sculptor

mission, with an address by Thomas Condit Miller, the unveiling by Frances Pierpont Siviter, the acceptance of the statue on behalf of the State of West Virginia by Gov. William Ellsworth Glasscock, a poem by Frances Pierpont Siviter, followed by an address by Hon. John W. Mason and a benediction by Rev. Ulysses G. B. Pierce, D. D. The exercises in Statuary Hall were preceded on March 8, 1910, by formal concurrent resolution of acceptance in the Senate. This resolution was the first reference to the statue of Francis H. Pierpont, and in the House of Representatives on April 2, 1910, a resolution was agreed to which fixed the reception and acceptance of the statue of Pierpont as the special order for Saturday, April 30, 1910, at 3 o'clock p. m. In the Senate following the exercises in Statuary Hall addresses were made by the following Senators: Stephen B. Elkins, of West Virginia; Jonathan P. Dolliver, of Iowa; Welden B. Heyburn, of Idaho; George T. Oliver, of Pennsylvania; Nathan B. Scott, of West Virginia; and in the House of Representatives addresses were made by the following Members: William P. Hubbard, of West Virginia; J. Warren Keifer, of Ohio; Sereno E. Payne, of New York; Joseph Holt Gaines, of West Virginia; Samuel W. McCall, of Massachusetts; and George Cookman Sturgiss, of West Virginia.

Maryland furnished statues of Charles Carroll of Carrollton and John Hanson in the year 1903. Both of these statues are of bronze and are excellent examples of the work of the sculptor Richard Edwin Brooks, who was born in Braintree, Mass., October 28, 1865. His art instruction was received in the studios of T. H. Bartlett, Boston, Mass., and Jean Paul Aubé and Antonin Injalbert, Paris. Among his works are busts of Gov. William E. Russell (bronze) and Col. Gardener Tufts (marble), Boston statehouse, and O. W. Holmes (1897) and Gen. F. A. Walker, Boston Public Library; statues of John Hays and Roger Ludlow, Hartford, State capitol; statues and monuments of Col. Thomas Cass, Boston Public Garden; W. H. Seward, Seattle, Wash.; and J. M. Hood, Baltimore, Md.; medallions of 15 mayors of Boston, mayor's office, Boston; statue of Robert Treat Paine, Taunton, Mass.; statue of John Harte McGraw, Seattle, Wash.; and several nude statues, of which one received honorable mention at Paris Salon, 1895. His awards include gold medal, third class, Paris Salon, 1899; gold medal, first class, Paris Exposition, 1900; gold medal, first class, Pan-American Exposition, Buffalo, N. Y. Mr. Brooks also served as chairman of the jury of awards on sculpture at the World's Fair, St. Louis, 1904. He died in Boston, Mass., May 2, 1919.

The acceptance of the statues from Maryland was commenced in the House of Representatives December 17, 1902, and in the Senate December 20, 1902, at which times the tender of the statues was referred to and the exercises fixed for Saturday, January 31, 1903. In the House of Representatives a resolution was offered providing for the admission to the floor of the House of Representatives of the Maryland Statuary Commission and for the reservation of the southeast and southwest ladies galleries for the relatives of Charles Carroll of Carrollton and John Hanson "and for such citizens of Maryland as may attend these ceremonies." In the Senate on January 31, 1903, Mr. McComas, of Maryland, asked unanimous consent that the gentlemen who constituted the Maryland Statuary Commission be admitted to the floor and that the descendants of Charles Carroll of Carrollton and John Hanson, with the ladies and others of their party, have the privilege during the exercises of occupying the gallery reserved for the families of Senators. This request was agreed to. In the Senate, addresses were made by Mr. McComas, of Maryland; Mr. Hoar, of Massachusetts; Mr. Dolliver, of Iowa; Mr. Depew, of New York; Mr. Bacon, of Georgia, and Mr. Wellington, of Maryland. In the House,

STATUE OF CHARLES CARROLL OF CARROLLTON (MARYLAND)

Richard E. Brooks, sculptor

STATUE OF JOHN HANSON (MARYLAND)

Richard E. Brooks, sculptor

addresses were made by Mr. Pearre, of Maryland; Mr. Dalzell, of Pennsylvania, and Mr. Schirm, of Maryland.

In 1905 Illinois tendered its second statue, that of Frances E. Willard. Proceedings in relation to the acceptance of this statue were instituted in the Senate on January 12, 1905, when a communication from the Governor of the State of Illinois requesting that a date be fixed for the acceptance by Congress of the statue of Frances E. Willard was laid before the Senate and referred to the Committee on the Library and ordered to be printed. The Committee on the Library reported January 13, 1905, and Mr. Cullom, of Illinois, asked that the communication might lie on the table for the time being. On January 17, 1905, Mr. Cullom called up the communication from the Governor of Illinois, which was read at the desk. He then offered the following resolution, which was considered by unanimous consent and agreed to:

Resolved, That the exercises appropriate to the reception and acceptance from the State of Illinois of the statue of Frances E. Willard, erected in Statuary Hall in the Capitol, be made the special order for Friday, February 17, at three o'clock.

A similar resolution was offered in the House of Representatives January 19, 1905, considered by unanimous consent, and agreed to. On February 17, 1905, the resolution of acceptance and thanks was introduced in the Senate by Mr. Cullom, of Illinois, and addresses were made by Mr. Cullom; Mr. Beveridge, of Indiana; Mr. Hopkins, of Illinois, and Mr. Dolliver, of Iowa, after which the concurrent resolution was unanimously agreed to. In the House of Representatives on the same date a concurrent resolution was presented by Mr. Foss, and addresses made by that gentleman; also by Mr. Graff, of Illinois; Mr. Littlefield, of Maine; Mr. Rainey, of Illinois; and Mr. Brooks, of Colorado. The sculptress of this statue, Helen Farnsworth Mears, was born in Oshkosh, Wis., 1878; studied at the Art Institute of Chicago under Lorado Taft and while there received a commission for a 9-foot marble statue, the Genius of Wisconsin, from the women of her native State. This statue was exhibited at the Chicago World's Fair and received an independent prize of $500. It was subsequently placed in the rotunda of the capitol at Madison, Wis. In 1894 Miss Mears went to New York and studied at the Art Students League under Saint-Gaudens for two years, entering Saint-Gaudens's studio as assistant after the first year. Her studies were continued in Paris under Alexandre Charpentier, Collin, and Merson at Académie Viti, and at Julien's under Puech. While in Paris she worked as assistant in Saint-Gaudens's private studio. In 1898 she won in competition a commission to execute a marble statue of Frances E. Willard, presented from the State of Illinois to the National Statuary Hall. Her large wall fountain, The Fountain of Life, was given a place of honor and received a silver medal at the St. Louis Exposition of 1904. Other important works are: Marble portrait bust of President George Albee, of Oshkosh Normal School; bronze bas-reliefs of Edward MacDowell, composer (a replica of which is installed at the Metropolitan Museum, New York City, and one at the rooms of the MacDowell Club, Metropolitan Opera House), Louise Collier Wilcox, Augustus Saint-Gaudens, Margaret Adams, Richard Porter Hackett, and Elizabeth Mears; group, The New Year Borne in Triumph by the Months, designed and executed for Mrs. F. F. Thompson, New York City; bronze bust of Gen. George Rogers Clark, for the Milwaukee Public Library; bronze bust of William T. G. Morton, M. D., for the Smithsonian Institution; and bronze crouching figure, Echo, for Mrs. William Scofield, Cambridge, Mass. Miss Mears was a member of the National Sculptural Society, the MacDowell Club, New York City, and the Circle of the Friends of the Medallion. She died in New York February 17, 1916.

STATUE OF FRANCES E. WILLARD (ILLINOIS)

Helen Farnsworth Mears, sculptress

First statue of a woman to be placed in Statuary Hall

STATUE OF JOHN J. INGALLS (KANSAS)

Charles H. Niehaus, sculptor

In the same year, 1905, the statue of John J. Ingalls, the first statue tendered by the State of Kansas to Statuary Hall, was received. In the Senate on December 13, 1904, Mr. Long, of Kansas, submitted a resolution fixing the date for the exercises appropriate to the reception and acceptance of this statue as a special order for Saturday, January 31, 1905, after the conclusion of the routine morning business. On the 16th of December, 1904, Mr. Curtis, in the House of Representatives, offered the resolution fixing the date for the exercises of acceptance as a special order for Saturday, January 31, 1905, at half past 3 o'clock p. m. In the Senate on the day set apart for exercises addresses were made by Mr. Long, of Kansas; Mr. Allison, of Iowa; Mr. Cockrell, of Missouri; Mr. Platt, of Connecticut; Mr. Gorman, of Maryland; Mr. Spooner, of Wisconsin, and Mr. Daniel, of Virginia. In the House of Representatives addresses were made by Mr. Curtis, of Kansas; Mr. Clark, of Missouri; Mr. Gibson, of Tennessee; Mr. Bowersock, of Kansas; Mr. Wiley, of Alabama; Mr. Hamilton, of Michigan; Mr. Scott, Mr. Campbell, Mr. Miller, Mr. Calderhead, and Mr. Murdock, of Kansas. This statue is the work of the sculptor Charles H. Niehaus, whose biography has previously been given in connection with other work in the Capitol.

The statues of Sam Houston and Stephen F. Austin were presented by the State of Texas in the year 1904. The action taken in the direction of acceptance of these two statues was in the House of Representatives, where the ordinary resolutions of acceptance were introduced by Mr. Burleson, of Texas, April 2, 1904. In the Senate on April 18, 1904, the Presiding Officer laid before the Senate the concurrent resolution passed by the House on April 2, and it was agreed to. The date was fixed by the House of Representatives at the session of January 20, 1905, at which time a special order was made for the exercises appropriate to the reception and acceptance for the 25th of February, at 3 o'clock p. m. On that date in the House of Representatives addresses were made by Mr. Cooper, of Texas; Mr. Richardson, of Tennessee; Mr. Burgess, of Texas; Mr. Clark, of Missouri; Mr. Stephens, of Texas; Mr. Gibson, of Tennessee; Mr. Field, Mr. Wallace, Mr. Gillespie, and Mr. Slayden, of Texas.

The sculptress of these two statues, Elisabet Ney, was born in Westphalia, Germany, 1835. Her father was a nephew of Napoleon's marshal, her mother a descendant of Polish political exiles. At 17, in spite of bitter opposition, being the first woman to apply for admission, she entered the Munich Academy of Art. At 19, upon the recommendation of the sculptor Rauch, she was admitted after opposition to a scholarship in the Berlin Academy of Art. Her unique personality and genius brought her recognition in the literary, scientific, and art circles of Berlin, and upon the death of her champion, Rauch, when she was 20 years of age she became the portrait sculptor of a notable list of eminent people, among them Von Humboldt, Von Liebig, Jacob Grimm, Schopenhauer, Garibaldi, King George V of Hanover, King Leopold II of Bavaria, Joachim, and Bismarck. Her life-size statue of King Leopold is in the gardens of the Castle of Lindenhoff. She married Dr. Edmund Montgomery, a Scotch scientist, but retained her maiden name. Shortly after the Civil War, in company with a band of German enthusiasts, she came to the United States with the expectation of founding a colony based upon Utopian principles in the State of Georgia. Upon the failure of this enterprise she, with her husband, settled upon a plantation near Hempstead, Tex. In 1890 she established a studio in Austin, Tex., and began her series of sculpture of distinguished Texans. Her memorial to Albert Sidney Johnston at the instigation of the Daughters of the Confederacy was placed by the State over his grave in the State cemetery at Austin, Tex. Among her works are busts of Senator Reagan and Governors Lubbock, Roberts, and Sayers. Through the efforts of

STATUE OF STEPHEN F. AUSTIN (TEXAS)

Elisabet Ney, sculptress

{ 409 }

STATUE OF SAM HOUSTON (TEXAS)

Elisabet Ney, sculptress

{ 410 }

the Daughters of the Republic of Texas the State made the necessary appropriation for placing the statues of Houston and Austin in Statuary Hall, United States Capitol, and replicas in the statehouse at Austin, Tex. After the death of the sculptress her studio and grounds were purchased by her friend, Mrs. Joseph B. Dibrell, through whose efforts appropriations had been secured for the artist's public works in the United States. In this studio has been collected a large number of the models made by Miss Ney, among them her model for the statue of Leopold II. The studio will be used as a museum to the memory of this eminent sculptress, who died in Austin, Tex., June 29, 1907. Her statues of Austin and Houston in Statuary Hall as examples of the sculptor's art have many features of attractive quality, but are somewhat lessened in sculptural worth by the fact that the statues are probably less or possibly not more than life size, while the statues surrounding them are of heroic size. This has a tendency to give an impression of slenderness or to impart a feminine quality to the celebrated persons whom they are intended to portray.

In 1907 the statue of Jabez Lamar Monroe Curry was placed in Statuary Hall as a gift from the State of Alabama. A concurrent resolution of acceptance was introduced in the Senate on December 21, 1907, and in the House of Representatives on the same date. The report from the Committee on the Library was presented by Mr. McCall, of Massachusetts, on February 14, 1908, and on February 15 the concurrent resolution was agreed to in the House of Representatives. On February 18 the concurrent resolution passed by the House of Representatives was laid before the Senate by the Vice President, referred to the Committee on the Library, and that committee reported through its chairman, Mr. Wetmore, of Rhode Island, on April 6, 1908, at which time the resolution was agreed to by unanimous consent.

The sculptor of this statue, Dante Sodini, was born in Florence, Italy, August 20, 1858, and began his art studies in that city; elected member of Fine Arts Academy in Florence in 1885; awarded gold medal at International Exposition in Paris in 1889. Among his works are a portrait medallion of Queen Victoria in the new hospital at Birmingham, England; portrait medallion from life of Hon. W. E. Gladstone; Savonarola memorial in Piazzi Signoria, Florence, Italy; a colossal statue of St. Simon Stock at Putney, London; statue of Christ in St. Miniato's Cemetery, Florence; portrait medallion from life of the Lord Mayor of London, 1909; portrait bust from life of Hon. J. L. M. Curry, in library at Richmond, Va.; and statue of J. L. M. Curry, in Statuary Hall, United States Capitol, this being the only work in the Capitol executed by this sculptor.

In the year 1908 there were two statues presented by the State of Virginia to Statuary Hall. The statues selected as the contribution by the State are those of Washington and Robert E. Lee. The statue of Washington is a replica in bronze of the marble statue in the statehouse at Richmond, Va., the work of Jean Antoine Houdon, and in its general composition resembles the plaster cast of Washington in the rotunda of the Capitol. The statue of Robert E. Lee is the work of Edward V. Valentine, a distinguished sculptor from the State of Virginia, who had lived in the same city and had had a personal acquaintance with this distinguished general.

Mr. Valentine was born in Richmond, Va., November 12, 1838; educated in private schools and by private tutors. He studied anatomy at the Medical College of Virginia. In 1859 he went to Paris and studied drawing under Couture; was also a pupil of Jouffroy; studied in Florence under Bonianti and under Kiss in Berlin, where he remained until the death of that sculptor; was also while in Berlin a pupil of the Royal Academy of Arts. Returning to the United States in 1865 he opened a studio in Richmond, Va. Among his prominent works are a bronze statue of Gen. Thomas J. (Stonewall) Jackson, Lexington,

In Statuary Hall

STATUE OF JABEZ L. M. CURRY (ALABAMA)

Dante Sodini, sculptor

STATUE OF GEORGE WASHINGTON (VIRGINIA)

Modeled after the marble statue by Houdon in the State capitol, Richmond, Va.

STATUE OF GEN. ROBERT E. LEE (VIRGINIA)

E. V. Valentine, sculptor

{ 414 }

Va.; bronze statue of Vice President Breckinridge, Lexington, Ky.; bronze statue of Gen. W. T. Wickham, Marion Park, Richmond, Va.; recumbent statue of Gen. Robert E. Lee, Washington and Lee University, Virginia; marble statue of Thomas Jefferson, Jefferson Hotel, Richmond, Va.; statue of John J. Audubon, Audubon Park, New Orleans, La.; classic group, Andromache and Astyamax, exhibited at the Columbian Exposition; marble statue of The Blind Girl; ideal figures, Judas and Grief; bronze busts of Commodore Matthew F. Maury, John F. Minor, Prof. J. Randolph Tucker, Col. John S. Mosby, Gen. Albert Sidney Johnston, and William Wirt Henry; bronze statue of Jefferson Davis; and allegorical female figure symbolical of the South, for Richmond, Va.

The chronological arrangement has been somewhat broken by our neglect to have referred to in its proper order the statue of Father Marquette, the gift of the State of Wisconsin. This statue has the peculiar distinction of being the only statue in which a joint resolution has been passed giving to the State the right to place a statue in Statuary Hall. It is only proper to state that there were those who made objection to this statue being placed in Statuary Hall both upon the ground of the religious faith of Father Marquette, although that probably was not cited as a reason, but the principal reason advanced seemed to be that Father Marquette was not a citizen of the State of Wisconsin, and the invitation by the President sent to the different States, while it gave to the State the liberty of choice, contained this qualification:

And the President is authorized to invite all the States to provide and furnish statues in marble or bronze not exceeding two in number for each State of deceased persons who have been citizens thereof, and illustrious for their historic renown or for distinguished civic or military services such as each State may deem to be worthy of this national commemoration.

In the House of Representatives on March 11, 1892, Mr. Mitchell, of Wisconsin, introduced the following joint resolution:

Resolved, by the Senate and House of Representatives of the United States of America in Congress Assembled, That the State of Wisconsin be and is hereby authorized and granted the privilege of placing in Statuary Hall at the Capitol the statue of Pere Marquette, the faithful missionary whose work among the Indians and explorations within the borders of said State in early days are recognized all over the civilized world.

This resolution was reported favorably from the House Committee on the Library on April 5, 1892; was called up on April 9, 1892, and passed the House; received in the Senate and referred to the Committee on the Library April 11, 1892, and reported by Mr. Voorhees from the committee and passed by the Senate on March 3, 1893, but was not signed by the President. On September 6, 1893, a similar resolution was introduced in the House of Representatives by Mr. Brickner, of Wisconsin. This resolution passed the House October 11, 1893, was debated, amended, and passed the Senate on the same date; on the 12th of October, 1893, the House concurred in the Senate amendment, and October 21, 1893, it was approved by the President. It was not, however, until April 29, 1896, that the customary resolution of acceptance and thanks were introduced in the Senate. At this time the resolution was not acted upon in the House of Representatives, but on January 30, 1904, a concurrent resolution of thanks and acceptance was introduced in the House of Representatives and agreed to, and on February 1, 1904, these resolutions were unanimously agreed to in the Senate. From March 11, 1902, until February 1, 1904, at intervals this question had been before the Congress, and by this action of February 1, 1904, the question was finally disposed of.

The sculptor of this statue, Gaetano Trentanove, was born in Florence, Italy, December 21, 1858; educated at Fine Arts Academies of Florence and Rome; knighted by the late

STATUE OF JAMES MARQUETTE (WISCONSIN)

Gaetano Trentanove, sculptor

{ 416 }

GAETANO TRENTANOVE (LEFT) AND LARKIN G. MEAD (RIGHT)

Trentanove is represented by the statue of James Marquette (Pere Marquette)
Mead is represented by the statue of Ethan Allen

King Humbert of Italy; became an American citizen in 1892. Among his works are a statue of James Marquette, Statuary Hall, United States Capitol; statue of Daniel Webster, Washington, D. C.; statue of Albert Pike, Washington, D. C.; Kosciuszko equestrian statue, Milwaukee, Wis.; The Last of the Spartans, Layton Art Gallery, Milwaukee, Wis.; soldiers' monument, Oshkosh, Wis.; Chief Oshkosh statue, Oshkosh, Wis.; monument to Confederate soldiers, Springfield, Mo.; soldiers' monument, Appleton, Wis.; and many other works for private citizens in the United States and in Europe.

In 1909 the statue of Gen. Lew Wallace was executed by Andrew O'Connor and presented to Statuary Hall by the State of Indiana. The ceremonies in Statuary Hall occurred at 10.30 a. m., January 11, 1910. The chairman of the commission, Capt. John P. McGrew, also acted as the chairman of the ceremonies in Statuary Hall. The

27

STATUE OF GEN. LEW WALLACE (INDIANA)

Andrew O'Connor, sculptor

invocation was offered by Rev. George F. Dudley, and the statue was unveiled by Lew Wallace, jr., a grandson of Gen. Lew Wallace. Following the unveiling the presentation of the statue to the State of Indiana was made in an address by Mr. William Allen Wood of the General Lew Wallace Statue Commission. The acceptance of the statue on behalf of the State of Indiana was made in an address by Gov. Thomas R. Marshall. Following the address by Governor Marshall, Indiana's poet, James Whitcomb Riley, read a poem entitled "General Lew Wallace," from which we quote the second verse:

> Aye, still he lives—where harvests hum
> And days of bounteous peace are ours;
> Or at the sudden whirring drum
> When battle-tempest lowers—
> He lives and moves, through war's alarm,
> A sensate spirit, leading still
> His legions with waving arm
> And an unwavering will.

The reading of the poem was followed by an address by Hon. Albert J. Beveridge, after which the representative of the Government of Turkey, Rustem Bey, spoke briefly upon the character of Gen. Lew Wallace as displayed while General Wallace served as an American representative at Constantinople from 1881 to 1885. Hon. W. H. Andrews brought his tribute from the Territory of New Mexico, over which Lew Wallace ruled as governor from 1878 to 1881. The benediction was pronounced by Rev. Lloyd Douglas.

The sculptor of this statue, Andrew O'Connor, born in Worcester, Mass., June 7, 1874, a pupil of his father, was employed at the Chicago World's Fair in 1891 and 1892 and by sculptors and painters in London from 1895 to 1898, inclusive; established in Paris in 1904, where he maintained a studio for many years; awarded medal, second class, Paris Salon of 1906. Among his works are the decoration of main porch, St. Bartholomew's Church, New York; decoration of Essex County courthouse, New Jersey; statue of General Lawton, Indianapolis, Ind.; statue of Inspiration, St. Louis, Mo.; statue for tomb of General Liscum, Washington, D. C.; portrait statue of Gen. Samuel Thomas, New York; and statue of Gen. Lew Wallace, United States Capitol, Washington. For some time subsequent to his stay in Paris Mr. O'Connor maintained a studio in Washington, D. C. During this time he executed a statue of Lincoln from material showing Lincoln's face without a beard, a statue designed to convey a portrait of Lincoln as he appeared prior to his election to the Presidency.

At about this same period there was placed in Statuary Hall as a contribution from the State of Iowa the statue of James Harlan, distinguished as a statesman and a man of great learning. He also served as a United States Senator and Secretary of the Interior. This bronze statue, the first contribution of the State of Iowa to Statuary Hall, is the work of Nellie V. Walker, who was born in Red Oak, Iowa, December 8, 1874. Her art education was received in the Art Institute of Chicago and in the studio of Lorado Taft of that city. Her works consist chiefly of private memorials, and at the time of the erection of the statue of James Harlan this was her second public commission.

In the year 1909 there was placed in Statuary Hall a marble statue of George Laird Shoup, this being the first statue to be sent to Statuary Hall from the State of Idaho. The customary concurrent resolutions of acceptance and appreciation were introduced in the House of Representatives on January 15, 1910, at which time a date was selected for the exercises of reception and acceptance of the statue. Addresses were made by Mr. Hamer, of Idaho; Mr. Hull, of Iowa; Mr. Stevens, of Minnesota; Mr. Mondell, of Wyoming;

STATUE OF JAMES HARLAN (IOWA)

Nellie V. Walker, sculptress

Mr. Needham, of California; and Mr. Graham, of Pennsylvania, all Members of the House of Representatives. Exercises in the Senate upon the House concurrent resolution were held on January 17, 1910, at which time the following Senators addressed the Senate upon the life and character of former Senator Shoup: Senators Heyburn, Perkins, Clark, Warren, Penrose, Beveridge, Scott, Gamble, Smoot, Carter, and Borah. This statue is the work of Frederick Ernst Triebel, whose biography will be given in connection with another statue of which he is also the sculptor.

The next to be erected was the statue of S. J. Kirkwood, which, like that of Iowa's other statue, is also in bronze, it being the second statue contributed by that State to Statuary Hall. Mr. Kirkwood was a lawyer by profession and served as minister to Denmark, United States Senator, Governor of Iowa, and as Secretary of the Interior in the Cabinet of President Garfield. He was born in 1813 and died in 1894. The sculptor of this statue, Mrs. Vinnie Ream Hoxie, has been referred to before and her biography given in connection with her marble statue of President Lincoln, the first commission given her by the Government.

CHAPTER XXII

STATUES IN STATUARY HALL (CONCLUDED)

ATE in the year 1909 South Carolina contributed her first statue—that of John C. Calhoun—to Statuary Hall. Exercises were held in Statuary Hall on March 12, 1910, at which time addresses were made by Gov. M. F. Ansel and Hon. W. L. Mauldin, and the unveiling of the statue was accomplished by Mrs. R. Moultrie Bratton and Miss Maggie A. Gist. The customary resolutions of acceptance and appreciation were introduced in the Senate on January 12, 1910, by Senator Tillman, of South Carolina, and called up and agreed to by unanimous consent on March 12, 1910. The exercises in the Senate included addresses of Senators Lodge, of Massachusetts, and Smith, of South Carolina; in the House the exercises relating to the acceptance of the statue occurred at 3 o'clock upon March 12, 1910, at which time addresses were made by Mr. Johnson, of South Carolina; Mr. McCall, of Massachusetts; Mr. Lever, of South Carolina; Mr. Ellerbe, of South Carolina, Mr. Lamb, of Virginia; Mr. Aiken, of South Carolina, and Mr. Finley, of South Carolina.

This marble statue is the work of Frederic Wellington Ruckstull, who was born in Breitenbach, Alsace, France, May 22, 1853. He arrived in St. Louis with his parents when about a year old; educated in public schools of St. Louis and for eight years studied art in Paris; received honorable mention in the Paris Salon for his work in 1888; was awarded a grand medal at the World's Columbian Exposition in 1893; member of fine arts jury at the Atlanta International Exposition; member of the advisory board of Charleston Exposition in 1902; secretary of the committee of National Sculptural Society, having in charge the sculpture decorations of Buffalo Exposition; chief of department of sculpture, St. Louis World's Fair (resigned); first secretary of the National Sculpture Society; second vice president of the New York Architectural League; secretary of committee which erected the Dewey Naval Arch in 1898; secretary of committee having in charge the sculptural decorations of the new appellate court building, New York City; second vice president Municipal Art Society, New York; member of National Institute of Arts and Letters of America, of the National Arts Club, and the Lambs Club. His principal works are Evening (life-size female marble statue), Metropolitan Museum, New York; Mercury Amusing Himself (bronze heroic group), Portland Palace, St. Louis; Victory (bronze heroic size) on soldiers' and sailors' monument, Jamaica, Long Island; Solon (heroic bronze), Library of Congress, Washington, D. C.; Franklin, Goethe, and McCaulay (colossal granite head), façade, Library of Congress; equestrian statue of Brig. Gen. John F. Hartranft, Capitol Hill, Harrisburg, Pa.; Wisdom and Force (two colossal marble statues), appellate court house, New York; Glory of Victis (heroic bronze group), Baltimore Confederate Monument; Defense of the Flag, Confederate Monument, Little Rock, Ark.; Phœnicia (colossal marble), customhouse, New York; equestrian statue of Lieut. Gen. Wade Hampton, for Columbia, S. C.; bronze statue of color guard for Petersburg Battle Field Monument; Woman's Monument, Columbia, S. C.; and monuments to Dr. Charles B. McIver, Gov. W. R. Graham, and Senator M. W. Ransom, Raleigh, N. C.

The second statue from the State of Michigan, that of Zachariah Chandler, was placed in Statuary Hall in 1913, and the exercises of unveiling occurred on June 30, 1913.

STATUE OF JOHN C. CALHOUN (SOUTH CAROLINA)

Frederic Wellington Ruckstull, sculptor

FREDERIC WELLINGTON RUCKSTULL
Represented by the statues of John C. Calhoun and Uriah M. Rose in Statuary Hall

{ 425 }

Senator William Alden Smith, of Michigan, acted as chairman at the unveiling exercises. The opening prayer was offered by Rev. Henry N. Couden, D. D. The opening address was by Senator William Alden Smith, of Michigan. The statue was unveiled by Mr. Chandler Hale, a grandson of Zachariah Chandler. The unveiling was followed by an address of the chairman of the statue commission, Mr. Arthur H. Vandenberg, of Grand Rapids, Mich. This was followed by an address by Lieut. Gov. John Q. Ross, of Michigan. The statue was accepted by Senator Jacob H. Gallinger, of New Hampshire, a Senator from the State where Zachariah Chandler was born. The exercises accompanying the passage of the resolutions of acceptance occurred in the Senate at different periods from June 21, 1913, to April 24, 1914. There appears to have been but one address made in the Senate, that of Senator Charles E. Townsend, of Michigan. In the House on June 24, 1913, the date of Monday, July 28, 1913, was fixed for the exercises appropriate to the reception and acceptance of the statue. For some reason, probably due to the pressure of other business, it does not appear that the exercises occurred upon that date. It does appear, however, that on March 10, 1914, in the House of Representatives, Samuel W. Smith asked for and obtained unanimous consent for the setting apart of Sunday, April 12, 1914, for the exercises relating to the acceptance of the statue, and that upon the same date Representative Smith obtained a change of the date to Sunday, April 19, 1914, for the reason that Easter Sunday occurred upon April 12. It also appears that on Sunday, April 19, the Speaker of the House of Representatives designated Mr. Doremus, of Michigan, as presiding officer at the ceremony in honor of the late Senator Chandler, and upon this occasion addresses were made by the following Members: Messrs. Hamilton, Fordney, J. M. C. Smith, Cramton, MacDonald, and Samuel W. Smith, all of Michigan.

An innovation in the commemoration of a citizen on account of his services to humanity was made when Florida in the year 1914 presented the marble statue of Dr. John Gorrie. The life period of Doctor Gorrie was from 1803 to 1855. He was an eminent physician, and through his devotion to his patients he was led to the invention of machinery for mechanical refrigeration in order that the temperature of the sick room might be lowered for fever patients. He was the first to invent and patent ice-making machinery, and this was done not for the purpose of the manufacture of ice for commercial purposes but that those who were ill and intrusted to his care might be treated with greater success through the use of this invention. Exercises were held in Statuary Hall at 10 o'clock a. m., April 30, 1914, at which time the presentation of the statue was made by Hon. George W. Dayton, the chairman of the statue commission. This was followed by an address by Hon. George H. Whiteside, the secretary of the statue commission. He was followed by the Hon. T. F. West, attorney general of the State of Florida and also a member of the statue commission. The acceptance was by Hon. Emmett Wilson, Member of Congress from the State of Florida. The unveiling of the statue was performed by Miss Mary Louise Stewart, of Bagdad, Fla., a great granddaughter of Doctor Gorrie. So far as is known the exercises in Statuary Hall were the only exercises held in connection with the installation of this statue.

The statue is the work of C. Adrian Pillars, who was born in Rantoul, Ill., July 4, 1870, son of John Adrian Pillars and Ella Lee (More) Pillars; educated in the public schools of Illinois and in the University of Illinois, where he was unable to complete the full collegiate course; first commenced to model at the age of 13, when he first met Lorado Taft, who was then engaged upon sculpture at Champaign, Ill. Taft encouraged the lad to continue the study of art, and in later years he became a student of Taft, also a pupil

STATUE OF JOHN GORRIE, M. D. (FLORIDA)

C. Adrian Pillars, sculptor

C. ADRIAN PILLARS

Represented by the statues of John Gorrie and Gen. E. Kirby Smith, in Statuary Hall

STATUE OF GEORGE W. GLICK (KANSAS)

Charles H. Niehaus, sculptor

{ 429 }

at the Chicago Art Institute; remained with Lorado Taft as pupil and studio assistant for nine years; was engaged for 18 months upon the colossal statuary of the Columbian Exposition, the larger part of the time under the direction of Daniel Chester French, although much of his work at this time was in connection with other sculptors; he did independently decorative relief work and modeled the Dancing Faun for the horticultural building; moved to Florida in 1894, where he has executed many commissions in portrait work, relief work, and decorative sculpture for private individuals. Among his better known works are the ideal composition, The South; Shield and Tablet for the Battlefield, Florida; and a fountain for Jacksonville, Fla. In addition to the Gorrie Statue, Mr. Pillars is the sculptor of the bronze statue of Gen. E. Kirby Smith, also a contribution from the State of Florida.

In 1914 the second statue from the State of Kansas, that of George W. Glick, formerly a governor of that State, was placed in Statuary Hall. Upon the occasion of the installation of this statue the former location of the statue of John J. Ingalls was changed so that the statues of Kansas guard the corridor leading from Statuary Hall to the Hall of the House of Representatives, complementing in this manner the location of the statues from New Hampshire, which guard the entrance from Statuary Hall to the rotunda of the Capitol. There were no public exercises held in Statuary Hall upon the occasion of the installation of the statue of Governor Glick, but on June 24, 1914, a resolution was presented in the Senate fixing the date of the exercises relating to the reception and acceptance of this statue for Saturday, July 18, 1914, and upon that date addresses were made by Senators Thompson, of Kansas; Bristow, of Kansas; Stone, of Missouri; Reed, of Missouri; and Thomas, of Colorado. In the House of Representatives exercises appropriate to the reception and acceptance of this statue were held upon the same date at 3 o'clock p. m., and addresses were made by Representatives Campbell, Taggart, and Murdock, of Kansas.

The statue, in marble, is the work of Charles H. Niehaus, who attempted the somewhat difficult sculptural interpretation of the subject in the act of speaking. How well he succeeded can only be judged, however, by the comparison of this work with other work where the same form of sculptural expression has been attempted. The biography of Mr. Niehaus has been previously given.

In 1916 the State of Minnesota presented its first statue, that of Henry Mower Rice, in marble. Unveiling exercises were held in Statuary Hall on February 8, 1916. At these exercises Mr. Frederick G. Ingersoll, the secretary of the Rice Statue Commission, acted as chairman, and after prayer by Doctor Montgomery the secretary made a brief statement concerning the work of the commission, after which Miss Matilda Whitall Auerbach, a granddaughter of Mr. Rice, unveiled the statue. Addresses were made by Mrs. Charles R. Davis, representing the Daughters of the American Revolution of Minnesota, who placed a wreath at the foot of the statue upon the conclusion of her remarks; Senator Nelson, of Minnesota, who also served as the chairman of the Rice Statue Commission; Senator Clapp, of Minnesota; and the Vice President, Thomas R. Marshall. In the Senate exercises were held on February 19, 1916, at which time customary resolutions of acceptance and appreciation were presented. Addresses were made by Senators Nelson, of Minnesota; Underwood, of Alabama; Harding, of Ohio; Gallinger, of New Hampshire; and Clapp, of Minnesota. In the House of Representatives exercises were held on March 11, 1916, when resolutions of acceptance and appreciation were introduced. Addresses were made by Representatives Davis,

STATUE OF HENRY MOWER RICE (MINNESOTA)

Frederick E. Triebel, sculptor

STATUE OF GEORGE L. SHOUP (IDAHO)
Frederick E. Triebel, sculptor

STATUE OF ZEBULON B. VANCE (NORTH CAROLINA)

Gutzon Borglum, sculptor

Steenerson, Miller, Volstead, Smith, Lindberg, Van Dyke, Schall, Anderson, and Ellsworth, all of Minnesota.

The sculptor of this work was Frederick Ernst Triebel, who also executed the statue of George L. Shoup. Mr. Triebel was born in Peoria, Ill., December 29, 1865; was educated in the public schools of Peoria, Ill., and in the Royal Academy of Fine Arts, Italy; has followed the profession of sculptor since 1888. His statue Mysterious Music, exhibited at World's Columbian Exposition 1893, was purchased by the Japanese Government for the Imperial Museum at Tokio; member Circolo Artistico, Florence, Italy; l'Associazione Artistics Internazionale, Rome, Italy; National Sculpture Society; and the Architectural League, New York.

In 1916 the State of North Carolina presented to Statuary Hall the bronze statue of Zebulon B. Vance, the work of Gutzon Borglum, whose biography has been given in connection with another work by this artist. Proceedings of unveiling and presentation were held in Statuary Hall, June 22, 1916. Hon. William Alexander Hoke, chairman of the Vance Statue Commission, presided at the unveiling ceremonies, and after a brief report from the chairman the statue was unveiled by Miss Dorothy Espey Pillow, aged 6, a great-granddaughter of Senator Vance, and the Hon. Clement Manly, of North Carolina, a member of the statue commission, then presented for the commission the statue. The Hon. Locke Craig presented the statue on behalf of the State of North Carolina to the Government, and the address of acceptance was made by Vice President Thomas R. Marshall. After the acceptance of the statue palms, wreaths of pine, and rhododendron sent by the patriotic women of North Carolina and presented by representatives of the Daughters of the Confederacy were placed about the statue. In the Senate on Saturday, June 3, 1916, the date of June 22, 1916, was fixed for the exercises appropriate to the reception and acceptance of the statue by that body, and on June 22 addresses were made by Senators Overman, of North Carolina; Lodge, of Massachusetts; and Smith, of Georgia In the House of Representatives on June 23 the customary resolutions of acceptance and appreciation were introduced, and on July 25, 1916, the date of July 29 was fixed for the exercises. Upon this date the following Representatives spoke upon the life and character of Senator Vance: Mr. Small, Mr. Hood, Mr. Pou, Mr. Stedman, Mr. Britt, Mr. Doughton, Mr. Webb, Mr. Godwin, and Mr. Kitchin, all of North Carolina.

The next statue to be given a place in Statuary Hall was the gift of the State of Arkansas, represented by the marble statue of Uriah M. Rose. This statue was erected March 29, 1917. There were no unveiling exercises held in Statuary Hall, and so far as has been learned no action toward the acceptance of this statue has ever been taken by either House of Congress. The sculptor of this statue, F. W. Ruckstull, has been referred to and his biography given in connection with the statue of John C. Calhoun.

In 1917 the first contribution from the State of Oklahoma was erected in Statuary Hall. This is a bronze statue of Sequoyah by the sculptor Vinnie Ream Hoxie, who was given a commission for this work and had made her model, but died before the work had been executed in bronze. Public ceremonies of unveiling were held in Statuary Hall on June 6, 1917, at which time the statue was unveiled by Miss Ahnawake Hastings and addresses were made by Senator R. L. Owen and others from the State of Oklahoma. The presentation on behalf of the State of Oklahoma was by Gov. R. L. Williams. The acceptance of the statue for the United States was by Speaker Champ Clark. On June 2, 1917, the customary resolution of acceptance and appreciation were introduced in the House of Representatives, and upon that occasion Mr. Slayden, for the Committee on the

STATUE OF URIAH M. ROSE (ARKANSAS)

Frederic Wellington Ruckstull, sculptor

STATUE OF SEQUOYAH (OKLAHOMA)

Vinnie Ream Hoxie, sculptress

STATUE OF GEN. E. KIRBY SMITH (FLORIDA)

C. Adrian Pillars, sculptor

Library, presented a report which, on account of the important information relating to Sequoyah which this report includes, is considered worthy of a place in this work:

Sequoyah, whose statue it is proposed to accept from the State of Oklahoma, was born in the State of Georgia about 1770. He was the son of a full-blooded Cherokee woman and a German trader by the name of George Gist, who dealt in contraband articles, and who abandoned his wife before Sequoyah was born.

Sequoyah grew up to young manhood among the Cherokees in Georgia and became a leader in the affairs of his tribe. He not only took an active part in hunting and fishing, as well as sports, but became a trader, silversmith, blacksmith, and philosopher, and later the inventor of the Cherokee alphabet, upon which his chief claim to fame rests. This invention is most remarkable when it is known that he never attended school and could neither read nor write the English language.

Following the invention of the Cherokee alphabet, consisting of 85 characters, in 1821, it was accepted by the tribe and he was voted a silver medal in 1824 as a mark of distinction. In 1828 an iron printing press was purchased by the Cherokees with Cherokee and English type, from which the Cherokee Phoenix was published at New Echota, Ga. It was the first newspaper printed in the Indian language. The paper was discontinued about 1835 and another, the Cherokee Advocate, was established in the Indian Territory, west, now a part of Oklahoma, in 1845. It ceased publication during the Civil War and was reestablished in 1870 and published until 1905, both in English and Cherokee.

The effect of this alphabet upon the future advancement of the Cherokee Indians and all other Indian tribes is difficult to fully appreciate. Immediately after its invention not only were newspapers published in the Indian language which could be read by all, but the New Testament, hymns, tracts, and books of various kinds were published, resulting, no doubt, in the adoption of the first written Indian constitution in 1827, modeled after that of the United States and the several States, and the formation of a government with three distinct branches—legislative, executive, and judicial—similar to the government of the surrounding States.

Sequoyah came to Washington as one of the representatives of the western tribes of Indians in 1828, when his invention was recognized by Congress and an appropriation of $500 was made for his benefit. Additional appropriations were made by Congress for the education of the children of the tribe.

In 1823 he moved from Georgia with other members of the Cherokee Tribe west, first into the Territory of Arkansas and later to the Indian Territory, now a part of Oklahoma.

While in Washington he conceived the idea of inventing another alphabet by means of which all Indians upon the American Continent speaking different languages could communicate with each other. In the early forties he started out on a western tour to visit the western Indian Tribes and further this plan, but he never lived to accomplish the end sought. He died in the far West about 1845, near San Bernardino, the exact spot being unknown.

Sequoyah's English name was George Guess, a corruption of Gist, and the word Sequoyah means "guessed it." The Cherokee Tribe in the Indian Territory west further recognized his great services by voting him a pension and naming one of its counties for him, and this honor was continued by the State of Oklahoma. Under the act of Congress authorizing each State to place two statues representing distinguished men in Statuary Hall, the first to be presented on behalf of the State of Oklahoma is that of Sequoyah, the Cherokee Cadmus.

In the Senate on June 4, 1917, the resolutions of the House were concurred in. There was no other action taken by either the Senate or House with reference to this statue.

The second statue from the State of Florida was that of Gen. Kirby Smith. This bronze statue is the work of the sculptor C. Adrian Pillars. The statue was erected August 25, 1918. There were no unveiling exercises held in Statuary Hall. Some four years later reference was made in the House and the customary resolutions of acceptance were introduced, but the general proceedings accompanying such resolutions, with addresses upon the life and character of the person commemorated by the statue, seem to have been omitted in this case with the exception of a few brief remarks by one of the Florida delegation, Hon. William J. Sears, in the House of Representatives on January 25, 1922.

The second statue to be erected in Statuary Hall from the State of Arkansas was that of James P. Clarke, a former Senator of the United States. This marble statue, the gift of

STATUE OF JAMES P. CLARKE (ARKANSAS)

Pompeo Coppini, sculptor

the State of Arkansas, is the work of the sculptor Pompeo Coppini. The statue was installed in Statuary Hall May 20, 1921. There were no public exercises of unveiling in connection with this statue. The sculptor, Pompeo Coppini, was born in Moglia, Province of Mantua, Italy, May 19, 1870, son of Giovanni and Leandra (Raffa) Coppini. He was educated in the schools of Florence, Italy. His father, a musician, was in favor of Pompeo becoming a civil engineer and for some time he followed a course of study to fit him for that profession. His love for art led him to desert the study of engineering, and in 1886 he entered the Academy of Fine Arts of Florence as a pupil of Augusto Rivalti, graduating from this institution with high honor. Following his graduation he entered the military service and secured his release therefrom in 1892. Opening a studio in Florence, he secured some notable commissions and executed many portrait busts, among them being busts of Senator Bovio, Senator Manteganzza, Professor Giglioli, and Prof. Hugo Shiff. Sailing for the United States, he landed in New York March 5, 1896, and secured employment among the sculptors; assisted Hinton Perry in the Neptune Fountain fronting the Library of Congress, Washington, D. C. In November, 1901, he moved to San Antonio, Tex., where he modeled five statues for the Confederate monument for the capitol grounds at Austin, Tex. Remained in that city for the following 15 years and received in competition many commissions, among these being an equestrian statue, The Texas Ranger, also on the capitol grounds at Austin; equestrian statue of John H. Morgan for Lexington, Ky.; and a statue of George Washington for the City of Mexico, a gift from the American colony. Moved to Chicago in the fall of 1916, where he executed an equestrian group for Charles Noyes and received the commission to execute a $250,000 war memorial for the University of Texas. Returned to New York in 1922, where he erected a studio adapted for the work at hand. In 1898 was married at New Haven, Conn., to Elisa de Barbieri. Became an American citizen in 1902.

On March 12, 1925, the bronze statue of Gen. Joe Wheeler was unveiled in Statuary Hall with public exercises attended by a large gathering of people. Many tributes were paid by the speakers on that occasion to the memory of the man who had served as an officer in two wars, that of the War between the States and the War with Spain. His long service in the House of Representatives was also called to the attention of the audience and his ability as a legislator and statesman given proper credit.

The sculptor of this statue, Berthold Nebel, was present at the unveiling exercises. Mr. Nebel was born in Basel, Switzerland, April 19, 1889, and received his art education at the American Academy in Rome, and in this country was a pupil of James E. Fraser. He has designed a medal for the Bureau of Mines to be awarded for rescues and first aid; exhibited a plaster group, The Wrestlers, in Pittsburgh, Pa. Other work by this sculptor includes busts for private parties and decorative sculpture for public and private buildings.

Concluding the list of statues in Statuary Hall, we mention the statue of Dr. Crawford Williamson Long, unveiled in Statuary Hall March 30, 1926, with exercises of a public character. This statue is the first contribution of the State of Georgia, and Doctor Long is represented by a statue carved from Georgia marble. As the discoverer of ether anæsthesia, the subject of this statue had reached great prominence in the medical profession, and members of different branches of the profession were represented in the exercises of the unveiling. The statue is the work of J. Massey Rhind, born in Edinburgh, Scotland, in 1858; educated at the Scotch Academy and at the Royal Academy in London; established himself in New York as a sculptor in 1889, and is represented in Washington by the Grand Army of the Republic memorial and by the statue of Doctor

STATUE OF GEN. JOSEPH WHEELER (ALABAMA)

Berthold Nebel, sculptor

{ 441 }

STATUE OF CRAWFORD W. LONG (GEORGIA)

J. Massey Rhind, sculptor

Long above referred to. Mr. Rhind is a member of the Architectural League, National Sculpture Society, Municipal Art Society, the Players' Club, and the Home Club.

It is possible that some one may ask the question, Why have the persons who are represented by statues in Statuary Hall been selected by the States by which the contributions have been made? It will be remembered that there was this requirement:

for historic renown or for distinguished civic or military services such as each State may deem worthy of this national commemoration.

and in order that this question may be answered as briefly as possible, the following information is given concerning the persons commemorated, arranged alphabetically by States:

Alabama.—J. L. M. Curry (1825–1903) and Joseph Wheeler (1836–1906). Mr. Curry was distinguished as a Member of Congress of the United States, also the Confederacy; served in the Confederate Army; was United States minister to Spain and an author.

Gen. Joseph Wheeler, a graduate of West Point, served in the Confederate Army and attained the rank of senior Cavalry officer; he also served in the United States Army during the War with Spain as a major general of Volunteers and was retired with the rank of brigadier general in the Regular Army; his service as a Representative in Congress included the Forty-seventh, Forty-ninth, and the seven following Congresses.

Arkansas.—Uriah M. Rose (1834–1913) and James P. Clarke (1854–1916). Mr. Rose was a lawyer of international reputation; chancellor of the State; charter member of American Bar Association, serving as president in 1901. In 1907 he was appointed by President Roosevelt as one of the delegates to the Peace Congress of The Hague and was given the rank of ambassador upon that mission.

James P. Clarke was also a lawyer, attorney general, Governor of Arkansas, and United States Senator from March 4, 1903, until the time of his death, October 1, 1916.

Connecticut.—Roger Sherman (1721–1793) and Jonathan Trumbull (1710–1785). The former was a signer of the Declaration of Independence, a Delegate in the Continental Congress and in the Constitutional Convention. He was also a Member of the House of Representatives and of the United States Senate.

Trumbull was chief justice and Governor of Connecticut in colonial times, the only colonial governor who espoused the cause of independence.

Florida.—Dr. John Gorrie (1803–1855) and Gen. E. Kirby Smith (1824–1893). Doctor Gorrie was an eminent physician and inventor of the ice machine and mechanical refrigeration. This device was invented for the purpose of lowering the temperature in the rooms of fever patients and not in the interest of the manufacture of ice for commercial purposes.

Gen. E. Kirby Smith was a soldier in the war with Mexico, a general in the Confederate Army, and in civil life a distinguished educator.

Georgia.—Dr. Crawford Williamson Long (1815–1878), a distinguished physician whose discovery of ether anæsthesia in the year 1842 gave him a prominent place among the physicians of his native State and throughout the entire medical profession.

Idaho.—George L. Shoup (1836–1904), distinguished as a pioneer and for disinterested patriotism; colonel in the Union Army in the Civil War; Governor of Idaho Territory and also the State of Idaho; served in the United States Senate from 1890 to 1901.

Illinois.—James Shields (1810–1879) and Frances E. Willard (1839–1898). Shields served in the Mexican War and was a Union officer in the Civil War; also a statesman, and served in the United States Senate.

STATUE OF DANIEL WEBSTER (NEW HAMPSHIRE)

Carl Conrads, sculptor

Frances E. Willard was distinguished in reform movements; was president of the Woman's Christian Temperance Union and editor of the Chicago Evening Post. She founded the Woman's Christian Temperance Union, also the World's Woman's Christian Temperance Union, of which she was its corresponding secretary, and she was the head of purity work of the World's and National Woman's Christian Temperance Unions.

Indiana.—Oliver P. Morton (1823–1877) and Lew Wallace (1827–1909). Morton was the greatest of the war governors of the Civil War and later a great constructive statesman, foremost in the United States Senate.

Wallace was distinguished as a Union general in the Civil War and the author of A Fair God, Ben Hur, and The Prince of India.

Iowa.—James Harlan (1820–1899) and Samuel Jordan Kirkwood (1813–1894). James Harlan was distinguished as a statesman and a man of great learning; United States Senator and Secretary of the Interior.

Kirkwood was a lawyer by profession, minister to Denmark, United States Senator, Governor of Iowa, and Secretary of the Interior in the Cabinet of President Garfield.

Kansas.—John J. Ingalls (1833–1900) and George Washington Glick (1827–1911). Ingalls was a lawyer, scholar, and statesman, the fearless peer of those with whom he served in the United States Senate three terms.

Glick was a lawyer, farmer, successful politician, and Governor of the State of Kansas. He was also a soldier in the Union Army in the War of 1861; and although he enlisted in the Mexican War, hostilities had ceased before he saw active service.

Maine.—William King (1768–1852). Was Maine's first governor and always active and influential in her politics; likewise a successful banker and business man.

Maryland.—Charles Carroll of Carrollton (1737–1832) and John Hanson (1715–1783). Carroll was educated by French Jesuits; was for independence of the Colonies; belonged to the council of safety of his State; a Delegate in the Continental Congress; and was the last surviving signer of the Declaration of Independence.

Hanson was a patriot of the Revolution, President of the Continental Congress, and encouraged enlistment in the Army in the War for Independence.

Massachusetts.—Samuel Adams (1722–1803) and John Winthrop (1588–1649). Adams was a patriot of the Revolution and of special fame in securing the independence of the Colonies and in launching the constitutional government. He was governor of his State.

Winthrop was a colonial Governor of Massachusetts, an author, believed in evangelizing the Indians, opposed democracy, and believed superior minds, though always in the minority, should rule.

Michigan.—Lewis Cass (1782–1866) and Zachariah Chandler (1813–1879). Cass was a statesman of renown, a United States Senator, a Cabinet officer, and held other high official positions covering long periods of this country's history. He left the Cabinet of President Buchanan when secession was imminent.

Chandler served as United States Senator, Secretary of the Interior, chairman of the Republican National Executive Committee, and died while in office as a Senator.

Minnesota.—Henry Mower Rice (1816–1894); pioneer, Delegate in Congress from Minnesota Territory, United States commissioner in making Indian treaties, and one of the first Senators from the State of Minnesota.

Missouri.—Francis P. Blair (1821–1875) and Thomas H. Benton (1782–1858). Blair was a soldier in the Civil War, an editor, and prominent in the political life of the country for a long time.

Benton was a Senator, statesman, and author; a warm supporter of President Jackson and other great patriots of that day.

New Hampshire.—John Stark (1728–1822) and Daniel Webster (1782–1852). Stark achieved fame as a soldier in the French and Indian wars and in the War of the Revolution.

Webster, a son of New Hampshire, was a lawyer and statesman in his adopted State, Massachusetts. In the United States Senate he combated by an unanswerable argument the doctrine of the right of secession.

New Jersey.—Richard Stockton (1730–1781) and Philip Kearny (1815–1862). Stockton was an important factor upon the side of the Colonies during the period of the Revolution.

Kearny was a major general in the Union Army; lost an arm in battle, and was afterwards killed at the Battle of Chantilly in the Civil War.

New York.—Robert R. Livingston (1746–1813) and George Clinton (1739–1812). Livingston was an early Governor of New York, a Delegate in the Continental Congress, and a signer of the Declaration of Independence.

Clinton was a soldier in the French and Indian and Revolutionary Wars, was a Delegate in the Continental Congress, several times Governor of New York, and was Vice President of the United States.

North Carolina.—Zebulon Baird Vance (1830–1894); lawyer, Representative in Congress from North Carolina, colonel in the Confederate Army, Governor of the State of North Carolina, and United States Senator.

Ohio.—James A. Garfield (1831–1881) and William Allen (1807–1879). Garfield was a major general of Volunteers in the Civil War; served for many years in the House of Representatives, and was President of the United States.

Allen was a United States Senator and Governor of Ohio. Prominent for a long time in the politics of his State.

Oklahoma.—Sequoyah (1770–1845); a Cherokee Indian, whose father was a German trader; a leader in the affairs of his tribe; was a trader, silversmith, blacksmith, philosopher, and the inventor of the Cherokee alphabet.

Pennsylvania.—J. P. G. Muhlenberg (1746–1807) and Robert Fulton (1765–1815). Muhlenberg was a distinguished minister of the gospel, a colonel in the Revolutionary War, and a Member of the House of Representatives in the First, Third, and Sixth Congresses.

Fulton, although an artist of merit, achieved his greatest distinction for his adaptation of steam power to the propelling of boats and ships.

Rhode Island.—Nathanael Greene (1742–1786) and Roger Williams (1599–1683). Greene was a Revolutionary general of renown.

Roger Williams was an early Puritan pioneer minister of the gospel in the Colonies and among the Indians, famed for his zeal and ability, especially in the cause of religious liberty, and the founder of Providence and Rhode Island Plantations.

South Carolina.—John C. Calhoun (1782–1850); the leader of a school of earnest men who believed secession was warranted or at least permissible under the Constitution of the United States because not expressly forbidden. He served his country as Secretary of War, Secretary of State, Vice President of the United States, and United States Senator.

Texas.—Stephen F. Austin (1790–1836) and Samuel Houston (1793–1863). Austin was a Texas revolutionist and did much to win the freedom of Texas from Mexico.

Houston was distinguished for his services in liberating Texas from Mexico, served as President of the Republic of Texas, Governor of Texas, and Member of the House of Representatives.

JOHN QUINCY ADAMS
who,
after fifty years
of public service,
the last sixteen
in yonder Hall,
was summoned thence
to die in this room,
23 February 1848.

In the office of the Clerk of the House of Representatives

BUST OF JOHN QUINCY ADAMS

John Crookshanks King, sculptor

Vermont.—Ethan Allen (1737–1789) and Jacob Collamer (1791–1865). Allen was an officer in the Revolutionary War. It was he who demanded and received the surrender of Ticonderoga.

Collamer was an illustrious statesman, a justice of the supreme court of the State, Member of the House of Representatives, Postmaster General, and at the time of his death a United States Senator.

Virginia.—George Washington (1732–1799) and Robert E. Lee (1807–1870). Washington's record and right to a place in Statuary Hall is so well known that to attempt to explain the reasons why the statue was placed there is entirely unnecessary.

Lee was a distinguished officer of the Confederacy and a citizen who, following the close of the war, did much for the building up of his native State.

West Virginia.—John E. Kenna (1848–1893) and Francis H. Pierpont (1814–1899). Kenna, while quite young, saw service in the Confederate Army. He was a Member of the House of Representatives and a Senator of the United States.

Pierpont in 1861 was chosen by a convention Provisional Governor of Virginia, its governor and lieutenant governor having declared for the Confederacy. He acted as Governor of Virginia until 1868. He was known as one of the war governors and assisted in the mobilization and sending to the front of more than 40,000 Union troops during the war.

Wisconsin.—James Marquette (1637–1675). A French Jesuit priest, a missionary among the wild tribes of Indians of the northern country, and a discoverer and explorer, including in his explorations the course of the Mississippi River. Although not a native of Wisconsin or a citizen of that State, the right of the State to commemorate the services of Marquette was established by a joint resolution of Congress approved October 21, 1893.

We should not forget that although the work of art to which we now invite attention is not contained in Statuary Hall, it is so closely associated with events occurring in that hall that it seems appropriate that it should be mentioned at this time. We refer to the bust of John Quincy Adams, which has been placed upon a bracket in the room at present occupied by the Clerk of the House of Representatives. It will be remembered that although Mr. Adams had served as President of the United States, he was subsequently elected a Representative from Massachusetts to the Twenty-second Congress and successively reelected eight times. The exact spot where Mr. Adams fell when stricken with the malady which resulted in his death is marked by a star and an inscription in Statuary Hall. He died February 23, 1848, in the room then occupied by the Speaker of the House of Representatives, now the office of the Clerk of the House of Representatives. The marble bust of John Quincy Adams is the work of John Crookshanks King, who was born in Hilwinning, Ayrshire, Scotland, October 11, 1806. His tendency toward art matters was shown while in school from the age of 6 to 15. During this period his lack of attention to other studies and his preference for drawing was strongly marked. He was taught the trade of his father, that of a machinist, and remained in his native country until the month of November, 1829, when, in company with his brother William, he sailed for the United States. Landing at New Orleans, he proceeded from there to a plantation where he remained on a visit for five months, and then moved to Cincinnati, Ohio, where he remained for a year and a half. In the year 1832 he met and became acquainted with Hiram Powers, in whose work he showed such deep interest and such an appreciation that Powers assured him that he could become a sculptor if he would only set himself about it with determination. About this time he commenced modeling in clay, but seemed to have accomplished little except in the formation of a

STATUARY HALL, LOOKING EAST

29

STATUARY HALL, LOOKING WEST

STATUARY HALL, LOOKING SOUTH

purpose to at some time take up sculpture as a life work. During the succeeding four years but little is known of his art studies or progress, although he returned to New Orleans and after a short time in that city moved to Louisville, where he remained until 1836. During this year he returned to New Orleans, where he made busts of Rev. Theodore Clapp, James H. Caldwell, and Pierre Soule. In 1840 he located in Boston and continued his art work. Here he produced busts of Daniel Webster, John Quincy Adams, Dr. Samuel Woodward, and Commodore Morris, the last-named bust being owned by the Corcoran Gallery of Art. In the year 1853 Mr. King was greatly disheartened by the burning of his studio and the destruction of casts and other material. He died in Boston, Mass., April 22, 1882.

This completes the list of statues in Statuary Hall, as well as the brief summary of some of the reasons impelling the States to commemorate those of whom statues have been installed. The information furnished in this short recital is probably sufficient to give to those who may want to pursue the history of different individuals something upon which to base a foundation upon which research may be carried as far as desired. We should not, however, leave Statuary Hall without calling attention to the plaster model of Liberty, the work of Enrico Causici, a native of Verona, Italy, and said to be a pupil of Canova. Concerning this plaster model it is stated by some writer that Causici had hoped to be able to reproduce it in marble, but died before this work could be done. It is stated by others that his death occurred in Habana, Cuba, but the date of death is not given. This statue of Liberty suffers greatly from its elevated position and from the fact that it is poorly lighted and probably in the course of the years which have elapsed it has been restored until it does not convey an adequate representation of the intention of the sculptor.

In addition to what has been previously written concerning the eagle, by Valaperti, which occupies a position upon the frieze at the south side of Statuary Hall, it may be stated that Valaperti must have been a sculptor of more than ordinary ability and came to this country or to Washington in the hope of securing commissions. From letters written by Thornton and Latrobe, previously referred to, it is shown that his reputation as a sculptor was of the best—in fact, Latrobe recommended him as the sculptor for the statue of Washington contemplated for the State capitol of North Carolina. It appears that this eagle, which all concede to be an excellent work of art, was the only commission awarded to Valaperti about the Capitol, and being in poor health he became suspicious of those who cared to befriend him and convinced himself that those who commended his work were not sincere in their commendation. It seems unfortunate that circumstances were so unfavorable at such a crisis in the life of this sculptor. Early in March, 1917, he disappeared from the house in which he occupied a room and left upon the table a will by which he disposed of all of his personal effects and named therein his wife and children as the beneficiaries and in the event of their death before the will became operative his personal effects were bequeathed to one of the Catholic churches in Washington. Valaperti was never heard of afterwards. It has been rumored that a body supposed to have been his was found in the Potomac River, but careful examination of the newspapers of that period does not disclose anything upon which to base such a conclusion. After more than a year had elapsed the executor named in the will presented the document for probate and proved the handwriting of the testator, and through the United States consulate the proceeds of the sale of the sculptor's personal effects were paid to his wife and children, who then resided near Genoa, Italy. In this manner the sad story of Giuseppe Valaperti comes to a close.

CHAPTER XXIII

IN THE Hall of the House of Representatives one may see an aisle commencing at the northern entrance to the Hall and continuing southward to the desk of the Speaker. This marks the separation of the two great political parties, the Democrats and the Republicans; east of it the Democratic forces are assembled, while on its west may be found those adhering to the Republican Party. It should not be presumed, however, that this aisle divides friendship, for upon each side of it are to be found many who are firm friends of those upon the other side, while upon a political question they may vote in opposition to each other. It was therefore appropriate that two of the celebrated leaders of the different parties, Champ Clark, of Missouri, formerly a Speaker of the House, and James R. Mann, of Illinois, the floor leader of the Republican Party during the period of Democratic ascendancy, should be commemorated by busts of marble, which are placed opposite to each other at the outer portal—the House connection—of the House wing of the Capitol. Here they may be found, one upon the Democratic side, the other upon the Republican side of this entrance, as though not only keeping alive the traditions of the two parties but also continuing the warm friendship which existed between these two great leaders. These busts, the first to be placed in the House wing of the Capitol of former prominent Members, were unveiled on February 28, 1925, at which time public exercises were held and eloquent tributes paid to the memories of these truly great Americans. It was probably the first time that exercises of this character were held in this corridor, where there is but limited space for a public gathering, and the large numbers who assembled on that occasion demonstrated the affectionate regard with which Mr. Clark and Mr. Mann were held by those who had known them in official and in private life. The bust of Mr. Mann is the work of the sculptor Herbert Adams, and in this example he has given us a portrait in which the genial qualities and the calm reasoning powers of the individual are well represented. Mr. Adams is represented in the Senate wing of the Capitol by a portrait bust of Vice President Gerry, and a biography of Mr. Adams has been presented in connection with this last-named work. The bust of Champ Clark is the work of Moses A. Wainer-Dykaar, heretofore referred to as the sculptor of the bust of Vice President Marshall and whose biography has been given in connection with that work. In the bust of Speaker Clark Mr. Wainer-Dykaar has given a clever likeness of the former Speaker, and in it is shown the calm attitude so often noted at times when the merits of a question were being determined in something of a judicial manner. It is to be hoped that this idea of commemorating with marble busts great leaders of the House of Representatives may be continued from time to time in order that coming generations may feel that the services of our legislators are not only appreciated but publicly honored.

Another sculptural work which should not be passed unnoticed is a small bust of Henry Clay, which for many years occupied a place in the room of the Senate Committee

BUST OF CHAMP CLARK

Moses A. Wainer-Dykaar, sculptor

BUST OF JAMES R. MANN
Herbert Adams, sculptor

on the Library and is now in the office of the Architect of the Capitol. This bust, although small, is conceded to be a fine sculptural production and it is worthy of a prominent location, where its beauty can be seen and appreciated. The history of this bust is of more than usual interest for the reason that the sculptor was comparatively unknown and that in order to secure the necessary information for a biography the quest led to different cities in Kentucky, and through these inquiries it was learned that members of the sculptor's family were living in Washington. Albert P. Henry, the sculptor, was born in Versailles, Ky., January 8, 1836. When a small boy his parents settled in Princeton, Ky. His first art work was commenced when but a mere boy. He carved from a block of marble thrown from a steamboat an ambitious group comprising an Indian girl holding a dove, while a wolf is creeping up to snatch the bird from her grasp. While crude, the proportion and perspective were well expressed. His business life commenced as a clerk in the Hillman Iron Works, where he occupied his leisure in modeling small portrait busts and casting them in iron to be used as weights to keep doors open. At the breaking out of the Civil War young Henry recruited a company for the Fifteenth Kentucky Cavalry and was commissioned as its captain. After the fall of Forts Fisher and Donelson he was promoted to the rank of lieutenant colonel and given the command of a regiment to guard these forts. In a skirmish near Fort Henry his horse was shot from under him. He was captured by the enemy and taken to Libby prison, where he was confined for nine months. While in prison he devoted much of his time to carving upon the bones of oxen, used in soup making. He managed to smuggle from the prison in a wooden box with a false bottom some of these carvings, among them a cup made from the bone of an ox upon which he had carved The Prisoner's Dream, showing the interior of the cell, an armed sentry at the door, while the prisoner is sleeping on the floor, using his boots for a pillow. Following the close of the war he was appointed consul at Anconia, Italy. Prior to his leaving the United States he had executed his bust of Henry Clay, now in the Capitol, and a bust of Abraham Lincoln from life, now in the customhouse, Louisville, Ky. While in Italy he spent considerable time in Florence, where he studied art under Powers and Joel T. Hart. Henry's most ambitious production is an ideal bust of Genevieve, placed in the historic courthouse in the room in which U. S. Grant was received on the occasion of his official visit to Louisville. He also made a bust of Senator Guthrie, of Kentucky, and a bust of Senator Garrett Davis. He was a man of many friends and a personal friend of Hart, the sculptor, who wrote to the artist's mother at the time of his death saying:

I sympathize with you and yours for the loss in his prime of a son so ardent in his love for his parents, his friends, and his profession; industrious, cordial and kind to all.

He died in Paris, Ky., November 6, 1872.

We have now reached that period in the history of the art development of the Capitol where it becomes necessary to take up the remaining art work, the portraits in the Speaker's lobby, which have been placed there under the provisions of House Resolution 163 (61st Cong., 2d sess.). Before this resolution was adopted it passed through an interesting period of debate. The question of precedent was raised, for the reason that the attempt was made, and properly so, to provide for the placing in the Speaker's lobby of portraits in oil to take the place of a large number of crayon portraits which were then hanging in the lobby. It was contended by some that as this resolution, or the subject matter thereof, was under the jurisdiction of the House Committee on the Library and as that committee had no money appropriated for its use, to take the money from the contingent fund of the House under the control of the Committee on Accounts was not permissible, since no authority existed for the purchase of portraits by the latter committee. It was, however, very wisely decided that, while the Committee on Accounts could not purchase portraits, it was within its right to employ painters to paint portraits and to pay such artists for their services. The bill originally provided for 17 portraits, but seems to have been amended or construed to include a larger number, as 19 portraits were purchased under the enactment referred to. The Committee on the Library of the House on March 3, 1911, passed the following resolution:

Resolved, That under and by virtue of House Resolution 163 of the Sixty-first Congress, Second Session, authorizing and directing the Committee on the Library to employ artists of reputation and ability to paint oil portraits of certain former Speakers of the House of Representatives, the said Committee hereby employs:

Miss Rebecca Polk to paint portrait of ex-Speaker J. K. Polk.
Mrs. W. B. Newman to paint portrait of ex-Speaker John Bell.
Miss Lucy M. Stanton to paint portrait of ex-Speaker Howell Cobb.
W. D. Murphy to paint portrait of ex-Speaker John W. Davis.
Charles A. Gray to paint portrait of ex-Speaker M. C. Kerr.
Freeman Thorp to paint portrait of ex-Speaker Schuyler Colfax.
R. N. Brooke to paint portrait of ex-Speaker Robert M. T. Hunter.
Spencer B. Nichols to paint portrait of ex-Speaker Andrew Stevenson.
Miss Kate F. Edwards to paint portrait of ex-Speaker Philip Barbour.
J. B. Sword to paint portrait of ex-Speaker J. W. Jones.
Hugo Ballin to paint portrait of ex-Speaker John G. Carlisle.
Gerard Barry to paint portrait of ex-Speaker John White.
Stanley Middleston to paint portrait of ex-Speaker Linn Boyd.
Henry Harrison to paint portrait of ex-Speaker Jonathan Dayton.
A. Edmonds to paint portrait of ex-Speaker J. L. Orr.
Hal Morrison to paint portrait of ex-Speaker Langdon Cheeves.
R. D. Gauley to paint portrait of ex-Speaker Nathaniel Macon.
Joseph Lauber to paint portrait of ex-Speaker Wm. Pennington.
Charles A. Gray to paint portrait of ex-Speaker J. Warren Keifer.

The price of each portrait, including a suitable frame, to be five hundred dollars, and each of said portraits to be delivered to the Chief Clerk of the House of Representatives on or before June 30, 1911; provided, however, that said Committee reserves the right to reject any portrait.

It will be noted that the foregoing resolution and the assignment of commissions was adopted on March 3, 1911, practically the last day of the Sixty-first Congress. The change in the political control of the House of Representatives resulted, as usual, in an entire change in the House Committee on the Library, so that the incoming committee had but little information and less preparation to meet the conditions which were brought about by the allotment of commissions for the 19 portraits. In numbers this was the largest commission for art works ever awarded at one time in the history of the Capitol, and as may well be imagined a number of artists were soon seen about the Capitol for the purpose of examining the portraits in oil which had theretofore been placed in the Speaker's lobby and also the crayon portraits which were to be replaced. As far as possible the artists were required to secure the best obtainable material other than the crayon portraits from which to paint the portraits assigned to them. In some cases this request was complied with, but in other cases it was claimed that no material existed except the crayon portraits. It has therefore happened that in many instances the oil portraits are but copies of the crayon portraits, and the usual objection to copies of this kind obtains in such instances.

With but two exceptions the artists to whom these commissions were given accepted and furnished the portraits which had been assigned to them. Hugo Ballin, who had been awarded the commission to paint the portrait of John G. Carlisle, failed to comply, and this commission was finally awarded to Ellen Day Hale. Miss Hale was born in Worcester, Mass., February 11, 1855. She studied art with Doctor Rimmer, William Morris Hunt, and Mrs. H. M. Knowlton in Boston and at the Académie Julien in Paris; exhibited at the Centennial Exposition in Philadelphia, 1876, at the Paris Salons of 1883 and 1885, and at the Columbian Exposition in Chicago in 1893. For many years she resided in Washington, D. C. Her portrait of John G. Carlisle, according to personal acquaintances of Mr. Carlisle, is an excellent likeness, but depicts the subject at an earlier period than that of his active life in Congress.

The other portrait, that of J. L. Orr, originally awarded to A. Edmonds, was painted by his daughter, Esther Edmonds. This was due to the fact that the commission arrived too late for Mr. Edmonds to comply with its terms. Miss Edmonds was born in New York City, September 16, 1888, and commenced her art studies with her father, A. Edmonds, a painter of rare ability. She followed this instruction by courses of study at Cooper Union and the Art Students League of New York, graduating with honor from these schools. After completing her studies she became associated with her father, assisting in his work. In 1910 her father opened a studio in Columbia, S. C., where Miss Edmonds continued to work with him. She has continued her profession of a portrait painter since the death of her father and has painted many portraits of prominent men.

The House Committee on the Library, realizing that it would be placed in the position of passing judgment upon portraits for which the commissions had been given by a preceding committee, concluded that it would not be forced into the position of possible hostility to the selection of painters made by a previous committee; and as it was necessary before payment could be made that an acceptance should be made of the works submitted, the committee very wisely delegated its authority to accept or reject to Mr. F. D. Millet, who at this time occupied a studio in Georgetown, D. C. Mr. Millet not only rendered valuable aid to the Government but to the committee and the artists. If portraits were submitted which did not meet with his approval, the artist was sent for and the defects in the portrait were pointed out and opportunity was afforded to make necessary corrections. Not a few of the artists who submitted their work and received compensation therefor are indebted to the good offices of Mr. Millet, who very often had the portraits brought to his studio, where the artists were permitted to correct, under his supervision, the objectionable features and to complete them in such a manner that he could conscientiously say they were worthy of places in the Speaker's lobby. The friendliness and the helpfulness of Mr. Millet and his earnest desire not only to encourage the artists but to accomplish through his efforts the completion of suitable pictures are entitled to the highest commendation. With him it was a matter of friendliness to the artists and a matter of patriotism in his attitude toward the Government, for his services were given no other compensation than the gratification of being permitted to serve.

The portrait of James K. Polk, painted by Rebecca Polk, gives us an impression of a man of swarthy complexion, and it seems possible that the color scheme of this portrait might have been improved. It was painted by a relative, however, and the material was probably the best obtainable. One thing can be said: Whether the portrait be

PORTRAIT OF HOWELL COBB (GEORGIA)

Lucy M. Stanton, painter

of the best or not, it is interesting on account of its being the only portrait of a Speaker of the House of Representatives who became a President of the United States. With two honors of this character it may be permissible to have a portrait which does not appeal to one as being attractive.

The portrait of John Bell, of Tennessee, was painted by Mrs. W. B. Newman. Mrs. Newman was born in Murfreesboro, Tenn., and began her art studies at the Art Museum of Cincinnati, Ohio, where she was awarded a scholarship entitling her to three years' instruction abroad. She exhibited in the Paris Salon from 1891 to 1900, when she was awarded honorable mention for a portrait of the daughter of Consul John K. Gowdy as representative of the South; awarded the medal of Académie Julien in 1903 for drawing of the nude; also awarded the only medal ever given by Nashville Art Club. Among her works are Passing of Holy Bread, now owned by Philadelphia Museum; Fisherman's Daughter, owned by Cincinnati Museum; Repose in Bretagne, owned by C. M. Schwab; Le Repas Frugal, in private gallery of W. K. Bixby; portraits of Vice President Sherman, Bishop Galloway, of Vanderbilt University, and several portraits of beautiful women of the South.

Howell Cobb, of Georgia, Speaker of the Thirty-first Congress, is represented by a portrait painted by Miss Lucy M. Stanton. The portrait is broadly painted, sketchy in its effect, and forms a pleasing variation to the ordinary type of closely painted portraits. Miss Stanton was born in Atlanta, Ga., May 22, 1875; studied painting in New Orleans, La., when a child. In 1896 she went to Paris, France, where she studied under M. Koopman and at the Académie Colarossi. In 1905 she made a second trip to Paris, where she studied under Lucian Simon and Blanche. She exhibited at the Salon de la Société National Des Beaux Arts; also at the Pennsylvania Academy of Fine Arts; member of Pennsylvania Society of Miniature Painters and New York Society of Miniature Painters.

The portrait of John W. Davis, of Indiana, who served as Speaker of the Twenty-ninth Congress, was painted by William D. Murphy. The portrait is the only example of the work of this veteran painter in the Capitol. Mr. Murphy was born in Madison County, Ala., March 11, 1834; son of a farmer, passing his early life on a plantation. His education was received at Cumberland University, Lebanon, Tenn.; followed teaching for eight years and later for several years was a photographer; received his first art education from William Cooper, a portrait painter of Nashville, Tenn.; continued his work as a photographer in several of the smaller cities of the South until 1876, when he moved to Philadelphia, where he remained until 1883, thence removing to New York, following principally his work as a photographer during these years; married Harriet Anderson, a pupil of Lorenz and William Morgan, October 31, 1887. Since that time Mr. and Mrs. Murphy have been continuously engaged in portrait painting, their work being conducted jointly. The list of works from their studio contains the portraits of many eminent public men, including President Lincoln, President McKinley (this portrait being the official portrait in the White House), President Roosevelt, Admiral Dewey, Admiral Schley, and other well-known public men.

Michael C. Kerr, of Indiana, served as Speaker for the first session of the Forty-fourth Congress and died four days after the adjournment of that session. His portrait is the work of Charles A. Gray, who also painted the portrait of J. Warren Keifer, of Ohio, who served as Speaker of the Forty-seventh Congress. The painter, Charles A. Gray, was born in Keokuk County, Iowa, June 25, 1857; son of James Dudley Gray, surgeon

PORTRAIT OF J. WARREN KEIFER

Charles A. Gray, painter

PORTRAIT OF THEODORE M. POMEROY
George L. Clough, painter

PORTRAIT OF CHIEF JUSTICE MARSHALL

Richard N. Brooke, painter

of the Twenty-fifth Iowa Volunteers, Civil War; began painting portraits for a living at 15 years of age; took instruction in painting from Ronde, Paris, France; passed the examination for West Point in 1875, but concluded not to accept the appointment; was connected with the editorial and art department of the Chicago Herald and the Chicago Tribune, 1889–1900; has painted portraits of President McKinley (from sittings in the White House), President James A. Garfield, Eugene Field (the poet), Opie Read (the author), Hon. Frank Vanderlip, Hon. Joseph G. Cannon, Hon. J. Warren Keifer, and Chief Justice Seevers of Iowa; also many people of prominence in Chicago, St. Louis, New York, and Washington.

The portrait of Schuyler Colfax, of Indiana, Speaker, during the Thirty-eighth, Thirty-ninth, and Fortieth Congresses, is the work of Freeman Thorp, who is repre- sented by many works of art in the Capitol Building and whose biography has heretofore been given. The resignation of Mr. Colfax as Speaker during the Fortieth Congress provided an opportunity for the election of another person during the remainder of the term, which was practically only one day. The Congress elected to fill the vancancy Theodore M. Pomeroy, of New York. It is believed that this is the only instance of the election of a Speaker for such a short period of time.

Notwithstanding the fact that the Hon. Theodore M. Pomeroy was Speaker for only one day, his portrait is included in the collection of portraits in the Speaker's lobby. This portrait is the work of George L. Clough, who was born in Auburn, N. Y., September 18, 1824, and died in that city February 20, 1901. As a child he showed an aptitude for drawing, and at 10 years of age he had but little interest in anything but drawing. At this time a wagon painter gave him a few colors on a bit of shingle, and using a smooth board as a substitute for a canvas he produced his first oil painting. Entering the employ- ment of a local physician, he was given such leisure that a part of his time was devoted to painting. When 18 years of age he was given some lessons in portrait painting by a painter named Palmer and a year later he commenced painting for a livelihood. About 1844 Charles L. Elliott visited Auburn to paint a portrait of Governor Seward, and Clough was able to secure from him valuable aid in the direction of his art studies; later visiting New York and continuing his studies under Elliott, he was able to secure some commissions, and in 1850 visited Europe and copied pictures in the principal conti- nental galleries. After his return to this country he found a ready sale for his work. For seven years he was president of the Brooklyn Art Club.

Robert M. T. Hunter, of Virginia, served as Speaker of the House in the Twenty-sixth Congress. His portrait is the work of Richard N. Brooke, who was born in Warrenton, Va., October 20, 1847. He entered the Pennsylvania Academy of Fine Arts, Philadelphia, October, 1865, where he was art instructor in three colleges until 1871, when he was called to the chair of Fine Arts, Virginia Military Institute; was United States consul at La Rochelle, France, from 1873 to 1876, subsequently entering the studio of Leon Bonnat in Paris; came to Washington in 1880 with the well-known negro picture, A Pastoral Visit, now owned by the Corcoran Gallery of Art; painted by order of the Library Com- mittee in 1880, from the original by W. D. Washington, the full-length portrait of Chief Justice Marshall, now in the House gallery, west side, facing the large mural decoration Westward the Course of Empire Takes Its Way; received a medal and honorable mention at Atlanta Exposition; is represented by many portraits of public men; was president of the Society of Washington Artists and vice principal of the Corcoran School of Art. He died at Warrenton, Va., April 25, 1920.

PHILIP P. BARBOUR

From a crayon portrait formerly in the Speakers lobby; now replaced by a portrait in oil

The portrait of Andrew Stevenson, of Virginia, who served as Speaker in the Twentieth, Twenty-first, Twenty-second, and Twenty-third Congresses, is the work of Spencer Baird Nichols, who received his art education in Washington, D. C., and who followed his profession in that city for many years.

Philip Pendleton Barbour, a Representative from Virginia, served as Speaker of the House of Representatives in the Seventeenth Congress, and after a life of political prominence was appointed Associate Justice of the Supreme Court of the United States and continued in that position until his death in Washington, D. C., February 25, 1841. His portrait is the work of Miss Kate F. Edwards, who was born in Marshallville, Ga., July 29, 1877; daughter of Joseph A. Edwards and Emma Miller Edwards; pupil of Art Institute of Chicago under Frederick Warren Freer; has painted portraits of many prominent people of the South and of many residing in the vicinity of Chicago.

In the Twenty-eighth Congress John Winston Jones, of Virginia, served as the Speaker. His portrait was painted by James Brade Sword, who was born in Philadelphia, Pa., October 11, 1839; early life spent in Macao, China; received his education in the public schools of Philadelphia, graduating from the Central High School in 1855; took up civil engineering on the enlargement of the Union Canal from Lebanon to Reading, Pa.; after completion of the canal he was connected with the United States Coast Survey in 1857 and served on the steamer *Walker* in the making of the survey of Atchafalaya Bay, La.; after his return in 1858 was engaged in building a railroad tunnel through Broad Mountain to the Mahanoy Valley, Pennsylvania; engaged in art as a profession about 1863; served for a number of years as vice president and director of the Art Club of Philadelphia, president of the Philadelphia Society of Artists, and as president of the Artists' Fund Society of Philadelphia; is represented by portraits and paintings in many public institutions; was one of the founders of the Art Club of Philadelphia. He died in Philadelphia, Pa., December 1, 1915.

John White, of Kentucky, served as Speaker of the House during the Twenty-seventh Congress. His portrait was painted for the collection in the Speaker's lobby by Gerard Barry, who was born in County Cork, Ireland, in 1864; began to study art at Paris, France, in 1885, at the Académie Julien, and studied under Lefebvre, Boulanger, and Carolus Duran; exhibited in the Paris Salon of 1885 and 1886 and at the Royal Academy, London, England, in 1887; came to the United States in 1888 and after remaining for 18 months returned to study under Carmon, returning to the United States, where he has remained ever since; engaged in portrait painting with the exception of occasional trips in Europe for vacation purposes.

Linn Boyd, a Representative from the State of Kentucky, served as Speaker of the House of Representatives in the Thirty-second and Thirty-third Congresses. His portrait is the work of Stanley Grant Middleton, who was born in Brooklyn, N. Y., in 1852; son of John N. B. Middleton, a merchant, in whose office he commenced work and continued for some three years. During this period his sketches of several sea captains induced his father to encourage him in following art as a profession. Commencing his study under Alfred C. Howland, he afterwards spent nine years in Paris, where he was under the instruction of the Académie Julien, Jacquesson de la Chevreuse, Harpignie, Benjamin Constant, and Dagnan Bouverat; exhibited portraits and landscapes at the Paris Salon, the Centennial Exposition, Philadelphia, 1876, and received honorable mention for his exhibit in the Pan-American and the Charleston Cotton States Expositions; is a member of the Lotus Club, the Salmagundi Club, and the Artists' Fund Society, New York.

Jonathan Dayton, of New Jersey, served as a Representative from New Jersey in the Second, Third, Fourth, and Fifth Congresses and as Speaker of the House of Representatives during the Fourth and Fifth Congresses. His portrait is distinctive in that it is from very early material, when the dress infallibly marks the time of the portrait. The portrait was painted by Henry Harrison, who was born in Nottingham, England, September 14, 1844; came to the United States with his parents when 6 years of age. His art work began as a decorative painter; studied portrait painting under Daniel Huntington and LeClear; at the age of 18 went to Munich, where he spent six years in study; while in Munich studied under Courader and Piloty; returning to New York he has followed portrait painting exclusively and has painted many portraits of prominent people as well as of those in private life.

In the Thirteenth Congress Langdon Cheves, of South Carolina, was elected as the Speaker during the second session, following Henry Clay, who served as Speaker in the first session. The portrait of Langdon Cheves was painted by Hal Morrison.

The portrait of Nathaniel Macon, Speaker of the Seventh, Eighth, and Ninth Congresses, from the State of North Carolina, was the last portrait of the original 19 portraits ordered in 1911 to be placed in the Speaker's lobby. Concerning this portrait some controversy has arisen, as it has been claimed by some that Nathaniel Macon had never sat for his portrait. The portrait in question, however, now in the Speaker's lobby, is one the material for which was obtained from an earlier portrait, and this early portrait, it is claimed, was one which was never taken from life, the theory being that an amateur painter was told that Nathaniel Macon resembled strongly some person who could be obtained as a model and that from this substitute model the portrait was painted, which was afterwards used as the basis for the portrait in the Speaker's lobby. Whether this is a correct statement or not, it probably matters very little at this time.

The painter, Robert David Gauley, was born at Carnaveigh, County Monaghan, Ireland, March 12, 1875; came to America with his parents in 1884; studied with Denman W. Ross, Cambridge, Mass., Edmund Tarbell, and Frank Benson, Museum of Fine Arts, Boston, and with Bouguereau and Ferrier, Académie Julien, Paris; awarded bronze medal, Paris Exposition, 1900; honorable mention, Buffalo Exposition, 1901; bronze medal, St. Louis Exposition, 1904; Isador portrait prize, Salmagundi Club, 1907, 1912; Thomas B. Clarke prize, Academy of Design, 1908; third best figure exhibit, Appalachian Exposition, Knoxville, Tenn., 1910; associate of the National Academy of Design, 1908, and a member of the American Water Color Society.

The portrait of William Pennington, Speaker of the Thirty-sixth Congress, from the State of New Jersey, is the work of Joseph Lauber, who was born in Meschede, Westphalia, Germany, August 31, 1855. He was brought to this country when but 9 years of age, and, although apprenticed to a jeweler, studied art in Cooper Institute at the night session, afterwards studying at the Art Students' League, New York; studied sculpture with Karl Mueller and painting with Walter Shirlaw and W. M. Chase. After working for a year with John LaFarge on the decorations of the Cornelius Vanderbilt residence he went abroad for study and upon his return executed several etchings, besides displaying paintings in several exhibitions. His greatest interest has been in the direction of mural paintings, including the modern development of stained glass. Executed mural paintings and windows in appellate court, New York; Trinity Lutheran Church, Lancaster, Pa.; Scranton railroad station; and Hudson County courthouse; also in many private dwellings; in 1906 painted a figure of the Christ, which became widely known; director,

PORTRAIT OF JOSEPH G. CANNON
W. T. Smedley, painter

In the Speaker's lobby

PORTRAIT OF FREDERICK H. GILLETT
Edmund C. Tarbell, painter

National Society of Mural Painters; vice president, Architectural League, New York, 1906–1908; president Artists' Aid Society, New York.

Other portraits of former Speakers which have been obtained by special appropriations therefor since the general resolution of March 3, 1911, are the portraits of Joseph G. Cannon, Champ Clark, and Frederick H. Gillett.

The portrait of Joseph G. Cannon is the work of William T. Smedley, who was born in Chester County, Pa., March 26, 1858; pupil of the Pennsylvania Academy of the Fine Arts, also a student in Paris under Laurens; associate of National Academy in 1897, academician, 1905; Society of American Artists, 1882; member of American Society of Water Color Artists, Mural Painters and Century Association; awarded Evans prize, American Water Color Society, 1890; bronze medal, Paris Exposition, 1900; bronze medal for painting and silver medal for drawing, Pan-American Exposition, Buffalo, 1901; Proctor prize, National Academy of Design, 1906; Carnegie prize, National Academy of Design, 1907; Maynard prize for portraits, National Academy of Design, 1916; represented in the National Gallery, Washington, D. C., by the painting One Day in June. The portrait of Mr. Cannon is one which combines the qualities of an admirable likeness with those of a technique which is thoroughly attractive. Mr. Smedley died in Bronxville, N. Y., March 26, 1920.

The portrait of Champ Clark is the work of Boris Gordon, a painter concerning whom biographical data have not thus far been obtainable. The portrait has been criticized by some as failing in the elements of a pleasing likeness to this popular Speaker. There is a wide diversity of opinion in all art criticism. It is said that Thomas B. Reed when he saw his portrait as painted by Sargent exclaimed, "I hope now that my enemies will be satisfied." It is quite evident that while the many friends of Mr. Reed, who presented this portrait, were pleased with it, Speaker Reed himself did not coincide with their opinions. In the case of the Clark portrait, while the friends of Mr. Clark do not appear to be pleased with this work, it appears that Speaker Clark was satisfied and approved of it, and inasmuch as he was pleased the opinion of others is perhaps a secondary matter.

In the portrait of Speaker Frederick H. Gillett we have an admirable example of marked ability in portrait painting. The portrait is a forceful presentation of an active, able statesman. It may have lost some of the genial expression which some have noted in the subject, but if so this has been sacrificed in the effort to present a man who thinks clearly, acts rapidly, and that upon mature judgment. This portrait is the work of Edmund C. Tarbell, who was born in West Groton, Mass., April 26, 1862. He is a pupil of Grundmann and also Boulanger and Lefebvre. For many years he has been an instructor in drawing and painting in the Boston Art Museum and has occupied a like position in the Corcoran Gallery of Art, Washington, D. C. His prizes for paintings include Clark prize, National Academy of Design, 1890; Shaw fund, Society of American Artists, 1893; first Hallgarten prize, National Academy of Design, 1894; Walter Lippincott prize, Pennsylvania Academy of the Fine Arts, 1895; first prize, Worcester Museum, 1900; bronze medal, Paris Exposition, 1900; medal of honor, Pennsylvania Academy of Fine Arts, 1908; gold medal of the National Academy of Design, 1908; first prize, Carnegie Institute, 1909; first William A. Clark prize and Corcoran gold medal, 1910. He is a member of the Ten American Painters, academician of the National Academy of Design, and his portrait of Mr. Gillett has been favorably received at different art exhibitions in this country where it has been publicly shown.

CHAPTER XXIV

PORTRAITS IN THE ROOM OF THE COMMITTEE ON APPROPRIATIONS
OF THE HOUSE

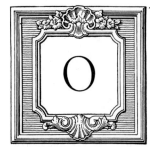 THER works of art in the House wing of the Capitol may be found in the room of the House Committee on Appropriations. Here are portraits of Joseph G. Cannon and James A. Taweny, by Freeman Thorp, and of James A. Garfield, by Cornelia Adele Fassett. These portraits are of large size and are excellent examples of the work of these artists, whose biographies have been given in connection with other works of art in the Capitol Building. It should be understood that those whose portraits are in these rooms are thus honored because of their service as chairmen of the House Committee on Appropriations.

Other chairmen who have been honored are John J. Fitzgerald, whose portrait was painted by Kenyon Cox, one of the distinguished portrait painters of his period. This portrait and other portraits which have been added are of smaller size than the portraits of Garfield, Cannon, and Tawney.

It was fortunate that the friends of John J. Fitzgerald were able to secure the services of Kenyon Cox to paint the portrait of Mr. Fitzgerald. Mr. Cox was born in Warren, Ohio, October 27, 1856. His art education was commenced in Cincinnati, Ohio, continued in Philadelphia, Pa., and completed in Paris, France, where he was a pupil of Carolus Duran, and Gérôme from 1877 to 1882, when he returned to New York.

As a painter of portraits and figure studies he was both successful and eminent. His ability as a draftsman and a colorist gained for him a foremost position among his fellow artists; his work as a mural painter made him prominent with those who used this form of art expression; his ability as an art writer and lecturer upon art subjects brought him conspicuously before a large circle of art readers and introduced him to appreciative audiences in many cities of this country.

Among his works as a mural painter are decorations in the Library of Congress; decorations in Bowdoin College, Maine; decorations in the appellate court, city of New York; Minnesota State capitol; Iowa State capitol; Essex County courthouse, New Jersey; Luzerne County courthouse, Wilkes-Barre, Pa.; and the public library, Winona, Minn.

Among the many portraits painted by Mr. Cox, his portrait of Saint-Gaudens is considered as one of the best, and his portrait of John J. Fitzgerald is an admirable example of a keen appreciation of all that is commendable in portrait painting. Mr. Cox died in New York City on March 17, 1919.

The portrait of J. Swagar Sherley was painted by Charles Sneed Williams, and the criticism has been made by some of Mr. Sherley's associates that the portrait gives an impression of Mr. Sherley at a much younger period than that covered by his services as chairman of this important committee. The portrait is well painted and satisfactory to Mr. Sherley. The artist was born at Evansville, Ind., May 24, 1882; studied in New York under William M. Chase, in Scotland under George Harcourt, A. R. A., and in London and on the Continent; has exhibited his works in the Paris Salon and in many

In the room of the House Committee on Appropriations

PORTRAIT OF JOHN J. FITZGERALD
Kenyon Cox, painter

In the room of the House Committee on Appropriations

PORTRAIT OF JAMES W. GOOD

John C. Johansen, painter

British and American exhibitions; won four years' residential scholarship, Allan-Fraser Art College, Scotland, 1902; has painted many portraits in Scotland, London, and the United States.

The last portrait to be added to this collection is that of James W. Good, who preceded the present chairman, Mr. Madden, as the leader of this important committee. In regard to this portrait it was not a matter of Mr. Good's approval and the disapproval of his friends, but the question has arisen as to whether the artist has seized upon a period in the life of Mr. Good which is reminiscent of his service as the chairman of this committee. The artist has given us a picture of a highly intellectual man under an apparent excessive nervous tension. There are qualities about this portrait which are exceedingly attractive. It may fail to satisfy those members of the committee who remember the genial personality of Mr. Good, but it can not fail to impress the casual observer as being an extremely attractive example of portrait painting. The artist, John C. Johansen, was born in Copenhagen, Denmark, November 25, 1876; brought to the United States when 6 months of age, his education and surroundings have thoroughly identified him with American life, traditions, customs, and progress. His art education was received in the Art Institute of Chicago, also as a pupil of Frank Deveneck and of the Académie Julien, Paris; was at one time instructor in painting and composition in the Chicago Art Institute. He is represented in the following galleries: Art Institute of Chicago; National Gallery, San Diego, Chile; Richmond Art Gallery; Gallery of Dallas, Tex.; Conservatur Club, Glasgow; Syracuse Art Institute; Herron Art Institute, Indianapolis; National Gallery, Washington, D.C. Awarded Saltus gold medal, Academy of Design, 1911; gold medal, International Fine Arts Exhibition, Buenos Aires, 1910; gold medal, Panama-Pacific Exposition; Norman W. Harris silver medal, Chicago; silver medal, Chicago Society of Artists; and bronze medal, St. Louis Exposition, 1904. He is a member of the National Academy; Century Club, New York; National Arts Club, New York.

This concludes the list of portraits in oil in the room of the House Committee on Appropriations. It should not, however, be assumed that the chairmen who have been thus honored are the only ones who have served the committee in that capacity. Some of the earlier chairmen are represented by photographic portraits, and one of them, Samuel J. Randall, is represented by a crayon portrait. The custom of providing portraits of chairmen of committees is not confined to the House Committee on Appropriations. The House Committee on Ways and Means, this committee room being located in the House Office Building, has several portraits of those who have served as chairmen. The first to be placed in this room was that of Sereno E. Payne, who served as chairman of that committee as early as the Fifty-sixth Congress. His portrait is one of distinction, having been painted by Cecilia Beaux, who was born in Philadelphia, Pa., in 1863. Her first lessons in drawing were received from Mrs. Thomas A. Janvier, and she was also a pupil of William Sartain. Her Last Days of Infancy was her first work to receive recognition through an award. For this work she received the first prize for a resident woman artist at the Pennsylvania Academy of the Fine Arts in the exhibition of 1885. She also won a similar prize in 1887, 1891, and 1892. In the winter of 1889–90 she studied at the Académie Julien under Bouguereau, Robert Fleury, and Benjamin Constant; also at the Académie Colarossi, where her drawings were criticized by Courtois and Dagnan-Bouveret. In 1893 she won the gold medal of the Philadelphia Art Club, also the Dodge prize at the National Academy of Design, for her portrait of Mrs. Stilson. Elected associate, National Academy of Design, in 1894, being the third woman to gain admission. She was elected a full member in 1902. By many she is considered to be the greatest living woman painter.

Another portrait in this committee room is that of Oscar W. Underwood. This portrait is the work of Michel Jacobs. The portrait is one of pleasing qualities and the color seems to be thoroughly suited to the subject. A biography of this artist follows.

Michel Jacobs was born in Montreal, Canada, September 10, 1877. His art education was received at the National Academy of Design, New York, the École de Beaux Arts, the Académie Julien, Paris, and as a pupil of Jean Paul Laurens. Among his portraits are those of Senator Oscar W. Underwood, former Speakers Champ Clark and Joseph G. Cannon, William Jennings Bryan, Ossip Gabrilówitsch, Mischa Elman, Terressa Carrenno, Fritz Kreisler, Anna Pavlowa, Duc de la Chartre, and the late Admiral Peary. He served in the World War from April, 1917, to May, 1919, and was promoted from the rank of lieutenant until he received the rank of lieutenant colonel. Is the author of Art of Color and The Study of Color.

The portrait of William McKinley, painted many years ago and presumably from life, is the work of Freeman Thorp. The portrait is dignified in its appearance and gives us an idea of Mr. McKinley that is in strict accord with the conventional pictures which are known so well as belonging to a period of 25 years ago. Mr. Thorp also painted the portrait of Claude Kitchin. The latter portrait is not as pleasing as the portrait of McKinley and does not seem to be in Mr. Thorp's customary manner. It may be, however, that he was handicapped in this work by the desire of Mr. Kitchin to be portrayed as a younger man than he actually was at the period of his chairmanship of this committee.

There is one more portrait in this room, and it can not be understood why the members of the committee should have selected a firm of photographers to provide the portrait of Joseph Warren Fordney. The work, however, is an excellent example of the photographer's art, and in addition to the accuracy of photographic drawing it has been carefully colored, so that we have in this instance a large colored photograph as the subscription portrait of Chairman Fordney. Surely no one can say while viewing this portrait that it is not an accurate likeness. The subject has been well posed and the expression seems wholly natural.

During the building of the House Office Building and the Capitol power plant the chairman of the House Office Building Commission, Hon. Joseph G. Cannon, was not only active in the work of the preliminary legislation making these new buildings possible but he also kept closely in touch with the construction of those buildings. It was felt by some of his fellow Members that his services were worthy of special recognition, and accordingly a marble bust was procured through subscription and placed in a niche in the wall of the central staircase of the House Office Building.

The sculptor of this bust, Albert Jaegers, was born in Elberfeld, Germany, March 28, 1868; died in Suffern, N. Y., July 22, 1925; came to the United States when a boy; started his art career in Cincinnati, Ohio, as a carver of church statuary and decorations; studied modeling in the academy there for a short time, otherwise largely self-taught; moved to New York in 1890; won several competitions inaugurated by the National Sculptors' Society; in 1907 was commissioned by the United States Government to design and erect the Baron von Steuben Monument in Washington, D. C., a replica of which was presented by Congress to the German Emperor in 1911. The United States Government commissioned him in 1913 to build the monument commemorating the German colonists and founders of Germantown, Pa.; was member of National Sculptors' Society and Institute of Arts and Letters.

It will be remembered that it was the intent of the Government to decorate the committee rooms of the House Committee on Military Affairs and the House Committee on Indian Affairs with paintings in oil by Seth Eastman. At the time of the employment of Brigadier General Eastman both committee rooms were in the Capitol Building, but with the erection of the House Office Building the House Committee on Military Affairs was given a committee room in this new building, and consequently the paintings (framed pictures of medium size) were taken to the committee room in its new location. It seems unfortunate that these very excellent works—17 paintings of United States forts— should be in a place where so few have an opportunity of inspecting them. The work was seriously done and the paintings are meritorious, and although hidden in a committee room it is not possible to determine where, if taken from this room, they could be hung so that the general public might have an opportunity of seeing them. As historical records they are valuable, as well as being fine examples of the work of a prominent painter of his period.

In the manner in which the description of the art development of the Capitol has been written it seems almost impossible to refer in chronological order to the production and placement of all the works of art in the Capitol Building. One of the most celebrated examples of portraiture in the Capitol Building was added during the year 1924. This is the portrait of Carlo Franzoni, now hanging in the office of the Architect of the Capitol. Carlo Franzoni has before been referred to, but in addition to what has been stated it may not be amiss to give some brief genealogical and historical statements concerning this gifted sculptor.

He was born in Cararra, Italy, in 1789. He belonged to a family of artists. His father was connected with the Cararra Art Museum; his brother, Giuseppe Franzoni, was a sculptor who came to this country in 1806 in company with Giovanni Andrei. Andrei was a brother-in-law of Giuseppe Franzoni, who died in Washington, D. C., in 1815. In that same year Andrei returned to Italy for the purpose of contracting for the carving of 24 Corinthian capitals for the restored House of Representatives. Andrei was also commissioned to employ one or more sculptors to accompany him on his return to this country, and as a result Francisco Iardella, a cousin of the Franzoni's, and Carlo Franzoni came with him, reaching here sometime in 1816. In 1818 this portrait of Carlo Franzoni was painted in the city of Washington, D. C., by Pietro Bonanni, also a native of Cararra and a student of the art academy, where he had studied under J. B. Desmarias. Having won a prize in this academy, he proceeded to Paris for further study and while there became a pupil of J. L. David. His period of study in Paris covered the years 1812 to 1814, after which he visited Rome and executed work in that city and in Cararra before coming to Washington, D. C., about 1816 or 1817. Bonanni was employed at the Capitol as a decorator and in this capacity decorated the half dome ceiling of the old Hall of the House of Representatives, now Statuary Hall. This ceiling was of wood and was painted in light and shade, so that it resembled the ceiling of the Pantheon in Rome, and so skillfully was it painted that engravings of this work give the effect of actual relief. The ceiling remained until the year 1901, when it was removed and a fireproof ceiling erected in its place. The present ceiling carries out in actual relief the pattern of the ceiling which formerly existed. Bonanni died in Washington, D. C., June 15, 1821. Carlo Franzoni died May 12, 1819.

PIETRO BONANNI
Self-portrait

Represented by the portrait of Carlo Franzoni and mural decoration
of the ceiling of the old Hall of the House

The portrait in question remained in the Franzoni family from the time of its execution until given to the Government by a great grandson of the sculptor Carlo Franzoni.

Thus far but little has been said concerning the bronze doors of the three eastern
entrances to the Capitol. While they form a portion of the architectural scheme of the
building, it must be recognized that they also belong to the general classification of works
of art. The Senate doors are from the models of Thomas Crawford, concerning whom
much has been written earlier in this book. It was at first contemplated that one of these
doors should be cast at the Royal Bavarian Foundry in Munich and that the other doors
should be cast in this country. The death of Thomas Crawford in 1857 and the subsequent occurrence of the Civil War caused many of the plans concerning these doors to
be changed. The doors were finally cast at Chicopee, Mass., by James T. Ames, and the

COMMENTO DEL BOCCACCIO

Example of work of Pietro Bonanni, painting now in Carrara, Italy

expense was far greater than was anticipated at the time when it was planned to have the work done in this country. Each of these Senate doors consists of three panels and a medallion picturing the events of the Revolutionary War. The right-hand valve contains in its upper panel a representation of the death of General Warren at the Battle of Bunker Hill. Below is the rebuke of Gen. Charles Lee by General Washington at the Battle of Monmouth. The lowest panel pictures the storming of the redoubt at Yorktown by Alexander Hamilton. The medallion at the bottom represents a conflict between a Hessian soldier and a New Jersey farmer. The medallion upon the left-hand valve represents Peace and Agriculture. Next above this is a panel showing General Washington passing beneath an arch of flowers at Trenton, N. J., while on his way to New York City to be inaugurated first President of the United States. The middle panel represents Washington taking the oath of office administered by Chancellor Livingston, who officiated in that capacity for the reason that at this time the Supreme Court was not organized, and the oath, therefore, could not be administered by the Chief Justice. The top panel gives a representation of Washington laying the original corner stone of the Capitol on the 18th of September, 1793.

The doors forming the eastern entrance to the rotunda, and known as the Rogers bronze doors, are the work of Randolph Rogers, whose biography and much information in connection with these doors have been given earlier in this book. The Rogers doors are by far the most elaborate of any of the doors in the Capitol. By some they are called the Columbus Doors, and each door, or valve, is composed of four panels. The top of the door or transom is in the form of a lunette and represents the landing of Columbus in the New World on October 12, 1492. The lowest panel on the left pictures Columbus before the council of Salamanca. Then follows his departure from the Convent of La Rabida. The next is the audience before Ferdinand and Isabella, and the last upon the left the sailing from Palos on the first voyage. The top panel on the right represents the first encounter with the Indians; below that the triumphal entry into Barcelona. Then follows Columbus in chains, and the lower panel on the right depicts the death of the discoverer. On the border of the door is a decorative scheme composed of anchors, rudders, and armor; four figures in low relief typify Asia, Africa, Europe, and America. The borders of the separate doors contain each eight figures representing prominent personages of the fifteenth century.

The House doors resemble in general outline and arrangement the bronze doors of the Senate. Each door consists of three panels and a medallion picturing events in American history. The design is apparently that of Thomas Crawford, but the modeling and completion of the idea of Crawford's was intrusted to William H. Rinehart, and the doors after being transported to this country remained for a long time in storage and were finally cast by M. H. Mosman at Chicopee, Mass., who had succeeded to or continued the business organization of James T. Ames, by whom the Senate doors were cast. The doors were installed in the autumn of 1905, the cost to the Government being $45,000. The subjects portrayed upon the House doors are: Upper panel, left-hand door, the massacre of Wyoming, July 17, 1778; center, the Battle of Lexington, April 19, 1775; lower, presentation of flag to Gen. William Moultrie for his defense of Sullivans Island, Charleston Harbor, June 28, 1776; and the medallion at the bottom shows the death of General Montgomery, December 31, 1775. The upper panel of the right-hand door depicts the Declaration of Independence; below this the Paris treaty of peace between the United States and Great Britain, September 3, 1783; the next, Washington's farewell to his officers at New York, December 4, 1783; and the medallion at the bottom of the door contains a seated figure of Franklin.

The sculptural contracts awarded to Thomas Crawford included a group over the Senate entrance on the main floor, entitled "Justice and History"; the statue of Freedom surmounting the dome; bronze doors for the Senate and House wings of the Capitol; and the sculpture for the Senate pediment. All of the cutting of the marble of the sculpture for the pediment was executed in the shops near the Capitol by Italian workmen who were employed during the years 1856 to 1858 upon this and other sculptural works. Among the names of those employed we find those of Gagliardi, Butti, Casoni, Vincenti, and others who apparently were of lesser importance. As the work progressed, from time to time the separate figures were placed about the Capitol Grounds where they could be viewed by those who cared to inspect them. The subject of the pediment is a portrayal of the advancement of the white race and the decadence of the Indian. In the center of the group stands America, a majestic goddess, crowning the central space of the pediment and with head extending above the upper margin. On her right are the soldier, merchant, youth, schoolmaster, pupil, and mechanic, with the anchor and wheat sheaf completing that section of the sculptural decorations. On the left, the march of civilization is typified by the pioneer, who is represented as felling a tree; then the hunter, the Indian brave, the Indian mother and child, and completing this portion of the decoration is an Indian grave. The marble from which these statues are carved came from quarries in Lee, Mass. It was an experiment calculated to test the qualities of native marble as compared with the different specimens of marble from Italy, and which has proved the superior quality of American marble for withstanding the action of the weather.

It was evidently the intention that the contract for sculptural decorations of both the House and the Senate pediments should be awarded at practically the same time. We have before related the lack of inclination upon the part of Hiram Powers to accept a commission for either pediment. From time to time others applied for commissions for doing this work, and at one time it seems to have been the intention to have awarded this commission to Erastus Dow Palmer, whose sketch model illustrating the subject, the Landing of the Pilgrims, was paid for by the Government, but the decision was reached that under the existing form of the appropriation money could not be expended for the exterior decoration of the building. In this manner the House pediment was left incomplete, although from time to time sketches were submitted and models prepared by different sculptors in the hope that Congress might be induced to take some action toward the completion of this portion of the Capitol. It was not until 1908 when definite action was taken. At that time the following legislation was enacted:

Be it enacted by the Senate and House of Representatives of the United States of America in Congress assembled, That the expenditure of seventy-five thousand dollars, or so much thereof as may be necessary, be, and the same is hereby, authorized for the purpose of completing the pediment of the House Wing of the Capitol by placing suitable statuary therein, said expenditure to be made under the direction of the Speaker of the House, the Joint Committee on the Library, and the Superintendent of the Capitol. (Approved April 16, 1908.) (Stats. L., vol. 35, p. 63.)

The authorization contained in the foregoing legislation fixes the personnel of the committee intrusted with the carrying into effect of the act of April 16, 1908. Acting under the advice of the National Sculptors Society, the committee was led to select as the sculptor for this important commission Paul W. Bartlett, who early in the year 1909 presented for the inspection of the committee his sketch model for this work. This model was accepted and the work commenced. Many delays occurred because of the general disturbance in all sections of the world owing to the war with Germany, and Mr. Bartlett, whose studio was in Paris, was obliged to reconstruct some of the models for this statuary on account of the difficulty of transporting them from France to this country. Work was carried on in spite of numerous interruptions until its completion in the year 1916. August 2, 1916, was designated by the House of Representatives as the date for the unveiling of the pediment. The exercises upon that occasion were in charge of the chairman of the House Committee on the Library, inasmuch as this statuary belonged to the House wing of the Capitol. Arrangements were made to hold the unveiling exercises upon the east lawn of the Capitol at that portion nearest to and in view of the pediment to be unveiled. The decorations for the occasion were in charge of Mr. F. D. Owen, of the office of the Commissioner of Public Buildings and Grounds. In addition to the flags covering the sculptural work, Mr. Owen arranged a number of code flags which, reading by the code signals from left to right, spelled "House of Representatives." Hon. James L. Slayden, chairman of the House Committee on the Library, presided and addressed the assembled guests from a small rostrum which had been erected in the shade of the large trees on the lawn. Following his introductory remarks the unveiling of the statuary occurred, the Marine Band at this time furnishing appropriate music. Mr. Slayden then introduced Paul W. Bartlett, the sculptor, who made a brief address explaining the purpose of decorative sculpture of this character and referring to the problems met with in carrying out the completion of

PAUL W. BARTLETT

Represented by the statuary of the House pediment

PEACE PROTECTING GENIUS
Central group of House pediment

PEDIMENT ON THE HOUSE WING

Paul W. Bartlett, sculptor

PAUL W. BARTLETT

At the unveiling exercises of the statuary for the House pediment

this work. The address of Mr. Bartlett was followed by an address by Hon. Champ Clark, Speaker of the House of Representatives. The address of Mr. Clark was well calculated to arouse the enthusiasm and the patriotism of all who were fortunate in hearing it. Mr. Clark in his address stated:

How many new propositions do you suppose our system of Government rests on? On three. There are two of them in the Declaration of Independence and one in the Constitution. "All men are created equal." That is one of them. "All governments derive their just powers from the consent of the governed." That is two, and they form the basis of republican institutions. The third one is—hardly anybody ever reads it—the preamble to the Constitution, one of the finest sentences ever written and one of the most comprehensive: "We, the people of the United States, in order to form a more perfect Union, establish justice, insure domestic tranquility, provide for the common defense, promote the general welfare, and secure the blessings of liberty to ourselves and our posterity, do ordain and establish this Constitution for the United States of America." There it all is. That is our chart and our creed. What courtship is to marriage, what the flower is to the fruit, what youth is to manhood, that is what the Declaration of Independence is to the Constitution of the United States. [Applause.] Since Washington on Yorktown's blood-stained heights made good Jefferson's declaration thrones have been crumbling, crowns have been tumbling, and dynasties have been fleeing for their lives. [Applause.]

The exercises concluded with a benediction by Rev. Forest J. Prettyman, D. D., the Chaplain of the Senate.

The exercises will long be remembered by those who were so fortunate as to be present. The day was cloudless but not too warm. The picture of this assembly seated upon the greensward of the Capitol lawn, with flag decorations on the pediment, music by the Marine Band, and the general inspiration growing out of the exercises of the morning marked an occasion such as Washington has rarely known.

The address of Mr. Bartlett is summarized, in so far as the description of the pediment is concerned, in the following extract:

An allegorical group of two figures, "Peace Protecting Genius," fills the center of the pediment. "Peace," an armed "Peace," stands erect, draped in a mantle which almost completely hides her breast-plate and coat of mail; her left arm rests on her buckler, which is supported by the altar at her side; in the background the "olive tree of peace."

Her right arm is extended in a gesture of protection over the youthful and winged figure of "Genius," who nestles confidingly at her feet and holds in his right hand the torch of "Immortality."

The composition is completed by two other groups, symbolizing and typifying the two great fundamental living powers of labor, the two great sources of wealth—Agriculture and Industry.

The most modest of our farmers and laborers can find in these groups the symbol of his own self and of his endeavors. He may even find there his own resemblance, and he will see that his helpmate, his children, his cattle, and the harvest from his fields have been exalted and carved in marble forms.

The printer, the ironworker, the founder, can do the same, and enjoy the same profound satisfaction. The toiling factory girl, weaver or spinner of textiles, will observe that she has not been forgotten, and those who are devoted to the sea can discover a group which will remind them of the joys of their vocation.

A wave terminates the sculpture at either end of the pediment, and is meant to indicate that all this humanity, all its power and energy, are comprised between the shores of the two oceans—the Atlantic and Pacific.

The sculptor, Paul Wayland Bartlett, was born in New Haven, Conn., January 24, 1865. At an early age he was taken abroad, and his art education was received in the city of Paris, where he was a student in the studio of Frémiet. At the age of 14 Mr. Bartlett exhibited in the Salon a bust of his grandmother. Dating from that time his work was a record of progressive successes. He was awarded honorable mention in the Salon of 1887, and at the exposition in Paris in 1889 he received the medal of honor and as a member of the jury was placed hors concours. He was awarded a gold medal in 1901, chevalier of the Legion of Honor in 1895, and an officer in 1908. A great portion of Mr. Bartlett's art life was passed in Paris. He had, however, for many years maintained a large studio in Washington, D. C., where the greater portion of the models for the sculpture of the pediment were developed. In addition to this work, while in this country he erected the sculptural decoration surmounting the frieze of the New York Public Library and also produced before his return to Paris a notable statue in bronze of Benjamin Franklin. Mr. Bartlett is also represented in the visitors' gallery of the reading room of the Library of Congress by bronze statues of Michaelangelo and Columbus. One of his notable works in Paris is his equestrian statue of General Lafayette.

In the Speaker's lobby directly underneath the portrait of Speaker Muhlenberg is a bronze tablet designed by Mr. Bartlett for this location. The tablet contains the following inscription:

Speakers of the House of Representatives of the United States.

Chosen by the people, honored by the preferment of their associates, these makers of history are memorialized as a tribute of their worth to the Nation.

For some years Mr. Bartlett had resided in Paris; in 1924 France conferred upon him the title of commander of the Legion of Honor. He returned to this country in May, 1925, and remained for about a month before his return to Paris. He died in Paris, France, September 20, 1925.

One of the most conspicuous examples of statuary about the Capitol Grounds is to be found upon the west plaza of the Capitol, where the seated statue of Chief Justice John Marshall was unveiled on May 10, 1884. Chief Justice Marshall died in Philadelphia on the 6th of July, 1835, and on the 7th day of July, at a meeting of the bar of Philadelphia, resolutions were offered setting forth the grief of the bar at the death of the late Chief Justice and expressing a sense of the great public loss sustained and recommending to the bar of the United States cooperation in erecting a monument to the memory of the Chief Justice at some suitable place in the city of Washington. On the 10th of August, 1835, a circular letter setting forth the purpose of collecting funds for erecting a monument was sent out to members of the bar in different sections of the country.

It was the purpose of the committee having in charge the collection of funds to be devoted to the erection of a monument to Chief Justice Marshall to limit the amount of subscriptions to the sum of $10 from each individual, and as the sum thus received failed to reach an amount considered necessary the receipts were carefully invested in the name of trustees of the Marshall Memorial Fund, so that in the year 1882 the sum thus invested had grown to an amount approximating $20,000.

At this time it was felt that the bar might be disposed to use this sum and such other moneys as might be subscribed and complete the project. Congress, however, supplemented the effort of the bar of Philadelphia by the enactment of the following legislation:

Be it enacted by the Senate and House of Representatives of the United States of America in Congress assembled, That the President of the Senate and the Speaker of the House of Representatives do appoint a joint committee of three Senators and three Representatives, with authority to contract for and erect a statue to the memory of Chief Justice John Marshall, formerly of the Supreme Court of the United States; that said statue shall be placed in a suitable public reservation, to be designated by said joint committee, in the city of Washington; and for said purpose the sum of twenty thousand dollars, or so much thereof as may be necessary, is hereby appropriated out of any money in the Treasury not otherwise appropriated. (Approved March 10, 1882.) (Stats. L., vol. 22, p. 28.)

The program upon the date of unveiling consisted of music by the Marine Band; prayer, Reverend Doctor Armstrong; music; address, the Chief Justice; music; oration,

AIRPLANE VIEW OF PENNSYLVANIA AVENUE

Showing the United States Capitol in the distance

Inaugural processions pass from the Capitol to the White House along this historic avenue

William Henry Rawle, Esq.; music; benediction.   Chief Justice Morrison R. Waite in his address gave a history of the steps taken to secure the necessary funds for the erection of this memorial.   In the course of his remarks reference was made to Justice Story, who sat upon the Bench of the Supreme Court for 24 years, and whose son, William Wetmore Story, had been selected as the sculptor of the memorial they were then met to dedicate. He also referred to an address delivered by Justice Story upon the occasion of the death of John Marshall, in which he referred to "those exquisite judgments, the fruits of his own unassisted meditations from which the court has received so much honor."   The Chief Justice, in explanation of this statement of Justice Story, referred to the fact that when Chief Justice Marshall took his seat on the bench in February, 1801, the court had then been in existence but 11 years and in that time less than 100 cases had passed under its judgment, so that there was but little to guide the decisions and judgment of the distinguished Chief Justice Marshall other than "the fruits of his own unassisted meditations."   The remarks of Chief Justice Waite were followed by an oration by William Henry Rawle, Esq., of Philadelphia, who spoke at length upon the life and character of Chief Justice Marshall.   The address carried along in consecutive order the important events in the life of Chief Justice Marshall in their relation to the courts and the judicial procedure during the period of his service.   It was a masterly effort—a splendid tribute to one who has been popularly enshrined as the expounder of the Constitution of the United States.

The biography of the sculptor, William Wetmore Story, is given on page 374.

CHAPTER XXV

MURAL DECORATIONS IN SENATE AND HOUSE WINGS

NOTHER work of art belonging to the exterior of the building, although its erection has not been accomplished and at the present time it is impossible to conjecture when its erection may be expected, is the Amateis bronze doors. This work consists of a transom and two doors inclosed in an ornamental frame of bronze. These doors are nearly 8 feet in width and more than 13 feet in height. They were contracted for May 18, 1904, and have been completed for nearly 15 years.

It was expected at the time the contract was awarded that it was probable that structural changes would be made in the central portion of the Capitol Building; that the eastern front of the Capitol would be extended, so that the dome would be centrally located between the east and west fronts of the building; and that the entire central portion of the building, constructed of Aquia Creek sandstone, would be faced with marble, so that the Capitol would be in its entirety a marble structure. Legislation providing for the expense of estimates and reports upon this project had been enacted, and it was supposed that this work would be completed in time to receive the Amateis bronze doors, but this plan having been indefinitely suspended left the western main entrance to the Capitol, for which these doors were intended, in the same condition that existed when the doors were contracted for. The installation has never been completed, for the reason that it has been deemed inadvisable to make such structural changes as would be required for the installation of these doors because of the possibility of the entire western front being changed by the facing of marble which had been contemplated in the general scheme of reconstruction of the central portions of the building. Upon completion, therefore, the doors were placed upon exhibition for some years in the Corcoran Gallery of Art, where they remained until removed to the New National Museum, where they have been installed as exhibition pieces in one of the vestibules of the north entrance to that building. It is believed, however, that the contemplated changes in the central portion of the building will be made and when made that the Amateis doors will be installed, and for this reason it seems appropriate that a description of the doors should be contained in this work

The transom panel represents America seated in a chariot drawn by lions, typical of strength, led by a child, signifying the superiority of the intellectual over brute force. At the sides of the chariot are figures representing education, architecture, literature, painting, music, sculpture, mining, commerce, and industry. At one side of the transom panel stands Thomas Jefferson and at the other Benjamin Franklin. The medallions at the four corners of this panel represent Peabody, founder of educational institutions; Emerson, philosopher and thinker; Horace Mann, educator; and Hopkins, merchant and philanthropist. In the eight panels, four on each side of the doors proper, are scenes depicting jurisprudence, science, art, mining, agriculture, iron and electricity, naval architecture, and commerce. About the panels are statuettes and medallions of famous Americans.

Jurisprudence is represented on the top panel of the left side of the door by a scene showing a meeting of the Supreme Court of the United States, presided over by Chief Justice John Marshall. A bust of Washington is shown over the chair of the Chief Justice. The statuettes represent Madison, writer of the Constitution, and Daniel Webster, one of its chief exponents. Around it are medallions of Rufus Choate, Chief Justice Taney, and Patrick Henry.

{ 489 }

In the science panel is a group of the world's greatest scientific workers, from the Egyptian astronomer, Hipparchus, inventor of the planiscope, down to Darwin. At the sides are figures of Oliver Wolcott Gibbs, America's greatest chemist, and Joseph Henry, the physicist. The medallions are of Dana, geologist; Simon Newcomb, astronomer; Alexander Graham Bell, of the telephone; and Morse, of the telegraph.

On the third panel, art is represented in a group in which are Homer, Virgil, Dante, Shakespeare, Goethe, Hugo, Palestrina, Beethoven, and Rossini. Above them is a flying figure of Genius. Statues: Edgar Allan Poe, writer, and William Thornton, architect of the original Capitol. Medallions: Stuart, painter; W. H. Brown, sculptor.

Mining is represented by a scene in a mine. On one side of this panel stands James W. Marshall, discoverer of gold in California, and on the other, Alexander W. Holley, the mining engineer. E. B. Case, A. Hewitt, and Clarence King are on medallions.

The top panel on the right side of the door shows a harvest scene, typical of agriculture. At one side is Samuel G. Morton, the ethnologist, and at the other Secretary of Agriculture Wilson. The medallions are of the late Senator Morrill and I. P. Norton and Bussey, founders of agricultural chemistry.

The iron and electricity panel has a scene in which iron and electric workers are shown. Peter Cooper stands at one side of this panel, and on the other is H. A. Rowland. Medallions show Baldwin, founder of locomotive works, and Edison, the inventor.

In the engineering scene workers are shown laying tracks for a railroad. In the background is a long iron bridge. James B. Eads, builder of the St. Louis Bridge, stands at the right; opposite him is Gen. Thomas L. Casey, the famous Army engineer. One medallion is of Roebling, builder of the Brooklyn Bridge, and another is of Stevens, of transcontinental railroad fame.

Naval architecture and commerce are represented by a figure typical of naval architecture, showing to commerce, industry, and agriculture on a globe held by a youth the places where they can dispose of their wares. The seller is represented by a sailor holding a flag with a liberty cap on top, significant of an open-door policy. At one side of this panel stands Fulton and on the other Ericsson, inventor of the *Monitor*. On the medallions are Cyrus W. Field, layer of the first Atlantic cable; Eli Whitney, of cotton gin fame; Howe, the sewing machine; Fremont, "the Pathfinder"; and J. Lenthall.

The sculptor of these doors, Louis Amateis, was born in Turin, Italy, December 13, 1855. He was educated in the schools of that city and a graduate of the Institute of Technology and the Academy of Fine Arts at Turin, where he was awarded a gold medal upon his graduation. His first sculptural work of importance was a bas-relief purchased by a committee of sculptors for the Art Gallery of Turin. In a competition he was awarded the commission for the sculptural decorations for the Palace of Fine Arts of Turin. He came to this country in 1884 and became a naturalized citizen. After living for some time in New York he moved to Washington, D. C., where he maintained a studio and executed many works of note. He was the founder of the School of Architecture and Fine Arts of the Columbian University (now George Washington University), Washington, D. C., and a member of the National Sculpture Society. Among his works are Baldwin memorial for cemetery in Milford, Conn.; monument to heroes of Texan Revolution, Galveston, Tex.; soldiers' monuments for Houston, Corsicana, and Galveston, Tex.; Heurich memorial at Hyattsville, Md.; portrait busts from life of President Arthur, General Hancock, General Logan, Gen. B. F. Butler, Secretary Carlisle, Secretary Bayard, and James G. Blaine. Mr. Amateis died in West Falls Church, Va., March 16, 1913.

It may occur to some that but little attention has been given in the course of this work to the mural decorations in the Capitol Building. An occasional reference has been made thereto, but beyond this no particular attention has been given to this branch of art. It may be that these decorations in themselves do not form an attractive portion of the art work of the Capitol to many who visit that building, and, on the other hand, it may be that a larger proportion of the visitors will be interested in this work. The ordinary visitor who goes about the building under the leadership of one of the Capitol guides will invariably be taken to the President's room in the Senate wing of the Capitol. The frescoes in this room are probably examples of the best work of Constantino Brumidi and can be viewed with greater satisfaction than his large fresco painting in the ceiling of the dome of the Capitol. In the President's room we find upon the walls portraits of Cabinet officers. The portrait of Henry Knox, Secretary of War, a native of Massachusetts and a member of Washington's first Cabinet, occupies a place upon the northern section of the east wall of the President's room. Upon the southern section of the east wall is a portrait of Alexander Hamilton, of New York, Secretary of the Treasury in Washington's first Cabinet. On the south wall we find the portrait of Thomas Jefferson, of Virginia, who was Secretary of State in Washington's first Cabinet, and on the west wall upon the southern section of the wall the portrait of Edmund Randolph, of Virginia, Attorney General in the same Cabinet. Upon the northern section is a portrait of Samuel Osgood, of Massachusetts, who served as Postmaster General in the same Cabinet. These not only are portraits of distinguished men but they are portraits of distinction, and a careful examination leads one safely to conclude that among the decorations of Brumidi there is none better than those contained in the President's room. In particular, the portrait of Thomas Jefferson gives us a conception of Jefferson as a much younger man than as usually portrayed. There is something about this portrait that is reminiscent of the portrait of Jefferson found in the large painting, The Declaration of Independence, by John Trumbull, in the rotunda of the Capitol. Of course it is not positively known that Brumidi used Trumbull's portrait of Jefferson for his material for the portrait in the President's room, but there is enough resemblance upon which to base a theory that Brumidi was at least influenced by the work of Trumbull. There are other portraits in this room which are worthy of mention and of careful consideration. In the northwest corner of the ceiling is a portrait of Vespucius, the navigator; in the northeast corner a portrait of William Brewster, the Elder Brewster shown in Weir's painting, The Embarkation of the Pilgrims, found in the rotunda of the Capitol. In the southeast corner is a portrait of Christopher Columbus, and in the southwest corner a portrait of Benjamin Franklin, which at once is easily recognized as containing all of the characteristics of the many portraits and statues of Franklin which are generally known. A small decorative portrait of Washington, high up on the south wall of the room, may have been inspired from the portrait of Washington by Rembrandt Peale. There are other decorations in this room which will appeal to those fond of conventional schemes, and on the whole one feels that the artist did his best to make the room of the Chief Executive in the Capitol the best example of his skill to be found in this great building.

In the room of the Committee on the District of Columbia, which was originally designed for the Senate library, there may be found in the vaulted ceiling frescoes of history, geography, science, and invention. These frescoes are the work of Brumidi, and, while not equal in character to those in the room of the President, they are, as a group, entirely pleasing and form an attractive feature of the room. The original studies for these ceiling frescoes were recently sold at public auction with other sketches and effects of Brumidi.

The public reception room is decorated in oils and frescoes by Brumidi. On the south wall is a painting of President Washington in consultation with his Secretary of State, Thomas Jefferson, and Alexander Hamilton, Secretary of the Treasury. Allegorical decorations of War, Peace, Liberty, Plenty, Power, Temperance, Prudence, and Justice are pictured in the vaulted ceiling of this room.

On the basement floor of the Senate wing in the different corridors are contained a great variety of decorations, such as allegorical figures, birds and game, traceries of vines and foliage, and some very interesting fruit studies. It should be understood that many of these committee rooms were decorated with reference to the committee at that time occupying the room. This has been noted in the case of the room of the Committee on the District of Columbia which was originally decorated for the Senate library.

The room now occupied by the Senate Committee on Appropriations contains five frescoes, the work of Brumidi. These frescoes represent the Boston Massacre, the Battle of Lexington, the death of Wooster, Washington at Valley Forge, and the storming of Stony Point.

Adjoining the room containing these frescoes is a room which was decorated by Carl Rakeman. The decorations are lunettes, containing portraits of Gen. George Washington, Gen. Joseph Warren, Gen. Anthony Wayne, and Gen. Horatio Gates, with flags of the Revolutionary period as accessories. These decorations are modern as compared with those in the adjoining room by Brumidi. Carl Rakeman was born in Washington, D. C., April 27, 1878. He studied in Europe and was a student at the Royal Academy in Dusseldorf, Germany, for two years, after which he went to France and resided for a year in Paris. Upon returning to Germany he continued his studies at the Royal Academy at Munich and during the following year returned to the United States. His art expression is not confined to any one medium, as he is an etcher, a painter in water colors, in oils, and of frescoes. He has, however, occupied himself in the field of mural decorations. He exhibited in the contemporay exhibition of American oil paintings at the Corcoran Gallery of Art, and his works are to be found in various private collections.

There are also found in the corridor of the basement floor of the Senate a number of portraits of prominent people connected with the early history of the United States. In the north-south corridor, starting at the south end and going north, on the left are found portraits of R. L. Livingston, John Jay, and Charles Carroll of Carrollton, and on the right, portraits of John Hancock, Francis Hopkinson, Roger Sherman, Charles Thompson, and Robert Morris. In the east-west corridor, starting at the elevator at the west end and going east, on the left are portraits of Thomas Jefferson, Richard Montgomery, Silas Deane, Horatio Gates, and Daniel Morgan, and on the right are portraits of Benjamin Franklin, Joseph Warren, Thomas Mifflin, Israel Putnam, and Jonathan Trumbull. These portraits are painted in imitation of relief in monochrome, the circle around them being 20 inches in diameter, inclosed in a molded frame having eight points, these points being connected by a segment of a circle. The portraits are far more interesting than the decorative frames surrounding them.

On the House side of the Capitol but little has been done in the way of decoration of the committee rooms. The corridors of this wing bear no resemblance to those of the Senate wing. There is one notable exception and that is the room formerly occupied by the Committee on Agriculture, which was the first room in the Capitol Building to be decorated by Brumidi. This room contains two large lunettes, the one on the east wall picturing the calling of Cincinnatus from the plow, and on the west wall is found the summoning of Putnam to his part in the Revolutionary War. In the ceiling are decorations typifying spring, summer, autumn, and winter. Portraits of Washington and Jefferson, who were both farmers, are contained upon the north and south walls of this room.

The adjoining room to the south was at one time occupied by the Committee on Insular Affairs and contains mural decorations of a modern date, typical and illustrative of former and present conditions in the insular possessions of the United States. These decorations are in the form of lunettes and cemented to the walls. The decorator, Henry Lyman Sayen, is probably seen at his best in these decorations, two of which, Tyranny and The Rule of Justice, are the most conspicuous for their dramatic composition and illustrative qualities. They were made at a period before Mr. Sayen had become so strongly impressionistic, with marked tendencies in the direction of the cubist form of art. Mr. Sayen was born in Philadelphia April 25, 1875, and began his career as an electrical engineer. He received a diploma from the Columbian Exposition, Chicago, 1893, for designs and inventions of instruments for physical research; inventor of self-regulating X-ray tube; studied art under Thomas Anshutz, 1899 to 1903, at the Pennsylvania Academy of the Fine Arts; designer and sculptor of the Jennie Sesnan gold medal awarded each year by the Pennsylvania Academy of the Fine Arts for the best landscape exhibited in the annual exhibition held by this institution. His most conspicuous art works are the four lunettes for the room of the Committee on Insular Affairs, now one of the rooms of the subcommittee of the House Committee on Appropriations. From 1906 to 1914 Mr. Sayen resided in Paris, where he studied under different masters. He died in Philadelphia, Pa., April 28, 1918.

Another decorator who assisted in the decorations of the Capitol was Joseph Rakemann, who was born in Melle, Germany, April 26, 1832, and came to America in the year 1856. He was identified with the decorative work in the early days of the Capitol and one of the associates of Brumidi in the decorations of the dome and the committee rooms. Later his work was extended to the decoration of the Speaker's lobby, House of Representatives, and in some of the corridors in the House wing of the Capitol and the connecting corridor to Statuary Hall. His work is well known in the various Government buildings and private residences of the city of Washington. He died in Washington, D. C., September 30, 1917.

It probably will be apparent to the visitor in Statuary Hall that although but 52 statues have been installed, the hall is overcrowded; further, that the installation of 46 additional statues, which will occur if every State is represented by two statues, is seemingly an impossibility. This problem is one which is not easily solved, for it must be plain to all that each State has an equal right with the other States to be represented in this hall by two statues. Of course it may be possible to enact legislation prohibiting the placing of more than a certain number of statues, possibly 60, in this hall, but that would hardly be just to those States which are without representation or are represented by only one statue. It may also be possible to enact legislation enlarging the space to be occupied by statues from the States, so that in the corridor and spaces adjacent to Statuary Hall other statues might be located, but it is doubtful if such States as were obliged to place their statues outside of Statuary Hall would feel satisfied with the locations afforded them. It has also been suggested that the statues might be removed to the crypt of the Capitol, where the suffrage group is now located, and that in this large room there would be sufficient space to give all States the representation to which they are entitled, but this location would not be desirable unless an entirely new system of lighting could be installed and the crypt properly decorated, so that it might seem as though some special preparation had been made for its occupancy by the statues now in Statuary Hall. Those favoring this plan have suggested the restoration of

PHOTOGRAPHIC VIEW OF WASHINGTON, D. C., FROM AN AIRPLANE

In this photograph may be seen the Capitol and to the east and a little south the Library of Congress; to the south and east, the House Office Building; to the north, a building with three sides, the Senate Office Building; to the north, with railroad tracks seen in the rear, is the Union Terminal Station; to the west, the city post office, a building with many columns; and farther to the west and to the north, at the margin, the Government Printing Office, a building with many windows, and the largest printing office in the world

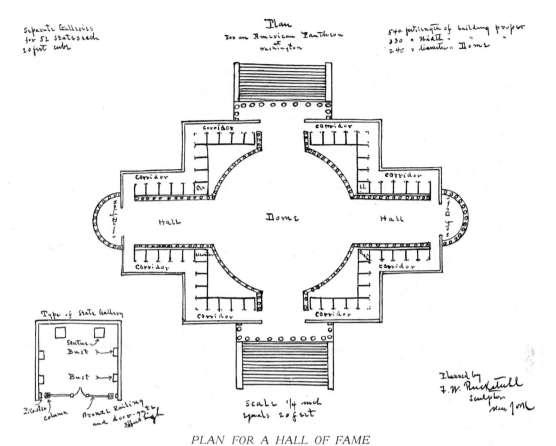

PLAN FOR A HALL OF FAME

With a separate room for each State, thereby relieving the crowded condition of Statuary Hall

Sketch by Frederic Wellington Ruckstull

Statuary Hall in so far as possible to the condition existing at the time when the House of Representatives held its sessions in this historical location.   Such a use of Statuary Hall would give to the visitors of the Capitol an ample opportunity to compare the former conditions in this legislative chamber with the conditions now existing in the present Hall of the House.   Of course, to do this we must return to the primitive mode of lighting and to some other conditions which are now obsolete.   There is yet another plan which has been suggested, and although it may be a long way in the future it is worthy of serious consideration.   This plan includes the construction of a special building to be used as a pantheon, a hall of fame, or a national statuary building for the States—the name is not important.   The plan was suggested by F. W. Ruckstull, of New York, who, during a conversation with the writer in the year 1915, was given the idea of the need of a building which would furnish a separate room for each of the States, so that in this large collection of statuary there might be no appearance of a crowded condition and the comparison of the works contributed by one State with those contributed by another would be avoided.   Mr. Ruckstull has prepared a sketch of a building 540 feet in length, 340 feet in width, and with a dome 240 feet in diameter. This proposed building in its ground plan represents a square with projections to the north and south terminating at the end in a half dome. A spacious hall leads from this half dome on the north to the half dome on the south, and another hall leads from the east entrance to the west entrance, both of these corridors crossing in the center of the dome. These corridors are bounded, as well as the dome, by separate rooms 20 feet square, of which there are 52 in this plan. Each of these rooms opens upon a corridor, so that it is possible to go around the entire outside of these tiers of rooms in all portions of the building without entering any of the rooms. The rooms fronting on the corridor are each separated from it by a bronze railing and gate. The walls of each room completely separate the inclosure from adjoining rooms. In the plan provision has been made for two statues at the end of each room opposite the entrance gate, and there are also places upon the side walls upon which four busts, two upon each side, may be placed. The advantages of this plan may be briefly summed as follows: It gives to each State an equal amount of floor space in a room equally as well lighted as all other rooms and in which their contributions to this national hall of fame can remain without being overcrowded or suffering from comparison with the works contributed by States which possibly may be fortunate enough to incur an unusual expense in furnishing statues for their representation. It also provides for a building which shall be devoted entirely to the commemoration of the notable citizens of our country, where care can be given to its upkeep, such as is commonly given to the best art institutions in the land. It also provides in the spacious hall and great dome an ample opportunity to honor such citizens of our country as really belong to the country at large rather than to the States in which they were born or of which they were citizens. It also provides a meeting place for such great gatherings as are of national or international importance, for upon such occasions all of the bronze gates opening into the rooms assigned to the States could be closed and the public would only be admitted to the corridors and to the space under the great dome, which with its diameter of 240 feet would afford room for such meetings.

The plan of Mr. Ruckstull may not be perfect, and it may not be such a one as Mr. Ruckstull would himself commend at this time. However, it forms a basis for study, and it is hoped that this matter may be considered by those who care for our common country to such an extent that they will not be satisfied until the overcrowded conditions of Statuary Hall have been remedied, and the statues of those now installed and those hereafter to be installed may be given a location worthy of the States making this contribution and of the Union of States of which these contributing States form a part.

It may be that the manner in which the art works of the Capitol have been described will be to some confusing, and that, having read this book, they may fail to have a clear idea of the art of the Capitol as a whole; and for the benefit of those who may be possessed of a statistical turn of mind I will state that in the Senate wing of the Capitol there are 42 examples of statuary, of which number 28 are busts of Vice Presidents, 3 busts of Presidents, and 2 full-length statues. The remaining statuary, which does not belong to the classes given above, may be described as international in its character, comprising portrait busts of distinguished individuals found in the east corridor of the Senate gallery. In addition to the statuary referred to, there are in this wing 26 portraits, 8 historical paintings, and 3 large landscapes. There should also be included in this list a painting by W. F. Halsall, entitled "The First Fight of Ironclads," which on account of its size is now being stored, as there is no available space in the Senate wing where it can be displayed. The works of art therefore in this wing of the Capitol are 80 in number.

In the Supreme Court section of the Capitol there are 12 marble busts, 10 portraits of Chief Justices, 2 portraits of Associate Justices, 8 portraits of clerks of the Supreme Court, 9 portraits of court reporters, 1 portrait group, and 1 group in bas-relief, making a total of 43 works of art in the Supreme Court section of the Capitol.

In the central portion of the Capitol, which includes the rotunda and committee rooms and office rooms, there are 8 historical paintings, 6 statues, and 3 busts in the rotunda; in the architect's office, 2 portraits, 1 bronze fountain, and 1 bust, that of Henry Clay; in the House Committee on Indian Affairs, 9 paintings, depicting life among the Sioux Indians; and in the crypt of the Capitol, the suffrage group, which includes the busts of Susan B. Anthony, Lucretia Mott, and Elizabeth Cady Stanton. The collection, therefore, of works of art in the central portion of the Capitol numbers 35.

In that section of the Capitol known as Statuary Hall there are 52 statues, 1 group, the Car of History, and a plaster model of Liberty, and in the office of the Clerk of the House of Representatives there is 1 bust, that of John Quincy Adams. We must therefore credit this section of the Capitol with 55 works of art.

In the House wing of the Capitol there are 5 historical paintings, 1 by Emanuel Leutze, 2 by Bierstadt, 1 by Carpenter, and 1 by Brumidi, the last named being a fresco in the southwest corner of the Hall of the House of Representatives. There are in the Speaker's lobby 37 portraits of former Speakers. In the Hall of the House of Representatives are 2 full-length portraits. On the east gallery front, facing the Emancipation Proclamation, are 3 portraits, and on the west gallery front, facing Leutze's Westward the Course of Empire Takes Its Way, is 1 portrait, a full-length seated portrait of Chief Justice Marshall. In the room of the House Committee on Appropriations there are 6 portraits. There are also in this section of the Capitol 1 bronze bust, 1 marble statue, a marble bust of Champ Clark, and a marble bust of James R. Mann, making a total of 58 works of art in the House wing of the Capitol.

In the House Office Building there are 17 paintings by Seth Eastman, showing the forts of the United States, and in the room of the Committee on Ways and Means are 5 portraits. There is also in the main staircase of this building a marble bust of Joseph G. Cannon, who acted as the chairman of the House Office Building Commission at the time of the erection of the building. There are therefore 23 works of art in the House Office Building.

There should also be added to the total number of works of art owned by the Government 2 paintings which have never been assigned to space on account of their size, and these, added to the number enumerated above, brings the total number of art works belonging to the Government to 296.

It must be understood that this does not include such works of art as the bronze doors, the statue of Freedom, which surmounts the dome, the statues of Peace and War, occupying niches in the east portico of the Capitol, the Rescue and Discovery groups, occupying spaces upon the blocking of the steps of the east front of the Capitol, the group of Justice and History over the main entrance door of the Senate, nor the statuary in the pediments of the Senate wing, the central portion, and the House wing of the Capitol. Nor does the enumeration include the bronze statue of Chief Justice Marshall at the west front of the Capitol terrace, nor have the many frescoes and mural decorations in different portions of the Capitol been included in this list.

It may seem to have been the duty of the writer or compiler of the information disclosed in this work to have included a more critical estimate of the art value of the works described. This has purposely been avoided, and sufficient reasons appear to justify the omission. Many of the works of art have been presented to the Government and it may show a lack of courtesy to discuss gifts received in this manner. Many of the works belong to an early period of the art history of this country, and it seems unjust to attempt a criticism of such works from the standpoint of present-day estimates. In addition to this there is a wide difference of opinion as to what constitutes real merit in a work of art. The people having these opinions differ in art education from those who simply say they "know what they like" to those who are professional artists, art critics, or connoisseurs, and it is evident that art criticism must, under such circumstances, be largely a matter of individual opinion. It is possible that those who "know what they like" will receive as much satisfaction in their acquaintance with works of art as those who really are expert and upon whose opinion the most learned can place confidence. Among all of the standards of art and among all of the rules upon which we may determine the merit of an art work, I am inclined to agree with Frederic Wellington Ruckstull, who states as a definition—

every human work made in any language with the purpose of expressing or stirring human emotions is a work of art; and a work of art is great in ratio of its power to stir the highest emotion of the largest number of cultured people for the longest period of time.

And so to those who find pleasure in some of the art of the Capitol which to others may seem of little value, and to those who are looking for better things in art, and to those who only admire the best in art, I wish to say this is our Capitol, and may you be able to find in it something which will renew and stimulate your patriotism and love of country, with a reverent feeling toward those who have striven through the art of architecture, the art of sculpture, and the art of painting to make our Capitol worthy of the Nation it represents.

INDEX

{ 500 }

{ 504 }

{ 509 }